SMALL ARMS SURVEY 2001

Profiling the Problem

May 2000

To Fred:

with best wishes
& looking forward to
working together in
the future

About the Small Arms Survey

The Small Arms Survey is an independent research project located at the Graduate Institute of International Studies in Geneva, Switzerland. Established in 1999 with the generous financial support of the Swiss Federal Department of Foreign Affairs, it currently receives additional funding from Belgium, Canada, Denmark, the Netherlands, Norway, Sweden, and the United Kingdom.

The objectives of the Survey are: to be the principal source of public information on all aspects of small arms; to serve as a resource centre for governments; policy makers, researchers, and activists; to monitor national and international initiatives (governmental and non-governmental) on small arms; and to act as a clearing house for the sharing of information and the dissemination of best practices. The Survey also sponsors field research and information-gathering efforts, especially in affected states and regions.

The project has an international staff with expertise in security studies, political science, law, economics, development studies and sociology who work closely with a worldwide network of researchers and partner institutions.

Small Arms Survey

Graduate Institute of International Studies

12, Avenue de Sécheron

CH-1202 Geneva, Switzerland

Tel. (41 22) 908 57 77

Fax (41 22) 732 27 38

Email. smallarm@hei.unige.ch

Website. www.smallarmssurvey.org

SMALL ARMS SURVEY 2001

Profiling the Problem

A Project
of the Graduate Institute
of International Studies, Geneva

HEI

OXFORD
UNIVERSITY PRESS

Great Clarendon Street, Oxford OX2 6DP

Oxford University Press is a department of the University of Oxford.
It furthers the University's objective of excellence in research, scholarship,
and education by publishing worldwide in Oxford New York
Athens Auckland Bangkok Bogotá Buenos Aires Calcutta - Kolkata
Cape Town Chennai Dar es Salaam Delhi Florence Hong Kong Istanbul
Karachi Kuala Lumpur Madrid Melbourne Mexico City Mumbai
Nairobi Paris São Paulo Shanghai Singapore Taipei Tokyo Toronto Warsaw
with associated companies in Berlin Ibadan

Oxford is a registered trade mark of Oxford University Press
in the UK and in certain other countries

Published in Great Britain
By Oxford University Press Inc., Oxford

British Library Cataloguing in Publication Data
Data available

Library of Congress Cataloging in Publication Data
Data available

ISBN 0-19-924670-X
ISBN 0-19-924671-8 (Pbk.)

Typeset in Garamond Light Condensed
by Iseman Creative with Raymond Geary & Associates and Logan Smith

Printed in Great Britain
on acid-free paper by
Bath Press Ltd, Bath, Avon

Acknowledgements

This first edition of the *Small Arms Survey* has benefitted from the input and advice of a vast number of researchers, government officials, activists, experts, and friends. This volume is a collective product of the staff of, and contributors to, the Small Arms Survey project. All chapters have been researched, written, peer reviewed, edited, revised—and immeasurably enhanced—by the knowledgeable critiques and supportive comments received from colleagues around the world.

The main contributors to the *Survey 2001*, as well as the principal chapter authors, are: Peter Batchelor (Products and Producers), Aaron Karp (Stockpiles), Maria Haug (Legal and Illicit Transfers), Deborah Berlinck and Spyros Demetriou (Brokers), Robert Muggah (Effects), and Glenn McDonald (Measures).

The principal chapter authors were assisted by a large number of in-house and external contributors, who also wrote or drafted sections for the relevant chapters. These include: Pete Abel, Anatole Ayissi, Eric Berman, Ignacio Cano, Martinho Chachiua, Elisabeth Clegg, Robin Coupland, Wendy Cukier, Andreas Danevad, Pablo Dreyfus, Sami Faltas, Virginia Gamba, William Godnick, Ettienne Hennop, Clare Jefferson, Brian Johnson-Thomas, Tara Kartha, Kai Kenkel, Jeremy King, Judit Kiss, Katherine Kramer, Etienne Krug, Edward Laurance, Andrew McLean, David Meddings, Kevin O'Brien, Geraldine O'Callaghan, Johan Peleman, Daniel Plesch, Ruslan Pukhov, Camilla Waszink, and Brian Wood.

Peter Batchelor and Keith Krause were responsible for the overall planning and organization of this volume. Keith Krause also wrote the introduction. As the project manager for the *Survey*, Adrea Mach was responsible for copy editing and co-ordinating with the chapter authors and design team. Layout and design was done by Iseman Creative with Raymond Geary & Associates and Logan Smith. Derek Miller headed the production process in Geneva with help from Erick Waldman.

In addition to those mentioned above, comments on chapters were provided by: Michael Brzoska, Owen Greene, Lora Lumpe, Peggy Mason, Sarah Meek, Michael Renner, Elisabeth Sköns, Reinhilde Weidacher, Pieter Wezeman, Steve Wright, and Herbert Wulf. Support at Oxford University Press was provided by Dominic Byatt and Amanda Watkins.

Staff and infrastructure support was supplied by Delphine Zinner, Kai Kenkel, Silvia Cattaneo, Fridrich Strba, and other personnel of the Graduate Institute of International Studies, in particular Peter Tschopp, and staff members Edgardo Amato, Wilfred Gander, Nicole Mouthon, and Marielle Schneider.

As the overall project that produces this annual report of the same name, the Small Arms Survey itself would never have seen the light of day without the generous financial and overall support of the Swiss Government, in particular of Raimund Kunz, Stefano Toscano (thanks for the title!), Lukas Schifferle, and Theodor Winkler. Generous financial support was also provided by the Governments of Belgium, Canada, Denmark, the Netherlands, Norway, Sweden, and the United Kingdom. In all cases, the support and encouragement of several key individuals (who shall remain unnamed) was crucial, especially for the launch of the *Survey*.

In Geneva, our Survey staff also received support and expert advice from David Atwood, John Borrie, Christophe Carle, Helen Gates, Jozef Goldblat, Martin Griffiths, Olivier Guerot, Peter Herby, Philippa King, Alexander Kmentt, Steffen Kongstad, Patricia Lewis, Bennie Lombard, Joel McClellan, and Jennifer Milliken. Beyond Geneva, support was forthcoming from a host of colleagues in partner institutions. In addition to those mentioned above, we would like to thank: Péricles Gasparini Alves, Antonio Rangel Bandeira, David Biggs, Paul Eavis, Rubem César Fernandes, Björn Hagelin, João Honwana, David Jackman, Kate Joseph, Jakkie Potgieter, Yeshua Moser-Puangsuwan, and Greg Puley. Other individuals who contributed their time or insights include: Ian Anthony, Kathi Austin, Chris Smith, Rachel Stohl, Terrence Taylor and Alex Vines.

Keith Krause
Programme Director
Small Arms Survey

Table of Contents

Chapter 5: Crime, Conflict, Corruption:
Global Illicit Small Arms Transfers

Chapter 6: After the Smoke Clears:
Assessing the Effects of Small Arms Availability

Chapter 7: Tackling the Small Arms Problem:
Multilateral Measures and Initiatives

Notes to Readers/Photo Credits

Introduction

At least 500,000 people are killed each year by small arms and light weapons. They die in an astonishingly diverse number of ways: as combatants in internal and inter-state wars; as participants in gang fights and criminal battles; as casualties of government-sponsored or condoned violence and terror; as innocent civilians trapped in deadly wars and social conflicts; and as victims of suicide, homicide, or random acts of violence.

The causes of the violence behind these deaths are complex and multi-faceted, and the easy availability and misuse of small arms and light weapons is only one part of the story. Still, this statistic—half a million deaths each year—ought to catch our eye. After all, it is higher than the number of deaths in almost all recent wars. Thus, it is no exaggeration to call small arms and light weapons 'the real weapons of mass destruction'. While they may not devastate entire cities or populations within a space of a few seconds, they are implicated in more than 1,300 deaths each day.

Small arms and light weapons are the real weapons of mass destruction, taking well over a thousand lives each day, more than half a million lives each year.

Aside from their direct role in armed conflicts and violence, small arms and light weapons are also widely used in 'peacetime' situations to terrorize individuals, to control or subdue groups and communities, to influence politics, to profit and amass personal gain, and to undergird and maintain power. Throughout the world—in both poor countries and rich ones—socially marginalized or desperately impoverished people may resort to violence in order to survive or to gain a tenuous foothold in society. At the same time, others—driven by power or greed—may use weapons to consolidate and build their positions. Over time, the result is a pervasive sense of social danger, insecurity, and anxiety, exacerbated by self-perpetuating cycles and cultures of violence. In worst-case scenarios, the end result is a totally corrupt or collapsed state. Only more effective national, regional, and international measures to regulate various aspects of the small arms and light weapons problem can help break this vicious circle.

Concerted international action

Against this backdrop, governmental and non-governmental efforts have been galvanized to counter the proliferation and destabilizing accumulation of small arms and light weapons in recent years. Yet effective long-term policy requires reliable and comprehensive information and analysis on all aspects of the problem—something that has been relatively rare to date. The *Survey* is intended to fill this gap.

Such a contribution is sorely needed since several characteristics of small arms and light weapons make them an uncommonly difficult and politically contentious issue for the international community to address. These include:

The Survey's primary goal is to fill the small arms information and analysis gap.

- The *nature* of the weapons—lethal, easy to use and transport, difficult to track, and relatively simple to maintain in circulation for a long time;
- The large *number* of producing companies and countries, which makes supply-side control a difficult logistical challenge;
- The legitimate *use* of these weapons for national and/or individual security and defence, and the acquisition or retention of such weapons when governments fail to guarantee the physical safety of their citizens;
- The 'grey' and 'black' *markets* in such weapons, which are often linked to transnational crime and drug trafficking, and to the activities of non-state actors;
- The *relationship* between light weapons flows, situations of economic insecurity and deprivation, and the ensuing social and political conflicts;

- The disarmament *requirements* of post-conflict settings, including the demobilization and re-integration of ex-combatants; and
- The differing national *norms* for firearms possession, use, and reporting.

Small arms constitute a relatively new issue on the international agenda. So it is not surprising that there is still little agreement on the precise contours of the problem. It has been variously defined as an arms control and disarmament issue, a human rights and humanitarian law issue, a public health or economic development issue, a problem of post-conflict disarmament, or as an issue of terrorism and criminality. In the absence of a broad overview, each perspective focuses a different lens on the problem and advocates different solutions. There is also no agreement on which weapons are of greatest concern: pistols and revolvers, which are most numerous; military assault rifles, which are widely used in conflict situations; or hand grenades and high-tech portable military equipment, which cascade into civilian hands.

Whatever the perspective, three issues are clear:

First, controlling small arms and light weapons—which are responsible for most of the deaths and injuries, especially of civilian non-combatants, in recent wars—is of vital importance to the contemporary international security agenda. Precisely because small arms are so ubiquitous and have legitimate military and civilian uses, efforts to regulate and control them must be carefully crafted.

Second, as much of the work in the *Survey* shows, small arms and light weapons are more than just an arms control and disarmament issue. In his *Millennium Report* (2000), UN Secretary-General Kofi Annan pointed out that:

> *Small arms proliferation is not merely a security issue; it is also an issue of human rights and of development. The proliferation of small arms sustains and exacerbates armed conflicts. It endangers peacekeepers and humanitarian workers. It undermines respect for international humanitarian law. It threatens legitimate but weak governments and it benefits terrorists, as well as the perpetrators of organized crime.*

Finally, small arms and light weapons do not proliferate by themselves. Rather, they are designed, produced, and procured in response to demand by governments and/or civilians. They are sold, re-sold, perhaps stolen, diverted, and maybe legally or illegally transferred several more times. Ultimately they are used and re-used, during or after conflicts. At each juncture in this complex chain of legal and illicit transfers, people—brokers, insurgents, criminals, government officials, and/or organized groups—are active participants in the process. Regulation and control of small arms and light weapons must proceed from this simple fact.

Goals and objectives of the *Small Arms Survey*

Small arms and light weapons do not proliferate by themselves.

The primary goal of the *Small Arms Survey* is to provide reliable information and analysis on all aspects of the problem of small arms and light weapons proliferation. Persuaded that transparency is a cornerstone of national and international accountability—as well as an indispensable element in effective policy-making—the *Survey* is an *independent transparency mechanism* that serves many audiences. Our work is based on the conviction that greater transparency for all small arms and light weapons issues will improve international, regional, national, and human security.

Yet the task will not be easy. Until recently, such an initiative would have been considered virtually impossible. Even today, the available data are far from complete. Still, enough information exists with which to sketch an outline of the situation and to provide a 'roadmap' showing the way forward.

The Survey is committed to collecting and analyzing the best available open-source data, and to sponsoring primary and field research that will generate new data. The Survey also carefully assesses and verifies the reliability of data before using it in its publications, and our research work is governed by four principles:

- **Using a multidisciplinary approach:** The problem of small arms and light weapons must be approached from a broad, multidisciplinary perspective. Proliferation and misuse are not purely an arms control and disarmament issue. Equally important (and context-specific) are the crime control, humanitarian law, economic development, and public health perspectives.
- **Studying the multiple societal effects:** Far greater attention must be paid to the economic, social, and human costs and consequences of small arms and light weapons proliferation and use. Only when the costs in terms of lost growth, stalled development, and distorted allocation of government or household investment are quantified will the opportunity cost of inaction become irrefutably clear, and the benefits of even simple regulatory measures evident.
- **Examining different levels of the problem:** Small arms proliferation is not exclusively an international issue. It is also one with important regional, national, and local dimensions.
- **Engaging multiple actors:** Small arms proliferation and control is no longer simply an issue for governments. Increasingly, non-governmental actors, including researchers and advocates, have a crucial role to play in shaping and developing policies in this area. Indeed, they are often the *essential actors* in the grassroots implementation of various global, regional, or local measures.

The Survey is an independent transparency mechanism.

What role might the newly launched *Small Arms Survey* play? A significant one, we hope. But this publication is only the most visible product of the activities of the Small Arms Survey project as a whole. Since its establishment in 1999, our Geneva-based resource centre has served as a node in the network of small arms research-based activities that includes field projects, occasional papers, conferences, workshops, and other outreach activities. Our overall aim is to become a well-utilized international centre of excellence and expertise on all small arms and light weapons issues.

The Survey's overall aim is to become a respected and well-utilized international centre of excellence and expertise on small arms issues.

Introducing the Small Arms Survey 2001: Profiling the Problem

The seven chapters in this year's *Survey* address many of the most prominent small arms and light weapons issues. In this first edition, subtitled 'Profiling the Problem', we have chosen to present a broad overview of the state of the world's knowledge and awareness on different aspects of these wide-ranging issues.

In many cases, through a combination of comprehensive data collection, careful estimation techniques, and best judgement where sources conflict or are unclear, we have sought to fill a few large gaps in our collective knowledge. Such a global overview is the first step in identifying more specific problem areas, topics for future research, and additional 'missing links' that can be supplied in future editions.

Chapter One *(Products, Producers)* concentrates on production, identifying more than 600 firms in at least 95 countries that produce small arms, light weapons, and/or associated ammunition and parts. These figures are significantly higher than previous estimates. The major producers include: Austria, Belgium, France, Germany, Great Britain, Israel, Italy, the Russian Federation, Switzerland, the United States and—although hard data are difficult to come by— probably China. Although an estimate of the global value of annual production is still premature, available information suggests that, despite an increase in the types of small arms being produced, the market itself is not expanding. It may, in fact, be shrinking as a result of the recent downsizing of global armed forces and consolidation of defence industries. Nevertheless, the re-circulation of existing small arms and light weapons, and their longevity, suggests that global stockpiles continue to grow.

Chapter Two (Stockpiles) seeks to estimate global stockpiles of small arms and light weapons. It focuses on individual-use firearms, including military-style weapons belonging to armed forces, handguns and sidearms used by national police forces, and guns in civilian possession. Based on extrapolations from limited existing data, it concludes that, worldwide, there are *at least* 550 million small arms and light weapons, not including illicit civilian weapons. About 41 per cent of these —226 million weapons—are in the arsenals of national armed forces, while 56 per cent— some 305 million weapons—are in legal civilian possession. Only three per cent are held by the world's police forces, and most surprisingly, less than one per cent of such weapons are in the hands of insurgent groups.

Small arms production may be shrinking but global stockpiles continue to grow.

Chapter Three (Brokers) highlights the crucial role played by arms brokers, dealers, transport agents, and their associated networks in transferring small arms and light weapons. In the past, most brokers operated under the tacit or explicit aegis of state security apparatuses. Today they have increasingly taken on the role of independent private actors who exploit loopholes in laws and regulations, and sidestep the weak regulatory capacities of some states, to provide arms to conflict zones. The lack of harmonized national or international legal instruments, in addition to the absence of information-sharing arrangements between states, makes it particularly difficult to catch brokers directly engaged in illegal activities since transactions are carefully designed to circumvent, bend, or break the fewest laws. The Survey's research does suggest, however, that the number of people engaged in arms brokering and shipping is actually quite small, and that they often operate in complex, fluid, and opaque networks.

Worldwide, there are more than 550 million small arms and light weapons.

Chapters Four and Five (Legal and Illicit Transfers) present an overview of the legal, grey, and black markets in small arms and light weapons. The *Survey* estimates the annual value of the legal small arms trade at between US\$ 4-6 billion. The top exporters for which reliable information is available are: the United States, the Russian Federation, Germany, and Brazil. Other less transparent states that are likely to be major players include Bulgaria, China, and Israel, for whom reliable information is not yet available. In all, more than 60 states are involved in the legal export of small arms while almost *all* the world's countries are importers of varying quantities of small arms and light weapons.

The illicit trade in small arms—transfers that engender 'crime, conflict and corruption'—while far more difficult to assess, appears to comprise less than 20 per cent of the total trade. The so-called 'grey market'—covert transfers conducted by governments or government-sponsored entities— appears significantly larger than the wholly illegal 'black market'.

The annual value of the legal trade in small arms is estimated at US\$ 4-6 billion.

Chapter Six (Effects) focuses on the social and economic impacts of small arms and light weapons proliferation and availability 'after the smoke clears'. It documents the relationship between availability and use, and highlights the similarities and differences between the direct and indirect effects of small arms use in the North and the South. The chapter also documents a broad array of indirect effects, including increasing insecurity for humanitarian relief workers and operations, the privatization of violence, strains on public health systems, increased violent criminal activity, and reduced economic activity and socio-economic development. The Inter-American Development Bank (IDB) estimated the direct and indirect costs of violence at US\$ 140-170 billion a year for Latin America alone. Such a figure clearly indicates the pressing need for further research on the effects of small arms and light weapons' use and availability.

Chapter Seven (Measures) surveys the wide array of proposed or partially implemented multilateral measures at the global, regional, and sub-regional level to 'tackle the small arms problem'. The aim is not to present a comprehensive analysis of all existing measures and initiatives, but to provide an introduction and overview of major efforts, to guide readers to other sources, and to lay a foundation for further in-depth studies. This chapter focuses especially on the recent development of regional instruments in the Americas, Africa, and Europe, as well as specific multilateral efforts within such bodies as the OSCE, NATO, and the UN (e.g. the *Firearms Protocol* being negotiated within the Crime Commission of the ECOSOC). It also sets out the major issues identified for the July 2001 *UN Conference on the Illicit Trade in Small Arms and Light Weapons in All Its Aspects.*

The challenges ahead

This first edition of the *Small Arms Survey* raises as many questions as it answers. Future issues will be devoted to addressing them. They will not present annual 'snapshots' detailing changes over the previous calendar year since the available data and nature of the problem make such a year-to-year survey inappropriate. Instead, the *Survey* will focus on particular issues and regions; refine the analysis and estimates of stockpiles and transfers; follow the development of regional and global initiatives; and highlight problem areas that warrant greater policy attention. Two important issues the *Survey* will focus on in future editions are the humanitarian and developmental impacts of small arms and light weapons proliferation and use.

In addition to refining our estimates of global weapons stockpiles, future editions will provide regional and sub-regional breakdowns to highlight areas of concern. We will also broaden the scope to include stocks and flows of other small arms and light weapons, including larger, more sophisticated weapons that are not in wide circulation, but nevertheless pose grave security risks. Efforts to track transfers will also focus on specific regions and sub-regions, especially those most seriously affected by conflicts and instability.

As an increasing number of states become able and willing to furnish reliable information on their transfers of small arms and light weapons, there will be an urgent need to present these data in the clearest, most comprehensive, and most harmonized fashion. Future editions of the *Survey* will analyze the strengths and weaknesses of existing national reporting practices and present suggestions for common definitions and standards to increase the utility and comparability of information. The *Survey* will also treat the growing problem of weapons brokering, and the link to other lucrative activities (e.g. trade in diamonds, drugs, tropical timber, and other 'conflict goods'), analyzing case studies, as well as providing details on the activities of prominent arms brokers.

Activities undertaken in the context of the July 2001 *United Nations Conference on the Illicit Trade in Small Arms and Light Weapons in All Its Aspects* will also be examined in next year's *Survey,* especially since this groundbreaking conference is likely to shape policy initiatives and priorities for years to come. Finally, such issues as marking and traceability, stockpile management and security measures, plus newer issues, such as the relevance of international instruments covering the transport of dangerous goods and the tracing of domestic production chains, will be covered in subsequent issues of the *Survey.*

Ultimately, the concerted efforts of all actors in this important disarmament arena will be successful only if the use of such weapons in peacetime, conflicts, wars, and post-conflict struggles abates, and if individuals and communities can live their lives in greater safety and security. The role of the *Small Arms Survey* will be to monitor and report on these efforts, to raise awareness of their relevance, and to provide policy benchmarks in the years ahead.

For Latin America alone, the direct and indirect costs of violence amount to between US$ 140-170 billion a year.

International small arms control efforts will be successful only if individuals and communities can live in greater safety and security.

1

Small Arms, Big Business:
Products and Producers

Introduction

The production of small arms is a big, and growing, business—at least in terms of the number of countries that produce them. Based on existing information, small arms are legally produced in more than 600 companies in at least 95 countries worldwide—even more if those countries in which illicit production takes place are included.

Map 1.1   The world's legal small arms producers

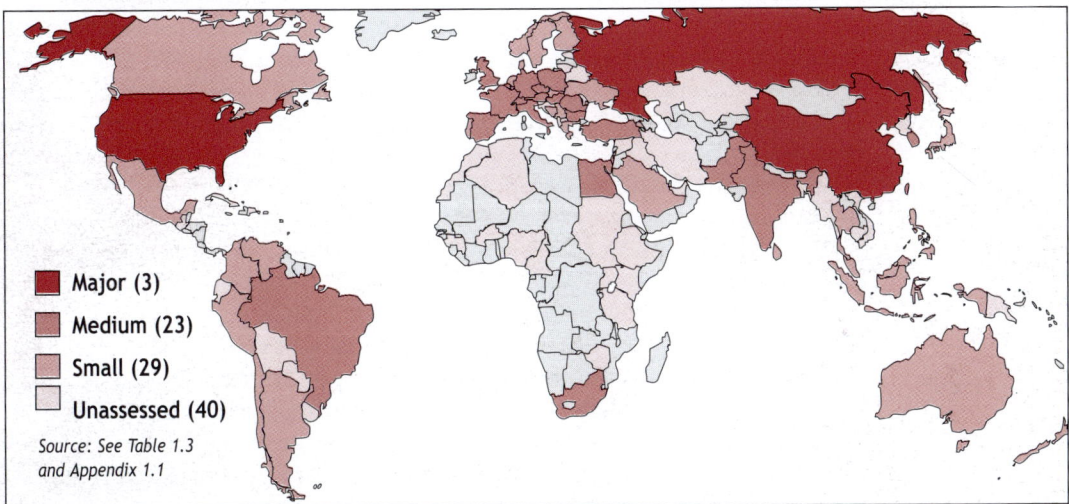

Major (3)
Medium (23)
Small (29)
Unassessed (40)

Source: See Table 1.3 and Appendix 1.1

The myriad problems—security, humanitarian, and developmental—associated with the widespread proliferation, availability, and use of small arms are often blamed on the re-circulation of existing stocks or the sale of surplus weapons. But that is only half the story.

New and better small arms products are also contributing to these problems. These weapons—lighter, more accurate, easier to operate, and sometimes cheaper—are appearing on the international arms market at an alarming rate. In addition, new production of weapons and ammunition continues unabated in a large, and growing number of countries and companies, thus contributing to the ever expanding global supply of small arms.

The small arms industry is the most widely distributed sector of the global defence industry. While its absolute size, in terms of capacity, has declined in recent years, the number of actors, both companies and countries, that manufacture small arms, has increased since the end of the Cold War. Furthermore, most production now takes place in private companies, thus reducing the ability of governments to control the manufacture, possession, and trade in small arms.

The growing number of small arms products and producers, both legal and illicit, has far-reaching consequences. First, in terms of sheer numbers, the diffusion of small arms makes their

Small arms are legally produced in more than 600 companies in at least 95 countries worldwide.

New and better small arms products are appearing on the international arms market at an alarming rate.

Box 1.1   Defining small arms and light weapons

The definition of small arms and light weapons used by the *Small Arms Survey* covers both military-style weapons and commercial firearms (handguns and long guns). It follows the guidelines set out in the 1997 *Report of the Panel of Governmental Experts on Small Arms* (United Nations document A/52/298, 27 August 1997):

- **Small arms:** Revolvers and self-loading pistols, rifles and carbines, assault rifles, submachine guns, and light machine guns;
- **Light weapons:** Heavy machine guns, hand-held under-barrel and mounted grenade launchers, portable anti-tank and anti-aircraft guns, recoilless rifles, portable launchers of anti-tank and anti-aircraft missile systems, and mortars of less than 100mm calibre.

The *Survey* uses the terms 'small arms', 'firearms', and 'light weapons' interchangeably. Unless otherwise noted, there is no distinction to be made between commercial firearms (e.g. hunting rifles), and small arms and light weapons that are designed for military purposes (e.g. assault rifles).

The small arms industry is the most widely distributed sector of the global defence industry.

accessibility, even to civilians, an issue of concern. For example, in the United States, there is the equivalent of one weapon for every one of the country's 250 million residents (STOCKPILES, EFFECTS). Secondly, this burgeoning growth threatens to undermine attempts to control their legal manufacture and trade. Some of the countries allegedly committed to dealing with the small arms proliferation problem are also some of the world's major producers. Thus, it is important for governments to be held accountable for both the legal and illicit production of small arms that takes place within their territories.

Any analysis of this critical aspect of the small arms issue is inhibited by a lack of data. This absence of official and unofficial information about companies, countries, and the value and volume of global production makes it difficult to produce a clear picture of the nature and scope of the global small arms industry.

On the basis of current information and research, this chapter attempts to provide a comprehensive survey of global small arms production. It analyzes the world's small arms industry in terms of its geographic distribution, key trends, and patterns, and provides some estimates of the current value and volume of global production. It identifies the most important producer countries and offers a tentative ranking of all the world's known and assessed legal small arms producers. It provides information on some of the world's most widely-distributed and popular small arms products—specifically handguns, assault rifles, sub-machine guns, and machine guns—that are in the hands of government forces, rebel groups, and/or individuals. [1]

The global small arms industry is not homogenous. There are significant differences between the nature of production in different areas of the world. This chapter, therefore, also presents a number of regional and country case studies, as well as information about particular companies, to illustrate some of the key characteristics of the global small arms industry. The following questions are addressed:

Some of the countries allegedly committed to dealing with the small arms proliferation problem are also some of the world's major producers.

- **What is the nature and scope (i.e. defining features, size, distribution, trends, and major producers) of the global small arms industry?**
- **How many countries legally produce small arms? Who are the major producers?**
- **What are the world's most popular legal and illicit small arms products in terms of numbers produced and distribution?**
- **In which countries does illicit production of small arms occur?**

All the material presented in this chapter is based on information obtained from open public sources, including official information, annual and specialized defence publications, corporate and

---

Box 1.2   Types of small arms production

Legal Production: This includes production, or assembly of, small arms from components or parts that are legally acquired, or production with a license from a competent governmental authority; it may also include licensed production.

Licensed Production: A company in country A contracts with a company in country B to undertake the legal production of its products (e.g. weapons). In terms of a licensed production agreement, the licensing company in country A usually provides technical data or copies of the products to be produced in country B, and sometimes provides machine tools or assists in the setting up of production facilities.

Illicit Production: This refers to the production, or assembly of, small arms from components or parts that are illicitly acquired, or production without a license from a competent governmental authority. It may include craft or homemade production. In some cases, the state itself engages in illicit production, by manufacturing another country's or a company's products without permission.

Craft/homemade Production: This type of production occurs in small private workshops or homes without any legal (i.e. governmental or company) authorization. This type of production tends to be crude and small-scale (e.g. single weapons or small batches) and is usually done by hand rather than via complex manufacturing processes (e.g. production lines). Most craft production involves the manufacture of simple single-shot weapons, and/or illicit copies of existing types of small arms.

---

non-governmental information services, defence exhibitions, company promotional information, and primary field research in selected countries and regions.

The global small arms industry

Much has been written about the global defence industry, particularly the major producers of conventional weapons. However, far less attention has been focused on the global small arms sector, which is part of the defence industry in general, but is also distinctive in many ways.

This section analyzes the defining features of the global small arms industry. It focuses on the distribution of production (i.e. the number of countries and companies that produce small arms), general trends and patterns, and the size and scope of the industry (i.e. the value and volume of production). It also identifies the world's most significant small arms producers and presents a tentative ranking of all known arms-producing countries.

Distribution

The production of small arms has been a growing worldwide industry since the 1960s, even predating the global production of many types of conventional weapons. In recent years, a number of studies have attempted to quantify the worldwide distribution of small arms production.[2] According to information supplied by 77 countries to the United Nations (UN) *International Study on Firearm Regulation* (1999), 45 countries acknowledged that firearms, components, and/or ammunition were legally produced in their territories for domestic and/or export markets. The 1999 report of the UN Group of Governmental Experts stated that small arms 'continue to be produced in large numbers, mostly in developed countries, although they are now manufactured in over 70 countries' (UN, 2000b, p.8).

One study estimated that there were at least 385 companies in 64 countries producing small arms in the 1990s, compared to 196 companies in 52 countries in the 1980s (Abel, 2000). However,

The production of small arms has been a growing worldwide industry since the 1960s.

recent data from the 1997 US Census of Manufacturers provide information on 304 US small arms and ammunition companies. This, combined with more recent Canadian data, suggests that the total number of companies is closer to 600 (See Fig. 1.1).

The data in Figure 1.1 suggest a substantial increase in the number of companies and countries producing small arms between the 1980s and the 1990s. The greatest increases occurred in Europe, with slight increases in Africa and the Middle East. The increase in the number of producers does not necessarily indicate an increase in the global production capacity for manufacturing small arms (Abel, 2000, p. 83). In fact, in terms of the volume of production, the global small arms industry was smaller in the 1990s than it was in the 1980s.

Figure 1.1   Global distribution of small arms production, 1980s and 1990s

Region	1980s		1990s	
	Countries	Companies	Countries	Companies
Africa	5	10	7	22
Asia Pacific	14	23	14	31
Europe/CIS	22	100	30	203
Middle East	4	6	6	13
South/Central America	5	15	5	17
North America	2	42	2	99
Total	52	196	64	385*

* More recent data from the 1997 US Census of Manufacturers provide information on 304 US small arms and ammunition companies. This, combined with more recent Canadian data, suggests that the total number of companies is closer to 600. (See section 3 for further details)

Source: Abel, 2000

Based on current information and research, it is estimated that small arms are legally produced in at least 95 countries (see Appendix 1.1). The global distribution of producer countries is given in Figure 1.2.

The increased number of producing countries, compared with earlier studies, reflects the creation of a number of 'newly independent states' following the break up of the Soviet Union, including states in Eastern Europe and the Balkans. It is also related to the desire of a growing number of countries, particularly developing countries, to be self-sufficient in small arms production.

Figure 1.2   Global distribution of small arms producing countries, 2000

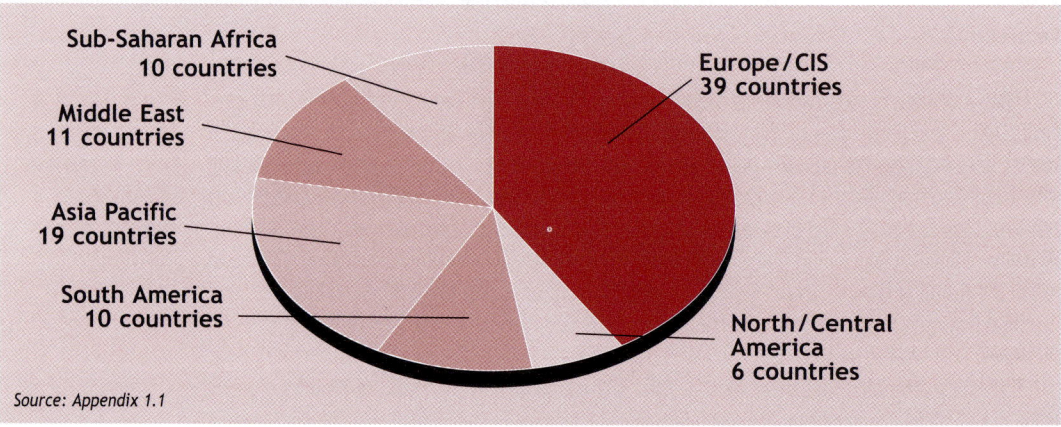

Source: Appendix 1.1

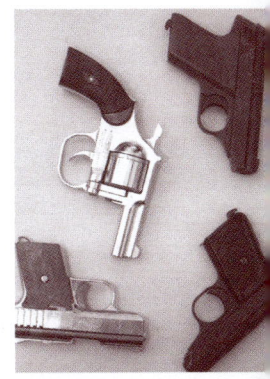

Figure 1.2 shows that the largest geographic concentration of producer countries—over 40 per cent—is in Europe and the Commonwealth of Independent States (CIS).

This estimate of the total number of small arms producing countries should be treated with caution. In some countries (e.g. Cambodia, Ethiopia), the lack of reliable information, both official and unofficial, makes it difficult to ascertain whether small arms production is taking place, and if so, whether it occurs consistently or only on an *ad hoc* basis. Some countries are only involved in the production of components, rather than final products; while in others, small arms production involves relatively marginal activities, such as loading or filling ammunition cartridges.

The total number of companies that produce small arms is much more difficult to quantify. This is because it is often difficult to distinguish between end producers that sell final products (e.g. rifles) to buyers, and intermediate producers—companies that produce parts or components for small arms that are then sold by end producers. In addition, small arms are often produced in different divisions, subsidiary companies, or plants that are part of a larger company. Thus, the total number of *end producers* is likely to be much lower than the total number of producers, including intermediate producers.

There are more than 600 companies worldwide that are involved in some aspect of small arms production.

Based on current information and research, it is estimated that there are more than 600 companies worldwide that are involved in some aspect of small arms production, either as intermediate and/or end producers.[3] This is an increase on estimates during the 1990s, largely because of the release of more recent information about the small arms industry in the United States, where more than half of all the world's small arms companies are located. The rest are concentrated in Europe and the CIS with smaller numbers in Latin America, sub-Saharan Africa, the Middle East, and the Asia Pacific region.

The types of companies are extremely diverse, ranging from small family-owned businesses to subsidiaries or business units of large, multinational, defence-industrial conglomerates. Some firms produce thousands of arms annually, while others produce as little as one gun a year. The size of the companies ranges from establishments with less than 20 to over 1,000 employees. In the US, for example, only 55 out of a total of a 191 small arms producers have more than 20 employees (BATF, 2000a).

The United States is home to more than half of all the world's small arms companies.

The diversity of countries and companies in which small arms production takes place means that it is difficult to generalize about the nature and scope of the global small arms industry. The regional survey in Section 3, which includes country and company case studies, attempts to provide a more detailed picture of the industry's distinguishing features.

Trends and patterns

What have been the major trends and patterns in the global small arms industry in the last decade? Has the size of the industry increased or decreased since the end of the Cold War?

In general terms, the global defence industry has experienced a dramatic process of downsizing, restructuring and consolidation over the last decade.[4] Total employment in arms production during the period 1988–98 declined by more than 50 per cent (BICC, 2000, p. 68). The downsizing of the global defence industry was prompted by the more than 30 per cent cuts in defence spending that have occurred since the late 1980s (BICC, 2000; SIPRI, 2000). These aggregate figures do not, however, capture the significant variations in defence industry employment that have occurred at the regional, sub-regional, and national levels; nor does it reflect the sectoral differences (e.g. small arms) within the overall defence industry.[5]

The global defence industry has experienced a dramatic down-sizing over the last decade.

This downsizing has certainly affected the size of the global small arms industry, at least in terms of employment and manufacturing capacity. However, given the significant country and regional variations, and the lack of detailed information about the value and volume of small arms production, it is impossible to quantify its impact precisely.

At first glance, the increasing number of countries and companies that produce small arms might indicate that the global small arms industry has been growing in recent years. However, more suppliers do not necessarily translate into an increase in the size of the industry, as measured by the value and volume of global small arms production, or manufacturing capacity. In fact, the current estimates for both the value and volume of small arms production suggest that the absolute size of the world's small arms industry has actually shrunk in recent years.

The absolute size of the world's small arms industry has actually shrunk in recent years.

During the Cold War, small arms production was largely confined to state-owned factories. As a result of restructuring and privatization in many parts of the world (e.g. Australia, Western Europe, East Central Europe, South Africa), it now takes place increasingly in private firms. Privatization, together with the trends in licensed production, has important implications for national and multilateral attempts to regulate and control the legal, as well as illicit, manufacture and transfer of small arms.

The technology needed to produce small arms is relatively mature and there are few technical obstacles to entering the small arms market. This has meant that a growing number of countries, including developing countries, have been able to establish their own domestic production capabilities with relative ease—a development that has had a negative impact on the markets of established small arms producers in the Russian Federation, the US, and Europe.

Licensed production is an important feature of the global small arms industry, and has been occurring since the 1960s. In many countries, particularly developing countries, legal production of small arms involves the licensed production of foreign weapons.[6] According to current information and research, companies such as FN Herstal (Belgium) and Heckler & Koch (Germany/UK) are among the world's most significant small arms licensors; their products are produced under license in a large, and growing number of countries.[7]

Between 1960 and 1999, at least 14 countries established small arms licensed production agreements with some 46 countries.

Some countries, such as China and Croatia, have emerged as extremely sophisticated copiers of various small arms products, and tend to produce very good copies of existing products, rather than under license from the original producer (licensor). Some studies have documented the increase in licensed defence production, including small arms, in developing countries.[8] From 1960-99, at least 14 countries established small arms licensed production agreements with some 46 countries (Abel, 2000, p. 88).

Value and volume

How many small arms are currently produced *per annum* by the global small arms industry, and how does this compare with the previous decade? What is the value and volume of small arms production relative to the production of its ammunition? Detailed information is difficult to obtain, however, a commercial market-analysis company, Forecast International, in their Ordnance and Munitions Forecast (October 2000) provides some estimates for past, current, and future volumes of small arms production.[9]

Volume: Forecast International (2000) estimates that more than 43 million military-style small arms of all types were produced in Europe, the Russian Federation, and all other countries, *excluding the US,* between 1980-99, and that 778,000 such weapons were produced during the year 2000. This figure is significantly less than the annual average production of 2.1 million during the period 1980-99 (see Table 1.1).

These estimates of global production have to be treated with a high degree of caution as it is not possible to verify their accuracy or reliability. In addition they exclude the production of commercial style small arms, including handguns and long guns, and thus may underestimate quite significantly the total number of small arms produced. Furthermore, many of the countries and companies identified as current small arms producers (see Appendix 1.1) are not included in these estimates. They also are not comparable with other figures which suggest that at least 150 million military-style small arms have been produced since 1945 (see Table 1.4).

Table 1.1   Estimated global production of military-style small arms (excluding US), 1980-2000 [1]

	Total 1980-99	Average: 1980-1999 [2] excluding the US	Total 2000
Military Sidearms (Pistols/Revolvers)			
Europe	6,292,200		272,000
Other countries (excl. US)	3,937,100		249,000
Total	10,229,300	511,465/year	521,000
Military Rifles			
Europe	20,102,700		65,700
Other countries (excl. US)	5,218,700		102,370
Total	25,321,400	1,266,070/year	168,070
Sub-Machine Guns			
Europe	2,242,300		14,700
Other countries (excl. US)	1,363,429		29,300
Total	3,605,729	180,286/year	44,000
Machine Guns			
Europe	2,965,700		23,440
Other countries (excl. US)	1,121,300		21,600
Total	4,087,000	204,350/year	45,040
Total	**43,243,429**	**2,162,171/year**	**778,110**

Notes: (1) Figures exclude the United States. (2) Includes sidearms (pistols and revolvers), rifles, sub-machine guns and machine guns.

Source: Forecast International, 2000

According to Forecast International (2000) more than 1.4 million military-style small arms of all types were produced for the armed forces in the US between 1970-99, including more than 650,000 of various models of the M-16 series assault rifle (FN Manufacturing and Colt's Manufacturing) and 240,000 of the M-9 pistol (Beretta). It is estimated that 37,000 small arms were produced for the US armed forces during 2000, which is significantly less than the average of 46,000 per year during the period 1970-1999. These estimates highlight the fact that the market for military-style small arms in the US has declined in recent years, and may continue to decline in the coming years.

The military market for small arms in the US may be in decline, but private sales are increasing.

While the military market for small arms in the US may be in decline, private sales are increasing. According to information from the Bureau of Alcohol, Tobacco and Firearms (BATF), nearly 127 million firearms[10] were produced in the US during the period 1970-98 with an average of 4.37 million firearms *per annum* (BATF, 2000a).

Given the premise that at least 40 million small arms were produced in Europe, the Russian Federation, and other countries (excluding the US) between 1980-98 (Forecast International); and that over 78 million firearms were manufactured in the US during the same period (BATF, 2000a), then it is possible to assume that at least 120 million small arms were produced worldwide during the period 1980-98, with an average of 6.3 million per year. Extrapolating these figures, it is estimated that at least 347 million small arms were produced worldwide between the end of World War II in 1945 and 2000 (STOCKPILES).[11]

Nearly 127 million firearms were produced in the US during the period 1970-98 with an average of 4,37 million firearms per annum.

Reflecting the recent downturn in production, it is estimated that, during the year 2000, around 4.3 million small arms were produced worldwide. This includes at least 3.5 million in the US— substantially down from its peak production period of over 5 million per year in 1993-94 (BATF, 2000a)—and roughly 800,000 from producers in Europe, the Russian Federation, and other countries, based on estimates from Forecast International.

Value: The value of global small arms production is also difficult to estimate, given the lack of detailed information from small arms producers. According to the latest information from the BATF,

The value of global small arms production in 2000 was at least US$ 1.4 billion.

the total value of small arms shipments (production) in the US in 1997 was US$ 1.2 billion, and the total number of new firearms produced in that year was 3.5 million. This means that the average price of each firearm produced in the US in 1997 was US$ 335.[12] Using this figure as a rough proxy, it is possible to assume that the value of global small arms production in 2000, based on the production of roughly 4.3 million units, was at least US$ 1.4 billion.

According to Forecast International (2000) the total international market for small arms ammunition has declined in the last ten or more years, and is considerably smaller than it was during the Cold War period.

With regard to ammunition, it is estimated that at least 15 billion units of all types and calibres were produced worldwide in 2000, a number which is significantly lower than the annual average of 21 billion units for the period 1980-99 (Forecast International, 2000). While it is difficult to verify the accuracy or reliability of these figures, they do suggest that the volume of production for small arms ammunition among producers in the US, Europe, and the Russian Federation beyond 2000 is likely to be lower than the average levels of production during the period 1980-99.

Table 1.2 Estimated global production of small arms ammunition, 1980-2000

Region	Figures in billions of units of all types and calibres		
	Total: 1980-1999	Annual Average: 1980-1999	Total: 2000
Europe/Russian Federation	204.9	10.2/year	8.7
US	105.5	5.2/year	1.0
Other countries (1)	115.6	5.7/year	5.7
Total	**426.0**	**21.1/year**	**15.4**

Note: (1) Includes all countries outside Europe, the Russian Federation, and the US.
Source: Forecast International, 2000

Again, according to Forecast International (2000), while the volume of production in Europe, the Russian Federation, and the US is expected to decline in the coming years, the volume of production in other countries is forecast to remain relatively constant in relation to the annual average level of production during the period 1980-99.

The value of global small arms ammunition production in 2000 was worth at least US$ 2.6 billion.

Detailed information, including estimates, on the value of global small arms ammunition production is much more difficult to obtain. The BATF estimates that the total value of small arms ammunition shipments (i.e. production) in the US in 1997 was US$ 859 million. If we assume, based on the estimates from Forecast International, that roughly 5 billion units of small arms ammunition were produced in the US in that year, then the estimated average cost of each unit of ammunition was 17 US cents. Using this figure as a rough proxy, it is possible to assume that the value of global small arms ammunition production in 2000, based on the production of at least 15 billion units, was worth at least US$ 2.6 billion.

These estimates highlight the fact that the value of global ammunition production was almost double the value of global small arms production. This is not surprising, and demonstrates the importance of focusing on the production and control of ammunition as a critical measure to control the trafficking in, and proliferation of, small arms.

The total value of small arms production, including ammunition, in 2000 was estimated at US$ 4 billion. However, this figure should be treated with caution as it may underestimate the value of global small arms production, given the lack of detailed information about major producers such as the Russian Federation and China.

While these figures seem, at first glance, to be inconsistent with the US$ 4-6 billion estimate of the annual global legal trade in small arms (LEGAL TRANSFERS), these apparent inconsistencies between global production and global trade can be explained as follows:

- The lack of detailed information on the value of production means that it is not possible to calculate the profit margin between the total value of global production and the total value of global export sales;
- Information on the value of small arms exports from a number of countries, including the US, is not consistent, and therefore may under- or overestimate the actual value of arms exports;
- In some countries, the figures for small arms exports reflect the value of authorizations rather than value of actual deliveries; and
- In some countries, the value of annual small arms exports includes categories of weapons that are not defined as small arms (e.g. missile launchers, howitzers, heavy-calibre ammunition).

The world's major small arms and ammunition producers

During the Cold War, the global market for small arms was dominated by the former Soviet Union and the US, leaving a few European countries (e.g. Belgium, Germany) to squabble over the 'spoils'. Since the mid-1990s, the market has become much more fragmented and thus competitive. Although the two former major producers retain their pole positions, the rest of the global market is now hotly contested by a number of established European actors, plus a group of other countries as far-ranging as Brazil, China, India, Israel, Pakistan, Singapore, South Africa, and Taiwan (*International Defence Review*, 1 October 2000).

Despite changes in the size and structure of the global small arms industry that have occurred in the last decade, it is still dominated by a handful of countries—Austria, Belgium, Brazil, China, France, Germany, Israel, Italy, the Russian Federation, Spain, Switzerland, the UK, and the US. These countries are consistently identified as the most important small arms producing countries worldwide.

The global market for small arms ammunition, which is worth more than the market for small arms, is dominated by a handful of companies in the US, the Russian Federation, and Europe, including Nordic Ammunition (Norway), Steyr-Mannlicher (Austria), Dynamit Nobel (Germany), Giat Industries (France), FN Herstal (Belgium), and Royal Ordnance (UK) (Forecast International, 2000). A group of other countries, including Brazil, China, Pakistan, and Singapore are also significant actors in the international market for small arms ammunition (Forecast International, 2000).

Based on a qualified assessment of existing official and unofficial information, it is possible to produce a preliminary ranking of 55 of the world's 95 known legal small arms producing countries based on the following criteria:
- Value and volume of production;
- Total employment;
- Range of small arms products, including ammunition;
- Number of companies; and
- Global distribution and use of products.

The global small arms industry can be divided into at least four categories—major producers, medium producers, small producers, and unassessed producers. At least three countries—China, the Russian Federation, and the US—can be identified as major producers.[13] Another 20 or so countries, mainly in Europe and Asia, can be identified as medium-sized producers.

Brazil and South Africa are the most significant medium-sized producers outside of Europe and Asia. Many of these medium-sized producers, including Austria, Belgium, Brazil, Czech Republic, France, Germany, Hungary, Italy, and Spain, are among the major foreign suppliers to the US domestic small arms market (Diaz, 1999).

Nearly 30 countries can be identified as small producers. Some of them (e.g. Yugoslavia) are

The US, the Russian Federation, and China are the world's major small arms producers.

Brazil and South Africa are the most significant medium-sized producers outside of Europe and Asia.

Table 1.3 **Ranking of world's small arms producers**

Major	Medium	Small	Unassessed*
China	Austria	Argentina	Albania
Russian Federation	Belgium	Armenia	Algeria
United States	Brazil	Australia	Bangladesh
	Bulgaria	Canada	Belarus
	Czech Republic	Chile	Bolivia
	Egypt	Colombia	Bosnia and Herzegovina
	France	Croatia	Burkina Faso
	Germany	Denmark	Cambodia
	Hungary	Finland	Cameroon
	India	Greece	Cuba
	Israel	Indonesia	Cyprus
	Italy	Japan	Dominican Republic
	Pakistan	Luxembourg	Ecuador
	Poland	Malaysia	Estonia
	Romania	Mexico	Ethiopia
	Singapore	Netherlands	Guatemala
	South Africa	New Zealand	Guinea
	South Korea	Norway	Iran
	Spain	Peru	Iraq
	Switzerland	Philippines	Kazakhstan
	Taiwan	Portugal	Kenya
	Turkey	Saudi Arabia	Lithuania
	United Kingdom	Slovakia	Macedonia
		Slovenia	Malta
		Sweden	Moldova
		Thailand	Monaco
		Ukraine	Morocco
		Venezuela	Myanmar
		Yugoslavia	Nigeria
			North Korea
			Papua New Guinea
			Paraguay
			Sudan
			Syria
			Tanzania
			Uganda
			United Arab Emirates
			Uruguay
			Vietnam
			Zimbabwe
3	**23**	**29**	**40**

* Inadequate information currently available to permit ranking.
Source: Appendix 1.1

potentially medium-sized, but are ranked as small producers because of a lack of detailed information about current production. In most cases, these countries produce only to meet their domestic requirements. At least 40 countries are identified as unassessed producers, because there is insufficient information to rank them.

Box 1.3 The Kalashnikov assault rifle: The world's most widely distributed weapon

The AK-47 is named after its designer, Mikhail T. Kalashnikov, a Red Army staff sergeant with limited formal engineering training, who began designs for a new assault rifle in 1941. It began mass production in 1947 at the Izhmash plant in Izhevsk, in the former Soviet Union, and entered into service in 1949.

While the term 'AK-47' is often used to mean the entire family of Kalashnikov-designed weapons, over the course of the last five decades numerous derivatives and copies have emerged. The Soviet AK-47 was modernized in 1959, becoming the AKM, and in 1974, becoming the AK-74 which, together with its derivatives, is today thought to be the world's most widely distributed single weapon model. There are more than 160 derivatives of the various models of the AK series. These include assault rifles, light machine guns, sub-machine guns, carbines, rifles, grenade-launching sub-machine guns, sporting rifles, sniper rifles, and shotguns in at least eleven calibres.

None of the designs underlying the AK family were ever patented until Izhmash finally attempted to do so in 1998. Thus, copies of the AK family have been produced in at least 19 countries, including China, Bulgaria, Egypt, Finland, Yugoslavia, and Iraq. The original AK series assault rifle is no longer produced in its country of origin, and no new AK series rifles have been manufactured by the Izhmash plant since 1995, although the plant is producing various sporting and commercial derivatives, including shotguns. The AK series rifle is still produced in Bulgaria, China, and Romania (*International Defence Review*, 1 October 2000).

Estimates of the total number of AKs in circulation range as high as 100 million (*National Defense*, January 2000). According to a recent study (Walter, 1999), more than 70 million AK series assault rifles have been produced worldwide. AKs and their derivatives are held in the inventories of more than 80 countries; the Russian Federation armed forces alone possess ten different versions (Jane's Infantry Weapons, 2000-01). The national flag of Mozambique, as well as six national coats of arms, bear an AK image.

Due to their ease of production, their excellent performance under adverse conditions, and especially their ease of use and disassembly, the models of the AK family have achieved unparalleled levels of availability on the global arms market. The simplicity of Kalashnikov's design has been exploited to devastating effect; with only nine moving parts, this 4.5kg assault rifle is easily handled by child soldiers. Such is the ubiquity of the AK that it has become a symbol for resistance and guerrilla movements worldwide, including Afghanistan's mujahideen, the African National Congress, the Irish Republican Army, UNITA, and the Kosovo Liberation Army.

Estimates of the mean price of a Kalashnikov on the black market range from US$ 200-1,000.[14] According to Russian Federation sources, the current export price of an Izhmash AK-74 is US$ 100; this is still two to three times more expensive than those produced in Asia (e.g. China). In areas of high availability, such as Southern Africa, the price can drop to as low as US$15—the equivalent of one large sack of maize (Boutwell and Klare, 2000a).

Sources: Kenkel, 2000a; Walter, 1999

The AK-47 and its derivatives is the world's most widely distributed single weapon model. Estimates of the total number of AKs in circulation range as high as 100 million.

Wth only nine moving parts, the AK-47 assault rifle is easily handled by child soldiers.

Popular small arms products

In recent years, there has been a noticeable increase in the number of types and models of small arms that are currently available on the international market. According to Terry Gander, the editor of *Jane's Infantry Weapons,* 'as a new millennium begins the number of infantry weapons types and models seems to be expanding ... the infantry weapon scene has probably never been busier ... the number of products on offer is seemingly greater than ever' (*International Defence Review,* 1 October 2000).

Austria, Belgium, Brazil, China, France, Germany, Israel, Italy, the Russian Federation, Spain, Switzerland, the UK, and the US dominate the global market for both commercial and military-style small arms.

This section provides information on a selection of the most popular types of small arms products, both legal and illicit, that are in service with government forces and in the hands of rebel groups and/or private individuals. It focuses specifically on handguns (pistols and revolvers), rifles, sub-machine guns, and machine guns. Light weapons will be examined in subsequent editions of the *Small Arms Survey*.

Legal products

Despite the lack of detailed information about small arms producers, there is a considerable amount of public information about the types of small arms that are legally available for sale to companies and private individuals and/or that are in service with various countries' security forces. For example annual publications, such as *Jane's Infantry Weapons, Jane's Ammunition Handbook, Jane's World Armies* and the *IISS Military Balance,* together with other specialist defence publications (e.g. *Military Technology's World Defence Almanac*) provide extensive details of the various types of small arms in the inventories of national defence forces. Information on the most popular commercial products for sale to private individuals is readily available from the companies themselves, as well as in a number of commercial publications, such as *Guns & Ammo, American Rifleman,* and *Small Arms Review.*

The world's most popular military-style handgun, in terms of sheer numbers, is the Makarov 9mm pistol, produced by the Izhmash plant in the Russian Federation for at least 50 years.

A selection of the world's most popular small arms is presented in Table 1.4. Based on current information and research, it is clear that the world's most popular small arms products, in terms of numbers, distribution, and use originate from a relatively small number of countries. Austria, Belgium, Brazil, China, France, Germany, Israel, Italy, the Russian Federation, Spain, Switzerland, the UK, and the US dominate the global market for both commercial and military-style small arms. Another group of countries, namely the Czech Republic, India, Pakistan, South Africa, Singapore, and Taiwan are also regarded as significant or emerging actors in the international small arms market.

Handguns (pistols/revolvers): The global market for handguns (pistols/revolvers) is dominated by a number of European and US companies. The world's most popular military-style handgun, in terms of sheer numbers, is the Makarov 9mm pistol, produced by the Izhmash plant in the Russian Federation for at least 50 years. However, the 9mm Browning Series pistol, produced by FN Herstal (Belgium), is the most widely distributed handgun. Glock (Austria), Beretta (Italy and US) and Sturm, Ruger & Co (US) are some of the world's largest suppliers of handguns, both for the military and commercial markets.

Assault rifles: The market for assault rifles is dominated by three weapons—the Kalashnikov AK series (The Russian Federation), the M-16 series (US), and the FN-FAL (Belgium). Rivals to the three 'giants' include the following rifles: G3 (Germany), SIG 540 Series (Switzerland), AUG (Austria), the Galil (Israel), and the FAMAS (France). Other new, or emerging producers of assault rifles include Brazil, China, the Czech Republic, India, Singapore, South Africa, and Taiwan (*International Defence Review,* 1 October 2000).

Sub-machine guns: The world's most popular sub-machine guns (SMG) are produced by companies in Germany, Israel, and the UK. The 9mm Sterling SMG was originally produced by the

Box 1.4   The Uzi sub-machine gun

The standard 9mm Uzi sub-machine gun was designed in the years following Israel's wars for independence. Regular production began in 1953, and it entered into regular service two years later (Jane's Infantry Weapons, 2000-2001). The Uzi is produced by Israel Military Industries (IMI) near Tel Aviv. A miniature version dubbed the 'mini-Uzi', as well as a semi-automatic model, have been in production since 1987; the even smaller 'micro-Uzi' entered production in 1994. IMI also produces a pistol based on the Uzi design (Jane's Infantry Weapons, 2000-2001).

Throughout its 47-year history, the Uzi has been either copied or produced under license in several countries. Belgium's FN Herstal ceased licensed production in the 1970s. The 9mm S-1, a copy of the standard Uzi, was produced by LIW of South Africa as a reserve weapon for that country's National Defence Forces. China's Norinco produces an unlicensed Uzi-based 9mm SMG for export. The 9mm ERO SMG produced by Croatia's RH-Alan is in essence an unlicensed copy of the standard Uzi. RH-Alan's 9mm MINI ERO appears to be an amalgam of 'mini' and 'micro' versions of the Uzi. There are also reports of the unlicensed production of Uzi-type weapons in Eastern Europe. IMI has authorized the assembly of Uzis in Estonia (*International Defence Review*, 1 March 1994).

Estimates of the number of Uzis produced are made difficult by its copying and unlicensed production. IMI itself claims that 1 million standard Uzis have been produced in Israel alone since 1953. A recent estimate suggests that a total of 1.5 million units of the entire Uzi family have been produced (*Jane's Defence Weekly*, 3 November 1999). However, estimates of total global production range as high as 10 million (Renner, 1999). IMI claims to produce 20,000 units a year across all models. The standard 9mm Uzi is in service in at least 50 countries, while the mini-Uzi is in service in Israel and in eight other countries (Jane's Infantry Weapons, 2000-2001).

Given their high fire rate, reliability, and the ease with which they can be concealed, Uzis are popular with soldiers in non-combat roles, special forces, commandos and law enforcement agencies. The price of an Uzi varies widely. In the US, where a ban on automatic weapons is in effect, pre-ban Uzis are valued at no less than US$ 1,300. In the war-zones of Africa, they can cost at least US$ 500. In Western Europe, governments, the sole legal buyers, pay between US$ 1,100-1,700, while civilians pay half that sum on the black market. Forecast International estimates that the current price for the latest model Uzi is US$ 708.

Source: Kenkel, 2000b

Estimates of total global production of the entire Uzi family range as high as 10 million.

Sterling Armament Company (UK) but the rights were bought by Royal Ordnance (BAE Systems) in 1988. It is no longer in production in the UK but has been produced under license in India and Canada and is in service in more than 90 countries (Jane's Infantry Weapons, 2000-2001). The 9mm MP5 SMG is produced by Heckler & Koch (Germany). It is also produced under license in Greece, Iran, Mexico, Pakistan, Saudi Arabia, Turkey, and the UK and is in service in over 50 countries (Heckler & Koch Company Information).

Machine guns: The world's most popular machine guns are manufactured by companies in Belgium, Germany, the Russian Federation, and the US. The FN 7.62mm MAG is manufactured by FN Herstal (Belgium). It is also produced under license in Argentina, Egypt, India, Singapore, the UK, and the US. An estimated 150,000 - 200,000 have been produced and are in service in over 90 countries (Jane's Infantry Weapons, 2000-2001). The 7.62mm MG1/2/3 series is manufactured by Rheinmetall (Germany). It is produced under license in Greece, Iran, Italy, Pakistan, Portugal, Spain, and Turkey and is in service in 13 countries.

The Browning M2 heavy machine gun is manufactured by Saco Defense (US). It is produced under license by FN Herstal (Belgium) and Manroy Engineering (UK), and is in service in over 30

The world's most popular machine guns are manufactured by companies in Belgium, Germany, the Russian Federation, and the US.

Table 1.4 The world's most popular small arms products

	Original Producer	Licensed Producers	Number Produced	In Service
Handguns				
FN 9mm Browning Series	FN Herstal (Belgium)	Argentina, Bulgaria, Canada, India, Israel, China, Venezuela	> 1.3 million	64 countries
Glock 9mm Series 17	Glock (Austria)		> 1 million	> 50 countries
Beretta 9mm 92 Series	Beretta (Italy/US)	Brazil, Egypt, France	n/a	> 15 countries
Makarov 9mm	Izhmash (Russian Fed.)	Bulgaria, China	20 million	14 countries
Assault Rifles				
Kalashnikov AK Series	Izhmash (Russia)	19 countries incl. China, Bulgaria, Egypt, Finland, Yugoslavia, Iraq	70-100 million	> 80 countries
M-16 Series	Colt's Manuf. (US)	Canada, Philippines, South Korea, Singapore	> 7 million	67 countries
G3	Hechler & Koch (Germany)	18 countries incl. Myanmar, Greece, Iran, Mexico, Pakistan, Portugal, Saudi Arabia, Sweden, Turkey, UK	> 7 million	> 64 countries
FN-FAL	FN Herstal (Belgium)	15 countries incl. Argentina, Australia, Brazil, India, Indonesia, Mexico, South Africa, UK, US, Venezuela	5-7 million	94 countries
AUG	Steyr-Mannlicher (Austria)	Australia, Malaysia		24 countries
SIG 540	SIG Arms (Switzerland)	Chile, France, Portugal		> 20 countries
Galil	IMI (Israel)	Estonia, Italy, South Africa	> 500,000	15 countries
FAMAS F1	Giat Industries (France)		400,000-500,000	6 countries
Sub-Machine Guns				
Uzi	IMI (Israel)	Belgium, China, Croatia, Estonia, South Africa	1-10 million	> 50 countries
Sterling	Sterling Armament Co.(UK)	Canada, India		> 90 countries
MP5	Hechler & Koch (Germany)	Greece, Iran, Mexico, Pakistan, Saudi Arabia, Turkey, UK		< 50 countries
Machine Guns				
7.62 MAG	FN Herstal (Belgium)	Australia, Argentina, Egypt, India, Israel, Singapore, Taiwan, UK	150,000-200,000	> 90 countries
7.62 MG1/2/3	Rheinmetall (Germany)	Greece, Iran, Italy, Pakistan, Portugal, Spain, Turkey		13 countries
Browning M2	Saco Defense (US)	Belgium, UK		> 30 countries
HK21 Series	Heckler & Koch (Germany)	Greece, Mexico, Portugal, Thailand		14 countries
7.62 RPK	State Factories (Russian Fed.)	Bulgaria, Iraq, Romania		> 30 countries

Sources: Ezell, 1995; Ezell, 1988; Gander, 2000; Gander and Cutshaw, 2000; Reed, 2000; Renner, 1999; Brom and Shapir, 2000; Heyman, 2000; Forecast International, 2000; OMEGA Foundation Company Database; Company Information.

Box 1.5 Popular small arms in South Africa[15]

As of August 1999, there were 4.5 million registered small arms in South Africa, excluding those weapons in service with the military and police. The most popular type is the 9mm parabellum pistol, with 155,517 licensed in 1998, and over half a million in total licensed between 1994 and 1998. Other popular types include the 9mm short pistol, the 7.65mm pistol, the .38 special revolver, and the 6.35mm pistol (Chetty, 2000, p. 37). The most popular makes of small arms, in terms of numbers licensed to civilians, are manufactured in Brazil, China, Spain, South Africa, the Czech Republic, and the US (Chetty, 2000, p. 38). Foreign types of small arms, especially those made by Norinco (China) dominate the local civilian market.

Table 1.5 Top manufacturers of civilian firearms, South Africa, 1997-99

Year	1st	2nd	3rd	4th	5th
1997	Lorcin 107,920	Norinco 55,453	CZ 16,837	Rossi 10,963	Vektor 8,685
1998	Norinco 72,669	Lorcin 39,451	Astra 18,750	CZ 16,641	Vektor 10,960
1999*	Norinco 41,574	CZ 12,469	Lorcin 10,952	Vektor 6,123	Astra 3,416

Note: * 1 January - mid-November 1999
Source: Chetty, 2000

countries (Jane's Infantry Weapons, 2000-2001). The HK21 series machine gun was originally produced by Heckler & Koch (Germany). It is no longer produced in Germany, but has been produced under license in Portugal, Greece, Mexico, and Thailand and is in use in 14 countries (Renner, 1999). The 7.62mm RPK light machine gun is manufactured by various state factories in the Russian Federation. It is also produced under license in Bulgaria, Iraq, and Romania and is in service in at least 30 countries (Jane's Infantry Weapons, 2000-2001).

Illicit products

Information on the most popular small arms products in illicit hands—whether used by rebel forces or criminals—is obviously much more difficult to obtain. However, in some countries, such as Brazil and South Africa, the police publish information on the types and makes of illicit small arms that are seized or collected as a result of police operations. In the US, annual figures on the types of weapons used to commit crimes provide some indication of the most popular 'crime guns', some, not all, of which are illicit.

South Africa: There are no accurate figures for the numbers and types of illicit small

Table 1.6 Illicit small arms seized by the South African Police, 1994-99

Firearms	Total	% of Total	Annual Average
Rifles (1)	13,436	12	2,239
AK-47s	6,121	6	1,020
Pistols (2)	52,802	50	8,800
Revolvers	17,026	16	2,838
Homemade Weapons	16,781	16	2,797
Total	**106,166**	**100**	**17,694**

Ammunition			
7.62mm all types	284,309	21	47,385
Other	1,040,842	79	173,474
Total	**1,325,151**	**100**	**220,859**

Notes: (1) Includes all rifles (except AK-47s), shotguns, sub-machine guns, and carbines. (2) Includes machine pistols.
Source: Chetty, 2000

arms in circulation in South Africa. However, it is estimated that there are 500,000 illicit firearms in circulation, of which at least 200,000 have been 'lost' by the state, including theft from state armouries (e.g. SANDF, SAPS). Other estimates of the number of illicit firearms in circulation range from 400,000 to 8 million (Oosthuysen, 1996).

Between 1994 and 1999, the Illegal Firearm Investigation Unit of the South African Police Service (SAPS) seized over 106,000 illicit small arms, an average of over 17,000 *per annum*. Home-made weapons account for 16 per cent of the total. Handguns (pistols and revolvers) account for 66 per cent of the total number of illicit firearms seized by the police. The numbers and proportions of handguns (e.g. pistols) have been increasing in recent years. These trends are similar to the trends for small arms apprehended by the police in Rio de Janeiro, Brazil.

The total number of illicit small arms seized by the police has increased quite significantly since 1997. It is unclear whether this trend is related to better reporting, police efficiency, or an actual increase in the total number of illicit weapons in circulation. The number of small arms lost or reported stolen increased from 15,309 in 1994 to 30,220 in 1998, an increase of 97 per cent. The total number of small arms lost and/or reported stolen between 1994 and 1998 is 112,692. During the same period 63,703 (56 per cent) were found or recovered (Chetty, 2000, p. 40).

The type of small arms used/preferred by criminals depends on the type of crime. In most countries in Southern Africa, including South Africa, handguns (pistols and revolvers) are the weapons of choice in most crimes, although assault rifles tend to be used in specific crimes, such as cash-in-transit heists. For example, during 1998 handguns were used in 49 per cent of all reported murders, and 85 per cent of all robberies (Chetty, 2000, p. 18).

Brazil:[16] A non-governmental organization, the Institute for Religious Studies (ISER), in partnership with the police force in the state of Rio de Janeiro, Brazil has analyzed the numbers and types of small arms apprehended by the police since 1990. These include weapons used in crimes, weapons from security companies that have closed down or gone bankrupt, illicit weapons, or weapons that are legal but not allowed to be visibly displayed/carried.[17] Currently, the police database in the Division of Weapon and Explosive Control[18] contains records for a total of 72,769 weapons for the period January 1990-August 1999.[19] In analyzing the data, a number of trends are evident.

Over 80 per cent of the small arms apprehended by the police in Rio are handguns: 65 per cent revolvers and 15 per cent pistols. This contradicts the prevailing perception in Brazil that automatic

Figure 1.3   Apprehended small arms by country of origin, Rio de Janeiro, 1990-99

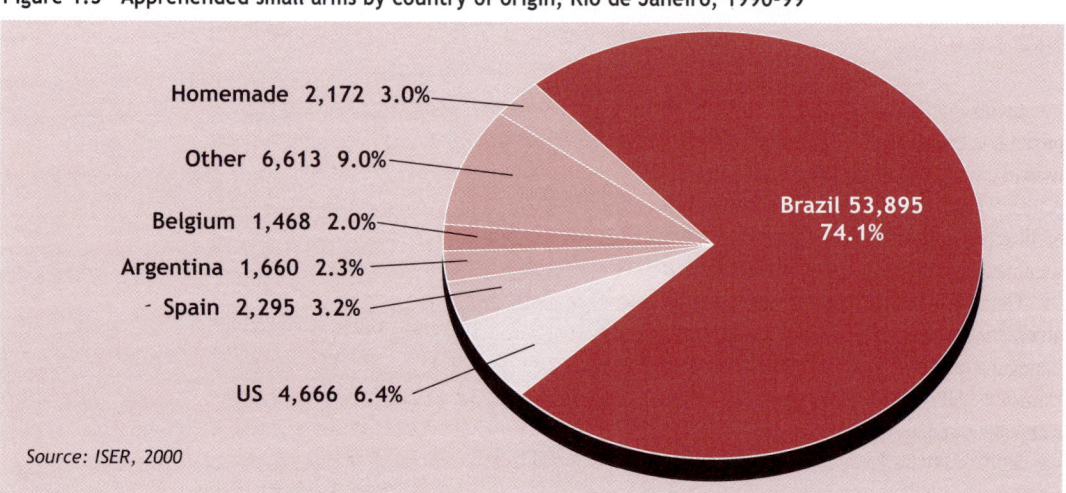

Homemade 2,172 3.0%

Other 6,613 9.0%

Belgium 1,468 2.0%

Argentina 1,660 2.3%

Spain 2,295 3.2%

US 4,666 6.4%

Brazil 53,895
74.1%

Source: ISER, 2000

weapons, such as assault rifles, are responsible for most of the crimes committed in the country. Automatic weapons do obviously exist, and are used in certain crimes, but they are a minority of the weapons apprehended by the police in Rio.

Nearly 75 per cent of small arms apprehended by the Rio police are made in Brazil. This evidence contradicts another perception that the weapons used in crime tend to be foreign weapons illegally smuggled into the country, whereas the arms produced and sold legally in Brazil are used mostly for purposes of self-protection. The other major supplier countries include Argentina, Belgium, Spain, and the US. At least three per cent of the weapons apprehended are home-made, suggesting the presence of a significant home-made weapons industry in Brazil and in surrounding countries.[20] Most of the revolvers (85 per cent) that are apprehended are manufactured in Brazil, whereas pistols and other types of small arms are more divided between domestic and foreign producers. Sizeable proportions of the apprehended automatic weapons are manufactured in the US.

Half of the small arms apprehended by police are manufactured by two Brazilian companies: Taurus (27.1 per cent) and Rossi (23.5 per cent). In addition, there are also other local and foreign manufacturers that account for a significant amount of the weapons apprehended by the police (see Table 1.7).

Nearly 75 per cent of small arms apprehended by the Rio police are made in Brazil.

Table 1.7   Apprehended weapons by manufacturer, Rio de Janeiro, 1990-99

Company	Country	Number	Per cent
Taurus	Brazil	19,687	27.1
Rossi	Brazil	17,130	23.5
US Repeating Arms	US	8,891	12.2
INA	Brazil	2,122	2.9
Beretta	Brazil, Italy, US	1,535	2.1
Smith & Wesson	US	1,370	1.9
Colt's Manufacturing	US	1,135	1.6
Castelo	Brazil	1,108	1.5
FN Herstal	Argentina, Belgium, Brazil, Mexico, US, Venezuela, and others	980	1.3
IMBEL	Brazil	912	1.3
Other		17,899	24.6
Total		72,769	100.0

Source: ISER, 2000

Crime guns in the US: The 1999 Crime Gun Trace Report in the US issued by the BATF provides detailed information regarding the types of firearms (handguns and long guns) that are used to commit crimes in that country. According to information for both 1998 and 1999, nearly 13 per cent of crime guns were manufactured outside the US (BATF, 2000b, p. 6). More than 20 per cent of all small arms sold in the US in 1998 were imported (BATF, 2000b). This suggests that local guns were more likely to be used to commit crimes than foreign guns.

The most popular type of handgun used to commit crimes in the United States is the 9mm semi-automatic pistol. This type of weapon is used in more than 20 per cent of all crimes committed with handguns in the US. The top domestic manufacturer of crime handguns is Smith & Wesson.[21] The company's .38 revolver is the top crime handgun, used in nearly six per cent of all crimes committed with handguns during 1999. The company's 9mm semi-automatic pistol is the 5th most popular crime handgun. The major foreign manufacturers of crime handguns include Taurus of Brazil (.38 revolver), Glock of Austria (9mm semi-automatic pistol), and Rossi of Brazil (.38 revolver) (BATF, 2000b).

Table 1.8   Handguns: top US crime guns by manufacturer, calibre, and type, 1999

No.	Manufacturer	Calibre	Type	Number of Crime Guns	Percentage of Crime Guns
1	Smith & Wesson	0.38	Revolver	2,968	5.9
2	Lorcin Engineering	0.380	Semi-Automatic Pistol	1,911	3.8
3	Sturm, Ruger & Co.	9mm	Semi-Automatic Pistol	1,636	3.2
4	Raven Arms	0.25	Semi-Automatic Pistol	1,394	2.8
5	Smith & Wesson	9mm	Semi-Automatic Pistol	1,376	2.7
	All Handguns			**50,676**	**100.0**

Source: Bureau of Alcohol, Tobacco and Firearms, 2000

The most popular type of long gun used to commit crimes in the United States is the 12GA Shotgun. This type of weapon is used in more than 35 per cent of all crimes committed with long guns in the US. The top domestic manufacturer of crime long guns is Mossberg. The company's 12GA Shotgun is used in over nine per cent of all crimes committed with long guns. Norinco of China is the most common foreign supplier of crime long guns. The company's 7.62mm rifle is used in six per cent of all crimes committed with long guns (BATF, 2000b).

Table 1.9   Long guns: top US crime guns by manufacturer, calibre, and type, 1999

No.	Manufacturer	Calibre	Type	Number of Crime Guns	Percentage of Crime Guns
1	Mossberg	12GA	Shotgun	1,287	9.3
2	Marlin	0.22	Rifle	907	6.6
3	Norinco (China)	7.62mm	Rifle	873	6.3
4	Remington Arms	12GA	Shotgun	705	5.1
5	Winchester	12GA	Shotgun	639	4.6
	All Long Guns			**13,822**	**100.0**

Source: Bureau of Alcohol, Tobacco and Firearms, 2000

Regional survey of small arms producers

The global small arms industry is not homogenous, and the production of small arms and ammunition varies considerably between countries. Some countries have been producing small arms for more than a century, while others have only recently established production facilities for the manufacture of small arms, components, and/or ammunition. In some countries, production takes place in state arsenals or state-owned companies, while in other countries it occurs in private companies that are often part of larger, local, or multi-national defence-industrial companies.

Production in some countries occurs in modern, technologically advanced, manufacturing facilities using sophisticated production processes, while in others it occurs in small, craft facilities using fairly basic production processes. Furthermore, the quality of information, both official and unofficial, concerning small arms production in specific countries and regions also varies considerably. In some countries there is little or no information, or the information is of such poor quality that it is unclear whether production is taking place at all. As a result, it is difficult to make generalizations about the nature and scope of the global arms industry.

Based on the distribution of small arms producing countries listed in Appendix 1.1, this section undertakes a regional survey of small arms producers, and provides some case studies of particular countries and companies. The case studies are illustrative rather than comprehensive and are intended to highlight some of the general and specific patterns and characteristics of the global small arms industry. While it is not possible for this regional survey to be comprehensive, given the constraints of existing information, those companies, countries, and regions that are not covered in this chapter will be dealt with in future editions of the *Survey*.

The Americas

North and Central America: All the countries of North America—Canada, Mexico, and the US—have well-established domestic small arms industries. Most countries in Central America do not possess a domestic small arms production capability, given the low levels of economic and industrial development in many parts of the region. Guatemala has a state-owned small arms production facility in Alta Verapaz (*Jane's Sentinel Security Assessment*, 11 June 1999). There is some uncertainty regarding current production in Cuba and the Dominican Republic. In Central America, most production of small arms takes place in state-owned companies, while in North America, with the exception of Mexico, small arms are manufactured by private companies.

Map 1.2 Small arms producers: North and Central America

CANADA

US

MEXICO

CUBA

DOMINICAN REPUBLIC

GUATEMALA

■ Known producers

■ Uncertainty regarding current production

Source: Appendix 1.1

The United States: The US, together with China and the Russian Federation, is one of the world's major producers of small arms. Over 300 companies, all privately-owned, serve both the commercial and military small arms markets. According to the US Department of Commerce there were 191 small arms companies in the US in 1997, of which only 55 had 20 or more employees. In the same year, there were 113 ammunition companies in the US, of which only 19 had more than 20 employees (Department of Commerce, 1997a; 1997b). Three states alone—Connecticut, Massachusetts, and New York—were the largest domestic producers (by volume) of small arms, accounting for 77 per cent of the total volume of domestic small arms production between 1975 and 1997 (Violence Policy Center, 2000).

The small arms industry is not a particularly significant sector of the US economy. Total employment amounted to 16,770 people in 1997, comprising 9,907 in small arms producers, and 6,863 in ammunition producers. The total value of production (shipments) was US$ 2.059 billion (US$ 1.2 billion for small arms and US$ 859 million for ammunition) (Department of Commerce, 1997a; 1997b). Thus, the small arms business is worth about US$ 2 billion a year to the American economy.[22]

The small arms business is worth about US$ 2 billion a year—not a particularly significant amount—to the American economy.

*Between 1980-98,
a total of 78
million small arms
were produced
in the US—
an average of 4.1
million per annum.*

According to a recent study, the domestic small arms industry in the US is 'like a pyramid in terms of companies, and an upside-down pyramid in terms of volume ... a few giant manufacturers make most of the guns ... [and an] assortment of many other small manufacturers make the rest, some as few as one gun a year' (Diaz, 1999, p. 23).

The BATF's Firearms Manufacturing and Export Report (1998b) provides detailed statistics on the numbers of small arms manufactured and exported by US companies. In 1998 a total of 3.7 million small arms were locally produced, of which less than six per cent (215,096) were exported. More than 1.2 million (34 per cent) of the total number of firearms produced were handguns (pistols/revolvers), the most popular being the 9mm pistol (284,374). Over 1.3 million rifles (36 per cent) were produced. Total domestic production in 1998 increased slightly over the previous year, but was significantly lower than the peaks of over five million *per annum* in 1993 and 1994, which were the highest levels of production since 1990 (BATF, 2000a). Between 1980 and 1998 a total of 78 million small arms were produced in the US, with an average of 4.1 million *per annum* (BATF, 2000a).

Figure 1.4   Total numbers of small arms produced (US), 1998

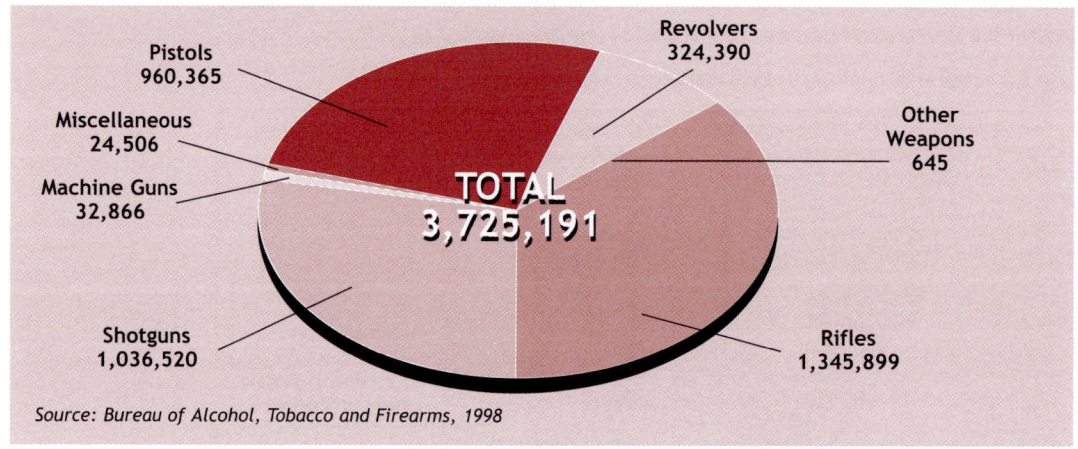

Source: Bureau of Alcohol, Tobacco and Firearms, 1998

*In the US, Sturm,
Ruger & Co is the
largest producer
of pistols and
rifles. Smith &
Wesson is the
largest producer
of revolvers while
Remington Arms
is the largest
producer of
shotguns.*

Three companies constitute the core of the US military's small arms industrial base. They are Saco Defense (part of General Dynamics), Colt's Manufacturing, and FN Manufacturing (part of Groupe Herstal of Belgium). Saco Defense produces the M-2, M-19, and M-60 machine guns. Colt's Manufacturing produces the M-4 carbine and the M-16 rifle. FN Manufacturing produces the M-16 rifle, the M-249 light machine gun, and the M-240 medium machine gun (Jane's Infantry Weapons, 2000-2001).

The commercial small arms market in the US is dominated by a few well-known and well-established firms, such as Sturm, Ruger & Co., Smith & Wesson, Beretta US Corp. (a subsidiary of Beretta of Italy), The Marlin Firearms Co., Remington Arms Co., US Repeating Arms Co. (part of Groupe Herstal of Belgium), H&R 1871, and O.F. Mossberg & Sons (Diaz, 1999). Sturm, Ruger & Co. is the largest producer of pistols and rifles in the US. Smith & Wesson is the largest producer of revolvers, while Remington Arms is the largest producer of shotguns (see Figure 1.5). The ranking of major domestic producers has not changed significantly in recent years. In 1995 the major producers were: pistols (Smith & Wesson); revolvers (Smith & Wesson); rifles (Sturm, Ruger & Co.); and shotguns (Remington Arms) (BATF, 1995).

A number of foreign producers are also major suppliers to the US domestic market. At least 1 million firearms (handguns, rifles, and shotguns) were imported into the country during 1998. During the period 1980-98, foreign suppliers accounted for over 20 per cent of the total sales of firearms in the US domestic market (BATF, 2000a). The leading suppliers of handguns (pistols and

Figure 1.5 Major US domestic small arms producers, 1998

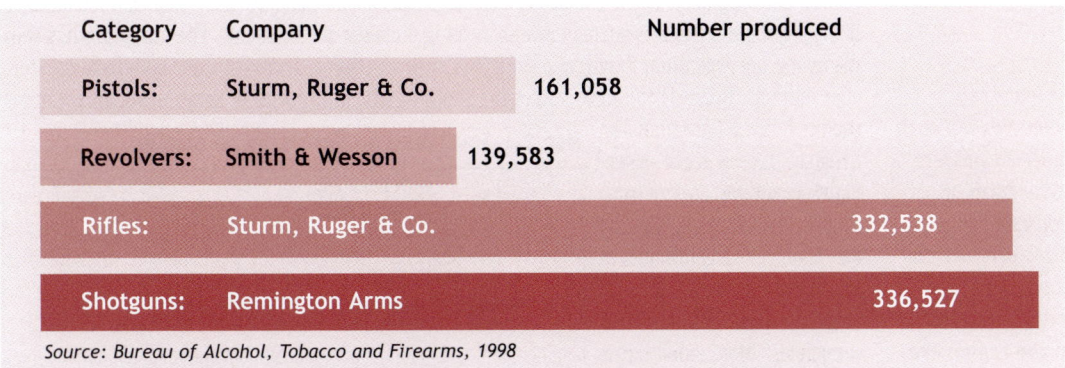

Category	Company	Number produced
Pistols:	Sturm, Ruger & Co.	161,058
Revolvers:	Smith & Wesson	139,583
Rifles:	Sturm, Ruger & Co.	332,538
Shotguns:	Remington Arms	336,527

Source: Bureau of Alcohol, Tobacco and Firearms, 1998

revolvers) to the United States between 1991-96 were Austria, Belgium, Brazil, Germany, Italy, and Spain. China was one of the major suppliers of rifles (e.g. SKS assault rifles) to the US during the period 1987-94, accounting for more than 40 per cent of total US rifle imports, including military-style weapons (Diaz, 1999, p.73).

Most military-style small arms ammunition is produced at state-owned plants, which are usually operated by private sector companies. Alliant Techsystems (ATK) manages the Lake City Army Ammunition Plant in Independence, Missouri. The plant, which supplies all the US Army's requirements for small-calibre ammunition, has the capacity to produce an average of 450 million rounds of small calibre ammunition per year (*Defence Systems Daily*, 16 August 2000). ATK is the largest supplier of small arms ammunition to the US military and one of the largest small arms companies in the world (SIPRI, 2000).

ATK is the largest supplier of small arms ammunition to the US military and one of the largest small arms companies in the world.

Primex Technologies, which was recently acquired by General Dynamics for US$ 520 million, is also one of America's most important small arms ammunition producers. ATK and Primex dominate the US military market for small arms ammunition. ATK employs more than 6,000 people, and in 1999 had a turnover of over US$ 1 billion (Extel Cards Database, 2000). However, its small arms business is worth approximately US$ 100 million *per annum* (*Defence Systems Daily*, 16 August 2000). Primex employs more than 2,800 people and in 1999 had a turnover of US$ 544 million, of which approximately half came from its arms business (SIPRI, 2000).

Canada: Canada's defence industry has experienced a dramatic process of restructuring and consolidation in recent years (Edgar and Haglund, 1995). The manufacture of small arms is concentrated in a few companies, including Diemaco (assault rifles), Para-Ordnance (pistols), Savage Arms (sniper rifles), and Armament Technology (tactical rifles). Diemaco is the major supplier of small arms to the Canadian Department of National Defence. Most small arms for domestic purposes are produced under license to American (e.g. Colt's Manufacturing) or European (e.g. FN Herstal of Belgium) companies. SNC Industrial Technologies, Royal Canadian Cartridge and Munitions Corp., Challenger Ammunition, and Wolf Bullets are Canada's major small arms ammunition producers.[23] SNC is the major supplier of small arms ammunition to the Canadian armed forces, and is a major exporter (NISAT, 2000).

Canada's SNC is the major supplier of small arms ammunition to the country's armed forces, and is a major exporter.

Mexico: Mexico has a relatively small, but well-established domestic defence industry. Various types of small arms, some of them of indigenous design, have been manufactured since the beginning of the 20th century. The country's major small arms producers include the state-owned Fabrica de Armas Nacionales (rifles) and the Departamento de Industrias Militares. Private companies include Productos Mendoza (machine guns) and Industrias Technos Aquila.[24]

South America: At least ten countries in South America possess some form of domestic small arms production capability. Some countries, such as Ecuador, manufacture only ammunition and, in many cases, production is geared towards meeting domestic requirements. The major producers in the region are Argentina, Brazil, and Chile, where production is geared towards both local and foreign markets. Brazil is the most successful South American exporter of small arms. In countries such as Bolivia, Paraguay, and Uruguay there is some uncertainty regarding current production of small arms. With the exception of Argentina and Brazil, most production of small arms takes place in state-owned companies. Most small arms products are manufactured under license from European companies such as FN Herstal (Belgium), SIG (Switzerland), and Beretta (Italy).

Map 1.3 Small arms producers: South America

Legend

Known producers

Uncertainty regarding current production

Source: Appendix 1.1

Argentina: One of Latin America's oldest and largest small arms producers, Argentina has been manufacturing small arms since the 1930s (Dreyfus, 2000; Solingen, 1998). During the 1980s, there were more than 20 private sector small arms producers, in addition to the various production facilities that were part of Dirección General de Fabricaciones Militares (DGFM) (sec box 1.6).

The major private producers include Bersa, Rexio, and Mahely Ind. & Co. All three companies are located in Buenos Aires Province and produce a wide range of products for civilian and military markets. A large number of private sector producers went out of business in the late 1980s and early 1990s, brought down by the collapse of Argentina's traditional arms export markets (Middle East), the liberalization of the Argentine economy, and the introduction of stricter domestic gun control legislation.

According to industry sources, during the 1980s and early 1990s, the private sector industry produced over 300,000 units *per annum,* but since 1994, the industry has been producing an average of only 24,000 units a year (Dreyfus, 2000). Argentina's state-owned small arms industry, which is part of DGFM, is currently in deep crisis and its future is unclear (see Box 1.6).

Brazil is South America's largest small arms producer and has been manufacturing for both local and export markets since the early 1960s (Solingen, 1998). Its defence industry emerged as one of the major developing countries' arms producers in the 1970s and 1980s, accounting for eight per cent of the global arms market (*Jane's Defence Weekly*, 21 June 2000). In the last decade the local defence industry has been struggling to survive, largely as a result of the loss of its major export markets in the Middle East. Many of the major companies have disappeared or exited the defence business in the last few years.

Box 1.6 Dirección General de Fabricaciones Militares (DGFM)

In 1941 the Argentine Government created the state-owned military industrial complex, Dirección General de Fabricaciones Militares (DGFM). The DGFM was placed under the control of the Army Command, and, by the early 1990s, included 12 factories, whose output was directly linked to meet the requirements of the Argentinian armed forces.

In 1946 the first production plant for small arms, Fabrica Militar de Armas Poratiles Domingo Mattheu (FMAP), was established and began to produce Mauser carbines and Colt pistols. During the 1950s and 1960s, the FMAP produced various types of small arms under license from FN Herstal (Belgium) and Beretta (Italy). Until the early 1990s production was concentrated in three DGFM factories: FMAP (small arms) located in Rosario, Sante Fe; Fabrica Militar Fray Luis Beltran (ammunition) located in Fray Luis Beltran, Sante Fe; and Fabrica Militar Rio Tercero (light weapons) located in Rio Tercero, Cordoba.

Since the early 1990s, DGFM has been restructuring as part of a larger government policy of privatization of public enterprises. In 1996, it was placed under the control of the Ministry of Finance, and FMAP closed and merged with the Fray Luis Beltran (FLB) ammunition factory. The merging of the two plants took three years, and the new plant is now producing FN 9mm pistols, FMK5 rifles, FMK3 sub-machine guns, and .22 sports carbines. In addition, the factory still provides general maintenance and produces parts for the various types of weapons produced under license from FN Herstal (Belgium) for the Argentinian armed forces.

In 1999, the FLB produced 200 carbines (350 in 1998) and 4,500 pistols (1,800 in 1998), and current production is estimated at 400 pistols per month. Turnover in 1999 was US$ 5.2 million (US$ 5.4 million in 1998), of which 41 per cent was sales to the Argentine security forces (34 per cent in 1998). The Fabrica Militar Rio Tercero (FMRT) factory is still active, having produced various types of mortars for the Argentinian armed forces in the past. However, the plant has no current orders for production.

Future prospects for Argentina's local small arms industry are uncertain as a result of budgetary constraints, including cuts in defence spending, the abolition of conscription in 1994, competition from Brazil's industry, and the fall-out from DGFM's illicit arms sales to Croatia and Ecuador in the early 1990s (Dreyfus, 2000, p. 21).

During 2000 the Argentine Congress established an *ad hoc* commission to examine future options for the DGFM. It appears clear that privatization is inevitable. However, the capability to produce small arms and ammunition is considered strategically and logistically indispensable so it is possible that the state may retain a controlling interest or share in FLB.

Source: Dreyfus, 2000

The major ammunition producers in Brazil include Fábrica Nacional de Cartuchos e Munições in São Paulo, Companhia Brasileira de Cartuchos (CBC) in São Paulo, and Fabrica Realengo in Rio de Janeiro. CBC is the largest and oldest ammunition producer in Brazil, and is considered one of the largest ammunition producers in the developing world. In 1999 it employed 900 people and had total sales of US$ 35 million (Worldscope, 2001). Brazil's major small arms producers include the state-owned Indústria de Material Bélico Brasil (IMBEL) and a number of private companies including Companhia de Explosivos Valparaiba (grenades, mortars), Condor SA Indústria Qúimica (grenades), Mekanika Indústria e Comércio (machine guns), Forjas Taurus (handguns and sub-machine guns), Amadeo Rossi (handguns), Viera de Mello (machine guns and sub-machine guns), and Indústria Nacional de Armas (INA) (sub-machine guns).[25]

IMBEL, which was established in 1974 as part of the Ministry of Defence, manufactures FAL assault rifles under licence from FN Herstal (Belgium), and a wide range of small arms. IMBEL is a non-quoted, state-owned company, and currently employs 2,220 people (The Major Companies Database, 25 July 2000). IMBEL and CBC have a joint venture with Royal Ordnance (UK) in South

CBC, the largest and oldest ammunition producer in Brazil, is also considered one of the largest ammunition producers in the developing world.

American Ordnance. Forjas Taurus produces pistols under licence from Beretta (Italy), as well as a range of small arms for both domestic and export markets. It has 1,620 employees and total sales of US$ 74 million in 1999 (Worldscope, 2001). Exports account for nearly 50 per cent of the firm's turnover. Rossi has 1,354 employees and had total sales of US$ 3.9 million in 1999 (Worldscope, 2001). More than 40 per cent of the company's production is sold in the US. Both Rossi and Taurus are major suppliers of small arms to the US and other foreign markets. In 1996, Brazil was the second largest supplier of handguns to the US, having been the largest supplier throughout the period 1991-95 (Diaz, 1999, p. 76).

The main Brazilian small arms companies (CBC, IMBEL, Taurus, Rossi, INA) currently employ 4,153 people, and in 1999 total revenues for the five companies amounted to US$ 110 million (*São Paulo Valor*, 16 August 2000). In July 2000, the Brazilian Ministry of Defence effectively 'closed' the local small arms market to foreign competitors, in an attempt to protect the local small arms industry (*Sao Paulo Valor*, 12 July 2000).

Chile: Chile has a long history of producing small arms. Its local defence industry expanded considerably during the 1970s, when many countries imposed an arms embargo against it in response to the overthrow of the Allende government.[26]

Chile's small arms industry is dominated by the state-owned organization, Fabricas y Maestranzas del Ejército (FAMAE), which is part of the Ministry of Defence. FAMAE employs 3,000 people in factories distributed around the country and produces ammunition and various types of small arms (mortars, pistols, sub-machine guns, and assault rifles) for the domestic and export markets (*Jane's Sentinel Security Assessment*, 6 August 2000). The company produced the FN-FAL assault rifle under licence from FN Herstal (Belgium) until the early 1980s. Since 1991, it has been producing the SIG 540 series assault rifle under licence from SIG (Switzerland) (Jane's Infantry Weapons, 2000-2001). The company also produces mortars under licence from TDA (France). FAMAE has a strategic alliance with Forjas Taurus (Brazil) to produce machine guns (based on the SIG 540 assault rifle) for the security forces in Brazil. There are only two private small arms producers:Complejo Quimico Industrial del Ejercito (CQIE) is involved in ammunition assembly filling and ordnance retrieval and recycling;[27] and Metalnor Industria, which is part of the large private defence company, Cardoen Industries, produces hand grenades.[28]

Europe and the CIS

There are at least 39 countries in Europe and the CIS that currently produce small arms. The Russian Federation, one of the world's major producers, and most of the world's medium-sized producers (including Austria, Belgium, France, Germany, Italy, Spain, Switzerland, and the UK) are located in this region (Hébert, *et al.*, 2000). There are also a number of well-established producers in East Central Europe and the Balkans. There is some uncertainty regarding current production in Belarus, Estonia, Kazakhstan, Lithuania, and Moldova.

Over 200 companies, at least one-third of the total number of known companies in the world that produce small arms, are found in this region. Some of the most important small arms producers include: Glock (Austria), Steyr (Austria), FN Herstal (Belgium), Giat Industries (France), Beretta (Italy), Rheinmetall (Germany), Santa Barbara (Spain), Celsius (Sweden), SIG (Switzerland), Heckler and Koch (UK/Germany), and Royal Ordnance (UK).[29] The major ammunition producers include FN Herstal (Belgium), Giat Industries (France), Nammo (Norway), Rheinmetall (Germany), Bofors (Sweden), and Royal Ordnance (UK) (Hébert, *et al.*, 2000).

Western Europe: The defence industry in Western Europe has been undergoing a major process of re-structuring and consolidation since the end of the Cold War (BICC, 1998; Brzoska and Markusen,

In 1996, Brazil was the second largest supplier of handguns to the US, having been the largest supplier throughout the period 1991-95.

There are at least 39 countries in Europe and the CIS that currently produce small arms. Eight of the world's 13 top producers are located there.

Map 1.4 Small arms producers: Western Europe

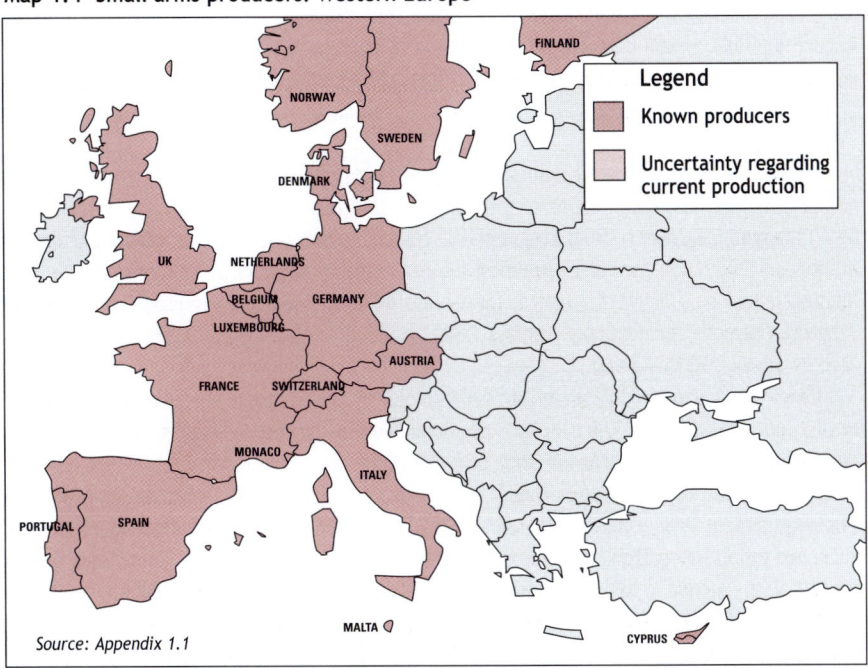

Legend

- Known producers
- Uncertainty regarding current production

Source: Appendix 1.1

2000). Much of this restructuring has included downsizing and privatization initiatives, while consolidation has involved a series of company mergers and acquisitions (Hébert, et al., 2000). These processes have also had an impact on the size and structure of the small arms industry in the region.

Austria: Glock and Steyr-Mannlicher are the two major small arms producers in Austria.[30] Glock produces a wide range of pistols, including nearly 40 different models in various sizes and eight calibres. Since its founding in 1963, Glock has supplied more than 2.5 million pistols to security forces and civilians in more than 100 countries. The Glock 17 series pistol is in service in more than 5,000 police departments and agencies in the US, and over half a million pistols are carried daily as service handguns in the US (Jane's Infantry Weapons, 2000-2001). Steyr-Mannlicher, in which Daewoo (South Korea) has a controlling interest, produces a comprehensive range of small arms including the AUG 5.56mm assault rifle, which is in service in at least 24 countries and is produced under license in Australia and Malaysia (Jane's Infantry Weapons, 2000-2001).

Belgium: FN Herstal is one of the world's most famous small arms producers, and the most important producer of small arms in Belgium. The company is part of Groupe Herstal, which was, until 1997 owned by Giat Industries (France), but since then has been owned by the Walloon Regional Government (Mampaey, 2000). FN Herstal was established in 1889 to produce German Mauser rifles under license for the Belgian Army.

Today FN Herstal produces 450,000 weapons in nine countries every year. Its products include pistols, rifles, sub-machine guns, and machine guns. The company recently stated that 'two-thirds of the American Army's "portable" arms are made (by FN Herstal) in Belgium' (*Groot Bijgaarden De Standaard*, 7 December 2000). In 1999, FN Herstal employed 940 people and had a turnover of US$ 93 million, which represented 22 per cent of the total turnover of the Groupe Herstal (Mampaey, 2000). The Groupe Herstal has a subsidiary in the US, FN Manufacturing, that produces assault rifles (M-16 series) and machine guns, mainly for the US armed forces.

France: Despite being a major producer of conventional arms, France does not enjoy such a high profile as a producer of small arms as certain other countries in Europe, such as Belgium,

Over 200 companies, at least one-third of the total number of known companies in the world that produce small arms, are found in Europe and the CIS.

Germany, and Italy. Small arms production in France is dominated by the state-owned defence company, Giat Industries. [31] The company produces a wide range of small arms and ammunition, including pistols, assault files (FAMAS F1 Series), and grenades, and is the major supplier of small arms to the French armed forces. The company has experienced a number of financial problems in recent years, and has posted losses of about US$ 2.7 billion in the last ten years (*Jane's Defence Weekly*, 10 May 2000).

Despite improving financial figures, the company is still losing money, and remains heavily reliant on government bail-outs to keep production lines moving. Since 1998, the company has been undergoing a major restructuring. This has resulted in the closure and/or rationalization of a number of production facilities, including the ammunition facilities at Le Mans, Salbris, and Rennes. It sold its share in the Herstal Group in 1997 to the Walloon Regional Government in Belgium. Currently the company employs 7,800 people, down from over 10,000 in 1998 (*Jane's Defence Weekly*, 10 May 2000).

Italy: Small arms production in Italy is dominated by one company—Beretta, which is owned by Giat Industries of France (36 per cent), and Beretta family interests (64 per cent). Beretta owns a number of Italy's other major small arms producers, including Luigi Franchi (shotguns, machine guns) and Benelli Armi (shotguns) (*Jane's World Defence Industry*, 2000). [32] Beretta has over 1,800 employees and, in 1999, recorded total sales of US$ 233 million. The company produces rifles, shotguns, and pistols. Its sporting arms account for 75 per cent of total production. Over 70 per cent of production is exported to almost 100 countries. Beretta also has a subsidiary in the US, Beretta US Corporation, which has 170 employees and registered sales of US$ 30 million in 1999 (Directory of Corporate Affiliations, 2000).

Germany: In recent years, Germany's small arms industry has become increasingly consolidated in one company—Rheinmetall. [33] The company's small arms business is concentrated in Rheinmetall DeTec, and produces a wide range of small arms and ammunition (Lock, 2000). The company has also begun to dominate the European small arms market in recent years as a result of a number of local and cross-border acquisitions. The company recently acquired a number of other well-known local producers, such as Mauser Werke (rifles, machine guns) and Buck Werke (mortars). During 1999 it increased its stake in Eurometaal, a Dutch small arms producer, to 66 per cent; and, in 2000, acquired 100 per cent of Oerlikon Contraves (Switzerland). In 1999 Rheinmetall DeTec had annual sales of US$2 billion and employed about 11,500 people (*Jane's Defence Weekly*, 7 June 2000).

Spain: In Spain, the major small arms producers include Empressa Nacional Santa Barbara (ENSB), which is state-owned, and a number of private companies including Astra-Unceta y Cia, Llama Gabilando, and Star. ENSB produces various types of small arms and ammunition including machine guns, rifles, and grenade launchers, and is the main supplier to the Spanish armed forces (Jane's World Defence Industry, 2000). The company, which employs around 2,000 people at nine locations, has been experiencing severe financial difficulties in recent years. In 2000, it had projected losses of US$ 22 million, 85 per cent higher than the previous year (*Jane's Defence Weekly*, 18 October 2000). The Spanish government has acknowledged that ENSB is 'technically bankrupt', and has accumulated losses of over US$ 800 million in the past decade. It is currently the target of a take-over tug of war between the US's General Dynamics Group and Germany's Rheinmetall and Krauss-Maffei (*Defense Daily*, 13 November 2000). Astra and Star, the major private sector producers of military-style handguns have recently consolidated their operations under the ASTAR name (Forecast International, 2000).

Switzerland: Although a neutral country, Switzerland supports a fairly significant domestic small arms industry, which is helped by the structure of its militia army. The major ammunition producer is Oerlikon Contraves, which is 100 per cent owned by Rheinmetall (Germany) and employs about 2,400 people (Jane's World Defence Industry, 2000). The Swiss Ammunition Enterprise (SM)

According to FN Herstal, 'two-thirds of the American Army's "portable" arms are made in Belgium.'

Small arms production in Italy is dominated by one company—Beretta. Over 70 per cent of its production is exported to almost 100 countries worldwide.

and the Swiss Ordnance Enterprise (SW), both of which are located in Thun, are important local producers of grenades, mortars, and machine guns. Both operate as independent companies within the state-owned RUAG Suisse Group (*Military Technology*, May 2000).

Schweizerische Industrie-Gesellschaft (SIG) based in Neuhausen Rheinfalls, produces a wide range of pistols, rifles, and grenade launchers, including the famous Mauser and Sauer brands. The company has facilities in Germany (SIG Arm Sauer in Eckernforde), Switzerland, and the US. The SIG540 series assault rifle is in service in more than 20 countries (including ten countries in Africa), and is produced under license in Chile, France, and Portugal. In October 2000, the small arms division of SIG, which employs over 700 people, was sold to two private German investors (*Agence France Presse,* 4 October 2000). Thus, two of Switzerland's most significant small arms companies are now foreign owned.

Two of Switzerland's most significant small arms companies are now foreign owned.

The United Kingdom: The UK is one of Western Europe's largest defence producers. The major small arms and ammunition producer is Royal Ordnance (RO), which is part of the BAE Systems Group.[34] RO has owned Heckler & Koch (Germany) since 1991 and has plants in both the United Kingdom and Germany.[35] It employs about 4,000 people and its products are sold in more than 50 countries. Its main small arms production facility in the United Kingdom is in Nottingham and employs 450 people. The facility is slated for closure during 2001, following the awarding of a contract to modify 200,000 faulty SA-80 rifles to Heckler & Koch's plant in Obendorf, Germany (*Daily Mail,* 5 October 2000). Heckler & Koch had a turnover of US$ 130 million in 1999 and employs about 700 people. Early in 2000 BAE Systems tried unsuccessfully to sell Heckler & Koch to Colt's Manufacturing (US).

CIS and the Baltic States: During the Cold War, the Soviet Union was one of the largest small arms producers in the world, with production taking place in many republics of the Soviet Union. Since the end of the Cold War, the Soviet Union's defence industry has been affected by the break-up of the Soviet Union, and has been forced into a dramatic process of downsizing and restructuring (BICC, 2000; Gonchar, 2000). A number of the CIS states have maintained, or expanded, their Soviet-era small arms production capabilities.

The Russian Federation: The Russian Federation inherited the bulk of the former Soviet Union's small arms industry. The industry is still largely state-owned, and production takes place in a large number of state-owned factories.[36] The two major production centres are in Tula (Tulsky Oruzheiny Zavod), near Moscow, and in Izhevsk (Izhmash Joint Stock Company) in the Republic of Udmurtia. Other facilities include the Kovrov Mechanical Plant (sub-machine guns and machine guns) and the Degtyarev Plant, both located in Kovrov; the Molot Joint Stock Company (pistols, revolvers, and machine guns), located in Vjatskie Poliany, and the Central Scientific Research Institute of Precision Machinery Construction (Tsniitochmash) in Klimovsk, near Moscow.

During the Cold War, the Soviet Union was one of the largest small arms producers in the world.

The cites of Tula and Izhevsk, both 'closed' during the Soviet era, are dominated by the production of small arms. There are numerous production facilities in both, usually with different names, indicating the type of weapon produced and/or developed. Plants in both cities manufacture various types of small arms, including the 9mm Makarov pistol and various commercial and sporting derivatives of the original AK series assault rifle. In the early 1990s, 70-80 per cent of Izhmash's income came from small arms sales, but this has been reduced significantly in recent years. In 1999, exports were worth US$ 39.1 million. The enterprise is currently experiencing severe financial problems, largely due to five years of payment arrears from the Russian Federation Department of Defence (Gonchar, 2000). Izhmash's small arms have been sold in more than 45 countries, although many of its products, especially handguns, are still restricted from being sold in the US (*National Defense,* January 2000).[37]

Map 1.5 Small arms producers: CIS and Baltic States

Source: Appendix 1.1

Other states, including Armenia, Belarus, Estonia, Moldova, Kazakhstan, Lithuania, and Ukraine are known to have limited small arms production capabilities.[38] However, there is a lack of information regarding current production activities in many of these countries.

East Central Europe:[39] All the countries of East Central Europe[40] were significant arms producers during the Cold War era (Kiss, 1997a; Anthony, 1994). Poland and the former Czechoslovakia had the largest defence industrial sectors, based on the number of people employed in defence production.[41] The structure and size of arms production in each country was determined by the requirements of the Warsaw Treaty Organisation (WTO). Most products were produced according to Soviet designs, but with some local adaptations and developments.

Since the end of the Cold War, the defence industry in East Central Europe has experienced a dramatic process of downsizing, restructuring, and consolidation (Kiss, 1997a). Between 1990 and 1994, output levels fell to 10-30 per cent from their 1988 peak. During this period, many companies retrenched large numbers of people. The total number of people 'formally' employed in the defence industries of East Central Europe declined by 70 per cent from 510,000 in 1988 to 150,200 in 1998 (BICC, 2000).

The defence industry in East Central Europe experienced a dramatic downturn between 1990 and 1994, with output levels falling to 10-30 per cent from their 1988 peak.

The reasons for this dramatic collapse in East Central Europe included:

- The end of the Cold War and the resulting dissolution of the Warsaw Pact organization, which had provided lucrative, protected markets and cheap inputs for defence production;
- The collapse of the related economic trading system;
- International sanctions and embargoes on traditional markets (e.g. Libya, Iraq, Syria, and Yugoslavia);
- Significant cuts in defence spending as part of more general processes of economic and political transformation; and
- The many economic problems associated with the introduction of market forces.

By the late 1990s, the crisis in the East Central Europe defence industry was largely over, and the

Map 1.6   Small arms producers: East Central Europe

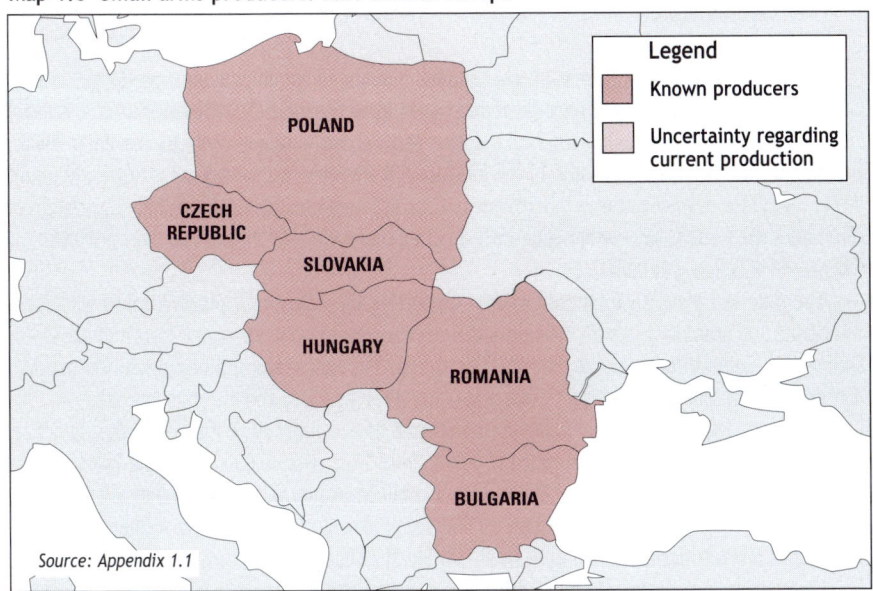

Source: Appendix 1.1

sector had embarked upon a process of consolidation, although the eventual outcome still remains uncertain. In the Czech Republic, Hungary, and Slovakia, local defence companies began to show modest increases in output and profitability. However, in other countries, such as Bulgaria, Poland, and Romania, output continued to fall and many defence companies were doomed to failure in the absence of state intervention.[42] High levels of 'technical unemployment' and huge arrears in wages in the defence industry have prompted violent workers' protests in recent years in Bulgaria, Poland, Romania, and Slovakia.

The stabilization of the defence industry in East Central Europe was helped by a number of factors, such as macroeconomic recovery in most countries (with the exception of Romania), and invitations to join the North Atlantic Treaty Organization (NATO) 'Partnership for Peace' programme and become members of NATO (Czech Republic, Hungary, and Poland). This has prompted increases in defence spending and military modernization programs. It has also renewed government support for defence industry restructuring. Privatization, international co-operation, and new export markets have also played a crucial role.

In response to the crisis situation, the defence industries of East Central Europe implemented two general types of adjustment strategies, albeit with certain variations between countries. In Slovakia, defence industry adjustment was state-led and inward-oriented. Bulgaria and Romania utilized similar strategies, but were more export-oriented. In Hungary, defence industry adjustment was largely industry-led, and export-oriented. The Czech Republic and Poland followed similar strategies, but with more state involvement.

By the late 1990s, a vastly reduced number of small arms producers were operating in East Central Europe as a result of defence industry restructuring, privatization, and consolidation. Ammunition producers had more difficulties than small arms producers. This was largely due to the fact that the conversion and/or maintenance of production capabilities was a more complex challenge for the former. The future prospects for the defence industry, including small arms producers, in East Central Europe will be determined by the following factors:

- The upgrading and modernization of existing arsenals/defence forces to meet NATO standards;
- Creation of hybrid systems that use both NATO and WTO parts, and can be sold in both markets;

Privatization, international co-operation, and new export markets have played a crucial role in stabilizing East Central Europe's defence industry.

- International co-operation through joint ventures and technology transfers; and
- New export markets.

Czech Republic: The former Czechoslovakia was one of the largest arms producers in East Central Europe in the 1980s, and the bulk of the country's defence industry was located in what is today Slovakia. The Czech Republic's defence industry experienced a major crisis in the early 1990s. However, in recent years the position of the industry has strengthened considerably. Currently, about 90 per cent of the defence industry is in private hands, although the state retains a share in several key companies. In some cases, former state-owned companies were sold through coupon privatization schemes (e.g. Sellier and Bellot).

The former Czechoslovakia was one of the largest arms producers in East Central Europe in the 1980s.

The state still plays an important role in supporting the industry by placing orders with local companies and promoting exports.[43] Some of the most important small arms producers include: Ceska Zbrojovka[44], Caliber Praha, Holek, and the LCZ Group. The major ammunition producers include: Zbrojovka Vsetin, Policske Strojirny, Sellier and Bellot, Prototypa ZM, and the State Arsenals.

Hungary: Hungary's defence industry has shrunk considerably since the end of the Cold War. Total employment in 1998 was estimated at 5,000, down from over 30,000 in the late 1980s (BICC, 2000). During the Warsaw Pact era, the country's small arms producers had a relatively privileged position. According to Hungarian military guidelines, all personal equipment for soldiers, including small arms and ammunition, had to be produced locally. This situation continued during 2000.

The key problems facing Hungarian small arms producers include a lack of state orders, which limits income and undermines the companies' export potential, and tough external market conditions. On the other hand, Hungary's recent admittance into NATO, which will be accompanied by increased defence spending and a modernization programme for the armed forces, will certainly benefit the country's local small arms producers.

During the late 1980s, Poland had the largest defence industry in East Central Europe.

Poland: During the late 1980s, Poland had the largest defence industry in East Central Europe. By the late 1990s the industry was struggling to survive, despite the country's impressive macro-economic growth. In 1998 the industry employed about 70,000 people (BICC, 2000). Privatization of the defence industry only began in 1999, and most companies remain in state hands, under the control of the state industrial development agency. Some of the privatization that has occurred has taken place through debt equity swaps. In recent years the government has provided significant financial assistance and placed orders with domestic companies to help the industry to survive.

The country's major small arms producer is Zaklady Metalowe Lucznik, which employs some 1,600 people. In September 2000, the Polish Government placed an order worth US\$ 1.8 million with the company for 4,000 assault rifles for the country's border guards in an attempt to prevent the company from closing down (*NewsEdge Corporation,* 7 September 2000).[45] The major small arms ammunition producers include the government-owned Zaklady Metalowe Mesko and Zaklady Tworzyw Sztucznych Pronit.

The Balkans: Many countries in the Balkans, including Albania, Bosnia and Herzegovina, Croatia, Greece, Macedonia, Slovenia, and Yugoslavia, have well-established domestic small arms industries. However, most countries in the region have experienced long-running civil wars in recent years, largely as a result of the break-up of the former Yugoslavia. This has had a negative effect on domestic production capabilities.

Bosnia and Herzegovina: This country (a province of the former Yugoslavia) was a major producer of small arms prior to the civil war of 1992-95. Many factories were destroyed during that conflict, although some production of small arms (e.g. mortars and ammunition) continued to take place (Jane's World Armies, 2000). Since the end of the war in 1995, production facilities have been re-established and, in recent years, Bosnian companies have exported various types of small

Box 1.7   Hungary's small arms producers

During the 1980s, small arms production in Hungary was concentrated in two companies—the FEG Company (Fegyver es Gazkeszulekgyar) and Danuvia Gepipari Rt. Both employed several thousand people and had a long tradition of producing small arms and other dual-purpose products. Danuvia received its last order from the Hungarian army in 1988. In early 1990, the company liquidated its defence-related activities, and now concentrates solely on its civilian business, which includes hydraulic supply sources, machines, and spare parts.

FEG, which is still the largest and most significant small arms producer in Hungary, is owned by the State Privatisation and Asset Managing Agency (AVRT). The company produces assault rifles and a range of pistols for Hungary's military and police forces, and a number of foreign clients. During the 1990s, an average of 75 per cent of the company's output of self-defence and sports pistols was exported to a number of countries, including the US.[46] In 1999, however, 60 per cent of the company's output was sold on the domestic market, due to the weakening of its export market and a large order worth US$ 500,000 from the Hungarian Interior Ministry for 4,000 Parabellum pistols. Inno-Coop, which was established in the early 1990s, has developed a capability to produce high-tech mines, fuses, and river bombs. Batori Epszol, owned by the town of Nyirbator, produces various types of semi-automatic rifles.

During the 1980s Hungary's small arms ammunition producers included Nitrokemia, Eszak Magyarorszagi Vegyimuvek (EMV), Matravideki Femmuvek (MFS), and Mechanikai Muvek. Both EMV and Nitrokemia came close to bankruptcy during the 1990s. EMV was privatized and currently 100 per cent of its sales are civilian. Nitrokemia was kept afloat through various restructuring initiatives and state intervention strategies.

Nike-Fiocchi, which is a joint venture with the Italian company, Fiocchi Munizioni, was established in 1991 as part of the restructuring of Nitrokemia. It is now one of the most successful defence companies in Hungary. In 1999, it had a turnover of US$ 5 million, with a staff of 75. The company's main product is hunting ammunition, sold in Germany, Finland, Norway, Japan, and the US. Less than 10 per cent of its output is military-related.

MFS's ammunition division, MFS Magyar Loszergyarto was established as an independent company in 1994. The company was initially privatized, but was bought back by the AVRT in 1997. More than 90 per cent of the company's output is military and about 90 per cent of production is exported to countries such as Germany, Italy, Lebanon, and the US. Private Hungarian interests have recently purchased the company, which went insolvent in 1999. Mechanikai Muvek produces a range of artillery and mortar ammunition, technical explosive devices, and hand and gun grenades. During 1999, the company became insolvent and was bought by a consortium of Hungarian and American interests.

Source: Kiss, 2000

arms to Croatia, Turkey, and Azerbaijan (*Jane's Defence Weekly*, 25 March 1998).[47] It is estimated that about 6,000 people were employed in the local defence industry in 1998, down from 30,000 in 1992 (BICC, 2000).

Croatia: Croatia has a well-established defence industry, and produces a wide-range of small arms and ammunition. It is estimated that 12,000 people were employed in the industry in 1998, down from 50,000 in 1994 (BICC, 2000). Many of the weapons produced in Croatia are copies of well-established designs, mainly Soviet, while others are of indigenous design (*Jane's Sentinel Security Assessment,* 23 August 2000).

The major small arms producer is the RH Alan company, which is owned by the Ministry of Defence. The company, which is located in Zagreb, produces a wide range of small arms and ammunition and is currently in discussion with IMI about the licensed production of the 5.56mm Tavor assault rifle. RH Alan has produced unlicensed copies of a number of foreign designs, including the 9mm Mini ERO submachine gun, a virtual copy of the 9mm Uzi (*Jane's Sentinel Security Assessment,* 23 August 2000).

Greece: Greece's small arms industry is dominated by two state-owned companies—Greek Powder and Cartridge Company (Pyrkal), and the Hellenic Arms Industry (EBO)—and a few private companies.[48] It is estimated that at least 15,000 people were employed in the local defence industry in 1998 (BICC, 2000). Pyrkal produces various types of ammunition and mortar bombs. EBO was established in 1977 and comprises five plants. It employs about 1,700 people, produces pistols, rifles, sub-machine guns, machine guns, and mortars, and is the major supplier to the Greek armed forces. It has a number of co-production programmes with various foreign defence companies, including Bofors (Sweden), Colt's Manufacturing (US), Dynamit Noble (Germany), and Heckler & Koch (Germany/UK) (*Jane's Defence Weekly*, 30 September 1998). Both Pyrkal and EBO are slated for privatization in the near future.

Map 1.7 Small arms producers: The Balkans

Legend

Known producers

Uncertainty regarding current production

SLOVENIA
CROATIA
BOSNIA-HERZEGOVINA
YUGOSLAVIA
MACEDONIA
ALBANIA
GREECE

Source: Appendix 1.1

Yugoslavia: During the NATO airstrikes, most of Yugoslavia's defence production facilities were destroyed. Prior to the war, the local defence industry had consisted of 15 plants with about 30,000 employees (*Jane's Sentinel Security Assessment*, 10 December 1999). Today the major domestic small arms producer is the state-owned company Zastava, which was founded in 1853, and is located in Belgrade, Serbia (*International Herald Tribune*, 6-7 January 2000). The company produces cars (the Yugo) and a wide range of weapons, including pistols, rifles, sub-machine guns, and machine guns. The company has reportedly begun production of three new variants of the AK series assault rifle (*Jane's Sentinel Security Assessment*, 10 December 1999).

The Middle East

A large, and growing, number of countries in the Middle East have domestic small arms industries. Currently, there are at least eleven countries in the Middle East that produce small arms although there is some uncertainty regarding current production in Algeria, Iraq, and Sudan.[49] The major producers are Egypt, Israel, and Turkey.

Most small arms production takes place in state-owned companies, and most products are produced under license from European companies, including Beretta (Italy), FN Herstal (Belgium), Rheinmetall (Germany), and Heckler & Koch (Germany/UK). The most significant producers of licensed weapons in the region include Egypt, Iran, Saudi Arabia, and Turkey (Jane's Infantry Weapons, 2000-2001).

The major Middle East producers are Egypt, Israel, and Turkey.

Egypt: Egypt has one of the largest and oldest defence industries in the Middle East (Feiler, 1998). The National Organisation for Military Production (NOMP) was founded in 1949. Saudi Arabia, Qatar, and the United Arab Emirates provided US$ 1 billion in 1975 for the founding of the Arab Organisation for Industrialisation (AOI), whose plants are located in Egypt (Jane's World Defence Industry, 2000, p. 4). The Gulf States withdrew from the AOI in 1979 following the Camp

Map 1.8   Small arms producers: The Middle East

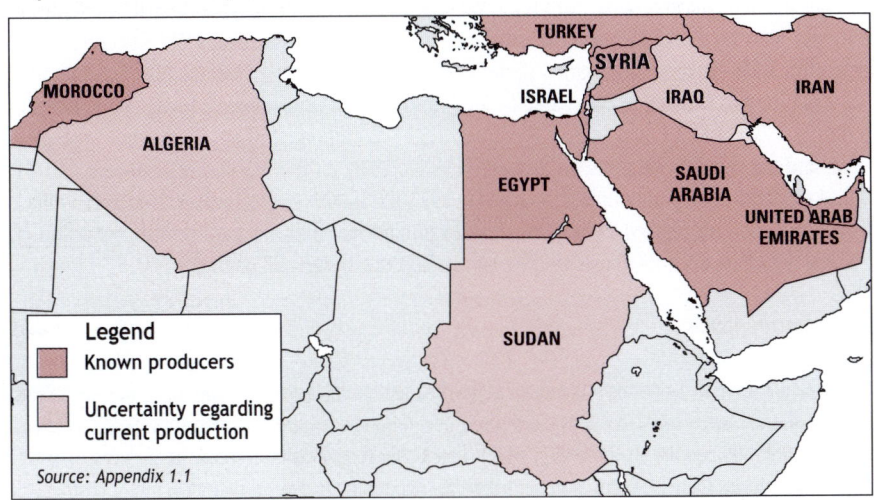

Source: Appendix 1.1

David Accords. Egypt has maintained the AOI since then, and both it and the NOMP are under the control of the Ministry of Military Production (MMP), which was itself placed under the Ministry of Defence in 1993.

The NOMP controls 16 factories, 14 of which also produce civilian goods.[50] The AOI controls nine factories. The factories of the NOMP and the AOI produce a wide range of small arms and other defence equipment. The NOMP was estimated to employ 50,000 in the 1980s; the AOI currently employs some 20,000 workers. The MMP controls six small arms and ammunition manufacturing plants; the best-known is Factory 54, the Maadi Company for Engineering Industries. It was founded in 1949 to produce rifles and machine guns under license. It currently produces the Misr 7.62mm assault rifle (a copy of the Kalashnikov AKM) and a variety of pistols, rifles, sub-machine guns and machine guns (e.g. FN Herstal MAG) (Jane's Infantry Weapons, 2000-2001). Five other factories produce small arms of various calibres, mostly under licence from the former Soviet Union.

Israel: Israel is one of the most important producers of small arms outside the US, Europe, and the Russian Federation (Klieman, 1998). The country's main small arms producer is Israel Military Industries (IMI).[51] It was a subsidiary of the Defence Ministry until 1991, when it became a state-owned company. IMI is located near Tel Aviv and currently employs 4,300 people, down from 11,000 in 1990. It produces pistols, the Uzi family of sub-machine guns (see Box 1.4), the Galil, and Tavor families of assault rifles, light machine guns, anti-armour weapons, grenades, and ammunition. Its products are exported to more than 80 countries (Jane's Infantry Weapons, 2000-2001).

Israel is one of the world's more important producers of small arms.

IMI accumulated massive financial losses between 1985 and 1995, largely as a result of declining export markets and cuts in Israel's defence spending, but returned to profit in 1996. However, in 2000, the company slid back into the red after two years of profits. In 1999, total sales were US$ 485 million, down from over US$ 500 million in the previous year (*Jane's Defence Weekly,* 25 October 2000).

Turkey: As a NATO member state, Turkey receives large amounts of cascaded Western defence equipment, and thus its own arms production capacity remained very limited until the late 1980s. However, in recent years, the local defence industry has expanded considerably. The Under Secretariat for Defence Industry (SSM) was established in 1985 to reduce Turkish dependence upon procurement from abroad. A substantial part of the country's defence production results from licensed production (e.g. Heckler & Koch) and joint ventures. These joint ventures involve manufacturers from NATO member states, as well as Israel.

As a NATO member state, Turkey receives large amounts of cascaded Western defence equipment.

The major producer of small arms is the state-owned company MKEK (Makina ve Kimya Endüstri Kurumu–Machinery and Chemical Industry Board). Over 20 factories are under MKEK's control. They produce a wide range of small arms under license, including the G3 assault rifle and the MP5 sub-machine gun (Heckler & Koch) and the MG3 machine gun (Rheinmetall) (Jane's World Defence Industry, 2000). MKEK's total sales in 1998 were US$ 570 million, of which 77 per cent were arms sales, and the company employs 9,120 people (SIPRI, 2000, p. 331). As part of a 10-year, US$ 31 billion modernization programme announced in 1997, the Turkish Government decided in early 1998 to award a contract, reputed to be worth US$ 18 million, to MKEK for the licensed production of 500,000 Heckler & Koch HK33 assault rifles (Jane's Defence Weekly, 27 January 1999).[52]

Sub-Saharan Africa

Given the low levels of economic and industrial development on this part of the continent, most countries in sub-Saharan Africa (SSA) do not possess their own domestic small arms industries. South Africa is currently the only country in the region which has a well-developed indigenous small arms industry, although countries such as Nigeria and Zimbabwe are attempting to develop their fledgling industries.

Map 1.9   Small arms producers: Sub-Saharan Africa

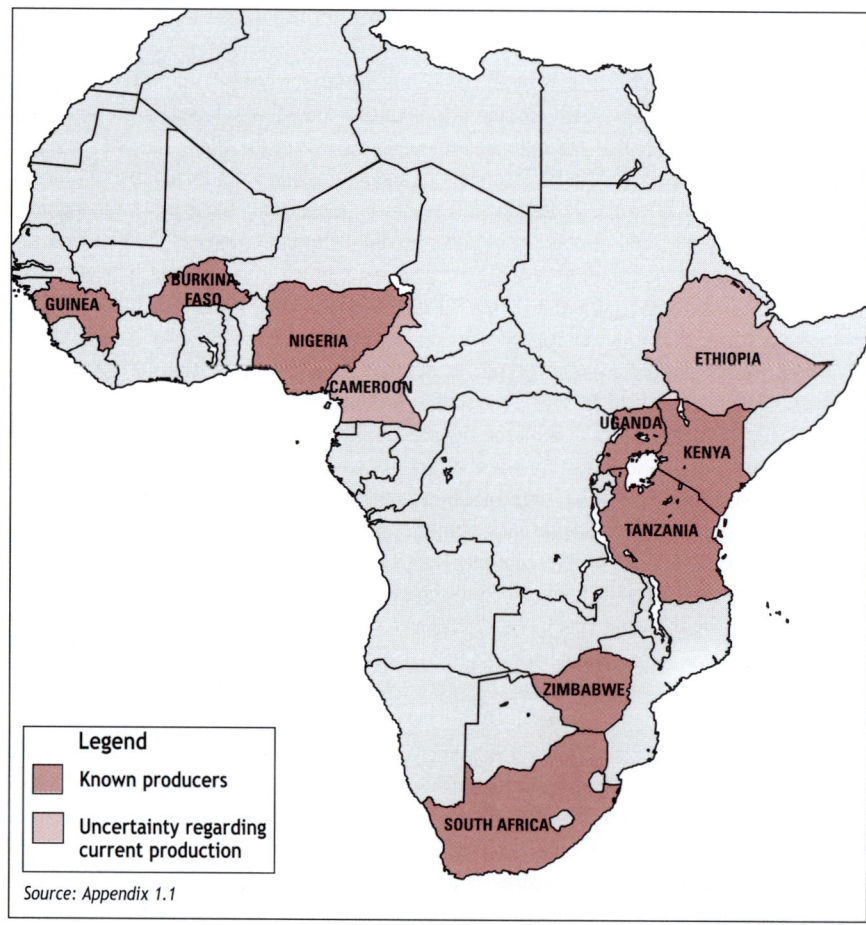

There are currently at least ten countries in sub-Saharan Africa that produce small arms.

Legend

Known producers

Uncertainty regarding current production

Source: Appendix 1.1

There are currently at least ten countries in SSA that produce small arms, although there is some uncertainty regarding current production in Cameroon and Ethiopia. With the exception of South Africa, there is very little information, official or unofficial, about the size and scope of small arms production in SSA. Most small arms producers in SSA (e.g. Tanzania, Zimbabwe) only manufacture components for small arms or small arms ammunition, or have basic facilities for filling ammunition. Most production, with the exception of South Africa, takes place in state-owned factories.

Nigeria: Nigeria's defence industry is concentrated in one state-owned arms company, Defence Industry Corporation of Nigeria (DICON). The company was established in 1964 with assistance from Belgium (FN Herstal) and Italy (Beretta), and is located in Kaduna (*Africa News,* 3 June 2000). In 1987, the company was removed from under the direct control of the Ministry of Defence and transformed into a state-owned company in an attempt to force it to become commercially viable.

DICON produces small arms ammunition for domestic use, although there are unconfirmed reports of exports to other countries in West Africa such as Liberia (Forecast International, 2000). The company also produces the NR-1 military rifle and rifles and pistols under license from Beretta (Italy), and has produced 18,778 rifles to date (*BBC Monitoring,* 18 October 1999). DICON has suffered in recent years due to budgetary constraints and a lack of orders from the Nigerian military. The late President Sani Abacha spent US$ 17 million on imported rifles, despite the fact that DICON had large amounts of rifles in its inventory (*BBC Monitoring,* 18 October 1999). In June 2000, the company was closed, and the staff sent on indefinite leave without pay, due to the company's financial crisis (*Africa News,* 3 June 2000).

South Africa: South Africa has the largest and most diversified defence industry in sub-Saharan Africa. The industry was established in the period after the World War II and expanded considerably during the 1970s and 1980s when South Africa was subject to a UN arms embargo (Batchelor and Willett, 1998). The country is totally self-sufficient in the production of small arms and associated ammunition. Since 1990, the local industry has been forced into a process of downsizing, rationalization, and consolidation as a result of the significant cuts in the national defence budget, particularly the procurement budget (Batchelor and Dunne, 1998). These broader processes of defence industrial downsizing and restructuring have had an impact on its local small arms producers. However, South Africa remains one of the world's most important developing country small arms producers and exporters.

South Africa remains one of the world's most important developing country small arms producers and exporters.

The most important local small arms producer is Vektor, a division of Denel, the large state-owned defence company. Private sector companies include: Hausler Scientific Instruments (pistols, rifles, mortars), Milkor (grenade launchers), Neostead (shotguns), Republic Arms (riot guns), Reutech Defence Industries (pistols, shotguns), and Truvelo Armoury Division (rifles). In recent years, a number of small arms producers have closed down, including Musgrave (formerly part of Denel and absorbed into Vektor) and the private company Aram.[53] Local small arms ammunition producers include: Pretoria Metal Pressings, which is also a division of Denel, and a private company, New Generation Ammunition. Another private company Ammu-Tech, which previously produced small arms ammunition, closed in 1998.[54]

Zimbabwe: Zimbabwe's local defence industry was established in the early 1980s to reduce the country's reliance on external suppliers, and to preserve scarce foreign currency (Mlambo, 1998). The state-owned Zimbabwe Defence Industries (ZDI) manufactures various types of small arms ammunition. At its filling plant outside Harare, it fills mortar shells, and has the capacity to fill artillery shells, rocket launchers (RPG-7), and fragmentation hand grenades. In recent years ZDI has attempted to export some of its products, but with limited success. It has been reported that ZDI has sold ammunition and other military equipment to a small number of countries including the Democratic Republic of Congo and Sri Lanka (*Jane's Sentinel Security Assessment,* 10 October 1999).

Map 1.10   Small arms producers: Asia Pacific

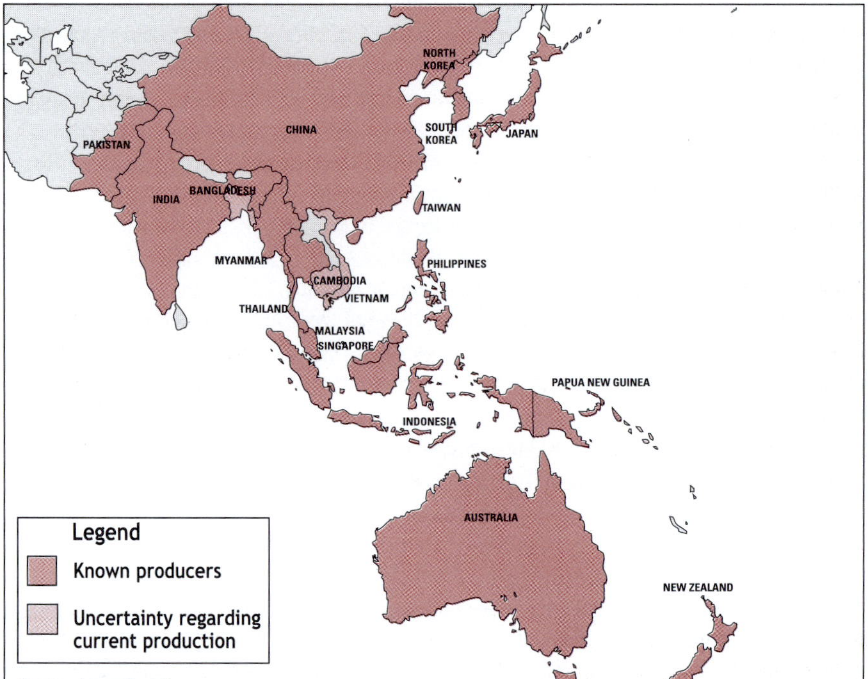

Legend

Known producers

Uncertainty regarding current production

Source: Appendix 1.1

Asia Pacific

Currently there are at least 19 countries in the Asia Pacific region that produce small arms. One of the world's major producers—China—and a number of medium-sized producers including India, Pakistan, Singapore, and Taiwan are located in this region. There is some uncertainty regarding current production in Bangladesh, Cambodia, and Vietnam. In most countries production of small arms takes place in both private companies, and/or in state-owned factories.

South Asia: India and Pakistan are the most important small arms producers in South Asia, and in both countries a wide range of small arms are produced in large, state-controlled Ordnance Factories. There is some uncertainty regarding current production of small arms in Bangladesh (Hussain, 2000). 55 Bhutan, Nepal, and Sri Lanka do not possess their own small arms industries.

   India: India is one of the largest developing country arms producers. The Department of Defence Production was established in 1962 and currently includes 39 Ordnance Factories that produce pistols, rifles, machine guns, mortars, grenades, anti-tank systems, and various types of ammunition. The Ordnance Factories, which employed 155,000 people in 1997, had a turnover of US$ 737 million and total arms sales of US$ 640 million (SIPRI, 2000, p. 330).

   The Ordnance Factories manufacture products under license from Belgium, Sweden, and the United Kingdom, as well as their own designs (Jane's Infantry Weapons, 2000-2001). They have also received technical assistance from the United States (*Jane's Defence Weekly,* 26 August 1998). There have been reports of production problems, sometimes due to financial and/or technical constraints, and in general it is considered that the Ordnance Factories are 35-40 per cent underutilized. This has prompted the Indian Government to recently invest US$ 642 million to upgrade the factories to increase production and efficiency (*Jane's Defence Weekly,* 7 April 1999).

Pakistan: In 1950 Pakistan established its first small arms production facility. Since then the country has strived to become self-sufficient in small arms and ammunition. The domestic small arms industry comprises a number of private companies and the state-owned public enterprise, Pakistan Ordnance Factories (POF), which is under the Ministry of Defence Production. POF comprises 14 plants and eight subsidiary companies, and employs more than 30,000 people (*Military Technology,* March 2000). The company manufactures a wide range of small arms, most of which are produced under license. It manufactures G3 assault rifles and MP5 sub-machine guns under license from Heckler & Koch (Germany) and MG3 machine guns under license from Rheinmetall (Germany) (Jane's Infantry Weapons, 2000-2001).

ASEAN: Almost all the member states of ASEAN, with the exception of Laos, produce small arms.[56] Small arms have been domestically produced in South East Asia since the first local production facilities were established in the 1950s and 1960s. Many countries began to manufacture licensed designs of assault rifles and ammunition with assistance from Western producers including Germany, Italy, Sweden, the UK, and the US.

With few exceptions, production has expanded to include a wide range of small arms, light weapons, and ammunition, including indigenous designs. The aim for most countries is to become less reliant on outside sources to meet their domestic defence requirements. The most important small arms producers include Indonesia, Malaysia, Myanmar, the Philippines, Singapore, and Thailand.

Indonesia: Indonesia has only one domestic small arms producer, PT Pindad, which produces small arms, light weapons, and ammunition. Pindad took over the existing production facilities from the Indonesian military in 1983. Production falls into two categories, military and non-military. All military production is controlled by the Ministry of Defence and all non-military production is controlled by the Indonesian police. Most of Pindad's production goes towards supplying Indonesia's Armed Forces, police, and forest patrol, although some production is for domestic civilian use as well as for export. Pindad operates two plants on Java, one that manufactures cartridges for small arms, shells and missiles for light weapons, hand grenades, pyrotechnics, and riot control equipment; and another that manufactures pistols, rifles, carbines, assault rifles, sub-machine guns, mortars, and grenade launchers. Most production is under license from countries such as Belgium, Finland, Israel, and Singapore (Jane's Infantry Weapons, 2000-2001).

Malaysia: Malaysia's first arms production facility was established in 1972. Defence production is largely integrated within the commercial sector as there are few companies solely dedicated to defence production. Currently there are four local small arms producers: Munora Holdings and SME Technologies, which produce assault rifles under license from Steyr (Austria); SME Ordnance, which produces a wide range of ammunition from cartridges for small arms to mortar bombs as well as pyrotechnics; and Kerambit Industries, which produces shotgun cartridges (Forecast International, 2000; Jane's Infantry Weapons, 2000-2001).

Myanmar: Myanmar's domestic defence industry was established in the early 1950s. In 1957, the German company Fritz Werner, in co-operation with Heckler & Koch, built an arms factory in Yangon to produce G-3 automatic rifles (*Jane's Intelligence Review,* 1 December 1998). Another factory was built near Prome to produce small arms ammunition. These factories are managed by Defence Products Industries (Ka Pa Sa) and are under the direct control of the Ministry of Defence. In February 1998, Myanmar acquired a prefabricated small arms factory designed and built by Chartered Industries of Singapore with the assistance of Israeli consultants (*Jane's Intelligence Review,* 1 December 1998). Ka Pa Sa factories now produce assault rifles and light machine guns of indigenous design, as well as landmines and various other types of small arms. Recent reports suggest that Norinco of China is planning on building a factory near Yangon to produce various types of small arms and ammunition (*Asia Defence Yearbook,* 1999-2000; *Asian Defence Journal,* April 2000).

Almost all ASEAN member states, with the exception of Laos, produce small arms. The most important include Indonesia, Malaysia, Myanmar, the Philippines, Singapore, and Thailand.

Philippines: The Philippines has a number of local small arms producers, who produce for both commercial and military markets. Local producers have the capacity to manufacture pistols, shotguns, rifles, carbines, assault rifles, mortars, cartridges for small arms, and shells and missiles for light weapons. From the late 1970s to 1983, the company Elisco Tool produced the M-16 assault rifle under license from Colt's Manufacturing (US). Later production has been undertaken by the government arsenal in Limay, Bataan (Forecast International, 2000). Arms Corporation of the Philippines (Armscor), which produces various types of small arms, recently signed a contract with Denel of South Africa to produce the Vektor SP-1 9mm pistol. Armscor will license-build 10,000 pistols for the Philippines National Police and market the weapon commercially (*Jane's Sentinel Security Assessment,* 28 September 1999).

Singapore has the most diverse and well developed arms industry in South East Asia.

Singapore: Singapore has the most diverse and well-developed arms industry in South East Asia. The Ministry of Defence (MINDEF) controls all local arms production through Sheng-Li Holding Company. Singapore Technology Corporation (STC), through its subsidiary Chartered Industries of Singapore (CIS), is the major local producer of small arms. In early 2000, CIS was reorganized and renamed Singapore Technologies Kinetics (STK). STK's products include cartridges for small arms, hand grenades, landmines, mortar bombs, shells, and missiles for light weapons, rifles, carbines, assault rifles, light and heavy machine guns, grenade launchers, mortars, anti-tank guns, surface-to-air missiles and launchers (STK Company Information).

Most products are produced under license from Austria (Steyr), Belgium (FN Herstal), Germany (Heckler & Koch), Italy (Beretta), Sweden (Bofors), UK (Sterling), and the US (Colt's Manufacturing). In addition to supplying Singapore's Armed Forces, STK has become an aggressive competitor in the export market, particularly in certain categories such as mortars and light machine guns (Forecast International, 2000).

Thailand: Domestic production of small arms began in Thailand in 1969. The primary vehicle for this was a private company called Thai Interarms, which received substantial government aid. The company consists of four sub-units and manufactures small arms, ammunition, gunpowder, and other explosives (*Asian Defence Journal,* April 2000). Other private companies include: Bullet Master Company Ltd., Rungphaisal Industry Company (rifles), Thai Arms Company, and Thai Melon Company. In addition, the Royal Thai Army has a production centre in Lophuri, which manufactures various types of small arms and ammunition. During 1999, the Army's production centre exported about US$ 2 million worth of military equipment, with most of its sales (including 60mm and 81mm mortars and various types of ammunition) going to Singapore and the Philippines (*The Straits Times,* 12 December 2000).

China is one of the world's major producers of small arms and employs three million people in its overall national defence industry.

East Asia Pacific: The major small arms producers in East Asia and the Pacific region include China, one of the world's major producers of small arms, Taiwan, Japan, North and South Korea, Australia, and New Zealand.

China: The Chinese defence industry is estimated to employ over three million people (BICC, 2000).[57] However, there is very little official or unofficial information about domestic small arms production. China started to export weapons in 1950 and between 1964-78 exported weapons to more than 60 countries, including 4.2 million small arms and 4.3 billion rounds of small calibre ammunition (Jane's World Armies, 2000, p. 149).

During the late 1980s and early 1990s, China became one of the major foreign suppliers of small arms to the US domestic market. It accounted for over 40 per cent of all rifles (including assault rifles) imported into the US between 1987 and 1994, and 15 per cent of total firearms imports during the same period (Diaz, 1999, pp. 73-74).[58]

China North Industry Corporation (Norinco) is the most significant local producer of small arms and ammunition, and produces a wide range of products for both domestic and export markets.

The company was established in 1980 and falls under the Ministry of Machinery and Electronics (MME) (Jane's World Defence Industries, 2000). It incorporates 160 enterprises and employs more than 700,000 personnel. It currently controls about 30 research institutes and more than 200 plants.

Between 1980 and 1990 Norinco earned a total of US$ 12 billion from arms exports, and throughout the 1990s, total sales of military and civilian products have averaged about US$ 2 billion per year (Jane's World Armies, 2000, p. 150). However, weapons account for only 20-30 per cent of overall production, while civilian products account for the remaining 70 per cent (*Jane's Sentinel Security Assessment*, 29 September 2000). PolyTechnologies, another state-owned company, together with Norinco, are the dominant suppliers of small arms to the lucrative US firearms market (Diaz, 1999, p.72). Norinco has been known to license its products for production abroad, including Albania, Egypt, and Pakistan. In addition, the company has provided technical assistance to both Pakistan and Myanmar's defence industries.

Australia: Australia Defence Industries (ADI), established in 1989, is the country's most important producer of small arms. Previously government-owned, it was sold to Thomson-CSF and Transfield, in 1999 (*Asia-Pacific Defence Reporter*, Oct/Nov 2000). ADI has a number of production facilities in different parts of the country, including an explosives site at Mulwala, a munitions site at Benalla, Victoria, and a small arms facility at Lithgow, New South Wales. ADI produces a light machine gun under license from FN Herstal (Belgium) and an assault rifle and grenade launcher under license from Steyr-Mannlicher (Austria).

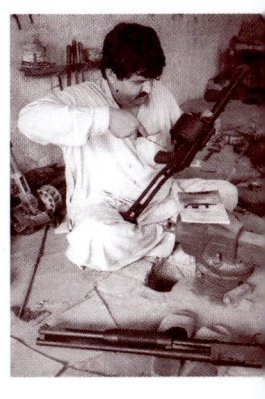

Illicit production

In addition to legal production in complex manufacturing processes (production lines), small arms are also produced illicitly in small private workshops, or in larger production lines. Illicit production, including craft/homemade production of small arms, takes place in many countries, including in some, like Trinidad and Tobago, that do not possess a legal small arms manufacturing capability. In some countries the state itself may engage in illicit production, by manufacturing another country's or company's products without permission (e.g. China).

Illicit production of small arms, including craft/homemade production, takes place in at least 25 countries.

According to information supplied by governments to the UN, illicit production of small arms, including craft/homemade production, takes place in at least 25 countries (UN 1999a). These include: Argentina, Brazil, Cambodia, Canada, Chile, China, Colombia, the Czech Republic, Indonesia, India, Japan, Pakistan, Papua New Guinea, Philippines, South Africa, Trinidad and Tobago, the UK, and the US.[59]

Detailed information on the value and volume of illicit global production is not available. Thus, it is not possible to assess whether the incidence and scope (value and volume) of illicit production is on the increase or not. However, the following case studies from South Africa, South East Asia, and South Asia provide some illustrative examples of the different dimensions of illicit small arms production. Illicit production is not confined to developing countries: it also occurs in many developed countries, including Canada, Japan, the UK (including Northern Ireland), and the US.

South Africa[60]

Before 1983, the South African Government prohibited the granting of firearm licences to 'Black' South Africans (those people classified as Blacks, Coloureds, and Asians). Between 1983-94, only a handful of Blacks were granted firearm licences. Only after the country's first democratic elections in 1994 were Blacks able to obtain firearm licences on a non-discriminatory basis. The difficulties in obtaining these licences, together with the history of armed struggle, led to the development of a homemade firearm industry in South Africa, particularly during the later years of the liberation struggle in the 1980s.

The types and quality of homemade firearms vary considerably, with some displaying a high level of craftsmanship. The most common type of homemade firearm is the 'pipe gun'. These firearms do not circulate among different users as much as other commercially produced firearms, since they are usually manufactured by the actual users and not mass-produced.

There are no official figures on the numbers of homemade firearms in circulation. The Joint Investigation Team of the SAPS estimated in 1997 that there were between 20-30,000 homemade firearms in circulation in South Africa. Between 1994 and 1999 the Illegal Firearm Investigation Unit of the SAPS retrieved a total of 16,781 homemade firearms (including rifles, pistols, and revolvers). This amounted to 16 per cent of the total number (106,166) of illicit firearms seized by the police. The vast majority of seized homemade firearms were pistols and revolvers (Chetty, 2000, p. 43). While the numbers of seized homemade firearms has remained relatively stable during the period 1994-99 (an average of nearly 2,800 per annum), this does not provide any clear indication of whether the incidence of homemade production is increasing or not.

South East Asia[61]

Illicit production of small arms occurs throughout South East Asia. In countries, such as Indonesia, Laos, Malaysia, and Thailand, most illicit production is geared towards simple, low technology and low quality hunting rifles. However, in the Philippines, illicit production has become an important industry, providing arms for local criminal elements, as well as in other countries such as Japan.

Most of the illicit production in the Philippines is centred in the south, in Cebu and Danao, although there have been reports of arms production in Sara as well. There has been some discussion within the government on trying to control illicit production by granting licenses to organizations such as the Worker's League of Danao Corporation, which acts on behalf of a number of individual gunsmiths (*Asiaweek*, 19 January 1996).

Groups operating in countries such as Myanmar and the Philippines are also known to have the capacity to produce various types of small arms. The Moro Islamic Liberation Front (MILF) alters rifles and produces rocket-propelled grenade launchers and shells, as well as anti-aircraft guns (*Business World*, 29 June 1999). The Karen National Liberation Army and Karenni Army operating in eastern Myanmar are known to have produced landmines and mortars. The former Mong Thai Army had a foundry and weapons production centre at its base in Shan State until it capitulated to the Myanmar government in 1996 (*Jane's Intelligence Review*, 1 November 1998).

India and Pakistan have had thriving 'cottage industries' in illicit arms production since the era of the British Raj.

Illicit production in South Asia[62]

India and Pakistan have had thriving 'cottage industries' in illicit arms production since the era of the British Raj. The traditional centres of the industry are: Darra Adam Khel in Pakistan's Northwest Frontier Province and Bihar in India. In India, illicit production also occurs in Uttar Pradesh, West Bengal, Andhra Pradesh, Punjab, Coimbatore, and Tamil Nadu (Behera, 2000).

Numerous clandestine factories manufacturing guns, pistols, revolvers, and hand grenades are operating in different parts of India. The largest illicit arms workshop is believed to be in Bihar, where observers have noted that gun making seems to be the only industry that thrives in many villages. An unofficial study conducted in 1987 revealed that there were 1,500 illicit arms manufacturing workshops in the region, and police records for the same year suggested that there were 200 illicit factories in Nalanda district of Bihar alone (Behera, 2000; Chandran, 2000). Uttar Predesh also has a significant amount of illicit workshops and factories. Bamhaur is well known for the weapons it produces, and products from local workshops can be found all over the country. Gunsmiths take great pride in their work and often inscribe 'Made in Bamhaur' on their products (Behera, 2000).

Weapons manufactured illicitly in India primarily arm private armies, criminals, caste groups, and individuals. Bihar arms can sell for US$ 5-7 each. In Bamhaur, arms can range in price from US$ 47-116. Factories in Coimbatore and Tamil Nadu are reported to have provided arms to the LTTE in Sri Lanka until they were discovered during state-wide raids in 1991 (Behera, 2000).

India's illicit gunsmiths are poor cousins when compared to those of Darra Adam Khel in Pakistan. Darra is the heart of Pakistan's notorious 'arms bazaar' and it is here that one can acquire practically any small arm desired at low cost—Kalashnikovs, M-16s, Uzis, and even guns hidden in walking sticks and ballpoint pens (*The Nation,* 2 August 1998). Some are originals left over from the war in Afghanistan; others are copies made in back alley workshops, repaired originals, or copies made from cannibalized parts. Often the only difference between original and local designs is that locally manufactured barrels are made from an inferior quality of metal (Kartha, 2000). Original AK-47s sell for about US$ 320, but an identical copy starts at US$ 50 (*The Guardian,* 15 December 2000).

Darra's gunsmiths are famous for their skills and expertise, which have been passed down from father-to-son for generations. Before the Soviet invasion of Afghanistan in 1979, they produced mainly rifles and shotguns in addition to a wide range of pistols (Malik, 2000). Now, they are adept at producing authentic copies of any light weapon desired in a matter of days. They have been known to make imitation Chinese laser-sight pistols and Japanese pen pistols down to the finest detail (Kartha, 2000). Some of Darra's elder craftsmen have also invented their own designs, for example a shotgun that works like a revolver with a chamber holding six shells (*The Nation,* 2 August 1998).

Darra's gunsmiths are keenly aware of market trends. At one point, they supplied Afghan *mujahideen* rebels in their struggle against Soviet occupation. Now they are the main suppliers of guns to Kashmir and to Pakistan's troubled provinces of Punjab and Sind. Darra's shops and factories offer home-delivery anywhere in the country and are known to have also sold arms to guerrillas from Northern Ireland and the Middle East (*The Nation,* 2 August 1998).

Recent reports suggest that the Pakistani Government is planning on incorporating Darra's illicit gunsmiths into the legal fold (*The Guardian,* 15 December 2000). In India, the government has also made some attempts to curtail illicit production through sporadic and routine raids, which do little to stem the phenomena. However, it has been difficult to enforce the law when many of these illicit production facilities are funded and run by ministers or ruling party officials (Behera, 2000; Kartha, 2000).

Working in the heart of Pakistan's notorious 'arms bazaar', Darra's gunsmiths are famous for their skills and expertise, which have been passed along for generations.

Conclusions

This chapter has provided an initial survey of global small arms production. It has identified the countries and companies that currently produce small arms, and provided global estimates of the value and volume of their production. It has also profiled some of the world's most popular legal and illicit small arms products, ranging from handguns to machine guns.

It is difficult to assess the size and economic significance of the global small arms industry due to the current lack of detailed and reliable information. Greater transparency is urgently needed to gain a better understanding of the scope of global small arms production—and especially its implications for the security, development, and humanitarian problems associated with their widespread proliferation, availability, and misuse

While the volume of small arms production is currently less than it was during the last years of the Cold War, millions of these types of weapons are still being produced every year. Certainly, there is no global shortage of small arms. The production of new, and ever more sophisticated, small arms is spreading to an increasing number of countries and companies throughout the world. Simultaneously, large numbers of surplus small arms continue to re-circulate from one country to another and from one conflict to the next.

Based on estimates presented in this chapter, the *value* of global small arms production, including ammunition, for the year 2000 was estimated to be worth at least US$ 4 billion. In terms of *volume,* it is estimated that roughly 4.3 million new small arms were produced in 2000, down from an annual average of 6.3 million during the period 1980-98. This represents a decline in production of at least 30 per cent. While it is possible that the current volume of global small arms production is less than a decade ago, this does not necessarily mean that we are witnessing a long-term decline in the size of the international small arms market.

While the demand for new small arms may be declining, based on the estimates of the volume of global production, the supply side of the market seems to be expanding. Every day new, cheaper, and more lethal types of small arms appear on the international market, driven by technological and industrial developments (e.g. new types of materials and production techniques), and by the changing nature of warfare and military doctrine.

In addition to these new types of small arms, there has also been a marked increase in the number of countries and companies that legally produce small arms since the mid-1990s.

The number of companies has more than tripled in less than two decades, from 196 in the 1980s to about 600 today. The number of countries is growing too: add to the 95 countries that are legal small arms producers, those others that produce illicitly, and it becomes clear that well over half the world's countries are small arms producers. An increasing number of these producers are developing countries in parts of Asia, Africa, and Latin America that have recently developed their own local small arms industries for a variety of nationalistic, strategic, and often unconvincing economic reasons.

The combination of shrinking demand, and the increasing number of suppliers has made the international small arms market intensely competitive, with the result that many companies have been forced into selling their products at low, and often unprofitable, prices. This has meant that a number of companies, both state-owned and private, in countries such as Argentina, France, Hungary, Poland, South Africa, Spain, Switzerland, and the US, are experiencing severe financial problems. Some have gone bankrupt or left the small arms business altogether, while others are forced to rely on *ad hoc* government contracts and subsidies to survive.

The highly competitive nature of the international arms market and the increasing number of actors, together with other key features of the global small arms industry (e.g. licensed production and the incidence of illicit and craft production), could jeopardize attempts by governments and the international community to tackle the small arms proliferation problem.

Furthermore, the ongoing intra- and inter-state conflicts in many parts of the world, together with attempts by the international community (e.g. UN, NATO) to deal with them, means that the demand for new small arms from governments and non-state actors will continue. Added to this, the presence of new and increasing numbers of companies and countries that produce small arms—and who are willing to sell to anyone, anywhere, at any price—means that it is now easier for authoritarian governments, non-state actors, terrorists, and criminals to obtain weapons that are newer, more sophisticated, and more lethal than ever before. The need for government control of small arms production has become an urgent international security issue.

For further information and current developments on small arms issues please check our website at www.smallarmssurvey.org

1   List of Abbreviations

ADI	Australia Defence Industries
AOI	Arab Organisation for Industrialisation
ATK	Alliant Techsystems (US)
AVRT	State Privatisation and Asset Managing Agency (Hungary)
BATF	Bureau of Alcohol, Tobacco and Firearms (US)
BICC	Bonn International Center for Conversion
CIS	Chartered Industries of Singapore
CIS	Commonwealth of Independent States
DGFM	Dirección General de Fabricaciones Militares (Argentina)
DICON	Defence Industry Corporation of Nigeria
EBO	Hellenic Arms Industry (Greece)
ENSB	Empressa Nacional Santa Barbara (Spain)
FAMAE	Fabricas y Maestranzas del Ejercito (Chile)
HK	Heckler and Koch
IISS	International Institute of Strategic Studies
IMBEL	Industria de Material Belico Brasil
IMI	Israel Military Industries
ISER	Institute for Religious Studies (Brazil)
LTTE	Liberation Tigers of Tamil Eelam
MKEK	Makina ve Kimya Endustri
MMP	Ministry of Military Production (Egypt)
NATO	North Atlantic Treaty Organization
NISAT	Norwegian Initiative on Small Arms Transfers
NOMP	National Organisation for Military Production (Egypt)
POF	Pakistan Ordnance Factories
RO	Royal Ordnance
SAPS	South African Police Service
SIG	Schweizerische Industrue-Gesellschaft (Switzerland)
SIPRI	Stockholm International Peace Research Institute
SM	Swiss Ammunition Enterprise
SMG	Sub-machine Gun
SSA	Sub-Saharan Africa
SSM	Under Secretariat for Defence Industry (Turkey)
STC	Singapore Technology Corporation
STK	Singapore Technologies Kinetics
SW	Swiss Ordnance Enterprise
UK	United Kingdom
UN	United Nations
UNITA	União Nacional Para a Independência Total de Angola
US	United States
WTO	Warsaw Treaty Organization
ZDI	Zimbabwe Defence Industries

1 Endnotes

1 Due to a lack of information this chapter does not examine in any detail light weapons products such as mounted grenade launchers, portable anti-aircraft and anti-tank guns, or the companies or countries that produce them.

2 Two reports published in the mid-1990s estimated that between 250-300 companies in 50-70 countries produced small arms (Abel, 2000).

3 The number of companies is based on the following sources: Jane's Infantry Weapons (2000-2001), Jane's Ammunition Handbook (2000-2001), Jane's World Defence Industry (2000), Abel (2000), Forecast International (2000), US Economic Census (1997), company information, visits to defence exhibitions, and the OMEGA Foundation company database.

4 Globalisation has also had a significant impact on the process of defence industry restructuring. See study by Bitzinger (1999).

5 See also the recent study by Inbar and Zilberfarb (1998).

6 A report in 1995 estimated that licensed production was taking place in at least 21 developing countries, 16 of which were also exporting the small arms they manufactured (Klare, 1995).

7 Based on information obtained from Jane's Infantry Weapons (2000), Forecast International (2000) and company material.

8 See studies by Sanders (1990), US Office of Technology Assessment (1991), Klare and Andersen (1996), and Keller (1995) on licensed production.

9 It is difficult to verify the reliability of the information presented by Forecast International, with the exception of the information presented for the US, which contains details of recent US government procurement contracts, and information from the Bureau of Alcohol, Tobacco and Firearms.

10 The term firearms includes handguns (pistols and revolvers) and long guns (rifles and shotguns), but excludes machine guns and other weapons that are often classified as 'small arms' (BATF, 2000a, p. 6).

11 This figure is significantly lower than the figure of 550 million that is given in the chapter on stockpiles. This is because the figures from Forecast International do not include many of the weapons produced for private use. The fact that the annual average of 6.3 million for the period 1980-98 is much lower than the annual average during the period 1945-80, given the higher production levels of small arms during the 1960s and 1970s, might also explain the difference.

12 The average production costs for small arms in the US may be higher than for developing countries, given higher wage costs in the US relative to costs in countries in Asia, Africa, and Latin America. However, the efficiency of production means that non-labour production costs may actually be lower in the US than in certain developing countries.

13 There is almost no official, or unofficial information on the size and scope of domestic arms production in China and the Russian Federation. This makes it impossible to undertake an objective comparison of the size and scope of small arms pro-

duction in these countries as compared to the US.

14 According to *The Guardian* (15 December 2000) original AKs sell for between US$ 315-360 in Darra Adam Khel in Pakistan while cheap copies sell for US$ 45.

15 Information obtained from Jane's Infantry Weapons (2000), Jane's World Armies (2000), the Arms Management Programme (AMP) of the Institute for Security Studies (ISS) in South Africa and McKenzie (1999).

16 The information in this section is from ISER (2000).

17 Since 1997 it has been a crime to display/carry certain types of weapons in public.

18 This department—*Divisao de Fiscalizacao de Armas e Explosivos*—registers legal guns sold to civilians, issues gun permits, and keeps all weapons and explosives apprehended by the police.

19 Approximately 3000 records exist for 1989, but these have not been entered into the database.

20 Chile for example has a well-known and long tradition of homemade arms (*armas hechizas*) which are manufactured in the poor areas (*poblaciones*) south of Santiago de Chile (Dreyfus, 2000).

21 The top domestic producers of handguns include Sturm, Ruger & Co (pistols) and Smith & Wesson (revolvers) (BATF, 1998b).

22 By comparison the tobacco industry in 1997 had shipments (production) worth US$ 28.3 billion, while the alcohol industry had shipments worth US$ 27.7 billion during the same year (BATF, 2000a).

23 Information from Norwegian Initiative on Small Arms Transfers (NISAT), Jane's Infantry Weapons (2000), Jane's Ammunition Handbook (2000)and Forecast International (2000).

24 Information from Jane's Infantry Weapons (2000), Jane's Ammunition Handbook (2000) and Forecast International (2000).

25 Information from Jane's Infantry Weapons (2000), Forecast International (2000), and company promotional material.

26 See study by Dreyfus (2000).

27 See Jane's Infantry Weapons (2000) and Forecast International (2000).

28 See Jane's Infantry Weapons (2000) and Forecast International (2000).

29 Information from Jane's Infantry Weapons (2000), Forecast International (2000), and company promotional material.

30 Other producers include Kufsteiner Waffenstube, Hirtenberger, Dynamit Nobel, and Arges Armaturen (*Military Technology*, July 2000).

31 Other major small arms producers include Titanite (grenades), Manufacture d'Armes Automatiques de Bayonne (MAB) (pistols), PGM Precision (sniper rifles), Lacroix Defense (light support weapons), and SAE Alsetex (tactical shotguns, grenades). Major ammunition producers include Gevched (ammunition), SFM Defense (ammunition), and Athena

(ammunition) (Jane's Infantry Weapons, 2000-2001).

32 Other small arms producers include Bernardelli (shotguns and pistols), Fabarm (shotguns), Fratelli Tanfoglio (pistols), Fiocchi Munizioni (ammunition), Europa Metalli (ammunition) (Jane's Infantry Weapons, 2000). Alenia Difesia, which is 100 per cent owned by Finmeccanica, the partially state-owned defence group, produces mortars. BPD Difesa e Spazio, which is 100 per cent owned by the Fiat Group, produces various types of small arms ammunition.

33 Other small arms producers include Dynamit Nobel, Carl Walther Waffenfabrik, and the Diehl Group.

34 Other major small arms producers include Armalon (rifles), Accuracy International (rifles), FR Ordnance (rifles), BMS Trading Limited (rifles), Manroy Engineering (machine guns), SF Firearms (pistols), John Slough of Londond (pistols), Victory Arms (pistols), Parker-Hale (rifles), and Haley and Weller (grenades) (Jane's Infantry Weapons, 2000).

35 The acquisition of Heckler and Koch in 1991 gave Royal Ordnance access to 74 per cent of the European small arms market, and a significant share of the world market (Forecast International, 2000).

36 See studies by Walter (1999) and Cutshaw (1998) for details of Russian small arms and ammunition.

37 In 1996 President Clinton imposed voluntary restrictions on the import of certain types of Russian small arms and ammunition, including SKS assault rifles and Makarov pistols (Diaz, 1999).

38 Information from Jane's Infantry Weapons (2000), Jane's Ammunition Handbook (2000), and Forecast International (2000).

39 The information on East Central Europe is based on Kiss (2000, 1997a, 1997b).

40 The countries of East Central Europe include Bulgaria, Czech Republic, Hungary, Poland, Romania, and Slovakia.

41 In 1988, there were 220,000 people employed in the defence industry in Poland, and 140,000 in Czechoslovakia (BICC, 2000).

42 According to a recent study, only three out of 45 defence-related companies in Poland were in a sound financial condition in 1999 (Kiss, 2000).

43 In April 2000, the Czech government placed a US$ 15.5 million order with Ceska Zbrojovka to provide 46,000 pistols to the Czech police over the next four to five years (*The Prague Post,* 26 April 2000).

44 The company Ceska Zbrojovka has emerged as a highly successful small arms producer in recent years, thanks to its role as traditional supplier to the Czech armed forces and police. The company is also a successful exporter, and a large proportion of its output is exported to the US (Diaz, 1999).

45 Other small arms producers include Dezamet, Kombinat Przemyslu Narzedziowego, Widezewskie Zaklady Masyn Wlokienniczych, Zaklady Mechaniczne Tarnow, Osrodek Badawaczo, and Zaklady Sprzetu Precyzynego.

46 Hungary exported more than 200,000 handguns to the US between 1991 and 1996 (Diaz, 1999).

47 The major production facilities include Igman (small arms and ammunition), Pretis (mortars), Pobjeda (ammunition), Bratstvo (mortars, rifles), Slavko Rodic (mortars, grenades), and Iron and Steel works (small arms, ammunition) (*Jane's Sentinel Security Assessment,* 10 December 1999).

48 Private companies include Advanced Weapons Technologies (rifles), Elviemek (grenades), and Matren (rifle magazines).

49 There is some speculation that Libya also produces small arms, including the Makarov 9mm pistol. However, the Middle East Military Balance 1999-2000 does not provide any information on domestic small arms production in Libya.

50 For details of the factories under the control of the NOMP see study by Feiler (1998).

51 Private sector producers include KSN Industries (pistols), Soltam (mortars), and the Kalia Israel Cartridge Company (ammunition).

52 However, production of the rifles has been held up by German export regulations because of Turkish transgressions against the country's Kurdish minority.

53 The closure of Aram in 1999 was linked to financial problems and the results of a police investigation, which revealed that the company was operating outside the conditions of their licence.

54 The closure of Ammu-Tech was linked to the results of a police investigation concerning illegal arms exports. There are unconfirmed reports that Ammu-Tech was also involved in an abortive attempt to establish a small arms ammunition reloading facility in Kigali, Rwanda.

55 It is reported that Bangladesh has a small arms manufacturing plant that was built by China in the late 1960s. The plant was damaged during the war for independence and was refurbished in the late 1970's to produce semi-automatic 7.62mm SKS rifles and ammunition. The factory was later upgraded with Chinese assistance to produce variations of the AK-47 assault rifle (*Jane's Sentinel Security Assessment,* 28 May 1999).

56 The information on small arms producers in ASEAN countries is based on Kramer (2000a).

57 See studies on China's defence industry by Shichor (1998) and Brömmelhörster and Frankenstein (1997).

58 China's exports of firearms to the US was stopped in 1994 when President Clinton imposed a ban on Chinese firearms imports (Diaz, 1999, p. 75).

59 Some information on craft production is reported in the 1999 *UN International Study on Firearm Regulation.*

60 Information in this section is from the Arms Management Programme of the Institute for Security Studies, South Africa, and Chetty (2000).

61 Information in this section from Kramer (2000b).

62 Information in this section from Kramer (2000b), Kartha (2000), Malik (2000), and Chandran (2000).

1 Appendix

Appendix 1.1 Small arms producers

No	Country	Small Arms (1)	Ammunition	Sources (2)
1	Albania	x	x	Jane's Sentinel, 10 December 1999
2	Algeria	x		Middle East Military Balance,1999-2000
3	Argentina	x	x	
4	Armenia	x	x	Jane's Sentinel, 16 July 1999
5	Australia	x	x	
6	Austria	x	x	
7	Bangladesh	x	x	Jane's Sentinel, 28 May 1999
8	Belarus	x	x	
9	Belgium	x	x	
10	Bolivia		x	Jane's Sentinel, 4 February 2000
11	Bosnia and Herzegovina	x	x	
12	Brazil	x	x	
13	Bulgaria	x	x	
14	Burkina Faso	x	x	
15	Cambodia	x	x	Jane's Sentinel, 6 April 2000
16	Cameroon		x	
17	Canada	x	x	
18	Chile	x	x	
19	China	x	x	
20	Colombia	x	x	Jane's Sentinel, 4 February 2000
21	Croatia	x	x	Jane's Sentinel, 23 August 2000
22	Cuba	x	x	Jane's Sentinel, 11 June 1999
23	Cyprus		x	
24	Czech Republic	x	x	
25	Denmark	x	x	
26	Dominican Republic	x	x	
27	Ecuador		x	
28	Egypt	x	x	Middle East Military Balance 1999-2000
29	Estonia	x		Jane's Sentinel, 3 April 2000;
30	Ethiopia	x		Jane's Sentinel, 22 February 2000
31	Finland	x	x	
32	France	x	x	
33	Germany	x	x	
34	Greece	x	x	
35	Guatemala		x	Jane's Sentinel, 11 June 1999
36	Guinea	x	x	
37	Hungary	x	x	
38	India	x	x	
39	Indonesia	x	x	
40	Iran	x	x	Middle East Military Balance 1999-2000
41	Iraq	x	x	Middle East Military Balance 1999-2000
42	Israel	x	x	
43	Italy	x	x	
44	Japan	x	x	
45	Kazakhstan	x		Jane's Sentinel, 31 May 2000
46	Kenya		x	Jane's Intelligence Review, 1 February 1998
47	Korea, North	x	x	
48	Korea, South	x	x	
49	Lithuania	x		Jane's Sentinel, 3 April 2000
50	Luxembourg	x		

No	Country	Small Arms (1)	Ammunition	Sources (2)
51	Macedonia		x	Jane's Sentinel, 12 April 2000
52	Malaysia	x	x	
53	Malta		x	
54	Mexico	x	x	
55	Moldova	x		Jane's Sentinel, 9 November 1999
56	Monaco	x	x	
57	Morocco	x	x	Middle East Military Balance, 1999-2000
58	Myanmar	x	x	Jane's Intelligence Review, 1 March 2000
59	Netherlands		x	
60	New Zealand	x	x	
61	Nigeria	x	x	Africa News, 3 June 2000
62	Norway	x	x	
63	Pakistan	x	x	
64	Papua New Guinea	x		
65	Paraguay		x	Jane's Sentinel, 24 August 2000
66	Peru	x	x	
67	Philippines	x	x	
68	Poland	x	x	
69	Portugal	x	x	
70	Romania	x	x	
71	Russian Federation	x	x	
72	Saudi Arabia	x	x	Middle East Military Balance, 1999-2000
73	Singapore	x	x	
74	Slovakia	x	x	
75	Slovenia	x	x	
76	South Africa	x	x	
77	Spain	x	x	
78	Sudan	x	x	
79	Sweden	x	x	
80	Switzerland	x	x	
81	Syria		x	Middle East Military Balance, 1999-2000
82	Taiwan	x	x	
83	Tanzania		x	Africa News, 15 May 2000
84	Thailand	x	x	
85	Turkey	x	x	Middle East Military Balance, 1999-2000
86	Uganda		x	Africa News, 2 October 2000
87	Ukraine	x	x	
88	United Arab Emirates		x	Jane's Sentinel, 26 April 2000
89	United Kingdom	x	x	
90	United States	x	x	
91	Uruguay		x	Jane's Sentinel, 4 February 2000
92	Venezuela	x	x	
93	Vietnam		x	Jane's Sentinel, 6 April 2000
94	Yugoslavia (Serbia)	x	x	
95	Zimbabwe		x	Jane's Sentinel, 10 October 1999

Notes: (1) Includes firearms (handguns and long guns) and small arms and light weapons.

(2) If no information from other sources listed below, then alternative source listed in this column.

Sources: United Nations, 1999b; Gander and Cutshaw, 2000; Reed, 2000; Brom and Shapir, 2000: Heyman, 2000 ; BICC, 2000; Ezell, 1995; Ezell, 1988.

1 Bibliography

Abel, Pete. 2000. 'Manufacturing Trends: Globalizing the Source.' In Lora Lumpe, ed. *Running Guns: The Global Black Market in Small Arms*. London: Zed Books.

Anthony, Ian, ed. 1994. *The Future of Defence Industries in Central and Eastern Europe*. SIPRI Research Report No. 7. Oxford: Oxford University Press.

Anthony, Ian, ed. 1998. *Russia and the Arms Trade*. Oxford: Oxford University Press.

Banerjee, Dipankar, ed. 2000. *South Asia at Gun Point: Small Arms and Light Weapons Proliferation*. Colombo: Regional Centre for Strategic Studies.

Batchelor, Peter and Susan Willett. 1998. *Disarmament and Defence Industrial Adjustment in South Africa*. Oxford: Oxford University Press.

Batchelor, Peter and Paul Dunne. 1998. 'The Restructuring of South Africa's Defence Industry.' *African Security Review*, Vol. 7, No.6.

Behera, Ajay Darshan. 2000. 'Domestic sources of diffusion of light weapons in India.' In Dipankar Banerjee, ed. *South Asia at Gun Point: Small Arms and Light Weapons Proliferation*. Colombo: Regional Centre for Strategic Studies.

Berrigan, Frida and Michelle Ciarrocca. 2000. *Weapons at War: Profiling the Small Arms Industry*. New York: Arms Trade Resource Center.

Bitzinger, Richard. 1999. 'Globalisation in the Post-Cold War Defence Industry: Challenges and Opportunities.' In Ann Markusen and Sean Costigan, eds. *Arming the Future: A Defence Industry for the 21st Century*. New York: Council on Foreign Relations.

Bonn International Center for Conversion. 1998. *Conversion Survey 1998: Global Disarmament, Defence Industry Consolidation and Conversion*. Oxford: Oxford University Press.

Bonn International Center for Conversion. 2000. *Conversion Survey 2000: Global Disarmament, Demilitarization and Demobilization*. Baden-Baden: Nomos Verlagsgesellschaft.

Boutwell, Jeffrey and Michael Klare. 2000a. 'A Scourge of Small Arms.' *Scientific American*. June, pp. 48-53.

____. 2000b. *Light Weapons and Civil Conflict: Controlling the Tools of Violence*. New York: Rowman and Littlefield.

Brom, Shlomo and Yiftah Shapir, eds. 2000. *The Middle East Military Balance 1999-2000*. London: The MIT Press.

Brömmelhörster, Jörn and John Frankenstein, eds. 1997. *Mixed Motives, Uncertain Outcomes - Defence Conversion in China*. Boulder, Colorado: Lynne Rienner.

Brzoska, Michael. 1998. 'Too Small to Vanish: Too Large to Flourish: Dilemmas and Practices of Defence Industry Restructuring in West European Countries.' In Efraim Inbar and Benzion Zilberfarb, eds. *The Politics and Economics of Defence Industries*. London: Frank Cass.

Brzoska, Michael and Ann Markusen eds. 2000. 'Military Industrial Conversion: Special Issue.' *International Regional Science Review*, Vol.23, No.1.

Chandran, Suba. 2000. 'Meeting the Demand: Illegal Production in India.' In Dipankar Banerjee, ed. *South Asia at Gun Point: Small Arms and Light Weapons Proliferation*. Colombo: Regional Centre for Strategic Studies.

Chetty, Robert, ed. 2000. *Firearm Use and Distribution in South Africa*. Pretoria: National Crime Prevention Centre.

Craft, Cassady. 1999. *Weapons for Peace, Weapons for War*. London: Routledge.

Cutshaw, Charlie. 1998. *The New World of Russian Small Arms and Ammo*. Boulder, Colorado: Paladin Press.

Diaz, Tom. 1999. *Making a Killing: The Business of Guns in America*. New York: The New Press.

Dreyfus, Pablo. 2000. *Small Arms Producers in the Southern Cone Countries of Latin America*. Background Paper. Geneva: Small Arms Survey.

Edgar, Alistair and David Haglund. 1995. *The Canadian Defence Industry in the New Global Environment*. Montreal: McGill-Queen's University Press.

Ezell, Virginia. 1995. *Report on International Small Arms Production and Proliferation*. Alexandria, Virginia: Institute for Research on Small Arms and International Security.

Ezell, Edward. 1988. *Small Arms Today Second Edition*. London: Arms and Armour Press.

Feiler, Gil. 1998. 'The Military Industries of the Arab World in the 1990s.' In Efraim Inbar and Benzion Zilberfarb, eds. *The Politics and Economics of Defence Industries*. London: Frank Cass.

Forecast International, 2000. *Ordnance and Munitions Forecast (October)*. Newtown, Connecticut: Forecast International.

Gander, Terry and Charles Cutshaw, eds. 2000. *Jane's Ammunition Handbook: 2000-2001*. Coulsdon: Jane's Information Group.

Gander, Terry and Charles Cutshaw, eds. 2000. *Jane's Infantry Weapons: 2000-2001*. Coulsdon: Jane's Information Group.

Gonchar, Ksenia. 2000. *Russia's Defence Industry at the Turn of the Century*. Brief No. 17. Bonn: Bonn International Center for Conversion.

Hussain, Neila. 2000. 'Problems of Proliferation of Small Arms in Bangladesh.' In Dipankar Banerjee, ed. *South Asia at Gun Point: Small Arms and Light Weapons Proliferation*. Colombo: Regional Centre for Strategic Studies.

Hébert, Jean-Paul, Yves Bélanger and Peter Lock. 2000. *Naissance de l'Europe de l'Armement*. Cahier d'Etudes Stratégiques, Nr. 27. Paris: CIR-PES.

Heller, Mark. 1998. *The Middle East Military Balance 1996*. New York: Colombia University Press.

Heyman, Charles, ed. 2000. *Jane's World Armies, Issue Eight*. Coulsdon: Jane's Information Group.

Hogg. Ian, ed. 1989. *Jane's Infantry Weapons: 1989-90*. Coulsdon: Jane's Information Group.

Hogg, Ian. 1998. *The World's Sniping Rifles*. London: Greenhill Books.

Inbar, Efraim and Benzion Zilberfarb, eds. 1998. *The Politics and Economics of Defence Industries*. London: Frank Cass.

Institute for Religious Studies (ISER). 2000. *Small Arms Apprehended in Rio de Janeiro*. Background Paper. Geneva: Small Arms Survey.

Institute for Research on Small Arms in International Security. Various years. *Small Arms World Report*. Alexandria, Virginia: Institute for Research on Small Arms and International Security.

Jauhianinen, Jussi, Luc Mampaey, Joachim Schuster et al. 1999. *Post Cold War Conversion in Europe: Defence Restructuring in the 1990s and the Regional Dimension*. Les Rapports du GRIP.

Bruxelles: GRIP.

Kartha, Tara. 2000. *South Asia: A Rising Spiral of Proliferation*. Background Paper. Geneva: Small Arms Survey.

Keller, William. 1995. *Arm in Arm: The Political Economy of the Global Arms Trade*. New York: Basic Books.

Kenkel, Kai. 2000a. *Kalashnikov Assault Rifle*. Background Paper. Geneva: Small Arms Survey.

____. 2000b. *Uzi Sub-machine Gun*. Background Paper. Geneva: Small Arms Survey.

Klare, Michael. 1995. 'Light Weapons Diffusion.' In Jasjit Singh, ed. *Light Weapons and International Security*. Delhi: Pugwash Conferences on Science and World Affairs.

____. 1997. 'The New Arms Race: Light Weapons and International Security.' *Current History*. April.

____. 1999. 'The Kalashnikov Age.' *The Bulletin of the Atomic Scientists*. Vol. 55, No.1. January/February.

Klare, Michael and David Andersen. 1996. *A Scourge of Guns: The Diffusion of Small Arms and Light Weapons in Latin America*. Washington, DC: Federation of American Scientists.

Kiss, Yudit. 1997a. *The Defence Industry in East Central Europe: Restructuring and Conversion*. Oxford: Oxford University Press.

____.1997b. *The Transformation of the Defence Industry in Hungary*. Brief No. 14. Bonn: Bonn International Center for Conversion.

____. 2000. *Small Arms Producers in East-Central Europe*. Background Paper. Geneva: Small Arms Survey.

Klieman, Aharon. 1998. 'Adapting to a Shrinking Market: The Israeli Case.' In Efraim Inbar and Benzion Zilberfarb, eds. 1998. *The Politics and Economics of Defence Industries*. London: Frank Cass.

Kramer, Katherine. 2000a. *Small Arms Producers in ASEAN*. Background Paper. Geneva: Small Arms Survey.

____. 2000b. *Illicit Small Arms Production in South Asia and ASEAN*. Background Paper. Geneva: Small Arms Survey.

Lock, Peter. 2000. 'Rheinmetall: un paradigme de la restructuration du secteur de la défense en Allemagne.' In Jean-Paul Hébert, Yves Bélanger and Peter Lock. *Naissance de l'Europe de l'Armement*. Cahier d'Etudes Stratégiques, Nr. 27.

Paris: CIRPES.

Lumpe, Lora, ed. 2000. *Running Guns: The Global Black Market in Small Arms*. London: Zed Books.

Malik, Salma. 2000. 'Domestic Production, Illegal Manufacture and Leakage of Small Arms - A Case Study of Pakistan.' In Dipankar Banerjee, ed. *South Asia at Gun Point: Small Arms and Light Weapons Proliferation*. Colombo: Regional Centre for Strategic Studies.

Mampaey, Luc. 1998. *L'Industrie Belge de Défense*. Les Rapports du GRIP, No.1. Bruxelles: GRIP.

Mampaey, Luc. 2000. *Groupe Herstal S.A: L'Heure des décisions*. Les Rapports du GRIP, No. 6. Bruxelles: GRIP.

McKenzie, Katharine. 1999. *Domestic Gun Control Policy in Ten SADC Countries*. Report Commissioned by Gun Free South Africa. Johannesburg: Gun Free South Africa.

Mlambo, Norman. 1998. 'The Zimbabwe Defence Industry: 1980-1995.' *Southern African Centre for Defence Information Working Paper*, No. 2.

Norwegian Initiative on Small Arms Transfers. 2000. *Canadian Small Arms Industry and Products*. <http://www.nisat.org>

Oden, Michael. 1998. 'Defence Mega-Mergers and Alternative Strategies.' In Gerald Susman and Sean O'Keefe, eds. *The Defence Industry in the Post Cold-War Era*. New York: Pergamon.

Oosthuysen, Glenn. 1996. *Small Arms Proliferation and Control in Southern Africa*. Johannesburg: South African Institute of International Affairs.

Rana, Swadesh. 1995. *Small Arms and Interstate Conflict*. Research Paper No. 34. Geneva: United Nations Institute for Disarmament Research.

Reed, John. ed. 2000. *Jane's World Defence Industry: Issue Six*. Coulsdon: Jane's Information Group.

Renner, Michael. 1995. *Small Arms, Big Impact*. Washington, DC: Worldwatch Institute.

Renner, Michael. 1999. 'Arms Control Orphans.' *The Bulletin of the Atomic Scientists*, Vol.55, No.1. January/February.

Sanders, Ralph. 1990. *Arms Industries: New Suppliers and Regional Security*. Washington, DC: National Defense University Press.

Shichor, Yitzhak. 1998. 'Conversion and Diversion: The Politics of China's Military Industry after Mao.' In Efraim Inbar and Benzion Zilberfarb, eds. *The Politics and Economics of Defence Industries*. London: Frank Cass.

Sköns, Elisabeth and Reinhilde Weidacher. 2000. 'Arms Production.' In Stockholm International Peace Research Institute. *SIPRI Yearbook 2000: Armaments, Disarmament and International Security*. Oxford: Oxford University Press.

Solingen, Etel. 1998. 'The Rise and Fall of Arms Industries in Argentina and Brazil.' In Efraim Inbar and Benzion Zilberfarb, eds. *The Politics and Economics of Defence Industries*. London: Frank Cass.

Stockholm International Peace Research Institute. 2000. *SIPRI Yearbook 2000: Armaments, Disarmament and International Security*. Oxford: Oxford University Press.

Susman, Gerald and Sean O'Keefe, eds. 1998. *The Defence Industry in the Post Cold-War Era*. New York: Pergamon.

Walter, John. 1999. *Kalashnikov - Machine Pistols, Assault Rifles, and Machine Guns: 1945 to the Present*. London: Greenhill Books.

Wood, Brian and Johan Peleman. 1999. *The Arms Fixers: Controlling the Brokers and Shipping Agents*. Oslo: PRIO.

United Nations. 1997. *Report of the Panel of Governmental Experts on Small Arms*. A/52/298. 27 August.

____. 1999a. *United Nations International Study on Firearm Regulation*. New York: United Nations.

____. 1999b. *Report of the Group of Governmental Experts on Small Arms*. A/54/258. 19 August.

____. 1999c. *Report on the Feasibility of Restricting the Manufacture and Trade of Small Arms to Manufacturers and Dealers Authorized by States*. A/54/160. 6 July.

____. 1999d. *Report of the Group of Experts on Ammunition and Explosives in all their aspects*. A/54/155. 29 June.

United States Department of State. 1999. *World Military Expenditure and Arms Transfers 1998*. Washington, DC: US Department of State, Bureau of Arms.

United States Office of Technology Assessment. 1991. *Global Arms Trade: Commerce in Advanced Military Technology and Weapons*. Washington, DC: US General Publications Office.

US Bureau of Alcohol, Tobacco and Firearms. 1995. *Annual Firearms Manufacturing and Export*

Report. Washington, DC: Department of the Treasury.

____. 1998a. *Department of the Treasury Study on the Sporting Suitability of Modified Semi-Automatic Assault Rifles*. Washington, DC: Department of the Treasury.

____. 1998b. *Annual Firearms Manufacturing and Export Report*. Washington, DC: Department of the Treasury.

____. 2000a. *Commerce in Firearms in the United States*. Washington, DC: Department of the Treasury.

____. 2000b. *Crime Gun Trace Reports (1999)*

National Report. Washington, DC: Department of the Treasury.

US Census Bureau. 1997a. *Small Arms Manufacturing - 1997 Economic Census*. Washington, DC: Department of Commerce.

____. 1997b. *Small Arms Ammunition Manufacturing - 1997 Economic Census*. Washington, DC: Department of Commerce.

Violence Policy Center. 2000. *Firearms Production in America, 1975-1997*. Washington, DC: Violence Policy Center.

2

Half a Billion and Still Counting ...
Global Firearms Stockpiles

Introduction

One of the characteristics of the rise of international civil society is the enormous growth in the amount of previously sensitive information that is now in the public domain. In innumerable fields of public policy, information previously considered proprietary or secret must now be revealed to all. Weapons and military technology, once the ultimate area of secrecy, are not immune to this trend.

In this climate of increasing transparency, international efforts have led to increasingly accurate assessments of the scale and dimensions of the diverse range of weapons jeopardizing international peace and security. However, small arms and light weapons remain an exception to this trend, one of the last areas where policy is seriously hindered by a lack of basic information.

Although it might seem bizarre, more is known about the number of nuclear warheads, stocks of chemical weapons, and transfers of major conventional weapons than about small arms. While several countries have declared how many firearms are legally owned by their private citizens, only a handful have revealed the number of small arms and light weapons in the inventories of their police or armed forces. Moreover, there is still no systematic method of determining the number of illegally owned small arms in private hands. In lieu of systematic reports from official sources, this chapter explores the dimensions of the global small arms problem, asking:

- **How many small arms and light weapons are there?**
- **Who owns them and where are they concentrated?**
- **Has the problem grown, or spun completely out of control?**
- **Are there some aspects that are more amenable to intervention than others?**

Although there is a need to quantify all aspects of the world's small arms problem, this chapter focuses on one in particular: the global quantities and the distribution of firearms—the handguns, rifles, shotguns, and machine guns that are the most visible aspect of the small arms problem. It reviews differences in the distribution of firearms in selected countries, then estimates the global total of firearms owned by police, government armed forces, insurgencies, criminal organizations, and private owners.

New research has revealed that there are at least 550 million firearms around the world. This figure emphasizes readily identifiable military, police, and some private firearms. A comprehensive total, covering all firearms in circulation around the world—including all privately and illegally owned firearms—would be significantly greater, by tens to hundreds of millions more. It was not possible, for example, to include any information on privately owned guns thought to be in major countries like China, France, India, or Pakistan. Nor do the estimates here include illegally owned weapons. These missing categories of firearms, along with other types of small arms, will be examined in subsequent editions of the *Small Arms Survey*.

There are at least 550 million known firearms around the world. If all privately and illegally owned firearms were included, the number would be significantly greater, by tens to hundreds of millions more.

The elusiveness of small arms data

Small arms may be the most commonly used and the most deadly of all armaments, but they have never received the degree of attention lavished upon major conventional weapons, much less weapons of mass destruction. The number of major weapon systems like armoured vehicles, aircraft, guided missiles, and naval vessels around the world is also generally well-known. With official and unofficial statistics on annual production of major weapon systems readily available from several sources, the number of strategic nuclear weapons deployed by the Russian Federation and the United States (US) has been public knowledge for almost a decade, following the signing of the first *Strategic Arms Reduction Treaty* (START) in 1991. Even inventories of chemical weapons have become known in recent years through the 1993 *Chemical Weapons Convention*.

Unfortunately, the same cannot be said of small arms. For example, the total number and global distribution of small arms remains one of the greatest enigmas in the field of international peace and security. The automatic rifle—the small arm *par excellence*—has been in continuous production for more than 50 years; yet there are no reliable overall statistics on global production or international transfers. Only a handful of governments have made any data available on their own procurement and transfers.

It is remarkable that the number of weapons responsible for most of the deaths and destruction in crime and conflict remain concealed, whether through official secrecy or bureaucratic neglect. To be sure, for many years now, the types of small arms and light weapons deployed by armed forces around the world—including government forces and insurgencies—have been well-known. But the numbers of automatic rifles, machine guns, mortars, grenade and rocket launchers, whether they are linked to national defence, communal conflict, policing, or other uses, remain a matter of conjecture.

The shifting tides of international priorities account for some of the shortcomings. Small arms were almost completely overlooked in Cold War discussions of peace and security so governments had little reason to gather or reveal statistics on them. Even studies of criminality tended to focus exclusively on particular aspects of small arms. More fundamental factors are also at work. Inquiries undertaken for this chapter revealed, not one big data problem, but innumerable small ones. Much of the problem is due to simple ignorance; few governments have comprehensive data on all public and official small arms available to share in the first place. In many cases, the problem is official secrecy, itself the result of habit as much as anything else. In the few cases where data are available, such as on public firearms ownership, no effort has been made to combine the many categories of ownership to arrive at a total figure.

The total number and global distribution of small arms remains one of the greatest enigmas in the field of international peace and security.

This chapter demonstrates that the scope and contours of small arms proliferation *can* be established. However, the quantification problem will not be solved easily, what with small arms and light weapons in the hands of some two hundred governments, hundreds of insurgencies, and thousands of organized criminal groups, as well as hundreds of millions of individual owners. To keep the problem to manageable proportions, this chapter focuses exclusively on the number of firearms existing in the world today. It emphasizes weapons like rifles and carbines, revolvers and pistols, shotguns and machine guns—in part because they are the most ubiquitous of all small arms. Their distribution is also easier to trace, following a common set of rules to make it easier to estimate. Subsequent editions of the *Survey* will devote greater attention to the global diffusion and inventories of other small arms and light weapons like grenades and grenade launchers, mortars, and rocket launchers.

The need for comprehensive numbers

Confronted by a crippling paucity of reliable data, analysis, and policy-making on small arms diffusion have, of necessity, relied instead on reasoning, historic examples, and anecdotal evidence.

While examples of individual small arms transfers are legion, thorough case studies of such transfers in the course of a single conflict are few and incomplete.[1] Nevertheless, many of these examples are highly illuminating and suggestive, illustrating the ways small arms spread around the world and the kinds of processes involved. As these insights accumulate, a broader and more nuanced image of the nature of the global small arms problem is emerging.

The lack of systematic and fully reliable data on the number and global distribution of firearms does not prevent incisive research, nor should it inhibit policy-making. But whether such methods will enable those concerned to accumulate enough information to create a comprehensive, overall picture of what is going on and what most needs to be done is more elusive. We have a growing wealth of ideas and experience, but little basis for sound judgment.

This tension makes it increasingly difficult to determine when to act and when not to, which problems are readily solvable, which will require long-term efforts, and which solution is appropriate to which problem (see Box 2.1). In other words, while we are rapidly becoming experts on specific trees, the forest remains more of a mystery.

Comprehensive or aggregate figures will help define and shape the future of small arms policy and studies. They will clarify the scale of the problem, guide analysis and policy-making, and focus public interest. Not only will such figures provide an impression of the nature of the phenomenon; they will also contribute to the way it evolves. They can help identify where the dangers are greatest and where most discrete. Such perceptions will contribute to decisions among policy-makers and analysts on whether to deal with the problem through universal principles and global approaches, or through approaches tailored to specific regions and types of problems.

Box 2.1 Specific reasons for addressing small arms data problems

1. **Scientific value:** Accurate numbers have an intrinsic scientific value, establishing standards of measurement and evaluation and benchmarks for measuring future progress.
2. **Systematic study:** A firm evidence base permits systematic study of trends in small arms issues over time.
3. **Comparative assessment:** Data collection paves the way for comparative assessment between the scale of the problem in different regions and situations, as well as between various cases over time.
4. **Influence on attitudes and choices:** In small arms, as in all areas of public policy, perceptions of the scale of the problem will influence attitudes and choices about what to do.
5. **Catalyzation of interest:** Tangible figures will catalyze interest, giving even those with only a marginal or passing interest in the problem of small arms proliferation deeper insight into the challenge before us.

The data void

The small arms issue is not new. Antecedents to current studies date back to the late 1970s when researchers first endeavoured to develop data for the international trade in small arms, aspiring—unsuccessfully—to create insights comparable in strength and utility to the readily available data on the trade in major weapons systems. Despite the expenditure of considerable energy, the small arms field still is a unique kind of *terra incognita*. Compared to the sophistication of quantitative information available in closely related fields, information about international small arms proliferation remains statistically primitive and underdeveloped. There are no small arms counterparts to the Stockholm International Peace Research Institute (SIPRI) Arms Trade Data Base, the *United Nations Arms Register,* the reports filed under the *Treaty on Conventional Forces in Europe,* or the *Chemical Weapons Convention*. There is no regular information to explain how global production of firearms fluctuates from year to year. There are few reports on the numbers acquired by major buyers. While there are statistics on some aspects of purchases by private buyers, there are no published statistics on the quantities of small arms and light weapons in military and police arsenals.

Although officials in many countries maintain that their governments keep excellent records on particular aspects of small arms within their territories, this information is rarely, if ever, released publicly. In no international aspect of this phenomenon is there reliable quantification. As a prominent United Nations study noted a few years ago, 'Quantifying the illicit trade in small arms and light weapons is difficult, because the activity is by nature clandestine and outside the law. In addition, while various reporting mechanisms have been established with respect to the legal trade of major conventional weapons...no such mechanisms have been created which cover the legal trade in small arms.'[2]

To date, the only general estimate of the global spread of firearms originated with the Indian defence expert, Jasjit Singh, who wrote in 1995 that 'another dimension [of the problem of small arms and light weapons] is the phenomenal spread of guns, 500 million of which are in circulation in the world...'[3] This was a personal conjecture, but a reasonable one.[4] Even so, the exact meaning of this statement has provoked debate. Another Indian analyst, for example, maintains that the figure refers, not to all firearms, but is meant more narrowly, pointing out that there are 'over 500 million Kalashnikovs estimated to be in circulation around the world.'[5] Contributing to the confusion, the *1999 Report of the Secretary-General* interpreted the same figure to mean not just guns, but all small arms, stating that 'Globally, it has been estimated that more than 500 million small arms and light weapons are in existence,' apparently combining weapons like mortars and rocket launchers in the total.[6]

Despite its status as the ubiquitous symbol of post-Cold War conflict, even the automatic rifle is veiled in statistical secrecy. The most influential estimate came from the late firearms expert, Edward Ezell, and was based on his study of the AK-47. Since its designer, Mikhail Kalashnikov himself, had no idea how many copies of his famous rifle had been manufactured, Ezell was forced to arrive at an estimate using a surrogate indicator. His assessment was arrived at by comparing the size of armies known to use the weapon.[7] Applying a sense of dimension developed through a lifetime of professional study, Ezell extrapolated this example to other major families of automatic rifles. In each case, he relied largely on the size of the armies deploying each weapon, creating figures later updated by his wife, the firearms expert, Virginia Ezell.[8] This led to an estimate of global production of major types of automatic rifles during the years 1945-90, which ranged from 55 to 72 million such weapons (see Table 2.1). Even this figure appears to be conservative. Its author recently offered a significantly higher figure of up to 100 million AK-47s alone (Ezell, 2000).

The estimate of 500 million guns and 55 to 72 million automatic rifles have served as benchmarks in the field for a long time.

This estimate, too, has won wide acceptance, including in United Nations studies, albeit mostly for want of any alternative.[9] The limited information available about production of other types of automatic rifles is enough to show that these estimates were far from complete.

Both the estimate of 500 million guns and 55 to 72 million automatic rifles have served as benchmarks in the field for a long time. Yet, both are no more than informal estimates; their exact meaning is ambiguous, and they appear to be based on professional guesswork. Current data suggest that approximately 90 to 122 million modern military rifles have been produced (see Table 2.1). Other figures in routine use are less plausible. The most dubious are the incredibly large figures that regularly appear in the media, exaggerating the number of firearms in a particular country or region. For example, it has been reported that Mozambique alone has six million or more AK-47s, which would be roughly half the number thought to be in all of the Russian Federation (see Box 2.2).

Table 2.1   Global production of major assault rifles

Original Designation	First Service	Other Versions	Total Production (1995)	Prominent Users
AK-47/74	1947	M-62, M-76, Type-56, Type-68	70-100 million	Russia, China, Vietnam, Poland
M-16	1962	C-7, Type-65	>7 million	US, Canada, South Korea, Philippines
G-3	1959	G-36	>7 million	Germany, Sweden, Angola, Mexico
FAL		L1A1	5-7 million	Belgium, UK, Argentina, India
AR70	1968	AR70/223		Italy, Jordan, Malaysia
FAMAS F-1		FAMAS G2	>400,000	France
Galil			>500,000	Colombia, Israel, South Africa
L85A1	1986		323,920	UK, Jamaica
SAR 80	1978			Singapore
SIG540	1984	SIG 550-552		Switzerland
AUG	1978			Austria, Australia
Total			**90-122 million**	

Sources: Ezell, 2000 and Gander, 2000.

Today it is widely recognized that Afghanistan is the world's leading center for unaccounted weapons, with at least 10 million in circulation within the country.[10] The Afghan war against the Soviet Union was long and brutal, as was the civil war that followed. Even so, it is not easy to reconcile such an estimate with a total population of only about seven million Afghani men aged 18 to 52, especially considering that this figure also includes millions of Afghani men still living in Iran and Pakistan.

In the most extreme example of all, in early 2000 it was widely reported that the people of Yemen owned an estimated 60 million guns, most of them Kalashnikovs, and virtually all of them in civilian hands.[11] This would be more than seven weapons for every Yemeni male, whether infant, adult, or elderly. While no one questions that all of these countries suffer from cultures of violence and excessive firearms ownership, such figures probably obscure more than they clarify. Exaggerated figures are also counter-productive, in that they discourage taking action to address the problems that actually may be more readily dealt with than such inflated numbers suggest.

Box 2.2 Mozambique's dangerous numbers

A poignant example of the scale and seriousness of the data problem was illustrated by Mozambique in the early 1990s, where uncertainty about the number of small arms in the country after the long civil war probably inhibited and/or undermined disarmament initiatives. Although this war was fought by a government with traditional Cold War suppliers against an insurgency that was also dependent on foreign sponsorship, there is no consensus on how many small arms seeped into the country during some 20 years of fighting.

When the Portuguese left Mozambique in 1974, they took their equipment with them, leaving the country with the modest military capabilities inherited from a revolutionary war that never involved more than 10,000 Frente de Libertacão de Moçambique (FRELIMO) independence fighters.[12] Only after independence, as fighting gradually intensified against Resistencia National Moçambicana (RENAMO) rebels sponsored by South Africa, did arms acquisitions become steadier.

How much equipment was imported? According to accepted estimates, the troops on both sides never numbered more than 92,000 altogether. Even allowing for considerable wastage, it is unlikely that their combined small arms requirements rose to more than a half a million firearms; even that is feasible only if the vast majority were lost or permanently broken.

Only after the war ended in 1992-93 was there serious interest in the weapons left over. Ironically, it was South Africa that tried hardest to determine the number of small arms that reached Mozambique during its civil war, motivated by concerns that unlicensed weapons were pouring across their shared border. With violent crime reaching crisis proportions, and thousands of former Mozambican weapons ending up in the hands of the South African police, they needed to gauge the potential seriousness of the problem. Thus, South Africa began to develop a special interest in small arms proliferation.

In lieu of reliable figures, estimates quickly ballooned due to inflation. According to the first reports in 1993, during the course of the war, the Mozambique Government handed out 1.5 million AK-47s to civilian self-defence organizations. At a 1994 Interpol conference, one presentation asserted that 1.5 million AK-47s came from the Soviet Union alone.[13] A 1995 press report estimated there were six million AK-47s left in the post-war country.[14] Subsequent analysis increased these estimates to 10 million weapons.[15]

However, the entire population of Mozambique was no more than 16 million when the fighting ended. Only some 2.7 million were men of typical military age (18 to 37 years old), and many of them were among the refugees forced to flee the country.[16] That between two and five automatic rifles were distributed to each and every one strains credulity. Even the Provincial Militia—for whom the reported 1.5 million rifles were supposedly intended—was expected to reach only 300,000 in number and there is no evidence that this goal was actually achieved.[17] Upon reconsideration, at least one analyst revised his estimate of AK-47 imports down to between 500,000 and one million weapons.[18]

One effect of this exaggeration was to trivialize disarmament efforts. Why collect a few hundred thousand firearms when millions more remained at large? These perceptions were exacerbated by tales of automatic rifles being traded in Mozambique for the equivalent of US$ 15 and in nearby Swaziland for US$ 6.[19] South African black marketeers were quoted as complaining that they could not get rid of the things at a profitable price.[20]

In retrospect, it appears that the United Nations (UN) probably collected an unprecedentedly high proportion of the small arms belonging to the 91,570 uniformed troops when both sides demobilized. The rival armies turned in a combined total of roughly 168,000 firearms.[21] Under the likely misapprehension that they had collected only a small share of the huge Mozambican national arsenal, officials had no incentive to destroy these weapons. The widespread trading in excess weapons—and the flow of large numbers of them to criminals in South Africa—began only when these reclaimed guns were later dumped on the market.

Five categories of firearms

Although general estimates are useful for drawing attention to the global spread of small arms and light weapons, careful analysis can do much better, especially when it comes to the extremely important role of firearms. Ideally, figures should come from manufacturers, governments, and buyers. However, until that becomes possible, much can be determined through careful use of published reports, extrapolation from selected examples, and formal modelling.

The rest of this chapter carefully examines the kinds of information available about particular categories of firearms to arrive at more useful cumulative estimates. The task has been divided into five categories, based on firearms ownership. These are:

1. Police firearms
2. Government armed forces firearms
3. Insurgent and other non-state actor firearms
4. Private legal firearms
5. Private illegal firearms

Each category harbours unique statistical problems requiring equally unique solutions. For example, the kinds of information provided on government armed forces' firearms are very different from the data available on privately licensed weapons. The analytical procedures required to fill in the gaps are different as well. In the long run, this means that different kinds of data reporting will be needed to establish how guns are distributed. In the short run, there is no alternative to distinctive estimating procedures, each tailored to the special characteristics of each major category.

Three important areas excluded from this assessment should be acknowledged at the start. First, it has not been possible to assess manufacturers' stocks or the inventories of brokers and dealers. Second, obsolete weapons—such as old revolvers, semi-automatic, or bolt-action military rifles—still in military storage—are not systematically included. And third, it is currently not feasible to produce systematic estimates of the number of illegally held private weapons.

The distribution of firearms ownership

Although the proliferation of firearms is a global phenomenon, their distribution varies dramatically from region to region, and country to country. Countries like Colombia, El Salvador, Israel, Switzerland, the United States, and Yemen have well-deserved reputations for widespread gun ownership, while other countries like Japan and the United Kingdom are equally well-known for their scarcity of firearms. Going beyond these clichés to establishing just how many guns they have is actually another matter entirely.

None of the countries consulted or studied by the Survey report systematically on their total number of firearms. Typically, no more than one or two categories—if any—are known; others must be estimated. In lieu of a systematic list of countries and their firearms inventories, it is revealing to examine some of the handful of countries—the US, New Zealand, Argentina, and the United Kingdom—for which reasonably complete firearms statistics are available. By combining data from gun registration, official inventories, public surveys, and official statements, a useful portrait begins to emerge. To be sure, these four countries may not be highly representative of global firearms owner-ship, but they do illuminate an impressive range of variations. [The data in this section (pp. 9-12) are taken from the material analyzed in the following section of this chapter].

With a total of at least 230 million firearms, the US has the world's largest known arsenal of firearms, constituting almost half of all known firearms in the world. This amounts to approximately 84 guns for every 100 people. A precise figure is impossible to calculate since there is no central gun

With a total of at least 230 million firearms—84 guns for every 100 people—the United States has the world's largest known arsenal of firearms, constituting almost half of all known firearms in the world.

registry in the US; weapons can be owned legally without being registered. Indeed, most civilian firearms in the US are not licensed or registered and thus can be estimated only through public surveys. Nor are police weapons centrally tracked; although they are usually registered, this is done locally, without reporting to the federal government. Even the United States' armed forces do not make their total firearms inventories public. Although they attempt to keep extremely precise records of each and every gun under their control, most of their five armed services do not reveal the details of their records. However, this is beginning to change.

Instead of relying on official data, a picture of gun ownership in the US has to be assembled bit by bit. Using sources discussed later in this chapter—including published surveys of public gun ownership, police firearms inventories, and figures released by the US Army—a broad picture of the distribution of the roughly 230 million firearms in the US emerges (see Fig. 2.1).

This assessment reveals that gun ownership in the United States is overwhelmingly a civilian matter, with some 98 per cent of all firearms in private hands. In contrast to many countries, where illegal gun ownership is a serious problem, this is not the case in the US; since it does not register or license most guns, virtually all are fully legal. The significant exception comprises weapons that have been stolen from their original owners.

The total quantity of civilian firearms in the United States is comparable to— or even greater than —the total firearms of all the armed forces in the entire world.

The US armed forces own only approximately two per cent of the country's firearms, and the police roughly one-third of one per cent. The US public not only owns far more firearms than their armed forces, as shown below, but the total quantity of civilian firearms in the United States is comparable or even greater than the total firearms of all the armed forces in the entire world. In addition to owning the vast majority of United States' firearms, its citizens are also better armed in terms of quality than many official agencies. For example, while the public owns a large proportion of rifles (including military-style automatic and semi-automatic rifles) and shotguns, the overwhelming majority of police weapons are mere pistols. Despite florid language from some activists, in the US it is far and away the public that dominates the tools of violence; the government is a small player by comparison.

Nor is the United States alone in this regard. Although few countries come close to the US in the total number of their firearms, the tendency for civilian ownership to overwhelm official stocks seems to be the norm. A few other countries—such as Switzerland and Yemen, and possibly Belgium and Israel—may match or approach the United States' rate of gun ownership, but they appear to be exceptional.

More typical of many wealthy societies is New Zealand, with approximately 25 firearms for every 100 people, virtually all in private hands (see Figure 2.2). Canada also has a very similar pattern of gun ownership, with some 25 firearms for every 100 people as well. Although comprehensive data are

Figure 2.1 Firearms in the United States, 2001

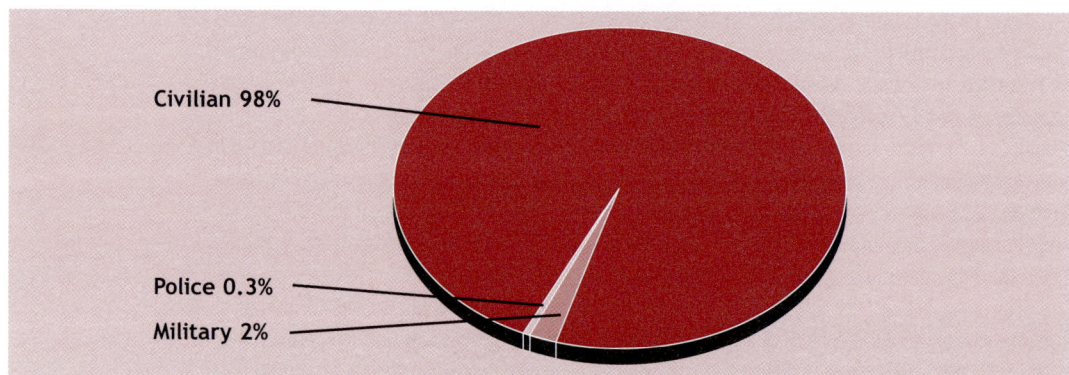

Civilian 98%

Police 0.3%

Military 2%

missing, the same proportion appears to hold for countries like Germany, France, and Sweden, with roughly one gun for every four people and civilian guns outnumbering military and police weapons by large proportions. This same general trend appears to hold even for some poorer countries like Colombia or South Africa.

Figure 2.2   Firearms in New Zealand, 2001

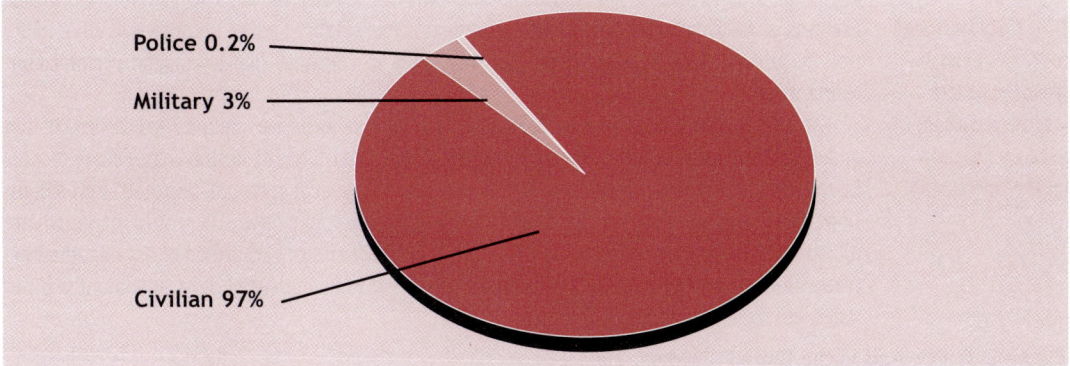

Another group of countries is exemplified by Argentina, where firearms ownership is neither rare nor atypical, even in rural areas. In Argentina, there are roughly 14 firearms for every 100 people. Since gun-owners in even moderately wealthy societies often have two or three firearms (typically a rifle, a shotgun, and a handgun), the proportion of individuals and households with a gun probably is significantly lower, on the order of one in 10 or even less. This appears normal for moderately wealthy and poorer countries with large urban populations. Many other countries of Latin America, as well as Eastern Europe, the Russian Federation, and other former Soviet states appear to fall into this category.

In Argentina (as illustrated in Figure 2.3) this means that, while the overall proportion of people owning guns is lower than countries like the United States or New Zealand, civilians still own far and away most of the country's guns. The figures on Argentina also illustrate an important nuance: the extent of illegal as opposed to legal gun ownership. As a country requiring guns to be licensed, Argentina has a large proportion of firearms outside legal ownership. The numbers estimated here are based on public surveys.

Finally, there are those countries where public gun ownership is considered unusual, with the United Kingdom (UK) as a prominent example. Even though guns are uncommon there, and

Figure 2.3   Firearms in Argentina, 2001

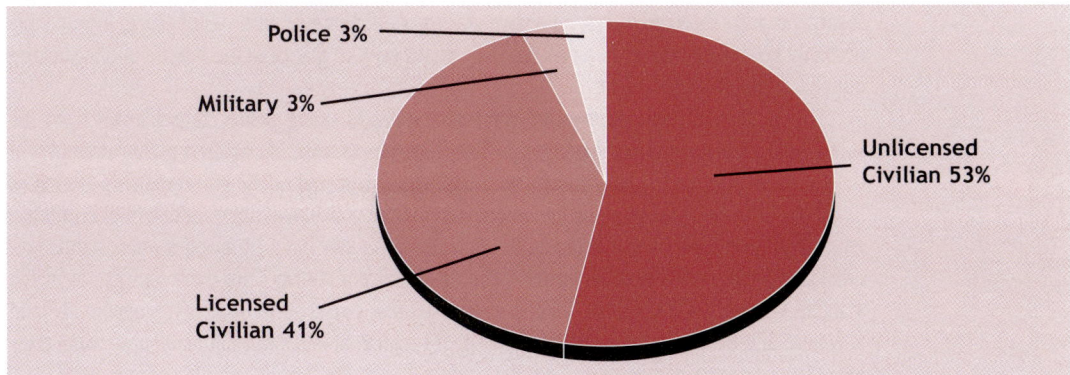

The United Kingdom has by far the largest share of guns in military and police hands— roughly 28 per cent of its total national stockpile. Even so, official guns are massively outnumbered by those in civilian possession.

many regional constabularies still send their police officers on patrol unarmed, there is more myth than truth to the image of an unarmed United Kingdom. With approximately six firearms—largely shotguns and single-shot rifles—for every 100 people nationally, the rural areas of the UK are reportedly especially well-armed. However, since there are fewer guns in absolute terms, the relative proportion of those that are unregistered and illegally owned is more important than in many other countries (see Figure 2.4). The figure of 25 per cent illegally owned firearms is widely accepted but, given the comparatively smaller total of firearms overall, it could well be greater. Similar proportions probably apply to countries like Japan and perhaps even China as well.

Another tendency illustrated by the United Kingdom is the inverse relationship between civilian and official firearms. Of all the countries reviewed here, the UK has by far the largest share of guns in military and police hands, roughly 28 per cent of its total national stockpile. Revealingly, however, even in such a modestly armed country like the UK, official guns are massively outnumbered by those in civilian possession. Centuries of orthodox assumptions and conventional wisdom about the well-armed state appear to be in need of reconsideration. It is not states, but societies that are well-armed.

Figure 2.4 Firearms in the United Kingdom, 2001

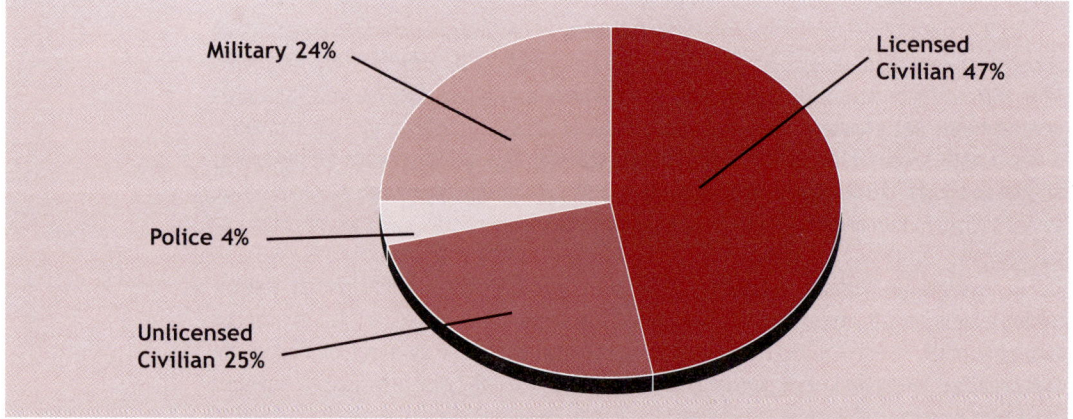

Military 24%

Licensed Civilian 47%

Police 4%

Unlicensed Civilian 25%

Police weapons

Ironically, those small arms most often seen by the largest number of people in the world are also those that are least numerous and probably least dangerous. Small arms proliferation is dominated by the chaos and destruction caused by the weapons of petty criminals and organized crime, insurgents and rebels, as well as repressive governments. However, in times of peace, most people probably never come closer to a firearm than an occasional glance at the handle of one sticking out of a police officer's holster.

The problem of determining the number of firearms under police control arises from the secrecy natural to most police departments. They have ample reason to suppress public awareness of their weapons inventories. In countries with relatively widespread public gun ownership—such as Brazil, the Russian Federation, or the United States—the police may not want potential criminals, especially organized crime or terrorists, to know how *little* they have. In societies where public gun ownership is unusual—such as Japan or the UK—police authorities are more sensitive to media scandals created by the image of 'killer cops'.[22] Like other armed authorities, police apparently tend to believe that too much transparency about their firearms arsenals will not necessarily make their job of law enforcement any easier—on the contrary—and are thus resistant to sharing details.

Since they cannot be ascertained through official sources, police firearms have to be estimated. This draws the focus to a major theme throughout this chapter: the overwhelming importance of people in estimating numbers of small arms. Although little may be known about the number of firearms, much more is known about the number of people who carry them. Since the guns cannot be counted, the next best thing is counting the people and multiplying the result by the number of firearms believed to be available to each of them. For police officers, the number usually appears to be relatively low, averaging between one and two weapons per person. As will be shown, however, for government armed forces, it can be as high as four to five per soldier. And for large groups of private owners, it may be ten guns per person or more.

US police firearms policy is illustrative. Although every police department in the highly decentralized United States is separately administered and regulated, most appear to follow fairly consistent armament policies, based on issuing each sworn officer with one weapon for which he or she is personally responsible. Reserve stocks are small. In the departments polled for this research, reserves amounted to approximately five to eight per cent additional weapons, intended primarily to cover breakage. Shotguns are also a standard US police weapon, with police forces usually buying enough to equip their patrol cars on call, although the procedures and quantities vary considerably. In addition, officers on patrol normally carry one or two less lethal weapons, typically a baton and pepper-gas.

In times of peace, most people probably never come closer to a firearm than an occasional glance at the handle of one sticking out of a police officer's holster.

Aside from their normal everyday armament, modern police forces often stock special weapons. These military-style weapons kept in reserve include automatic rifles, sub-machine guns, sniper rifles, and sometimes even grenade launchers, the latter usually intended for firing tear gas. In the United States, these other lethal weapons are usually reserved for specially trained teams, typically found in larger cities. In the cities polled, these units averaged some 18 personnel (part-time officers normally assigned to other duties) with a total of approximately 24 special weapons in all (a mixture of sniper rifles, carbines, sub-machine guns, and a grenade launcher).

Table 2.2 Police weapons in Belgium, 2000

Category	Type	Sub-Total	Total
Revolvers	Smith & Wesson .38	10,130	
	Various .357	1,349	11,479
Pistols	FN	5,645	
	Glock	1,939	
	Various	2,300	9,884
Shotguns			1,286
Sub-machine guns	Uzi	588	
	Heckler & Koch	300	
	Steyr	245	
	Various	88	1,221
Automatic rifles	FN FAL	30	
	Various	10	40
Sniper rifles	Ruger	6	
	Steyr	5	
	Various	8	19
Ceremonial rifles	US M-1	24	24

Total Belgian police firearms: 23,953 for a 17,767-man police force

Source: Commission Permanente de la Police Communale en Belgique, 2000

To be sure, police in many countries carry sub-machine guns or automatic rifles. To date, the country most forthcoming with its police weapons statistics is Belgium, which reported a total of 23,953 firearms for 17,767 sworn police officers as of July 2000 (see Table 2.2). Most Belgian officers carry a handgun, either a pistol or a revolver, as well as less lethal weapons, usually a baton and pepper-gas. Additional firearms include a stockpile of shotguns, ostensibly for riot control; sub-machine guns, primarily for security details protecting VIPs; automatic rifles; a few dozen sniper rifles; and even two dozen weapons of World War II vintage, presumably for ceremonial duties. While some police forces, such as the Belgians, are better armed quantitatively, there is less evidence that the police in such countries are better armed qualitatively.

Based on survey data, it is possible to estimate the total number of US official police firearms, averaging the number of weapons per police officer in known cities and subsequently multiplying by the total number of officers nationally, including other sworn officers, such as those in sheriffs' departments, state police, and federal officers. This results in a national figure of approximately 813,000 American police firearms of all types. It should be emphasized that these are official weapons: most American police departments 'officially permit and unofficially encourage' their officers to carry private back-up weapons. Typically, this is a small handgun in a back or sock holster. Since these are privately owned weapons, their numbers are covered in the private gun ownership statistics that follow.

In a world with six billion people there are 10 to 20 million police officers, armed with 12 to 30 million firearms.

Available data from three other countries—Belgium, Norway, and South Africa—suggest that the US example should probably be placed towards the middle of the spectrum of global trends for police armament (see Table 2.3). This is shown by comparison with the countries that have released official information on the numbers of both police officers and weapons. Norway, with a confirmed total of 9,000 police firearms, has a police force of 7,500 officers and, with only one police officer for every 600 citizens, is lightly policed [23] compared to the United States, where there is one police officer for every 421 citizens. Similarly, Belgium, with a total of 17,767 police offers, has one officer for every 570 people. South Africa, by comparison, is a heavily policed nation, with one officer for every 290 people. Despite this important difference, the ratio of officers to firearms is much closer in these four countries, ranging from 1.2 guns per officer in Norway, to 1.45 per officer in South Africa.

Extrapolated to the rest of the world, the experiences of these countries suggest that, in a world with six billion people, there are a total of approximately 10 to 21 million police officers. The same logic leads to the conclusion that they are armed with a global total somewhere between 12 and 30 million official police firearms (see Table 2.4). Assuming that there is a global average of one armed police officer for every 421 citizens—which would correspond to the high but not extreme level in the United States—the global total number of police firearms would be no higher than approximately 18 million.

Table 2.3 Police weapons in selected countries

Country	Population	Sworn Officers	Handguns	Shotguns	Special Weapons
Norway*	4,500,000	7,500	6,000	–	3,000
Belgium*	10,100,000	17,767	21,363	1,286	1,221
South Africa**	40,000,000	137,500	200,000	?	?
United States***	270,000,000	641,000	680,000	131,000	20,000

Source: Military Balance 1999-2000

* Official government statistics made available to the *Small Arms Survey*.
**All South African Police Service (SAPS) weapons, including shotguns and special weapons. Estimated by Jakkie Polgieter, private correspondence, April 2000.
*** *U.S. Crime Statistics 1998*, p. 291. All US police firearms figures are estimates based on surveys by the author.

Table 2.4 Calculating global police firearms

Country	Officers/ Population	Weapons/ Officer	Equivalent Global Officers	Equivalent Global Police Firearms
Norway	1/600	1.2	10,000,000	12,000,000
Belgium	1/570	1.3	10,500,000	13,650,000
United States	1/421	1.3	14,000,000	18,200,000
South Africa	1/290	1.45	20,700,000	30,015,000

Small arms of government armed forces

Unlike police weapons inventories, which are a relatively small proportion of the global small arms stockpile, the weapons of armed forces constitute a very large proportion. This is not because active-duty soldiers are more numerous than police officers; on the contrary, their numbers around the world appear to be generally comparable. Rather, it is due to the fact that armed forces are inherently better armed and maintain larger reserves. Why is this necessary?

While deadly force is the exception for the police, whose individual operations seldom last as long as a day, the armed forces prepare as if deadly operations were the norm to be conducted over a period of weeks or months. This preparing-for-the-worst approach holds true even if much of their actual activities consist of peacekeeping or police-type duties. Soldiers generally carry rifles instead of pistols and reserve stocks tend to be more plentiful to compensate for much greater anticipated breakage or other losses. The armed forces also stock a much wider variety of lethal small arms, including grenades, machine guns, mortars, anti-tank, and anti-aircraft weapons. Finally, armed forces carry ammunition primarily for sustained and highly intense combat operations rather than intermittent encounters.

Another major difference is the importance of reserve stocks in military planning. This stems from the way many states prepare to meet challenges to their highest national interests, which compels them to prepare to mobilize a far greater military force than they could afford to sustain in peacetime. Beginning with the European arms races in the second half of the 19th century, when pressure to maximize mobilization led to the creation of the *Nation in Arms,* in which all physically fit men of military age were expected to serve, reserve forces have been essential to military planning in many countries.[24] Reserves vary greatly in proficiency and utility—some are highly professional, others are just glorified drinking clubs—but all require basic small arms to retain any credibility. Even when the troops were little more than imaginary—just something to plan for—the weapons had to be real.

At their apogee in the mid-1980s, some countries maintained reserve forces five or even ten times the size of their standing armies (see Table 2.5). Since the end of the Cold War in Europe in 1989 and the decline of extreme threats to national security among most states elsewhere as well, reserve forces have atrophied even faster than active duty contingents. In some cases, their weapons have since been transferred abroad to permit poorer countries to modernize their own reserves. Except for a few highly publicized cases, though, the weapons originally procured for reserve forces remain, swelling national inventories.

A final factor contributing to the much greater dimensions of military small arms inventories are paramilitary forces. These are special forces, under the authority of the Ministry of Defence or the Ministry of the Interior, usually responsible for domestic security. They operate primarily at home against major threats to the state, often in situations constitutionally forbidden to the armed forces. Well-known examples include the French *Gendarmerie,* India's elite *Rashtriya* and *Assam Rifles,*

Table 2.5 Examples of Cold War era active, reserve, and paramilitary forces, 1987 and 1999

Country	Active Duty	Reservists	Paramilitary	Total 1987	Total 1999
USSR/Russia	5,130,000	6,265,000	530,000	11,925,000	3,978,000
Vietnam	1,052,000	4,000,000	3,600,000	8,652,000	9,000,000
Spain	275,000	2,400,000	66,000	2,741,000	710,000
Switzerland	20,000	625,000	0	645,000	388,000
India	1,262,000	460,000	672,000	2,394,000	2,791,000
Israel	149,000	554,000	4,500	707,500	604,000
Cote d'Ivoire	7,000	12,000	7,800	26,800	33,000

Sources: The Military Balance 1987-1988, The Military Balance 1999-2000.

or the Italian *Carabinieri*. In many countries, these forces can also be much larger than the traditional armed forces. The largest essentially are reserve forces intended to counter a foreign invasion, like Cuba's *Territorial Militia* with over one million members, and Vietnam's *People's Militia* with four to five million members. The least reputable are *ad hoc* forces, personal armies raised by local warlords that are outside official command structures and frequently beyond the pale of the law. Typically tolerated by the state instead of being organized by it, such paramilitaries lie at the juncture between government forces and insurgents.

Barriers to transparency: Secrecy and ignorance

Although there is reliable and detailed information on the major weapons systems of virtually all armies of the world, there is virtually no public information on the number of small arms at their disposal. As is usually the case in discussions of small arms, information tends to be exclusively about types, not quantities. While many governments release precise statistics on the number of major conventional weapons their forces deploy, very few provide comparable data on their small arms. The only quantitative information tends to be from procurement contracts and export orders, which many countries make public. While it is possible to determine the quantities of small arms being acquired in selected countries with information like this, it is quite different from establishing how much they already have.

It appears that some governments themselves do not even know the size of their major weapons stocks, let alone their small arms inventories. An extreme example is Kazakhstan, where an export scandal involving the recent unlicensed sale of MiG-21 fighters to North Korea led the Defence Minister to confess that 'Unfortunately, up to now, we do not have a full inventory and do not know how many arms we own.'[25] Under such circumstances, it would be optimistic to expect such a country to command the details of its small arms arsenal. If a country does not even know how many aircraft—each worth millions of dollars—it has, what can be expected of its inventory of small arms, worth no more than a few hundred dollars each?

Determining the size of government armed forces' small arms inventories cannot be separated from the broader issue of transparency. Despite the fully established place of the small arms issue in international affairs and the broad international participation in a variety of initiatives to address the issue, very few countries are willing to share statistics on the small arms inventories of their own armed forces. Some governments maintain that national sovereignty and security require such reticence. Others are unable to produce relevant data. In yet other cases, civil servants or military officers have volunteered that their ministries or armed services were simply 'uncomfortable' with the idea.

Official discomfort is much different from compelling national interest. For many governments, the problem appears to be more a matter of habit than motives. In lieu of strong arguments against releasing detailed information, it seems likely that a commitment from national decision-makers would be enough to break through traditional attitudes.

The same thing has already happened in other areas of national security previously shielded by official secrecy—areas much closer to unambiguous national interests. For example, over the last decade, most countries have concluded that national security is better served by sharing (rather than concealing) data on nuclear delivery systems and warheads, chemical weapons, transfers of major conventional weapons, and even anti-personnel landmines, which most countries now declare in compliance with international agreements. Most of the European Nations, as well as Canada and the United States, already declare their major conventional armaments under the 1993 *Treaty on Conventional Forces*. The field of small arms may just be awaiting its turn.

Examples of data on the total firearms of government armed forces

Until that happens, the best general impression of the number of small arms of government armed forces around the world may come through formal estimations, based on applying the number of weapons per soldier in a few well-understood cases to arrive at global totals. Unfortunately, there is a serious shortage of cases to use for estimation. The best-documented examples tend to be historical. For example, in World War II, the US Army procured a total of 12.6 million rifles, 1.8 million sub-machine guns, and 2.8 million handguns of all kinds. When added to a pre-war stockpile of some 1.5 million firearms, this gave a total of almost 19 million firearms for an army that crested at 8,267,958 troops in 1945—some 2.3 firearms per soldier and aviator (the US Air Force became independent only in 1947).[26] The ratio of firearms per soldier—revealing, albeit dated—illustrates the fact that firearms, which will last for decades in proper storage, need to be replaced rapidly when used in actual combat. A few contemporary examples provide the following somewhat sketchy information:

- **Norway:** The Norwegian Ministry of Defence has reported that its inventories include 28,270 handguns ('one-hand weapons') and 266,800 rifles ('two-hand weapons'). Whether these include all types of firearms, such as machine guns or stockpiles for reserve forces, is not clear.[27]
- **South Africa:** The South African National Defence Forces have not revealed official information either, but they are understood to keep a total of some 450,000 modern rifles, 17,000 pistols, and thousands of machine guns, although this, too, does not include extensive war reserves.[28]
- **Sweden:** The Ministry of Justice revealed that the country's armed forces control 920,000 firearms but, without a breakdown by type and service, this is only suggestive.[29]
- **United States:** The number of M-16 rifles owned by the US Army and US Air Force reportedly stands at 720,000 and 220,000 respectively.[30] These figures do not appear to include obsolescent weapons nor are there figures for the other services—the US Coast Guard, Marines Corps and Navy—or for reserve units and the National Guard (see Box 2.3).

The only comprehensive official military small arms figures to be shared so far come from the Canadian Department of National Defence (see Table 2.6). The Canadian data are highly revealing since they cover all the armed services and reserve organizations. They show not only the number of weapons needed to equip standing forces, but the extent of one NATO ally's preparations for war time losses and its preparedness for combat losses today. With a total of 233,949 firearms of all types to supply a combined force of 60,600 active-duty military personnel and 43,300 reservists (i.e. 103,900 all together), Canada has 2.25 firearms per uniformed soldier, sailor and aviator. The ratio of 2.25 firearms per combatant is virtually the same as the ratio of US firearms procured for each uniformed soldier during World War II, a fact of more than coincidental significance.

In World War II, the US Army procured a total of almost 19 million firearms for a force of 8,267,958 troops —some 2.3 firearms per soldier and airman.

Box 2.3 Small arms wear wings and anchors

Official military small arms involve much more than each country's army. Although the land forces are the best known, and usually the largest armed forces customer for small arms, they are not the only ones. All branches of the armed services are usually large buyers. Only the Marines—with their mission of projecting force from ship to shore—require a full suite of the various types of small arms as well. Other services tend to focus on firearms.

Air Forces require large guard units to insure the safety of their aircraft and facilities from terrorists or special forces attacks. Navies and Coast Guards must not only protect their shore installations; in addition, every ship must be able to defend itself from hostile boarding attacks. Many countries also have large independent forces of border guards, paramilitary, and/or gendarme forces for domestic security. Although exact information is lacking, it appears that the needs of the other services combined makes up roughly half of many countries' military small arms procurement.

Other armed services can also take major initiatives in small arms development. Depending on budgetary politics, they may be in a position to buy more advanced small arms ahead of the Army or Marines. In some cases, exceptional leadership may lead them into pioneering roles. The best known example is the US Air Force under the leadership of Chief of Staff General Curtis LeMay, who supported the development of the M-16 and began equipping his service with it in 1962, a move that eventually convinced the US Army to overcome its resistance to the 'plastic toy rifle' which it adopted in 1967.[31]

In Canada, there are a total of 233,949 firearms for a combined force of 60,600 active-duty military personnel and 43,300 reservists—that is, 2.25 firearms per uniformed soldier, sailor and airman.

With so few bases for comparison, it is no small irony that two of the only other sources left concern the armed forces of countries which no longer exist: East Germany and the former (pre-1991) Yugoslavia. While most current states continue to shield accurate data about their official small arms inventories, non-existent states have no interests to protect. Although the data for these former states are not comprehensive in specific categories—especially for firearms—it is highly revealing about the kinds of inventories governments tend to maintain.[32]

However, both the former German Democratic Republic (GDR) and the pre-1991 Yugoslavia were weak states with questionable legitimacy, even among their own people. Both of their armed forces were unique manifestations of the Cold War.

Table 2.6 Small arms of the Canadian Department of National Defence, 2000

Firearms Type	Quantity	Other Small Arms	Quantity
Pistols	25,125	40mm grenade launcher	336
Rifles & carbines	169,053	60mm mortar	440
Sub-machine guns	25,563	81mm mortar	142
Sniper rifles	487	Carl-Gustav LAW	921
Shotguns	700	Eryx SRAAW	435 launchers
Light machine guns	6,932	TOW	147 launchers
Medium machine guns	4,735	Javelin SAM	110 launchers
Heavy machine guns	1,354		
Total firearms	**233,949**		

Source: Canadian Departments of National Defence, and Foreign Affairs and International Trade, 2000.

- East Germany needed large armed forces both to show the Soviet Union that it could maintain domestic order and to pre-empt expansion of Soviet forces into its territory (at the end of the Cold War in 1989, the Soviet Union still had over 400,000 troops posted there). On the other hand, its forces also were limited by Moscow, which kept them from growing too large and potentially independent.
- Yugoslavia required large forces of its own, both to deal with potential separatism and to ensure its independent position as a non-aligned Marxist state. President Tito's personal commitment to guerrilla warfare—he was an expert guerrilla leader during World War II— led to even greater stockpiling (see Box 2.4).

While one must be cautious when generalizing from these examples, it appears that East Germany was more typical of the way most states arm themselves, while Yugoslavia was a massively-armed state, representative only of the most extreme end of the small arms spectrum.

A preliminary global estimate

From these detailed examples, it is possible to extrapolate the number of small arms in official military hands around the world today. Dividing the number of weapons in each example by the total number of soldiers, sailors, and aviators produces a multiplier that can be applied globally. Although caution is clearly called for, when used with care, this approach generates a useful estimate of the minimum number of firearms likely to be stockpiled by government armed forces around the world.

Box 2.4   Stockpiles and strategies: The former East Germany and pre-1991 Yugoslavia

Sometimes the best way to get solid information is a *post mortem*. Beginning in 1990, a series of reports were compiled, initially by the German Democratic Republic (GDR) and subsequently by the united Federal Republic of Germany. They grew in scale and quality as additional stockpiles were discovered and added. The data used here, based on 1994 information sources, are probably not comprehensive; however, they provide unique insights into the evolution of one country's small arms inventories. In both the East German and Yugoslav cases, there is a strong relationship between the number of small arms available and the number of personnel in uniform (see Table 2.7). East Germany's stocks of AK-74 rifles (a more advanced version of the better known AK-47, using lighter ammunition) were reserved for its standing armed forces.[33] They totalled about 171,925 AK-74s, compared to a total of 137,700 active-duty personnel of the New People's Army.[34] The much larger stockpile of older AK-47s— approximately 783,217—is more than double the total of armed forces reservists and Ministry of Interior border troops, some 364,000 altogether. The total ratio is 1.9 firearms per uniformed soldier.

The small arms inventories of the Yugoslav People's Army (YPA) and the reservist Territorial Defence Army (TDA) appear to have been proportionately much larger. Although its standing forces were not exceptionally large for the times—with some 195,000 personnel on active duty, including Ministry of Defence border guards—the large reserves of some 510,000 were typical of a country relying on rapid mobilization for territorial defence, such as Finland, Israel, and Sweden.[35] With a total of 2,330,000 rifles for 705,000 readily mobilized troops, Yugoslavia maintained a vast stockpile.[36]

Specific strategies may account for the differences. Although East Germany had to be well-armed, it was planning for a short war in which it would fight together with the entire Warsaw Treaty Organization, while Yugoslavia was planning for a long war which it might have to fight alone.

At the same time, attention must be called to certain dynamic factors in operation since the late 1980s. Since then, there has been a steady decline in the number of soldiers, sailors, and aviators in uniform around the world, as most countries trimmed the number of active and reserve troops. While troop numbers have gone down, the guns bought when forces were bigger have not disappeared. Thus, a mirror image of post-Cold War troop cuts has been the accumulation of large stockpiles of excess equipment. Some of them have been stored; many have been transferred abroad, allowing regional militaries to complete the modernization of their forces. But—significant to note— *very little of this excess weaponry has been destroyed.*

The ideal basis for estimating the number of global military firearms would be to calculate it using the maximum military strength of all military units in the world in recent years. This approach would stress, not the number of troops actually assigned, but the authorized strength for which most units are equipped. In lieu of such detailed information, the best surrogate for the maximum dimensions of the world's militaries is the number of troops in uniform during the year of greatest military expansion around the world, which was 1987.

Although there are approximately 22,300,000 military personnel on active duty today, back in 1987 there were some 28,300,000 soldiers, sailors, and aviators serving on active duty the world over.[37] To this figure must be added official paramilitary forces, which increase the total number of full-time troops at that time to almost 35 million. In addition, there were a total of approximately 55 million reservists ready for mobilization for combat duty. All in all, at their maximum level of military preparedness, the governments of the world were in a position to mobilize 90 million combat troops for military service, with weapons on hand to equip them.[38]

The year of greatest global military expansion was 1987 when the governments of the world were in a position to mobilize 90 million combat troops for military service, with weapons on hand to equip them.

Of the countries for which adequate data could be compiled—the former East Germany, pre-1991 Yugoslavia, contemporary Canada, and Norway—Canada appears to offer the most suitable basis for comparison. The Yugoslav example, at the high end of the spectrum, would be applicable only to those countries with intensive military preparations, stressing the nation in arms and people's wars, such as China, Cuba, or Vietnam. At the other extreme, the Norwegian example is incomplete, based as it is on only partial stockpile data. Even so, Norway's modest military preparations as revealed here resemble countries prepared to fight only skirmishes or the shortest of conflicts.

Only a handful of comparable nations, apparently prepared only for minimal use of military force, come to mind: certainly countries like Costa Rica and Panama, which have no armed forces, only *gendarmes*, and the Baltic States (i.e. Estonia, Latvia, and Lithuania). This leaves the other two examples—the former GDR and Canada—as most suitable for global comparisons, with Canada approaching the lower end of the likely range of international military firearms inventories.

Using Canada, therefore, as a benchmark, and assuming global levels of armaments proportional to Canadian levels in the late 1980s, there were at least 202,000,000 official military firearms in the world, including automatic rifles and sub-machine guns, pistols, light and medium machine guns (see Table 2.7). Given the relatively modest levels of Canadian stockpiles, this figure can safely be regarded as a minimal estimate. Actual figures are likely to be higher. Virtually all of these guns remain in existence today.

An exception must be made, though, for attrition. Some of the firearms in existence at the peak of global armed forces' presence in the mid-1980s have been lost through normal attrition. Although most military firearms are amazingly durable, designed to withstand not just the rigours of combat, but also the imaginative abuses that soldiers routinely inflict upon them, most attrition appears to occur when weapons are broken beyond repair in training. Operational tempo is crucial to the rate of attrition, another facet illustrated by the Canadian example. Although its forces have not fought in combat since Korea, Canada actively contributes to UN and NATO peacekeeping operations, be they in the Middle East, Somalia, Bosnia, Kosovo, or elsewhere. As a result, its ground troops undoubted-

Table 2.7 Estimating global official military firearms inventories of the late 1980s, selected examples

Weapon	Country Multipliers			
	1989 Yugoslavia	1990 GDR	2000 Canada	2000 Norway
Automatic rifle multipliers	3.26	1.91	1.63	1.49
Est. world military total at 1987 troop levels	293 million	172 million	147 million	134 million
Pistol multipliers	0.74	0.55	024	0.16
Est. world military total at 1987 troop levels	67 million	48 million	22 million	14.4 million
Light/medium Machine gun multipliers	0.39	0.11	0.11	–
Est. world military total at 1987 troop levels	35 million	10 million	10 million	
Total firearms multipliers*	4.53	2.56	2.25	1.65
Est. world military total at 1987 troop levels	407 million	230 million	202 million	149 million

Note: *Also includes multipliers for sub-machine guns, shotguns and sniper rifles, when available

Sources: Gorjanc, 1988; Military Balance 1986-87

ly have lost additional firearms. The impact of attrition on total global military stockpiles is important, but it is also difficult to assess, depending on highly idiosyncratic factors like maintenance, intensity of training, and the extent of their operational deployment.

To the earlier cited figure of 202 million official military arms worldwide must be added subsequent military procurement of newly manufactured firearms since 1987, the base year for calculation. According to the most detailed estimate available, production of military firearms remained at a level of roughly 3 million annually from 1987 through 1991, falling to an average of approximately one million per year thereafter, beginning with 1992 (PRODUCERS). This would mean that the global stockpile of military firearms has risen by an additional total of some 24 million small arms. Taken together, and assuming that attrition losses have not been very significant, the likely minimum Cold War stockpile plus subsequent production would place the current (January 2001) global stockpile of government-owned military firearms at approximately 226 million or greater, minus any attrition.

The firearms of insurgents and organized crime

The essential rule of guerrilla warfare holds that—by taking advantage of the surprise factor, striking when the risks are low and retreating when the risks are high—a small insurgency force can tactically dominate a much larger conventional army. The same also holds true for guerrilla weapons. Although their numbers may be far smaller than those of their conventional, government-armed adversaries, insurgent arsenals tend to be far more deadly and destructive. While all small arms and light weapons have the potential to cause needless death and suffering, these are the weapons most likely to be used to harm.

Not only are the armaments of non-state actors likely to be more deadly, they also tend to be far more elusive. The problem of determining the quantity of military small arms pales in comparison to the problem of quantifying the small arms of insurgents and other non-state actors. While placing greater demands on the accuracy of outside observers, the smaller size of rebel forces also makes transactions harder to spot and track. Voluntary statistics are unlikely. Not only is it hard

As of January 2001, the global stockpile of government-owned military firearms was conservatively estimated to number about 226 million.

to imagine arms control co-operation with most ongoing insurgencies and other violent groups, many major insurgencies are so secretive, decentralized, or disorganized that they themselves may not have anything beyond a general sense of their own weapons inventories.[39]

Despite their elusiveness, however, insurgent weapons are often those of most immediate importance internationally. These are the small arms at the nexus of the greatest political instability, threatening violent challenges to the authority of states, and creating immediate dangers to the lives and welfare of civilians. They are also the weapons upon which many governments at the 2001 *United Nations Conference on the Illicit Trafficking in Small Arms and Light Weapons in All Its Aspects* focus. Even if they do not constitute a major share of the global small arms arsenal, these considerations make it essential to examine their numbers very carefully.

To be sure, one must avoid exaggerations or misleading comparisons; as political scientists like Barry Buzan and Ken Booth have shown, more people are threatened by the misrule of states than are endangered by challenges to state authority.[40] Nevertheless, the chaos and disorder of intra-state warfare makes a better understanding of this aspect of the small arms phenomenon essential.

Trends in communal and intra-state conflict

The armaments of non-state actors are heavily influenced by the intensity of organized sub-state violence and other forms of communal warfare. The most important trend affecting small arms flows to these factions had been the decline of communal warfare and other forms of sub-state conflict since the mid-1990s. While there was a widely perceived rise in communal conflict, it is increasingly clear that this was more apparent than real, dominated by wars ignited by the disintegration of the Soviet Union and Yugoslavia. 'Many observers mistook these wars for the start of a new trend', wrote the political scientist Yahya Sadowski, but he concluded that, on the contrary, 'the state-formation wars that accompanied the "Leninist extinction" now appear to have been a one-time event—a flash flood rather than a global deluge.' [41]

This trend can be traced in data on the number of wars (conflicts with 1,000 or more battle deaths), which declined from 37 in 1990 to between 25 and 27 in every year since 1995.[42] The reason for the decline is surprisingly simple. As noted by the scholar of communal conflict, Ted Gurr, 'Two-thirds of all new campaigns of protest and rebellion since 1985 began between 1989 and 1993; few have started since. The decline in new protest movements foreshadows a continued decline in armed conflict. Since the number of new communally-based protest campaigns has declined— from a global average of ten per year in the late 1980s to four per year since 1995—the pool of potential future rebellions is shrinking.' Most on-going conflicts are also de-escalating, as rebels demand, not independence, but autonomy, which states are more willing to offer.[43]

However, as shown below, there is a strong regional component in these assessments. The focal point of sub-state warfare has shifted increasingly toward sub-Saharan Africa, the one region where the problem is unambiguously growing worse, bringing trends in insurgent gun trafficking with it.

Although the decline in new protest movements foreshadows a continued decline in armed conflict, sub-Saharan Africa is the one region in the world where the problem is unambiguously growing worse.

The special problems of quantifying insurgency weapons

Although there is no shortage of reports about the weapons of insurgents, most of this is highly anec-dotal. Even so, such accounts help illuminate the dynamics of black and grey market transfers of small arms and light weapons to secessionists and other non-state factions (ILLICIT TRANSFERS). Typical reports note the types of weapons used in armed conflict, observed in the field, or seized by police and the armed forces. Quantitative information on arms deliveries or factional arsenals becomes available only under special circumstances and, even when sufficiently detailed, such reports are questionable at best. Some of the best information comes from actual brokers' contracts, but these are rarely revealed. As a result, we know a lot about the kinds of weapons involved and the transfer processes at work, but relatively little about the quantities being shipped. This kind of research is ultimately too idiosyncratic to form a cumulative portrait of global processes.

Under these challenging circumstances, the best way to estimate the full scale of insurgent small arms is through formal modelling. This may be the only way to arrive at a global figure covering all small arms inventories and acquisition by insurgents. While formal modelling cannot determine exactly how the world's insurgents are armed, it can give a useful sense of the scale of the problem. The most important characteristics to be identified are the size of a guerrilla or other fighting organization and its tempo of activity. With this information in hand, the likely small arms acquisitions of such fighting groups can be calculated. When this is done for all known insurgencies and other non-state armed forces, a global picture of the illicit trade in small arms for violent conflict emerges (see Box 2.5).

Using news reports and reference works believed to be most reliable, as well as the advice and comments of regional experts, the total number of active or full-time non-state combatants in 1999—the latest year for which complete data were available—was approximately 184,000. In addition, another 480,000 people carried arms for secessionist insurgencies or other non-state armed forces; of these, some were more intermittently active troops, while others were uninvolved in actual fighting (see Table 2.8).

If each of these combatants carried a rifle and one-quarter of them carried a handgun as well, then they controlled as many as 728,000 rifles and 182,000 handguns, or some 910,000 in all. This includes a stockpile estimated at ten per cent. Of this, an estimated 300,000 were new. Insurgent firearms appear to constitute approximately two-tenths of one per cent of all global firearms.

Geographically, the data suggest that the greatest flow of additional small arms to insurgents went to sub-Saharan Africa, the region with more active non-state combatants than the rest of the world together. Europe was a surprising second, with a large number of active non-state combatants and the largest concentration of armed militiamen. Although Western Europe has several small rebel and terrorist groups, Europe's global salience comes almost entirely from Kosovo and regions on the periphery of the former Soviet Union, including Chechnya and Nagorno-Kharabhak, as well as Turkey. The changes mentioned above also explain the declining salience of the Middle East. North America and Northeast Asia appear to be the regions least touched by the flow of weapons to illegal organizations.

Table 2.8   Insurgent and other non-state combatants and militia in 1999

| Region | Combatant Status | | | |
	Active	Semi-Active	Inactive	Militia
Sub-Saharan Africa	102,000	36,350	17,000	54,000
Europe	27,800	4,225	23,180	74,300
Latin America	22,500	2,400	5,000	5,000
South Asia	10,500	2,400	0	0
Central Asia	10,000	36,600	0	0
South East Asia	7,200	23,700	34,500	32,400
Middle East	3,750	39,450	14,000	63,550
North East Asia	0	5,000	0	0
North America	0	300	100	5,000
Total:	**183,750**	**150,425**	**93,780**	**234,250**

Insurgent stockpile problems

One shortcoming of the approach used above is its omission of major insurgent stockpiles of excess or reserve equipment. In practical terms, such stockpiles are almost impossible to estimate without complete reports on the flows of weapons reaching these groups and, granted, most groups appear to have only relatively modest stockpiles. This is largely because they do not control territory where large stockpiles can be safely stored. But it is also due to military pressures that compel them to arm as many combatants as possible. Several major groups, on the other hand, do effectively control territory or have safe havens on the soil of neighbouring countries where they can and do stockpile weapons:

- The Kurdish factions, benefiting from the UN Air Exclusion Zone and their *de facto* autonomy from Baghdad, effectively control about 25 per cent of northern Iraq;
- Palestinian groups in Lebanon and Syria reportedly are permitted to maintain bases for their own use;
- The Liberation Tigers of Tamil Eelam (LTTE) in Sri Lanka reportedly stockpiles weaponry in the Indian state of Tamil Nadu;
- In Colombia, both the National Liberation Army (ELF) and the Revolutionary Armed Forces of Colombia (FARC) control regions where government troops are forbidden.

Because insurgent stockpiling is almost entirely covert and becomes evident only when the weapons are actually used, the figures shown here are inherently incomplete.

In the late 1990s, the greatest flow of additional small arms to insurgents went to sub-Saharan Africa, the region with more active non-state combatants than the rest of the world together.

Box 2.5 Estimating insurgent small arms

The scale of insurgent small arms arsenals has been estimated by multiplying the number of non-state troops against a value for their probable maximum weapons consumption. The model owes its basic assumptions largely to the pioneering work of Trevor Dupuy, who devoted much of his career to studying the relationship between armaments and military effectiveness.[44] Although the use of a formal model—even one as succinct as that employed here—may seem unusual, it is worthwhile to recall the observation that virtually all analysis is based on a model, whether we acknowledge it or not.[45]

The number of armed members of non-state factions has been determined from monographs, press clippings, and reference works such as *Defence and Foreign Affairs Global Information System*, *Jane's Insurgencies*, *The Military Balance*, and *The Middle East Military Balance*. These have been accumulated and evaluated for the most reliable figures. Complete tables listing over 135 insurgencies, as well as the work sheets covering all insurgent and non-state groups covered in this report, are available on the Small Arms Survey website at www.smallarmssurvey.org.

Unless otherwise defined, total forces are assumed to consist of one-quarter full-time soldiers and three-quarters support forces and militiamen, the latter typically equipped at one-fourth the level of the former. In other words, active troops are engaged in regular fire or training, accelerating the loss and necessitating routine replacement of their equipment. The equipment of support troops and militiamen has a slower rate of breakage due to wear and tear. The following assumptions govern this model:

- **Active troops** are full-time or nearly full-time soldiers. They spend most of their time in military activity, including tactical operations, training, and garrison duties. They are assumed to be involved in two or more fire-fights per year. They consume small arms and ammunition rapidly and their equipment suffers from high rates of breakage and wastage. For present purposes, they are assumed to replace their weapons annually.
- **Semi-active troops** operate occasionally but typically spend a large part of their time in cantonments or at civilian work. Their military activity is mostly patrolling. Although they may occasionally fire their weapons, they usually get into no more than one fire-fight per year. Their weapons use is less intense, leading to replacement approximately every four years, or

Fluctuations in insurgent activity and demand

The scale of insurgent small arms is influenced by the level of conflict around the world. While government armed forces benefit from annual budgeting and long-term procurement planning, insurgencies are much more sensitive to the ups and downs of internal war and communal conflict. Since the demand for guerrilla weapons is determined largely by the rise and demise of fighting factions, there is an enormous effect on small arms transfers when groups are defeated, reduce the tempo of their operations, abandon armed struggle, become dormant, or emerge victorious and overthrow governments.

The effects of these vicissitudes on small arms demand is clearest in the massive scale insurgent wars of the 1990s (i.e. civil wars in Afghanistan, the Bosnian and Kurdish secessionist wars) which dwarfed all other current internal conflicts during that period. Within months of reaching their crescendos of violence, these conflicts either ended or began to recede. For example:

- **Bosnia:** Fighting in Bosnia, which involved some 300,000 combatants, ended with the 1995 *Dayton Accords,* which also gave the country a legitimate right to arm itself.
- **Afghanistan:** The total number of fully active Afghan guerrillas was estimated by the London-based International Institute for Strategic Studies at approximately 500,000 at the height of the fighting in the early and mid-1990s. Today the number of active Afghan resistance fighters has reportedly declined to some 40,000.[46] While Afghanis may be replenishing their private weapons stockpiles, they clearly are not using them on a scale remotely comparable to before.

25 per cent annually.
- **Inactive troops** are those who have not been involved in armed clashes during the previous year. They train and may patrol and retain personal control over their arms. Their weapons are assumed to last ten years, requiring replacement of only ten per cent annually.
- **Support troops and militiamen** are not active combatants. Instead, they support combat elements or participate in occasional exercises and drills. They are trained in the use of personal weapons that are allocated to them. The weapons may be stored in a garrison arsenal so they have no personal control over them. These weapons are assumed to last ten years as well, requiring replacement of ten per cent annually.

Active troops—including guerrilla fighters—must replace their equipment regularly to remain fully capable of offensive action. It is a myth that small arms last forever. While this may hold true for weapons that are properly stored and cared for, with heavy use, small arms suffer breakage which can usually be repaired only by a professional armourer. Multiple repairs render most weapons unreliable and, ultimately, unusable. Even light use, when combined with regular carrying or drill, will eventually wear out a weapon, leading to frame cracks or other damage that eventually necessitates its replacement.

Losses among insurgents are likely to be much greater than for government armed forces, both because insurgents tend to be much more active, losing or breaking their weapons at a faster tempo, but also because they are less likely to have the ability to repair damaged equipment. For the purposes of this model, which tries to reflect likely maximum insurgent firearms procurement, it is assumed that active insurgent combatants replace all their firearms every year.

Rather than risk minimizing time problems, the approach used here intentionally errs in favour of exaggerated actual weapons consumption. Most guerrilla weapons do not appear to be replaced this often. Very few insurgents and other sub-state armed forces are engaged as heavily as the active troops described here. Contemporary groups that meet this high involvement level are the Kurdish PKK (until it suspended most fighting in mid-1999), the RUF of Sierra Leone and the LTTE of Sri Lanka. Other groups, even many with deservedly vicious reputations, are much less active by comparison. Many of the world's rebel armies, moreover, do very little besides routine patrolling punctuated by intermittent raids.

It is a myth that small arms last forever.

- **Kurdish insurgency:** Similarly, the Kurdish wars, when at their height in the early 1990s, involved a total of 80,000 full-time fighters in the three largest Kurdish rebel groups engaged in major campaigns against the Governments of Iraq and Turkey. As they arrived at understandings with their adversaries (as the Iraq-based Kurds did) or abandoned combat operations (as the PKK did in Turkey), they ceased to be fully active armies and evolved instead into part-time militias. Today there appear to be no more than 5,000 full-time combatants in their combined ranks and even these are not fully active.

As of January 2001, the Afghan and Kurdish conflicts had declined and their armies appear to have greatly diminished; whether through desertion or organized disbandment is not clear. Although neither region could be described as 'at peace', the tempo of fighting has obviously diminished, as shown by the retirement of hundreds of thousands of Afghani, and tens of thousands of Kurdish, soldiers. Although many undoubtedly retain their personal weapons and could be drawn into renewed fighting at quick notice, as of January 2001 they were militarily inactive, engaging in no more than occasional training, patrolling, or assemblies. Called back into action, they could immediately inflate local demand for arms and ammunition enormously, but they do not appear to be engaged in systematic re-armament today nor should they be considered a major market for re-armament in the near future.

Even quiescent factions may be using times of relative peace to re-group and re-arm. Especially those factions in effective control of territory can use conflict 'down time' to continue buying arms and accumulating stockpiles. But such peacetime procurement is virtually impossible to estimate. This problem points to a major rule governing our appreciation of the trade in small arms: in most cases, an unused weapon is a secret weapon, its existence unknown to the outside world. While the number of firearms used in combat can be inferred from the number of troops engaged, it is much harder to estimate stockpiles that are not used.

A major rule governing estimates of all small arms trade is that an unused weapon is a secret weapon, its existence unknown to the outside world.

From rebels to statesmen

These examples also reveal the statistical importance of groups 'graduating' through victorious campaigns or political successes that catapult them into power. Finding themselves suddenly in control of the state transforms them from fighting factions into politically legitimate governing authorities. Victory changes factions in innumerable ways. Of most relevance here, they gain control of much greater resources, not only enabling them to acquire much more military equipment, but also to acquire it legitimately and stockpile it freely. Although their arsenals usually begin to grow exponentially, they no longer appear among global insurgent holdings. Illegal weapons suddenly become legal—although the weapons themselves have not changed at all; only the nature of their ownership has. Thus it is that 'overnight', the illegitimate firearms of criminals and subversives become the bulwark of the new national defence.

When several major factions gain power at once, the effect can be to swiftly reduce the level of overall global insurgent armaments—on paper at least. In actuality, the change is more apparent than real, a legal distinction, as their holdings are shifted from insurgent to state categories. However, the effect on the two categories is not proportionately the same. Global insurgent armament inventories are relatively small and highly sensitive to the departure of a major faction, which can sharply reduce the overall global total. But global state-owned armaments are much more numerous, and the shift of even the very largest insurgent movements into the state category has only a negligible effect on the overall global level of official state armaments.

The effects of these vicissitudes were prominent in 1994-95, when several major insurgencies and rebel movements suddenly acquired legitimate political power. The change was especially dramatic for the Afghan Taleban, which took control of most of the country in 1994. With victory, their 25,000 fighting men ceased to be guerrillas and became government soldiers overnight.

A different version of the same phenomenon is illustrated by the police and paramilitary forces of the Palestinian Autonomous Areas, which include approximately 35,000 armed police, security, and intelligence officers. Most of these were drawn from the ranks of former Palestinian guerrilla factions that, partially as a direct consequence, have declined dramatically in size. In both cases, the demand for small arms has not declined—quite the opposite, new roles have led to even more intense weapons procurement—but it has become legal.

Shifting regional insurgent demand for small arms

Even though some insurgencies are acquiring less military equipment, others clearly are using more. The arms trade largely follows the armies. In the late-1980s and early-1990s, the illegal trade in small arms was directed largely toward conflicts in Afghanistan, Europe (Bosnia and Nagorno-Kharabhak), the Middle East (Palestinians and Kurds) and, to a lesser extent, to Africa (Angola, Liberia, and Sudan). Today small arms traffic is drawn overwhelmingly to the concentration of insurgent fighting in sub-Saharan Africa, especially to the Great Lakes Region and Sierra Leone, as well as to Angola and Sudan (BROKERS, ILLICIT TRANSFERS).

The greatest demand for small arms among non-state forces today is in sub-Saharan Africa, home to more than 60 per cent of the world's fully active non-state combatants. Totally displacing Central Asia and the Middle East, the region of sub-Saharan Africa is the most likely destination for most of the world's black and grey market small arms.

Surprising perhaps to those accustomed to associating violent conflict with less developed regions, Europe is the world's second most deadly region for secessionist fighting. This reflects the unsettled nature of Europe's periphery where wars resulting from the collapse of Yugoslavia and the Soviet Union continue in the Balkans and the Caucasus.

In Latin America and South East Asia, the level of conflict is relatively stable, although the most serious war sites have changed during the previous decade; in Latin America, from Peru to Colombia; and in South East Asia, from Myanmar to the Philippines. The regions least touched by conflict are Northeast Asia, where the problem is limited mostly to Russian organized crime groups, and North America, where Mexican revolutionary groups are active. The well-armed North American militia groups—which get so much media attention—are not included here. This is partially because they appear to acquire most of their weapons legally and because, despite their fearsome rhetoric, none have engaged in organized violence. The closest approximation to that was the network of friends and acquaintances responsible for the 1995 Oklahoma City bombing.

Private firearms: Legal and illegal

In most parts of the world, the gravest daily danger of armed violence comes neither from repressive use of government weapons nor from the weapons of insurgent rebels. Rather, it is the misuse of privately owned weapons that translates directly into the crime statistics driving much of the concern with small arms proliferation.

Determining the number of firearms in private hands is made difficult by the diversity of national laws regulating gun ownership; by different licensing and reporting practices; by differences in national customs regarding gun ownership; and by the problem of illegal gun ownership. Although private gun ownership is regulated in most countries, many are unable to determine the number of private firearms at large in their societies. Small arms proliferation may be a definitive example of the way globalization is transforming the world, but globalization has yet to make inroads against the diversity of national policies regarding gun regulation.

When guerrillas become government soldiers 'overnight', the demand for more small arms generally does not decline—it just becomes legal.

The greatest demand for small arms among non-state forces today is in sub-Saharan Africa, home to more than 60 per cent of the world's fully active non-state combatants.

The seriousness of rising numbers of firearms in private hands is beyond dispute, but their numbers are the most elusive of all. There is such a severe shortage of hard data in this area that the estimating procedures employed elsewhere in this chapter cannot be applied to private small arms. The simple methods used above are based on correlations between people and their weapons: the number of police to the number of police firearms; the number of soldiers to the number of military small arms, etc. This reflects the underlying fact that, in order to do their job, the police require a certain number of weapons while soldiers need a different but still readily determined number. In each of those cases, national population or the number of gun owners, be they police or soldiers, is used as a substitute for the total number of firearms involved.

The risk of rising numbers of firearms in private hands is beyond dispute, but their numbers are the most elusive of all. If small arms proliferation is a definitive example of the way globalization is transforming the world, it has yet to unite national policies regarding gun regulation.

For privately held weapons, however, there are no universal rules of thumb. Each country has its own firearms culture, in which the various types of small arms have their distinct niche. Whether private firearms ownership is perceived as high or low, normal or exceptional, is a judgment call that each society renders in accordance with its own traditions.

Therefore, rather than rely on the types of generalizations that facilitated earlier estimations of police or military firearms, private guns have to be quantified through a country-by-country building-block approach. Currently, there is simply no alternative to adding up the numbers in each country to cumulatively arrive at regional and global totals. At this point in time, however, the building blocks— the specific national statistics—are missing in most countries. Creating them will be possible only through a co-ordinated international effort, probably relying on a combination of forthright official declarations, backed up by country-by-country public surveys, as discussed below.

Licensed private firearms and the United Nations International Study on Firearm Regulation

The most important effort thus far to collate available information on private firearms ownership is the *United Nations International Study on Firearm Regulation.* Undertaken in 1995-97 and updated in 1999 by the Vienna-based UN Commission on Crime Prevention and Criminal Justice, this is a collection of responses from national governments outlining their policies.[47] Submissions were received from 69 governments, but not all presented data on the specific question of the number of privately owned guns.

Updated data released by the Commission in 1999 included numerical data on firearm ownership from a total of 49 countries. Many lacked accurate data on private firearms ownership while others could account only for the number of owners—who require licenses in many countries—but not their actual guns. An even greater number of countries failed to offer any useful data at all. Some just failed to co-operate. Other holdouts, however, were governments that participated in other aspects of the study. Their explanations are often highly revealing about the nature of gun laws and the existence of relevant data within their societies. For example:

- **Chile:** Chile reported that data were 'not available because the system does not separate civilians from the military.'[48]
- **France:** French officials have said unofficially that their Government cannot supply information on private gun ownership because such information is confidential and cannot be released except in response to specific requests from the courts.[49]
- **Germany:** Germany explained that 'accurate figures are not obtainable since registration of entitled persons takes place at the lowest administrative level and is not centrally collected.' Instead, the German Government offered a 'realistic guesstimate' of 10 million licensed firearms owners but provided no estimate for actual firearms. The most recent estimates of actual firearms, from 1972, put the number in the range of 15 to 25 million. Moreover, the 'guesstimate' on gun owners and the old range for actual guns covered only the territory of the former West Germany; records for the former East Germany reportedly 'were deliberately destroyed'.[50]

- **Others:** A few countries, lacking accurate statistics from registrations, instead offered widely accepted estimates of national gun ownership. When based on the professional judgment of knowledgeable experts, these are a helpful substitute, as was the case with New Zealand's estimate of one million privately owned firearms. Other estimates, reflecting little more than journalistic speculation, may be highly misleading.

Testifying to the difficulty of co-operation between rival government agencies, a few countries—including Ecuador and Papua New Guinea—explained that their representatives were unable to secure the necessary co-operation from officials in other ministries of their own governments. Others, like Austria, Belgium, Estonia, and the Netherlands, reported that official data basically did not exist. And these countries, it should be noted, have been among the most co-operative. Several others, including governments that participated in other parts of the study—most prominently China and India—simply ignored the request for private gun statistics.

Adding all the actual submissions of privately owned and licensed firearms, including estimates for specific states, produces a total of almost 40 million firearms in public hands in 49 countries. In other words, the *United Nations International Study on Firearm Regulation* generated some useful information, but mostly served to confirm the lack of data in general and the widespread confusion over how to use the available data. No less revealing was the final submission by the United States. The US advised that it was unable to present formal information on licensed gun ownership since it has no national gun licensing for most firearms. Only eleven out of its 50 states require gun registration of any kind. Instead, the US presented the results of a major public survey—a 'scientific, privately conducted poll'—which indicated that US citizens owned approximately 192 million guns in 1994.[51] While the survey approach is less reliable than official numbers, where such figures do not exist, it may be the most effective way—shy of changing existing legislation—to answer basic questions.

Government data are available on US firearms production, imports, and exports, and this is very important for filling the gaps left by surveys. These data reveal that the US typically produces about 3.5 million guns annually for domestic customers and imports an additional 1.5 million (PRODUCERS). Adding these figures together suggests that, by the end of the year 2000, there were about 226 million private guns in the United States. Similar surveys have been undertaken in other countries. Prominent examples are:

- **Australia:** A survey revealed that in 1996 there were roughly 3.5 million privately owned firearms in the country. Since then, this number has decreased, largely through the prohibition of public ownership of semi-automatic rifles and shotguns. Indicative of the weaknesses of surveys, however, another survey, undertaken by the private *Newspoll* group and released by the Australian Attorney-General in 1997, concluded that the nation's citizens owned just 2.5 million private firearms.[52]
- **Canada:** A Government-sponsored study showed the country to have approximately 7.1 million private guns. At the time the survey was completed, gun registration was just beginning, so these were almost all legally unlicensed weapons.[53]

Ultimately, the only way to determine the number of guns in private hands is either through comprehensive reporting by the world's governments or through global surveys. Until this is possible, the easiest alternative is adding together available numbers. This approach is far from ideal, since it mixes registration and licensing data with official estimates and survey reports, often from different years.

Adding the available and reasonably reliable reports shows that there are at least 305 million privately owned firearms in the world today (Table 2.9). This, however, is a very conservative estimate. It underestimates gun ownership in many countries, most clearly in countries like Germany and whole regions like Eastern Europe and the former Soviet Union. It completely leaves out the world's two most populous countries—China and India—as well as other countries with widespread gun ownership, including Afghanistan, France, Switzerland, Yemen, and most African states.[54]

One clear impression from the study is the overwhelming role of the United States in the world's private firearms arsenal. US dominance of private gun ownership is almost certainly exaggerated by the fact that other countries thought to have large civilian firearms inventories are not included in the *UN International Study on Firearm Regulation*. The addition of illegally owned firearms in other countries would also reduce the disparities. Nevertheless, the United States' essential prominence seems irrefutable. These results—incomplete as they are—also show that the majority of all the world's firearms—at least 55 per cent—are in private hands.

Illegal firearms in private hands

Legal firearms are only part of private gun ownership. How many illegal firearms are there in the world? The only truthful answer is that no one has any idea. Reminded daily by the rising dangers of illegal weapons use, journalists and even seasoned observers are tempted to indulge in guessing. In Brazil alone, it has been estimated that there are approximately 12 million unlicensed firearms out of 18.5 million total.[55] While the Government of the Russian Federation reports having 3.6 million registered private firearms, unofficial sources reportedly believe the illegal figure to be closer to 30 million. One estimate for all of South Asia—Bangladesh, Bhutan, India, Pakistan, Nepal, and Sri Lanka—posits that there are at least 73 million unlicensed firearms throughout the region.[56] A more cautious estimate from South Africa notes that 'an estimated 4.1 million firearms are licensed to civilians in South Africa, with ... estimates of illegal weapons ranging from 800,000 to 4 million.'[57]

National submissions to the United Nations International Study on Firearm Regulation indicate that there are currently a total of almost 40,000,000 firearms in public hands in 49 countries. As there are some 200 countries in the world, this survey is clearly incomplete.

Table 2.9 Total known private firearms

Source	Year(s)	Millions of guns
UN Firearm Study total (non-US)	1996	39
United States 1994 survey	1994	192
Subsequent US private gun purchases	1994-2000	34
Official estimates for Brazil, Germany and South Africa	1970-2000	40
China, France, India, Switzerland, and others		unknown
Total		**>305**

Sources: Commerce in Firearms in the United States, 2000; Cook and Ludwig, 1997; UN International Study on Firearm Regulation, 1999

When it comes to unlicensed weapons, vague figures are not the only problem. Very specific ones are no more credible. This is illustrated by the example of the Philippines, the only government to release detailed information about illegal firearms ownership. In 1996, the Philippine police identified 160,750 unlicensed firearms in the country. By 1998, this figure had increased to 329,985 unlicensed firearms in the hands of enthusiasts, criminals, private armies, and rebel groups.[58] Given the nature of the problem, these seemingly precise numbers must be regarded with scepticism.

In fact, none of these figures should be regarded as anything other than suggestive. The problem of illegal gun ownership is serious and observers naturally want to associate the problem with a serious-looking number. But even the relationship between legal and illegal firearms ownership is often very slippery. An exception is the United States, where, for the most part, only stolen weapons are illegal. Canada, which historically had the same policy, is in the process of introducing national gun registration. One country without a history of firearms registration and rapidly mounting gun problems is Pakistan, which is in the process of trying to establish a legal framework for greater stability.[59] All such innovations, while beneficial, face problems of compliance. They tend to be more effective with the registration of new weapons, leaving the pool of older, unlicensed, and unregistered weapons untouched.

In the few countries where the scale of illegal firearms ownership is somewhat understood—especially Argentina and the UK—the approximate number of unlicensed firearms varies from half as much as the number of licensed guns in Britain to even more than the total number of licensed firearms in Argentina. Such estimates are too vague to establish a global figure. All that can be said is that the scale of the problem is very large indeed, probably amounting to several tens of millions of illegally owned firearms.

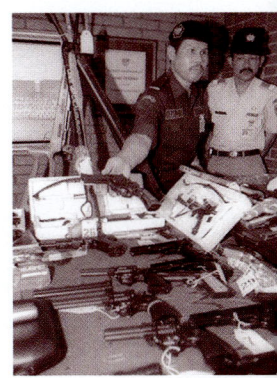

Answering the illegal and unlicensed firearms riddle

The most feasible method to estimate the global number of illegal and unlicensed firearms is either through residual estimates or public surveys. The residual method requires accurate information on the number of firearms in existence and on all other major categories of firearms ownership. If these can be firmly established, then unlicensed guns would be the only category left unaccounted for. This recipe sounds straightforward enough: if the total number of guns produced in recent decades can be determined, as well as the number destroyed over the years; and then the number currently belonging to the police, the armed forces or those licensed to private owners are deducted from the total, the remainder must be the total of unlicensed firearms. Lacking accurate information for any of the first five categories, however, there is no way to calculate a residual figure at this point in time.

Ultimately, the most promising way to develop a general sense of the global distribution of illicit firearms may be to copy the American example and rely on public surveys. The relevance of polling was revealed recently in Argentina, where a privately commissioned survey showed that, in addition to their 1.75 million legally licensed firearms, the people of Argentina have at least 2.57 million unlicensed firearms. As the authors of the survey were careful to point out, their findings were tentative, but the sense of direction and overall scale of the problem are clear enough.[60]

There are other obvious weaknesses to this approach, especially when it comes to undemocratic or recently democratized countries where there is considerable public suspicion concerning the purposes and anonymity of polling. Some governments that restrict expressions of public opinion, especially in the Middle East, China, and some other East Asian states, may not be willing to permit this kind of activity. Even in a co-operative environment, polling is an imperfect science, especially when it comes to highly sensitive subjects like (possibly illegal) gun ownership. Even so, a programme of standardized public surveys covering the largest gun-owning societies would do much to overcome legal barriers to the release of licensing information and the inevitable problem of unlicensed weapons.

The advantages of surveys and polling are relevant virtually everywhere. Where there are no official records of gun ownership, the benefits are obvious. For a country like France, polling offers a way around official confidentiality. For others like Germany or Switzerland, it may be the best way of circumventing official hesitancy and the lack of federal record-keeping. In the Nordic region and other countries which license owners rather than individual firearms, surveys can help establish the number of firearms per licensed owner and thus the total number of weapons in each country. And for countries like Brazil, India, the Russian Federation, or South Africa, it is the only way to account for the presumably large number of unlicensed weapons.

Conclusions

Small arms proliferation involves a large spectrum of different types of equipment designed to kill and maim. It is guns, however, that command the most attention. While this preoccupation should not lead observers and policy-makers to overlook other dangerous items, it may be appropriate nevertheless. Not only do firearms appear to cause the most death and injury, they also are the type of small arms that is most widespread, not just among armed forces, but also throughout much of civil society.

The above estimate resulting from this analysis—incomplete because several important categories are only partially included or left out altogether—reveals that there are at least 550 million firearms in the world today (see Table 2.10 and Figure 2.5). This amounts to at least one gun for every eleven of the world's people. Even though a large proportion of legally owned private guns are left out, as are all illegally owned private guns and all manufacturers' and dealers' stocks, it is still possible to clarify several critical questions. Above all, who controls most of the firearms in the world?

This analysis, tentative as it is, reveals that the results are not always consistent with the conventional wisdom:

There are at least 550 million firearms in the world today— one gun for every eleven people, including children.

- **Police stocks** appear to form a relatively small part of the total number of global firearms, often operating with modest reserves for breakage and special operations. The numbers derived from the small but diverse sample of countries used here show that there are approximately 18 million official police firearms globally—roughly three per cent of all known firearms.
- **Military firearms** is a category full of surprises. Experts, even in many Western and OECD states, often assume that the inventories of the armed services are kept close to the number of actual troops, with reserves only for breakage and minimal battlefield replacements. The examples here suggest that this assumption errs on the conservative side. Even countries with carefully controlled armed forces can have substantial small arms reserves of roughly double the nominal requirements, while some may have stockpiles of three or four times the basic requirements. The grand total for all kinds of government-owned military firearms in existence today is estimated at a minimum of 226,000,000 official military firearms, including automatic rifles and sub-machines guns, pistols, light and medium machine guns. This equals some 41 per cent of all known firearms. The largest concentrations appear to be among those countries with the largest armed forces and reserve organizations.
- **Private firearms** account for an enormous proportion of gun ownership. The total number currently is impossible to evaluate. The world's most populous countries—China and India—do not make data available. Nor do other countries with widespread public gun ownership like Afghanistan, France, Switzerland, and Yemen. Still others report only obviously incomplete

Table 2.10 Comparative distribution of known global firearms in 2001

Group	Estimated number of firearms	Percentage of total
Police firearms	18,000,000	3.3 %
Government armed forces	226,000,000	41.1 %
Private legally owned	305,000,000 +	55.4 % +
Insurgents and non-state forces	±1,000,000	0.2 %
Approximate total	550,000,000 +	100.0 %

Note: The above estimate does not include the large but indeterminate number of privately owned and illegal firearms for which no estimates are currently available.

Figure 2.5   Estimates of known global firearms, 2001

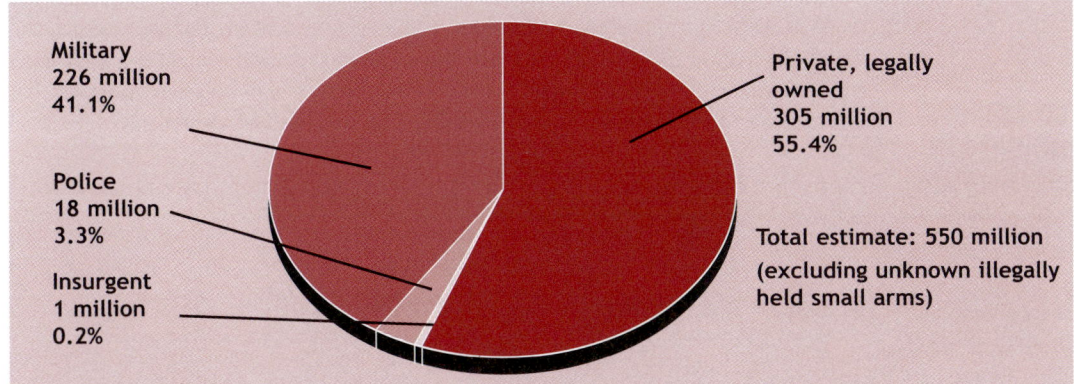

figures. But the existing data is sufficient to confirm that this is the largest single category of firearms, totaling a minimum of 305 million guns in the year 2000. This amounts to at least 55 per cent of all guns. With more complete reporting or surveys, both the total number of privately owned guns and their proportion of the global total undoubtedly would rise significantly.

- **Insurgent firearms** may provide the greatest surprise in terms of the relatively small size of stocks. The firearms under their control are estimated at approximately 910,000. The comparatively small scale of this figure, compared to the others developed in this chapter, partially reflects the declining incidence of communal warfare since the mid-1990s. Even more salient, the enormous havoc rebel factions can wreak upon life, welfare, and political stability does not require large weapons holdings—apparently as little as two-tenths of one per cent of all known firearms. The classic rules of insurgent warfare hold just as true for guerrilla weapons, enabling small rebel forces to tie up much larger forces sent to control their trepidations. Rebels with one-tenth the combatants and proportionately even less weaponry than their government adversaries still may be able to dominate the battlefields of internecine warfare.

- **Illegal private gun ownership** remains a serious and highly intractable problem for efforts at quantification. Compared to the small but systematic data developed for all other categories, the evidence developed so far is too anecdotal and too intermittent to be useful for broader generalization. All that can be said with certainty is that the total number of illegally owned firearms is in the range of tens—or possibly even of hundreds—of millions. The problem may be constructively addressed only through systematic international public surveys. Since illicit firearms have not been included in these estimates, the final figures shown here must be regarded as a substantial underestimate of the total number of guns in the world.

The cumulative portrait of the distribution of firearms around the world is highly tentative. All the numbers are estimates and will require constant revisions for years to come. The numbers themselves may be less consequential than the proportional distribution, which could prove highly relevant to the setting of political priorities for future national and international action, suggesting which problems are of greatest relative significance, which are most intractable, and which are most amenable to solution.

In conclusion, the most significant finding of this review is the overwhelming importance of official transparency and the advantages of public surveys as a substitute for comprehensive, official government statistics when the latter are unavailable. Only when governments and manufacturers begin to systematically share information on the number of small arms under their control, will it become possible to identify the trends in global small arms with greater accuracy. Meanwhile, without the availability of better information, governments and the international community will continue to encounter unnecessary difficulties, inhibiting agreement on priorities for action and identification of the most suitable solutions. This means that many important aspects of small arms proliferation will remain beyond control, not just because of the weapons themselves, but also as a direct result of excessive secrecy regarding their numbers and whereabouts.

The most significant finding is the overwhelming importance of official transparency and the advantages of public surveys.

For further information and current developments on small arms issues please check our website at www.smallarmssurvey.org

2 List of Abbreviations

ELF	National Liberation Army
FARC	Revolutionary Armed Forces of Colombia
FRELIMO	Frente de Libertacão de Moçambique
FRY	Former Yugoslavia
GDR	German Democratic Republic
LTTE	Liberation Tigers of Tamil Eelam
NATO	North Atlantic Treaty Organization
OECD	Organization of Economic Cooperation and Development
PKK	Kurdistan Worker's Party
RENAMO	Resistencia National Moçambicana
RUF	Revolutionary United Front
SIPRI	Stockholm International Peace Research Institute
START	Strategic Arms Reduction Treaty
TDA	Territorial Defence Army
UN	United Nations
UK	United Kingdom
USSR	Union of Soviet Socialist Republics
YPA	Yugoslav People's Army

2 Endnotes

1. One of the very best examples of what case studies can achieve is *Arming Rwanda: Arms Trade and Human Rights Abuses* (1994).

2. United Nations (1999b, para.12).

3. Singh (1995, p. ix).

4. Author's correspondence with Prakash Dikshit, November 2000.

5. Tara Kartha (1998, p. 19).

6. United Nations (1999a, para. 12).

7. Ezell (1986).

8. Ezell (1995, p. 9). Virginia Ezell provided additional comments on the origins of these estimates.

9. United Nations (1997, para. 35).

10. United Nations (1997, p. 31, Appendix III).

11. Allen (2000).

12. Chachiua (1999, p. 16-18).

13. Smith, Batchelor, and Potgieter (1996, p.36).

14. *Africa Confidential* (14 April 1995, p. 7).

15. The figure of 6 million is cited in Chachiua (1999, p. 21) and Jett (1999, p. 98). The estimate of 10 million appears in Mathiak (1997, p. 94), citing *The New York Times* (2 March 1997).

16. Population figures derived from IISS (1990, p. 139).

17. IISS (1990, p. 138).

18. Smith (1999a, p. 107).

19. Smith (1999b, pp. 47, 49).

20. Vines (April 1998, p. 19).

21. Based on data from Berman (1996 pp. 46, 48, 87-88). Berman's source is *Final Report of the Chairman of the Cease-Fire Commission*, 5 December 1994. Using the same raw data from Berman, Chachiua arrives at a total of 214,219 weapons collected. (Chachiua, 1999, p. 26). Most of the difference appears to be due to inclusion of 46,193 weapons collected after official demobilization.

22. This point was brought to the author's attention by Steve Shropshire.

23. This data was made available by Martin Langvandslien of the International Peace Research Institute, Oslo (PRIO).

24. The phrase was coined by the German General Baron Colmar von der Goltz, in the title of his book, *The Nation in Arms* (1913). See Carroll (1968).

25. *Baltimore Sun* (15 June 2000).

26. Thomson and Mayo (1960, pp. 156, 170, 174, 186). The size of the U.S. Army in 1945 is from Weigley (1967, p. 599).

27. Correspondence from Lt.Col. Ola Stubdal, Norwegian Defence General Staff, courtesy of Martin Langvandslien, PRIO, 20 September 2000.

28. Cock (1999, p. 160).

29. Justitiedepartementet (1999, p. 27, 36, 74, and 112-115).

30. Ezell (1999, p. 25) and Ezell (1998, p. 35).

31. Ezell (1969).

32. Nassauer (1995, p. 57) and Gorjanc (2000).

33. Ezell (1988, pp. 161-162).

34. IISS (1990, pp. 48-49).

35. IISS (1990, p. 95). The special characteristics of territorial defence are explored in Roberts (1976).

36. Gorjanc (2000).

37. Global troop levels from *World Military Expenditure and Arms Transfers 1998* (1999). According to BICC (1999, p. 162) the total number of armed forces personnel was 28.8 million in 1987 and 22 million in 1997. Both sources appear to refer exclusively to active duty personnel, including some paramilitaries.

38. Force levels derived from IISS (1987).

39. Cooper (2000).

40. Buzan (1991), Booth (1997).

41. Sadowski (1998, p. 13).

42. Sollenberg, Wallensteen, and Jato (1999).

43. Gurr (2000, pp. 52-64, quote from p. 53).

44 Dupuy (1990); and Dupuy (1987).

45. Epstein (1988, pp. 158-159).

46. IISS (1989, pp. 155-156); IISS (1999, pp. 159-160).

47. (United Nations, 1998). The study was mandated by a resolution of the UN Economic and Social Council (ECOSOC). Data was received from 69 participating governments.

48. United Nations (1999b). Updated Data, available at www.uncjin.org/Statistics/firearms/index/htm.

49. Private communication with Ed Laurance, December 1999.

50. United Nations (1999b).

51. The survey results are analysed in Cook and Ludwig (1997).

52 Harding (1996). The Newspoll survey is cited in Alpers (1997).

53. See *Focus on Firearms* (3 March 1999).

54. These figures are available in the document, 'Statistics on firearms ownership, public and private.' Available at www.smallarmssurvey.org.

55. Mathiak (1997, p. 94).

56. *Nezavisimoe Voennoe Obrozrenie* (April 2000 p. 7); *Hindustan* (23 April 2000, p. 6).

57. Meek (1999, p.165-166).

58. United Nations (1998), and Makinano and Lubang (2000, p. 1).

59. Rizvi (2000).

60. Der Ghougassian and Lapieza Spota (1999). The author would like to thank Pablo Dreyfus for bringing this source to his attention.

2 Bibliography

Nezavisimoe Voennoe Obrozrenie. 2000. 'Territorial FSS Departments Try to Suppress Illegal Arms Sales.' No. 14. (Agency WPS, 25 April).

Allen, Robin. 2000. 'President Fires a Warning Shot Across Yemenis' Guns and Drugs Culture.' *Financial Times*. 12-13 February.

Alpers, Philip. 1997. *Gun Policy Database*. 26 August.

Baltimore Sun. 2000. 'Kazakhstan Says There is No Inventory of Country's Weapons.' 15 June.

Batchelor, Peter. 1996. 'Disarmament, Small Arms and Intra-State Conflict.' In Christopher Smith, Peter Batchelor and Jakkie Potgieter. *Small Arms Management and Peacekeeping in Southern Africa*. Geneva: United Nations Institute for Disarmament Research.

Berman, Eric. 1996. *Managing Arms in Peace Processes: Mozambique*. Geneva: United Nations Institute for Disarmament Research.

Bonn International Center for Conversion. 1999. *Conversion Survey 1999: Global Disarmament, Demilitarisation and Demobilization*. Baden-Baden: Nomos Verlagsgesellschaft.

Booth, Ken. 1997. 'Security and Self: Reflections of a Fallen Realist.' In Keith Krause and Michael C. Williams, eds. *Critical Security Studies*. Minneapolis: University of Minnesota Press.

Bureau of Alcohol, Tobacco and Firearms. 2000. *Commerce in Firearms in the United States*. Washington, DC: Department of the Treasury.

Buzan, Barry. 1991. *Peoples, States and Fear*, 2nd Edition. Boulder, Colorado: Lynne Rienner.

Canadian Firearms Centre. 1999. *Focus on Firearms*. Ottawa: Canadian Firearms Centre. 3 March.

Caroll, Berenice A. 1968. *Design for Total War: Arms and Economics in the Third Reich*. The Hague: Mouton.

Chachiua, Martinho. 1999. 'The Status of Arms Flows in Mozambique.' In Tandeka Nkiwane et al., eds. *Weapons Flows in Zimbabwe, Mozambique and Swaziland*. ISS Monograph No. 34. Pretoria: Institute for Security Studies. January.

Cock, Jacklyn. 1999. 'A Sociological Perspective on Small Arms Proliferation in South Africa.' In Jayantha Dhanapala et al., eds. *Small Arms Control: Old Weapons, New Issues*. Aldershot: Ashgate.

Cook, Philip, and Jens Ludwig. 1997. *Guns in America: National Survey on Private Ownership and Use of Firearms*. National Institute of Justice Research Brief. Washington, DC: U.S. Department of Justice, Office of Justice Programs. May.

Cooper, Neil. 2000. 'Arming and Disarming Kosovo: A Structural Arms Control Perspective.' Paper presented at Conference sponsored by the United Nations Research Institute for Social Development. Geneva, 26-30 June.

Dupuy, Trevor. 1987. *Understanding War: History and the Theory of Combat*. San Francisco: Paragon.

____. 1990. *Attrition. Forecasting Battle Casualties and Equipment Loses in Modern War*. Fairfax, Virginia: Hero Books.

Epstein, Joshua. 1988. 'Dynamic Analysis and the Conventional Balance in Europe.' *International Security*, Vol. 12, No. 4. Spring.

Ezell, Edward Clinton. 1969. *The Search for a Lightweight Rifle: The M14 and M16 Rifles*. Ph.D. Dissertation. Pittsburgh, Pennsylvania: Case Western Reserve University.

____. 1986. *The AK-47 Story: Evolution of the Kalashnikov Weapons*. Harrisburg, Pennsylvania: Stackpole Books.

____. 1988. *Small Arms Today*, 2nd Edition. Harrisburg: Stackpole Books.

Ezell, Virginia Hart. 1995. *Report on International Small Arms Production and Proliferation*. Alexandria, Virginia: Institute for Research on Small Arms and International Security.

____. 1998. 'Rumors of Colt's Death Exaggerated.' *National Defense*. October.

____. 1999. '"Less Weight" is the Mantra for Infantry Weapon Makers.' *National Defense*. September.

____. 2000. 'Arms Guru B-Day Offers Policy Forum.' *National Defence*. January.

Hindustan. 2000. 'Frightful Web of Small Weapons.' 23 April, p. 6. (FBIS SAP-20000424000072).

Gander, Terry J. 2000. *Jane's Infantry Weapons 2000-2001*. Coulsdon: Jane's Information Group.

der Ghougassian, Khatchik and Hernan Lapieza Spota, 1999. 'Las armas livianas, la violencia y la seguridad: fundamentos y lineamientos para una investigacion.' Paper presented at the First Seminar on Security, Violence and Democracy. La Plata, Argentina, 10-11 August.

von der Goltz, Colmar Freiherr. 1913. *The Nation in Arms*. Translated by Philip Ashworth. London: H. Rees.

Gorjanc, Milan. 2000. 'Small Arms and Light Weapons and National Security.' Paper presented at the Workshop for Small Arms and Light Weapons. Ljubljana, 27 January.

Gurr, Ted Robert. 2000. 'Ethnic Warfare on the Wane.' *Foreign Affairs*, Vol. 79, No. 3. May-June.

Harding, Richard. 1996. *Numbers, Types and Distribution of Firearms in Australia, 1996*. Perth: University of Western Australia, Crime Research Centre. June.

Hennop, Ettienne. 2000. 'Illegal Firearms in Circulation in South Africa.' In Virginia Gamba, ed. *Governing Arms: The South African Experience*. Pretoria: Institute for Security Studies.

Human Rights Watch. 1994. *Arming Rwanda: Arms Trade and Human Rights Abuses*. Vol.6, No. 1. Washington, DC: Human Rights Watch.

International Institute for Strategic Studies. 1987. *Military Balance 1987-88*. London: International Institute for Strategic Studies.

____. 1989. *The Military Balance 1989-90*. London: Brassey's.

____. 1990. *The Military Balance 1990-1991*. London: Brassey's.

____. 1999. *The Military Balance, 1999-2000*. Oxford: Oxford University Press.

Interpol. 1994. Third International Symposium on Firearms and Explosives. Lyon, 7-9 September.

Jett, Dennis. 1999. *Why Peacekeeping Fails*. New

York: St. Martin's Press.

Justitiedepartementet. 1999. *Regeringens Proposition 1999/2000:27, En Skaerpt Vapenlagstiftning*. Stockholm: Justitiedepartementet. 18 November.

Kartha, Tara. 1998. *Wars and Civil Society: The Rising Threat from Small Wars*. PSIS Occasional Paper No. 2/1998. Geneva: Graduate Institute of International Studies, Programme for Strategic and International Security Studies.

Makinano, Merliza and Alfred Lubang. 2000. 'Disarmament, Demobilization and Reintegration: the Mindanao Experience.' Paper presented at the RCSS Conference. Colombo, Sri Lanka, June.

Mathiak, Lucy. 1997. 'The Light Weapons Trade at the End of the Century.' In Virginia Gamba, ed. *Society Under Siege: Crime, Violence and Illegal Weapons*. Pretoria: Institute for Security Studies.

Meek, Sarah. 1999. 'New Democracies Under the Gun: Small Arms in Southern Africa.' In Abdel-Fatau Musah and Niobe Thompson, eds. *Over a Barrel: Light Weapons and Human Rights in the Commonwealth*. London: Commonwealth Human Rights Initiative.

Mozambique Cease-Fire Commission. 1994. *Final Report of the Chairman of the Cease-Fire Commission*. 5 December.

Nassauer, Otfried. 1995. 'An Army Surplus—the NVA's Heritage.' In Edward Laurance and Herbert Wulf, eds. *Coping with Surplus Weapons*. Brief No. 3. Bonn: Bonn International Center for Conversion.

Rizvi, Shamim Ahmed. 2000. 'Government's "Arms Control" Campaign.' *Pakistan and Gulf Economist*. 18 September.

Roberts, Adam. 1976. *Nations In Arms*. London: International Institute for Strategic Studies.

Sadowski, Yahya. 1998. 'Ethnic Conflict: Think Again.' *Foreign Policy*, No. 111. Summer.

Singh, Jasjit. 1995. 'Introduction.' In Singh, ed. *Light Weapons and International Security*. New Delhi: Pugwash Conferences and BASIC.

Smith, Christopher. 1996. 'Light Weapons and the International Arms Trade.' In Christopher Smith,

Peter Batchelor and Jackie Potgieter. *Small Arms Management and Peacekeeping in Southern Africa*. Geneva: United Nations Institute for Disarmament Research.

____. 1999a. 'Areas of Major Concentration in the Use and Traffic of Small Arms.' In Jayantha Dhanapala et al., eds. *Small Arms Control: Old Weapons, New Issues*. Aldershot: Ashgate.

____. 1999b. 'Light Weapons Proliferation: a Global Survey.' *Jane's Intelligence Review*. July.

Sollenberg, Margareta, Peter Wallensteen and Andrés Jato. 1999. 'Major Armed Conflicts.' In Stockholm International Peace Research Institute. *Sipri Yearbook 1999*. Oxford: Oxford University Press.

Thomson, Harry C. and Lida Mayo. 1960. *United States Army in World War II: The Technical Services: The Ordnance Department: Procurement and Supply*. Washington, DC: Department of the Army, Office of the Chief of Military History.

Africa Confidential. 1995. 'Underpaid, Underfed and Unruly.' Vol. 36, No.17. April.

United Nations. 1997. *Report of the Panel of Governmental Experts on Small Arms*. A/52/298. 27 August.

____. 1998. *United Nations International Study on Firearm Regulation*. New York: United Nations.

____. 1999a. *Small Arms: Report of the Secretary-General*. A/54/404. 24 September.

____. 1999b. *United Nations International Study on Firearm Regulation*. On-line database. 30 August. <http://www.uncjin.org/Statistics/firearms/index.htm>

United States Department of State. 1999. *World Military Expenditure and Arms Transfers 1998*. Washington, DC: U.S. Department of State, Bureau of Arms.

Vines, Alex. 1998. *The Struggle Continues: Light Weapons Destruction in Mozambique*. BASIC Occasional Papers No. 25. London: BASIC. April.

Weigley, Russel. 1967. *History of the United States Army*. Bloomington, Indiana: University of Indiana Press.

3

Fuelling the Flames:
Brokers and Transport Agents in the Illicit Arms Trade

Introduction

Arms brokers occupied a prominent place in 20th century military commerce (Silverstein, 2000b, pp. 53-55). Although the legal trade in military goods has, for the most part, been the mainstay of arms brokers, post-Cold War developments have increased the demand for their expertise in the illicit global arms trade markets as well.

Today brokers and their associated networks of intermediaries and sub-contractors are increasingly involved in the transfer of new and surplus weaponry into contemporary conflict zones. Most of these transfers have dubious legitimacy, contravening national and/or international law and occurring in the grey and black markets of the global arms trade.

The cloak of secrecy surrounding most illicit weapons transfers results in a paucity of easily accessible public information on the scope, nature, and magnitude of both the grey and black arms markets (ILLICIT TRANSFERS).

In recent years, the important role that arms brokers and their intermediaries play in the illicit trade has been the subject of some in-depth studies (Wood and Peleman, 1999). All of them suggest that these 'go-betweens' are far more critical to the illicit arms trade than first meets the eye. As a result, the United Nations, various governments, researchers, and activists have begun to focus more intently on the issue of illicit arms brokering in an attempt to find ways to regulate and control the activities of these actors.[1] This chapter attempts to answer the following questions:

- What are the defining characteristics of arms brokers in today's world?
- What is the role of brokers in contemporary illicit arms transactions?
- What is the role of transport agents and their relationship with brokers?
- What national and international initiatives are underway to address the problems of illicit arms brokering?

Several important caveats must be kept in mind when studying the arms brokering profession and its overall implications for the illicit arms trade: *First,* it is important to recognize that arms brokering can be a perfectly legal profession. By focusing on illicit brokering, the objective is not to stigmatize legal brokers, but to understand the critical role they may play in the illicit trade in small arms. *Second,* the information that has emerged to date on illicit arms brokering is fragmentary and anecdotal at best, and cannot be used to arrive at general statements.

At this stage, it is impossible to know what percentage of illicit arms deals are brokered, how many brokers operate in today's world, or what the overall significance of brokering in illicit arms deals is. However, examining how brokers operate provides important insights into:
- the centrality of these actors in many illicit transactions;
- the various techniques and strategies brokers use to ply their trade and ensure that their transactions remain undetected; and
- the means by which their activities contribute to shaping and sustaining contemporary arms markets and exacerbating violent conflict.

Arms broker, Afghanistan (SIPA Press Agency/P. Evrard)

Drawing on open-source information and investigative research, particularly in Africa, this chapter attempts to explain the phenomenon of brokering by delineating certain patterns and common features. While illicit arms brokering is not limited to Africa, its conflicts and their massive humanitarian consequences have drawn more attention from analysts and researchers than other regions of the world. Focusing on Africa should not imply that illicit arms brokering is unique to that continent; rather, that it is currently the best source of information on the issue. Other regions of the world will be the subject of research in subsequent editions of the *Small Arms Survey*.

This chapter is divided into three main sections:

Section 1 defines illicit arms brokering and discusses the diverse activities that brokers undertake on behalf of parties to a weapons deal. By exploring brokers' strategies and techniques, it illustrates how existing arms control laws and regulations can be circumvented and exploited. Moreover, examining the world of bartering or commodity concessions and private military companies reveals how arms brokers operate at the interface of various networks that, together, sustain and shape many contemporary conflicts.

Section 2 focuses specifically on the way brokers arrange for weapons transports. It explains how, at least in the air cargo industry, brokers contract dedicated transport agents to arrange the physical transfer of weapons cargoes to destinations throughout the world. In so doing, they draw on large networks of specialized support personnel to minimize detection. Case studies, particularly in Africa, provide vital insights into the various actors and services involved in the structure, logistics, and functioning of transport networks, and the way several large networks fuel current conflicts in many parts of the world.

Section 3 reviews a number of national arms control systems (i.e. the body of laws and regulations that govern the import, export, and transit of military and paramilitary goods) and highlights how, in many countries, the issue of brokering is inadequately addressed in national legislation. It also provides a brief survey of current international initiatives in the United Nations and other intergovernmental organizations that are attempting to regulate and control illicit brokering. Future editions of the *Survey* will undertake a more in-depth review of national arms control systems to identify inadequacies with regard to brokering activities, including the lack of enforcement and monitoring capacity.

Arms brokering in the post-Cold War era

Simply by picking up a telephone, an arms broker in a western European city can negotiate an arms deal, procure large quantities of weapons from one country, arrange for their transportation to a country on another continent, and organize payments through front companies and secret bank accounts in offshore finance or 'tax havens'. Given the right contacts and a good knowledge of the market, a single individual can—without ever physically taking possession of the weapons—bring together suppliers and recipients who would otherwise have remained separated by the dictates of legality and geographical distance.

Although small arms and their associated ammunition represent only about five per cent of the total value of global arms exports (LEGAL TRANSFERS), more than 80 per cent of contemporary conflicts are fought with them. Thus, it has been observed that brokers operating in this area play a potentially more pernicious role than middlemen organizing conventional weapons sales. By arming combatants in both intra- and inter-state conflicts, their destabilizing role in geopolitical affairs assumes a far greater magnitude than their small numbers might suggest (Silverstein, 2000). Moreover, unlike conventional weapons, there is currently no international mechanism (e.g. *UN Register of Conventional Arms*) to monitor the production, stockpiling, and/or transfer of small

Although small arms and their ammunition represent only about five per cent of the total value of global arms exports, more than 80 per cent of contemporary conflicts are fought with them.

arms. Finally, the secrecy that is the trademark of this business plays right into the hands of brokers operating in the 'grey' and 'black' sectors of the illicit small arms market.

Several factors underlie the prominence of brokers in contemporary illicit arms transfers:

- **Changing demand patterns:** It appears that governments may be increasingly outsourcing the organization of covert arms transfers to private actors, as opposed to relying on security agencies and payrolled companies (Silverstein, 2000b). This is primarily to conceal the chain of accountability, to avoid potentially damaging public scrutiny, and/or to overcome their lack of expertise or capacity to obtain arms on the global market (Silverstein, 2000b, p. 59).

  Moreover, most contemporary conflicts tend to be internal, involving a multitude of state and non-state actors. According to SIPRI, of the 27 major conflicts in 25 countries in 1999, the vast majority were intra-state wars in Africa and Asia (SIPRI, 2000). These conflicts have generated increased demand for weapons, particularly small arms. This, in turn, has created a market for brokers whose clients dominate today's warfare 'market'—illegitimate or repressive government forces, rebels, militias, and ethnic, religious, or guerrilla groups— who usually cannot afford expensive conventional arms. Compounding this situation is the spillover of many intra-state conflicts into surrounding countries (e.g. the spillover of the Rwandan and Burundian conflicts into the Democratic Republic of Congo). A final significant factor behind changing demand is the increasingly transnational scope of organized crime (e.g. drug trafficking, terrorist activities), sometimes even abetted by persons in official positions. This situation has created ample opportunities for brokers, notably in states with little centralized authority.[2]

- **Changing supply-side factors:** Since the end of the Cold War, the ready availability of massive surplus arms stocks from the West and the former Soviet bloc, together with new production, has created a flourishing 'buyer's market' (PRODUCERS). Likewise, it has increased brokers' opportunities to clinch deals at advantageous prices for actors involved in conflicts (BICC, 1997, pp. 142-173; Wood and Peleman, 2000). At the same time, Western governments have started downsizing their military operations and infrastructures now that there is no longer the pressing need to counteract the Warsaw Pact's conventional arms capabilities.

Of the 27 major conflicts in 25 countries in 1999, the vast majority were intra-state wars in Africa and Asia.

Box 3.1   A time of plenty for illicit arms suppliers

Today brokers enjoy considerably greater access to supplies of new and surplus weapons than during the Cold War era. As countries downsize their defence sectors,[3] massive arms surpluses are 'dumped' onto the markets, usually at bargain basement prices. In many cases, these weapons end up in conflict zones. For example, it has been reported that Russian officials sold rebels in Tajikistan massive amounts of arms from Soviet stockpiles between 1992-97 (Pirseyedi, 2000, pp. 46-48).

In Eastern Europe, the collapse of the communist bloc and the deterioration of state control over various sectors of the economy have undermined the power to regulate the behaviour of the private arms industry and the movement of military goods. As a result, many of these companies are now free to supply the highest bidder (Laurance, 1998). The most conspicuous pattern that has emerged in the 1990s involves West European-based arms brokers obtaining supplies from cheap stocks, primarily in Eastern Europe, and delivering them, primarily by air, to warring state and non-state forces in poorer countries (Wood and Peleman, 1999).

Much of this offloading of small arms has been prompted by a combination of factory over-production, poorly managed stockpiles, inadequate export controls, and corruption. Finally, brokers and their intermediaries also obtain weapons directly out of conflict situations. In regions plagued with endemic warfare, brokers often transfer military leftovers from one conflict to another (BICC, 1997, p.150).

As a result, many former employees of security agencies and defence forces have sought work in the private sector, either as arms brokers, dealers, or 'security service' providers. They have brought their insider contacts, technical expertise, and know-how inherited from the covert Cold War arms markets with them to this new calling.

- **Arms and the opportunities of globalization:** The forces of globalization, catalyzed by advances in communications and information technology, are creating unprecedented opportunities and altogether new forms of economic activity. In this interlinked world, the privatization of many defence industries and the rapid growth of transnational business, finance, and transport networks have facilitated the ability of brokers to match weapon supplies with demand, allowing them to surmount geographic and legal barriers. As in other areas of cross-border commerce, international co-operation to regulate the transnational movement of military goods has yet to catch up with the realities of the globalized economy. Consequently, brokers exploit loopholes in national legislation and international law, taking advantage of areas in which regulatory capacity is either lacking or inadequate.

Contemporary arms brokering: Actors and services

The secrecy surrounding illicit arms transfers often makes it difficult to identify the actors involved and the services they provide. In any business relationship, potential parties to a deal must first establish contact, negotiate a contract, arrange financing and payment, and carry out the deal. In the arms business—as in most other businesses—specialized agents provide a crucial supporting role. This is where the brokers come in.

Identifying who is, in fact, the 'broker' in a given arms transaction and outlining the scope and nature of his activities is not a simple task. Arms transactions involve a fluid constellation of actors whose roles, activities, and identities overlap and shift in form over time, and whose degree of influence varies widely. Drawing overly rigid distinctions between 'dealers', 'brokers', or 'transport agents' could prove counter-productive.

The important distinction to make—and the basis on which to identify an actor as either a dealer or broker—is the extent to which one set of activities is emphasized over the other. A dealer is an actor who *primarily* purchases weapons for subsequent resale; a broker is an actor who *primarily* works to facilitate weapons transactions. In the world of illicit trafficking, it is arguably brokering, and not dealing, activities that play the most critical role in ensuring a timely and usually cheap flow of weapons to embargoed states, insurgent groups, and other actors.

Defining brokers: The definition of brokering used in this chapter is based on the *essence* of arms brokering—the facilitation and organization of transactions on a relatively autonomous basis, and for some form of compensation or material reward (e.g. financial commission on the deal).[4]

Arms broker: an individual who facilitates and organizes arms transactions on behalf of suppliers and recipients for some form of compensation or financial reward.

On this basis, several characteristics of brokering can be identified from actual practice:

- **Invisibility:** Considering the transient, intangible, and invisible nature of facilitating and arranging deals, brokers often do not even see, much less take concrete possession of, the weapons they procure. As a result, they cannot easily be held legally accountable under contractual arrangements based on the notion of ownership.
- **Autonomy:** Most brokers act independently as middlemen, which is what the term 'broker' implies. By bringing together buyers and sellers, they could, in principle, be said to bear equal responsibility for the arms transactions they facilitate. Because parties to an illicit weapons deal rarely take recourse to contract litigation, brokers often serve as arbitrators or neutral third-party witnesses to minimize violations of the deal.
- **Expertise:** Brokers are a source of sophisticated expertise for arms suppliers and buyers who might not otherwise know how to negotiate the dark corridors of illicit market deals. They

often possess considerable technical and marketing know-how, keep themselves current on the easiest and most reliable transport routes and financial modalities, and utilize a large network of contacts, collaborators, and experts 'in the business'. The 'bigtime brokers' are not infrequently key players in broader networks involving foreign military interventions and economic activities.

- **Management:** Superior management skills are practically a prerequisite in this 'profession'. Since brokers are usually the ones responsible for setting up and maintaining the structure of arms transactions, they play a vital role in maintaining the complex network of intermediaries and sub-contractors that comprise any given transaction. In addition, brokers' abilities to secure the expertise of financial and transport agents and to ensure the timely flow of goods, documents, and payments illustrates their managerial skills in providing knowledge and know-how at the same time they are running covert, continent-spanning, military-style operations.

'The broker's world' (see Figure 3.1) shows in schematic form the nature of arms brokering activities: the broker's relationship to other parties in a given transaction (i.e. the producer or initial supplier, and the recipient or end-user); and the links between brokers and other intermediaries (e.g. dealers, financial agents, government officials, and transport agents). In organizing and facilitating arms transactions, brokers provide the following series of services (see Fig. 3.1):

Figure 3.1   The broker's world

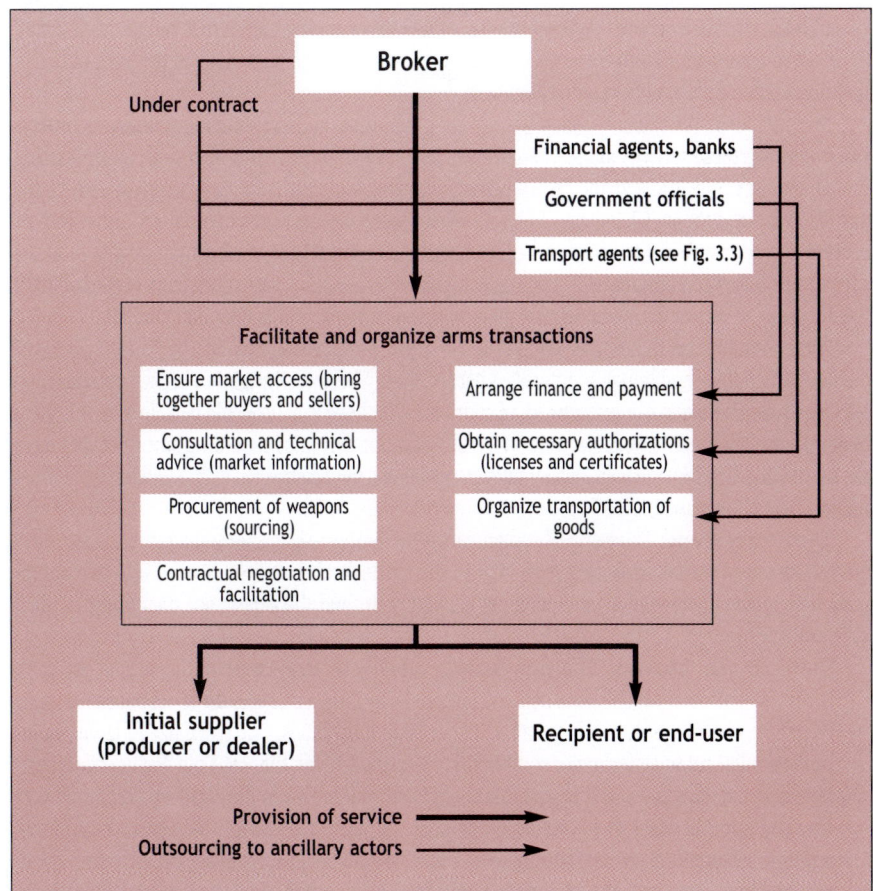

1. **Prospecting:** At the outset, brokers prospect for clients, investigating or responding to demand in different parts of the world and identifying willing suppliers. Their value-added lies in their ability to bring buyers and sellers together and ensure market access.
2. **Offering technical advice:** Having established relations between potential suppliers and end-users, brokers offer important consultative and technical advice on the 'nuts and bolts' of the deal. This includes advice on appropriate weapons systems, possible modalities for transport and financing, appropriate contacts, and strategies for the overall transaction.
3. **Sourcing:** Once the contours of a deal begin to emerge, brokers identify the desired type and quantity of weaponry, and obtain information on pricing, payment schemes, and so forth.
4. **Mediating negotiations:** Subsequently, brokers play a key mediating role in the contractual negotiations, in planning and facilitating communication between the parties, and in acting as a buffer to conceal evidence of their interaction.
5. **Financing:** Once a deal has been struck, brokers are instrumental in arranging financing and payment of arms transactions, and securing appropriate lines of credit.
6. **Obtaining authorizations:** In addition, brokers often arrange for official documentation authorizing the transaction, either through legal or illicit channels, and often with the assistance of conniving government officials.
7. **Organizing transports:** At the same time, they also organize the transport of the ordered goods—either by air, sea, or overland cargo—and take steps to ensure that it reaches its final destination.

In return for their services, brokers receive some form of compensation that ranges from a 'cut' or financial commission from the arms sale, or even payment 'in-kind', usually in the form of highly lucrative commodities, such as oil or diamonds.[5]

Because arms transactions vary greatly in magnitude and complexity, individual brokers rarely perform these services alone. Sometimes, they work in partnership on a deal, co-ordinating complementary roles and activities, while other brokers backstop activities undertaken directly by the parties to a transaction (Peleman, 2000a).[6] Where weapons are first acquired by arms dealers, brokers can be contracted to seek out willing buyers or, conversely, to contract dealers, as in Africa where arms have been purchased by mining companies on behalf of non-state actors at the behest of their brokers, in return for promises of a share of future mineral profits (Berman, 2000).

Sometimes brokers themselves act as dealers, acquiring stocks of arms on the basis of perceived demand which they then broker to interested parties. Geda Mezosy, a Hungarian broker, obtained and later purchased weapons using a network of couriers in the hope that he would be able to re-sell them to prospective clients. The weapons were supplied by Croatian militias exploiting surplus stocks from the Bosnia and Herzegovina war. Mezosy's illegal operations were discovered by the Belgian authorities in May 1996 (Peleman, 2000a).[7]

The broker scene: The world of contemporary brokering revolves around a rather small, select group—a sort of insider brokering elite. Within this circle, brokers can be divided into two groups according to their professional and personal backgrounds, and the experience they bring to illicit arms trafficking.

- **The Cold War brokers:** This first group is actually already somewhat a relic of the past, comprising brokers who became rich and famous by facilitating large-scale arms transfers for one or more governments during the Cold War.[8] For these individuals, who specialize in large, multi-million dollar contracts for major conventional weapons systems, the post-Cold War era offers business as usual, plus the added opportunities of globalization. Driven primarily by profit, and now liberated from the ideological dictates of the Cold War, these high-profile players maintain long-standing relationships to state procurement networks and sources. More importantly, they retain and assiduously cultivate the trust and confidence of government officials at the highest levels.

Investing their cumulative profits in lucrative businesses associated with their principal occupation (e.g. oil or mineral concessions, transport, and financing enterprises), this calibre of brokering tends to become an institution in its own right with vast numbers of employees and contacts. Notable members of this elite group include: Monzer Al-Kassar who built his career during the Cold War, thanks to his connections with intelligence services on both sides of the Iron Curtain;[9] Sarkis Soghanalian, a long-time CIA agent who counted France and China among his clients (Public Education Center, 1998, p. 2); and Adnan Kashoggi, a former Lockheed agent and key player in the Iran-Contra Affair (Wood and Peleman,1999, p.8).

- **The 'newcomers':** The second group of brokers includes former mid-level government officials and personel from agencies or national security armed forces. Entering the private sector more recently, and usually as smaller-scale operators, these individuals often use their prior experience, government contacts, or military careers as springboards to launch private brokering practices. Many of them operate in or near conflict zones, in offshore banking or 'tax havens', or in supply centres, such as Eastern Europe where they combine their expertise with access to already glutted weapons markets. While, in the past, only brokers with ample financial and political assets could deal in markets involving such high-powered deals as million dollar credits, current demands— from rebel armies, gangs, or even corrupt governments—have created a new 'climate' where these smaller brokers can slip into the market mainstream.[10]

In contrast to the popular stereotype of the lone gun runner, arms brokering is increasingly becoming a networking activity.

Overall, in contrast to the popular stereotype of the lone gun runner, arms brokering is increasingly becoming a networking activity, intertwined with the provision of private military services, drug trafficking, money laundering, organized crime, and the trade in commodities (e.g. oil, timber, and 'conflict diamonds').

Brokering strategies and techniques: The 'rules of the game'

Illicit arms transactions are scarcely a new phenomenon. The nature of contemporary conflicts, involving both internal actors and foreign intervenors (including individuals and corporations), has created a new dynamic that has expanded the weapons market far beyond the regulatory frameworks of existing national and international arms controls. In order to conceal arms transfers from unauthorized parties, circumvent geographical barriers, and ensure that complex logistical and human resource requirements are met, illegally operating brokers employ a wide variety of strategies and techniques.

Operating in the shadow of the 'grey weapons market': In order to maximize opportunities and earnings, some brokers prefer to operate in the opaque and fitfully controlled grey and black areas of the illicit arms market. Here the legal status of transactions is ambiguous at best and deliveries are carried out on a covert basis (ILLICIT TRANSFERS). In pursuing this path, brokers hope to avoid, not only the watchful eye and punitive force of national or international law, but also the visibility that accompanies such brazen flouting of the laws that is characteristic of black marketeers.

Grey market transactions are less brazen. They are commonly understood to encompass only those small arms transfers that are legally endorsed or not regulated or those that take place covertly, with either the tacit or explicit support of governments. Covert (secret) transactions may be either legal or illicit, depending on whether they have violated the sanctioning state's laws or it can be foreseen that the arms will be transferred to forces using them for serious violations of international law.[11] Either way, organizing arms transfers beyond the pale of the law—yet not in open violation of it— is a form of expertise that only the most astute brokers possess. They can bring this to the negotiating table in at least two ways.

Organizing arms transfers beyond the pale of the law—yet not in open violation of it—is a form of expertise that only the most astute arms brokers possess.

- First, many brokers depend on either the active or passive complicity of governments and officials to obtain the necessary authorizations for a given arms transaction, regardless of its legal status.

A recurrent motive for the alleged involvement of government officials in illicit small arms transfers is— pure and simply— profit.

The most obvious government involvement occurs when some countries try to conceal their weapons purchases to keep them out of public expenditure budgets that are monitored by donor countries or multilateral organizations. Moreover, while most arms-producing countries do not supply military specification weapons to rebel movements, others might. Acting through brokers can disguise the true nature of the relationship between the supplier and the recipient.[12] Another motive for the alleged involvement of government officials in illicit small arms transfers is— pure and simply—profit. Thus, some will allow weapons to traverse their territories, or even provide the necessary end-user certification, in exchange for a cut of the deal's value or some other payback. As a result, these brokers move arms through state-authorized channels placed at their disposition. This serves as a near perfect camouflage for illicit transactions.

Box 3.2   Breaking an international arms embargo: Argentina, Croatia, and the role of Diego Palleros

Between 1991 and 1995, Diego Palleros, a retired Argentine Army colonel, allegedly arranged, together with several high-ranking Argentinian government officials, a shipment of 6,500 tons of Argentinean small arms, light weapons, and ammunition to Croatia—breaking an international arms embargo in the process (BBC Summary of World Broadcasts, 23 March 1999).

The scandal tainted the image of the Menem Government just at a time when the administration was presenting Argentina as a reformed country that respected international law. As a result, a minister and several high-ranking officials resigned, and at least three key witnesses in the case died prematurely during the investigations. The broker himself went into hiding in South Africa (*Latin America Weekly Report,* 1 September 1998). The weapons shipment, included 20,000 9mm pistols ordered for Panama's 'police and security forces'—but it never reached Panamanian soil. Instead the weapons were shipped to Croatia. Palleros reportedly said that President Carlos Menem and other high-ranking members of his government had known all along about the arms sales (*Latin America Weekly Report,* 1 September 1998).

The way Palleros had organized the transaction illustrates the key role brokers play in bringing suppliers and recipients together. Having been informed by a relative in South Africa about a possible deal in Croatia, Palleros allegedly consulted with the management of Argentina's major weapons producer, the Dirección General de Fabricaciones Militares (DGFM), which gave the green light for the deal (Santoro, 1998, pp.133-134). In order to avoid any embarrassment to the Government, Palleros bought Debrol International Trade in Uruguay, a fake company with no offices or telephones. He then obtained an end-user certificate from Panama, for which he allegedly paid US$ 50-80,000 (Santoro, 1998, p.136).

This end-user certificate originally stated that the weapons were destined for the Panamanian National Guard, despite the fact that this agency no longer existed. Palleros wrote to the Argentine weapons producer, informing him that the end-user certificate would be sent from Panama to Buenos Aires by courier and that payments were to be made through the Deutsche Bank (Santoro, 1998, p.137). At the last minute, however, the Panamanian in charge of preparing the document decided to increase the price. Because Croatia was in a rush to receive the weapons, the Argentine Government reportedly issued a decree on 27 August 1991, approving the sales without documentation. A last minute end-user certificate was produced by Palleros with the official stamp and signature of an official at the Panamanian Embassy in Buenos Aires. The Panamanian official later claimed in court that his signature had been forged (Santoro 1998, pp.138-141).

The UN Security Council had approved an embargo on weapons sales to any of the former Yugoslav republics on 25 September 1991, five days after the first shipment of arms from Argentina arrived in Croatia. Despite the embargo, Argentinian shipments continued, even after 800 Argentine soldiers had joined the UN Protection Force (UNPROFOR) in parts of former Yugoslavia (Santoro, 1998, pp.147-162).

Box 3.3   Edwin Wilson: Arming Qadhafi, CIA style

During his time with the CIA, Edwin Wilson, who left the Agency in 1976, made large sums of money setting up front companies for a top secret Navy intelligence unit. With his insider contacts, Wilson was able to broker weapons and mercenaries for military dictators and shady regimes, including Augusto Pinochet's secret service, DINA, and the regime of Muammar Qadhafi in Libya.[13] Living in a seaside villa in the Libyan capital of Tripoli, Wilson became Qadhafi's private broker, enlisting former CIA agents and firms he had used as covers in his CIA heyday to run a multi-million dollar operation for the Libyan dictator.

Forged US State Department export certificates and international shipping documents were used to ship arms and explosives to Libya. When Qadhafi placed an order for hundreds of thousands of timer devices and detonators, Wilson and his associates had no trouble finding them through traditional CIA contractors in the US. Several companies, although selling the devices at highly inflated prices, reportedly thought Wilson's orders were part of an authorized CIA operation (Goulden, 1984, p. 460; *International Herald Tribune*, 18 June 1981).

A first investigation by the US Justice Department, begun in 1977, was dropped later that year when it was concluded that, despite the 'nefarious business activities' of these former CIA-agents, no US laws had been violated (*International Herald Tribune*, 25 June 1981). At that time, Wilson and a host of US companies had been shipping weaponry and explosives via Europe to Libya and had been recruiting various experts for operations and training in that country.

Four years later, when Wilson was finally arrested, the US Internal Revenue Service demanded US$ 21 million in back taxes and penalties from the estimated US$ 50 million he was thought to have made between 1977-81. In 1980 alone, tax court files showed that Wilson's dealings with Libya had generated a gross income of US$ 22.9 million dollars. More than half of this revenue reportedly came from a contract to supply rifles, small arms, and ammunition to the Libyan Armed Forces (*International Herald Tribune*, 30 July 1983).

Source: Peleman, 2000

Wilson became Qadhafi's private broker, enlisting former CIA agents to run a multi-million dollar operation for the Libyan dictator.

Depending on the degree of leverage they exert, brokers can also bring about states' 'passive' involvement in their activities, usually through a policy of non-interference, or acts of omission. Some brokers with powerful political clout, like Kashoggi, are virtually 'untouchable' insofar as their relationships and dealings involving government officials at the highest echelons go. Any persecution of these brokers, or denunciation of their activities as illicit, could result in the incrimination of states, or the exposure of embarrassing covert activities by the governments themselves.

Sarkis Soghanalian, a former CIA employee who represented the French and Chinese governments (Public Education Center, 1998, p. 2), was allegedly involved in the arming of the Christian militias in Lebanon in the 1970s and 1980s and the Argentine military *junta* during the Falklands war (Peleman, 2000a). Arrested in 1991, he was convicted in the United States of conspiring to circumvent federal requirements to set up a US$ 100 million arms deal, supplying South African arms to Iraq in 1983, using Austria as a transit country. After serving two years in prison, he assisted US authorities in cracking a counterfeit ring in Lebanon. He was released and became a registered arms dealer in France, with offices in Paris and the Middle East. According to a defence correspondent based in Africa, Soghanalian has been linked in recent years to procurement and military assistance services on that continent, including to the warring parties in Congo-Brazzaville (*International Defence Review*, 1 August 1998).

- The second technique brokers use to operate beyond the pale of the law involves exploiting loopholes and inadequacies in national and international arms control regulations. At present, many national arms control systems do not adequately address the activities of brokers and affiliated transport and financial agents. Because they cannot be prosecuted for the 'intangible' services

Box 3.4   Arms trafficking, offshore banking, and 'tax havens'

Strong client confidentiality for money transactions, lax regulatory systems, poor licensing procedures, inadequate enforcement capacity for customs controls, and the lack of income tax are some of the main characteristics of the so-called financial offshore 'tax havens'. Not surprisingly, they are often used by unscrupulous arms brokers, transport agents, and cargo charter companies as a convenient money laundering and tax evasion site. By constantly registering and closing down front companies, arms traffickers can evade accountability for their actions.

A freelance pilot who lived in the UK's Channel Islands reflected on his involvement in the delivery of arms to the exiled Rwandan forces and militia in April 1994: '... *as far as I understand it, the banking laws in this country make it an ideal place for the trade to actually take place without anything physically happening ... The brokerage of these flights, the provision of aircraft for them, and the financial facilitation for them, tends to take place in the UK, but the flights themselves do not originate within the UK or, for that matter, operate through the UK.*' [14]

A 1998 UK Government Home Office report found that an estimated 90,000 companies were incorporated in UK offshore 'tax havens', most of them by non-residents (Edwards, 1998). In these places, business can be conducted in relative secrecy without filing public accounts, annual reports, or publicly registering the names of their beneficiaries.

Several air cargo companies operating in conflict regions and contracted by brokers for illicit arms transactions have aircraft registered in 'tax havens'. These include:

- **Air Transport Office (ATO)**, implicated in transporting weapons to UNITA from Kinshasa, which has aircraft registered in the Bahamas;
- **Ibis Air International**, a group allegedly registered in the Bahamas with offices in Guernsey and Malta, and which has planes registered in Equatorial Guinea, that has flown cargo on behalf of Sandline and Executive Outcomes (Wood, 2000);
- **Jet-Lease International**, the transport agent used by Mil-Tec Corporation, Ltd. to deliver arms to the perpetrators of the Rwandan genocide in April, May, and July 1994. This company is reportedly registered in the Bahamas, but is run out of London (Wood, 2000). [15]

The UK Home Office report estimates that Channel Island companies hold around five per cent of the global offshore tax haven funds totalling some US$ 6 trillion—equivalent to almost half the GNP of the United Kingdom.

In one 1997 deal, the money for an oil-for-arms deal to Congo-Brazzaville, brokered by a German dealer based in South Africa, was laundered through a Barclays Bank account and a front company in Jersey. The dealer also used a trading company and a Barclays account in

they provide, brokers can set up illicit arms deals—as long as the physical weapons do not cross or enter the territory of the state in which they themselves reside (so-called 'third-country' brokering).[17] Edwin Wilson, a former CIA agent, used his contacts and know-how to broker weapons for Libyan President Muammar Qadhafi in the 1970s (Peleman, 2000a). Because Wilson had organized his activities outside US territory, however, an investigation launched into this deal by the US Justice Department was ultimately dropped after 1977 on the grounds that no US law had been violated (see Box 3.3).

Brokers often exploit discrepancies between national arms control systems, taking advantage of inconsistent documentation requirements, and ineffective verification mechanisms. For example, states commonly require end-user certificates—a document stating the destination of the weapons shipments, which, additionally, serves as the buyer's pledge that weapons will not be re-exported to third parties. As fool-proof as this sounds, brokers do not appear to have much difficulty obtaining or forging them. Sometimes genuine certificates are obtained and used to procure arms that are subsequently diverted to other destinations with the issuing government's approval.

London.[16] The arms were used in a civil war in which many thousands of civilians were indiscriminately killed and over 300,000 internally displaced. The bank was later accused of operating a lax screening system for large funds (Wood and Peleman, 1999; Barnett, 1999).

Suspiciously, since neither has a standing defence force, the Channel Islands of Jersey and Guernsey were also listed by the UK Government in 1998 as the destination points in 74 standard individual export licences for small arms, and also for seven of the UK's open export licences for a variety of equipment relating to small arms, military vehicles, naval vessels, and combat aircraft. Moreover, the UK Customs and Excise export data for 1998 show no arms movements for those Islands (*UK Annual Report on Strategic Export Controls*, 1997 and 1998; *Report of UK Defence, Foreign Affairs and International Development and Trade Select Committees*, 2000).

Source: Wood, 2000

Figure. 3.2 Thirty-five of the world's best known financial and 'tax havens'

Andorra	The Republic of the Maldives
Anguilla – Overseas Territory of the UK	The Republic of the Marshall Islands
Antigua and Barbuda	The Principality of Monaco
Aruba – Kingdom of the Netherlands	Montserrat – Overseas Territory of the UK
Commonwealth of the Bahamas	The Republic of Nauru
Bahrain	Netherlands Antilles – Kingdom of the Netherlands
Barbados	Niue – New Zealand
Belize	Panama
British Virgin Islands - Overseas Territory of the UK	Samoa
Cook Islands – New Zealand	The Republic of the Seychelles
The Commonwealth of Dominica	St. Lucia
Gibraltar – Overseas Territory of the UK	The Federation of St. Christopher and Nevis
Grenada	St. Vincent and the Grenadines
Guernsey/Sark/Alderney - Dependency of the British Crown	Tonga
Isle of Man – Dependency of the British Crown	Turks and Caicos – Overseas Territory of the UK
Jersey – Dependency of the British Crown	US Virgin Islands – External Territory of the US
Liberia	The Republic of Vanuatu
The Principality of Liechtenstein	

The relatively recent emergence of transnational business networks has also helped brokers organize transactions that span countries and continents, exploiting the laws where they are weakest. As a result, brokers can base their operations in European capitals, where they benefit from communications and business infrastructures or are close to suppliers and other service providers, while routing financial transactions through offshore 'tax havens', and using cargo companies based in or near conflict zones to effect the transport.

Brokering networks: Without brokers, the illicit weapons market would be far less accessible to buyers who, for example, may find themselves caught in the chaos of far-flung conflicts or blacklisted by the international community. Without brokers, private individuals and companies seeking access to diamond and oil 'war economies' would lose their most basic bargaining chip—the steady flow of weapons. Most importantly, without brokers, the illicit arms market would lose its form and structure, being deprived of one of its most important components: the very networks that sustain and channel the interactions of all involved.

Without brokers, illicit arms transfers would also be far more difficult and risky. Their ability to use large networks of contacts and intermediaries to facilitate a given weapons deal goes far beyond

> **Box 3.5   Jacques Monsieur: Iranian weapons for African wars—and more**
>
> Jacques Monsieur, a former Belgian army officer, had been a privileged middleman for Iranian weapons procurement for decades. In 1987 a Brussels prosecutor started investigating Monsieur's wheeling-and-dealing after the Belgian Minister of Justice was interrogated by a parliamentary commission of inquiry into embargo-trade via Belgium. Monsieur was at that time a middleman between Iranian officials and the Belgian sales agencies of international arms merchants and producers. Despite the Belgian investigation, he continued his deals via a Belgian-registered company until 1993.[18] None of the numerous criminal investigations instigated by the Brussels prosecutor ever led to any court cases, let alone convictions of Monsieur (*De Morgen*, 23 August 1999).
>
> Following the end of the Cold War, Monsieur reportedly began using his contacts in Iran to transform his former client state into a hub for his far-flung weapons deals with other countries like Serbia, Croatia, and the Republic of Congo (Brazzaville). As documents later seized at his premises revealed, he was using Iran this time as a supplier country for deliveries.
>
> In Africa, during the war in the Republic of Congo, Monsieur was reportedly a 'commercial consultant' to then President Pascal Lissouba. According to one source, Lissouba's rival Sassou N'Guesso (the current President) was also among his clients (*La Lettre du Continent*, 3 June 1999). Monsieur also reportedly supplied the West African country of Togo with ammunition in 1996 (*L'Express*, 24 June 1999). Despite a Belgian investigation and a brief period of detention in France, Monsieur kept operating freely, although in late 2000 he was arrested and detained, for unknown reasons, in Iran.[19]
>
> *Source: Peleman, 2000*

the mere provision of 'consultative' services. It is what gives their 'intangible' activities such significance. This is clearly illustrated in the activities of two brokers—Edwin Wilson and Jacques Monsieur (See Boxes 3.3 and 3.5).

Transactional complexities

Arms suppliers and recipients generally try to keep their transactions secret. Brokers involved in shady deals resort to various techniques to increase the number of sub-transactions and intermediaries involved. The goal is to make it virtually impossible to trace the chain of accountability to the principal parties. There are three main techniques:

Brokers involved in shady deals are experts in creating non-existent front companies, disguising money trails, and making ships and aircraft 'vanish into thin air'.

1. The first involves the proliferation of entities in a given transaction, many of which have no real or legal existence. It entails setting up numerous fronts, or holding companies, in jurisdictions with weak oversight over corporate activities and registration (see Box 3.4 and Fig. 3.2). Such companies, whose names appear on contracts, airwaybills, and other documents, conceal the actual entities involved.
2. The second technique involves disguising the 'money trail', usually through classic money laundering schemes using global financial networks (Lumpe, 2000, pp. 154-183).
3. Finally, brokers usually employ transport agents and cargo handlers who have substantial expertise in making aircraft and ships 'vanish into thin air' when delivering arms cargoes.

For example, the brokering of weapons from Israel to Colombia in the late 1980s by Yair Klein clearly illustrates how he (almost) managed to conceal this transaction by utilizing the above techniques. Arms destined for the paramilitary forces of Jose Gonzalo Rodriguez Gacha, leader of the Medellin drug cartel, were reportedly purchased from Israel Military Industries (IMI) (*The Jerusalem Post*, 15 March 1991). To conceal the identities of the ultimate end-users, Klein's private security company, Spearhead, claimed it was purchasing the weapons on behalf of the Panamanian government (*The Jerusalem Post*, 26 April 1991).

To disguise the nature of the payment, a complex money laundering scheme was developed. Between November 1988 and February 1989, two payments—in the amounts of US$ 98,132 and US$ 286,250 respectively—were reportedly made from Spearhead's Panamanian account in Banco Aleman-Panemeno to Philadelphia International Bank. These payments were then said to have been transferred to Manufacturer Hanover Trust Co., and on to the Bank Hapoalim account of IMI's commissioned sales representative in Miami Beach (*The Jerusalem Post*, 15 March 1991). From there, they were reportedly transferred to IMI in Israel. While no definitive proof has emerged that these payments were originally first made by the Medellin cartel into Spearhead's account, a further transfer of US$ 44,000 was reportedly made in early February 1989 to Luiz Meneses Baez, a retired Colombian army officer who mediated between the cartel and Klein, proving the existence of a Colombian connection (*The Jerusalem Post*, 15 March 1991). If the raid by Colombian police on the Medellin cartel headquarters on 15 December 1989 had not retrieved weapons whose serial numbers were traced to IMI, evidence of the weapons sale would never have been uncovered.

To cite another example, the Syrian Monzer Al-Kassar, a broker of Cold War fame who built a career on relations with intelligence services on both sides of the Iron Curtain, was a master of subterfuge. His claims to fame include his well-documented role as a supplier of arms to terrorist groups and a distributor of narcotics grown in Lebanon's Bekaa-valley; his role in the Iran-Contra Affair, which involved the transfer of large quantities of small arms from Polish state factories and the Portuguese company DEFEX, using a host of fake companies in Austria and Holland (*Final Report of the Independent Counsel for Iran-Contra Matters*, 1993); and his suspected role in having financed and supplied the explosives used to blow up the Israeli Embassy in Buenos Aires in 1992 (*Latin America Weekly Report*, 21 July 1998).[20]

In 1995, a Swiss prosecutor accused Al-Kassar of arms trafficking to the Balkans (Bosnia). The arms, hidden in sacks of sugar, had been shipped in 1992, in violation of the UN arms embargo against the former Yugoslavia. Al-Kassar allegedly set up the deal but the operation was run by a Polish state enterprise and a private Austrian company under the cover of the Embassy of South Yemen in Paris (Peleman, 2000). The Swiss prosecutor asked the Geneva court to seize US$ 6 million from Al-Kassar, saying that the funds had been obtained from drug trafficking and money laundering (*Agence France Presse*, 3 August 1995). Although Al-Kassar partially admitted the facts in court, he claimed that the weapons had been earmarked for South Yemen, a country that no longer legally existed at the time of the arms transaction.

The broader context: Globalizing the war economy

Today more than ever, brokers play a key role in the broader networks and activities that sustain and shape contemporary conflicts and, by implication, fuel the illicit arms trade. For example, in order to obtain weapons, rebels or other non-state actors set up business relationships with commodity traders to exploit and trade the resources in the areas they occupy. The trafficking and smuggling of raw materials, such as minerals, timber, palm oil, coffee, and other commodities, from war zones to international markets, call for a broker.

This is the context in which brokers organize the necessary contacts abroad to market these commodities or to set up supply lines of weaponry, ammunition, uniforms, medical supplies, and food for the warring parties. By interacting with diamond buyers, oil companies, drug cartels, and weapon suppliers, these actors—who have a dual role, both as commodity brokers and as weapons brokers—effectively link international markets to the warring parties in what has been described as the 'globalization of the war economy' (Kaldor,1999).

Brokers play dual roles, facilitating both commodities (e.g. diamonds, drugs) and weapons deals. In doing so, they link international markets to the warring parties, thus fuelling the 'globalization of the war economy'

> **Box 3.6   Brokers and the broader picture**
>
> The activities of Yair Klein, a former reserve Lieutenant-Colonel in the Israeli army, illustrate the adaptability of arms brokering skills in the broader picture.
>
> Between 1987-89, Klein allegedly provided paramilitary training to the death squads of the Medellin cartel in Colombia (*Agence France Presse*, 15 January 1999). In 1991, he was found guilty by an Israeli court of exporting 400 Galil rifles and 100 Uzi sub-machine guns without license to the same group in Colombia, routing the goods through Antigua (*Jerusalem Post*, 15 March 1991). Despite having been convicted in Israel, Klein went on to train RUF fighters based in Liberia in 1996, in return for which he allegedly secured the right to operate a rubber plantation and a diamond company (*Agence France Presse*, 5 February 1999). In March 1999, following his arrest by authorities in Sierra Leone, Klein admitted to acquiring Ukrainian and Libyan arms for the RUF (*Reuters*, 19 February 1999). In April 2000, Klein was acquitted under ambiguous circumstances and allowed to return to Israel (*The Jerusalem Post*, 24 April 2000).

The link between raw materials, the arms trade, and warfare is being increasingly acknowledged.

The link between raw materials, the arms trade, and warfare is being increasingly acknowledged within the United Nations. Following its investigations into the diamond and weapons trade in Angola and Sierra Leone,[21] the UN Security Council recently established a panel of experts to investigate the financing of the war in the Democratic Republic of Congo (DRC) (Security Council Resolution 1304, June 2000). The occupation by several armed non-state groups in East Congo of resource-rich, but protection-poor, bits of territory has lead to factionalism and internal fighting over the spoils of war. Angola, Namibia and Zimbabwe—the allies of the late President of the DRC, Laurent Kabila—all have troops deployed in the DRC and are exploiting this territory under their control to finance their efforts to resist the rebels that are supported by Burundi, Rwanda, and Uganda.

Case Study: Central Africa: Chinese arms companies, such as Norinco, have functioned as some of the largest small arms suppliers for brokered deals to Africa (PRODUCERS). Gradually, they have sought alliances with local partners, reaping their rewards from African mineral riches.

For example, in 1996 it was reported that President Mugabe's Government in Zimbabwe gave the then armed opposition leader, the late Laurent Kabila, US$ 5 million to finance his rebellion against Zaire's President Mobutu. Just before Kinshasa fell to Kabila, Zimbabwe Defence Industries (ZDI), a state-owned company, concluded a US$ 53 million three-way deal with China to supply Kabila with everything from food and uniforms to mortar bombs. ZDI was then used to spearhead Zimbabwe's economic penetration of the DRC. ZDI had been extremely secretive but in 1993, the last year when such information was provided, its directors included the head of Zimbabwe's army, General Vitalis Zvinavashe, and Perence Shiri, the former head of the notorious Zimbabwe 5th Brigade (*Focus Newsletter*, November 2000; ZBC Radio, 2000; *Le Monde*, 17 November 1998; *Sunday Telegraph*, 8 November 1998).

Gradually the efforts of Shiri, Zvinavashe, and other top officials in Zimbabwe have led to a lucrative network of intertwined commercial and military interests in the DRC. This follows a Chinese model centred on the supply of arms and the extraction of minerals. Zvinavashe and his brother are also directors of Operation Sovereign Legitimacy (OSLEG) that is viewed as the economic wing of the Zimbabwean armed forces. OSLEG wanted, above all, to acquire mining concessions that Kabila had promised. The first such venture was with Comiex-Congo, producing a new joint company, Cosleg. Then followed a joint venture with the Omani-owned Oryx Natural Resources to form Oryx-Zimcon. In January 2000, Oryx Natural Resources bought Petra diamonds and re-named it Oryx Diamonds (*Focus Newsletter,* November 2000).

Oryx has been partly owned by Zidco Holdings, a company run by the ruling Zimbabwean political party, Zanu-PF, which is, in turn, 55 per cent owned by another Zanu-PF company, M&S Syndicate. Zidco's directors are two Malawian Asian brothers, who have residence in the UK, and who have long

supported the Zanu-PF ruling party. The other two partners are politicians and businessmen—Emmerson Mnangagwa and Sidney Sekeramayi, both of whom are extremely close to President Mugabe—who have controlled Zimbabwe's Central Intelligence Organisation (CIO) ever since majority rule in the 1980s.

Mnangagwa also played a key role in the expansion of Zanu-PF's financial interests into the DRC. In May 1999, he admitted that he had introduced representatives of a Chinese arms company, two transport companies, a banking group, and a power company to Laurent Kabila and that they had all established businesses there. One of Zidco's subsidiaries, the First Bank Corporation, then set up in Kinshasa (*Sunday Telegraph*, 8 November 1998).

Other associates of Mnangagwa went into business ferrying arms and supplies between Zimbabwe and the DRC. The first was Billy Rautenbach's Wheels of Africa road haulage company, based in South Africa and several surrounding countries. The second was General Vitalis Zvinavashe, with his company, Zvinavashe Transport. Mnangagwa then helped to broker an arms deal for Kabila of 21,000 AK-47s and US$ 53 million worth of heavy arms, all from China. Mnangagwa also worked closely with John Bredenkamp, who has boasted of being the biggest single supplier of arms to the Congo (*Africa Confidential*, 5 November 1999).

In late 1998, Mugabe instructed Mnangagwa to oversee Zimbabwe's military operations in the DRC, giving him unparalleled military clout, which was allegedly used to help Billy Rautenbach gain a long list of mining concessions in the Congo. The DRC's Minister of Mines cancelled all deals with him in March 1999. In November 1999, the South African Office for Serious Economic Offences (OSEO) and Revenue Service raided Rautenbach's home and business premises, including Wheels of Africa, because of allegations of tax fraud, cross-border arms smuggling, and other illegal activities. Then, in September 2000, after Rautenbach had fled to Zimbabwe, the South African Justice Department seized US$ 5.7 million of assets from his companies, including an aircraft and a helicopter (*Mail and Guardian*, September 2000).

Private military companies: In addition to commodity trading, the provision of private military services, in which arms brokering plays a key role, also serves to sustain current conflicts. Since 1990, transnational companies designated as private military companies (PMCs) have claimed to offer—in the form of decisive military intervention—solutions to conflicts that the international community has been unable (or unwilling) to implement. By intervening in these conflicts, these companies became deeply involved in the small arms trade.

The best known PMCs include Defence Systems Limited (UK), Military Professional Resources Incorporated (MPRI) (US), Sandline International (UK), and the now defunct Executive Outcomes (South Africa). Other companies include Saladin Security, The Corps of Commissionaires (which has operated since the end of the 19th century), BDM/Vinnell Corp (US), AirScan (US), Levdan (Israel), and Gurkha Security Guards Limited (UK).

PMCs offer a wide spectrum of services that require a variety of skill sets and personnel. Though not comprehensive, their services could range from commercial security through military consulting and implementation; force training; the procurement or brokering of weapons systems; specialized or technical support; military operations support; and finally combat operations.

All of these roles mirror government military, foreign trade, and intelligence activities traditionally carried out by Western special forces and intelligence services for the covert or clandestine implementation of national foreign policy abroad. Increasingly, governments such as the US, the UK, Israel, or France 'outsource' activities in this sphere to an alliance of intelligence agencies and private sector companies, including PMCs.

The best known private military companies include Defence Systems Limited, MPRI, Sandline International, and the now defunct Executive Outcomes.

Box 3.7 Private military companies (PMCs) and arms brokering in Africa

The ways in which PMCs have become involved in arms brokering are legion. They have allegedly included the provision of arms brokering services in return for shares in natural resource exploitation through an elaborate network of companies. Moreover, PMCs have often provided advice to governments, as well as corporate clients, regarding what types of weapons to purchase, how to go about it, and where to obtain them.

PMCs can also organize the transport of weaponry, obtaining end-user certificates and bills-of-lading where necessary. They are often ideally placed—with links to governments, arms brokers, air cargo companies, and arms manufacturers—to provide the 'best service' in arms brokering and procurement. Several examples illustrate the role of PMCs in arms brokering:

Executive Outcomes (EO): Between 1992-96, the now defunct South African-based EO was contracted to support the Angolan Armed Forces (FAA) against UNITA, including procuring weapons systems for the FAA, with contracts worth US$ 40 million in 1993 and US$ 95 million in 1994, in addition to an undisclosed monthly fee (estimated at US$ 1.8 million/month) for the remaining months between 1995 and their withdrawal from Angola in January 1996. Altogether, more than 1,400 EO employees were involved in the Angolan contracts.

Later, during its 1995-97 involvement in Sierra Leone, EO provided training, armed forces, and procured weapons for the government's armed forces. These weapons, most of which originated in the former East Bloc, included small arms and crew-served weapons. While EO never purchased or owned the equipment and weapons it utilized—all of which had been purchased by the Sierra Leone Ministry of Finance—it did provide the government with advice and recommendations on purchases to meet its contract requirements.

Sandline International: Project 'Castle', Sandline's involvement in providing arms to Ahmad Tejan Kabbah's deposed Government of Sierra Leone, as well as to the ECOMOG regional peacekeeping force in 1997-98, led to the April 1998 'Arms-to-Africa' scandal in the UK.

Sandline (UK) had been retained by Kabbah to arm the more than 40,000 *Kamajor* militia, as well as elements of ECOMOG, to overthrow the military junta. In the autumn of 1997, the operation was cancelled after news of it leaked in the Canadian press. Later, a second smaller operation was planned by Sandline, together with British and Sierra Leonean government officials, to support the ECOMOG's February operations to derail the coup. It required Sandline to provide intelligence, logistical, and air support during the operation, as well as 35 tons of military equipment, purchased in Bulgaria, to the ECOMOG and *Kamajor* forces.

Supplying these arms may have been in violation of both the UNSC embargo (UNSC Resolution 1132, 8 October 1997) on Sierra Leone and the UK Government's Order-in-Council (1 November 1997), implementing this embargo.

Source: O'Brien, 2000

PMCs are often ideally placed—with links to governments, arms brokers, air cargo companies, and arms manufacturers—to provide the 'best service' in arms brokering and procurement.

Transport agents in the arms brokering industry

In addition to facilitating arms deals, brokers often organize the transport of weaponry from the supplier to the ultimate recipient.

In addition to facilitating arms deals, brokers are often responsible for organizing the transport of weaponry from the supplier to the ultimate recipient. Because such arrangements require a specialist's knowledge, as well as planning and financial acumen, brokers often contract a dedicated 'transport agent' for this purpose.

This section focuses on agents that organize the transportation of small arms by air.[22] In recent years, considerable evidence on the involvement of air cargo companies in transporting arms has been collected by investigative journalists, researchers, and international organizations, particularly in the conflict zones of Africa. This is partly due to increased UN scrutiny and several scandals involving individuals or governments. At the same time, the proliferation, and thus heightened visibility, of air cargo companies has come about as a consequence of the globalization of the aviation industry as a whole.[23]

While most of the evidence collected thus far is anecdotal and fragmentary in nature, enough 'pieces of the puzzle' exist to: illustrate various techniques and strategies of clandestine transport, as well as the basic structure and functioning of transport networks; and assemble profiles of several major transport networks supporting ongoing conflicts in sub-Saharan Africa.

Air transport networks

A transport agent is defined as an individual or organization that facilitates or organizes the transport of arms from the provider (manufacturer or dealer) to the buyer (or end-user) in exchange for some form of compensation. These individuals are dependent upon a network of industry professionals who can, in turn, be categorized into a number of actors and core services as the diagram below illustrates (see Figure 3.3).

- Actors serving as transport agents must obtain the use of freighter aircraft, usually through leasing or charter arrangements with the owner. Transport agents are usually cargo companies or air freight agencies.
- Transport agents must hire an air crew, either concurrent with the leasing of the aircraft (i.e. 'wet-leasing') or through other companies and arrangements (e.g. 'mercenary pilots' who offer their services independently).
- Transport agents must purchase, or otherwise obtain, the necessary overflight authorizations for the countries through which the goods will be transported.
- Detailed flight and routing plans must be charted and overseen to ensure adherence.
- Temporary storage for the goods must be rented, as well as facilities for the parking and maintenance of aircraft.
- Transport agents must organize the appropriate runway and fuelling facilities.

In any arms transaction, a variety of actors can act as transport agents. For this reason, the term 'transport agent' is loosely defined as the actor(s) with *primary* responsibility for organizing and managing a network of individuals and companies involved in the transport of a given stock of arms from the point of dispatch to its final destination.

Figure 3.3 Air transport: The arms brokers' preference

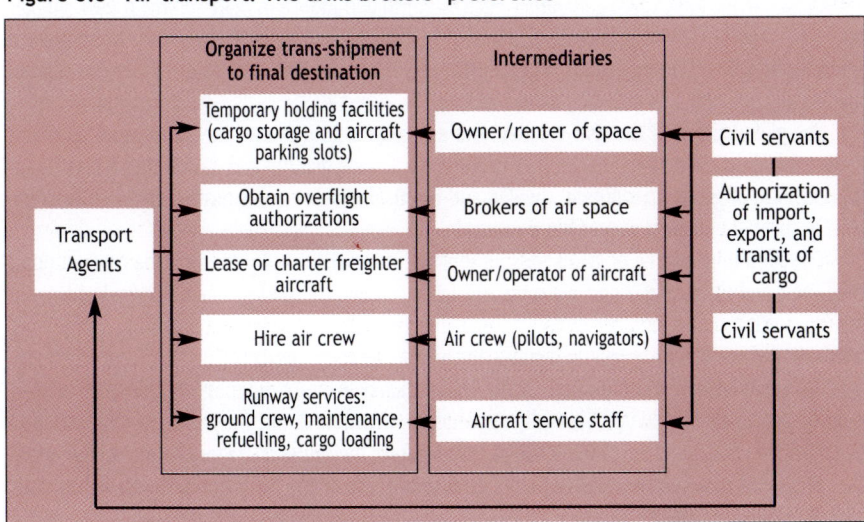

Each of the above activities involves a number of subsidiary or intermediate actors, not all of whom are aware of the nature of the cargo, its point of origin, or its final destination. These include the aircraft operators or owners; air crews and the agencies or organizations through which they are sub-contracted; government officials who may be complicit in the arms deal and provide the necessary overflight, landing, and other transport authorizations; owners of temporary cargo space and aircraft parking slots; and organizations that provide airport and ground services, such as refuelling, maintenance, and cargo loading.

Clandestine arms transport flights rarely fly directly to their destinations, but prefer circuitous routes involving multiple landings, refuellings, and/or changes of aircraft.

Because clandestine arms transport flights rarely fly directly to their destinations, but prefer circuitous routes involving multiple landings, refuellings, and/or changes of aircraft, a typical delivery will involve several interacting groups of intermediaries and fellow collaborators spread over several countries. In some cases (see Box 3.9), these groups cohere as loose alliances and partnerships with an interest in maintaining a working relationship. In others, especially where a transport network is used for multiple arms transfers, these clusters of collaborating individuals can coalesce to form parts of a larger corporate structure within which numerous companies are integrated (Peleman, 2000; Cilliers and Dietrich, 2000).

Techniques and strategies of air transport agents

Many contemporary conflict zones are not easily accessible by land and sea, a situation that has placed a premium on the air transport of goods and supplies, including weapons. Transport agents, and their associated networks of intermediaries, employ a range of techniques and strategies in order to avoid official scrutiny and legal regulations, all of which make the industry difficult to monitor and regulate. While these techniques have been honed and refined over the past decades—and thus are not a new phenomenon—the size and structure of the air cargo industry has changed significantly in recent years, including an increase in the number of companies (Whitaker, 1998).

Not only have the number of private companies increased, but the industry's market liberalization has also enabled aviation companies to organize across borders and continents. The resulting strong competition among cargo companies to offer an integrated package of services and destinations has made the industry increasingly dynamic and responsive to users' needs (Whitaker, 1998).

Transport agents use shrewd tactics to avoid official scrutiny and legal regulations, all of which make the industry difficult to monitor and regulate.

At the same time, various networks of transport companies have developed a presence and expertise in particular geographic or commodity markets (*South China Morning Post,* 8 November 1999, p. 2). While large cargo companies often establish dominance in high-volume routes, smaller operators may be drawn to peripheral areas with dubious customers. Propelled by technological innovation, regional specialization, and industry-wide economic pressures, some of these companies are literally 'pushed' into the illicit arms markets.

The globalization of the civil aviation and air cargo industries over the past several years has eroded the ability of national authorities to enforce adequate security and monitoring measures on the transport of goods. In addition, the demand for black market goods has increased at the same time as the cost of their transport has decreased.

The spiralling volume of goods passing through international airports, and the integration of road, rail, and marine transport networks in highly competitive markets, create heavy burdens on security institutions. A number of countries do not have the necessary accountability, technology, training, and resources to properly regulate the private air cargo market. Thus, arms suppliers can, and do, easily exploit this situation. While international bodies regulating air transport exist—notably the International Air Transport Association (IATA) and the International Civil Aviation Organisation (ICAO)—these have no real power to enforce their rules on national aviation authorities that retain ultimate authority over their national airports or the airlines registered within their territory (Peleman, 2000).

In this context, several techniques utilized by transport agents can be discerned:

- **Flight routing:** A few of the techniques transport agents use to conceal flight plans, routes, and destinations include unscheduled or 'emergency' landings in order to load or offload cargo, and the diversion of the aircraft from authorized flight paths. Other techniques involve 'relay' flights, whereby cargo is offloaded at a dispatch point and then shipped on to its final destination by other aircraft. The more trans-shipment points there are, and the more aircraft are involved, the better the points of departure and final destination of arms shipments can be obscured, making it harder for national authorities to identify and track suspect consignments, not to mention the actors involved.[24]

    The International Air Transport Association (IATA) and the International Civil Aviation Organisation (ICAO) have no real power to enforce their rules.

    Moreover, the routing of arms shipments is made even more complex by the practice of sub-leasing international overflight permissions in which one aircraft flies under the call sign of another, the filing of fictitious flight plans, and lax enforcement or scrutiny of flight details by airport and customs officials.

    While many of these strategies are technically legal, some (e.g. unauthorized diversions, landings, and cargo on- or offloading) clearly transgress national and international laws and regulations. Yet they are facilitated by the lack of international flight information sharing and the weakness of regulatory mechanisms, such as air traffic control systems.[25]

    As for the aircraft crews, they are seldom informed of the true nature of their payloads or their exact flight plans, which are conveyed to them mid-route, usually in the form of deviations from their original destinations. For example, following their release from prison in India, five Russian crew members involved in an arms transport to a religious sect in India organized by Peter Bleach (Wood and Peleman, 1999) described how they were forced at gunpoint to divert from their original flight plan and to fly at an altitude of 1,500 feet in order to evade radar detection (minimum safe flight altitude in the areas they were traversing was 4,700 feet). Because the cargo ramp onboard the Antonov 26 could be operated by one person, the crew was not involved in the actual weapons drop, only the arms dealer, Kim Davey. According to one crew member, 'When there is no accompanying personnel, the crew are responsible for keeping the boxes intact. But when there is an accompanying agent, he himself is responsible for placing the cargo correctly and for the documents being in order.' Moreover, the crew was not required to check the contents of the cargo, except for its weight (*Official Kremlin International News Broadcast*, 27 July 2000).

    Aircraft crews flying clandestine arms shipments are seldom informed of the true nature of their payloads or their exact flight plans.

- **Cargo and transport documentation:** Transport agents involved in illicit transfers of weaponry exploit weak cargo verification and inspection mechanisms by falsifying transport documentation. This involves transgressing laws and regulations that require cargo manifests and airwaybills to accurately describe the contents of a given payload, and identify the consignor and consignee. Often weapons are described as harmless equipment in order to conceal illicit payloads. In addition, transport documents often disguise the true entities involved in a given arms transaction by entering only the names of front or holding companies, the sales agents, or other interme-diaries—or simply the aircraft operators, who are often conveniently incorporated or registered in distant 'tax havens'.

    The falsification of transport documents is intended to deceive not only government officials but also, in certain cases, the owners or operators of the aircraft themselves. In a case documented by the UK-based NGO, Saferworld, and the British newspaper *The Guardian*, a Bulgarian Igla portable surface-to-air missile system sold to the Zimbabwean Government was brokered by a group of Dutch individuals who contracted TransBalkan Cargo Service, based in Amsterdam, to arrange the transport. They, in turn, leased a Boeing 707, registered in Liberia as EL-ACP, from Luxembourg-based Air Cargo Plus (ACP), and based their operations in the Ostend offices of Air Charter Service (ACS), a UK firm that had previously leased the same aircraft. On 3 November

    Transport documents often disguise the true entities involved in a given arms transaction.

1999, the aircraft was used to transport the weapons system—described on the cargo manifest as 'technical equipment'—from Bulgaria and Slovakia to Harare. In Harare, it was allegedly transferred to an Illyushin 76TD freighter and then flown to Kinshasa in the DRC, whereupon it was transferred to Zimbabwean forces fighting in the country. According to the director of ACS at Ostend, they had not been aware at the time that the aircraft had been used to fly weapons. Whether or not both ACS and ACP were aware of the nature of the shipment, the case clearly illustrates the lengths to which arms brokers and transport agents will go in order to conceal the true nature of their cargoes (*The Guardian*, 15 April 2000, p. 15).

Many suspect air cargo companies are registered in 'flags of convenience' countries—like Liberia, Lesotho, Malawi, Namibia, and Swaziland—which are characterized by lax implementation, or the non-existence, of laws.

- **Aircraft registration:** Another common practice, particularly in Africa, is the falsification of aircraft registration, or the placing of an aircraft on multiple registers, in order to allow its operators to change its identities at will (UN Sierra Leone Report, December 2000). With regard to the former, there have been many instances of aircraft changing registration numbers in mid-flight, or simply falsifying them. Other aircraft have utilized operating licenses that have been either entirely fictitious, long-expired, or revoked (Wood and Peleman, 1999, p. 59). Together, these techniques allow transport agents to conceal both the history and identity of an aircraft, making it very difficult to trace its flight path or, in cases where they have been stopped by national authorities, to track down the original owners.

Box 3.8   Victor Bout's air cargo empire

Air Cess is a group of companies that has been operating in many countries throughout Africa. Its operations illustrate the ease with which certain companies evade registration laws.

Owned by Victor Bout, a former KGB officer named in the UN's Report of the Fowler Commission, Air Cess is linked to many subsidiaries, sales agents, associated companies, sub-contractors, and representatives in Russia, Bulgaria, Moldova, Ukraine, Belarus, Belgium, France, the United Kingdom, Central African Republic, Equatorial Guinea, Sudan, Rwanda, Uganda, Liberia, Swaziland, South Africa, and the DRC. The network of companies is supervised from a business address in the United Arab Emirates.[26]

Owned by a former KGB officer, Air Cess' operations illustrate the ease with which certain companies evade registration laws.

Different branches of the Group may supply different warring parties simultaneously. The group's planes, although under different company names, have been identified in the UNITA area, as well as in flying cargo for the Angolan and the DRC governments.[27] In South Africa, Air Cess operated through a joint venture company called AirPass in partnership with Norse Air. When the South African authorities began to get tough with Air Cess and similar companies, it just moved its planes to other less monitored airports of convenience across the continent.

In Swaziland, the Air Cess group used different company names and fraudulent documentation to register more than 40 aircraft. Although registered in Swaziland, many of the planes operated from South African or other airports in the region. When the Swazi authorities received repeated allegations that their aviation register was being used for gun running, they found that irregularities had occurred in their files but had no idea of the whereabouts of most of the planes listed on their official register. Airports in the region where the planes were thought to be based were contacted and requested to ground them.

Even months after the Swazi aviation authorities had withdrawn Air Cess' flight authorization, its planes were still flying with Swazi registration numbers, delivering cargo in Central Africa (*The Swazi Observer*, 11 January 1999 and 21 May 1999).[28] The group subsequently moved its planes to registers in Equatorial Guinea and the Central African Republic.

Source: Peleman, 2000

Many air cargo companies transporting weapons and other potentially illicit shipments are registered in countries that serve as 'flags of convenience' due to the lax implementation, or non-existence, of laws regulating aircraft licensing and registration, corporate activity, and reporting. In the late 1990s, such countries have included Liberia, Lesotho, Malawi, Namibia, and Swaziland (Wood and Peleman, 2000, pp. 141-143).

While the companies and aircraft are registered in such countries, their actual bases of operation might be located in one or more countries. According to one source, 'a cargo aircraft might typically be registered in one country, then leased and chartered by companies registered in another, while their crews can be hired in yet other countries. In addition, the plane might be serviced and based for practical purposes somewhere else, with the main operating offices of the airline or the handling agency based in yet another country or countries' (Wood and Peleman, 2000, pp. 140).

- **Flying techniques:** In order to avoid detection by airport and other radar systems, air cargo pilots use a variety of flying techniques. The typical profile of such pilots and their contract crew is that of war veterans specialized in the risky jobs of supplying remote bases and bush strips or flying search-and-rescue missions behind enemy lines. The high level of expertise required for these operations automatically creates a niche market for pilots, crews, mechanics, or load-masters with a military background and, preferably, expertise in the region (Peleman, 2000). Unlike commercial flying, where the relevant manuals for aircraft type operations are strictly adhered to, this small number who practice the black art of clandestine flying have to know exactly how far they can push the parameters of safety.

Pilots who practice the black art of clandestine flying push the parameters of safety.

In order to avoid fixed and mobile radar systems, pilots transporting arms payloads intentionally fly devious routes and vary their altitudes. In high-risk areas, flights often take place at night, and most electronic navigational and radio systems are de-activated, forcing the pilot to rely on global positioning systems (GPS), a satellite-based navigational system independent of any terrestrial aids and ground landmarks like major rivers.

As one former gun runner explained, 'To me it's proper flying. It's not as tough as flying up and down the airways and talking to people; you don't talk to anybody. There is nobody to talk to. It's quite nice in a way because, you know, it's like being back in a Tiger Moth or something … we do a lot of map reading as well you know … (the GPS) packs up sometimes so we follow the rivers and things like that'.[29]

Most illicit arms flights land in airports and on unilluminated bush strips that are beyond the reach of national authorities, usually in rebel-held areas. In order to avoid enemy surface-to-air missile systems (SAMs), pilots approach the runways at extremely steep angles, usually by spiralling down. Thus, large aircraft like a Boeing 707 or a DC-8 manage to land on small airstrips with only half the recommended landing distance—and on runways that are often very narrow and potholed or without a proper surface. Even on these airstrips, it is quite possible to land with up to fourteen metric tonnes over the 'book' maximum landing weight.[30]

To avoid enemy SAMs, pilots approach the runways at extremely steep angles, usually by spiralling down.

Transport networks: The African connection

In Africa, from conflicts in the Horn to the interlinking conflicts of Central Africa and Angola, to the volatile situation in West Africa (i.e. Gambia, Liberia, Sierra Leone, Guinea-Bissau, and Senegal), transport agents and air cargo companies play a central role in the supply networks of the warring parties. They typically fly in small arms, ammunition, and associated goods that must be delivered as close to the actual combat zone as possible—either that, or else to remote areas that are inaccessible and/or poorly monitored.

This section provides two case studies.

- The first—focusing on arms supplies to the *União Nacional Para a Independência Total de Angola* (UNITA)—illustrates the fluidity and flexibility of transport networks, and the extent to which they are controlled by political interests in the region.
- The second—focusing on arms supplies to the *Revolutionary United Front* (RUF) in Sierra Leone—highlights the transnational nature and broad geographic reach of certain transport networks, as well as their propensity to coalesce into semi-institutionalized forms.

Due to their vested interest in ensuring the constant flow of diamonds and other resources in return for large quantities of weaponry, transport agents have helped to perpetuate conflicts.

Together, both cases studies illustrate how the illicit transport of arms is often integrated within larger regional and international networks that sustain war economies and are based on political alliances between governments and warring parties.

As the supply networks of UNITA and the RUF illustrate, numerous air cargo companies are contracted to transport arms, either by the warring parties themselves, or by friendly governments, arms dealers, and brokers, as well as by major foreign investors in mining concessions. Due to their vested interest in ensuring the constant flow of diamonds and other resources in return for large quantities of weaponry, transport agents have helped, directly and indirectly, to perpetuate these conflicts.

Case study 1: Angola and UNITA arms supply networks

Despite the 1994 signing of the Lusaka Accords between the Angolan Government and the rebel movement, UNITA, hostilities resumed in 1998. In a clear contravention of the Accords, which stipulated the disarmament and demobilization of its troops, and in violation of subsequent UN embargoes, UNITA continued to re-arm throughout the period 1994-98.[31]

Map 3.1   Arms supply routes to UNITA (1993-99)

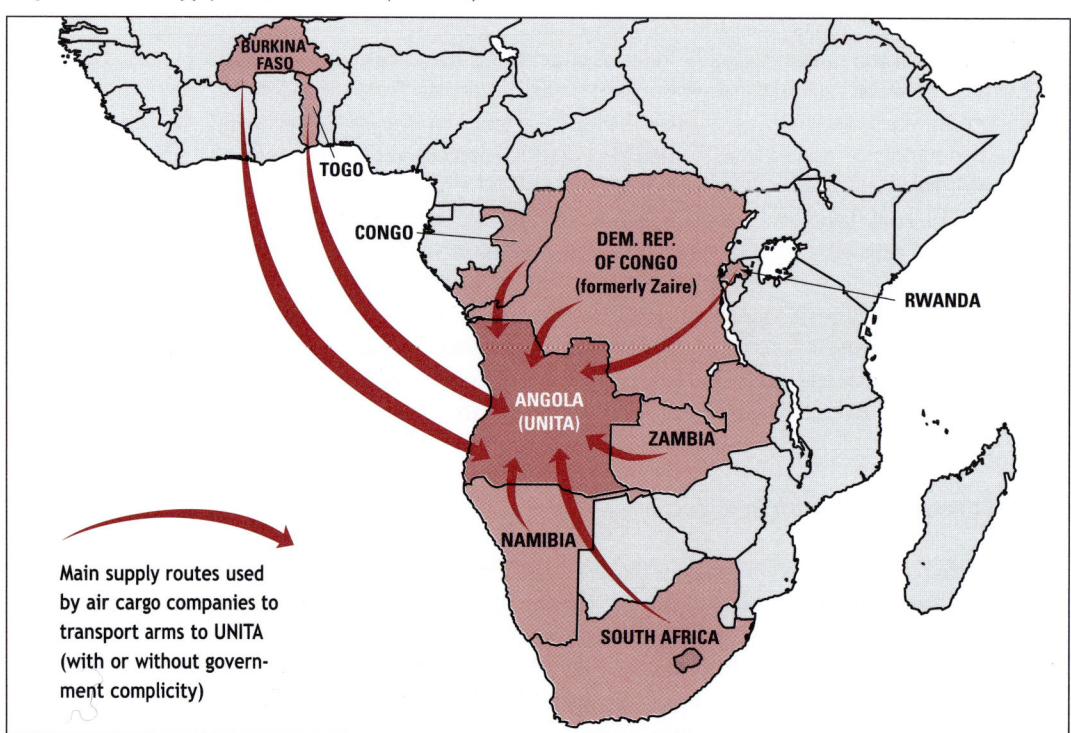

Main supply routes used by air cargo companies to transport arms to UNITA (with or without government complicity)

When UNITA's Cold War arms network ceased to exist, it was able to rebuild an extensive supply and procurement network for weapons and other needed materials. Its workings provide important insights regarding the role of transport agents.

Contrary to some beliefs, transport agents did not always act autonomously or in cohort with 'free-wheeling' brokers or dealers in an open market; instead, they were, in some cases, functioning as government agents within a larger network. Their foundations were the relationships between UNITA and a number of governments, such as Togo, Burkina Faso, and the former Zaire (now DRC).

Another major insight concerns the flexibility of the UNITA network in adapting to the shifting political alignments in the region. Despite the loss of political support from one government or another, and hence the shutting down of arms pipelines, UNITA was quickly able, in each case, to find alternative routes and air cargo companies for its weaponry. This reflects both the great availability of transport agents seeking such work, and their ability to move their bases of operation from one country to another in short order.

While a comprehensive list of transport agents working for UNITA is impossible to compile at this time, there is evidence of the existence of several dozen air cargo companies operating from neighbouring countries but based in Western and Eastern Europe, West Africa, and the former Soviet Union.[32]

UNITA, South Africa and the diamonds-for-arms pipeline: The activities of brokers and air transport agents, based in South Africa but working for UNITA, illustrate how the latter financed the procurement of arms, diesel fuel, and other war materiel through the sales of diamonds.

The report of the *United Nations Panel of Experts on Violations of Security Council Sanctions against UNITA*, the 'Fowler Report', cites two individuals—Ronnie Watson and Joe De Decker—as UNITA's primary brokers for arms and diamonds throughout the period 1993-94 (Fowler Report, 2000, paras. 16-17). Another individual, a South African businessman named Johannes Parfirio Parreira, was responsible for organizing arms flights to UNITA through his air cargo company, Northern Namibian Distributors, and air charter company Interstate Airways (Fowler Report, 2000, paras. 28-29). One of his pilots, Peter Britzke, admitted to flying over 300 covert flights to UNITA to supply arms and other military and mining equipment (Vines, 1999, pp. 117-118; *Africa News*, 18 April 2000).

According to Alex Vines, who cites officials from the South African police, arms flights from South African airports to UNITA-held territory ranged from a handful to a maximum of 50 a month throughout the 1990s (Vines, 1999, p. 116). Due to a lack of adequate air traffic control and customs regulations, many of South Africa's 36 international airports, including Mmabatho, Gateway in Pietersburg, and Lanseria, provided favourable flight conditions for UNITA-destined aircraft (Vines, 1999, p. 116). This situation changed only in mid-1998 with the installation of new air traffic monitoring systems, the introduction of tighter immigration controls, and a combined effort by aviation and law enforcement authorities to clamp down on smuggling activities.[33]

Zaire's involvement: Between 1994 and the demise of the Mobutu regime in May 1997, the former Zaire served as a major hub for arms trafficking to UNITA, with several of Mobutu's closest aides involved in arms purchases through their patronage of numerous brokers, dealers, and air transport agents. These activities were all part of lucrative triangular deals—involving speculation with black market currency, fuel, weaponry, and cash—that kept both UNITA and the ailing Mobutu regime running despite being isolated by the international community (*Washington Post*, 21 March 1997; *Associated Press*, 28 March 1997). Air transport agents operating from Zaire clearly illustrate both the complicity of the Government in arms procurement and their relationship to the other brokers and dealers involved.

The Government of Zaire not only allowed UNITA to stockpile weapons on its territory; it also purchased significant amounts of weapons on UNITA's behalf through the supply of end-user certificates.

Several dozen air cargo companies shipping arms to UNITA are based in Western and Eastern Europe, West Africa, and the former Soviet Union.

In the mid-1990s, Zaire served as a major hub for arms trafficking to UNITA. Lucrative triangular deals— involving speculation with black market currency, fuel, weaponry, and cash—sweetened the pot for arms brokers.

These were provided to a Lebanese arms broker named Imad Bakri (also known as Emad/Emat Bakir) in exchange for diamonds and cash supplied by UNITA leader Jonas Savimbi (The Fowler Report, 2000, paras. 18-20). During this period, massive amounts of weapons brokered by Bakri from Eastern European sources were transported to airstrips in UNITA territories via N'Djili airport in Kinshasa.[34]

The network in Zaire used for the procurement and transport of arms to UNITA consisted of several Lebanese, Portuguese, and other arms brokers and international diamond dealers, and a group of small airline companies. Each of them was directly under the patronage or ownership of several of Mobutu's closest aides, including his son, Mobutu Kongolo, the head of the Presidential Guard, General Kpama Baramoto, the head of the Special Council on Security Matters, Honoré N'Gbanda, the head of the Special Presidential Division, General Etienne N'Zimbi, the head of the secret police force, Tshimbombo Mukuna, and Bemba Saolana, a prominent businessman. In return for their protection, foreign brokers and air transport agents provided Mobutu's aides with a share of their profits (*Washington Post*, 21 March 1997).

Air Transport Office (ATO), one of the companies that had been operating under the protection of Mobutu's close security advisor, Honoré N'Gbanda, was identified as one of UNITA's most reliable suppliers. Human Rights Watch was able to identify several UNITA flights with ATO aircraft (Vines, 1999). On 20 February 1997, ATO (together with two other companies, Guila Air and Africair) was grounded by the Zairian Transport Minister for filing false flight plans and making illicit cross-border flights (*Washington Post*, 21 March 1997).

Until at least 1997, another air cargo company, Trans Air Cargo, was flying weapons almost exclusively between Zaire-based airports and the Cuango valley in Angola. Trans Air Cargo, run by a South African national, Dominique 'Kiki' Lemaire, one of the UNITA suppliers identified in the Fowler Report, also operated through a sales agent in Belgium (Wood, Peleman and Johnson-Thomas, 2000). According to Lemaire, cargo was flown to UNITA on behalf of David Zollman, an Antwerp-based diamond dealer with interests in Angola, DRC, and Namibia, and the owner of a mining company in Lubumbashi.[35] In 1998, Lemaire moved a number of his planes to the Lanseria and Rand airports in South Africa where they continued flying, albeit under a company renamed TAC Air Services (*Flight International*, 31 March 1999).[36]

Scibe Airlift, an airline owned by Bemba Saolano and (at least in 1985) Mobutu himself (*Forbes*, 18 November 1985), was also found to be transporting arms to UNITA when, in January 1996, an Antonov 32 crashed on take-off from Kinshasa en route to Angola, killing an estimated 370 people (*Agence France Presse*, 10 January 1996). The aircraft and crew, chartered by African Air from Scibe, had, in turn, been leased from Moscow Airways through Scibe's sales agent, Scibe CMMJ, in Ostend (*Washington Post*, 21 March 1997). In March 1997 one of Scibe's Boeing 707s was grounded in N'Djili, allegedly after refusing to allow a customs inspection of its cargo. Another airline, Air Excellence, owned by Mobutu's son Kongolo and Manuel Roque (part-owner of the Kwanza Sul diamond mine in Cuango Valley in Angola), was reportedly involved in transporting weapons and diamond workers (*Africa News*, 18 April 2000). Other airlines allegedly operating in UNITA territory from Zaire during this period included Service Air (under the patronage of General Kpama Baramoto), Guila Air, Africair, Trans-Service Airlift (owned by Belgian national Christian Vanoorschot), Express City Cargo, Skydeck, Fil Air, and Walt Air (Vines 1999, p. 112).

Arms transport after Mobutu: The role of Congo-Brazzaville and Rwanda: The case of UNITA also illustrates the ability of its transport and procurement networks to shift their areas of operation and thus adapt to changing political alliances and developments.

Following the signing of the 1994 Lusaka Protocol, the Government of the Republic of Congo (Congo-Brazzaville) also allowed UNITA to stockpile weapons, which were then progressively transported back into UNITA territory from Pointe-Noire (The Fowler Report, 2000, para. 23). Following the departure of Mobutu in May 1997, rebels captured most of the 30 aircraft serving the

Zairean-UNITA network but some, notably Trans-Service Airlift, Trans-Air Cargo, Fil Air, and Air Excellence, managed to shift their operations to Congo-Brazzaville in time (Vines, 1999, p. 114; *Le Nouvel Afrique-Asie*, July-August 1997). Air Excellence was reported to have resettled in Pointe-Noire and begun flights between Luzumba and Brazzaville. Finally, Air Cargo Express, a subsidiary of the Zairian-registered company Air Transport Office in which Savimbi is a part-owner, was also based in Congo-Brazzaville.[37] According to a UN report, 120 flights landed on UNITA airstrips in July 1997 alone (Wood and Peleman, 1999, p. 62).

Following the departure of President Pascal Lissouba from Congo-Brazzaville in October 1997, UNITA turned elsewhere for the procurement and transport of its arms supplies. In 1998, it allowed Rwandan troops trapped in the southwestern DRC to escape to freedom via Angola, initiating a period of co-operation during which the Rwandan government allowed UNITA to sell its diamonds in Kigali. In addition to allowing UNITA's former brokers and transport agents—notably Imad Bakri and Kiki Lemaire—to operate from Kigali, the Rwandan Government also allegedly encouraged UNITA to engage Victor Bout, whose air cargo empire—consisting of Air Cess, Air Pass, and TransAviation Network—serviced UNITA from South Africa and other locations in Africa (The Fowler Report, 2000, paras. 25-26; *Angolan Peace Monitor*, 3 April 2000; *Jane's Intelligence Review*, 1 May 2000). Given UNITA's support of anti-Kabila rebels in the DRC, it is alleged that Rwanda had been used by the former as a trans-shipment point. There have been reports of an attempted airdrop of weapons that originated in Kigali into UNITA territory in January 2000 (*Africa News*, 18 April 2000).

UNITA co-operation with other governments: Finally, the example of UNITA illustrates the extent to which its arms transport and procurement network was based on wide-ranging regional alliances, involving numerous governments.

For example, when the demise of Mobutu became imminent in early 1997, UNITA re-activated its working arrangement with Togo, and in particular with President Eyadema, whereby the latter imported weapons on UNITA's behalf (for a 20 per cent commission) and authorized the use of the country's airports as trans-shipment points (The Fowler Report, 2000, paras. 32-35). After May 1997, Togo became UNITA's main source of weaponry, providing end-user certificates to Eastern European (mainly Bulgarian) governments, once again through the intermediary of Imad Bakri. According to the Fowler Report, Bulgaria issued 19 permits authorizing the export of weapons from arms companies to Togo during 1997.[38] In one case, the weapons were transported by Victor Bout's company, Air Cess (The Fowler Report, 2000, para. 42; The Final Report of the Monitoring Mechanism on Angola Sanctions, 2000, paras. 36-38).

Burkina Faso has also been mentioned as a trans-shipment point for weapons from Eastern Europe to UNITA, through the airports at Ouagadougou and Bobo-Dioulasso. Furthermore, the UN Report on Angola mentions that weapons purchased legally by Burkina Faso were then transported to UNITA, raising the possibility that the former also issued end-user certificates for arms purchases.[39]

In recent years, the Government of Angola has repeatedly accused the Government of Zambia of assisting UNITA by providing airstrip facilities for the trans-shipment of arms and other war materials, including fuel.[40] While many of these claims have not been verified or substantiated, there is evidence that several companies made illicit flights into UNITA territory. Two aircraft belonging to Metex International, a firm registered in South Africa, were expelled from Zambia in June 1997 for having undertaken unauthorized flights to UNITA territory from Ndola airport (*Africa News*, 18 April 2000). Human Rights Watch subsequently confirmed that these flights transported arms (Vines, 1999, p. 124).

In July 1997 alone—in the short space of a month—120 flights landed on UNITA-controlled airstrips.

UNITA's arms network was dependent upon wide-ranging regional alliances involving numerous governments.

Case study 2: The case of Sierra Leone's Revolutionary United Front (RUF)

Despite the signing of the Lomé Peace Agreement between the Government of Sierra Leone and the Revolutionary United Front (RUF) in July 1999, fighting recommenced in May 2000 following

Map 3.2   Arms supply routes to the RUF in Sierra Leone

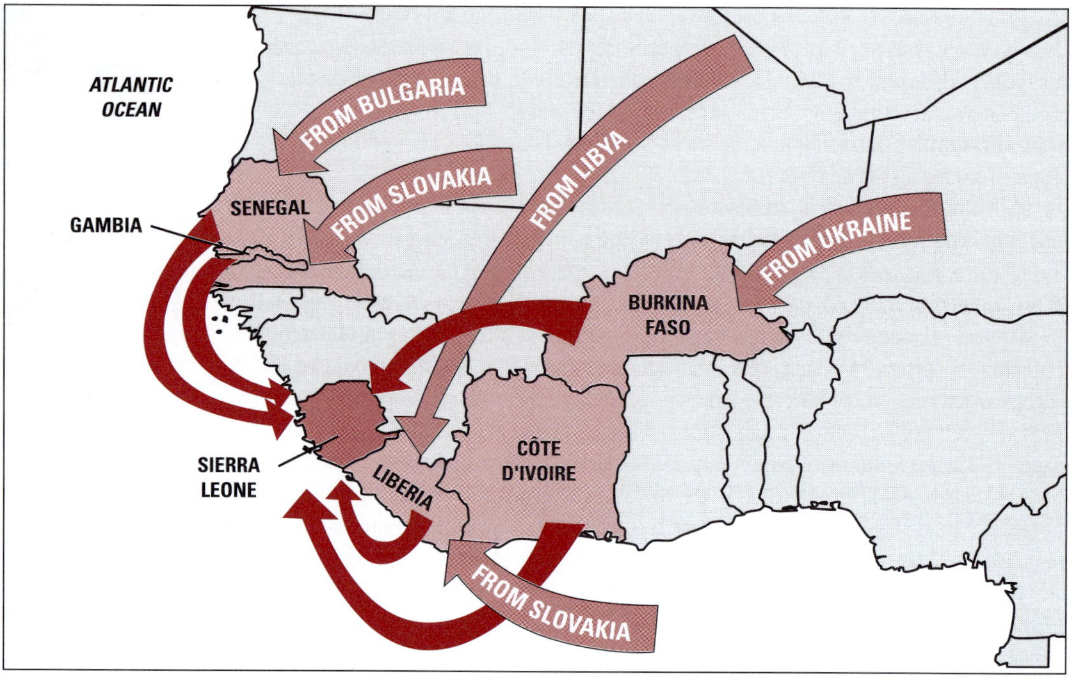

attempts by the UN peacekeeping mission (UNAMSIL) to disarm the RUF (Berman, 2000, p. 12). Despite the existence of a UN embargo on arms, petroleum, and related material to Sierra Leone, the RUF continued to receive weaponry through a clandestine supply network whose operations were financed by trafficking in diamonds.[41] The involvement of several prominent arms brokers, merchants, and air transport agents in this trade reveals how air transport networks are related to larger commercial syndicates and political alliances that span several countries in the region (UN Security Council, 2000c).

The core of the supply network in Sierra Leone—and the various diamond, arms brokering, and transport syndicates of which it is composed—are the ties of friendship and co-operation between the leader of the RUF, Foday Sankoh, the President of Liberia, Charles Taylor, the President of Burkina Faso, Blaise Compaore, and Libyan leader Muammar Qadhafi.[42]

Recent research has uncovered numerous cases of government complicity in the re-armament of the RUF through the sale of diamonds.[43] Aircraft from Burkina Faso have been sighted delivering weaponry to the RUF, and the US Ambassador to the UN, Richard Holbrooke, openly criticized the Burkinabe Government for providing arms and other assistance (*The Washington Post*, 16 October 1999; UN Security Council, 31 July 2000). Libya has also provided military assistance to the RUF, either in the form of training or arms supplies delivered to its strongholds in Kailahun and Pendembu (*Jane's Terrorism and Security Monitor*, 25 July 2000; Berman, 2000, p. 16). Finally, the President of Liberia, Charles Taylor, has provided critical support to the RUF in terms of arms and other materiel (despite a 1992 UN arms embargo on Liberia), while retaining up to 90 per cent of the latter's diamond profits.[44] Several key individuals worked alongside Taylor and the RUF, including Leonid Minin, who has been responsible for organizing the transport of weapons, and whose logging company was suspected to be a front for diamonds and arms (*The Washington Post*, 16 October 1999).[45]

Despite a UN embargo on arms, petroleum, and related material to Sierra Leone, the RUF continued to receive weapons through a clandestine supply network whose operations were financed by trafficking in diamonds.

Superimposed on the Sankoh-Taylor-Compaore-Qadhafi network are the activities of numerous arms brokers, diamond and other concessions, and air cargo companies. Because of the inaccessibility of most of its territory, arms destined for the RUF are usually transported via a complex relay system that entails trans-shipment from several countries and the en route transfer of cargo between one or more aircraft. The number of actors involved and the requirements of co-ordinating such operations necessitates a degree of knowledge, contacts, and logistical capacity that can only be handled by a few of the larger air cargo companies, operating in tandem with one another. While information on these transport networks is scanty, a few cases uncovered provide important insights into their structure and activities, as well as the complicity of several governments.

One example that clearly indicates how the RUF received military supplies with which to initiate the recent rounds of fighting is the case of Sky Air Cargo Services UK and Occidental Airlines. According to some reports, these airlines, the first registered in the UK, and the second in Belgium, jointly transported more than 400 tons of military weapons to the RUF between late 1998 and early 1999. The flights undertaken by both airlines originated in Bratislava (Slovakia). Although flight documents showed Uganda as the final destination, these aircraft were subsequently deviated to Liberia and Gambia. There, the cargo was switched to other aircraft that delivered it to its final destination, the Kenema airstrip in RUF-held territory in Sierra Leone (*The Sunday Times*, 10 January 1999).

While the identities of the aircraft flying the last leg of these relay flights have not been confirmed, reports indicate that, on at least some occasions, they belonged to Victor Bout, head of Air Cess. According to one crew member, 'I had to help transfer weapons from my aircraft to Bout's aircraft. One of his crew told me they were flying to (rebel) forces at an airstrip outside Kenema. Also we've flown weapons subsequently destined for Uganda and Rwanda directly to rebel Congo airstrips, especially Goma and Kisangani' (*The Sunday Times*, 10 January 1999).

The activities of these companies point to the transnational nature of the cargo companies transporting arms, their willingness to work together on the transport of particularly large weapons deliveries, and the regional scope of their activities. Indeed, Sky Air Cargo Services UK has been implicated, together with Air Cess and Air Atlantic Cargo (another UK company), in shipping an estimated US$ 10 million in arms to Nigeria (Wood and Peleman, 1999, p. 67). Air Atlantic Cargo has been spotted between 1997-99 delivering arms to the Sierra Leonean Government, UNITA, and both sides of the conflict in the DRC (*The Observer*, 31 January 1999). Moreover, Sky Air Cargo was the company hired by Sandline to deliver arms and materiel to the Sierra Leonean Government—with the alleged consent of the British Government—in 1998 (United Kingdom House of Commons, 27 July 1998).

Occidental Airlines, on the other hand, has been implicated in supplying military equipment to UNITA forces and transporting arms from Bulgaria to the rebel forces in the DRC in August 1998 (*The Observer*, 14 March 1999; *The Sunday Times*, 10 January 1999). By co-ordinating their activities and, in essence, operating as a single supply network, these four European companies—Air Cess, Air Atlantic Cargo, Sky Air Cargo, and Occidental Airlines—have maximized the scope of their activities throughout Africa. Sierra Leone is only the most recent market to have been targeted by them.

As this section illustrates, the sighting of a local aircraft operator delivering a consignment of weapons is only the last link in a complex chain of activities and actors. Based on the cases presented in the chapter, the following patterns and commonalities can be identified:

- **Airports:** Certain airports, including Entebbe in Uganda, N'Djili in the DRC, Monrovia in Liberia, Lanseria in South Africa (until 1998), Ostend in Belgium, and Sharjah in the United Arab Emirates, have served as central trans-shipment hubs or transit points for arms transportation, notably in countries where aviation regulations are vague or poorly enforced, or where the volume of cargo traffic is extremely high.

Liberia's President Charles Taylor has provided critical support to the RUF in terms of arms and other materiel while retaining up to 90 per cent of the RUF's diamond profits.

Sky Air Cargo (UK) and Occidental Airlines (Belgium) jointly transported more than 400 tons of military weapons to the RUF between late 1998 and early 1999.

Box 3.9   Big jets, big bucks: Supplying the RUF

Another revealing case highlighting the international and interconnected nature of the air transport networks serving the RUF in Sierra Leone involves the activities of the UK-based company, Air Foyle.

Implicated in the delivery of arms to the RUF in March 1999, Air Foyle has a prior history of arms deliveries, as well as connections to Victor Bout through Norse Air, a company in which he has a majority share, and which also served as Air Foyle's sales agent between June 1996 and May 1998 (*The Guardian*, 5 August 2000). Moreover, the case of Air Foyle illustrates the manipulation and deception so characteristic of the air transport of arms—both with regard to the entities involved, and the legal involvement of governments.

In terms of aircraft used, over the last decade, the Russian-manufactured Antonov 124 has played a pre-eminent role in the transportation of war materiel between producer and user, from Angola and Burundi to Yemen and Zimbabwe. Bigger than a Boeing 747, the Antonov 124 is by far the world's largest cargo aircraft and possesses the advantages of a rough airstrip capability.[46] The commercial success of the Antonov, however, has also been due to British companies, which provide both marketing skills and the expertise needed to obtain the requisite national and international permissions to operate these aircraft on a global basis.

In mid-2000, only 16 Antonov 124's were licensed to operate outside the Commonwealth of independant States (CIS) and thus available for international air charter. Of these, seven were owned and operated by the Anglo/Russian joint stock company, Heavylift Volga-Dnepr, based at London Stansted Airport, while six were owned by the Antonov Design Bureau (ADB) of Ukraine and operated on their behalf by Air Foyle from London Luton Airport.[47]

On 14 March 1999, an Antonov 124 registered as UR 82008, owned by ADB and operated by Air Foyle, delivered 68 metric tonnes of weapons and ammunition to Ouagadougou, the capital of Burkina Faso, for onward transmission to the RUF via Liberia (UN Security Council, 2000c). The documents show that a Gibraltar-based company, Chartered Engineering and Technical Ltd., bought weapons in Ukraine, in theory on behalf of the Government of Burkina Faso. The latter indeed issued an end-user certificate to the state-owned company, Ukrspetsexport. The Gibraltar company then contracted Air Foyle to fly the consignment—3,000 Kalashnikov assault

- **Carriers:** Due to the highly specialized and clandestine nature of air transportation of arms, there are relatively few transport agents and air cargo companies involved in large arms deliveries. Many are also involved in the transport of perfectly legal cargoes, including humanitarian aid, passengers, and commodities.[53]

- **Collaboration with would-be competitors:** Although ostensibly competitors, many transport agents provide assistance or work as partners through the lending of aircraft or crew, and the organization of segments of a transport route. This was clearly the case, for example, in the co-operation between Occidental Airlines and Sky Air, which linked up with Air Cess to deliver huge amounts of arms to the RUF.

- **Carrier ownership:** Many of the larger transport companies are owned by individuals and companies from Europe and the former Soviet Union. In many cases, however, aircraft purchased or leased by these companies are also operated through front companies by African nationals.

- **Clandestine networks:** Many of the better known transport agents and companies have long-standing relationships with governments, non-state actors, and transportation service providers, resulting in semi-institutionalized clandestine delivery networks and procedures. This was particularly the case in Zaire during its assistance to UNITA, where numerous air cargo companies were protected and assisted by aides close to Mobutu.

rifles, 50 machine guns, 25 RPG launchers, five Strela-3 surface-to-air missile systems, and five Metis ATGW systems, plus ammunition for them—to Burkina Faso.

Subsequent investigations in 2000 by the UN Panel investigating arms to the RUF revealed that the first onward shipment of these weapons via Liberia arrived at the Sierra Leonean airstrip of Kenema during the morning of 19 March 1999.[48] The registration of the delivering aircraft is recorded as EL-ALD.[49] This poses a conundrum, since the document produced relates to a BAC 1-11 aircraft flown out to Afghanistan in 1996 by a Briton—Christopher Barratt-Jolley—for the use of the Mazar-I-Sharif warlord General Abdul Rashid Dostum. However, it is also officially recorded on the main Liberian register as being an Ilyushin 18 aircraft operated by Viktor Sergeyivich Bout—a former KGB Major who owns Air Cess and has been named in the British Parliament for his gun-running activities in Africa (Sunday Times, 10 January 1999). Given the links between these companies and individuals, however, these revelations are not surprising.

Other sources paint a rather different picture of the sequencing of the transaction. According to the Report of the Expert Group on Sierra Leone (UN Security Council, 2000b and 2000c), the arms delivered by the Antonov 124 to Burkina Faso were trans-shipped to Liberia and then to the RUF via a series of flights by a BAC 1-11 aircraft with Cayman registration VP-CLM. This aircraft was allegedly owned by Leonid Minin who had previously placed the VIP-configured aircraft at the disposition of Charles Taylor.[50] Between 13 March (the date of the Antonov's arrival) and 27 March, the BAC 1-11 flew three flights between Ouagadougou and Liberia, and four flights from Bobo-Dioulasso and Liberia, where some of the weapons had been trucked following their arrival from Ukraine (UN Sierra Leone Report, 2000, paras. 208-210). While concrete evidence for the final transport of these weapons from Monrovia to the RUF has yet to surface, fragmentary and anecdotal accounts seem to indicate that most—if not all—were trucked into RUF territory throughout the course of 1999.[51]

Regardless of how the weapons were transported from Burkina Faso to Sierra Leone, the fact remains that Ukrainian-manufactured weapons were handed in under the terms of last year's Lomé Peace Accords. Moreover, the Small Arms Survey was able to verify that, in late May 2000, Ukrainian examples were present in the weapons storage compounds at Kenema, Lungli, and Port Loko.[52]

Source: Johnson-Thomas, 2000

Arms transport networks cohere on the fringes of armed conflicts, channeling material support from external governments and actors.

- **Key roles:** Finally, given the nature of the business, arms transport networks will always cohere on the fringes of armed conflicts, playing a crucial role in channeling material support from external governments and actors. They are, together with other provisioning systems, key support systems for contemporary conflicts (Peleman, 2000).

Measures: National controls and international initiatives

Brokers and transport agents involved in illicit transfers of small arms currently operate in favourable (i.e. legally lax) domestic and international environments. At the national level, many legal systems governing the trade in military goods either do not adequately regulate the activities of these actors, suffer from poor administrative and enforcement capacity, or are undermined by a lack of political will and transparency. At the international level, few initiatives to address the problem of small arms proliferation have explicitly addressed the activities of brokers and transport agents, though discussions in several fora (e.g. the UN) are making important progress in exploring possible solutions.

Brokers and transport agents involved in illicit transfers of small arms generally operate in legally lax environments.

For more details, see 'Overview of National Arms Controls' at *www.smallarmssurvey.org*

National arms control systems

A large number of illicit arms deals begin as legal transactions. Although national arms control systems have been relatively effective in regulating the trade in conventional weapons, they conceal important omissions and structural inadequacies that mask the activities of brokers and transport agents.

Arms brokers are usually able to provide their services with little or no official oversight or monitoring because national arms control laws do not directly address their activities. Most national arms control systems focus on the *physical* transfer of goods through the transaction chain, and even that, usually only within the home country's jurisdiction. They are not designed to capture the more intangible aspects of weapons deals.

Box 3.10   National arms control systems

Most states regulate their domestic arms trade through laws governing the import, export, and transit of military goods (including small arms and light weapons). Licensing or authorization schemes require arms manufacturers, dealers, and purchasers to seek government permission for transactions involving military goods specified in official 'control lists' across state borders. If approved, they must be acted upon within a specific timeframe and for a specific quantity and type of military goods:

- **Import licenses** permit the principal actor to physically bring such goods into the country granting the license;
- **Export licenses** permit the principal actor to export goods to a particular country from the country granting the license; while
- **Transit licenses** permit the principal actor to transport weapons across the territory of the country granting the license.[54]

In order to verify that the transaction is carried out properly, most governments require some form of evidence regarding the quantity and type of goods, the intended customer or end-user, proof of delivery, and ultimate use. In addition to invoices, bills of lading, and transport documents, such documentation also includes government-issued end-user certificates, which authorize the receipt of the goods on behalf of the purchaser or end-user, and which specify the intended use of the goods; and international import certificates that affirm the intent of the importer not to divert, re-export, or trans-ship the purchased goods.[55]

These are the most common elements of national control systems. Not all states require authorizations for every aspect of a given transaction (e.g. some governments do not require transit or import licenses) or require all the corroborating documentation mentioned above.

Due to the limited scope of some of these systems, western European arms brokers in particular are able to facilitate, negotiate, and organize what are ultimately illicit arms deals without transgressing any national laws (Wood and Peleman, 1999). Once a deal has been struck, they then arrange for the actual procurement and delivery by utilizing other loopholes in the legal architecture, or evading its jurisdictional reach by routing these operations through a third country. Of the 28 national control systems surveyed for this chapter, only seven have legislation that directly regulates arms brokers (Germany, Switzerland, the Netherlands, Luxembourg, Sweden, Israel, and the US). Another eight (Australia, Belgium, Canada, France, Hungary, Norway, Poland, and Ukraine) have legislation which indirectly addresses the activities of arms brokers. In many of these states, enforcement of these laws remains limited, especially where extra-territorial operations are concerned. This initial assessment is being clarified with further research.

The US appears to have the most comprehensive laws on arms brokers. The law on arms brokering introduced in March 1996 amended the existing *Arms Export Control Act*. According to this law, any US citizen, anywhere, and any foreign person residing in the US or subject to its jurisdiction, must obtain authorization to engage in brokering activity. In this law, arms brokering is defined as including 'the financing, transportation, freight forwarding, or taking of any other action that facilitates the manufacture, export, or import of a defence article or defence service, irrespective of its origin' (*International Traffic in Arms Regulations*, Part 129.2 [b]). Brokers are required to register with the Department of State, receive authorization for their brokering activities, and submit annual reports describing their activities.[56]

In France, by comparison, the law addresses arms brokers only indirectly through provisions governing the pre-negotiation, negotiation, import, export, and transit of weapons.[57] It does not, however, explicitly address dealers and brokers, although there are a number of clauses establishing a licensing regime for 'preliminary consent' to address their activities.

In addition to the problem of lax law enforcement of the main activities of arms brokers, many national control systems do not contain provisions on other brokering-related activities, such as the transportation and financing of weapons deals. While many national control systems contain provisions regulating the transit of military goods, a critical distinction must be made between the *transit* (or physical passage) of goods in or through the customs space of a country, and the *transportation* of goods involving the activities of 'transport' handlers and the specific routes and transport modalities involved.

Most transit licensing schemes limit the scope of authorization to the passage of goods from a point of production or stockpiling to the border designated as the export point, or vice-versa. Because transport agents, exact routes, and other modalities are not explicitly authorized or detailed under these schemes, brokers exercise considerable discretion in determining exactly how goods will leave or enter a given country. Coupled with weak inspection and oversight regulations at borders or over different transport sectors, this situation creates gaps exploited by some brokers to divert arms deliveries to unauthorized end-users.

The vast majority of existing national regulatory systems are inadequate in scope and/or poorly administered or enforced.[58] Given the transnational scope and nature of brokering and transport activities, one serious constraint of national control systems is their jurisdictional scope (the geographic extent to which a state's laws are applicable beyond its own borders). Few states possess controls that prohibit citizens or residents on national territory from arranging deals that are carried out in third or tertiary countries. Still fewer control the activities of their citizens regardless of their location.[59] As a result, most illicit arms transfers to contemporary conflict zones bypass the states with the most comprehensive control systems altogether. Out of the 28 national systems provisionally surveyed, 24 are limited to national jurisdictional scope, three possess 'extended' jurisdictional scope, while only one—the US—is truly extra-territorial in scope.

Another major inadequacy in many national arms control systems concerns the licensing and verification of arms transactions. Some import, export, and transit licenses are imprecise or vague, allowing for the manipulation or distortion of the contents of a given arms delivery. Others are open-ended in time or are liable to be used for multiple transfers, while still others lack sufficient information to enable authorities to track the details of a given arms deal (Wood and Peleman, 1999, pp. 117-131).

Moreover, there is a lack of consistency concerning the types of end-use, import, or delivery certification required by different states. This creates many loopholes that arms brokers and transport agents use to divert weapons to unauthorized end-users. Related to these problems are serious gaps in monitoring and verification. Because states do not share harmonized rules for recording and tracking cargo documentation, financial and corporate activity, and the registration of transport

The US appears to have the most comprehensive law on arms brokers.

Some small arms import, export, and transit licenses are imprecise or vague, allowing for manipulation or distortion.

There are serious gaps in monitoring and verification of small arms transfers.

activity—let alone procedures for sharing such information—brokers and transport agents are able to modify or falsify documentation and deliver their cargoes with considerable impunity.

A final inadequacy of many arms control systems concerns the lack of institutional memory. The absence of registers for arms dealers, brokers, and other entities involved in military transactions makes information-sharing between governments nearly impossible and internal control over known offenders difficult. Only five of the states surveyed (France, Poland, Latvia, Lithuania, and the US) possess registers for arms dealers or traders, and only one of them—the US—explicitly registers arms brokers and transport agents. In France, for instance, Articles 20-21 of Decree No. 95-589 of 6 May 1995 require arms traders to register their presence and transactions with appropriate authorities, while in the US, all brokers are required by law to register with the State Department before applying for authorizations covering their activities.

Shortcomings: Lack of co-ordination and harmonization

Lax customs inspection controls or corrupt customs and border officials prevent governments from effectively monitoring arms shipments .

National arms control systems need to be co-ordinated with a number of affiliated regulatory systems and institutions in order to implement, monitor, and enforce their provisions effectively. Thus, attention must also be given to current operational deficiencies. Lax customs inspection controls or corrupt customs and border officials, for instance, prevent governments from monitoring what leaves their countries. Inadequate air traffic monitoring and control systems prevent authorities from tracking the movements of transport aircraft within their airspace. By not requiring comprehensive details, some forms of cargo documentation make it extremely difficult to monitor and trace the movements of a weapons transfer. Similarly, lax supervision of transport and corporate registers, including the communication of information on registry violations to central authorities, prevents the identification of suspect brokers and transport agents.

Finally, the relatively few restrictions placed on financial transactions or corporate activity in certain countries, including offshore banking and so-called 'tax havens', further prevents the identification and monitoring of entities involved in arms transfers. In states in which the administrative structures are poor or lacking in the requisite personnel and skills, the consequences of poor regulatory co-ordination and harmonization are grave, providing almost unlimited freedom for brokers and transport agents to carry out their activities.

The political dimensions of transparency

The deficiencies of national arms control regulations also encompass a critical political problem. The provision of arms to conflict zones is big business—not only for private actors, but also for states. Some states have a vested interest in assisting brokers and transport agents in illicit arms deals for either financial or political gain. They will often provide legal channels for acquiring arms, together with the necessary authorizations.

These states are therefore culpable of having tapped into the grey market for profit, and hence deliberately crippling the effectiveness of their own national arms control legislation. Coupled with the traditional secretive attitude towards military matters, and the covert pursuit of interests in other parts of the world, the involvement of states in illicit arms transfers sustains the grey market for the activities of brokers and transport agents. This lack of transparency has the inevitable result that such transfers remain concealed from international scrutiny.

Recent international initiatives

Discussions on small arms at the international level, both within the UN and various other regional organizations, have recently begun to address the issue of arms brokers, transport agents, and other intermediaries for a number of reasons. For example:

- The increasing importance of small arms in ongoing conflicts means that brokering activities have also become more significant.
- The glut of surplus weapons created by the downsizing of armed forces at the end of the Cold War has opened up new opportunities for brokers.
- The ineffectiveness of UN arms sanctions illustrates the key role that brokers and transportation agents play in circumventing mandatory UN Security Council arms embargoes.

The glut of surplus weapons created by the downsizing of armed forces at the end of the Cold War has opened up new opportunities for brokers.

The recent focusing of attention on brokering activities—and especially transactions in the grey and black markets—is a reaction to changing transfer patterns. The brokering debate within the UN and the broader international community has to be seen as only one of several elements under consideration.

There are also calls for stricter, and better harmonized, transfer documentation, particularly end-use certificates; more transparency in the field of both legal and illicit transfers through information-sharing, the marking of small arms, light weapons, and munitions to facilitate tracking the flow of these weapons; and international co-operation in law enforcement.

Organization for Security and Cooperation in Europe (OSCE): The *OSCE Document on Small Arms and Light Weapons,* endorsed by the Ministerial Council in late November 2000, sets out a number of principles and measures for tighter control over small arms (MEASURES). In addition to advocating a number of common arms export criteria, greater co-operation among national arms control systems, and the need to increase information-sharing and technical assistance in the field of law enforcement, the *OSCE Document* also explicitly addresses the need to regulate the activities of brokers. In particular, Article 8 (D) recommends that governments require the registration of brokers within their territory; the licensing of their activities; or the disclosure of all authorizations, documentation, and the details of all brokers involved in particular transactions. The *OSCE Document* does not, however, offer a comprehensive definition of brokering activities, or mention transport agents or financiers.

The OSCE recommends that governments require the registration and licensing of arms brokers.

The European Union (EU): The EU's two major initiatives in the field of national arms control regulations are the *European Union Code of Conduct on Arms Exports,* adopted 8 June 1998 by the EU Council, and the EU *Joint Action,* agreed on 17 December 1998 (MEASURES). While the former agreement establishes an information-sharing and consultation mechanism for export control systems, it does not include provisions on brokers or transport agents. The *Joint Action,* which sets out a comprehensive programme of preventive and reactive measures to preclude or reduce the accumulations of small arms, in addition to a provision covering financial and technical assistance, is actually considered to be the potentially stronger initiative of the two (MEASURES).

The United Nations Firearms Protocol: In April 1998, the ECOSOC Crime Commission set up an *ad hoc* committee to negotiate a 'legally binding international instrument' to combat trafficking in firearms as a protocol to the forthcoming *UN Convention on Transnational Organized Crime* (MEASURES).[60] If agreed, the Protocol will become the first legally binding global mechanism to regulate international transfers of small arms and light weapons, albeit at the level of private activity and not state-to-state arms transfers. The *UN Firearms Protocol* establishes common standards for the import, export, and in-transit movement of weapons and procedures for international co-operation and information exchange. Moreover, a number of states have proposed key provisions that will affect the degree to which states control brokers, namely Article 18 bis.

On the basis of a US proposal, and as adopted by the *Ad Hoc* Committee for inclusion in the pre-session text of the Protocol for the 12th session, these provisions mirror almost exactly the provisions found in the OSCE text, with the notable difference that a definition of brokering might be included.[61]

The OAS does not address arms brokering in consistent fashion.

The Organisation of American States (OAS): The OAS has adopted a series of initiatives on tackling small arms proliferation. These, however, do not address arms brokering in a consistent

---

Box 3.11 The UN's role

The United Nations system began to consider the issue of brokering only relatively recently. The 1997 *Report of the Panel of Government Experts on Small Arms* (UN, 1997) addresses very broadly 'networks operating internationally' and recommends studying the feasibility of restricting the manufacture of, and trade in, such weapons to authorized persons only. The 1999 *Report of the Group of Government Experts on Small Arms* (UN, 1999), in contrast, specifically mentions the key role of arms brokers and concludes that inadequate national regulation systems constitute part of the leakage into the illicit realm. The report recommends undertaking a study of brokering activities relating to small arms and light weapons, which should also include transportation agents and financial transactions (UN, 1999).

The work of the UN Group of Experts: In May 2000, the UN Secretary-General appointed a panel of governmental experts from 20 countries—Argentina, Belgium, Brazil, Bulgaria, Canada, China, Egypt, France, India, Israel, Jamaica, Kenya, Mexico, Norway, Pakistan, Poland, Russia, South Africa, the UK and the US—to prepare a feasibility study for the 2001 *UN Conference on the Illicit Trade in Small Arms and Light Weapons in All Its Aspects* to evaluate the possible regulation of small arms brokering activities. This group defines the terms broker, dealer, transportation agent, financial activities, etc. 'Dealers', 'brokers', and/or 'agents acting' on behalf of manufacturers, suppliers, or recipients in arms means any person who acts as an agent for others in negotiating or arranging contracts, purchases, sales or transfers of arms, defence articles or defence services in return for a fee, commission, or other consideration.

After addressing the scope and nature of the problems of such brokering activities, the group lays out the options available for national governments, regional organizations, and the international community at large to control the manufacturing, stockpiling, decommissioning and surpluses, trade in (export, import, transit or re-transfer), and illicit circulation of, small arms and light weapons.

The options range from the authorization of manufacturers and brokers by simple registration, the requirement for government licenses, the introduction of specific legislation governing brokering, the marking of weapons, the registering of weapons, the harmonization of national regulations, politically binding codes of conduct, and international co-operation (including measures to strengthen the capacity of law enforcement agencies) to international information-sharing.

It is unlikely that the UN Group of Experts will come forward with any single recommendation on regulating brokering activities that could constitute an international norm or even provide standardized and harmonized regulatory mechanisms. Opinions on common international goals are too far apart. The options listed by the experts will, however, offer a menu from which governments can choose, so that, in the medium term, this area of widely uncontrolled brokering activities will become somewhat more regulated and more transparent, thus offering greater possibilities to preclude illicit deals. Just how constructively the various governments will co-operate on an international level remains to be seen. This will depend largely on the political and economic interests involved.

Source: Wulf, 2000

Opinions on common international goals related to small arms activities remain far apart.

fashion (MEASURES). The *Model Regulations for the Control of the International Movement of Firearms, their Parts and Components and Ammunition*, approved 4 November 1997, contain comprehensive guidelines for import, export, and transit licensing procedures, but make no reference to brokering. The *Inter-American Convention against the Illicit Manufacturing of and Trafficking in Firearms, Ammunition, Explosives, and Other Related Materials*, which was adopted on 14 November 1997 and entered into force in July 1998, also does not mention arms brokering. More recently, OAS Resolution 1642 (adopted on 7 June 1999) 'encourages … states to adopt such measures concerning arms brokering and transit as may be necessary'… while Resolution 1744 (adopted 5 June 2000) recommends undertaking a study on brokering and transit (article 5(a)).

Conclusions

This chapter has attempted to highlight some of the main features of contemporary brokering and transport activities in the illicit market for small arms. The findings presented should be taken as illustrative rather than comprehensive. Identifying overarching trends, patterns, and commonalities is not sufficient to illuminate the complex workings of the illicit arms market, nor is the African setting from which many of these cases have been extracted representative of other regions of the world.

With regard to the multiplicity of actors, services, strategies, and techniques discussed in this chapter, it is important to distinguish between the activities of dealers—who primarily purchase weapons stocks for resale—and brokers, who primarily facilitate and negotiate weapons deals, and who organize the necessary transport and financial services. Transport agents, in the form of freight forwarders, charter companies, or companies operating cargo vessels, are also usually distinct actors who play a pivotal role in the clandestine transport of goods, but some transport agents are also brokers.

Research has revealed how many illicit arms transfers start off as legal—or apparently legal—transactions that are subsequently diverted to unauthorized end-users or are used for abuses that constitute serious international crimes. That this downward spiral may have been foreseen, even intended, is in many ways a legacy of the Cold War where many covert transfers involved the complicity with, or reckless disregard of, one or more governments. Arms brokers and transport agents often cannot operate without some degree of government support. If they currently fuel the flames of the grey and black arms markets, it is partially because their activities are insufficiently regulated.

Contemporary brokers and transport agents also benefit from the advantages of globalization. The privatization of many defence industries, advances in communications technology, and the rapid growth of transnational business, finance and transport networks—all these developments have facilitated the ability of brokers to move weapons, exploit loopholes in national legislation and international law, and take advantage of areas in which regulatory capacity is either lacking or inadequate.

In this context, two main types of brokers can be distinguished: the 'Cold War brokers' and the new generation of brokers, who operate in or near conflict zones and combine specific know-how with access to markets glutted with surplus weaponry.

Investigations indicate that the world of arms brokers and transport agents is quite small; the same names keep reappearing. This means there is a network of brokers and transport agents who are known to each other and, though ostensibly competitors, often co-operate in the context of larger networks of illicit arms supply. They are often closely linked to government agencies (e.g. intelligence), private organizations (e.g. PNCs) and/or larger multinationals (e.g. diamond and petrol companies).

The world of arms brokers and transport agents is quite small; the same names keep reappearing.

National legislation and international initiatives on small arms transfers have only recently begun to address the problem of brokers and transport agents. Our research has highlighted several challenges in this regard:

- At the national level, many countries lack adequate laws on the manufacturing and export of military materials. While most have licensing provisions governing the trade in weapons, few adequately address the 'intangible' services provided by brokers and the role of transport agents. The exploitation of these loopholes is compounded by the limited jurisdictional scope of national legislation, which rarely addresses the activities of brokers and shippers operating from third countries. The transnational nature of brokering and shipping activities also permits the exploitation of discrepancies between legal systems through, for instance, the use of 'tax havens' and offshore banking, as well as transportation under 'flags of convenience'.
- At the international level, co-operation between states on monitoring and regulating arms brokering, transnational financial transactions, and transport activities is still at an embryonic stage. Because of this, many brokers and transport agents are able to conceal their operations and act with impunity.

Brokers and transport agents take advantage of the incapacity of certain states to monitor and enforce territorial borders and customs controls. This is particularly prevalent in conflict zones where borders are porous and authorities lack the necessary expertise and resources to regulate the traffic in goods and services. This lack of capacity is often compounded by the fact that, in many states, important sectors of activity are in the hands of corrupt officials, non-state actors such as rebel groups, private military companies, and other multinational organizations.

The problem of arms brokers and transport agents is also a political problem.

The problem of arms brokers and transport agents is also a political problem. The provision of arms to conflict zones can be big business, not only for private individuals, but also for states. In certain areas, states have a vested interest in assisting brokers and transport agents for either financial or political gain. Thus, they will often provide apparently legal channels for acquiring arms, together with the necessary authorizations. Coupled with their traditionally secretive attitude towards military matters, the involvement of states in the illicit activities of brokers and transport agents compounds attempts to regulate and control the legal trade in small arms.

Finally, it should be pointed out that there are important aspects of arms brokering that have *not* been covered in this chapter. These include arms brokering in other regions of the world (e.g. the former Soviet Union and Latin America); the relationship between arms brokering and other organized criminal activities (e.g. drug trafficking and prostitution); the techniques brokers use to arrange the financing of weapons transactions; the brokering of surplus versus 'new production' weaponry; and other forms of transport brokers use, notably sea and overland transport. Therefore, the findings and conclusions presented in this chapter should be seen as 'pointers' for subsequent research and investigation, to be further expanded upon, modified, and refined in light of more comprehensive data in future editions of the *Small Arms Survey*.

The provision of arms to conflict zones can be big business, not only for private individuals, but also for states.

For further information and current developments on small arms issues please check our website at www.smallarmssurvey.org

3 List of Abbreviations

ACP	Air Cargo Plus
ACS	Air Charter Services
ADB	Antonov Design Bureau
ATO	Air Transport Office
BBC	British Broadcasting Corporation
BICC	Bonn International Center for Conversion
CIA	Central Intelligence Agency (US)
CIS	Commonwealth of Independant States
CIO	Central Intelligence Organization (Zimbabwe)
DGFM	Dirección General de Fabricaciones Militares (Argentina)
DRC	Democratic Republic of Congo
ECOMOG	ECOWAS Monitoring Group
ECOSOC	United Nations Economic and Social Council
ECOWAS	Economic Community of West African States
EO	Executive Outcomes
EU	European Union
EUC	End-User Certificate
FAA	Angolan Armed Forces
GNP	Gross National Product
GPS	Global Positioning System
IATA	International Aviation Transport Association
ICAO	International Civil Aviation Organization
IMI	Israel Military Industries
MPRI	Military Professional Resources Incorporated
NGO	Non-governmental Organization
OAS	Organization of American States
OECD	Organization for Economic Cooperation and Development
OSCE	Organization for Security and Cooperation in Europe
OSEO	Office for Serious Economic Offences
OSLEG	Operation Sovereign Legitimacy
PMC	Private Military Company
RPG	Rocket Propelled Grenade
RUF	Revolutionary United Front (Sierra Leone)
SAM	Surface-to-Air Missile
SIPRI	Stockholm International Peace Research Institute
UK	United Kingdom
UN	United Nations
UNAMSIL	UN Mission in Sierra Leone
UNITA	União Nacional Para a Independência Total de Angola
UNPROFOR	United Nations Protection Force
UNSC	United Nations Security Council
US	United States
ZANU-PF	Zimbabwe African National Union - Patriotic Front
ZDI	Zimbabwe Defence Industries

3   Endnotes

1 The 1999 *Report of the UN Group of Governmental Experts on Small Arms* specifically mentions the key role of arms brokers and concludes that inadequate national regulation systems are partly to blame for the diversion of small arms into the illicit realm (UN Document A/54/258, 19 August 1999).

2 See, for instance, Martin and Romano (1992).

3 For example, at the beginning of the 1990s, the US had reduced force levels by nearly one-third. Moreover, the country had a surplus of outdated equipment, after the massive military modernization and build-up of the 1980s. As a result, vast quantities of weapons were retired and became surplus (Pineo and Lumpe, 1996).

4 According to the US definition (which is commonly considered the most comprehensive legal definition), brokers are 'any person who acts as an agent for others in negotiating or arranging contracts, purchases, sales or transfers of defense articles or defense services in return for a fee, commission, or other consideration.' Brokering activities cover 'acting as a broker as defined in Sec. 129.2(a) [above], and includes the financing, transportation, freight forwarding, or taking of any other action that facilitates the manufacture, export, or import of a defense article or defense service, irrespective of its origin.' (*International Traffic in Arms Regulations [ITAR]* 1996, Part 129.2 (a)—Registration and Licensing of Brokers).

5 For illustrative cases of these activities see Wood and Peleman (1999).

6 Brokers are also used to locate other brokers. According to 'Alex G.,' an influential Brussels-based broker in French-Africa involved in a deal for arms to the former president of Congo-Brazzaville, Lissouba: 'I am not involved in arms deals. When Lissouba needed weapons, the name of Jacques Monsieur [a Belgian broker] came up. I was the one who was asked to trace him in Brussels. I brought him to Brazzaville, I introduced him to the presidency and I received my commission. I was, however, never a party to Monsieur's deals with Congo-Brazzaville and I was never present when the contracts were negotiated, so I can hardly be considered an arms dealer. Moreover, I left Congo for Europe in February 1997, months before the civil war started. I just set up meetings, there's nothing illicit about that'. Interview by Johan Peleman, August 2000.

7 Court hearings, copies of police documents, and interviews with police officers on the case in Belgium and South Africa. Information and interviews by Johan Peleman, 2000.

8 See Silverstein (2000b) for detailed descriptions of many of these celebrity brokers.

9 Al Kassar was described by the US Drug Enforcement Administration as one of the most important figures in the international drug trade (Wood and Peleman, 1999, p.9).

10 The authors are grateful to Johan Peleman for information on this point.

11 The authors are grateful to Ambassador Peggy Mason, Emanuela-Chiara Gillard, and Brian Wood for clarification of this issue.

12 Communication from Brian Wood.

13 For details on Wilson's activities for Qadhafi, see US Marshal International Crime Alert, 1997; *International Herald Tribune*, 2 November 1981; *New York Times*, 3 November 1981; *Washington Post*, 21 December 1982; *Foreign Report*, 27 August 1981; *International Herald Tribune*, 18 June 1981; and Goulden (1984).

14 Interview conducted for Carlton Television, June 1995. The pilot in this interview claims he was tricked into the flight.

15 Testimony of aircrew who flew arms to Goma in 1994, 20/20 Television, 1994, and Carlton Television, 1995.

16 The Jersey company was Ibar Management and Trading and the London company was Winston Investments Ltd. Information from Johan Peleman, 2000.

17 For a discussion of national arms controls see Wood and Peleman, (1999).

18 The Brussels subsidiary of the American company C.I.C. reportedly played an important role in Monsieur's 1980s dealings with Iran through his company Matimco (*De Morgen*, 23 August 1999).

19 Interviews with Alex G. in Brussels and Budapest, August 2000. On Monsieur's arrest in Iran see *Africa Intelligence*, 8 January 2001.

20 In early 1995 Al-Kassar was acquitted of his role in the 1985 hijacking of the Achille Lauro cruise ship. His name also surfaced in the investigation of the 1988 downing of Pan Am flight 103 over Lockerbie, Scotland (Lemasson, 2000; Howe, 1999).

21 For the results of these investigations, see: UN Security Council. 2000. *Report of the Panel of Experts established by the Security Council pursuant to Resolution 1237, on violations of Security Council Resolutions against UNITA*, S/2000/203, 10 March; and UN Security Council. 2000. *Report of the Panel of Experts Appointed Pursuant to UN Security Council Resolution 1306 (2000), Paragraph 19 in Relation to Sierra Leone*. S/20.

22 There is considerable evidence of illicit weapons transfers by sea and overland transportation, but the scope of this chapter does not permit a full elaboration of these alternative means. Because data on the latter forms of transportation are less comprehensive, they will be the subject of future research by the *Small Arms Survey*.

23 UN Reports focusing on the illicit transport of small arms include the *Reports of the International Commission of Inquiry* (S/1996/67, S/1996/195, S/1997/1010, S/1998/63, S/1998/777, S/1998/1096); the *Panel of Experts on Violations of Security Council Sanctions Against UNITA* (S/2000/203); and the *Panel of Experts on Sierra Leone* (S/2000/1195).

24 See Wood and Peleman (1999) for a detailed description of the routes used by some transport agents to avoid detection (pp. 69-70).

25 Most of West Africa, according to the UN Report on Sierra

Leone (2000), is not covered by radar systems, allowing air-craft to utilize national airspaces with a minimal risk of detection. According to the report, 'at times, it is local authorities or even local individuals who contact them to inform them of an overflight. The military admit that they do not have the means to intercept such traffic, a common practice elsewhere' (paragraph 293).

26 Information on the Air Cess network compiled from: Hain, House of Commons Hansard Debates, 18 January 2000; Founding documents of NV Trans Aviation Network Group, Trade register of Ostend, enacted 17 March 1995; Documents of the registration of Air Cess Swaziland; Certificate of plane registration of Air Cess GE SA in Equatorial Guinea; Document of T.I.T. Insurance Company in Moscow for Air Cess planes; interviews with police and Aviation Authorities in Zambia, South Africa, Belgium, United Arab Emirates and Swaziland; and interview with former employee of Air Cess. Following the publication of the UN Report on Sierra Leone (2000), the British government in January 2001 requested the United Arab Emirates to shut down Bout's operations in Sharjah and Dubai, where he employs 100 Russian nationals (*Financial Times*, 23 January 2001).

27 The Small Arms Survey is in possession of documents showing an April 23, 1998 flight of Air Cess from Luanda to Kinshasa, and of lists of registration numbers of planes detected in UNITA-area 1997, 1998, and 1999, showing several planes belonging to the Air Cess group and associated companies.

28 List of planes obtained from the Aviation Authorities of Swaziland, August 1999; Interview and correspondence with director of civil aviation, Mbabane, Swaziland.

29 Brian Johnson-Thomas, note submitted to the Small Arms Survey, October 2000.

30 Brian Johnson-Thomas, note submitted to the Small Arms Survey, October 2000.

31 UN measures against UNITA include the oil and arms embargo imposed by Security Council Resolution 864 (15 September 1993); travel restrictions and the prohibition of flights of aircraft by UNITA imposed by Security Council Resolution 1127 (August 1997); and the freezing of the financial resources, funds and assets of UNITA, together with the banning of diamond sales not in the control of the government, imposed by Security Council Resolution 1173. The latter also prohibits all forms of supply or trade with UNITA save those of a humanitarian nature.

32 A list of cargo aircraft detected in the UNITA-area, made available to the UN in 1997, showed registration markings of airlines from Ukraine, Moldova, Russia, and Liberia. These included Trans Air Cargo, Moscow Airways, Renan, Khors Air, Flying Dolphin, HUK Hungarian-Ukrainian Airlines, InterOcean Airways, Air Cess, West Coast Airways, Impulse Aero, Veteran Airways, Air Ukraine, Ukraine Air Alliance, and Valan SRL (Wood and Peleman, 1999).

33 Subsequently, the number of airports used for international flights in South Africa was reduced from over 20 to ten, of which eight could still be used for international cargo transport (*Freight and Trading Weekly*, 16 May 1997).

34 James Rupert of the *Washington Post* reported that in October-November 1996, 450 tonnes of weapons were delivered to UNITA from Bulgaria, and that in July 1996, flights from Bulgaria averaged four a week (*Washington Post*, 21 March 1997).

35 Interview with Dominique Lemaire, *Le Soir* (15 March 2000).

36 Company documents obtained from the Belgian register of companies on Espace Aviation, Triple A Diamonds, and Barlak Development; additional interviews with law enforcement officers in Belgium. Interviews by Johan Peleman.

37 In August 2000, ATO and Air Cargo Express were still registered companies in the DRC and in Congo Brazzaville (*JP Airline Fleet Manual*, 1999-2000).

38 The Panel also received information concerning the involvement of Ukraine, Belarus, and Russia in the sale of arms to Togo, but none of these government replied to the Panel's queries (The Fowler Report, 2000, para. 43).

39 UN UNITA report, paras 21-22. Burkina Faso is also reportedly involved in the transportation of arms to the RUF in Sierra Leone. See also Human Rights Watch, 'Letter to President Compaore' (by Joost Hiltermann), 28 March 2000 and Final Report of the Monitoring Mechanism (UN S/2000/1225).

40 See the letter from the Angolan government to the UN Security Council, 9 March 1999.

41 For the UN arms and petrol embargo, see Security Council Resolutions 1132 (1997) and 1171 (1998). Furthermore, in its resolution of 5 July 2000 (1306) the Security Council prohibited the direct or indirect import of diamonds from Sierra Leone, unless accompanied by a Certificate of Origin issued by the Government.

42 Ties between these men date from the early 1980s, when Sankoh, Taylor, and Compaore trained at the latter's World Revolutionary Headquarters, and later matured into military and logistical support for each others' respective armed movements (*Washington Post*, 18 June 2000).

43 According to one commentator, 'the deal was that the RUF would help Taylor 'liberate' Liberia and afterward would provide a base for the RUF to enter Sierra Leone. When the RUF entered Sierra Leone there was a Burkinabe force under their command that Taylor arranged to send in. All the arms for Taylor and the RUF came from Burkina Faso, and were bought in Ukraine. The payment for all this was diamonds that went through Liberia, Burkina Faso, and the Ivory Coast. That basic route still works.' Quote from Ibrahim Abdullah, a historian at South Africa's University of the Western Cape (*Washington Post*, 18 June 2000).

44 For an in-depth analysis of Liberia's role in supplying arms and related materiel to the RUF, see Berman (2000, pp. 13-15).

45 Minin's company, 'Exotical Tropical Timber Enterprise' is based in Monrovia but exploits forests in Sierra Leone. According to one source, Minin used this company (which is under the protection of Charles Taylor) to supply the RUF with weapons in exchange for diamonds which were mis-labelled as Liberian in origin (*Le Soir*, 30 August 2000).

46 Air Foyle Press Release. 19 May 2000.

47 Air Foyle Press Release. 19 May 2000

48 Interview with UN peacekeeping force officer by Brian Johnson-Thomas, May 2000; UN Security Council Document, S/2000/1195 and *Report of the Panel of Experts Appointed Pursuant to UN Security Council Resolution 1306 (2000), Paragraph 19 in Relation to Sierra Leone*.

49 Liberian Government Certificate of Airworthiness, copy in possession of the Small Arms Survey.

50 According to some sources, the owner of Chartered Engineering & Technical—identified in the UN Security Council as a person of 'Eastern European origin'—was in fact Minin himself, though this has yet to be proved. Information received by Brian Johnson-Thomas.

51 For details, see Brian Wood's testimony to the UN Committee on Sierra Leone, 31 July.

52 Communication from Johan Peleman, September 2000.

53 Air Foyle, an air cargo agent based in the UK and implicated in the illicit transport of weapons to Sierra Leone, for instance, has operated its Antonov 124 on behalf of the UN peacekeeping mission to Sierra Leone, carrying British and Indian peacekeepers. See Brian Wood's testimony to the UN Committee on Sierra Leone, 31 July.

54 In some cases, transit licenses also embody agreements through to the final destination by all parties to a given transaction, and including all countries across whose territories the goods will transit. The authors are grateful to Ambassador Peggy Mason for her clarifications on this point.

55 These are the major documents used to verify that a given transaction meets the terms upon which its authorizations were based. Others include end-use statements (attesting the receipt and intended use of the goods), delivery verification certificates (attesting to the arrival of the goods to the intended beneficiary), and customs clearance certificates (attesting that the goods imported match those specified in the authorizations).

56 The US Office of Defence Trade Controls has thus far registered 137 brokers as authorized to facilitate arms transfers outside the US, while dozens have been refused. Moreover, the US has granted 200 licenses to undertake arms deals. Communication from Brian Wood, 8 December 1999.

57 Decree-law of 18 April 1939 *Creating a Regime Governing War Materiel, Arms and Munitions*; Decree No. 95-589 of 6 May 1995 Relative to the Decree-Law of 18 April 1939; and Order in Council of 2 October 1992 *Relating to Procedures for Importing and Exporting War Materials, Arms and Munitions, and Analogous Material.*

58 Indeed, as some have argued, increasing the scope of arms control systems to cover all the actors and intermediaries in a given transaction can be counter-productive by overburdening licensing systems and thus reducing their effectiveness. For a discussion of this point see Coflin (2000), p. 28.

59 According to Coflin (2000), three types of jurisdictional scope can be found in contemporary arms control legislation. Systems with 'national' jurisdictional scope limit their control to the activities of entities trading in arms from that country to second countries (the classic model of arms deals). Systems with 'extended' jurisdictional scope regulate the activities of entities that organize arms deals between second and third countries (where the arms do not pass through the territory of the regulating country). Finally, systems with 'extra-territorial' jurisdictional scope impose their control over their citizens arranging arms deals no matter where they reside, and regardless of the provenance and ultimate destination of the weapons. See also Wood and Clegg (1999).

60 For the text of the Draft Report on the *Revised draft Protocol against the Illicit Manufacturing of and Trafficking in Firearms, Their Parts and Components and Ammunition, supplementing the United Nations Convention against Transnational Organized Crime* (commonly referred to as the draft UN Firearms Protocol), see www.un.org/depts/dda/CAB/Program2.htm.

61 In the event a definition is deemed necessary for inclusion, the following text was discussed by delegates: 'Brokering' means the activities of a natural or legal person who acts as an agent or intermediary on behalf of others, in order to obtain, directly or indirectly, a financial or other material benefit, in negotiating transactions involving the international export or import of firearms, their parts and components or ammunition. For the full text of Article 8 bis of the draft Firearms Protocol, see UN Document A/AC.254/4/Add.2/Rev.6.

3 Bibliography

Africa Confidential. 1999. 'Zimbabwe/Congo-K — Rhodies to the Rescue.' 5 November.

Agence France Presse. 1995. 'Geneva Court Asked to Seize Six Million Dollars from Bosnian Arms Sales.' 3 August.

____. 1999a. 'Israeli Arms Merchant Reported Arrested in Sierra Leone.' 15 January.

____. 1999b. 'Colombia To Request Extradition Of Israeli Mercenary.' 23 January.

____. 2000a. 'Colombia Apprehends Alleged Arms Traffickers From Israel.' 28 May.

____. 2000b. 'Russian Pilots Jailed in India for Arms Drop Return to Homes in Latvia.' 2 August.

____. 2000c. 'Terrorism, Forced Marriage On Agenda For Jack Straw Visit to India.' 1 September.

Allio, Emmy. 2000a. 'Entebbe Mystery Plane Disappears.' *New Vision (Kampala)*. 9 July.

____.2000b. 'Mystery Planes Repainted at Entebbe Airport.' *New Vision (Kampala)*. 2 April.

Allio, Emmy and Grace Matsiko. 2000. 'Rwanda

Plane Linked to Entebbe Jet Racket.' *New Vision (Kampala)*. 26 April.

Austin, Kathi. 1999. 'Effectively Regulating Arms Brokering.' Paper presented at the Workshop on Small Arms Monitoring and Control. Geneva, 22-23 November.

Barnett, Antony. 1999. 'Barclays Held Cash For Massacre.' *The Observer*. 28 November.

van Berkel, Annemarie. 1999. 'Bulgaria's Arms Trafficking: An Issue Yet to Be Resolved.' *Weekly Defense Monitor*, Vol.3, No. 46. 2 December.

British American Security Information Council. 1998a. *The Struggle Continues: Light Weapons Destruction in Mozambique*. BASIC Papers No. 25. April.

____. 1998b. *Eastern Europe's Arsenal on the Loose: Managing Light Weapons Flows to Conflict Zones*. BASIC Papers No. 26. May

Bedi, Rahul. 2000. 'Russia Squeezes India Before Putin Visit.' *The Asian Age*. 25 July.

Berman, Eric. 2000. *Re-Armament in Sierra Leone: One Year After the Lomé Peace Agreement*. Occasional Paper No. 1. Geneva: Small Arms Survey.

de Bock, Walter. 1992. 'Wapenhandelaar in Boom had Stasi-konnektie.' *De Morgen*. 15 December.

Bondi, Loretta and Elise Keppler. 2001. *Casting the Net? The Implications of the U.S. Law on Arms Brokering*. Washington, DC: Fund for Peace, Arms and Conflict Program.

Bonn International Center for Conversion. 1997. *Conversion Survey 1997: Global Disarmament and Disposal of Surplus Weapons*. New York: Oxford University Press.

Bonner, Ray. 1998. 'Legal Loopholes Make Arms Shipments Easy.' *The Globe and Mail*. 15 July.

Boutwell, Jeffrey, Michael Klare and Laura Reed. 1995. *Lethal Commerce: The Global Trade in Small Arms and Light Weapons*. Cambridge: American Academy of Arts and Sciences, Committee on International Security Studies.

Bryson, D. 1997. 'Zairians Running Guns to Angolans.' *Associated Press*. 28 March.

Bulgaria. Government of Bulgaria. 2000. *Outline of Bulgarian Export Control Legislation and Institutional Arrangements Regarding Foreign Trade in Arms and Dual-Use Goods and Technologies*.

Cilliers, Jakkie and Christian Dietrich, eds. 2000.

Angola's War Economy. Pretoria: Institute for Security Studies.

Coflin, James. 1999. *State Authorization and Inter-State Information Sharing Concerning Small Arms Manufacturers, Dealers and Brokers*. Canada: Department of Foreign Affairs and International Affairs. January.

____. 2000. *Small Arms Brokering: Impact, Options for Controls and Regulation*. Canada: Department of Foreign Affairs and International Trade, International Security Bureau, International Security Research and Outreach Programme. May.

European Union (EU). Council of the European Union. 1998. *European Union Code of Conduct on Arms Exports*. 5 June.

____. 1999. *Annual Report in Conformity with Operative Provision 8 of the European Union Code of Conduct on Arms Exports*. Press release: 296 - Nr: 11651/99. Approved at the 2206th Meeting of the EU Council, Luxembourg, 11 October.

Crossette, Barbara. 1981. 'Role of Americans in Libyan Warfare Confirmed by US.' *New York Times*. 3 November.

____. 1999. 'Arms Trafficker With Army Connections.' *De Morgen*. 23 August. (FBIS-WEU-1999-0823).

Economic Community of West African States (ECOW-AS). 1998. *Declaration of a Moratorium on Importation, Exportation and Manufacture of Light Weapons in West Africa*. Abuja, Nigeria, 31 October. Reproduced in UN doc. A/53/763 – S/1998/1194 (Annex). 18 December.

____. 1999a. *Plan of Action for the Implementation of the Programme for Co-ordination and Assistance for Security and Development*. Bamako, 25 March. Reproduced in Jacqueline Seck, ed. 2000. *West Africa Small Arms Moratorium: High-Level Consultations on the Modalities for the Implementation of PCASED*. Geneva/Lomé: United Nations Institute for Disarmament Research/The UN Regional Centre for Peace and Disarmament in Africa.

____. 1999b. *Code of Conduct for the Implementation of the Moratorium on the Importation, Exportation and Manufacture of Light Weapons*. Lomé, 10 December. Reproduced in Jacqueline Seck, ed. 2000. *West Africa Small Arms Moratorium: High-Level Consultations on the Modalities for the Implementation of PCASED*. Geneva/Lomé: United Nations Institute for Disarmament Research/The UN Regional Centre for

Peace and Disarmament in Africa.

Edwards, Andrew. 1998. *Review of Financial Regulation in the Crown Dependencies: A Report. Part 1*. 24 October. <http://www.officialdocuments.co.uk>

Ehler, John. 1982. 'La Région Wallone a-t-elle Aidé Un Trafiquant D'Armes Arrêté?' *La Libre Belgique*. 8 April.

El Espectador. 1999a. 'Klein Si Cayo en Sierra Leone.' 23 January.

____. 1999b. 'Las Andanzas Del Israeli Yair Klein Por Africa.' 24 January .

Farah, Douglas. 2000. 'Liberia Reportedly Arming Guerrillas; Rebel Control of Sierra Leone Diamond-Mining Areas Crucial to Monrovia, Sources Say.' *Washington Post*. 18 June.

Focus Newsletter. 2000. November.

Foreign Report. 1981. 'Qaddafi's American Friends.' 27 August.

Gaetner, Gilles. 1999. 'Un Très Discret Marchand De Canons.' *L'Express*. 24 June.

Gerth, Jeff. 1983. 'US Seeks $21 Million From An Ex-CIA Agent.' *International Herald Tribune*. 30 July.

Gillard, Emanuela-Chiara. 2000. 'What's Legal? What's Illegal?' In Lora Lumpe, ed. *Running Guns: The Global Black Market in Small Arms*. London: Zed Books.

Golden, Tim. 2000. 'C.I.A. Links Cited on Peru Arms Deal That Backfired.' *The New York Times*. 6 November.

Grey, Stephen.1997. 'Arms-Deal Briton May Hang: Ex-Soldier Abandoned After Tipping Off Police.' *Sunday Times*. 28 September.

Harman, Danna. 2000. 'Yair Klein Released From Sierra Leone Jail.' *The Jerusalem Post*. 24 April.

Hersch, Seymour. 1981a. 'Export-Import, CIA Style: Ex-Agents Supply Arms to Qadhafi.' *International Herald Tribune*. 18 June.

____.1981b. 'How a CIA Ex-Agent Exposed Qadhafi Deal With US Arms Exporters.' *International Herald Tribune*. 25 June.

____.1992. 'US Secretly Gave Money To Iraq Early In Its War Against Iran.' *The New York Times*. 26 January.

Hirsch, Valérie. 2000. 'Un Belge d'Afrique du Sud nie soutenir les rebelles angolais.' *Le Soir*. 15 March.

Holbrooke, Richard. 2000. 'Remarks on Sierra Leone's Diamonds.' United Nations Security Council Sanctions Committee Public Hearing, 31 July.

Honigsbaum, Mark and Antony Barnett. 1999. 'UK firms in African arms riddle; Mystery of cargo planes and lethal trade that is fuelling a continent's murderous civil wars.' *The Observer*. 31 January.

Huisman, Roger. 1999. 'Antwerpse Douane Verijdelt Massale Trafiek Wapentuig.' *Gazet van Antwerpen*. 6-7 February.

Human Rights Watch. 1994. *Arming Rwanda: The Arms Trade and Human Rights Abuses in the Rwandan War*. Vol.6, No. 1.

____. 1995. *Rwanda/Zaire: Rearming with Impunity: International Support for the Perpetrators of the Rwandan Genocide*. Vol. 7, No.4.

____. 1999. *Bulgaria: Money Talks. Arms Dealing with Human Rights Abusers*. Vol.11, No.4.

International Law Enforcement Law Reporter. 2000. 'US Arrests Arms Merchant on International Bank Fraud and Money Laundering Charges.' February.

Itar-Tass. 1998. 'Itar-Tass Domestic News Digest.' 26 July.

Johnson-Thomas, Brian. 2000a. 'Anatomy of a Shady Deal.' In Lora Lumpe, ed. *Running Guns: The Global Black Market in Small Arms*. London: Zed Books.

____. 2000b. *Big Jets and Big Bucks—Flying Arms to the RUF*. Background Paper. Geneva: Small Arms Survey.

Kaldor, Mary. 1999. *New & Old Wars: Organised Violence in a Global Era*. Cambridge: Polity Press.

Kessler, Ronald. 1986. *The Richest Man in the World: The Story of Adnan Khashoggi*. New York. Warner Books.

Kestin, Hesh. 1985. 'God and Man in Zaire.' *Forbes*. 18 November.

Ku King, Alberto. 2000. 'Montesinos Es Un Espectro Que Perseguirá a Fujimori.' *La Republica*. 22 September.

Lallemand, Alain. 2000. 'Les 'Diamants de la Guerre' Perdent un Parrain.' *Le Soir*. 20 August.

Lashmar, Paul. 1999. 'British Arms Cargo Seized By Customs.' *The Independent*. 11 February.

Latin America Weekly Report. 1998. 'Death Adds Drama To Arms Sales Affairs: No Extradition For Dealer Who Implicate Menem.' 1 September.

Latin America Weekly Report. 1998. 21 July.

Laurance, Edward. 1998. *Light Weapons and Intrastate Conflict: Early Warning Factors and Preventive Action: a Report to the Carnegie*

Commission on Preventing Deadly Conflict. New York: Carnegie Corporation of New York.

Le Monde. 1995. 'Un Français Est Écroué Pour Trafic D'Armes De Guerre Avec Le Rwanda.' 2 February.

Lemasson, Eric. 2000. *Marchiani: L'Agent Politique*. Paris: Seuil.

Leppard, David and Brian Johnson-Thomas et.al. 1999. 'British Firms Arm Sierra Leone Rebels.' *Sunday Times*. 10 January.

Leppard, David, Gareth Walsh and Paul Nuki. 2000. 'Hague's Top Aide Paid by Arab Arms Dealer.' *Sunday Times*. 27 August.

Marcus, Raine. 1999. 'Ex-IDF Colonel To Be Tried This Week In Sierra Leone.' *The Jerusalem Post*. 21 September.

McGirk, Tim. 1996. 'Briton In Death Penalty Case Was MoD Spy; Arms Charges: MP's Letter Supports Defence.' *The Independent*. 16 September.

McLean, Andrew. 2000. *Tackling Small Arms in the Great Lakes Region and the Horn of Africa: Strengthening the Capacity of Subregional Organizations*. Pretoria: Institute for Security Studies.

Morgenstern, Henry, 1991. 'Making Friends Through Firepower.' *The Jerusalem Post*. 26 April.

Nairobi Declaration on the Problem of the Proliferation of Illicit Small Arms and Light Weapons in the Great Lakes Region and the Horn of Africa ('Nairobi Declaration'). 2000. Nairobi, 15 March. Reproduced in Andrew McLean. 2000. *Tackling Small Arms in the Great Lakes Region and the Horn of Africa: Strengthening the Capacity of Subregional Organizations*. Pretoria: Institute for Security Studies, pp. 74-77.

Naylor, R. 2000. 'Gunsmoke and Mirrors: Financing the Illegal Trade.' In Lora Lumpe, ed. Running Guns: The Global Market in Small Arms. London: Zed Books.

Norway. Department of Foreign Affairs. 1999. *The Second Oslo Meeting on Small Arms and Light Weapons: Elements of a Common Understanding*. 7 December.

O'Brien, Kevin. 2000. *Mercenaries and Private Military Companies in the Arms Trade*. Background Paper. Geneva: Small Arms Survey.

Official Kremlin International News Broadcast. 2000. Transcript of the press conference with the five Russian aircrew released from jail, 27 July.

Organization for Economic Cooperation and Development. 2000. 'Towards Global Tax Co-operation: Report to the Ministerial Council Meeting and Recommendations by the Committee on Fiscal Affairs.' Paris, 26 June.

Organization for Security and Cooperation in Europe (OSCE). 2000. *Document on Small Arms and Light Weapons*. 308th Plenary Meeting. FSC.DOC/1/00. 24 November.

Organization of African Unity (OAU). 2000. *Bamako Declaration on an African Common Position on the Illicit Proliferation, Circulation and Trafficking of Small Arms and Light Weapons*. SALW/Decl.(I). Bamako, Mali, 1 December.

Organization of American States (OAS). 1997. *Model Regulations for the Control of the International Movement of Firearms, their Parts and Components and Ammunition*. OEA/Ser.L/XIV.2.22 – CICAD/doc.905/97 Separata. Lima, Peru, 4 November. Washington, DC: General Secretariat of the OAS.

Oxfam. 1998. *Out of Control: The loopholes in the UK Controls of the Arms Trade*. Oxfam GB Policy Paper. Oxford. December.

Pallister, David. 1996. 'Britons Involved in Arms Running.' *The Guardian*. 15 April.

____. 2000. 'UK Air Firm Linked to Sanctions Buster.' *The Guardian*. 5 August.

Parker, Andrew. 2001. 'Britain tells UAE to close arms dealer's freight business.' *Financial Times*. 23 January.

Peleman, Johan. 2000a. 'The Logistics of Sanctions Busting: The Airborne Component.' In Jakkie Cilliers and Christian Dietrich, eds. *Angola's War Economy*. Pretoria: Institute for Security Studies.

____. 2000b. *Significant Arms Brokers of Past and Present*. Background Paper. Geneva: Small Arms Survey.

____. 2000c. *Small Arms and Private Military Companies*. Background Paper. Geneva: Small Arms Survey.

Pineo, Paul and Lora Lumpe. 1996. *Recycled Weapons: American Exports of Surplus Arms, 1990-1995*. Washington, DC: Federation of American Scientists.

Pirseyedi, Bobi. 2000. *The Small Arms Problem in Central Asia: Features and Implications*. Geneva: United Nations Institute for Disarmament Research.

Public Education Center. 1998. *Central Africa: The Influx of Arms and the Continuation of Crisis*. May.

<http://www.publicedcenter.org/nsns>

Rempel, William and Sebastian Rotella. 2000. 'Arms Dealer Implicates Peru Spy Chief In Smuggling Ring.' *Los Angeles Times.* 1 November.

Republic of Congo. Presidency of the Republic of Congo. 1998. Official correspondence. 24 February.

Rupert, James. 1997. 'Zaire Reportedly Selling Arms to Angolan Ex-Rebels.' *The Washington Post.* 21 March.

____. 1999. 'Diamond Hunters Fuel Africa's Brutal Wars.' *The Washington Post.* 16 October.

Russel, Warren. 1999. 'What If They Are Innocent?' *The Guardian.* 17 April.

Santoro, Daniel. 1998. *Venta de Armas: Hombres del Gobierno: El Escándalo de La Venta Ilegal de Arms Argentinas a Ecuador, Croacia y Bosnia.* Planeta: Buenos Aires.

Silverstein, Ken. 2000a. 'Licensed to Kill: Shadowing Our Government's Favourite Arms Dealer.' *Harper's Magazine.* May, pp.52-66.

____. 2000b. *Private Warriors.* London: Verso.

Smith, Chris. 1999. 'Light Weapons Proliferation: A Global Survey.' *Jane's Intelligence Review.* 1 July.

Smith, Philip. 1982. 'Wilson Gets 15-year Sentence For 'Calculated' Arms Scheme.' *Washington Post.* 21 December.

Soler, Francis. 1998. 'Conjoncture — Les Richesses Minieres au Coeur de la Guerre au Congo-Kinshasa.' *Le Monde.* 17 November.

States News Service. 1990. 'Shocking Report Sheds Light on Pan Am 103.' 19 November.

Stockholm International Peace Research Institute. 2000. *SIPRI Yearbook 2000: Armaments, Disarmament and International Security.* New York: Oxford University Press.

Sunday Telegraph. 1998. 'Fortunes of War — Mugabe's Money Mine.' 8 November.

Taubman, Philip, Jeff Gerth and Edward Pound. 1981. 'Former CIA-Agent's Efforts are Seen as Crucial to Libya Intervention in Chad.' *International Herald Tribune.* 2 November.

The Progress. 2000. 'High Court Acquits Foreign Mercenaries.' 20 April.

The Toronto Star. 1987. 'Air Firm Executive Faces Charge Over Weapons.' 4 December.

United Kingdom. 2000. *Report of the UK Defence, Foreign Affairs and International Development and Trade Select Committees.* February.

United Kingdom. Foreign and Commonwealth Office.

1997. *UK Annual Report on Strategic Export Controls.*

United Kingdom. Foreign and Commonwealth Office. 1998. *UK Annual Report on Strategic Export Controls.*

United Kingdom. United Kingdom House of Commons. 1998. *Report of the Sierra Leone Arms Investigation.* 27 July.

United Nations. 1997. *Report of the Panel of Governmental Experts on Small Arms.* A/52/298.

United Nations. 1999. *Report of the Group of Governmental Experts on Small Arms.* A/54/258.

United Nations General Assembly. 1999. *Report of a Consultative Meeting of Experts on the Feasibility of Undertaking a Study for Restricting the Manufacture and Trade of Small Arms to Manufacturers and Dealers Authorised by States.* A/54/160. 6 July.

United Nations Security Council. 2000a. *Report of the Panel of Experts established by the Security Council pursuant to Resolution 1237, on violations of Security Council Resolutions against UNITA.* S/2000/203. 10 March.

____ 2000b. *Hearings of the Committee on Sanctions on Sierra Leone.* July.

____. 2000c. *Letter dated 17 August 2000 from the Permanent Representative of the Democratic Republic of the Congo to the United Nations addressed to the President of the Security Council.* S/2000/810. 18 August.

____. 2000d. *Report of the Panel of Experts Appointed Pursuant to UN Security Council Resolution 1306 (2000),* Paragraph 19 in Relation to Sierra Leone. S/2000/1195. 20 December.

____. 2001. *Letter dated 16 January 2001 from the Secretary-General addressed to the President of the Security Council.* S/2001/49. 16 January.

United Press International. 1988. 'Suspected Marcos Coup Try Probed.' 27 May.

United States Marshal International Crime Alert. 1997. <http://www.ibb.gov/fugitives/terpiica.htm>

Venter, Al. 1998. 'Africa Greets Gun-Runners With Open Arms.' *International Defence Review,* Vol. 31. No. 8. 1 August.

Vines, Alex. 1999. *Angola Unravels: The Rise and Fall of the Lusaka Peace Process.* New York: Human Rights Watch.

Walsh, Lawrence. 1993. *Final Report of the Independent Counsel for Iran/Contra Matters.*

Vol 1. Investigations and Prosecutions.
Washington, DC: United States Court of Appeals for
the District of Colombia Circuit. 4 August.

Weekly Defense Monitor. 1999. 'Bulgaria's Arms
Trafficking: an Issue Yet to be Resolved.' Vol.3, No.
43. 2 December.

Whitaker, Richard. 1998. 'Airline Revolution Gathers
Pace.' *Airline Business*. August.

Wood, Brian. 2000a. 'Arms and Related Support for
the Rebels in Sierra Leone.' Testimony to the United
Nations Committee on Sierra Leone, 31 July –
1 August.

____. 2000b. *China's Search for Local Partners*.
Background Paper. Geneva: Small Arms Survey.

Wood, Brian and Elizabeth Clegg. 1999. *Controlling
the Gun-Runners: Proposals for EU Action to
Regulate Arms Brokering and Shipping Agents*.
BASIC/NISAT/Saferworld Briefing. London:
BASIC/NISAT/Saferworld. February.

Wood, Brian and Johan Peleman. 1999. *The Arms

Fixers: Controlling the Brokers and Shipping
Agents*. Oslo: PRIO.

____. 2000. 'Making the Deal and Moving the Goods:
The Role of Brokers and Shippers.' In Lora Lumpe,
ed. *Running Guns: The Global Market in Small
Arms*. London: Zed Books.

Wood, Brian, Johan Peleman and Brian Johnson-
Thomas. 2000. *Arms Brokers and Shippers*.
Background Paper. Geneva: Small Arms Survey.

Wulf, Herbert. 2000. *Regulating Small Arms
Brokering in the United Nations*. Background
Paper. Geneva: Small Arms Survey.

ZBC Radio. 2000. 'Zimbabwe Defence Industries
Outline 'Barter Trade' with DR Congo.' 20 August.
(BBC Monitoring Service, 26 August).

Zia, Amir. 2000. 'Gun Dealers on Pakistan Border
Chafe at Change in Rules.' *The Associated Press*.
22 July.

4

A Thriving Trade:
Global Legal Small Arms Transfers

Introduction

Based on both official and unofficial sources, the annual legal global trade in small arms and light weapons represents a brisk business, estimated at between US$ 4-6 billion. It accounts for at least 80-90 per cent of the total annual value of trade in small arms.

It is essential to emphasize that—initially at least—the overwhelming majority of small arms are sold and transferred legally. This is true for transfers both to governments and their agencies, and to private citizens. This legalized trade in small arms is a legitimate economic activity, based on the security, or other needs of states and individuals.

Figure 4.1 Small arms transfers: The legality spectrum

LEGAL TRANSFERS: These occur with either active or passive involvement of governments or their authorized agents, and in accordance with both national and international law.	**ILLICIT GREY MARKET TRANSFERS:** These happen when governments or their agents exploit loopholes or circumvent national and/or international laws or policy.	**ILLEGAL BLACK MARKET TRANSFERS:** In clear violation of national and/or international laws and without official government consent or control, these transfers may involve corrupt government officials acting on their own for personal gain.

Legal transfers—as opposed to grey or black market transfers (ILLICIT TRANSFERS)—are defined as those carried out by governments or their authorized agents in accordance with both international and national laws and with the policies of exporting and recipient states. Although officially authorized, available evidence suggests that even legal small arms transfers may, under unfavourable circumstances, contribute to destabilizing accumulations of weapons and provide a ready supply to the grey or black small arms markets. For this reason, any study of illicitsmall arms transfers should also examine their legal context.

There are several ways in which legal transfers of small arms can contribute to destabilizing small arms accumulations, as well as feeding into illegal markets. First, as they are replaced by newer models, older weapons can 'cascade' into the black or grey markets. Second, new weapons may add to already saturated stockpiles, driving prices down and increasing the market availability of small arms. Third, legal transfers can end up in countries where inadequate stockpile monitoring and security, as well as corrupt officials, may render these weapons easy targets for re-transfer into the illicit market.

In order to preclude, or at least mitigate, these circumstances, it is necessary to develop a comprehensive evidence base on the legal trade in small arms. With such a picture, states and their agencies are better equipped to ensure that the weapons they export stay within the legal market.

The global illicit small arms trade is examined in Chapter 5 of this Survey.

Unloading arms, Bosnia (Associated Press/Peter Andrews)

Box 4.1 Scrutinizing the scope of legal transfers

Legal transfers are defined as transfers that occur with the involvement, whether active or passive, of governments or government authorities, in accordance with both national and international law. 'Active' means that arms sales are initiated and officially carried out by governments; 'passive' means that governments license arms sales by private companies.

According to the 1997 *UN Report of the Panel of Governmental Experts on Small Arms*, 'legitimate trade occurs among Governments or among legal entities authorized by Governments'. With legal transfers, governments approve sales through legal instruments, such as export licences on the part of the seller, end user/end-use certificates on the part of the recipient, or through approval by national parliaments or specific government agencies. In many countries, the defence industry is nationalized; thus, any sale of small arms is implicitly a legal government sale.

Some legal transfers are less than transparent; however, this does not necessarily mean that they are illicit. Many countries maintain secrecy regarding such transfers due to national security or commercial confidentiality concerns. Such transfers fall under the heading of legal covert transfers; that is, transfers that are not necessarily in violation of any national or international law but that are nevertheless carried out in a clandestine manner.

To shed light on the ambiguous area of legal covert trade, it is helpful to look at the way the issue has been addressed by the UN, which has noted that 'during the Cold War ... States have secretly carried out transfers of small arms and light weapons. Such transfers are not necessarily illicit. Any transfer not approved by the competent authorities in the recipient State could, however, be classified by that State as interference in its internal affairs and therefore illegal' (United Nations, 1997).

A number of governments and researchers have identified sub-categories of legal transfers. The problem with such detailed definitions is that they are based on national legislation, gun laws, and reporting practices and are, in general, not universally applicable.

Each country has its own way of classifying arms transfers. For example, the United States, arguably the largest exporter by value of small arms and ammunition, categorizes three methods of legal transfers:

- Foreign Military Sales (FMS): Direct government-to-government sales of new or used weapons;
- Free or low-cost transfers of arms: These may take the form of grants, loans, or aid provided to countries with the express purpose of procuring arms. Such transfers usually take place when the importing country is unable to pay for the arms or if payment would put undue financial strain on the country of destination; and
- Direct Commercial Sales (DCS): Negotiated between the arms manufacturing industry and the buyer.

By way of comparison, Australia identifies the following legal small arms transfer forms:
- Government-to-government transfers, including in the form of aid;
- Commercial sales;
- Private imports: Individuals ordering and importing declared firearms;
- Private sales (e.g. through a firearms dealer); and
- Club armourers: selling or buying of firearms for, or on behalf of, club members (Mouzos, 1999).

By comparing and contrasting these American and Australian definitions, it can be seen that national classifications or definitions of legal arms transfers are generally based on domestic gun legislation or export control regulations and do not currently reflect any universally accepted norms or terminology.

It follows that these two examples of arms sales classifications are by no means applicable to the rest of the world. Even within the US, distinctions are made between trade in military small arms exports and trade in firearms although, for the most part, the UN definition of small arms covers both categories. Thus, it is clear that there is an urgent need to develop universally applicable and acceptable definitions, norms, and standards in the area of small arms and light weapons.

Each country has its own way of classifying arms transfers, based on national legislation, gun laws, and reporting practices.

In surveying the global legal trade in small arms and light weapons, this chapter addresses the following four questions:

- **What are the available sources of data on the worldwide legal small arms trade?**
- **How comprehensive and accurate are these data?**
- **What is the scope (i.e. volume, value, trade flow) of the global legal trade in small arms?**
- **Which countries are the major legal small arms suppliers and recipients?**

Data issues

In the field of small arms, many researchers contend that a comprehensive, accurate, and meaningful assessment of global trade is currently impossible.[1] To start with, precise dollar figures for the global small arms trade, both legal and illicit, have been virtually impossible to calculate. Now, however, the increasing quantity and quality of government export reports and UN statistics vastly exceeds that of ten, or even five, years ago. Every year, in fact, more countries reveal data on their arms exports. It is this statistical data on the small arms trade, along with some anecdotal media reports, that this chapter analyzes. It is expected that, as greater quantities of reliable data become available, a more accurate picture of the small arms trade will emerge. This, in turn, will open avenues to new policy options to stem the uncontrolled flow of small arms and light weapons and to reduce the destabilizing accumulations of these weapons.

Lack of uniformity in national reporting makes it difficult to estimate the global legal trade in small arms.

Major conventional weapons research: Collecting data on arms transfers is not new. Research institutes such as the Stockholm International Peace Research Institute (SIPRI) in Sweden and the International Institute of Strategic Studies (IISS) in the United Kingdom have supplied data on arms transfers and military spending for decades. *The UN Register of Conventional Arms* (UNRCA) is now entering its seventh year; 90 countries made submissions for its 1999 calendar year (United Nations, 2000).[2] However, data from these sources are concerned primarily with larger conventional arms rather than with small arms and light weapons.

Small arms trade research: In addition, a number of research institutions and NGOs have begun to collect information on small arms transfers in the last few years. Most notable is the Norwegian Initiative on Small Arms Transfers (NISAT), which has a searchable website (www.nisat.org) with extensive data on this subject. Others, such as the Institute for Security Studies (ISS) in South Africa, the Regional Centre for Strategic Studies (RCSS) in Sri Lanka, and the Institute for Defence Studies and Analyses (IDSA) in India, collect regional data on small arms transfers. However, such specialized institutions are hard put to produce comprehensive assessments of the value or volume of these transfers. Investigative reporting and analyses by a number of NGOs (e.g. Human Rights Watch, Oxfam), as well as reports in specialized defence and military publications, also contribute to the growing reservoir of information on both legal and illicit small arms transfers.

National reporting: As mentioned previously, in recent years, there has been a significant improvement in the quality and quantity of official information on small arms transfers. A small, but growing, number of countries have adopted more transparent policies by publishing regular arms export reports that include information on small arms transfers.

Unfortunately, official data on small arms transfers contained in these various government reports do not lend themselves to direct comparison since there is no universal definition, terminology, or reporting format. For example, a number of countries include hand grenades in the same export category as bombs and torpedoes. Some list ammunition in their small arms category while others list it separately, often in categories that include ammunition for major weapons systems. Such lack of uniformity makes it difficult to create an accurate picture of the global legal trade in small arms.

Inter-governmental monitoring: International organizations, such as the United Nations (UN), the European Union (EU), and the Organization for Security and Cooperation in Europe (OSCE), also contribute to the growing volume of information on small arms transfers.[3] For example, customs data are compiled under the auspices of the UN in its COMTRADE database (see below); an annual report in accordance with its Code of Conduct on Arms Exports is published by the EU; and fact-finding missions and field reports have been executed by the OSCE.

Small arms customs data: One of the only sources of comprehensive international data on the legal small arms trade is the COMTRADE database, which reports national customs trade data to the United Nations Statistical Division. However, even despite harmonized customs reporting systems, these data are not entirely comparable. In addition, only 33 countries currently submit data on exports of military firearms, pistols, and revolvers to this database—and they do not include a number of the world's major small arms exporters, such as Bulgaria, Israel, and the Russian Federation. Furthermore, the categories reported do not coincide with the previously cited definition of small arms formulated by the UN panel of experts. Finally, COMTRADE reports only data for countries that export over US$ 50,000 worth of arms per category ('military firearms' or 'pistols and revolvers') over a period of five years. Thus, reports from countries submitting data beneath this threshold are not reflected. And yet, inadequate as these data are for a variety of reasons, COMTRADE is virtually the only source for determining the financial magnitude of the small arms trade.

Small arms, light weapons, and associated ammunition may comprise only five per cent of the total value of legal arms exports; yet these weapons can account for up to 90 per cent of casualties in armed conflicts.

The scope of the legal global trade in small arms

The scope of the legal global small arms trade is described below in terms of financial value and physical volume.

Share: There are diverse and quite disparate estimates for the value of the annual legal global trade in small arms as a percentage of total arms trade. An analysis of available official statistics from government export reports suggests that the average annual value of legal small arms exports accounts for only about three per cent of total conventional arms exports; when associated ammunition is included, this figure climbs to about five per cent (see Table 4.1). Although a figure of 13 per cent, generated by the US Arms Control and Disarmament Agency (ACDA), is often cited as the value of annual trade in small arms and ammunition as a percentage of total arms exports (Renner, 1999), current research suggests that this estimate is substantially overvalued.

Table 4.1   Small arms and ammunition as a percentage of total legal arms exports

Country	ReportingYear	Value Total Arms Exports	Value Small Arms Exports	Small Arms as % of Total Arms Exports	Ammunition Exports	Ammunition as % of Total Arms Exports	Small Arms & Ammunition Exports	Arms & Ammunition as % of Total Arms Exports
Belgium	1999	$238.0 mil.	$33.0 mil.	14.0%	$23.0 mil.	10%	$56.0 mil.	24%
Canada	1998	$292.0 mil.	$6.0 mil.	2.0%	$13.0 mil.	4%	$19.0 mil.	6%
Finland	1998	$31.0 mil.	$0.5 mil.	2.0%	$4.0 mil.	13%	4.5 mil.	15%
Netherlands	1998	$369.0 mil.	$1.0 mil.	0.20%	$46.0 mil.	12%	$47.0 mil.	12%
Norway	1998	$130.0 mil.	$0.075 mil.	0.05%	$32.5 mil.	25%	$32.5 mil.	25%
Russian Fed.	1999	$3400.0 mil.	n.a.	n.a.	n.a.	n.a.	$100.0 mil.	3%
South Africa	1999	$178.0 mil.	n.a.	n.a.	n.a.	n.a.	$9.0 mil.	5%
South Korea	1997	$69.4 mil.	$5.3 mil.	8.0%	$38.3 mil.	55%	$43.6 mil.	63%
Sweden	1998	$413.0 mil.	$0.353 mil.	0.08%	$42.0 mil.	10%	$42.0 mil.	10%
United States	1998	$20000.0 mil.	n.a.	n.a.	n.a.	n.a.	$ 1000.0 mil.	5%
Weighted Averages				**3.0%**		**12%**		**5%**

Sources: Government reports and press reports

Small arms, light weapons, and associated ammunition—despite the fact that they comprise only an estimated five per cent of the total value of legal arms exports—may nevertheless account for up to 90 per cent of casualties in armed conflicts (EFFECTS).

Value: *The SIPRI Yearbook 2000* estimates that the global legal trade in conventional arms in 1998 was worth between US$ 35-49 billion. Applying the range of estimates of the small arms trade cited above (between 5-13 per cent) to the SIPRI data for conventional arms results in a range of US$ 2-6 billion annually. Other data, however, suggests that any figure below US$ 3 billion may be too low.

Although one study (Boutwell and Klare, 2000) estimated that the legal trade in small arms is worth between US$ 7-10 billion, existing data suggests that this figure is too high. Adding together existing information from both official sources (e.g. government export reports, customs data, UN data) and unofficial estimates cited in the press and elsewhere gives a figure of about US$ 3 billion for the total legal trade. However, official figures for several possible major small arms exporters, such as Israel and Bulgaria, are not available. In addition, figures available for a number of countries do not include light weapons or ammunition. If one includes estimates for the value of these countries' small arms exports, then the range of US$ 4-6 billion is an estimate substantiated by official export data figures.[4]

Attempts to estimate the value of the legal global trade in small arms are complicated by a number of other factors. The sales prices of small arms manufactured in China or the Russian Federation are not comparable to those made, for instance, in the US or Belgium. Furthermore, small arms are often donated or sold below market prices. Thus, the utility of trying to quantify the monetary value of the legal global trade in small arms without a better evidence base is questionable. Nevertheless, despite the limited value of current monetary estimates of the global trade in small arms, enough data—both official and unofficial, including media reports—does exist to identify trade patterns and provide illustrative accounts of transfers.

Volume: Quantifying the volume (i.e. actual quantities) of the legal global trade in small arms is considered by many researchers and policy-makers even more fundamentally crucial than the monetary value. Quantification refers to information on the actual numbers of guns and ammunition transferred and thus, indirectly, the military capabilities of given security forces. It is the volume that is more important when it comes to the leakage or diversion of small arms from legal to illicit markets.

With the exception of a few countries (e.g. Italy, the UK, the US), very little official information on the magnitude of the legal small arms trade, including ammunition, is available. Based on data currently available, it is therefore virtually impossible to calculate a 'fool-proof figure' for the total number of small arms and light weapons traded annually. Without more reliable, in-depth data, only an informed estimate is possible.

Based on the estimate of US$ 4-6 billion in legal transfers cited earlier, and adding an illicit trade estimate of less than US$ 1 billion annually, it is calculated that at least 80-90 per cent of the total world trade in small arms is legal (ILLICIT TRANSFERS). This is substantially greater than the 50-60 per cent estimate reported by the Office of the UN Secretary General in the year 2000 (Annan, 2000).

Small arms exporters

Small arms are produced in at least 95 of the world's 200-some countries (PRODUCERS). However, fewer than two-thirds of the states that produce small arms officially admit to exporting them. A recent study estimated that nearly 70 countries were exporting small arms as of the year 2000 (Lumpe, 2000). The Small Arms Survey positively identified at least 60 of them, using official and unofficial data. However, this figure did not include countries that are known sources of illicit small arms transfers, such as Albania, Libya, and Afghanistan. When such countries are also included, it is probable that more than 70 countries are involved in the export of small arms, both legal and illicit.

The annual legal global trade in small arms and light weapons is estimated to be worth between US$ 4-6 billion.

At least 80-90 per cent of the total world trade in small arms starts out legally.

According to information submitted to the 1999 *UN International Study on Firearm Regulation*, only 35 of a total of 78 reporting states officially admitted to having legal businesses within their territories that export firearms, small arms components, and/or ammunition.[5] In addition, the results are rendered incomplete by the fact that certain exporters, such as France, Iran, and Norway, which were part of the study, provided no information on legal firearms exports. Other states, such as Croatia, Indonesia, and Malaysia, which were also part of the study, denied any legal exports of firearms, despite submitting customs data to the COMTRADE database. Moreover, a number of well-known small arms exporters, such as Bulgaria, Italy, Israel, the Netherlands, Pakistan, and Portugal, did not respond to the study.

Thus, based on current information from all available sources, it appears that at least 60 of the 95 producer countries are involved in the legal export of small arms. What is not clear is whether the other 35 or so producers of small arms are also legal exporters, illicit exporters, or solely domestic producers? On the receiving end of the exports equation, it appears that a far larger number of states—in fact, virtually all countries in the world—are legal importers of small arms, for use by government security forces and/or by private individuals. This aspect of the legal small arms trade is treated later in the chapter.

At least 95 countries produce small arms. At least 60 countries admit to legally exporting them while as many as 200 countries legally import small arms for use by their security forces and/or by private individuals.

UN data on legal small arms exports

The COMTRADE database provides information on exports and imports of military firearms, pistols and revolvers. The category 'military firearms' does not include sporting firearms, revolvers, pistols, ammunition, or grenades, all of which fall under different categories.[6]

In the category of **military firearms**, according to COMTRADE's incomplete data, the total value of exports in 1998 was US\$ 709 million. While this figure is useful as a reference point for the total annual trade in small arms, it must be kept in mind that only 26 of the 60 or more countries that legally export small arms submitted data at least once during the period 1994-98. The top 1998 exporters, in descending financial value, were the USA, the Netherlands, the UK, China, and Canada.[7]

Twenty-seven countries also provided data over the 1994-98 reporting period to COMTRADE on the export of **pistols and revolvers**.[8] The total value of their exports for 1998 was over US\$ 148 million. The top five exporters in 1998, in descending order, were Germany, Italy, the US, the Czech Republic, and Switzerland. Taken together, these COMTRADE figures place the value of military firearms, pistols, and revolver exports that passed through customs during 1998 at over US\$ 850 million.

Countries that have exported an average of more than US\$ 1 million worth of small arms annually over the five-year period 1994-98 are listed in Table 4.2. Despite the insights provided by this table, there are a number of caveats with the COMTRADE data. *First*, COMTRADE does not include many of the world's major and mid-level small arms producers and exporters, such as Belgium, Brazil, Bulgaria, Pakistan, and the Russian Federation. *Second*, the data are mostly customs data; thus, many transactions are not covered (e.g. military transfers, such as 'donations' of surplus arms, which do not go through customs). *Third*, the data do not correspond to the UN definition of 'small arms and light weapons'. *Fourth*, a threshold of exports exceeding US\$ 50,000 over five years must be attained for the country to even be listed in the report.

The value of military firearms, pistols, and revolver exports that passed through customs during 1998 was over US\$ 850 million.

In addition to COMTRADE, there is also a significant amount of data from government export reports, industry reports, and other official and unofficial sources which permit a classification by value of the world's small arms exporters into major, mid-level, and minor categories. An additional 'shadow category' remains: the one for countries that are known to be legal small arms exporters but for which neither official nor unofficial data have been provided.

Table 4.3 uses a number of sources to classify countries as to their small arms exports by value.

Table 4.2 Average annual value of small arms exported through customs, 1994-98

Country	Military Firearms Value of exports	Country	Pistols and Revolvers Value of exports
United States	$367 million	Austria*	$57 million
Netherlands*	$140 million	Germany	$48 million
United Kingdom*	$57 million	United States	$42 million
China*	$23 million	Italy	$34 million
Switzerland	$16 million	Czech Republic*	$15 million
Romania*	$10 million	Spain	$13 million
Canada	$6 million	Canada	$8 million
Poland	$5 million	Switzerland	$8 million
Austria*	$3 million	Portugal	$6 million
		United Kingdom*	$5 million
		Argentina	$4 million
		China*	$4 million
		Poland	$2 million
		Rep. of Korea	$2 million

* Certain countries did not submit data for all five years but instead for a briefer period only: Austria (1994), China (1998), the Netherlands (1997-98), Romania (1995-96), the UK (1994-96, 1998), and the Czech Republic (1995-98).

Source: COMTRADE, UN Customs Data

It must be emphasized that the data available are not comparable in all respects. Still, they provide a general picture of global small arms exports. Some countries' figures, such as Sweden's, include exports of parts for small arms while others, such as Spain, cover only exports of pistols and revolvers based on COMTRADE data. The table's source legend provides additional information. While dollar values are available for two-thirds of identified legal exporters of small arms, no figures are available for the remaining third, which includes possible major exporters such as Bulgaria and Israel.

Official government data on legal exports of small arms

A growing number of countries now produce annual arms export reports, with comprehensive data on the value and, in some cases, the volume of exports to individual countries (SIPRI, 2000). In addition, some countries provide information on arms transfers as part of their national customs data. All told, nearly 30 countries provide public information, either from government or industry sources, on arms exports (SIPRI, 2000, pp. 436-440).

Countries such as Canada, Chile, Finland, South Africa, the UK, and the US also provide official data on the value of small arms exports, disaggregated by importing country. However, only Italy, the UK, and the US provide data on actual quantities of small arms exports. Other countries, such as Belgium, the Netherlands, Norway, and Sweden, provide data on small arms exports, but not disaggregated by country; or if so, then within a category that contains military exports other than small arms and light weapons.

As a result, there are a number of problems regarding the usefulness, reliability, and accuracy of such official data. As pointed out earlier, each reporting country has its own definition of 'small arms'.

Table 4.3 The 60 known legal small arms exporting countries

1. Major Exporters (More Than US$ 75 Million Annually)		2. Mid-Level Exporters (Between US$ 1 Million and US$ 75 Million Annually)		3. Minor Exporters (Less Than US$ 1 Million Annually)	4. Value Unknown
Country/Year	US$ Value/Source	Country/Year	US$ Value/Source	Country	Country
Brazil (99)	$100-150 million(D)	Argentina (98)	$3 million (B)	Australia (B)	Armenia (C)
Germany* auth (99)	$384 million(A)	Austria (94)	$60 million (B)	Chile (A)	Belarus (C)
Russian Fed.* (99)	$100-150 million(D)	Belgium (99)	$33 million (A)	Colombia (B)	Bosnia (C)
United States* auth(98)	over $1.2 billion (A)	Canada* (98)	$26 million (D)	Croatia (B)	Bulgaria (C)
4 Countries:	**Total: ±$2 billion**	China (98)	$27 million (B)	Denmark (B)	Cyprus* (E)
		Czech Republic* (99)	$59 million (C)	Japan (B)	Ecuador* (E)
		Finland* (98)	$5 million (A)	India (B)	Egypt (C)
		France (99)	$23 million (A)	Indonesia (B)	Greece (C)
		Italy (98)	$28 million (B)	Latvia (B)	Hungary* (E)
		Pakistan* (99)	$30 million (C)	Malaysia (B)	Iran (C)
		Poland* (99)	$40 million (C)	Mexico (B)	Israel (C)
		Romania (95,96 avg.)	$10 million (B)	Netherlands** (A)	Kazakhstan (C)
		Spain (98)	$7 million (B)	New Zealand (B)	Jordan (C)
		South Africa* (99)	$9 million (A)	Norway (B)	North Korea (C)
		South Korea* (97)	$43 million (A)	Philippines (B)	Singapore (E)
		Sweden* (98)	$40 million (A)	Portugal (B)	Slovenia* (E)
		Switzerland (98)	$10 million (B)	Slovakia (B)	Ukraine (C)
		United Kingdom (98)	$44 million (B)	Swaziland*** (A)	Zimbabwe (C)
		18 Countries:	**Total: $497 million**	Thailand (B)	**18 Countries:**
				Turkey (B)	**Unknown**
				20 Countries: less than $10 million total	**Value**

Source Code
A – National government reports
B – COMTRADE
C – Figures reported in the press
D – Calculation based on several reports
E – Declared exporter in firearms study
* – Includes ammunition
** – COMTRADE reported that US$ 187 million worth of military firearms, pistols, and revolvers passed through Dutch customs as exports in 1998
*** – Re-exports of commercial firearms, no domestic production
auth. – Authorized sales may not correspond to actual sales

So, while national efforts to increase transparency are to be commended, there are still serious gaps, as will be demonstrated below.

Nevertheless, reviewing each of these reports individually does provide valuable insights into the legal trade in small arms and light weapons. For most countries, the most recent data are from 1998, as it appears to take a year on average to compile data from the previous year. There are several reasons why an analysis of government reports of the legal small arms trade is useful:

- It illustrates the lack of norms and standards so essential for comparable data by highlighting the different definitions of small arms used by individual governments;
- It points out substantial data gaps while at the same time accentuating the usefulness of the data reported;
- It highlights patterns in legal small arms trade, both in terms of suppliers and recipients, and provides evidence of instances in which weapons are legally transferred to regions of conflict and instability, countries with records of human rights violations, or centres of illicit trafficking; and,
- It highlights the transparency of certain countries' reporting practices, providing impetus to others to improve their small arms transfers reporting standards and transparency.

The following section analyzes selected official government reports that are in the public domain. As will be seen, reporting methodology differs widely, with some countries concentrating on the volume of licenses, transfers, etc. while others focus on the financial value. These reports were chosen solely based on availability, easy access to the research community, and relatively comprehensive coverage of small arms and light weapons. A more detailed study of these reports will be presented in a forthcoming *Small Arms Survey Occasional Paper*.

Austria: The report on its military exports for 1998 listed export licences granted by weapons category and geographical export region. Austria granted a total of 14,258 licenses for small arms exports in 1998 and 2,735,751 licenses for ammunition exports. This is not to say that all these transactions took place, as they were only licenses granted, and not necessarily acted upon in 1998. At the time of the report, the monetary value of the licenses was not available. The primary recipients of Austrian small arms licenses were EU countries (5,065 licenses) and non-EU countries in Europe (8,692 licenses). The primary recipients for Austrian ammunition licenses in 1998 were Australia and the Pacific region (1,049,768 licenses). Licenses, however, give no actual indication of value or volume as they may be granted for one weapon only—or for thousands at a time.

Belgium: In terms of value, Belgium exported US$ 33 million (BEF 1.3 billion)[9] in 1999 under the category, 'military arms other than revolvers, pistols and swords', a marked decrease from the US$ 79 million (BEF 3.1 billion) exported in 1995. This category does not include military vehicles, motorized weapons, ammunition, or projectiles, which are listed separately.

Brazil: Value-related data on Brazil's small arms exports is available from the Brazilian Ministry of Industry and Commerce. Although all amounts cited below exclude pistols and revolvers, which constitute the majority of Brazilian small arms exports,[10] in 1999, Brazil exported US$ 44,883,106 worth of small arms. Previous years' exports of small arms were as follows: US$ 59,293,712 in 1996; US$ 47,445,181 in 1997; and US$ 42,729,865 in 1998.[11]

Canada: Since 1996, Canada has provided fairly detailed and easily accessible public information on its arms exports in the form of *The Export of Military Goods from Canada: Annual Report*. The Department of Foreign Affairs and International Trade (DFAIT) produces this report from its Export and Import Controls Bureau. Export data for 1998 lists the value of exports in Canadian dollars by importing country and military good component category. Category 2001 is defined as 'arms and automatic weapons with a calibre of 12.7 mm or less and accessories'. Unfortunately, actual quantities of weapons and accessories are not given, although there is an indication as to whether the exports were 'firearms' or 'parts'. Other categories, such as 2002, include light weapons as well as larger weapon systems, so it is difficult to assess Canada's actual exports of small arms and light weapons in terms of the UN definition based on the data provided by the Canadian Government.

The main drawback of the report is that it does not enumerate all Canadian small arms exports. Due to Canadian and US defence-sharing arrangements, exports to the US are not listed. The report does state, however, that 1998 military exports to the US accounted for about half of all Canadian military exports. Based on US customs import data, Canada exported to the US over US$ 17 million worth of pistols and revolvers and over US$ 3.5 million of military rifle parts between 1996 and 1998.

By value, the top six destinations for Canada's small arms exports between 1996-98 were: the United States, the Netherlands, Denmark, Germany, Thailand, and Italy. The top importers of Canadian small arms were Western countries, with the exception of Thailand and the Philippines.

The total value of Canadian small arms exports (Category 2001, not including ammunition and larger weapons systems and excluding US defence-sharing exports) for 1998 was US$ 6.5 million (CAD 9.4 million). This is a considerable drop from its 1997 small arms exports, which amounted to US$ 16 million (CAD 23 million).

Arms export licenses give no actual indication of value or volume as they may be granted for one weapon only—or for thousands at a time.

Canada's top six destinations by value for small arms exports between 1996-98 were: the US, the Netherlands, Denmark, Germany, Thailand, and Italy.

Chile: Chile reports its exports of firearms using customs data, which is accessible on the web at www.exportmall.cl.[12] While these data do not include government military exports, they do list commercial exports of military firearms, as well as pistols and revolvers. The Chilean commercial small arms export market is modest in comparison to others (only US$ 355,000 worth for 1997 and 1998 combined). Nonetheless, Chile has one of the more transparent small arms exports reporting practices. The major destinations for Chilean exports of firearms, by value, during 1997 and 1998 were the US, Canada, and the Cape Verde Islands.

Finland: Finland provides a very detailed report of its 'defence materiel exports', disaggregated by country. Category A is 'light weapons and their components' and is further broken down by type. For the most part, Finland's exports of small arms consist of sniper rifles. The Finnish report also details the export of 'ammunition shots, etc. and their components' under Category C. Value is given in Finnish marks in the official report; however, the actual quantity of weapons exported is not given. The Finnish small arms export industry by value is quite small, only US$ 417,000 (FIM 2,458,700) total exports in 1998 for Category A defence items. It has a larger market for its Category C ammunition: US$ 4.5 million (FIM 26,294,000) total exports in 1998. Finland's primary export markets in Europe are Germany, Norway, Denmark, Spain, and Sweden. Oman is its major non-European market.

Germany: In 2000, Germany published a comprehensive report on the values of its 1999 small arms export licenses, worth a total of $US 384 million (DM 746 million). For category A 0001 (firearms and parts), it issued 3,284 small arms export licenses worth US$ 237 million (DM 461 million) in 1999.[13] It also issued 1,138 licenses for ammunition (category A 0003) worth US$ 147 million (DM 285 million).

In 1999 Germany issued licenses worth US$ 384 million for the export of firearms and ammunition.

Germany lists total military export licenses by country. When a large number of exports fall under one category, that category's percentage of total exports is listed. This provides a partial view of which countries are importing small arms. For example, in 1999, Germany authorized firearms exports to the US worth US$ 174.4 million (DM 338.5 million)—the bulk of total German small arms exports. It authorized US$ 10.1 million (DM 19.7 million) for Switzerland, and US$ 7.5 million (DM 14.6 million) worth of firearms and parts for Spain. Other major authorizations for firearms exports included Lithuania with US$ 1.85 million (DM 3.58 million); Bulgaria, US$ 1.44 million (DM 2.79 million); and Thailand US$ 405,000 (DM 785,000). Germany reported exports under category A 0001 items to nearly every EU country although neither specific amounts nor percentages were provided. The German report can be found on the web at www.bmwi.de.

Italy: Data are regularly provided to the Italian Senate on authorizations and deliveries of overall arms exports. Unlike many other countries, quantities of weapons exported, by company, are also given in the report. According to this report, in 1998, Beretta alone exported 525 pistols worth US$ 300,000 (ITL 572 million) and parts worth US$ 200,000 (ITL 450 million). At the time of this writing, full details of the Italian report could not be accessed. However, these figures do not correspond at all to COMTRADE data which reflected US$ 28 million worth of pistols and revolvers exported by Italy in 1998.

Italy exported US$ 28 million worth of pistols and revolvers in 1998, according to COMTRADE data.

Netherlands: The Netherlands publishes details of its small arms exports in semi-annual and annual reports. In 1999, the Netherlands exported US$ 686,000 (NLG 1.5 million) worth of 'small calibre weapons ≤12.7mm'. Previous figures for this category were US$ 823,000 (NLG 1.8 million) in 1998 and US$ 640,000 (NLG 1.4 million) in 1997.

In comparison with data submitted by the Netherlands to COMTRADE, which reported over US$ 187 million worth of military firearms and pistols exports in 1998, glaring discrepancies are evident. However, the Netherlands has gone through a recent upgrade of its armed forces and purchased new small arms for its troops. Since replaced weapons were slated for destruction, it appears that these exports were not older weapons cascaded into other markets. One possible explanation for the far higher COMTRADE figures is that they represent small arms 'in transit' that have been held in customs warehouses in the Netherlands before being shipped elsewhere. Since many countries declare goods in transit that pass through their customs, the Netherlands could be following suit in supplying this information to COMTRADE. In any case, these data indicate the importance of the Netherlands as a major trans-shipment point for small arms.

Norway: Norway has been active in promoting transparency in the small arms trade, most notably through its support of NISAT. In its 1998 report on military exports, Norway reported US\$ 76,000 (NOK 609,000) in military small arms. It also exported US\$ 32.5 million (NOK 261 million) worth of ammunition and explosives in 1999. Norway's exports of hand grenades fall under the same category as exports of bombs, torpedoes, and rockets, which amounted to US\$ 1 million (NOK 8 million) in 1998.

South Africa: The South African Directorate Conventional Arms Control (DCAC) based in the Department of Defence has published data on South Africa's conventional arms exports since 1995. It divides them into five categories. Category B covers 'all types of infantry hand-held and portable assault weapons and associated ammunition of a calibre smaller than 12.7mm'. As is the case with all governments that provide such information, this definition does not correspond to the UN definition on small arms and light weapons. Light weapons of a calibre greater than 12.7 mm, as well as grenades and portable missiles, are covered under Category A, which also includes tanks and fighter aircraft.

South Africa's small arms exports have decreased somewhat since 1997, when a total of US\$ 15.2 million (ZAR 93.2 million) worth of Category B arms were exported. In 1998 South African exports of Category B arms totalled US\$ 8.4 million (ZAR 51.3 million), and in 1999 exports were up to US\$ 9 million (ZAR 55 million). The top recipients of South African small arms in 1999 were Singapore, Germany, Greece, Colombia, and Pakistan.

South Korea: South Korea published the value of its arms exports from 1990 to 1997 in its Defense Ministry White Paper. Although the categories of weapons were somewhat ambiguous, there were two—'guns' and 'ammunition'—that would logically cover small arms according to the UN definition. In 1997, South Korea exported US\$ 5.3 million worth of guns and US\$ 38.3 million worth of ammunition. The eight-year high for gun exports from South Korea was in 1995, when US\$ 12.2 million worth was exported. The total value of guns exported from South Korea from 1990-97 (inclusive) was US\$ 51.5 million, and for ammunition, US\$ 179.1 million.

Sweden: The Swedish Government has reported the value of its arms sales since 1993. The 1998 report stated that no small-calibre barrel weapons were exported in 1997 or 1998. However, Sweden does export small arms parts, the value of which was US\$ 705,000 (SEK 6 million) in 1997 and US\$ 352,000 (SEK 3 million) in 1998. These categories do not include ammunition, of which Sweden exported US\$ 16 million (SEK 138 million) worth in 1997 and US\$ 42 million (SEK 358 million) worth in 1998. One must take into account that Sweden's ammunition exports also include ammunition for larger weapons systems.

United Kingdom: In its 1999 *Annual Report on Strategic Export Controls*, issued in August 2000, the UK listed exports of small arms, by quantity, value, and country of destination, for the first time. Formerly, small arms were lumped together with other military items in a more general military equipment category. This report states that small arms data were derived from customs records for tariff codes 9301000 (military weapons), 93020010 (pistols), and 93020090 (revolvers).

The report indicates that the UK exported 4,471 'weapons and small arms' to countries outside the EU in 1999, including a donation of 10,000 self-loading rifles to Sierra Leone that was not declared through customs. The fact that these 10,000 rifles do not appear in the customs data highlights the limitations of depending exclusively on customs data to monitor a country's small arms exports. Another limitation of the UK report is that it does not list small arms exports to EU countries. Following Sierra Leone, which was far and away the largest recipient of small arms from the UK, the top 1999 importers were Chile, the United States, the Philippines, the United Arab Emirates, and Switzerland.

The Netherlands is a major trans-shipment point for small arms.

The top recipients of South African small arms in 1999 were Singapore, Germany, Greece, Colombia, and Pakistan.

United States: According to available data, the US is the world's largest exporter of small arms and light weapons in terms of value. A report by the General Accounting Office (GAO) in 2000 calculated that the US authorized the export or delivery of US$ 3.7 billion worth of small arms, light weapons and associated ammunition to a total of 154 nations for fiscal years 1996 through 1998 (GAO Report, 2000a).

The US Government provides arms export data through a multiplicity of reports from its various departments and agencies. The result is that, despite laudable efforts at transparency, data are often contradictory, incomplete, and not comparable.

- **The 655 Report:** To strengthen public oversight of arms trade data, the *655 Report*, prepared jointly by the Department of Defense (DOD) and the Department of State (DOS), is issued each year. However, each department prepares different sections of the report and each uses different reporting methods.

  For example, DOS reports authorized commercial sales, as opposed to actual deliveries. These approvals or licenses granted for commercial sales are valid for a period of four years. This time frame allows for interventions on the part of Congress or the public at large to intervene in the case of arms transfers which may be perceived as particularly dangerous. As a result, a number of announced arms transfers never actually take place. The US is one of the few countries that publishes data on proposed sales in a manner timely enough that such transfers can be stopped if concerns arise.

  In contrast to the State Department, the US Defense Department reports actual deliveries of foreign military sales, grants of 'Excess Defence Articles' (EDA),[14] and military assistance. As a result, there are two completely different reporting systems and sets of data on exports that are, consequently, not comparable. In addition, each department lists weapons systems in a different manner. For example, the DOD lists the category 'rifles' in its report while the DOS is more descriptive, sometimes distinguishing between models (e.g. M-16) and whether or not they are 'military' or 'non-military'. Further, even within the DOD, foreign military sales have a different reporting format and terminology than EDA transfers. The result is that, despite—or precisely because of—this profusion of facts and figures, there is little clarity on the actual number or nature of small arms deliveries.

  Still, the US is one of the few countries that reports quantities of actual weapons exported, or approved for export, by type. To its credit, the drawbacks of the *655 Report* have been acknowledged and steps taken to provide a more accurate picture of actual military exports. To improve monitoring, the *Foreign Relations Authorization Act for Fiscal Years 2000 and 2001* instructs actual deliveries of commercial sales of defence articles to be reported to the State Department in order that they be included in future *655 Reports*.

- **US Customs Data:** A secondary official data source on US arms exports is to be found in the form of customs data, compiled by the US Census Bureau, and provided, dating back to 1989, on CD-ROM. This customs data states that it includes FMS, as well as actual commercial deliveries of small arms. However, there is clear evidence that this is not always the case; for example, the inclusion of FMS under customs data appears to be by chance rather than by design. This may be due to the fact that arms are sometimes shipped through military transport channels and do not go through customs ports. However, in theory, as customs data supposedly include FMS, it should be listed in a subset. As the following evidence shows, this does not always occur.

- **BATF Reports:** A third source of US firearms export data is the Bureau of Alcohol, Tobacco and Firearms (BATF). In the BATF's 1998 annual report, available on their website at www.atf.treas.gov, firearms exports are listed by category. However, this weapons categorization does not appear to match customs categories, nor does it go into specific detail, as do the *655 Report* data. Nevertheless, in 1998, a total of 215,896 firearms were exported by the US according to BATF data. Of this figure, 29,537 were pistols, 15,788 revolvers, 65,807 rifles, 89,699 shotguns, 12,529 machine guns, 23 'other weapons', and 2,513 miscellaneous firearms.

Comparing the incomparable: The incomparability of data from the diverse reports cited above is best illustrated in the case of military rifles and machine guns exported to Israel from 1996 to 1998 (see Figure 4.2). A comparison of *655 Report* authorizations and customs data on deliveries for these three years reveals major discrepancies. As Direct Commercial Sales (DCS) licenses shown in the 655 Report are valid for four years, it is possible that previous *655 Reports* announced these transfers, although these data were not available.

In addition to the data in Figure 4.2, the 1998 *655 Report* also states that 127 'non-military rifles, all types' were authorized for sale to Israel under DCS in 1998, yet customs data shows that 3,926 'muzzle loading' and 'center fire' firearms were exported to Israel by the US in that year. These are not minor discrepancies; on the contrary, the figures involved are in a magnitude of thousands to tens of thousands of weapons exported. One possible explanation for these transfers is that Israel is a major centre for re-fitting small arms.

Transfers to Israel are not the only example that highlights the ambiguity, discrepancies, and incomparability of available data on small arms transfers from the US. Table 4.4 compares customs data on transfers from the US to Thailand of military rifles, shotguns, machine guns, and non-military rifles with data from the *655 Report* over a period of three years (no EDA transfers of small arms to Thailand were reported for this time period). Notable discrepancies appear with respect to transfers in all categories.

While customs data purportedly includes FMS, in fact, this is often not the case. In addition, free transfers of EDA also do not always appear in customs data. For example, in 1999 the US transferred 704 M-3 machine guns to Macedonia under an EDA grant; yet there is no record of this transfer in customs data. Under another 1999 EDA grant, the US transferred 40,000 and 40,500 rifles to Lithuania and Estonia respectively that were not recorded in customs data.

Figure 4.2 Discrepancies in export reporting: US small arms transfers to Israel, 1996-98

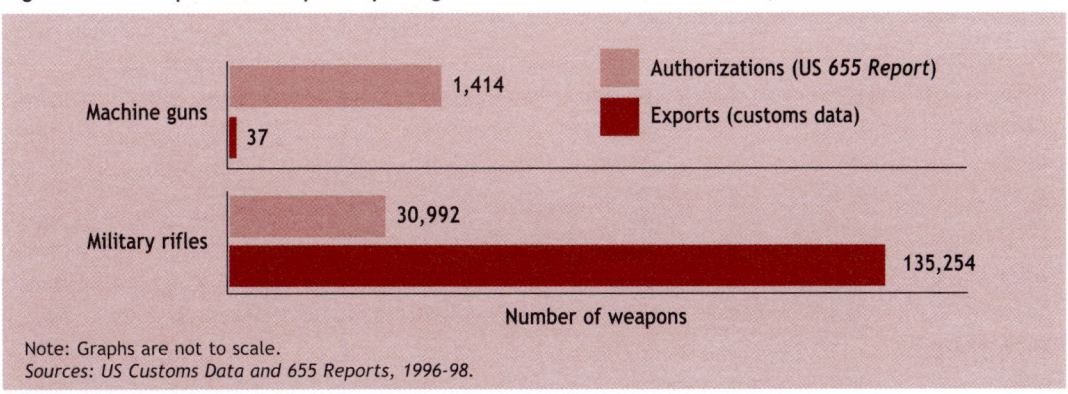

Note: Graphs are not to scale.
Sources: US Customs Data and 655 Reports, 1996-98.

In addition, customs data may contain parts for weapons being exported for further assembly or finishing in another country. Depending on customs practices in a given country, parts could be exported either as weapon parts or as a complete weapon. Also, when comparing the UK customs data for exports to the US against the US customs data on UK imports for the same shipment, the numbers seldom, if ever, tally. While figures may not vary widely, these inconsistencies nevertheless profile the problem of using non-standardized customs data.

Despite an agreed Harmonized Tariff Schedule used internationally by customs officials, different countries may classify weapons differently. In addition, due to transport and processing time lags,

Table 4.4 Discrepancies in reporting: US small arms transfers to Thailand, 1996-98

	US Customs Data				655 Report					
					DCS Authorizations				FMS	
Year	Military Rifles	Machine guns	Shotguns	Non-military rifles	Military Rifles	Machine guns	Shotguns	Non-military rifles	Military rifles	Machine guns
1996	510	–	3,646	1,628	–	–	221	1,622	39	292
1997	685	–	2,873	1,175	1,348	–	135	1,197	300	
1998	10,100	1	1,096	576	29	36	202	942	19	12
Total	11,295	1	7,615	3,379	1,377	36	558	3,761	358	304

Sources: US Customs Data and 655 Reports, 1996-98.

exports from a supplier country may not show up as imports in the recipient country until the following year. In end effect, the current analysis can only conclude that neither customs data nor *655 Reports* provide a complete picture of total actual US transfers of small arms and light weapons to other states. Table 4.5 presents the top importers of US small arms over a ten-year period, based on US customs data.

Even more worrisome than the data are the destinations of some of these small arms transfers— for example, to Israel, the Philippines, and Thailand (see Map 4.1)—countries already saturated with weapons. Despite all the facts and figures, the US Congress and the US public may not be receiving a totally transparent or accurate picture of the US arms trade. Certainly, greater concern and caution should be exercised in cases such as those cited here—and they are not the only ones.

Finally, to provide an overview of the quantity of weapons exported from the US, Table 4.6 presents total US exports of specific types of small arms over the last ten years, according to customs data. Again, inconsistencies with other reports crop up; for example, the BATF report reflects different figures (e.g. US exports in 1998: 45,325 pistols and revolvers, and 12,529 machine guns).

Table 4.5 Top importers of small arms from the United States (1990-99), by category

Military Rifles		Machine Guns		Pistols & Revolvers	
Israel	146,775	Lebanon	11,787	Belgium	276,967
Germany	66,449	Thailand	4,763	Thailand	164,718
Kuwait	56,723	Taiwan	4,015	Canada	164,690
Bosnia	42,637	Colombia	3,795	Germany	148,912
Taiwan	39,869	Italy	3,109	Philippines	82,269
Mexico	35,996	Turkey	2,894	Venezuela	80,423
U.A.E.	35,292	Kuwait	2,460	Turkey	76,444
Thailand	30,918	Egypt	1,876	Mexico	58,092
Philippines	27,671	Jordan	1,775	Taiwan	56,024
Brazil	21,477	U.A.E.	1,715	Italy	48,051

Source: US Customs Data

Other reports: There are other countries—for example, Australia, Portugal, and Spain — that report their military exports but provide no breakdown as to what percentage constitutes small arms and light weapons. Although these governments are clearly attempting to create a climate of transparency with respect to military exports, such reports provide little relevant information on the small arms trade. Denmark, Switzerland, and France published reports in early 2001. The data from these reports will be covered in a subsequent publication of the *Small Arms Survey*.

Table 4.6   Quantities of small arms exported by the United States (1990-99)

Year	Military Rifles	Machine Guns	Military Shotguns	Pistols and Revolvers
1990	22,633	3,079	4,482	191,44
1991	38,260	4,799	8,393	227,480
1992	28,997	6,238	11,390	207,211
1993	28,272	2,802	7,693	169,627
1994	67,452	12,780	21,680	195,874
1995	26,384	3,180	6,593	218,826
1996	110,973	2,828	20,233	193,676
1997	149,343	3,079	3,929	148,023
1998	105,159	6,434	4,561	124,295
1999	88,354	10,302	3,239	116,467
Total	**665,872**	**55,521**	**92,193**	**1,782,925**

Source: US Customs Data

Disturbing small arms transfers: Research sometimes reveals major small arms transfers going to states where caution should be the key word. Several top small arms importers deserve special attention. These are legal recipient states in which the accumulation or clandestine transfer of such weapons has historically greased the 'slippery slope' between legal and illicit dealing and, as a result, has had destabilizing effects on entire regions. Four cases in point:

- **Israel** is one of the most untransparent countries with respect to the reporting of small arms imports and exports. It is a regular recipient of major military small arms transfers from the US (and, in the past, South Africa), and it also has major domestic production facilities (for example, the Galil and Uzi series (PRODUCERS)). Moreover, Israel has, in the past, been implicated in several arms brokering deals, and some of its arms brokers have been caught evading sanctions by transferring arms to various non-state actors, such as the Liberation Tigers of Tamil Elam (LTTE) in Sri Lanka, drug lords in Columbia, and rebel forces in Sierra Leone (BROKERS).
- **The Philippines**, which receives substantial legal small arms transfers from the US, as well as from the UK, Canada, and South Africa, should be another source of concern. As a country saturated with weapons and prone to insurgencies within its own borders, the Phillipines poses a threat to the region (ILLICIT TRANSFERS).
- **Thailand** is another major small arms recipient, especially from the US, Canada, and Germany, with the dubious 'tradition' of having had a number of its nationals implicated in less-than-licit arms transfers. Thailand is a major source of illicit small arms transfers to non-state actors in the South Asia region (ILLICIT TRANSFERS).
- **Singapore:** South Africa's arms transfers to Singapore should also be scrutinized in greater detail as this country is reputed to be a source of black market weapons (US Department of Commerce, 1999).

In the period 1990-98, the US exported a total of some 666,000 military rifles, 56,000 machine guns, 92,000 military shotguns, and 1,800,000 pistols and revolvers, according to customs figures.

The examples above demonstrate the role of legal transfers in the destabilizing accumulations of small arms and suggest how such legal transfers can be diverted to the grey and black markets. There are recognized diffficulties in end-use monitoring of legal small arms sales. A US GAO report in the year 2000 strongly criticized the effectiveness of monitoring the end-use of weapons originating from the US; it is likely that these findings could be applied to virtually all the world's countries (GAO Report, 2000b).

Map 4.1 Legal arms transfers to countries of concern

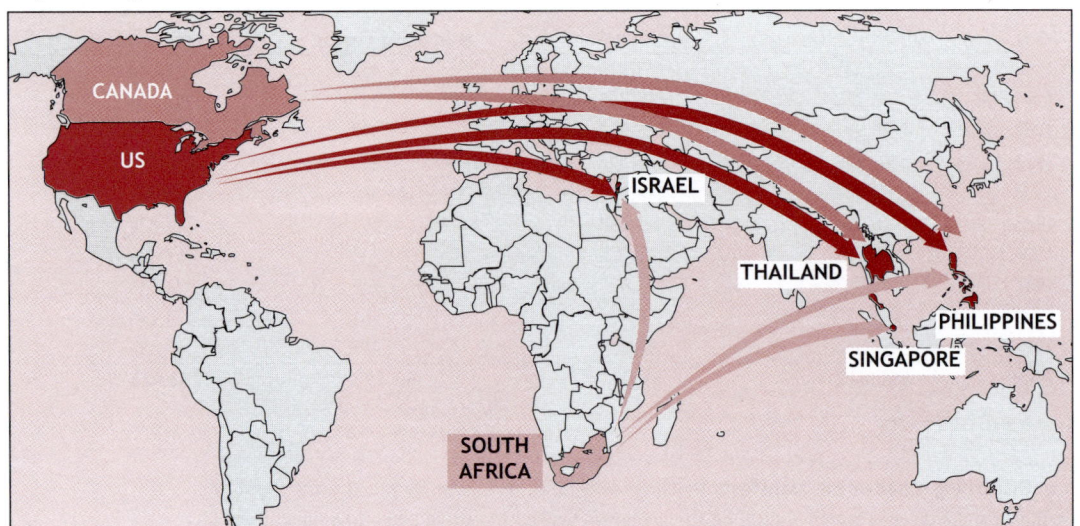

UN data on the world's major small arms importers

Import—as opposed to export—reports are another data source in determining the trade in small arms. Customs data is one of the most helpful information sources in this regard.

Among its many functions, the COMTRADE database also reports total military firearms imports by country. Again, the same limitations apply as for export data. According to COMTRADE, the top five recipients of military firearms in 1998 were the Netherlands, Turkey, South Korea, the UK, and Australia. For pistols and revolvers, the top five recipients were the US, Germany, the Philippines, Switzerland, and Turkey. The top five importers of military firearms, and pistols and revolvers over the longer five-year period 1994-98 are listed in Table 4.7.

According to COMTRADE, the top five recipients of military firearms in 1998 were the Netherlands, Turkey, South Korea, the UK, and Australia.

With regard to military firearms, pistols and revolvers, a far greater number of countries supply data to COMTRADE on imports than on exports. Again, the data threshold is US$ 50,000 worth of arms over a period of five years, so countries supplying data beneath this 'critical mass' would not be reflected. Currently, 68 countries have supplied data on imports of military firearms and/or pistols and revolvers: 40 have declared imports of military firearms while 62 have declared imports of pistols and revolvers.

As frequently pointed out in the course of this chapter, the problem with data, in this instance with the COMTRADE data, is that it is not a comprehensive reflection of the reality of the small arms trade. It is, however, a preliminary snapshot for legal small arms transfers for those countries able and willing to compile and publicly report such data. If more countries—particularly major weapons importers—followed suit, a more complete picture of the legal small arms trade would be available.

National customs data

Yet another data source in determining the trade in small arms is nationally reported customs data. The countries below had readily accessible customs data on small arms imports.

Table 4.7 Major small arms importers worldwide, 1994-98

Country	Military Firearms: Value of imports		Country	Pistols and Revolvers: Value of imports
Netherlands	US$ 320 million		United States	US$ 774 million
United Kingdom	US$ 161 million		Germany	US$ 109 million
Saudi Arabia	US$ 110 million		Thailand	US$ 81 million
United States	US$ 99 million		Turkey	US$ 74 million
Turkey	US$ 63 million		Switzerland	US$ 36 million

Source: COMTRADE

United States: Despite its position as one of the world's major small arms producers and exporters, the US also imports a significant amount of small arms. US customs data reveal information on large imports of military rifles from Eastern Europe and China since the early 1990s. While many of these weapons may be destined for US private markets, the numbers are truly staggering.

In the years 1990-97, the US imported more than 1.15 million military rifles from China although these imports dropped to zero after 1997 once the US ban on assault rifles went into effect. Similarly, during the period 1990-99, the US imported significant quantities of military rifles from the Russian Federation and countries in Central and Eastern Europe: 338,767 from Russia (after 1992), 138,750 from Ukraine, 114,876 from Romania, 91,690 from the Czech Republic (after 1993), 21,140 from Poland, and 3,060 from Bulgaria. In all, over the period 1990-99, the US imported more than 2.75 million military rifles from abroad—almost one for every ten US citizens.

Over the same time period, the US imported more than 8.29 million pistols and revolvers. In 1999 alone, more than 1.7 million guns, including hunting rifles, were imported into the US, whereas more than 3.7 million firearms were domestically produced (BATF, 1998). While a large number of these imports were probably for private domestic use, the final destination of many such firearms, particularly rifles, is unclear. There is evidence, however, that the large US domestic market for firearms is a ready source of weapons supply to the black market, notably in Mexico (Lumpe, 1997).

Australia: Based on 1999 customs data, Australia imported 20,351 firearms falling under tariff classifications 9301, 9302, and 9303, which are 'military weapons', 'pistols and revolvers', and 'other firearms', respectively (Australian Customs Service, 14 July 2000).

El Salvador: This country also reports firearm imports. In 1999 it provided the following commercial import authorizations: 17,741 pistols, 7,991 revolvers, 8,110 shotguns, 2,809 rifles, and 202 carbines.[15] The Ministry of Defence also reported that the following firearms were legally imported into El Salvador in 1998: 6,989 pistols, 5,950 revolvers, 3,117 shotguns, 1,431 rifles, and 61 carbines (Godnick, 2000).

Paraguay: According to customs data on small arms imports, between 1997-99 (inclusive), Paraguay legally imported 35,384 pistols and revolvers and 80 military firearms. The main exporter of pistols and revolvers to Paraguay for that time period was Brazil, which accounted for a total of 22,118 weapons. Of the 80 military firearms legally imported by Paraguay, 79 were for the National Police and one for the Supreme Court Justice Department (Paraguayan Customs Data).

Swaziland: In 1999 Swaziland registered 407 legal firearms imports. In addition, it registered 360 temporary importation permits for firearms granted to visitors or people transiting the country (Swaziland Embassy, 28 April 2000).

Uruguay: In 1999, Uruguay's customs data on civilian firearms imports revealed a total of 6,260 pistols and revolvers. The only suppliers were Argentina, Brazil, and the US (Uruguayan Customs Data).

Between 1990-99, the US imported more than 2.75 million military rifles from abroad—almost one for every ten of its citizens.

Unofficial information

A substantial amount of unofficial data on legal transfers of small arms comes from the print and electronic media, particularly specialized defence publications. In addition, national defence industry associations in many countries collect and publish information on exports and imports of small arms and light weapons. The problem with such unofficial data is that they are rarely comprehensive; transfers of small arms are often reported on an *ad hoc* basis. Below are some examples of reports from unofficial sources. Although not all of the countries below provide official small arms export information, some of the following media reports nevertheless cite official sources:

- **Croatia:** *Jane's Intelligence Review* reported that Croatia was supplying the French and Colombian militaries with small arms (Simunovic, 2000).
- **Poland:** The same *Jane's* report stated that Poland had annual exports of firearms and explosives worth approximately US$ 40 million.
- **Bulgaria:** Another press report claimed that Bulgaria would supply about 200,000 Kalashnikov-style[16] rifles to India in a deal struck in October 2000. A similar deal between Bulgaria and India for 100,000 assault rifles was agreed in 1994, but never took place (Raghuvanshi, 2000). No official confirmation of this agreement has been published.
- **The Czech Republic:** A November 2000 press report quoted a military spokeswoman of the Czech Republic detailing the country's exports of military equipment. She said that, in 1999, the Czech Republic exported over US$ 59.2 million worth of non-military weapons, ammunition, and explosives. Although unclear from the context of the press report, these non-military weapons probably consist of hunting and sporting weapons and may include pistols and revolvers (*CTK*, 10 November 2000).
- **Pakistan:** The official Associated Press of Pakistan reported that in 1999 the country's exports of machine guns, rifles, anti-tank rockets, mortars, and ammunition totalled US$ 30.2 million. It said that the value of Pakistani defence exports had doubled from 1997 to 1999 (*Khaleej Times*, UAE, 17 November 2000).
- **The Russian Federation:** According to domestic media reports, the Russian Federation supplied 4,000 Kalashnikovs to Indonesia in August 2000. Mention of this transfer was contained within a report of the sale of MI-17 helicopters to Indonesia. This is the way such transfers sometimes come to light and receive attention in the press—i.e. 'buried' within the report of sales of larger weapons systems (Novichkov, 2000). In addition, it was reported that the Russian Federation substantially increased its exports of Kalashnikov rifles to countries in Africa over the time period 1999-2000. It was estimated that the value of these transfers to Africa was in the tens of millions of dollars (Bull, 2000). Press reports also stated that Russian exports of small arms ammunition for the first six months of the year 2000 were 20 times greater than exports for the first six months of 1999. Countries importing Russian small arms ammunition during the first six months of 2000 were: Bulgaria, the Czech Republic, France, Germany, Kazakhstan, Latvia, Moldova, Mongolia, Singapore, Ukraine, the United Kingdom, and the US (Timergaliyeva, 2000).

In 1999-2000, the value of Russian exports of Kalashnikov rifles to Africa was estimated in the tens of millions of dollars.

Conclusions

In surveying data on the global legal trade in small arms and light weapons, one of the primary goals has been to draw together an initial evidence base. This has been facilitated by the fact that an ever increasing number of countries are producing annual reports on such transfers. This is a recent development to be encouraged. However, the utility of such reports in determining volumes, trends, or patterns in the global legal small arms trade still suffers formidable constraints. As with any statistics, data must be viewed as a trend indicator and only a rough approximation of reality.

Thus, while countries are to be commended for their increased transparency regarding military exports over the last decade, the data still do not provide a clear picture of the legal trade in small arms and light weapons nationally, much less globally.

In terms of imports, it is clear that certain Western countries are the major small arms importers. Others with a high level of demand for weapons due to their civilian gun culture, import substantial quantities of small arms. As to what happens to these weapons, any given country's stockpile security of military weapons and national gun legislation plays a major role in determining whether or not they may be diverted to the black market.

In terms of exports, it is also evident that large legal small arms transfers are going to areas of conflict and instability. While governments may cite political justifications for such transfers, countries should carefully assess small arms transfers to zones of war and conflict, taking into consideration what could happen to the weapons should the government of the receiving state collapse. There is also the ethical issue of small arms transfers to countries with records of human rights abuses, not to mention the political and strategic ramifications of exporting weapons to areas buffeted by political turmoil and civil unrest.

That is not all. Regional considerations—for example, countries acting as small arms suppliers or serving as a major source of illicit small arms transfers—must also be taken into account. Weapons replacement and the final disposal of old weapons also constitute crucial questions in terms of regional peace, security, and sustainable development.

Destabilization is another major issue. The role of legal transfers in augmenting and destabilizing small arms stockpiles must be carefully assessed, as well as the proclivity for legal transfers to be diverted into the grey or black markets. Then there are the recognized difficulties in end-use monitoring of legal sales of small arms.

Secrecy remains one of the overriding problems in assessing the legal trade in small arms. Many countries, including a few that are actively pursuing policies of greater transparency in arms transfers in the international arena, have been unwilling even to release customs data on military exports which they still classify as secret. Many others provide scant or no official data on their small arms exports.

Secrecy remains one of the persistent problems in assessing the legal trade in small arms.

And yet—a clear picture of the legal trade in small arms is an acknowledged prerequisite to assessing and addressing the far more pressing problem of illicit arms trafficking. This can be accomplished only if universal norms and standards for definitions and reporting formats are developed and implemented, including both explicit quantitative volumes and values for small arms and ammunition transfers. The most efficient way to promote transparency would be for all countries to publish their customs data on small arms, and to require that all legal transfers pass through customs. In this way, the COMTRADE database could become one of the most important international transparency initiatives.

Finally, the precedent set by many countries with respect to transparency in arms transfers should be followed and universalized. It is time to make those major small arms exporters that provide no official data on their exports aware of the changing international climate with respect to transparency.

The swiftest path to greater transparency in the international small arms trade: process all arms transfers through customs and make this data public.

However, until all the major small arms producers report on their small arms exports in a conscientious and consistent manner, using standardized terminology and reporting structures, the total volume and value of the global legal trade in small arms will remain elusive and only an 'educated guess'.

Future editions of the *Small Arms Survey* will provide updates of the reports analyzed here, as well as new data and reports that come to light. Through the compilation of an authoritative body of information on the legal small arms trade, it will be possible to define and better analyze trends over time. This chapter, indeed this volume, represents a significant first step.

For further information and current developments on small arms issues please check our website at www.smallarmssurvey.org

4 List of Abbreviations

ACDA	US Arms Control and Disarmament Agency
BATF	Bureau of Alcohol, Tobacco and Firearms
BEF	Belgian Francs
CAD	Canadian Dollars
COMTRADE	UN Customs Database (Commercial Trade)
DCAC	South African Directorate Conventional Arms Control
DCS	Direct Commercial Sales
DFAIT	Department of Foreign Affairs and International Trade
DM	Deutsche Mark
DOD	Department of Defense
DOS	Department of State
EDA	Excess Defense Articles
EU	European Union
FIM	Finnish Mark
FMS	Foreign Military Sales
FY	Fiscal Year
GAO	General Accounting Office
IDSA	Institute for Defence Studies and Analyses
IISS	International Institute of Strategic Studies
ISS	Institute for Security Studies
ITL	Italian Lira
NGO	Non-Governmental Organization
NISAT	Norwegian Initiative on Small Arms Transfers
NLG	Dutch Guilders
NOK	Norwegian Kroner
OSCE	Organization for Security and Cooperation in Europe
RCSS	Regional Centre for Strategic Studies
SEK	Swedish Kroner
SIPRI	Stockholm International Peace Research Institute
UK	United Kingdom
UN	United Nations
UNRCA	UN Register of Conventional Arms
US	United States
ZAR	South African Rand

4 Endnotes

1 Chris Smith wrote, 'Light weapons were, and still are, impossible to map and measure with the precision which the research community came to expect' (Smith, 1999).

2 During the year 2000, a UN group of governmental experts was established to study, for the third time, possibilities for expanding the scope of the UN Register of Conventional Arms, to include, among other things, transfers of small arms and light weapons (UN General Assembly Resolution, 53/77, 4 December 1998, section V).

3 For example, the UN 'Report of the Panel of Experts on Violations of Security Council Sanctions against UNITA' can be found at www.un.org/News/dh/latest/angolareport_eng.htm.

4 To further complicate matters, some figures include ammunition for, and export of, larger weapons systems that do not fall within the UN definition of small arms and light weapons.

5 The *1998 UN International Firearms Study* dealt only with commercial firearms, which includes handguns (e.g. pistols, revolvers), long guns (e.g. rifles, shotguns), and ammunition. It excluded military-style small arms and light weapons that are used by government security forces.

6 The definition of military firearms (category 9301), according to the Harmonized Tariff Schedule used internationally by customs officials, is as follows: Military weapons other than revolvers and pistols, to include, military rifles, military shotguns, howitzers, mortars, machineguns, grenade launchers, flame throwers, and others. Some countries in their own national customs reports give data for specific sub-categories, such as military rifles or machine guns. This category does not include weapons for

hunting or sport. Some weapons in the 9301 category are not small arms or light weapons, such as mortars over 100mm and howitzers.

7 The 26 countries that reported sales of military firearms at least once to COMTRADE during the period 1994–98 were: Argentina, Australia, Austria, Canada, Chile, China, Croatia, Denmark, Finland, Indonesia, Japan, Latvia, Malaysia, Netherlands, New Zealand, Norway, Poland, Portugal, Republic of Korea, Romania, Slovakia, Spain, Switzerland, Turkey, UK, and the USA.

8 The 27 COMTRADE countries reporting exports of pistols and revolvers at least once between 1994–1998 were: Argentina, Australia, Austria, Canada, Chile, China, Colombia, Croatia, Czech Republic, Denmark, Germany, India, Italy, Malaysia, Mexico, Netherlands, Philippines, Poland, Portugal, Republic of Korea, Spain, Sweden, Switzerland, Thailand, Turkey, UK, and the USA.

9 Currency conversions for all figures in this chapter that were listed in values other than US$ were calculated based on the inter-bank exchange rate of 1 January 2000. When values were for currencies other than US$, the original figure is given in parenthesis after the US$ figure.

10 For example, based on US customs data, in 1999 Brazil exported over US$ 25 million worth of pistols and revolvers to the US alone although it exports to many other countries as well.

11 These data were obtained from the Brazilian Government by the NGO Viva Rio.

12 These data are listed in US dollars, no conversion has been made.

13 Hunting and sporting rifles, as well as pistols and revolvers, are included in this category.

14 The US Government has a searchable website of all EDA exports and authorisations at www.dsca.osd.mil/programs/eda/search.asp.

15 This figure may not correspond to actual imports.

16 For the purposes of this study, the term 'Kalashnikov' will be used for all models of the Russian-made assault rifle. This is due to the fact that reports often use the term 'AK-47' even when it is clear that a newer model of the rifle (such as an AK-74 or AKM) was transferred. For Kalashnikov model rifles manufactured in countries other than the former Soviet Union, the term Kalashnikov-style will be used.

4 Appendix

Appendix 4.1   Publicly-available government arms export reports (deliveries and/or authorizations), and their information on the small arms trade

Country	Data on small arms exports and/or authorizations	Data on small arms exports and/or authorizations disaggregated by importing country
Australia	No	No
Austria	Yes	No
Belgium	Yes	No
Brazil	Yes	No
Canada	Yes	Yes
Chile	Yes	Yes
Denmark	Yes	Yes
Finland	Yes	Yes
France	Yes	Yes
Germany	Yes	Yes
Italy	Yes	No
Netherlands	Yes	No
Norway	Yes	No
Portugal	No	No
South Africa	Yes	Yes
South Korea	Yes	No
Spain	No	No
Sweden	Yes	No
Switzerland	Yes	Yes
United Kingdom	Yes	Yes
United States	Yes	Yes

4 Bibliography

Annan, Kofi. 2000. *We the Peoples: The Role of the United Nations in the 21st Century*. New York: United Nations Department of Public Information.

Austria. Government of Austria. 1999. *Report on the Export of Arms by the Republic of Austria for the Year 1998, Pursuant to Paragraph 8 of the Operative Provisions of the EU Code of Conduct for Arms Exports*. 23 June.

Boutwell, Jeffrey and Michael T. Klare. 1999. *Light Weapons and Civil Conflict: Controlling the Tools of Violence*. Lanham, Maryland: Rowman & Littlefield Publishers, Inc.

____. 2000. 'A Scourge of Small Arms.' *Scientific American*. June, pp. 48-53.

Belgium. Press Department of the Belgian Ministry of Foreign Affairs, Foreign Trade and International Cooperation. 1999. *Rapport sur l'Exportation d'Armes 1999*.

Bull, Kylie. 2000. 'Is Vladimir Putin the Salesman with a Hidden Agenda?' *Jane's Defence Industry*. 1 May.

Canada. Canadian Department of Foreign Affairs and International Trade (DFAIT). Import and Export Controls Bureau. 1996. *The Export of Military Goods from Canada: Annual Report*

____. 1997. *The Export of Military Goods from Canada: Annual Report*

____. 1998. *The Export of Military Goods from Canada: Annual Report*

Finland. Ministry of Defence. 1999. *Export of Defence Materiel*.

Germany. Bundesministerium für Wirtschaft und Technologie. 1999. *Rüstungsexportbericht 1999*.

Godnick, Bill. 2000. *Small Arms in Central America*. Background Paper. Geneva: Small Arms Survey.

Italy. Camera dei Deputati. 1999. *Relazione sulle Operazione Autorizzate e Svolte per il Controllo dell' Esportazione, Importazione e Transito dei Materiali di Armamento nonché dell' Esportazione e del Transito dei Prodotti ad Alta Technologia*.

Lumpe, Lora. 1997. 'The US Arms Both Sides of Mexico's Drug War.' *Covert Action Quarterly*. Summer, pp. 39-46.

Lumpe, Lora, ed. 2000. *Running Guns: The Global Black Market in Small Arms*. London: Zed Books.

The Netherlands. Ministerie van Economische Zaken. 2000. *Inhoudsopgave openbaar jaarrapport Nederlands wapenexportbelied 1999*.

Norway. Utenriksdepartementet. 1999. *Eksporten av forsvarsmateriell fra Norge I 1998*.

Novichkov, Nikolai. 2000. 'Indonesia to Buy 4 MI-17 Helicopters from Russia.' *Itar-Tass*. 12 September.

Raghuvanshi, Vivek. 2000. 'Bulgaria to Supply AK-47s to Indian Government.' *Defense News*. 20 November, p. 40.

Renner, Michael. 2000. 'Arms Control Orphans.' *Bulletin of the Atomic Scientists*. Vol.55, No.1. January/February.

Republic of Korea. Ministry of National Defense. 1999. *White Paper*.

Simunovic, Pjer. 2000. 'CEE Arms Exporters Making a Comeback.' *Jane's Intelligence Review*. 1 April.

Smith, Chris. 1999. 'Areas of Major Concentration in the Use and Traffic of Small Arms.' In Jayantha Dhanapala et al., eds. *Small Arms Control: Old Weapons New Issues*. Aldershot: Ashgate.

Stockholm International Peace Research Institute. 2000. *SIPRI Yearbook 2000: Armaments, Disarmament and International Security*. New York: Oxford University Press.

South Africa. Directorate Conventional Arms Control. 2000. *South African Export Statistics for Conventional Arms 1997-1999*.

Sweden. Ministry for Foreign Affairs. Strategic Export Control Division. 1999. *Swedish Arms Exports in 1998: A Government Report*. May.

Timergaliyeva, Daima. 2000. 'Russia: Export of Small Arms Ammunition Increases.' *Itar-Tass*. 17 October.

United Kingdom. Foreign Office. The Department of Trade and Industry and the Ministry of Defence. 2000. *Annual Report on Strategic Export Controls*. August.

United Nations. 1996. *Report of the Disarmament Commission, General Assembly*. A/51/42, Supplement No. 42, Annex I.

____. 1997. *Report of the Panel of Governmental Experts on Small Arms*. A/52/298.

____. 1998. *United Nations International Study on Firearm Regulation*. New York: United Nations.

____. 2000. *UN Register of Conventional Arms*.

A/55/299, Add. 3. 9 November.

United Nations Statistics Division. 1999. *PC-TAS Trade Analysis System*. CD-ROM for 1994-1998, based on the COMTRADE database.

United States. United States Department of Commerce. Bureau of Export Administration. 2000. *Annual Report: FY 1999*.

United States. United States Department of Commerce. Economics and Statistics Administration. U.S. Census Bureau. 1990-1999. *U.S. Exports History; U.S. Imports History*.

United States. United States Department of Defense. United States Department of State. 2000. *655 Report: US Defense Exports Authorizations and Sales FY 1999*.

United States. United States Department of the Treasury. Bureau of Alcohol, Tobacco and Firearms. 2000. *Commerce in Firearms in the United States*. February.

United States EDA (Excess Defense Articles). <http://www.dsca.osd.mil/programs/eda/search.asp>

United States General Accounting Office (GAO). 2000a. *Conventional Arms Transfers: U.S. Efforts to Control the Availability of Small Arms and Light Weapons*. July.

____. 2000b. *Foreign Military Sales: Changes Needed to Correct Weaknesses in End-Use Monitoring Program*. August.

5

Crime, Conflict, Corruption:
Global Illicit Small Arms Transfers

Introduction

It is the illicit trade in small arms, more than any other aspect of the global arms business, that exacerbates civil conflict, corruption, crime, and random acts of violence. The illicit arms trade is nothing new—gun smuggling has been a problem since the 19th century. And it may not be the largest aspect of the global spread of small arms; yet it is far and away the most infamous.

The illicit small arms trade is anything but transparent and, virtually by definition, the data are destined to remain forever incomplete and inadequately substantiated. Ironically—and perhaps for this very reason—it is also one of the most intensely scrutinized activities. For, while much of the trade in small arms and light weapons is accepted by governments as a legitimate economic and political activity, there is general consensus that the illicit trade is in need of aggressive remedial action at all levels of government, business, and civil society. Therefore, this chapter focuses on the following four questions:

- What is the worldwide scope of the illicit trade in small arms and light weapons?
- Which countries are the major sources or suppliers of illicit small arms?
- Which countries, non-state actors, or criminal entities are recipients of illicit small arms?
- Which regions are most seriously affected as a result of this illicit small arms trade?

The *Small Arms Survey's* analysis of the global illicit trade in small arms and light weapons utilizes field research, as well as information sources that are in the public domain.[1] It also employs case studies, focusing on certain regions and countries. This approach facilitates the understanding of how and why such transfers occur, and who the major suppliers and recipients are. Countries and regions not covered in this year's *Survey* will be addressed in future editions.

Defining illicit small arms transfers

The only available United Nations definition of illicit trafficking is from a 1996 UN report dealing with conventional arms transfers, which states that 'illicit arms trafficking is understood to cover that international trade in conventional arms which is contrary to the laws of States and/or international law' (UN, 1996).[2]

Encompassed within this term, 'illicit transfers' are two overlapping categories: the grey market and the black market (see Fig. 5.1). Though their borders are ambiguous and amorphous, distinguishing these categories is useful for the purposes of this chapter.

Figure 5.1 The overlapping legal, illicit, and illegal small arms trade markets

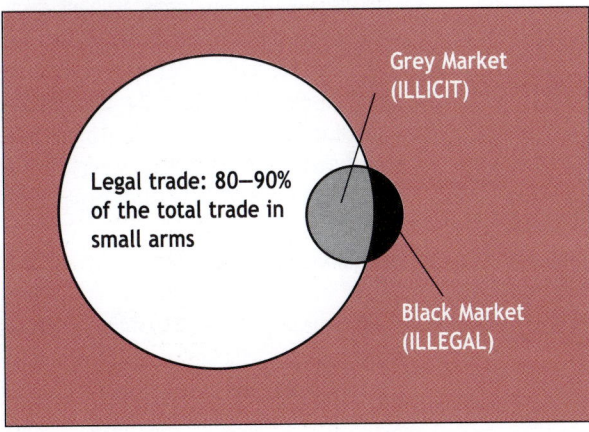

Grey Market (ILLICIT)

Legal trade: 80–90% of the total trade in small arms

Black Market (ILLEGAL)

Grey Market Transfers

Regulating the grey market in small arms poses perhaps the greatest challenge to the international community today.

An area without black-and-white clarity or transparency, grey market transfers are usually covert, conducted by governments, government-sponsored brokers, or other entities, that exploit loopholes or intentionally circumvent national and/or international law or policies.[3]

Grey market transfers include sales to recipient countries that have no identifiable legal government or authority (e.g. Somalia) and transfers by governments to non-state actors (i.e.

Terminology Tip-offs	
Transfers =	Span the legal and illicit spectrum
Trade =	Conducted by governments or with their knowledge
Covert trade =	Conducted clandestinely, whether legal or illicit
Trafficking =	Refers exclusively to illegal black market transfers

rebel and insurgent groups). In addition, there are cases where governments illegally hire brokers to transfer weapons (e.g. the 'Iran-Contra Affair'). Such transfers may be in violation of the supplier and/or recipient country's national laws or policies. They may also contravene international law. Regulating the grey market in small arms poses perhaps the greatest challenge to the international community today.

Black Market Transfers

The black market's distinctive feature is that it operates beyond the pale of the law and governments.

Although the black market is part of the overall illicit trade spectrum, its distinctive feature is that it operates beyond the pale of the law and governments. Indeed, this type of illegal arms 'trafficking' takes place in clear violation of national and/or international laws and policies, and without the government's official knowledge, consent, or control. As it is largely driven by a desire for personal gain, corrupt government officials are not infrequently both aware of, and actively involved in, such illegal transfers. Realistically, since substantial illegal small arms transfers could scarcely occur without some degree of government awareness, it is highly probable that the black market is but a small portion of the much larger illicit market, both in terms of its value and the volume of transfers.

The scope of the illicit small arms trade

The problem lies in the proof: that is, in assessing the scope of the illicit trade in small arms, irrefutable proof that such transfers actually take place is essential. Methods used to reveal illicit transfers frequently come under heavy attack by those nations implicated. Rarely will a nation admit to illegally supplying arms. Without rigorous reporting methodologies, countries implicated in illicit arms transfers can easily dismiss allegations.

The challenge is to accurately identify grey market transfers. Yet, their very nature implies duplicity and falsification, making the illicit transfer difficult to document. Then there are also devious practices, such as those employed by the United States (US) in the 1980s when it bought Warsaw Pact-produced arms and deliberately implicated other nations in their transfer (Silverstein, 2000). In sum, such transfers must be studied, keeping the validity of the source material constantly in mind.

Volume and Value

While the scope of the illicit trade—both in terms of value and volume—is by definition difficult to assess, such illicit transfers clearly contribute to destabilizing accumulations of small arms. The difficulty in detecting these transfers is likely to grow apace with globalization. According to a report by the US Coast Guard and Naval Intelligence, 'despite occasional seizures of illegal weapon

Box 5.1 Small arms transfers: The legality spectrum

Legal transfers: These occur with either the active or passive involvement of governments or their authorized agents, and in accordance with both national and international law.

Illicit grey market transfers: Governments, their agents, or individuals exploiting loopholes or intentionally circumventing national and/or international laws or policies.

Illegal black market transfers: In clear violation of national and/or international laws and without official government consent or control, these transfers may involve corrupt government officials acting on their own for personal gain.

Within the framework of UN definitions of the legal and illicit markets, there is room for a relatively broad interpretation of legal transfers but, in some cases, only a very narrow one for what is considered illicit trafficking. A number of governments interpret the phrase 'illicit trafficking in all its aspects' to include the entire spectrum of legal, grey, and black market trade; others say it includes only the black market. This more restrictive view poses serious problems to effectively addressing the issue of the destabilizing transfers of small arms and light weapons.[4]

A further distinction must be made between international and internal illicit arms transfers: international transfers refers to weapons crossing borders in violation of national and international law, internal transfers occur within a country and can involve theft, corruption, battlefield confiscations, and raids on armouries or stockpiles. Many governments (e.g. Colombia and Angola) also provide arms to local paramilitary organizations or individuals. Internal transfers can also occur when there is a breakdown of state authority (e.g. Albania and Somalia).

The grey market appears to have the greatest impact in situations of armed conflict—that is, when governments are actively or passively supplying weapons to non-state actors and are *de facto* involved in intra- or inter-state conflicts. In contrast, black market transfers tend to have a major impact on violence and criminality in civil society.

Identifying illicit maritime arms shipments will become increasingly difficult as the volume of commercial seaborne trade triples by 2020.

shipments, the full extent of maritime arms smuggling is unknown; identifying illicit arms shipments will become increasingly difficult as the volume of commercial seaborne trade triples by 2020.'

This is not to say that the actual quantity of the illicit small arms trade will increase over the next 20 years, but that this trade will become increasingly difficult to detect and intercept. Not only that, the global trend towards more open borders and greater trans-border traffic and trade will also make overland and airborne arms smuggling more difficult to deal with. The growing volume of legal trans-border trade in goods means that the actual detection of arms smuggling will require ever more manpower, experience, technology, and co-operation between law enforcement agencies, both nationally and internationally—not to mention a generous portion of luck.

A glimpse of the volume of the black market can be gleaned from police, border guards, and customs reports detailing seizures of illicit weapons and break-ups of arms trafficking rings. For example, it is estimated that about 300,000 rifles, handguns, and shotguns were newly added to the arsenals of insurgent forces in 1999 (STOCKPILES). These figures can be used to derive estimates of the value of the illicit trade in small arms.

The illicit trade accounts for 10-20 per cent of the total trade in small arms but is the prime culprit in fuelling crime, civil conflict, and corruption.

Based on existing information, the global illicit trade in small arms is estimated to be worth around US$ 1 billion annually. While it is not feasible to estimate the value of grey market versus black market transfers, all evidence points to the grey market being more significant both in terms of value and volume. When looked at in conjunction with estimates of the legal trade—US$ 4-6 billion annually (LEGAL TRANSFERS)—this illicit trade accounts for somewhere between 10 and 20 per cent of the total US$ 5-7 billion trade in small arms. Nevertheless, it is the illicit, rather than the legal, trade that contributes disproportionately to fuelling crime, civil conflict, and corruption.

Although one study estimated the illicit trade in small arms to be worth between US$ 2-3 billion annually (Boutwell and Klare, 2000), this figure cannot be verified and appears to be too high for two primary reasons:

- *First,* black market prices are usually much lower than those paid on the legal markets; and
- *Second,* illicit transfers of arms are much smaller in terms of quantity, as large shipments are not only too easily detected; financially, they are often beyond the purchasers' means.

The global illicit trade in small arms is estimated to be worth around US$ 1 billion annually.

In terms of value, extrapolating from intercepted grey and black market transfers, the figure of US$ 2-3 billion seems unrealistic. For example, a recent illicit transfer of 50,000 Kalashnikov assault rifles to the Revolutionary Armed Forces of Colombia (FARC) was reportedly worth US$ 5 million (Rempel and Rotella, 2000), making each rifle worth US$ 100. In order for US$ 1 billion worth of illicit transfers to occur annually, 200 comparable deals—all much larger than the norm for illicit transfers—would have to occur throughout the world each year. This is highly unlikely. Based on this benchmark calculation, one can assume that the value of the illicit trade in small arms is worth no more than US$ 1 billion annually.

Patterns and Characteristics

Pinpointing the precise value and volume of the illicit small arms trade presents its own problems, as seen above. Thus, it is easier to identify some of the common patterns and characteristics, using a regional analysis together with case studies, to identify some of the major weapons sources, suppliers, and recipients. Clearly the recipients, who are visibly in possession of these weapons, are easier to spot than the suppliers. And, not surprisingly, suppliers—whether governments or private individuals—try to stay behind the scenes and are reluctant to provide information about the destination of their illicit transfers.

The 'ant trade': cross-border illicit transfers from one state with lax gun purchasing requirements to another with stricter gun laws.

The information presented in this chapter shows that illicit arms flows follow a very different pattern from legal ones (LEGAL TRANSFERS). For example, a 1998 study analyzed patterns in arms acquisitions by 'ethnic groups in conflict' (Sislin *et al.*, 1998). It found that, for the most part, non-state actors involved in ethnic armed conflict obtained weapons, predominantly small arms, in three distinct ways: domestic procurement, indigenous production, and importation. Domestic procurement consists of theft, battlefield seizures, and raids on military and police facilities. Indigenous weapons production was found to be a rare but existing phenomenon. Weapons importation by such ethnic groups appears to take place primarily through the black market or through arms dealers.

An interesting and increasingly ubiquitous characteristic of the illicit arms trade has resulted in the coinage of a term that could be applied to illicit arms trafficking in many regions: the 'ant trade' —that is, cross-border transfers from one state with lax gun purchasing requirements to another with stricter gun laws. Guns purchased legally in one country are then smuggled, unregistered and illegally, across the border. Though minimal in terms of the scale of individual incidents—only one or two guns per person making the border crossing—when such practices become endemic, they add up. Such small-scale, cumulative trafficking can eventually push the numbers of weapons into the thousands—hence, the descriptive term, 'ant trade'.

Post-Cold War trends: One of the by-products of the Cold War was the ideologically driven arming of rebel groups throughout the world by the US and the Soviet Union. Today, many of these non-transparent and legally questionable (i.e. illicit) arms transfers carried out by governments have come back to haunt the original suppliers.

For example, the US is now engaged in a fight against Colombian drug lords who, ironically enough, are sometimes armed with the very weapons shipped to Central America by the US to fight communism in the 1980s. Even more dramatic is the situation of Afghanistan, where the US sent billions of dollars worth of military aid to radical Islamic fundamentalists in the 1980s, ostensibly to fight Soviet troops (Mathiak and Lumpe, 2000). Today, these same weapons are still in the hands of these groups, some having found their way into terrorist enclaves.

Today an ever stronger light is being shed on how these covert transfers worked, often with the intelligence community using brokers. For example, the US regularly purchased Warsaw Pact-produced weapons and equipment through brokers, which it then shipped, with the help of the Central Intelligence Agency (CIA), to the Afghanistan *mujahideen* (Silverstien, 2000). Some reports claim that the CIA supplied the *mujahideen* with some 400,000 Kalashnikovs during the Soviet-Afghan war (Vo, 1999).

While contemporary grey market transfers may lack the ideological underpinnings of the 1980s and, as a result of the end of the Cold War, be less prevalent, they do continue to occur. Today, especially in Eastern European and Commonwealth of Independent States (CIS) countries, suppliers' underlying motivations are more often financial and commercial rather than ideological. A number of state-owned (i.e. government-controlled) small arms manufacturers in Eastern Europe have been implicated in transfers to arms-embargoed nations or non-state actors. Although governments do not always sanction these transfers, they often know about them; thus, such transfers fall into the category of grey market transfers.

Regional and country case studies

In the following sections, the grey and black markets in small arms are analyzed using a regional and case study approach. The main objective of this analysis is to assess the movement, scale, and significance of the illicit trade in small arms. The political, ideological, and/or financial incentives of the source or supplier countries and recipients is not considered.

Since the end of the Cold War, the motives for supplying illicit small arms have become more financial and commercial than ideological.

Box 5.2 Cascading weapons: history tells ironic tales

During the Cold War, non-state actors in Central America were frequent recipients of large weapons shipments transferred illicitly, on the one hand, from the Soviet Union and its satellites and, on the other, from the US and its allies. Clearly, this was the result of fierce competition and jockeying for position by these two superpowers to influence the dominant political ideology in the region.

Specifically, the *Contra* rebels in Nicaragua received large quantities of small arms from the US prior to the mid-1990s. Israel also supplied them with Kalashnikov rifles confiscated from the Palestinian Liberation Organization (PLO). On the other side, Nicaragua's Sandinista Government obtained large quantities of weapons from the Soviet Union and Cuba that were subsequently cascaded to neighbouring insurgent groups.

Cuba was one of the region's most avid Cold War era suppliers. In Guatemala, Cuba provided the Guatemalan National Revolutionary Unit (UNRG) with US-made M-16s left in Vietnam after the US pulled out in the 1970s. To this day, many of these US-Vietnamese vintage rifles are circulating in Central and Latin America. Cuba also supplied Belgian-made FN FAL rifles purchased in the 1960s to the Farabundo Marti para la Liberacion Nacional (FMLN) in El Salvador, as well as 100,000 North Korean-made Kalashnikov-style assault rifles to Salvadoran guerrillas in 1987.

By the early 1990s, however, covert small arms sales in Central America had largely dried up, their ideological impetus dissolving with the demise of the Cold War. Today, though modest legal transfers of military small arms continue, there is little demand in a region already so saturated with small arms and light weapons that is now in the midst of a post-conflict peace-building process.

Source: Godnick, 2000

With respect to illicit small arms transfers, many governments are not accountable; many are irresponsible; and many are actively and/or passively supplying small arms to embargoed countries or non-state actors.

The focus is on conflict zones in an attempt to identify the most common sources, suppliers, and recipients of illicit small arms transfers. The grey and black markets are looked at in combination because it is often difficult to draw the line between them.

While the black market in small arms may constitute a major problem both nationally and internationally, it is the grey market that is predominantly responsible for supplying small arms to regions of conflict. Government involvement in such transfers is evident in almost every case, with most transfers occurring in violation of international and national laws. With respect to destabilizing small arms transfers, three conclusions are unavoidable:

- Many governments are not accountable;
- Many governments are irresponsible; and
- Many governments are actively and/or passively supplying small arms to embargoed countries or non-state actors.

Africa

In 1999, there were eleven major armed conflicts in Africa, ten of which were internal.

According to Stockholm International Peace Research Institute (SIPRI), there were eleven major armed conflicts in Africa in 1999 alone.[5] One of these, the war between Ethiopia and Eritrea, was interstate, the rest were intra-state—internal 'domestic'—conflicts, although the violence often has a spill-over effect into neighbouring states. Major conflicts raged in Algeria, Angola, Burundi, Democratic Republic of Congo (DRC), Guinea-Bissau, Republic of Congo, Rwanda, Sierra Leone, Somalia, and Sudan.

It may come as no surprise then that Africa is a major recipient of small arms. Its major suppliers are the countries of Eastern Europe and the CIS, and China. Also significant, however, are small arms transfers from western countries, as well as indigenous production of small arms within the region (PRODUCERS). While many small arms transfers to Africa may be technically legal, the lack of transparency with respect to countries such as China, the Russian Federation, Ukraine, and Bulgaria—as well as the fact that many weapons end up in areas of conflict or tension means that many of them may start out legal, but end up in the grey or black market.

Map 5.1   Africa, 'crucible of strife'

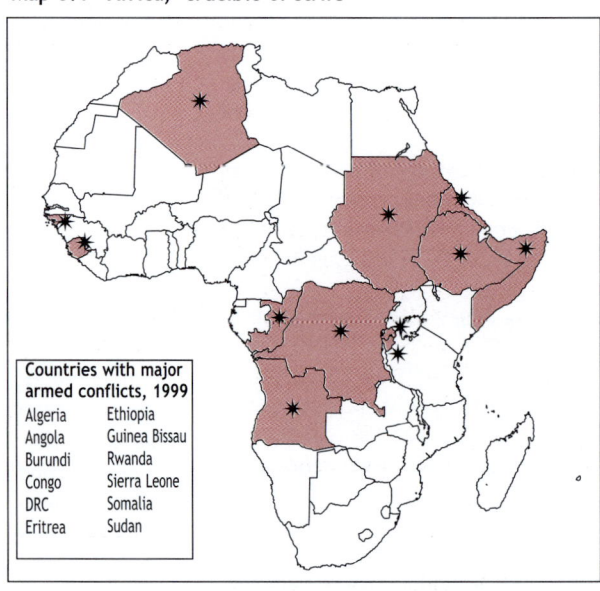

Countries with major armed conflicts, 1999

Algeria	Ethiopia
Angola	Guinea Bissau
Burundi	Rwanda
Congo	Sierra Leone
DRC	Somalia
Eritrea	Sudan

North Africa

Concrete data on small arms in North Africa is hard to come by. According to numerous reports, Libya is a significant source of weapons in the region and beyond. It is purportedly supplying the Goukouni Weddeyye rebels in Chad (Smith, 1999). It has also been implicated in supplying weapons to West African rebels, specifically in Sierra Leone (Berman, 2000). In addition, Libya has strong ties with Muslim rebels in the Philippines, a fact illustrated by its recent interventions—and alleged payment of high ransoms—to secure the freedom of a number of Western hostages held by rebels there (Channel News Asia, 12 September 2000).

In Egypt in July 2000 police confiscated 100 automatic rifles, 200 military style pistols, and 50 Israeli-made Uzis from three Egyptian nationals. One of the arrestees reportedly travelled frequently to Libya (Samir, 2000). This crackdown is indicative of Egypt's tougher stance on unregistered firearms and efforts to mitigate illicit trafficking. In 1999 Egyptian officials also confiscated 1,864 firearms, 1,200 of which were locally made revolvers. Four illicit production operations were raided in the same year (Al-Bindari, 2000). Chad is allegedly another source of illicit arms to Egypt, supplying weapons to terrorists in upper Egypt which have been smuggled in via Sudan (Al-Bindari, 2000). On the other hand, Egypt itself is a reported source of weapons smuggled into the Gaza Strip, as well as a supplier to Sudanese rebels (Smith, 1999).

Africa is a major recipient of illicit small arms.

In Algeria, press reports allege that indigenous terrorist groups are being supplied with small arms and financial assistance from Osama bin Ladin. In 1999 they groups were reportedly equipped with 'brand new Uzi sub-machine guns'. Israeli-made weapons are the most frequently confiscated weapons in Algeria. From 1993 to 1999, Algerian security services confiscated 400 Uzis and other Israeli-made weapons, in addition to other weapons of Belgian and Czech origin. According to Algerian sources, the arms trafficking networks supplying weapons in the country are based mainly in Germany, Italy, Poland, and the Czech Republic. 'Western intelligence services' are reportedly well-informed about these illicit arms deals, but 'choose, as regards Algeria, to turn a blind eye' (*BBC Summary of World Broadcasts,* 2 April 1999). Other reports claim that rebels in Algeria, specifically the Front Islamique de Salut (FIS), obtain weapons primarily from attacks on military and police depots, as well as from Sudan (Smith, 1999).

West Africa: The example of Sierra Leone

Sierra Leone is a worst-case scenario in the conflict-ridden West African region. This resource-rich, peace-poor West African country has been the scene of some of the most brutal small arms-driven violence on the continent, drawing in even small children as 'soldiers'.

Small arms transfers in Sierra Leone are driven in large part by the desire of rebel forces to control, and reap the rich financial benefits of, the country's diamond mines.[6] The Revolutionary United Front (RUF), the armed rebel group in Sierra Leone that controls a majority of the country's diamond mines, has committed some of the worst human rights abuses in recent times, including rape, abduction, murder, and—the group's signature instrument of terror—the hacking off of limbs of men, women, children, even infants.

Although difficult to verify, there are reports indicating that one of the major sources of weapons supply for the RUF is

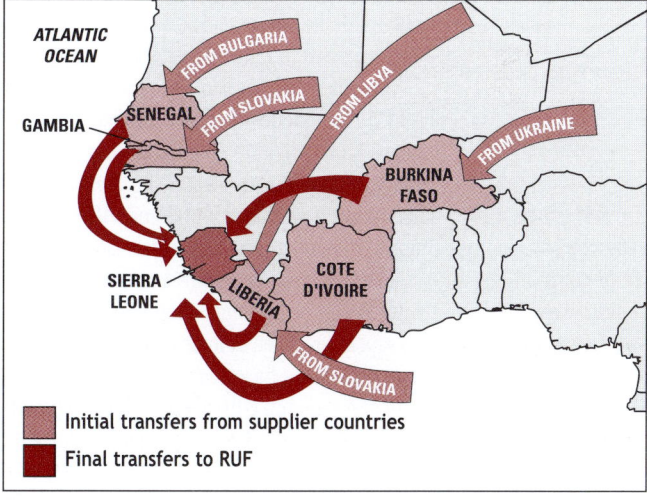

Map 5.2 Sierra Leone, driving West Africa's small arms violence

Initial transfers from supplier countries

Final transfers to RUF

through Liberia, specifically through the support of Liberia's President Charles Taylor. According to a statement by the US Ambassador Richard Holbrooke, the RUF finances its weapons purchases through the annual sale of an estimated US$ 30-50 million in diamonds, with approximately 60 per cent of them going through Liberia (Berman, 2000). Taylor's military support of the RUF has continued unabated from1991 up to the present, despite UN arms embargoes in force against the RUF and Liberia itself.

The RUF also has various other sources of small arms and light weapons. Libya allegedly flies air cargo arms shipments into Burkina Faso and then on to Liberia, where the arms are transferred to helicopters, air-dropped from small planes, or transported overland to RUF-controlled territory. Burkina Faso is a predominant conduit country in facilitating arms transfers to Liberia and Sierra Leone. Unconfirmed reports state that in 1998 numerous arms shipments were transported on a Burkina Faso-registered plane with flights originating from Rabat, Morocco, with a stopover in Ouagadougou, Burkina Faso and then on to Robertsfield, Liberia (HRW, 2000). Côte d'Ivoire has also been singled out as a source of military assistance to the RUF (Berman, 2000).

One of the best-documented recent cases of arms transfers to the RUF was in March 1999 when a shipment of small arms from Ukraine (including 3,000 Kalashnikov rifles, 50 machine guns, 25 grenade launchers, five SA-7s, five Metis anti-tank missiles, and associated ammunition) was sent to Burkina Faso (Wood, 2000). The shipment was facilitated by a Gibraltar-based firm, the Chartered Engineering and Technical Company, Ltd., and transported by a British airfreight company, Air Foyle, from Kiev to Burkina Faso. From there, the weapons went on to Liberia and the RUF (HRW, 2000). Charged with breaking the embargo, the Ukrainian Government defended itself before the UN Security Council in June 1999, presenting the documentation that it had shipped the arms to the Government of Burkina Faso only. It is worth mentioning that, in the absence of a special dispensation for the transfer, both Ukraine and Burkina Faso were breaking the Economic Community of West African States (ECOWAS) moratorium on small arms purchases in West Africa, to which Burkina Faso is a signatory.[7]

Western air cargo companies also appear to be involved in transporting arms to the RUF. There is evidence that British-based Sky Air Cargo and Belgian-owned Occidental Airlines have flown arms from Bratislava, Slovakia to Liberia and Gambia. Although the declared destination of these weapons was Uganda, they were in fact transferred to Sierra Leone, landing at a rebel-held airstrip in Kenema. The same route has been used to transfer arms to rebels in the Congo (Wood, 2000) (BROKERS).

In addition to small arms acquired from Ukraine and Slovakia, according to the US Government, the RUF has also received weapons from Bulgaria. In July 1999, a diamond dealer arranged for the transport of 68 tons of weapons from Bulgaria to the rebels. The Continental Aviation Company, based in Dakar, Senegal allegedly carried out the transfer of arms (Berman, 2000).

Not content to rely solely on the active and passive support from the aforementioned governments, the RUF also obtains weapons through theft and confiscations in battles with the Sierra Leone military. Small amounts of arms are also acquired through illicit trafficking from Guinea along the border with Sierra Leone. Reportedly, Guinean officials regularly confiscate arms from RUF rebels and others crossing the border into Guinea. However, there is an unofficial 'live and let live' policy between Guinean military and police officials along the Sierra Leone border and the RUF (Berman, 2000).

Yet another source of RUF weapons is those confiscated from the Economic Community of West African States' Monitoring Group (ECOMOG), as well as from UN troops in the area. While some of the weapons are taken by force in the thick of battle, there have been instances where ECOMOG troops simply abandoned their weapons while in retreat from the RUF.

Of grave concern is the alleged role of some UN peacekeeping troops in complicity with RUF rebels in Sierra Leone and the surrounding region.

Of grave concern is the alleged role of UN peacekeeping forces in the region. There have been reports of sales of weapons by UN troops; in particular, alleged cases of Nigerian ECOMOG troops selling arms and ammunition to the RUF in Liberia in exchange for cash, diamonds, food, and medicine (Berman, 2000). In a more significant transfer, Guinean United Nations Mission in Sierra Leone (UNAMSIL) troops were ambushed and relieved of 485 Kalashnikovs, 30 pistols, 24 light machine guns, 20 rocket-propelled grenade launchers (RPGs), ten 82mm mortars, ammunition, and larger pieces of equipment, including three armoured personnel carriers and several pieces of artillery. Unofficially, there is speculation among UN officials and Western diplomats that this transfer was the result of a payoff with the complicity of corrupt Guinean military officials (Berman, 2000). More recently, in May

2000, Zambian UNAMSIL troops were taken hostage by the RUF and were reportedly relieved of about 500 assault rifles, a few dozen machine guns, several mortars, and tons of ammunition. Indian and Kenyan UN peacekeepers have also had weapons forcibly taken from them by rebels (Berman, 2000).

In May 2000, a journalist viewing weapons depots containing arms confiscated from, or handed in by, rebels in Sierra Leone said that there were over 12,000 small arms and 389,877 rounds of ammunition at three separate depots. The majority of the rifles in the depots were said to be Kalashnikovs of Ukrainian origin, followed by Iranian made G3 rifles and Belgian made FN FALs (Wood, 2000).

Box 5.3 The UN Report on Violations of Security Council Sanctions against UNITA

In March 2000, a panel of investigative experts submitted a report (the Fowler Report) to the UN Security Council detailing how rebels from the Uniao Nacional Para a Independencia Total de Angola (UNITA) were able to break UN sanctions.[8] The findings of the report with respect to small arms procurement reveal complicity at the highest levels of government, including leaders from certain states in the region.

In the early 1990s, UNITA procured large amounts of arms, mainly manufactured in Eastern Europe, through a South African arms dealer, Ronnie De Decker. The purchases were financed with diamond sales reputedly worth US$ 4-5 million. Then, in the mid-1990s, UNITA began tapping into other sources of supply. From 1995 on, the then-president of Zaire, Mobutu Sese Seko, agreed to assist UNITA in its arms procurement. Weapons were shipped from Eastern Europe to Zaire and then passed on to UNITA. Mobutu provided UNITA leader Jonas Savimbi with Zairian end-user certificates and received diamonds and cash in return.

Zaire's Mobutu was not the only Head of Government involved in the supply of arms to UNITA. Following the overthrow of Mobutu, President Eyadema of Togo became UNITA's main arms supplier. It was agreed that Togo would keep 20 per cent of the arms shipments bound for UNITA, either in kind or in cash, in return for Togolese end-user certificates to purchase more arms. Once again, the majority of these weapons came from Eastern Europe. Other arms and military equipment have reached UNITA through Burkina Faso, Rwanda, and Congo. The original sources of arms implicated in the deals included Bulgaria, Belarus, Ukraine, and the Russian Federation.

Bulgarian arms manufacturers and Ukrainian flight crews were allegedly those most frequently involved in the supply of arms to UNITA. Bulgaria is accused of accepting end-user certificates at face value with little regard for where the weapons would eventually end up. Although the Bulgarian Government officially attacked the methodology of the UN-commissioned Fowler Report, which gathered much of its information from the testimony of UNITA defectors, it has launched an investigation into the matter. Other countries such as Ukraine and Belarus implicated in this report have either dismissed or not responded to the charges levelled against them.

Investigations of sanction-breaking small arms procurement for Angola's UNITA rebels reveal complicity at the highest levels of government.

The Horn of Africa and beyond: The case of Sudan

The war in Sudan is probably one of the most under-reported wars in the international media. Cast as a war driven mainly by conflict between special interest groups in the mainly Muslim north and the primarily animist and Christian south, it is the main factor in driving the demand for small arms in the country. Both sides have a long and pernicious record of human rights abuses, including slavery, rape, and arbitrary killings.

The Sudanese Government: Despite sanctions against the Government of Sudan by a number of states, many weapons, including small arms, continue to flow into the country. Western intelligence services estimate that the Sudanese Government spends US$ 485 million on arms each year, despite the fact that this country is one of the world's poorest. Recent weapons suppliers to the Sudanese Government allegedly include Libya, Qatar, and China (Lamb, 2000).

A well-documented case has proved the regular transfer of ammunition from Slovakia to agents for the Government of Sudan. The ammunition leaves Slovakia by plane, with an end-user certificate signed by the Defence Ministry of Chad, but lands instead in Khartoum, Sudan, where part or all of its cargo is offloaded (Johnson-Thomas, 2000).

Map 5.3 Arms flows to the Sudanese government and rebels

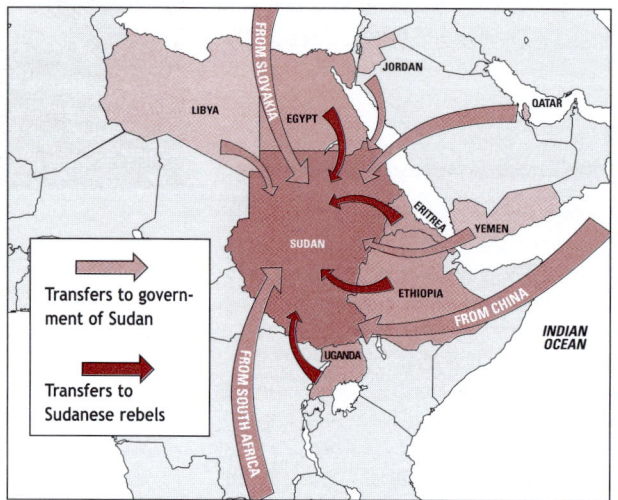

Where does the money to finance these arms purchases come from? The Sudanese Government is replete with revenues from its newly exploited oilfields in which the China National Petroleum Corporation is a leading international consortium partner, hence China's interest in supporting the government's control of the oilfields. Other partners include the Malaysian National Petroleum Corporation, and two Canadian companies, Arakis Energy Corporation and Talisman Energy. According to a Sudanese diplomat, arms are shipped to Sudan from China under the guise of oil exploration equipment from the Malaysian National Petroleum Corporation and the Chinese National Petroleum Corporation (HRW, 1998).

Despite the fact that Sudan is one of the world's poorest countries, its government spends an estimated US$ 485 million on arms each year.

Other alleged sources of small arms to the Sudanese Government include Iran, South Africa, Jordan, Yemen, and Qatar (Venter, 1999). A host of other nations, including Iraq, France, and several Eastern European states, have been implicated in sales of larger weapons systems, or sponsoring of military training and consultants to the Government of Sudan (HRW, 1998; Venter, 1999). In addition, Eritrea reports that the Sudanese Government receives arms purchased by independent Islamist financiers that are shipped through the United Arab Emirates using leased Russian cargo planes (HRW, 1998; Venter, 1999).

The Sudanese rebels: Persistent infighting among the Sudanese rebel forces based in the southern part of the country allows the government to pursue a strategy of 'divide and conquer', *inter alia* by supplying arms to various factions (Muggah and Berman, 2001). In addition, the National Democratic Alliance (NDA), a coalition of four rebel groups, has captured substantial quantities of small arms from Sudanese Government sources.

In terms of external suppliers, Uganda is allegedly a major source of weapons to the rebel forces, especially to the Sudan People's Liberation Army (SPLA), a member of the NDA. The Government of Uganda has officially denied these allegations. Other reported sources to rebel forces in Sudan are Ethiopia and Eritrea, both of which have large arms stocks previously supplied by the US and the former Soviet Union.

All the while, the world's major powers, including some of the largest arms producers and suppliers, are passively standing by. For example, since the US and Israel tacitly support the Sudanese rebels in their opposition to the Islamic government in Khartoum, there is little international condemnation of arms supplies to them. This fact was clearly illustrated by the lack of press coverage or public outcry in the summer of 2000, when the Government of Sudan bombed relief operations in the southern part of the country being carried out by the UN-sponsored agency Operation Lifeline Sudan (OLS) and the SPLA's humanitarian wing. The Sudanese Government protested that the relief operations were being used as a front for arms transfers to the SPLA. According to press reports, a UN official admitted that some organizations were using the relief mission as a cover for arms shipments (*Agence France Press,* 31 July 2000). However, certain Western governments apparently wanted to play down the incident.

Spreading regional instability: The civil war in Sudan—together with the conflicts in Somalia and Uganda, and the recently concluded war between Ethiopia and Eritrea—have constituted perhaps the deadliest cluster of conflicts in the world during the 1990s. All of them are closely interlinked, with cross-border arms flows spreading instability and undermining internal peace processes.

For example, in addition to arming Sudanese rebels, there is also evidence that Ethiopia and Eritrea are arming rival proxies in Somalia, in violation of the UN arms embargo on Somalia in force since 1992. Ethiopia has allegedly supplied the Somali warlord Musa Sudi Yalahow among others (*Agence France Press,* 21 January 2000), while Eritrea has allegedly supported Somali warlord Hussein Mohmed Aidid with arms since early 1999. It is reported that some of the weapons shipments were transported by Russian cargo ships chartered by Eritrea to the Somali port of Merca. One reported shipment from Eritrea to Aidid in 1999 consisted of 5,000 Kalashnikov rifles, machine guns, G3 rifles, ammunition, and explosives (*Jane's Intelligence Review,* 1 August 1999).[9]

One of the regional spillover effects has been increasing instability in Kenya. Lokichokkio Airport in Northwest Kenya is a significant trans-shipment point for arms into the region (Muggah and Berman, 2001). In the summer of 2000, Kenyan President Daniel Arap Moi highlighted the problem of illicit trafficking of arms into his country when he called on citizens in Kenya's North Eastern province to hand in illegally held weapons. To make good on his demand, Kenyan police broke up an arms trafficking ring operating in the North Eastern provinces, which border both Ethiopia and Somalia and face an influx of illegal weapons from both countries (*Xinhua,* 10 August 2000). Among the weapons seized was an M-16 rifle stamped 'Property of the US Government' (*The Nation,* 10 August 2000), probably originating from Somalia, where the US lost weapons during their 1992 intervention.

In May 2000, the UN placed an arms embargo on Ethiopia and Eritrea, and in August 2000 President Vladimir Putin banned Russian Federation arms exports to both countries. If these embargoes are enforced, they will hopefully reduce the weapons supply to the two warring countries and also limit their ability to ignite new rounds of conflict in the surrounding countries. Nevertheless, the large quantities of small arms and light weapons that have steadily flowed into the Horn of Africa over the last decades indicate that the region will remain saturated with small arms for the foreseeable future.

Europe

Europe and the CIS are major small arms supply sources. While the majority of their transfers are legal, a few teeter on the verge of being illicit while others have already slipped into the murky abyss of illegality. In other words, the region is a ready source of supply for the grey and black markets.

The small arms situation in Eastern Europe and the CIS must be viewed in the context of the overall political and economic hardships endured since the end of the Cold War, most particularly since the break-up of the Soviet Union in the early 1990s. In many cases, the arms industries in these struggling economies represent one of the few remaining competitive export sectors in the international market, not to mention their being a prime source of highly coveted hard currencies. For this reason, these governments feel an even greater incentive to promote these companies' survival at all costs.

Then there is also the basic national security incentive for many newly independent countries that want to extricate themselves from their former dependence on countries like the Russian Federation for their military hardware. Since these countries are, for the most part, too small to support a small arms industry based solely on national demand, exports are the route to economic viability.

While the majority of European and CIS countries have been able to preclude military-style weapons falling into the wrong hands, some others—such as Yugoslavia and Albania (Balkans), Georgia (Caucasus), and the Russian Federation (CIS)—have witnessed a burgeoning of black markets and stolen weapons seeping into the civilian population and/or into the possession of criminal organizations.

Eastern, Central, and Southern Europe

Since the end of the Cold War, Eastern European arms producers have been implicated in a number of grey market transfers. While the covert sales of the Cold War era were ideologically driven, sales today are for the most part purely economically driven. Most Eastern European producers are still either state-owned or heavily government-controlled. Thus, one could conclude that the vast majority of small arms exported from Eastern European countries, whether legal or grey market, occur with at least some official government knowledge.

As a case in point, in April 1999, Moldovan customs officials confiscated a Ukrainian cargo plane at the airport in Chisinau, Moldova, carrying 5,000 undeclared Hungarian-made pistols. The original flight plan followed a route from Budapest, Hungary on to Chisinau, followed by a stopover in Bulgaria and finally on to Yemen, where the weapons would be transferred to the Yemeni Defence Ministry. However, Moldovan officials suspected that the end-user certificate was false and that the actual destination of the guns was to be Yugoslavia (Demidetsky, 2000). As this publication went to press, the Ukrainian transport company was threatening the Moldovan Government with a lawsuit claiming unlawful seizure of this arms shipment.

While many Eastern European countries transfer weapons to Africa, other regions are also willing 'beneficiaries' of their sophisticated brokering and transfer system. Certain countries, such as Bulgaria, seem to be implicated more often than others as arms suppliers to non-state actors. As stated earlier, there are allegations of Bulgaria sending arms to the RUF in Sierra Leone and UNITA in Angola. Bulgarian arms have also been found in Albania. Slovak arms and ammunition are reportedly going to Sudan and the RUF in Sierra Leone, while the Czech Republic has allegedly armed Sri Lanka's Liberation Tigers of Tamil Eelam (LTTE).

The European Union is not immune to wrongdoing. For example, there are unconfirmed reports that the Kurdish Workers Party (PKK) in Turkey has received Stinger missiles from Greece, which are produced there under US license (Hunter, 1999). In turn, the PKK has allegedly passed on some of these Stingers to the LTTE in Sri Lanka.

The Balkans

The Balkans is one of the few regions in the world where the volume of the black market in arms may well rival that of the grey and legal markets combined.

The devastating ethnic wars in the Balkans throughout the 1990s have ruthlessly driven demand, as well as supply, of small arms and light weapons. This is one of the regions in the world where the black market in arms may well rival the grey and legal markets in terms of quantities of weapons, contributing to destabilizing accumulations. One of the major sources of illicit small arms in the region was the civilian looting of military depots in Albania in 1997, following a nation-wide panic after the collapse of pyramid investment schemes. More than 600,000 small arms were taken from Albanian army depots.[10] Of these, more than half a million remain in civilian hands (*CNN*, 7 September 2000). The Government of Albania has been trying to collect the weapons, but the instability of the country (both political and economic) plays a role in citizens' reluctance to turn in the weapons. The United States, Germany, and Norway are giving financial assistance to the Albanian Government for their collection and planned destruction programme. The Government of Albania has stated that it will destroy 100,000 small arms by the year 2002.

In the late 1990s, substantial weapons trafficking in the Balkans has involved the Kosovo Liberation Army (KLA), its organized crime networks, and sympathizers. While many KLA weapons came from looted Albanian military depots, Germany, Austria, and Switzerland—all countries with large Kosovar refugee populations—have also been a source of arms smuggled into the area. In a fairly typical case, Italian police confiscated 40 Austrian-made rifles at the port of Trieste that had been sold by a Swiss arms dealer to four Yugoslav nationals resident in Switzerland (*Die Presse,* 20 May 1999, p. 4).

With its large militia army and national gun culture, Switzerland is an obvious target as a source of weapons for such illicit weapons transactions. Another recent incident there involved the illegal use of the emblem of a Swiss aid organization on trucks supposedly filled with donations for Kosovar refugees that were actually used to transport arms. Switzerland has also been used as a financial centre for such transactions. For example, in the summer of 1999, a shipment of Bulgarian arms, including several hundred rocket launchers and several thousand grenades, was confiscated in Durres, Albania. When it was ascertained that the destination for these weapons was an African country, Swiss authorities arrested two individuals residing in Switzerland involved in the financing of the transaction and, as of August of 2000, had recovered US$ 440,000 (700,000 CHF) of the US$ 2.8 million (4.5 million CHF) deal (*Tribune de Genève,* 31 August 2000, p. 22).[11]

The weapons networks built up during the Kosovo conflict have spread small arms throughout the Balkan region. At one point in 1999, Macedonian police estimated that anywhere from 20-30,000 small arms were cached in the western part of the country by KLA operatives and sympathizers. Impoverished ethnic Albanians were reportedly selling Kalashnikov rifles in Macedonia for as little as US$ 25 a piece (Dimevski, 2000).

'Peace dividends' when conflict is over can also mean that weapons are 'freed up' for transfer to other regions. For example, it is reported that Bosnia and Herzegovina has become a source of surplus arms since the cease-fire (Simunovic, 2000). In July 2000, a shipment of portable rocket launchers, assault rifles, ammunition, and explosives was confiscated in Croatia. Croatian authorities, suspecting that the weapons originated in Bosnia and Herzegovina, conducted an investigation and concluded that the weapons were destined for the Real IRA (RIRA) in Northern Ireland (*Jane's Terrorism and Security Monitor,* 23 August 2000; Simunovic, 2000).

Conversely, on a positive note, the Balkans have been at the centre of some of the most ambitious and successful small arms and light weapons collection and destruction efforts. The North Atlantic Treaty Organization (NATO) has ongoing programmes in Bosnia and Kosovo, and the UN had collection programmes in Eastern Slavonia (Croatia) in 1997 and Gramsh, Albania in 1999. In addition, the Albanian Government has itself retrieved some of the weapons looted from state depots in 1997.

The Commonwealth of Independent States (CIS)

The Russian Federation: The Russian black market in arms has a strong economic component, appearing to be primarily driven by two factors: 1) economic hardship that encourages the Russian military to illicitly sell military weapons stocks; and 2) an unprecedented demand for weapons resulting from the wave of organized crime in the region.

Black market arms confiscation and theft data provide a disturbing glimpse into the quantities of arms in the Russian Federation's black market in recent years:

- In 1997, Russian border guards confiscated 1,300 firearms at Russian border control points.

The Russian black market in arms is driven by two factors: economic hardship that encourages illicit sales and an unprecedented demand for weapons by organized crime.

Russian armed forces may be the largest single source of stolen military equipment in the world.

- In 1998, there were 66,000 registered crimes involving illegal firearms trade, according to the results of a meeting of Russian federal law enforcement agencies convened to address arms trafficking (Allen, 1999); in the same year, there were 1,352 registered cases of firearms theft from Russian military units (IISS, 2000).[12] Most of these thefts were committed by Russian servicemen, mainly driven by economic incentives and connections to organized crime. In fact, some researchers claim that Russian armed forces are the largest source of stolen military equipment in the world (IISS, 2000).

- In 1998, the country's Federal Security Service (FSB, the successor to the KGB) confiscated 22,000 small arms, 6,500 grenades, and four tons of explosives on Russian territory (*Interfax*, 22 January 1999)—this, in addition to whatever was confiscated by other agencies.

- As of 1999, the Russian Ministry of the Interior reported that it was still trying to retrieve an estimated 36,000 weapons lost or stolen from the Russian Government. Of these, 13 were heavy rocket systems, 18 mortars and other artillery, and approximately 15,000 assault rifles (Allen, 1999). This figure does not include 40,000-plus small arms in the hands of Chechen rebels (see Box. 5.4).

Allegations are rife of the Russian mafia's involvement in arms trafficking to rebels beyond the Russian Federation's vast borders. For example, the Russian mafia, specifically the US-based branch, is rumoured to have been an important source of weapons for Colombian rebels, as well as paramilitary troops, at least since the mid-1990s. According to one report, more than 30 Russian organized crime groups operating out of the US, primarily in Florida and Puerto Rico, have collaborated with

---

Box 5.4 Arming Chechnya

Chechnya provides an intricate example of illicit small arms transfers. According to unofficial sources, the first such transfer occurred in May-June 1991, arranged between the ethnic Armenian militia in Nagorno-Karabakh and the National Congress of the Chechen People.

The militia in Nagorno-Karabakh began to arm itself with more modern small arms and light weapons obtained from Soviet military units stationed in the Caucasus. In turn, they got rid of their obsolete arms and those of inferior quality—for example, German rifles dating back to World War II and poor quality craft weapons turned out in Armenian metal working plants. Production of these Armenian craft weapons had begun in 1988 and, although virtually disposable due to their inferior quality, by 1990 the quantity manufactured already numbered in the thousands. Through Georgian paramilitary middlemen (Tengiz Kitovani and his deputy for armaments, Geli Lanchavi),[13] a significant number of Armenian small arms were traded for oil and oil products from Chechnya. The storming of the government offices of the Chechnya-Ingushetia Autonomous Soviet Socialist Republic (ASSR) and the seizure of Russian Federation military installations in Chechnya by armed Chechen rebels was actually carried out using these weapons of Armenian origin.

After the subsequent overthrow of the government of Doku Zavgayev and the proclamation of Chechen independence, the major source of small arms for the Chechen rebels was, ironically enough, the Russian Federation army itself. On 28 May 1992, the Russian Minister of Defence Pavel Grachev issued Directive No.316/1/030 ordering the hand-over to General Dzhokhar Dudayev of half of all the military armaments belonging to Russian Federation forces in Chechnya. Attempts to remove the other half failed and in June 1992, under the threat of attack from rebel forces, practically all these weapons were transferred to Dudayev's troops. According to official testimony, no more than 10,000 pieces of arms were evacuated from Chechnya at the time.

Archival documents from the Russian Federation Ministry of Defence and the federal counterespionage agency reveal that an investigation was made into the quantity of arms left on Chechen territory by the Russian Army when it pulled out in 1992. In addition to many military vehicles and armoured personnel carriers, it was determined that 40 pieces of various

---

Colombian drug traffickers, supplying Russian weapons in exchange for cocaine (Farah, 2000). According to Spanish intelligence reports, the Canary Islands are also reported to be a favoured arms transit point for the Russian mafia's deals in Africa (*El Mundo,* 2 November 1999).

Kazakhstan: Most of the successor states to the Soviet Union are dealing with a similar problem when it comes to theft of weapons from military arsenals. In 1999, Kazakhstan's Ministry of the Interior seized 1,095 weapons from organized criminal groups, 'nearly all' of which had been stolen from military depots. In the same year, there were 14 criminal cases involving arms thefts by soldiers (*Tass,* 1 January 2000).

Georgia, Armenia, Azerbaijan: The war in Chechnya aside, the South Caucasus is a region replete with conflicts and political tensions. Ethnic conflict, together with organized crime and a nascent gun culture—all pervasive characteristics of this region—fuel an ongoing demand for small arms. In Georgia, the war in Abkhazia continues while the cease-fire in Ossetia, although holding in general, continues to be breached by sporadic episodes of violence. Border clashes between Armenia and Azerbaijan also continue in connection with the dispute over the Armenian-controlled enclave of Nagorno-Karabakh in Azerbaijan. Add to this the many well-armed organized crime rings in the area that traffic in arms, drugs, and prostitution and a very volatile situation throughout the entire region emerges.

The former Soviet regional arsenals serve as the primary sources for small arms. Additionally, many weapons are acquired through theft and black market trafficking. However, there appear to be covert grey market sales as well. Armenia allegedly supplies the ethnic Armenian populace in

anti-aircraft missile launchers and artillery, and 590 pieces of modern anti-tank weapons, were left in Chechnya by Russian forces. However, the investigation report noted that the quantity of small arms left in Chechnya was practically impossible to assess. According to various estimates, the number is between 41,538 and 57,596 pieces. The Russian Defence Ministry has reported the following figures: 18,832 AK-74s; 9,307 AKMs, 533 Dragunov sniper rifles, 138 grenade launchers, 678 tank machine guns, 319 large calibre machine guns, and 10,581 pistols. Although equally difficult to pinpoint the quantity of ammunition left behind, it is believed that Chechen rebels acquired no less than 740 pieces of anti-tank munitions, about 200,000 hand grenades, and over 13 million rounds of ammunition.

There were also several other significant sources of small arms and light weapons transfers to Chechnya. For example, in the summer of 1994, Russian special forces troops attempted to transfer a substantial quantity of arms to the anti-Dudayev opposition; most of these, however, ended up in the hands of troops loyal to Dudayev.

In the course of the first Chechen conflict, Russian mass media reports stated that Chechen rebels were fighting with small arms and light weapons produced in 1995 and 1996. This suggests that another source of weapons for the armed conflict in the North Caucasus must have been the Russian arms industry itself.

From 1992 to 1993, Khankala airbase in the North Caucasus was used as a transit point for the transfer of Russian armaments to Armenia, Nagorno-Karabakh, and Abkhazia (Georgia). There is evidence that some of these arms in transit to Russian forces in Abkhazia and Armenia also ended up in Chechnya.

Finally, in the second half of the 1990s, the Chechen rebels' primary sources of arms were allegedly Turkey,[15] a number of Arab governments, and the Taleban Islamic fundamentalist movement. Other Islamic movements and countries that have Soviet-style arms and are likely current sources for the Chechen rebels include Egypt, the Autonomous Palestinian Territories, Libya, Iraq, and possibly Syria.
Source: CAST, 2000

Map 5.4 The Caucasus: A region replete with conflicts and political tensions

Nagorno-Karabakh and has initiated its own domestic production of small arms, mainly in response to the OSCE arms embargo on it. In violation of this embargo, Armenia received numerous weapons shipments from the Russian Federation in 1997. The investigation following the discovery of these shipments uncovered complicity at the highest levels of the Russian military. Although most of these 1997 transfers were not small arms but larger weapons systems, such as tanks and artillery, the incident underscores the Russian Federation's role in the region.

On the other hand, there are allegations that Azerbaijan, also under an OSCE arms embargo, is receiving small arms from Turkey (*Armament and Military Technology,* 27 May 1998).[16] In addition, it is reported that Azerbaijan has received weapons from Bosnia, Afghanistan, and Pakistan (Simunovic, 1999; *Armament and Military Technology,* 27 May 1998).

The situation in Georgia is exacerbated by tensions with the Russian Federation. Georgia has asserted that Russian military bases on its territory are a source of small arms for non-state combatants in the region, specifically for the Chechen rebels. For example, in January 2000, Georgian authorities intercepted a truck leaving the Russian military base of Vaziani (in Georgia) containing a 120mm mortar with ammunition and parts, 50 pistols, and 45,000 AK-74 cartridges. According to Georgian officials, this was the second such delivery from the Russian base destined for Chechen rebels in the North Caucasus. The Russian Federation officials categorically denied these allegations on both counts, saying Georgia itself was involved and that this was a media ploy fuelled by its animosity over the presence of these Russian bases on their territory (Gordon, 2000; *Itar-Tass,* 11 January 2000).

The whole region has fallen prey to a high level of organized crime, and a pervasive gun culture has developed rapidly since the break-up of the Soviet Union. For example, gun dealers in Tbilisi advertise the sale of Kalashnikovs with neon signs. All this is a relatively new development in the region since during the Soviet era it was impossible for such a gun culture to exist.

Asia and the Pacific

The scene in Asia and the Pacific is strewn with a series of armed conflicts and insurgencies in which the adversaries often obtain small arms from the same sources. While weapons from the 'Afghan pipeline' may not play as significant a role as they did earlier in the decade, the pipeline is still an important source of small arms in the region. Other alleged major supply sources include southeast Asian countries, such as Thailand, Cambodia, and Myanmar (Burma), as well as China and some CIS countries. Highly armed societies such as the Philippines also add fuel to the fire.

Central and South Asia

Between 1979 and 1989, the CIA channeled at least US$ 2 billion in weapons aid— an estimated 80 per cent of the agency's covert aid budget—to the mujahideen in Afghanistan.

Afghanistan, which received large amounts of weapons in the 1980s, remains a major source of small arms and light weapons in South and Central Asia. Between 1979 and 1989, the CIA channeled at least US$ 2 billion in weapons aid, or an estimated 80 per cent of the agency's covert aid budget, to the *mujahideen* in Afghanistan (Mathiak and Lumpe, 2000). The weapons were sent via Pakistan, which acted as a major transfer facilitator, despite estimates that only 30 per cent of the weapons ever reached their intended recipients (Smith, 1999). This so-called 'Afghan Pipeline' ran from Karachi or Rawalpindi in Pakistan, depending on whether the weapons arrived by sea or air, to Afghanistan (Smith, 1999).

Pakistan is a major source of small arms in South Asia.

Partly as a result of this practice of siphoning off a portion of the arms in transit, Pakistan has become a major source of small arms in South Asia, both in black market arms and in arms supplied covertly to insurgent groups in the region. While there are sometimes ideological incentives for transferring arms, some tribal groups (e.g. in Baluchistan) view these transactions mostly from a financial point of view.[17]

A vast array of military small arms is available in Pakistan, from M-16s and Uzis to Kalashnikovs of different makes, including Russian, Chinese, and Eastern European manufactures. There is clear evidence that small arms are transferred from Pakistan to rebel groups in the Indian states of Punjab and Kashmir. These transfers are carried out in conjunction with the military training camps operating in Pakistan, which train soldiers to fight in the war in Kashmir. If one takes the number of weapons seized by Indian Border Security Forces as an indicator, then such transfers appear to be increasing over time. For example, in 1987, the Indian security forces confiscated 33 rifles and 92 pistols while on border duties; in contrast, in 1996, they seized 16,772 Kalashnikov rifles alone (Kartha, 2000).

India's rebel groups also receive weapons originating in Pakistan. Three of the major insurgent groups in the northeastern part of the country (see Map 5.5) are the United Liberation Front of Assam (ULFA), the National Socialist Council of Nagaland (NSCN), and the National Democratic Front for Bodoland (NDFB). The ULFA and the NSCN have both received weapons through a pipeline originating in Pakistan (Dasgupta, 2000; Kartha, 2000) and the southeast Asian pipeline running through Thailand, Malaysia, and Singapore (*The Hindu,* 18 August 2000). In addition:

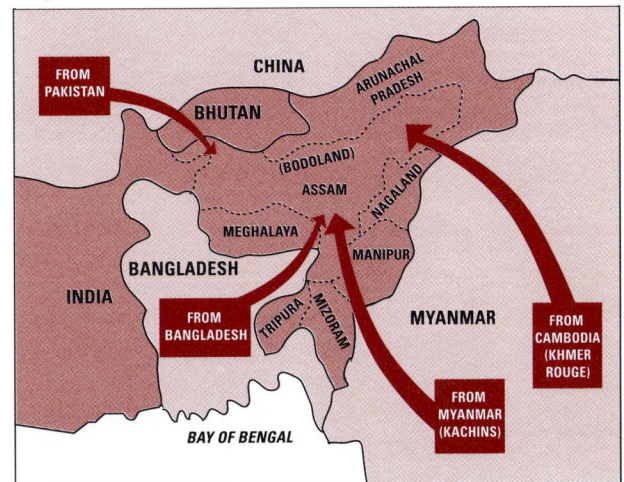

Map 5.5 Supplying insurgents in Northeastern India

- The **ULFA** is allegedly receiving direct support from the Bangladeshi Director-General of Foreign Intelligence, Indian intelligence sources claim. The same source asserts that China has now become a supplier to the ULFA as well. The arms are transported from China via merchant ships of various countries, including North Korea, to Cox's Bazar, a port in Bangladesh (*The Hindu,* 18 August 2000). The ULFA has developed contacts with Sri Lanka's LTTE, the rebels in Kashmir, the Kachins in Myanmar, and the Khmer Rouge in Cambodia (Dasgupta, 2000; *The Hindu,* 18 August 2000).

- The **NSCN**, which is the most heavily armed insurgent group in the region, has patronized armed insurgencies in the neighbouring states of Mizoram, Manipur, Tripura, and Assam (Dasgupta, 2000).

- The **NDFB**, an armed insurgency group in Assam, is receiving arms and training from Bangladesh. The NDFB also allegedly obtained weapons from the Khmer Rouge (Cambodia) and Kachin rebels (Myanmar) (*The Hindu,* 18 August 2000).

Myanmar has also played a major role as a supplier in the region, especially as a source of weapons for the LTTE and certain rebel groups in Northeast India. Though one of the world's most economically underdeveloped countries, Myanmar nevertheless has its own domestic small arms industry (PRODUCERS) and has also received significant quantities of weapons from China and Singapore (Huxley and Willet, 1999).

Bangladesh is a major transit point for arms in the region. Small arms come across to Bangladesh from Afghanistan and Pakistan on the one side, and from Thailand, Singapore, Myanmar, and Cambodia on the other. From there, the weapons usually go north to rebels in India's north-east or south to the LTTE.

Sri Lanka and the LTTE: The accumulation of small arms in Sri Lanka is driven by a bloody rebel secessionist movement led by the LTTE, fighting for independence from Sri Lanka in the northern part of the country. The LTTE has a sophisticated arms procurement network that includes obtaining weapons covertly from governments and through numerous black market channels. Weapons purchases are primarily funded by the Tamil diaspora in Switzerland, Canada, Australia, the US, the UK, and Scandinavia. One wealthy individual living in the US has allegedly given US$ 4 million to the LTTE over the past decade (Chalk, 2000). It is also reported that the LTTE derives funds from drug trafficking, primarily heroin. Thus, a well-heeled LTTE is able to purchase even quite sophisticated arms and equipment from various sources. Singapore and Hong Kong, with their strategic location and well-developed banking systems, serve as the financial nexus for LTTE weapons purchases (Chalk, 2000).

Map 5.6   South and South East Asia: The 'small arms road'

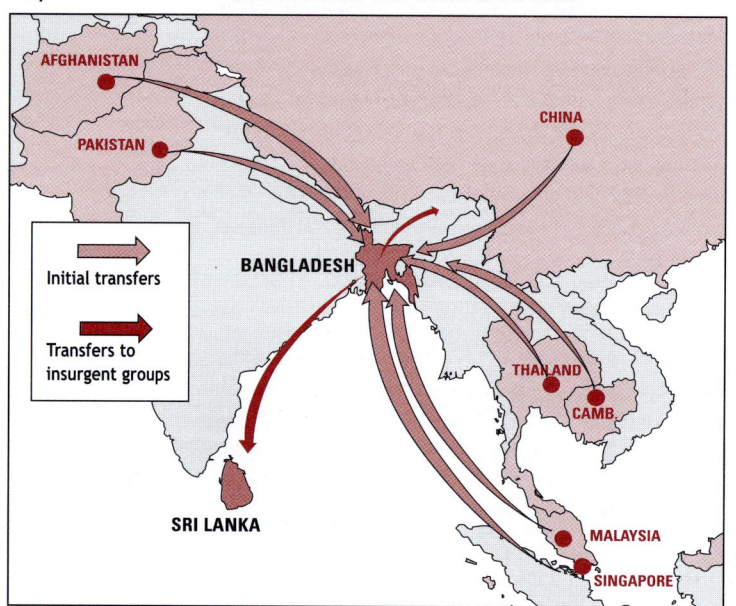

Since the 1980s, arms dealers in Lebanon, Cyprus, Singapore, Malaysia, and Hong Kong have purportedly facilitated arms purchases by the LTTE. They also received covert arms shipments from India up until 1987 when the transfers were officially stopped—even though, in fact, they allegedly continued until the assassination of former Indian Prime Minister Rajiv Ghandi in 1991. After the Indian arms flow dried up, they focused on building up other sources of supply. In the mid-1990s, the LTTE turned to Ukraine for weapons and explosives, submitting an end-user certificate signed by the Secretary of Defence of Bangladesh in at least one instance (Gunaranta, 2000). The LTTE has also received mortar rounds, surface-to-air missiles, and machine gun ammunition from Bulgaria and the Czech Republic (Davis, 2000). In 1997, Vietnam provided the LTTE with North Korean-made Igla man portable surface-to-air missiles. Vietnam is reported to have made more recent arms shipments to the LTTE as well (*Defence and Foreign Affairs Strategic Policy,* June-July 2000, p. 3; Gunaranta, 2000).

In 2000, there were reports that North Korea would be supplying the LTTE with small arms. While sporadic supplies of arms from North Korea had occurred in the past, there are allegations that the Government of North Korea is stepping up its sponsorship of the LTTE.

One well-worn transfer route for the LTTE is through Thailand, using an island near Phuket. The arms are trafficked from primarily Cambodia, and Myanmar, two countries with large stocks of arms in the region. Sri Lankan officials accused high-ranking Thai military officers of facilitating the transfers, although Thailand denied the accusations (*The Nation,* 29 March 2000). Other Thai regions likely being used by the LTTE for arms trafficking are Ranong and Satun (Davis, 1999).

In 1999, the Foreign Minister of Sri Lanka visited Cambodia to request the Government's assistance in shutting down that country's arms supply to the LTTE. Cambodian officials blamed the rebel Khmer Rouge as the culprits in the trade; however, evidence suggests that it is corruption among the Cambodian armed forces that is mainly to blame (Gunaranta, 2000).

In addition, there are assertions that the LTTE also gets arms from Africa, specifically from Nigeria, Zimbabwe, and South Africa (Chalk, 2000). Other sources include arms trafficked through the Afghan pipeline and Pakistan. There is sufficient evidence to lend credibility to a case reported in 1999 in which the LTTE obtained eleven Stinger missiles from the rebel PKK in Turkey—missiles manufactured in Greece under US licence (Hunter, 1999).[18]

Finally, perhaps the most ironic source of LTTE arms has been the Sri Lankan government itself. Indian sources allege that thousands of arms went to the LTTE in 1989, ostensibly so they could fight against the Indian Peacekeeping Force in Sri Lanka. More recently, sizeable amounts of weapons have been obtained from deserting Sri Lankan soldiers, as well as through thefts from government depots (Kartha, 2000).

The Philippines [19]

The Philippines is a hotbed of arms trafficking activities. A host of actors and armed groups within the country are engaged in transfers of small arms and light weapons, both legal and illegal. On the official government side are ranged the Philippine National Police (PNP), the Armed Forces of the Philippines (AFP), and the Citizens Auxiliary Force Geographical Units (CAFGU). Non-governmental actors include private citizens, private armies, criminal groups, legal and illegal manufacturers, smugglers, arms dealers, and armed insurgency groups operating in different parts of the country.

The Philippines has its own legal domestic small arms industry (PRODUCERS). In addition, in Danao there is a thriving illicit arms production industry that provides weapons to private individuals and criminal groups. There are also a number of criminal syndicates smuggling arms into the country. This is in addition to the arms flowing into the country to support the insurgency groups. It was reported that the Revolutionary People's Army, a Philippine communist insurgent group, received arms from China, although a spokesman for the group denied receiving foreign assistance, insisting that they relied on arms from domestic supporters (*Manila Times,* 4 March 2000; personal interview).

An Islamic secessionist movement in Mindanao, the Moro National Liberation Front (MNLF), which signed a peace agreement with the Philippine Government in 1996, received arms from Libya and Sabah, Malaysia. The Moro Islamic Liberation Front (MILF), an offshoot of the MNLF, is reported to receive arms from supporters in the Middle East through Malaysia (Garcia and Payumo, 2000; *The Strait Times Interactive,* 23 May 2000).

However, the vast majority of weapons procured by insurgency groups are obtained via the Philippine armed forces and national police. Many are captured during operations against the AFP or on raids of PNP supplies. The back-and-forth fluidity of arms between the government and insurgency forces is illustrated by the fact that the AFP frequently recovers these very same weapons lost in subsequent counter-operations. There are also cases where military officials and soldiers sell their arms outright to insurgency groups (*Manila Philippine Daily Enquirer,* 11 January 1999).

Insurgency groups also look to theft from landowners and kidnapping for ransom as a means to bolster their small arms arsenals. For example, Abu Sayyaf, an extreme Islamic group operating in Mindanao, made international headlines for months during the year 2000 after abducting dozens of tourists and locals from a diving resort in Malaysia and holding them for ransom. Intelligence sources report that the group received 'cash and guns in exchange for some of the freed hostages' (*South China Morning Post,* 2 August 2000). Libya reportedly paid US$ 1 million per hostage for each release (*Al-Sharq al-Awsat,* London, 12 September 2000), though a Libyan official stated that his government 'did not pay a ransom and that all that was agreed was that the Al-Qadhafi Charity Foundation would carry out some humanitarian projects' (*Channel News Asia,* 12 September 2000).

Not only do enormous quantities of arms flow into the Philippines; they flow out as well. Danao gunsmiths are known to export an undisclosed quantity of arms to criminal syndicates in Taiwan and are also a major source for Japan's Yakuza crime bosses (Seno, 1996; Perreño, 1995). There has also been speculation that Philippine-made arms are entering Indonesia's troubled Malukas via Mindanao.

The Pacific Region

A number of island states in the Pacific also find themselves beset with serious political and ethnic tensions. Major rebellions occurred in 2000 in Fiji and the Solomon Islands. In the latter case, rebels were reportedly armed with an array of small arms, ranging from World War II vintage weapons, to hunting rifles, to modern assault rifles apparently looted from police armouries (Blenkin, 2000).

Some of the most deadly armed groups in the Pacific operate in Papua New Guinea (PNG). In September 2000, press reports claimed that thousands of automatic and semi-automatic weapons were being smuggled in to PNG's criminal gangs and drug lords operating in the New Guinean highlands. The weapons are reportedly coming from Australia (those not turned in during Australia's gun amnesty period) and the Indonesian province of West Papua. Australian and Asian criminal gangs are primarily responsible for the transfers, but there are said to be connections with the Free Papua Movement (OPM) in West Papua, Indonesia. Analysts claim that the transfers not only threaten the security of Papua New Guinea, but also increase the chance of political tensions in West Papua becoming violent (Daley, 2000; *Stratfor.com,* 2000).

The Americas

Several fundamental factors are at work in the small arms situation in the Americas. First, some states, notably in Central America, are emerging from long periods of conflict and their left-over weapons are still in circulation in the region. Secondly, a number of armed conflicts continue in the region, most notably in Colombia. Thirdly, there are countries with high levels of crime and regions where the criminal drug culture is paramount. Finally, there are countries, such as the US and Brazil, with a highly developed gun culture among the civilian population. Not every country's experience with illicit trafficking in small arms is the same. While some of these factors may be of primary importance for the illicit small arms situation in certain countries, they may be virtually non-existent in others.

South America

Latin American illicit arms transfers have a number of unique features, as illustrated by the following examples.

Argentina has two main sources of black market arms: the illegal sale by Argentine arms producers of unregistered firearms, and the diversion of weapons from corrupt members of the military, police,

---

Box 5.5 Conditions conducive to illicit small arms transfers in the Americas

- Many small arms transfers are connected to narcotics trafficking and other organized crime activities;

- Rampant corruption among the military, police, and government officials in some countries facilitates such transfers;

- Cross-border trafficking is common due to the many porous, inadequately patrolled borders manned by poorly paid customs officials, many of whom are not averse to taking bribes;

- Some countries have a seemingly endless supply of weapons as a result of a history of covert transfers to the region;

- There are also a number of large indigenous small arms producers, including Argentina, Brazil, Canada, and the United States (PRODUCERS);

- Soaring crime rates in countries such as Brazil drive civilian demand for weapons intended primarily for personal protection; and finally

- Economic Free Trade zones, such as the Cayman Islands and Panama, provide ship registry flags of convenience for traffickers.

---

and security forces. One estimate of illegally-held firearms in Argentina puts the figure at more than 2.5 million (der Ghougassian and Lapieza-Spota, 1999). However, the director of operations of the National Arms Registrar (RENAR) estimates only between 50-200,000 illegal firearms. Foreign sources of illicit firearms in Argentina are minimal since its domestic arms industry prospered historically under protectionist policies (Dreyfus, 2000).

With respect to weapons diverted from corrupt government officials, there are three major sources. First, soldiers expelled from the military as a result of a series of failed military coups in 1987, 1988, and 1990 have formed criminal rings and obtain weapons from contacts remaining in the military. Secondly, active duty members of the armed forces, police, and security forces rent out assault rifles, semi-automatic pistols, and sub-machine guns to criminal gangs. Finally, local corrupt police officials sell confiscated weapons (der Ghougassian and Lapieza-Spota, 1999). Argentina does not have a major problem with weapons flowing into the country from outside sources; rather Argentina itself is a source of illicit weapons trafficked into neighbouring countries.

Chile, by comparison, has a relatively low level of corruption among officials. Still, in 1999, there were an estimated 600,000 illegally-held firearms in Chile, the primary sources being: cross-border smuggling, especially from Paraguay, where Argentina is used as the transit country, locally-produced homemade firearms, and small arms stolen from private individuals, police forces, and private security companies.

Chile has also had a number of minor insurgent organizations that were active until the mid-1990s, some of whose members have since turned to organized crime. These criminal groups, characterized by their possession of military assault weapons, are known for their penchant to rob banks and armoured cash transport vehicles. Recent police confiscations of their weapons have yielded US-made M-16s, abandoned in Vietnam when the US pulled out of the country in the 1970s, as well as Soviet-era sub-machine guns and assault rifles that were manufactured in Eastern Europe (Dreyfus, 2000).

Paraguay is a major source of assault rifles and other small arms in Latin America, most significantly for Brazil (see Box 5.6). Particularly Ciudad del Este, a Paraguayan city located in the tri-border region between Argentina, Brazil, and Paraguay, is known as a point of entry for automatic weapons, including Kalashnikovs, M-16s, G-3s, Galils, and Uzis. The weapons arrive at Guaraní

One estimate of illegally-held firearms in Argentina puts the figure at more than 2.5 million.

Airport, falsely labelled, and allegedly pass through customs for the most part without incident.[20] They are then transferred by air to clandestine landing strips in Colombia, Peru, and Brazil. Ciudad del Este also serves as an operations base for criminal gangs in the area, among them ethnic Chinese organized crime rings, Brazilian drug trafficking gangs, and ethnic Lebanese criminal organizations (Dreyfus, 2000).

Box 5.6   The booming Brazil-Paraguay 'ant trade'

A prime example of the previously described 'ant trade'—cross-border illicit trade from one state with lax gun purchasing requirements to another with stricter gun laws—is to be found in the Brazil-Paraguay small arms symbiosis.

Paraguay has relatively poorly-enforced gun purchasing laws in comparison to Brazil, making it easy for Brazilians to buy weapons there. In the 15-month period ending in May 2000, there were reportedly 1,779 weapons purchased in Paraguay by Brazilian nationals, the majority sold in towns along the Paraguayan-Brazilian border. Of these, 513 were 9mm pistols, which are illegal in Brazil except for military personnel, and therefore could not be legally registered.

Brazil, for its part, is one of the major legal small arms suppliers to Paraguay. Data from the Brazilian Ministry of Defence confirmed that 10,514 small arms were exported to Paraguay in 1998 alone—555 of them 9mm pistols produced by a single Brazilian manufacturer, Taurus. Since these 9mm pistols frequently find their way back illegally to their country of origin, the conclusion is that, using Paraguay as an intermediary, the Brazilian small arms industry is the source of a significant amount of illegally-held small arms within its own country.

To help combat such illicit small arms transfers, a co-operation agreement was recently concluded between the two countries, in which Paraguayan authorities promised to provide the Brazilian Government with data regarding the purchase of firearms by Brazilian nationals in Paraguay. However, the above data, a by-product of this agreement, reflect only those gun sales in which the official paperwork was filled out. Even this may be only 'the tip of the iceberg' as it is common that data provided by Paraguayan gun dealers to the authorities are incomplete or appear to be falsified. Only time—and better monitoring—will tell.

Source: ISER, 2000

On paper, Paraguay also imports large amounts of weapons from Brazil, although many of them never actually leave that country. The weapons are declared as exports to evade taxes, the legal loophole being that domestic sales are heavily taxed, while exported weapons are not. One estimate contends that only one-fifth of Brazilian weapons 'exported' to Paraguay actually arrive there. In one 1998 case, a shipment of 10,000 Glock automatic weapons destined for Paraguay was unloaded at the port of Santos, Brazil. The weapons were stolen and sold on the Brazilian black market to a group of bank robbers. According to Brazilian police, the weapons from this shipment continue to turn up, and be confiscated by the police, at least once a month (*O Estado de São Paulo,* 16 July 2000).

Only one-fifth of Brazilian weapons allegedly exported to Paraguay ever actually arrive there. It's about more than just tax evasion; it's also about crime.

There is also evidence that US-made weapons shipped to Paraguay end up being illegally trafficked to Brazil. In 1999, the Brazilian chief investigator for the Bank Hold-up Unit of the police requested information from US authorities on 120 US-manufactured rifles, sub-machine guns, and pistols. Of the 120 guns, US authorities provided information on only two guns that had been sold to a private dealer in Asunción, Paraguay (*O Estado de São Paulo,* 16 July 2000)— and this, despite the fact that the US supposedly stopped all small arms sales (with the exception of shotguns) to Paraguay in 1996. Nevertheless, reports have it that US-made weapons continue to enter Paraguay by way of Germany.

In Uruguay, there are 572,000 legally registered small arms, ten per cent of which are in the hands of the military or police. It is estimated that the country has an equal number of illegally-held arms. The black market in Uruguay is fed by arms smuggled from Brazil and Argentina, as well as the diversion of government and security forces' stocks through corrupt officials. In an interesting case, there is a record of Uruguayan peacekeepers returning from UN missions in the Balkans and Africa smuggling automatic weapons into the country. According to the Uruguayan Ministry of the Interior, the Uruguayan Army has declared that at least 800 weapons were smuggled into the country in this manner (Dreyfus, 2000).

In Colombia, the Government is combating a huge supply of military-style small arms from numerous sources. One of the major recipients of these weapons is the Revolutionary Armed Forces of Colombia (FARC), an armed guerrilla organization heavily involved in drug trafficking. Colombian officials maintain that there are over 20 international, and 30 national, routes used by guerrilla and paramilitary organizations to obtain arms (*El Tiempo,* 23 August 2000). Some of them have been identified in the process of intercepting illicit arms shipments.

For example, in 1999 Brazilian police arrested the leader of a criminal organization involved in trafficking arms from Brazil to Colombia through Suriname. The investigation allegedly implicated the former military dictator and current member of the parliament of Suriname, Desi Bouterse, who

Box 5.7 Guns for FARC, resignation for Fujimori

With much fanfare, Peruvian President Alberto Fujimori, along with the chief of the national intelligence service, Vladimiro Montesinos, announced in August 2000 that Peruvian police and intelligence services had broken up an arms smuggling ring responsible for arming the Revolutionary Armed Forces of Colombia (FARC). The ring had already supplied at least 10,000 Kalashnikov rifles of Jordanian origin to FARC in a series of four deliveries in March, June, July, and August of 1999. Fujimori declared that the Peruvian authorities had evidence implicating a Jordanian general in the transfers. However, the official version of the arms transfer soon unravelled, resulting in the issue of an arrest warrant for Montesinos.

The ensuing scandal began with the highly publicized arrests of a retired Peruvian army officer, two members of the Peruvian army, a Russian, and two Frenchmen (one a naturalized American, the other a naturalized Spaniard). However, later reports revealed that they had been set up as scapegoats for bigtime players such as Montesinos. An interview with Sarkis Soghanalian, the broker who arranged the deal, threw a harsh light on many of the less transparent aspects of the transfer.

It revealed that, in keeping with the original agreement with the Jordanian Government, the Peruvian military was to have purchased 50,000 AK-47 assault rifles manufactured in former East Germany at US$ 95 apiece (Rempel and Rotella, 2000).

The Peruvian Government provided the appropriate end-user certificates, and the US Embassy in Amman was informed of the deal. After initial difficulties, a Ukrainian-registered cargo plane with a Russian-Ukrainian crew flew the weapons via the Canary Islands, Mauritania, and Grenada, air-dropping them finally onto Colombian territory before landing in Iquitos, Peru.

According to the US State Department, the deal dissolved when the Jordanian Government discovered that the weapons were not going to Peru at all, but instead to FARC, and cancelled the contract (Rempel and Rotella, 2000).

Early reports claimed that the planes returned to Jordan with as much as 40,000 kilos of cocaine that went, in part, to Jordanian middlemen, in part to the former Soviet Union (Lackey, 2000). As official paperwork showed only an innocuous shipment of wood to Jordan, Peruvian investigators claimed that there was no evidence of cocaine smuggling. However, in October 2000, the Peruvian courts declared that the investigation into the affair would take months. It seems clear that the role of high-ranking Peruvian government officials in the transfer was one of the factors that led to President Fujimori's resignation in November 2000.

is wanted by the Dutch Government on charges of drug trafficking (*El Tiempo,* 23 August 2000). Between January and September 2000, Panamanian police intercepted four shipments of small arms and ammunition bound for Colombia—three from Costa Rica with weapons that had, for the most part, originated in Nicaragua and El Salvador (Gaynor, 2000).

By far the most publicized Colombian smuggling saga in 2000 involved several Peruvian army officers, Jordanian arms and Russian transport planes, all part of an arms ring operating out of Peru. The ensuing investigation is credited in part with bringing down Peru's President Alberto Fujimori (See Box 5.7).

Central America

Wedged, as it unenviably is, between the drug-producing centers of South America and their seemingly insatiable primary markets in North America, Central America has become a nexus for both drug traffickers and the illicit weapons which are the tools of their trade. Supplanting the 1980s heyday of the covert grey market arms transfers to rebel and insurgent groups, today it is the black market—characteristically linked to the drug trade spurred on by the high demand for narcotics in the United States—that has taken over in much of Central America. The links between drugs, thugs, and small arms is apparent in the examples below.

- Guatemala: Since 1991, the Ministry of Defence's Department of Control of Arms and Munitions (DECAM) has closed 52 firearms dealers and repair workshops for legal violations. In 1998 alone, there were 280 pending cases of registered arms dealers selling weapons to drug traffickers. In November 1999, DECAM had registered and authorized 78 commercial firearms dealers, 14 firing ranges, and 14 workshops for repair and modification (Godnick, 2000).

- Nicaragua-Colombia: In July 2000, a former Nicaraguan police chief, Roger Ramirez, was convicted of trafficking over 100 assault rifles and 215 kilos of cocaine, allegedly destined for paramilitary organizations in Colombia. Ramirez had been in charge of the Caribbean and Matagalpa regions, areas known for drug trafficking and re-armed ex-combatants, respectively.

Box 5.8 Honduras: Turning a blind eye to illicit arms resales

In December 1998, Mario Dellamico, a Cuban-American representative of the Panamanian-registered company Longlac Enterprises, Inc., attempted to illegally sell small arms to the Honduran civilian police force. Dellamico, no stranger to the illicit weapons scene, had been a CIA operative during the 1980s 'Iran-Contra Affair'. This time, the weapons subsequently confiscated at a military base storage facility near San Pedro Sula included 4,993 FN-FAL rifles, 790 Chinese-made AK style assault rifles, ammunition, anti-personnel landmines, and explosives.

The ensuing investigation brought to light the fact that Longlac Enterprises Inc., a private company, had contracted the Honduran military twelve years ago, in 1988, to store arms. However, the original inventory placed under contract for storage had consisted of 30 Yugoslav-made 20mm cannons, 548 RPG-7s, and 20mm and 7.62mm ammunition—a considerable discrepancy from the inventory seized in early 1999. Government investigations determined that various weapons from this storage facility had been transferred to the Czech Republic, Portugal, Guatemala, El Salvador, Nicaragua, Jamaica, the US, Yugoslavia, African rebel groups, and private security companies in Honduras.

Despite such blatant irregularities, a Honduran court ordered the weapons returned to Longlac Enterprises Inc. in February 2000. The company subsequently reported that an Iranian businessman in the US had offered to buy the weapons but that, as of November 2000, the deal had not yet taken place due to transport and financial complications.

Source: Godnick, 2000

An investigative report traced Kalashnikov assault rifles bought for as little as US$ 25 each in Nicaragua. These are smuggled across the San Juan River into Costa Rica or Panama where the price increases to between US$ 300-700, and then on to Colombia where they command a price of US$ 2,000 each, either in cash, its drug equivalent, or a combination of both (Godnick, 2000).

- Panama: This country's offshore banking facilities, Economic Free Trade (EFT) zones, and common border with Colombia make it uniquely positioned in the arms-drugs trade nexus. In 1998, the US Drug Enforcement Agency (DEA) uncovered a ring of Chinese and Colombian criminals, operating out of a Panamanian EFT zone, trafficking in drugs, assault rifles, and human beings. In June 2000, a joint Colombian-Panamanian police operation intercepted a Honduran-registered ship carrying 30 Kalashnikovs, 14 M-16s, and five Chinese-made rocket launchers that were thought to have originated in El Salvador or Nicaragua and were allegedly destined for guerrillas in Colombia (Godnick, 2000).

Not all illicit arms trafficking in Central America involves the drug trade; drugs are only one of the drivers, albeit a powerful one. Insurgencies are another. For example, in August 1998, Mexico accused ex-combatants from El Salvador of involvement in weapons trafficking and serving as mercenaries in the Chiapas region. In that same year, Honduran military officials were prosecuted in Mexican courts for allegedly supplying arms to the Zapatista rebels in 1994.

North America

The United States, with its huge stores of privately-held firearms, is both a source, a supplier, and a recipient of illegal small arms. Within the US itself, gun control is a hotly debated issue. Although it is beyond the scope of this chapter to look into these issues, illicit arms trafficking involving the US cannot be addressed without keeping this domestic context in mind.

Within the US, gun control is a hotly debated issue.

Recently, due to expanded arms trafficking activities by the Russian mafia and ethnic Chinese criminal gangs operating on US territory, illicit firearms trafficking in the US has taken a turn for the worse (Ward, 2000). Still, US arms trafficking activities are not limited to criminal gangs. It is difficult to quantify illicit arms trafficking in the US, as with any country or region; however, in 1998, US customs confiscated illegally trafficked arms or munitions in 728 separate seizures (US Customs Service, 1999).

Arms are also trafficked—occasionally in alarming quantities—across the US borders with Mexico and Canada. For example, in April 2000, one of the largest US-Canada trans-border smuggling cases ever was thwarted when Canadian and US police seized 1,709 M-1 Garand rifles and associated ammunition in Canada that had been smuggled from the US by two Americans who were later arrested. Although the weapons were of World War II vintage, they were supposedly all in good condition and working order (*Reuters*, 2 May 2000).

As for Mexico, the US is the largest source of illegal weapons for the country. The trafficking of arms between the two is often closely linked with the drug trade. Another characteristic arms trafficking pattern is the small arms 'ant trade'. According to a 1996 report by the Office of the Mexican Attorney General, a well-worn US-to-Mexico trafficking route originates in central Florida and moves through the Caribbean to Mexico's Yucatan Peninsula (Lumpe, 1997).[21]

The US is the largest single source of illegal weapons for Mexico.

Now a new facet of the arms trade is making its presence felt, both in the US and elsewhere: the illegal sale of firearms over the internet, a medium that is certain to become a major issue for policy-makers as this market expands. For example, the Irish Republican Army and its splinter groups have long been recipients of illegal arms from the US, financed and facilitated by sympathizers within the US. In late 1999, four Irish nationals were arrested for shipping dozens of small arms to terrorists in Northern Ireland, guns they had purchased through the internet (*Palm Beach Post*, 21 December 1999).

Conclusions

As crime experts have wryly noted, the best laws often inspire the worst kinds of ingenuity. In surveying the global illicit small arms trade, based on existing information in the public domain and using regional and country case studies to highlight it, the foregoing chapter has lent credence to this observation.

Granted that no review of the illicit trade in small arms can, by definition, be comprehensive, this chapter has focused on illustrating both the scope and a few of the innumerable forms that illicit activity can take. Those regions and countries that were not addressed, or only superficially mentioned in this chapter, will be examined in further detail in subsequent issues of the *Survey*.

What were the findings? While it is difficult to distinguish between grey and black market transfers, research has provided sound evidence that each market has its own unique characteristics. The *grey market* is generally much larger, both in terms of value and volume; its covert transfers tend to supply small arms to non-state actors (e.g. rebel groups) in countries or regions in war or conflict. The *black market* is usually much smaller than the grey market; its illegal transfers tend to supply arms to individuals and criminal organizations. Of course, there are exceptions to these rules. More research is needed to understand the characteristics and ever-changing dynamics of such markets.

Nevertheless, at the outset of this chapter, the close links between illicit small arms transfers and the crime, conflict, and corruption they spawn were stressed. A few concluding thoughts on how to deal with them are suggested below and will be the subject of future *Survey* editions.

Controlling crime: Examples of small arms-linked crimes abound—from lone Brazilian bank robbers armed with 'ant trade'-acquired pistols, to gun-toting gangs in Sierra Leone, Colombia, and the Russian Federation, to globe-spanning organized crime rings operating out of Asia or the US. Their way is paved through the continuing practice of covert grey market arms transfers. Acts of intentional omission facilitate this illicit trade; so do acts of commission, such as states knowingly and wilfully subverting their own, or recipient states' laws to facilitate such transfers.

The rule of law: To bring such criminals under control and, eventually, to justice, there is an urgent need for the rule of law, as well as its *de facto* enforcement, especially in the most seriously affected countries highlighted in this chapter.

Alleviating conflict: Both within and beyond national borders, armed conflict represents a source of international instability. More than 90 countries legally produce small arms, not to mention illicit production in a number of other countries. Thus, there will always be arms suppliers only too willing to instigate and fuel armed conflicts—either out of ideological zeal, for political reasons, or for financial gain.

Greater transparency: Transparency, both on the supply and demand side, is a crucial first step to minimize illicit grey market transfers that feed off of, and exacerbate, existing tensions.

Eradicating corruption: Corruption flourishes in environments devoid of transparency and accountability. As this chapter's case studies show, many supplier countries—even those with mature and otherwise orderly legal systems—currently have little effective control over their small arms exports. Cleaning up corruption among civil servants and customs authorities, who can be easily bribed to overlook suspicious exports, is essential to gaining control over illicit small arms transfers. Although economic factors are certainly not the only ones, they are undeniably one of the engines that drive the spread of crime and corruption. Overall, it is imperative to recognize the causal link between all three factors—crime, conflict, and corruption—and a country's fulfillment of its citizens' basic needs, such as survival, shelter, health care, and education. Still, it has been observed that while crime is often poverty-driven, corruption is not infrequently greed-driven.

Responsibility and accountability: In order to eradicate (combat) corruption, governments must exercise greater responsibility towards their own citizens (e.g. government employees), as well as greater accountability towards the international community. One of the first steps lies in acquiring evidence and information as a prerequisite for policy.

Ultimately, control over the global proliferation of small arms will be achieved only through greater information-sharing and transparency, which is absolutely essential to draw the line between what is legal and what is not. So long as even knowledgeable observers struggle to distinguish between a covert-but-legal deal and a totally illegal black market one, small arms will remain a perpetrator of international instability.

For further information and current developments on small arms issues please check our website at www.smallarmssurvey.org

5 List of Abbreviations

ABB	Revolutionary People's Army (Philippines)
AFP	Armed Forces of the Philippines
ASSR	Autonomous Soviet Socialist Republic
CAFGU	Citizens Auxiliary Force Geographical Units (Philippines)
CAST	Centre for Analysis of Strategies and Technologies
CIA	Central Intelligence Agency (US)
CIS	Commonwealth of Independent States
DEA	Drug Enforcement Agency (US)
DRC	Democratic Republic of Congo
ECOMOG	ECOWAS Monitoring Group
ECOWAS	Economic Community of West African States
FARC	Revolutionary Armed Forces of Colombia (Colombia)
FIS	Front Islamique de Salut (Algeria)
FMLN	Farabundo Marti para la Liberacion Nacional (El Salvador)
FN-FAL	Belgian assault rifle type
FSB	Federal Security Service (Russian Federation—Successor to the KGB)
HRW	Human Rights Watch
IISS	International Institute of Strategic Studies
ISER	Institute for Religious Studies
ISS	Institute for Security Studies
KLA	Kosovo Liberation Army (Yugoslavia)
LTTE	Liberation Tigers of Tamil Eelam (Sri Lanka)
MILF	Moro Islamic Liberation Front
MNLF	Moro National Liberation Front (Philippines)
NATO	North Atlantic Treaty Organization
NDA	National Democratic Alliance (Sudan)
NDFB	National Democratic Front for Bodoland (India)
NSA	Non-State Actors
NSCN	National Socialist Council of Nagaland (India)
OLS	Operation Lifeline Sudan
OPM	Free Papua Movement (Papua New Guinea)
OSCE	Organization for Security and Cooperation in Europe
PLO	Palestinian Liberation Organization
PNP	Philippine National Police
RENAR	Director of Operations of the National Arms Registrar (Argentina)
RIRA	Real Irish Republican Army
RPG	Rocket Propelled Grenade Launcher
RUF	Revolutionary United Front (Sierra Leone)
SIPRI	Stockholm International Peace Research Institute
SPLA	Sudan People's Liberation Army (Sudan)
SRRA	Humanitarian Wing of SPLA
UK	United Kingdom
ULFA	United Liberation Front of Assam (India)
UN	United Nations
UNAMSIL	UN Mission in Sierra Leone
UNITA	Uniao Nacional Para a Independencia Total de Angola (Angola)
UNRG	Guatemalan National Revolutionary Unit (Guatemala)
US	United States
USSR	Union of Soviet Socialist Republics

5 Endnotes

1 All the information presented in this chapter is obtained from open, public sources.

2 A number of experts have identified other typologies of arms transfers than those identified here. Michael Klare has identified four types of transfers: government to government transfers, government sanctioned commercial sales, covert or 'grey market' operations, and black market transactions and theft (Klare, 1999). There are several drawbacks to this typology with respect to the data in this study, although certain definitions are applicable. First, there is a distinction of two different types of legal transfers—government sales and commercial sales. This distinction, while it is applicable to a number of states, such as the US, is not applicable to the large number of states where the production of small arms is state-run or where no distinction is made between government sales and commercial sales. Second, there is a blurring of the definition of covert transfers, insinuating that they are all 'grey market'. A covert transfer is one that is simply non-transparent, it can be legal, grey market, or illicit, depending on the applicable laws. Finally, Klare's definition of black market sales stipulates that such transactions are carried out by 'private entities in knowing violation of established government laws or policies.' This is a helpful definition in better understanding the black market, in that it generally involves 'private entities' rather than governments.

3 The grey market may also include government-sponsored transfers that are illegal, but where the parties involved are acting on instructions from government officials. However, such transfers are viewed by some as clearly being black market transfers if they are in violation of any law.

4 Definitions of what is legal or illegal have become a highly politicized debate. Within the framework of negotiations on 'illicit trafficking in small arms and light weapons in all its aspects', some countries want to address the whole spectrum of small arms transfers, from legal to illicit, while others want to restrict negotiations to the black market only (i.e. exclusively those transfers occurring without government knowledge).

5 SIPRI defines a major armed conflict as one that involves the military forces of two governments or one government armed force and an organized armed group, and results in battle-related deaths of at least 1000 people, although in some cases in certain years less than 1000 deaths may occur. The incompatibility of the warring factions revolves around the control of territory or the government of the country (SIPRI, 2000).

6 See Berman (2000).

7 Such special dispensations are secret, so there is no public record if one was granted or not.

8 UN Security Council, 2000. This report is also known as the *Fowler Report*.

9 For a very detailed field report on the small arms situation in Somalia see Forberg and Terilinden (1999).

10 The breakdown is as follows: 351,000 rifles, 226,000 assault rifles, 25,000 machine guns, 38,000 pistols, 2,450 grenade launchers, and 770 mortars. In addition, 1 million anti-tank mines, 3.5 million hand grenades, and 1.56 billion rounds of small arms ammunition were stolen. (United Nations, 1998).

11 For an extensive analysis of the financing and transfers of arms to the KLA see Cooper (2000).

12 For an in-depth assessment of the Russian Federation military's involvement in arms trafficking see Turbiville (1995). For a very detailed study of the problems of small arms in Central Asia, focusing on Tajikistan, Uzbekistan, Kyrgyzstan, Kazakhstan, and Turkmenistan see Pirseyedi (2000).

13 Kitovani was at one time the Defence Minister of Georgia. He was sentenced to eight years in prison for establishing an illegal paramilitary force but was released early (in May 1999) on humanitarian grounds, due to ill health.

14 This was before Dudayev became the leader of the Chechen rebel movement. According to official reports, he was killed in a Russian bomb attack in 1996.

15 This allegation is especially interesting in light of the fact that Turkey received 347,000 Kalashnikov rifles in 1994 from former East German stocks, through NATO, after Germany's reunification.

16 See endnote 15.

17 These groups are also often heavily involved in the drug trade (Kartha, 2000; Siddiqa-Agha, 2000).

18 Evidence is based on reports of the transfer and also the fact that two helicopters of the Sri Lankan armed forces were shot down before they could take evasive action, indicating the use of Stingers rather than other, less accurate anti-aircraft missiles.

19 This section on the Philippines was researched and written by Katherine Kramer.

20 Many goods, including weapons, arrive first at the port of Paraguá, Brazil. Brazil and Paraguay have signed an agreement to allow Paraguay, a landlocked country, free use of an Atlantic port. That port is Paraguá. Goods destined for Paraguay arriving in Paraguá are marked 'in transit', and are not checked until they meet their final destination (by land or air) in Paraguay.

21 For a detailed look at small arms trafficking from the US to Mexico see Lumpe (1997).

5 Bibliography

Al-Bindari, Ahdaf. 2000. 'Report Examines Egyptian Legal, Illegal Weapons Market Prior to Elections.' *Al-Ahram*. 18 September, p. 13.

Allen, Nick. 1999. 'Anti-terrorism Search Operation Uncovers a Country at Arms.' *Deutsche Presse-Agentur*. 17 October.

Berman, Eric. 2000. *Re-Armament in Sierra Leone: One Year After the Lomé Peace Agreement*. Occasional Paper No. 1. Geneva: Small Arms Survey.

Blenkin, Max. 2000. 'Australian Supplied Patrol Boats Fire Shot in Anger.' *AAP Newsfeed*. 7 June.

Boutwell, Jeffrey and Michael Klare. 2000. 'A Scourge of Small Arms.' *Scientific American*. June, pp. 48-53.

Centre for Analysis of Strategies and Technologies (CAST). 2000. *Report on Armament within the Chechen Zone of Conflict*. Background Paper. Geneva: Small Arms Survey.

Chalk, Peter. 2000. *Liberation Tigers of Tamil Eelam's (LTTE) International Organization and Operations – A Preliminary Analysis*. Commentary No. 77. Canadian Security Intelligence Service. March.

Cooper, Neil. 2000. 'Arming and Disarming Kosovo: A Structural Arms Control Perspective.' Paper presented at Conference sponsored by the United Nations Research Institute for Social Development. Geneva, 26-30 June.

Daley, Paul. 2000. 'Australians in PNG Guns-for-Drugs Deals.' *Sydney Morning Herald*. 9 September.

Dasgupta, Anindita. 2000. 'Small Arms Proliferation in North-East India: A Case Study of Assam.' In Dipankar Banerjee, ed. *South Asia At Gun Point: Small Arms and Light Weapons Proliferation*. Colombo: Regional Centre for Strategic Studies.

Davis, Anthony. 2000. 'Bangkok Discovers LTTE Logistics Cell.' *Jane's Intelligence Review*. July, pp. 3.

Demidetsky, Valery. 1999. 'Moldavia detains Ukrainian plane loaded with hidden arms'. *Itar-Tass*. 13 April.

Dimevski, Sasko. 1999. 'Macedonia- An Illegal UCK Arms Depot?' *Skopje Utrinski Vesnik*. 13 September, p. 5.

Dreyfus, Pablo. 2000. *An Overview of the Modalities of Illegal Transfers of Small and Light Weapons in the Southern Cone*. Background Paper. Geneva: Small Arms Survey.

Farah, Douglas. 1997. 'Russian Mob, Cartels Joining Forces: Money-Laundering, Arms Sales, Spreading Across Caribbean.' *The Washington Post*. 29 September.

Forberg, Ekkehard and Ulf Terlinden. 1999. *Small Arms in Somaliland: Their Role and Diffusion*. Berlin: Berlin Information- center for Transatlantic Security. March.

Garcia, Cathy and Manolette Payumo. 2000. 'MILF Tells Gov't to Choose: Talk Peace or Resume War.' *Business World*. 22 February.

Gaynor, Tim. 2000. 'Gun, Drug Trades Thriving in Panama.' *Detroit Free Press*. 19 October.

der Ghougassian, Khatchik and Hernán Lapieza Spota. 1999. 'Las armas livianas, la violencia y la seguridad: fundamentos y lineamientos para una investigación.' Paper presented at the First Seminar on Security, Violence and Democracy. La Plata, Argentina, 10 to 11 August.

Godnick, William. 2000. *Transfers in Central America*. Background Paper. Geneva: Small Arms Survey.

Gordon, Michael. 2000. 'Russian Federation Arms in Pipeline to Chechnya, Georgia Says.' *New York Times*. 18 January.

Gunaranta, Rohan. 2000. 'Sources of Arms Supplies to the LTTE; Successes and Failures of the Sri Lankan State.' In Dipankar Banerjee, ed. *South Asia At Gun Point: Small Arms and Light Weapons Proliferation*. Colombo, Sri Lanka: Regional Centre for Strategic Studies.

Human Rights Watch. 1998. *Sudan: Global Trade, Local Impact: Arms Transfers to All Sides in the Civil War in Sudan*. New York. August.

_____. 2000. *Neglected Arms Embargo on Sierra Leone Rebels*. New York. May.

Hunter, Thomas. 1999. 'Tamil Tigers May Be Using Thai Bases.' *Jane's Intelligence Review*. 1 February, p. 5.

Huxley, Tim and Susan Willet. 1999. *Arming East Asia*. Adelphi Paper 329. London: The International Institute for Strategic Studies.

International Institute for Strategic Studies (IISS). 2000. 'Russian Federation's Armed Forces: Problems of Reform and Resettlement.' *Strategic Comments*, Vol. 6, Issue 7. September.

Institute for Religious Studies (ISER). 2000. *Profile of Weapons Sold to Brazilians in Paraguay*. Background Paper. Geneva: Small Arms Survey.

Johnson-Thomas, Brian. 2000. 'Anatomy of a Shady Deal.' In Lora Lumpe, ed. *Running Guns: The Global Black Market in Small Arms.* London: Zed Books.

Kartha, Tara. 2000. *South Asia- A Rising Spiral of Proliferation.* Background Paper. Geneva: Small Arms Survey.

Klare, Michael. 1999. 'The International Trade In Light Weapons: What Have We Learned?' In Jeffrey Boutwell and Michael Klare, eds. *Light Weapons and Civil Conflict.* Lanham, United States: Rowman & Littlefield Publishers, Inc., pp. 9-27.

Lackey, Sue and Michael Moran. 2000. 'Russian Federation Mob Trading Arms for Cocaine with Colombia Rebels.' 9 April. <http:www.msnbc.com>

Lamb, Christina. 2000. 'China puts "700,000 troops" on Sudan alert.' *The Telegraph.* 27 August.

Lumpe, Lora. 1997. 'The US Arms Both Sides of Mexico's Drug War.' *Covert Action Quarterly.* Summer, pp. 39-46.

Mathiak, Lucy and Lora Lumpe. 2000. 'Government Gun-Running to Guerrillas.' In Lora Lumpe, ed. *Running Guns: The Global Black Market in Small Arms.* London: Zed Books.

Muggah, Robert and Eric Berman. 2001. *The Humanitarian Impacts of Small Arms.* United Nations Inter-Agency Standing Committee.

Nkruma, Gamal. 1998. 'Small Arms for Big Wars.' *Al-Ahram Weekly.* 25 June.

Perreño, Disraeli. 1995. 'Danao City Bi Supplier of Yakuza Guns.' *Manila Chronicle.* 21 January.

Pirseyedi, Bobi. 2000. *The Small Arms Problem in Central Asia: Features and Implications.* Geneva: United Nations Institute for Disarmament Research.

Rempel, William and Sebastian Rotella. 2000. 'Arms Dealer Implicates Peru Spy Chief in Smuggling Ring.' *Los Angeles Times.* 1 November.

Samir, Samah. 2000. 'Israeli-made Weapons Seized in Al-Buhayrah.' *Cairo Rose Al-Yusuf.* 22 July.

Seno, Alexandra. 1996. 'Aiming for Legitimacy.' *Asiaweek.* 19 January, p. 29.

Siddiqa-Agha, Ayesha. 2000. 'Setting an Agenda for Regional De-Weaponization.' In Dipankar Banerjee, ed. *South Asia at Gunpoint: Small Arms and Light Weapons Proliferation.* Colombo, Sri Lanka: Regional Centre for Strategic Studies.

Silverstein, Ken. 2000. 'Licensed to Kill.' *Harper's Magazine.* May.

Simunovic, Tifani. 2000. 'Croatia Said to be Crossing Point for International Arms Smuggling.' *Fokus.* 21 July.

Sislin, John, Frederic Pearson, Jocelyn Boryczka, and Jeffery Weig. 1998. 'Patterns in Arms Acquisitions by Ethnic Groups in Conflict.' *Security Dialogue*, Vol. 29. No. 4.

Smith, Chris. 2000. 'Light Weapons Proliferation: A global survey.' *Jane's Intelligence Review.* 1 July.

Stockholm International Peace Research Institute. 2000. *SIPRI Yearbook 2000: Armaments, Disarmament and International Security.* Oxford: Oxford University Press.

Stratfor.com. 2000. 'Arms Smuggling Menace in Papua New Guinea.' *Global Intelligence Update.* 13 September.

Turbiville, Graham. 1995. *Mafia in Uniform: The Criminalization of the Russian Armed Forces.* Fort Leavanworth, Kansas: Foreign Military Studies Office.

United Nations General Assembly. 1996. *Report of the Disarmament Commission.* A/51/42, supplement No. 42, Annex I. 22 May.

United Nations. 1998. *Report of the Evaluation Mission to Albania.* 11-14 June.

United Nations Security Council. 2000. *Letter Dated 10 March 2000 from the Chairman of the Security Council Committee Established Pursuant to Resolution 864 (1993) Concerning the Situation in Angola Addressed to the President of the Security Council (Fowler Report).* S/2000/203. 10 March.

United States. US Customs Service. 1999. *FY 1998 Accountability Report.* p. 36.

United States. US Office of Naval Intelligence and US Coast Guard Intelligence Coordination Center. 1999. *Threats and Challenges to Maritime Security 2020.* 1 March.

Venter, Al. 1999. 'Sudan in Strife: A Catalyst for Conflict.' *Jane's Intelligence Review.* 1 December.

Vo, Minh. 1999. 'Getting a Handle on Small Arms.' *Christian Science Monitor.* 17 February.

Ward, Richard. 2000. 'The Internationalization of Criminal Justice.' In United States Department of Justice. *Boundary Changes in Criminal Justice Organizations: Criminal Justice 2000, Volume 2.* Washington, DC. US Department of Justice. July.

Wood, Brian. 2000. 'Arms and Related Support for the Rebels in Sierra Leone.' Testimony to the United Nations Committee on Sierra Leone, 31 July– 1 August.

6

After the Smoke Clears:
Assessing the Effects of Small Arms Availability

Introduction

Small arms and light weapons are made to maim and kill. Even conservative estimates suggest that well over half a million lives are lost to them each year: some 300,000 in armed conflict and another 200,000 from gun-inflicted homicides and suicides. The direct effects of small arms availability and use include death and injury. The opportunity costs of such small arms in terms of foregone investment, health costs and lost educational opportunities run into the billions of dollars. The broad array of indirect socio-economic impacts, while hard to measure, is devastating. These indirect effects emerge only gradually 'after the smoke clears'. Then it becomes obvious that the global spread of small arms and light weapons is exacerbating human insecurity, fuelling the creation of 'cultures of violence', and undermining the stability of states and entire regions. Indiscriminate arms use not only jeopardizes individual welfare and livelihoods, it also imperils broader sustainable development opportunities from the local to the international level. This chapter addresses the following three questions:

Small arms ... have damaged development prospects and imperilled human security in every way. Indeed, there is probably no single tool of conflict so widespread, so easily available and so difficult to restrict, as small arms.

Kofi Annan,
UN Secretary General

- Why are small arms so readily available?
- What is the relationship between their high availability and their actual use?
- What are their direct and indirect effects?

The chapter begins with a review of the process by which small arms find their way into civilian hands. Though only tentative conclusions can be drawn, their accessibility is linked to the liberalization of markets and the emergence of new brokering activities. Their availability is also a legacy of the Cold War and the recirculation of previously stockpiled arms. The chapter then goes on to assess the accessibility thesis, by demonstrating the association between easy access to, and ownership of, small arms with armed violence. Manifestations of armed violence range from suicide and domestic abuse to homicide and armed massacres. As the chapter shows, unregulated small arms availability has destabilizing implications, particularly in areas engaged in, or attempting to recover from, armed conflict.

The chapter identifies the direct effects of small arms availability—that is, mortality resulting from homicide, suicide, domestic violence, and armed conflict. Among the many direct effects common to the so-called North and South are the high rates of firearm-related homicide, suicide, and accidental death. However, Southern populations are subject to disproportionate levels of armed homicide while Northern societies experience higher rates of suicide committed with firearms. Conflict and post-conflict environments invariably generate unique situational variables that influence the scale of mortality and morbidity attributed to firearms. What is more, the unregulated availability of such weapons has made the (re)constitution of war accessible to both professional and amateur—the trained and the untrained—alike. Today we live in a world where even the poorest and most marginalized communities have access to military-style weapons capable of transforming a localized dispute into a bloodbath.

The chapter also distils a broad array of indirect effects—social and economic impacts resulting from small arms availability and use. Such effects range from deteriorating public health facilities and the rise of banditry and armed criminality, to the obstruction and diversion of humanitarian relief and reductions in overseas development assistance (ODA) to insecure regions. The resultant anxiety of individuals and communities in both the North and the South has encouraged the privatization of security and the resort to extra-legal forms of protection. The unregulated access to, and use of, firearms has adverse implications for public safety, peace-building and reconciliation, humanitarian aid and development, good governance and the rule of law.

Rates of armed homicide are proportionally higher in the South while suicide ranks higher in the North.

These direct and indirect effects are interconnected. The real or perceived threat of firearm death or injury clearly influences everyone's daily decision-making behaviour—from children to criminals to combatants. Furthermore, small arms-inflicted casualties reduce economic productivity and often strain public services that are already overextended. This has a self-perpetuating effect as, to cite just two examples, declining labour productivity and limited access to health clinics and hospitals can lead, in turn, to increased mortality and morbidity.

In its conclusion, the chapter calls for a shift away from a conventional demilitarization perspective. Instead, it stresses the multi-dimensional impact of arms-related insecurity on public health, exposure to criminality, access to, and impact of, humanitarian assistance, and the overall development of societies (see Figure 6.1).

In providing a comprehensive overview of the direct and indirect effects of small arms there are a number of caveats to be considered. *First*, there are real gaps, flaws, and omissions in both theory and data reliability. This is partly a result of the novelty of the subject matter, though it can also be attributed to under-reporting and poorly managed or under-financed data collection facilities. While such statistics are vital, quantitative precision is not necessarily as important at this stage as a solid qualitative appreciation of the magnitude of the effects.

Second, the plethora of competing views on the effects of firearms issuing from criminologists, in addition to gun-control, public health, humanitarian and disarmament constituencies, makes it impossible to record in detail every facet of every argument. Rather, the chapter endeavours to present a survey of the current 'state of knowledge' on effects—as a baseline for future editions of the *Small Arms Survey*.

Ultimately, the Survey's long-term goal is to develop and refine competing perspectives on small arms and to introduce new techniques to assess their impacts. In this regard, the following chapter raises more questions than it answers.

Figure 6.1 Mapping the effects of small arms and light weapons

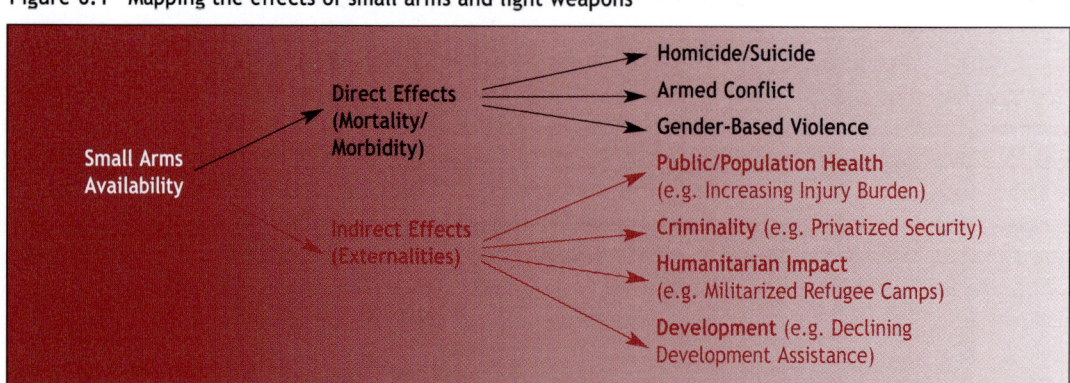

A global flood of small arms

Contemporary intellectual debate on the diffusion of small arms often begins with an abstract discussion of the catalytic role of globalization in the post-Cold War decade.[1] There have been ominous reports documenting the proliferation of millions of small arms and light weapons as the world's major military powers reduced their armed forces or, as in the case of the former Soviet Union, collapsed outright.

Defence economists and political analysts have documented how small arms availability has increased as a result of state manufacturers attempting to reconcile surplus production with decreased demand (PRODUCERS). Globalization, here defined as rapid market liberalization and the privatization of 'non-competitive' public arms industries, is purported to have contributed indirectly to accelerating the spread of such weapons.

Small arms proliferation is by no means a new phenomenon. Nor is there sufficient evidence to suggest that their availability is wholly attributable to globalization. It should be recalled that 40 years of the Cold War encouraged the diffusion of small arms throughout virtually all layers of society. The crackle of automatic gunfire has been background noise on the streets of San Salvador and Kabul for over three decades. In the US, as a result of Americans' demand for guns, there are more gun retail outlets than McDonald's restaurants and the equivalent of one weapon for every one of the country's 250 million residents. More often than not, the proliferation of small arms take place between local officials, formal and informal retailers, and civilians. But the effects can be deeply traumatic and are felt globally—from high-school massacres in Littleton, Colorado to large-scale genocide in Rwanda.

In the US, there are more gun retail outlets than McDonald's restaurants and the equivalent of one weapon for every one of the country's 250 million residents.

In the industrialized countries of the North, the state-sanctioned arming of civilian populations, such as reservists in Switzerland, Israel, or the US National Guard, was often conducted as part of a strategic project to bolster national defence against perceived or potential external aggressors. Alternatively, the arming of communities in the former Yugoslavia, Kenya, Colombia, and Albania ensured the presence of militia or paramilitary groups to shore up domestic authority. The consequences of widespread arms proliferation following economic and political state collapse have illustrated the perils of such strategies (Box 6.1). The resulting interpersonal trafficking of arms for profit and protection was inevitable.

What is different today is the sheer multiplicity of actors that have access to small arms—whether via illicit channels or not. Ours is a turbulent era during which many government and guerrilla armies are fragmenting, warlords are growing in financial and territorial influence, and the distinctions between various forms of violence (e.g. political, communal, religious, and criminal) are blurring. Paradoxically, this is also a time when guarantees of public security remain unfulfilled in large parts of the world. Rather, the provision of security—particularly of the kind administered by governmental institutions—is becoming a commercially tradable commodity.

Even were there a consensus on the actual number of small arms circulating in the wrong hands, many more questions would remain unanswered. Of urgent concern is a practical appreciation of precisely how small arms are made available and in what way they actually affect people. The international community needs to understand where they are affected geographically and who are the most vulnerable.

Also, a clearer appraisal is required of the relationship between the high availability of arms and their use. Particularly with regard to the latter point, the small arms debate has expanded to accommodate a range of perspectives that seek to clarify the positive association between these two variables.

Box 6.1 From Albania to Kosovo: A flood of arms

In the former Yugoslavia and throughout the Balkans, sweeping socio-economic transitions toward market deregulation and the development of democratic institutions have taken place in tandem with the diffusion of light weapons into civilian hands. Arms saturation—accompanied by acute unemployment, ineffective state control, corruption, and a weakened civil society—makes for a volatile mixture. Not only are armed attacks on refugees, internally displaced persons (IDPs), and minorities increasingly common, the availability of small arms discourages such vulnerable groups from returning to their original homes. Casualties resulting from armed attacks, even among peace-keeping personnel, have occurred repetitively in the course of United Nations (UN) operations in Croatia and Bosnia and Herzegovina and are of continuing concern to NATO and the UN.

Map 6.1 Illicit Albanian arms flows: When the dam bursts

During the Albanian crisis of March 1997, the country was brought to the brink of civil war. Angered over allegations that the regime of President Sali Berisha had defrauded thousands of their life savings through pyramid financial schemes, Albanian citizens pillaged massive weapons stockpiles built up during the dictatorship of Enver Hoxha. With a defence strategy premised on militia-partisan warfare, state collapse unleashed a flood of arms into civilian hands, since the location of fortification programmes and small arms depots installed in every city and rural district were well known.

As a result, an estimated 80 per cent of the country's military arsenal was pillaged, including 2,500 rocket-propelled grenades, 800 mortars (60mm), 1.5 billion rounds of ammunition (7.62mm), 3.5 million hand grenades, and 1.4 million anti-personnel mines (Smith, 2000). The

A relationship between arms availability and armed violence

Is there a relationship between arms availability and armed violence? The answer appears to be a qualified yes. It goes almost without saying that the risk of being killed as a result of armed violence is much greater in some parts of the world than in others—unsurprisingly, these locations frequently correlate with areas of high weapons availability.

For example, in parts of the Horn of Africa (e.g. Somalia), South Asia (e.g. Sri Lanka), Central America (e.g. El Salvador), and the Balkans (e.g. the former Yugoslavia), conflict and post-conflict environments jeopardize civilian security. Countries undergoing various forms of economic and political transition (e.g. the former Soviet Republics) are also susceptible to the mutually reinforcing effects of armed conflict and crime. In South East Asia (e.g. the Philippines) and Latin America (e.g. Colombia), transnational crime, armed violence, and insurgencies pose critical, intertwined threats to human security. Still other regions, particularly North America (e.g. USA) and Western Europe (e.g. Switzerland), find themselves grappling with how to prevent a different kind of tragedy: suicide committed with firearms.

absence of comprehensive small arms control policies, coupled with lax controls on collected surplus, led to black market trading from one simmering Balkan conflict to the next. For example, an estimated one million assault-rifles looted from state armouries and arms depots later resurfaced on the black market, selling for as little as US$ 15 apiece.

As the internal conflict intensified, the Albanian armed forces scattered, leaving the country at the mercy of mob rule. *The Sunday Times* (Loyd, 1997) reported, '... ten-year-old children scrambled with adults and local mafia gangs to seize whatever weapons they could, firing them in jubilation ... As car boots were loaded up with heavy machine guns, mortars and rockets, grenades, tossed like discarded fruit, exploded all over the base, and a teenager was killed by his brother as they grappled over an assault rifle.'

The consequences of state collapse for the region were recognized early on by scholars and policy analysts alike. Professor Tom Gallagher, University of Bradford (UK), predicted that the Albanian conflict had the potential to ignite the already-brewing revolt against Serb rule in adjacent Kosovo. Gallagher (1997) argued that the vast supply of arms in Albania would find its way across the Kosovo border, provoking the Milosevic regime that was 'looking for a diversion to dig itself out of the political hole it is in at home.' Indeed, analysts believe that more than 50 per cent of all pillaged weapons were taken out of the country.

Albania's smugglers quickly profited from the growing unrest in Kosovo, selling looted Kalashnikovs for US$ 150 apiece (Planck, 1997). An OSCE emergency meeting called in March 1997 supported an early military intervention to help end the chaos. Carl Bildt, the international community's top civilian representative in Bosnia at that time, said of such an intervention, 'It will send a signal to other parts of the region that Europe will deal more decisively with potential threats to stability than was the case at the beginning of the Yugoslav crisis. We must not fail again' (Malone, 1997).

One week later, the OSCE was engaged in negotiations concerning its possible involvement in collecting illegally possessed light weapons (Toth, 1997). The OSCE ultimately failed to take an active role despite the apparent humanitarian and strategic interests at stake. More than a year later, in June 1998, NATO officials stressed their concern over arms smuggling from Albania, where they estimated that 'half a million guns are still in the hands of civilians after last year's turmoil.' Much like the so-called 'war on drugs', government rhetoric in favour of eradication of illicit weapons trafficking substituted for active pragmatic measures. The Albanian experience provides yet another example of the need to control the use and spread of small arms and light weapons in conflict regions.

Source: King, 2000

The provision of security is becoming a commercially tradable commodity.

Civilian vulnerability to firearm injury and death varies from region to region and country to country. For example, in Latin America and the Caribbean, there are some 80 million household robberies and an estimated 140,000 murders (including homicides committed with firearms) *per annum*.[2] The regional homicide rate (all causes) is twice the world's average: 22.9 as against 10.7 per 100,000 (UNDP, 2000). For the Organization for Economic Co-operation and Developement (OECD), whose members comprise the world's most industrialized countries and have twice the aggregate population,[3] but only one-third the population growth rate of Latin America and the Caribbean, the rates and scale of homicide and armed robbery are significantly less.

Statistical discrepancies are similarly dramatic between individual states. According to a UN study (1998b), there were 54 firearm homicides per 100,000 inhabitants in Colombia, 27 in South Africa, 26 in Brazil, six in the US, and 0.13 in the UK. Further, the risk of firearm-related violence is differentiated within, as well as between, countries. Urban residents, especially those living in slums, or disenfranchised groups, minorities, and young men often suffer disproportionately from armed violence. For example, firearm homicide rates among young unemployed males in Bogota,

In Latin America and the Caribbean, where the regional homicide rate is twice the world's average, there are an estimated 140,000 murders each year.

Johannesburg, Rio de Janeiro, Washington DC, and London are at least double the national average in their respective countries.[4] The following sections explore some of the reasons why certain societies are more prone to armed violence than others.

The Accessibility Thesis—an emotive debate

Cultural traditions and institutions, both formal and informal, are of primary importance. Depending on a country's firearm legislation and enforcement capacities (e.g. formal institutions), citizens may be permitted to own and use everything from pistols and revolvers to hunting guns and military-style assault rifles. Naturally, behaviour and attitudes toward firearms (e.g. informal institutions) also condition their use. While impossible to verify with absolute certainty, experts agree that, while small arms availability is not their principal cause, it does positively influence the likelihood of homicide, as well as the 'success rates' of suicide, violent crime, domestic violence, the probability of accidents in gun-owning households, and armed conflict. Put another way, the availability—even the presence—of small arms increases the risk of both intentional and unintentional injury.[5] But the relationship is far from straightforward.

The accessibility thesis claims that the availability of guns is a risk factor for armed violence.

When comparing the availability and use of small arms and light weapons, determining a causal link poses a challenge. The *accessibility thesis,* which contends that the accessibility of guns facilitates violence, is frequently contested.[6] Gun advocates and proponents of gun control are polarized—arguing over increasingly divergent claims to the 'truth'. Drawing on Boccaccio's infamous aside in the 14th century secular classic, *The Decameron,* pro-gun advocates claim that it is not the weapons, but the people who do the killing.[7]

Indeed, pro-gun lobbyists argue that focusing on restrictive gun policies misses the point. They contend that, rather than introducing more restrictive gun ownership legislation, the structural or root causes of violence need to be addressed. They are adamant that there is little concrete evidence to substantiate a tangible relationship between liberal firearm policies and a higher-than-average firearm death and injury rate. Gun advocates have also claimed that there is insufficient data to even gauge firearm availability,[8] noting that some researchers have erroneously focused on the proportion of gun ownership per household rather than the number of guns in circulation *per se.*

'Weapons defend the lives of those who wish to live peacefully, and they also, on many occasion, kill [murder] men, not because of any wickedness inherent in them but because those who wield them do so in an evil way.'

Boccaccio,
The Decameron

Some analysts have attempted to prove that advance notice of imminent gun legislation has actually catalyzed surplus production and, as a result of lowered costs due to economies of scale, spurred unintentional diffusion. Furthermore, gun lobbyists, like the United States' *National Rifle Association* (NRA) and the *World Shooting Federation* (WSF), continue to insist that responsible gun owners and recreational users pose little threat to public safety.[9] A number of researchers have also argued that facilitating increased access to arms for self-protection (e.g. concealed weapons) may even reduce mortality and morbidity.[10] Ultimately, they argue, research studies attempting to confirm a positive correlation between weapons availability and increased mortality are biased, partisan, and unsystematic.

Not so, counter-proponents of gun control and representatives of the public health community. While conceding that not all gun owners and households are at equal risk, a series of epidemiological studies have detected a positive correlation between the rate of firearm ownership and the incidence of homicide and suicide (Wintemute *et al*, 1999; CDC, 1997). Research has also indicated that the risk of being murdered by an intimate partner increases with the availability of firearms (Kellerman, 1993). Without underemphasizing the importance of situational variables, social scientists have found overwhelming evidence that various types of violent crime are positively associated with gun ownership rates and availability.[11]

An assessment of the relationship between gun ownership and firearm deaths from a selection of Canadian provinces, the US, England and Wales, and Australia concluded that over 90 per cent of the variance in death rates could be explained by access to firearms (Miller and Cohen, 1997). Further, a standardized survey of victimization carried out in fifty-four industrialized countries indicates that high rates of gun ownership are significantly related to both increases in the incidence of robbery and sexual assault (Van Dijk, 1997). But while firearm ownership and availability may affect an individual's choice of method, it is clear that other factors, such as social and cultural norms, also play a role in the decision.

Figure 6.2   Firearm ownership and deaths in industrialized countries

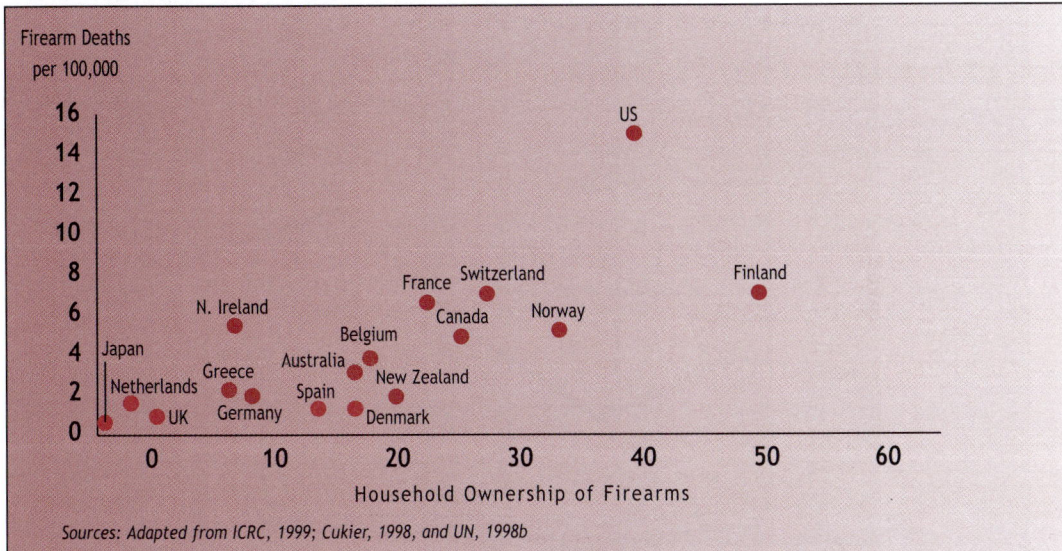

Sources: Adapted from ICRC, 1999; Cukier, 1998, and UN, 1998b

Figure 6.2 illustrates the relationship between legal household possession of firearms and recorded firearm deaths (e.g. homicides and suicides) among a sample of Northern countries. It draws upon aggregate population data from: the UNDP *Human Development Report 2000*; firearm death and household ownership rates in the *UN Firearms Study* (1998b), the ICRC's seminal study on small arms availability (1999), and Cukier (1998b). There is compelling evidence that, among industrializing societies, higher ownership rates result in higher mortality and morbidity rates (see Appendix 6.1). Although a precise determination of the relationship between illegal firearm possession and firearm death is impossible to calculate, it stands to reason that the association between illicit ownership and firearm death would hold.

The relationship is more ambiguous among states in the South. Indeed, there appears to be no statistical association between firearm ownership and firearm-related mortality. This is due, in large part, to an absence of reliable or standardized data on legal possession, firearm-related homicide, or suicide.

Social scientists have found overwhelming evidence that various types of violent crime are positively associated with gun ownership rates and availability.

The Accessibility Thesis and demographics

When national statistics on victims are disaggregated along demographic and socio-economic lines, even more compelling trends emerge. In the US, for example, the Bureau of Justice Statistics noted that indicators documenting homicide and crime in the country are higher than the industrialized country average. Compared with Canada, a country with more restrictive legislation on firearm ownership and use, the *per capita* rates of homicide committed without guns are roughly equivalent. However, the rate of homicide committed with handguns was 15 times higher in the US during the mid-1990s.[12] In a now famous study contrasting neighbouring cities, Seattle (US) and Vancouver (Canada), differences in the rate of gun ownership were described as the principal variable determining differences in the rates of mortality and morbidity (Sloan *et al*, 1988).

The rate of homicide committed with handguns was 15 times higher in the US than in neighbouring Canada during the mid-1990s.

The pervasiveness of guns in the US has had tragic consequences. Although almost a million people in the US have died from firearm-related injuries since the 1960s, certain population groups have been disproportionately affected. While firearm ownership tends to be concentrated among white middle-class adult males (Kates *et al*, 1994), gun-related mortality and morbidity affects all demographic sectors. The greatest increases in recent years have been among teens 15-19 years of age, young black males aged 20-24, and adults aged 75 and over (Figure 6.3 and Appendix 6.2). Young white males have also been particularly 'successful' at suicide.[13]

Figure 6.3 The demographics of homicide in the US

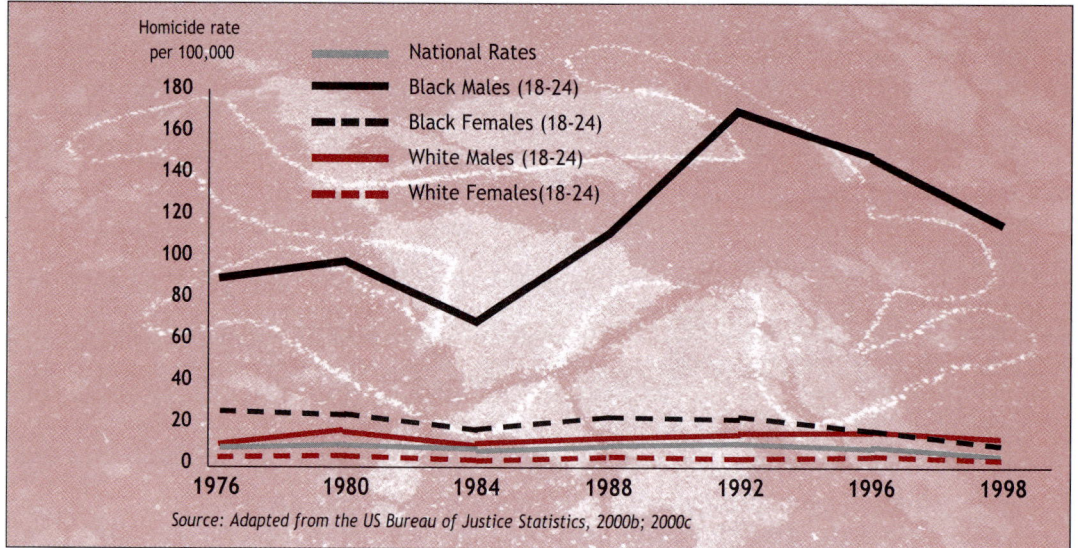

Source: Adapted from the US Bureau of Justice Statistics, 2000b; 2000c

Accessibility and the 'Trigger Effect'

With few exceptions, the more accessible the tools of violence, the more likely they are to be used, whether intentionally or accidentally. Even though certain humanitarian agencies are careful to distance themselves from the claim that widespread availability actually causes violations of international humanitarian law,[14] the accessibility thesis is supported in virtually all the peer-reviewed literature. Also, the positions of major public health and safety groups continuously emphasize the relationships between availability, acquisition, and (mis)use.[15]

The more accessible the tools of violence, the more likely they are to be used.

There is also ample evidence that small arms proliferation and poorly managed stockpiles of automatic weapons have contributed to the outbreak of complex humanitarian emergencies and severely hampered attempts at post-conflict reconstruction and development.[16] Availability, however, is distinct from 'acquisition'—where the triggering effect of increased transfers on conflict outbreak is more clearly defined.[17] But the two elements—availability and acquisition—frequently overlap. For example, the genocide in Rwanda, as well as the collapse of Somalia, Albania, and Afghanistan, all occurred in the context of new weapons acquisitions, coupled with systemic long-term availability. Also, the intensification of warfare and criminality in Colombia, Sri Lanka, and Democratic Republic of Congo (DRC) has been facilitated by ongoing acquisitions, in addition to accessible small arms stockpiles (see Box 6.2).

Recent studies exploring the symbolic and socially constructed value attached to small arms suggest that the argument is even more complicated. It is not only the availability of arms—it is the arms themselves that condition violence. The Kalashnikov rifle, for example, has been described as 'the most effective assault weapon in the world ... it has changed the way wars are fought forever ... (it) is an icon of the anti-establishment insurgent, the symbol of revolutionary resistance' (Cock, 2000, pp. 78-79).

Guns have in many cases acquired a symbolic resonance—much like a state's flag, a military chevron, or a combat infantry badge. In some cases, the gun itself embodies a symbol of emancipation and entitlement among widely disparate and otherwise unconnected groups, including so-called 'freedom-fighters' (e.g. Hezbollah) and 'pro-gun advocates' (e.g. the NRA).[18] Guns often retain a social and political dimension that far exceeds their utilitarian value. The Mozambican flag, for example, prominently displays an assault rifle crossed over a hoe. Seen in this light, Chairman Mao's famous dictum that 'political power grows out of the barrel of a gun' acquires an even more ominous tone.

Undoubtedly, the type of weapons, together with the psychological mindset of armed perpetrators, are factors conditioning the lethality and value attached to the arms themselves. The emboldening effect of weapons possession, particularly by those who are disenfranchised, either as a result of political or religious persuasion, race, sex, age, or who are under the influence of drugs, is significant. The legacy of small arms proliferation in South Africa, for example, has exacerbated confrontational social identities and a culture that accepts armed violence as a solution to social conflict, as well as a legitimate means of acquiring and retaining power and status.

Guns have acquired a symbolic resonance—much like a state's flag, a military chevron, or a combat infantry badge.

Creating cultures of violence

Survey after survey reveals that one of the key reasons why individuals acquire firearms in the first place is that they perceive a high or increasing level of gun-violence in their communities.[19] Even under conditions of 'imperfect information', there is evidence that individuals arm themselves because they see their neighbours doing the same. The faith of civilians in micro-deterrence and the social construction of demand are ironic, particularly in light of the overwhelming support among civil societies for rigid controls on gun ownership. The privatization of armed violence, then, can be interpreted as both a cause and effect of small arms availability. Where societies are subject to prolonged or protracted increases of small arms proliferation and use, 'cultures of violence' may emerge.

According to the UN (1999c)'... while not in themselves causing the conflicts in which they are used, the proliferation of small arms ... affects the intensity and duration of violence and encourages militancy ... we see a vicious circle in which insecurity leads to higher demand for weapons.' Part and parcel of cycles of armed violence, the manifestation of such cultures of violence can be conceived as the changing matrix through which attitudinal and behavioural norms are acted out in a given society. In this way, they are dynamic and conditioned by a range of situational variables.

For example, such cultures are purported to be influenced by 'consumerist militarism'—a reference to the banalization, even glorification, of war, weaponry, military force, and violence through TV, film, literature, song, sport, and recreation.[20] Naturally, the particular cause and expression of such 'cultures' varies from place to place. While the normalization of violence in British news and media may not have had a palpable or objective impact on homicide and crime rates, public perceptions of insecurity are growing throughout the UK.[21] Where cultures of violence find tangible expression in a society, the implications are more severe. At their worst, as in Sierra Leone or Liberia, cultures of violence glorify armed violence and small arms are elevated to the status of a totem.

The privatization of armed violence can be interpreted as both a cause and effect of small arms availability.

Box 6.2   Small arms availability in Rwanda: Triggering genocide?

In the course of a few horrific months in 1994, up to one million people were killed in Rwanda. Despite the fact that international covenants had been adopted to assure that genocide would never again take place, the international community not only failed to prevent the events in Rwanda; by seeking to actively support the economy, it actually facilitated the conditions that

Map 6.2   Recipe for genocide

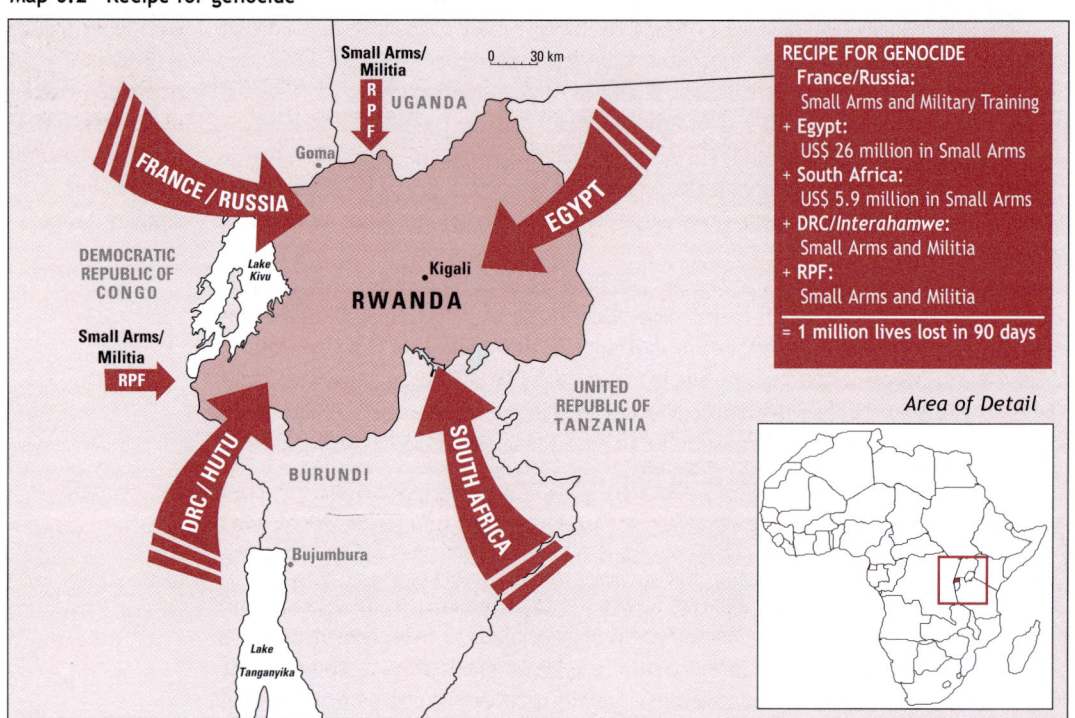

RECIPE FOR GENOCIDE
  France/Russia:
     Small Arms and Military Training
+ Egypt:
     US$ 26 million in Small Arms
+ South Africa:
     US$ 5.9 million in Small Arms
+ DRC/*Interahamwe*:
     Small Arms and Militia
+ RPF:
     Small Arms and Militia
= 1 million lives lost in 90 days

Area of Detail

made armed violence possible. More than a dozen nations helped fuel the Rwandan war, and both factions within the country purchased considerable weaponry through private sources on the open market. Furthermore, by its own admission, the Rwandan Government bankrupted its economy to pay for the weapons.

Secret arms deals between the Egyptian Government and the Hutu-led regime prior to the genocide amounted to US$ 26 million. The first deal, orchestrated by the then-Foreign Minister of Egypt, Boutros-Boutros Ghali, and guaranteed by a French Bank, amounted to US$ 5.8 million.

In Colombia, a country notorious for its culture of violence, someone is murdered every 20 minutes— a homicide rate higher than that of car theft.

In parts of Cambodia, for example, youth frequently threaten people with guns over traffic jams and even pastoral cattle tenders carry guns for protection. Government and NGO reports have documented the use of B-40 rocket launchers in simple robberies—weapons that, in the late 1990s, could be bought for as little as US$ 30. Victim surveys have repeatedly indicated that women fear that intoxicated men will turn their own guns on family members. Similar developments have been reported in northeastern and northwestern Kenya and throughout Nicaragua.

By way of comparison, in Colombia, a country notorious for its culture of violence, someone is murdered every 20 minutes—a homicide rate higher than that of car theft.[22] Even more disturbing, in

It was comprised of 60,000 grenades, three million rounds of ammunition, 18,000 bombs, 4,200 assault rifles, 16,000 60mm and 82mm mortar shells, 122mm D-30 howitzers, rocket-propelled grenades, plastic explosives, and rocket launchers. The consignment was shipped from Cairo International Airport to Kigali, Rwanda as 'relief materials'.

Still more weapons, including AK-47 assault rifles from Russia, mortars, and light artillery continued to flood into the country, complemented by military training of Hutu militia by France. According to Goose and Smyth (1994), 'in October 1992, on the heels of the Egyptian deal, Rwanda made a US$ 5.9 million purchase from South Africa'. This included '100 60-mm mortars, 70 40-mm grenade launchers with 10,000 grenades, 20,000 rifle grenades, spare parts and 1.5 million rounds of ammunition for R-4 rifles, and one million rounds of machine gun ammunition'.

'There was a seemingly unstoppable flow of arms to Rwanda' (Melvern, 2000). The weapons, Rwanda's President Juvenal Habyarimana argued, were needed to fight the three-year civil war against the Ugandan-supported Rwandan Patriotic Front (RPF). But how did the Rwandan Government, then virtually bankrupt, pay for the arms? Part of the answer is buried in the records of the IMF and the World Bank.

A 'Structural Adjustment Programme' (SAP) had been negotiated in the early 1990s and some US$ 260 million, complemented by bilateral contributions from France, Germany, Belgium, and the US, was forwarded directly to the Rwandan Government. Various EU governments, particularly the French, also provided in-kind support. But the acquisition of foreign currency from the SAP was not the only contributing factor to arms accumulation in the region. On the one hand, the economic 'shock-therapy' of Rwanda's SAP contributed to worsening economic conditions among its citizens, leading to a zero-sum game between Tutsis and Hutus. On the other hand, the Rwandan regime simultaneously exchanged tea, the country's second highest export earner, for small arms from the Egyptian Government.

Media coverage was perhaps responsible for the general impression that the 1994 genocide was committed primarily with machetes. This is a largely misguided assumption. Indeed, documents obtained in Kigali reveal that huge numbers of machetes, hoes, axes, knives, and razors were imported in the months preceding the genocide. However, just before the killing began, peacekeepers estimated that 85 tons of weapons had also been distributed throughout the country. The huge quantities of low-intensity weapons contributed to the number of victims and the speed of the killing. In the words of Goose and Smyth (1994), 'much of the killing was carried out with machetes, but automatic rifles and hand grenades were also commonly used. Their wide availability helped Hutu extremists carry out their slaughter on a horrendous scale. The huge piles of Tutsi bodies massacred in Rwanda since April are now juxtaposed with the huge piles of rifles in Goma, Zaire, that were confiscated from fleeing Hutu.'

In Gitarama, a town of 150,000 residents, there were an estimated 50,000 pistols and rifles. Six large massacre sites were later uncovered in the region. The relationship between weapons availability and use was emphasized in a Human Rights Watch report (HRW, 1994) issued just prior to the genocide, which warned 'it is impossible to exaggerate the danger of providing automatic rifles to civilians ... [and] of large numbers of ill-trained civilians equipped with assault rifles'.

Africa during the Rwandan genocide, Hutu militia (*Interahamwe*) were trained to murder 1,000 people every 20 minutes—a killing rate five times that achieved by the Nazis in World War II (Melvern, 2000) and unprecedented even with automatic weapons, much less with machetes and knives. In virtually all of today's internal conflicts, narcotics and alcohol are used to incite combatants, particularly child soldiers, to kill their neighbours and community members so as to destroy personal ties and sever pre-existing social networks.

Automatic military weapons have been frequently employed to increase the speed and scale of carnage. In some cases, after the bullets were used up, the barrels of assault rifles were used to rape women. As a result of their sheer fear and powerlessness, civilian interpretations of 'reasonable' or 'acceptable' thresholds of violence have been profoundly distorted. Indeed, the long-term psychosocial implications for witnesses of large-scale armed violence are only now being explored. In the short-term, however, it is clear that 'the greater the fear of armed assailants, the bitterness over lost lives and property, the desire for retribution, and the demand for weaponry, ... the more difficult it will be to achieve reconciliation and disarmament, and the longer the violence is likely to endure' (Faltas, 2000, pp. 1-2).

Direct effects

The most traumatic effect of firearm use is loss of life. On average, an estimated 300,000 intentional firearm deaths occur each year as a direct result of armed conflict. An additional 200,000 intentional firearm deaths also occur in 30 countries ordinarily classified as 'peaceful'.[23] Besides fatalities, millions more suffer life-threatening injuries, many of which reduce longevity. Firearms are also the most lethal instruments of suicide: 93 per cent of attempts are completed as compared to 30 per cent using other means.[24] What possesses people to kill each other, or indeed themselves? Why has the 20th century been the most violent in history? Understanding the root causes of mass violence is as complex as it is evasive.

Each year an average 300,000 intentional firearm deaths occur as a direct result of armed conflict. Another 200,000 occur in 30 countries ordinarily classified as 'peaceful'.

While not the focus of this chapter, the motives underpinning armed violence and conflict are varied and hotly contested. Observers have typically focused on a combination of factors: exclusion and inequality;[25] competition for economic resources (greed) and lack of access to social justice (grievances);[26] and the erosion or absence of democracy and institutions of governance. Others have emphasized a lack of respect for national and international norms,[27] communal or religious hatreds, and 'ideologies of exclusion' flaring up in a post-Cold War world.[28] Still other analysts have pointed to the socialization of violence among young males, the cultures of violence nurtured by patriarchal societies,[29] and the abundance of valuable (exploitable) primary commodities.[30]

It is clear that contemporary armed violence and internal conflict disproportionately affect the poorer countries of the South—though it has also been occurring with increasing frequency on the doorstep of wealthier countries. Even so, whereas the levels of firearm homicides are higher in the South, the rates of firearm-related suicides are frequently higher (in both absolute and relative terms) in so-called 'developed' countries (see Figure 6.4). In any hemisphere and during any era, however, the abundance of small arms during conflict situations is positively correlated with higher mortality rates.

Homicide and suicide

Firearm injury is already the leading cause of death among adult Afro-Americans; the prognosis is that it will surpass automobile accidents for the entire population by 2003.

There is a growing sense that people are more vulnerable to firearm injuries and death than ever before. While the direct effects are experienced in both the North and the South, developing countries affected by conflict or emerging from war suffer disproportionately from firearm-related mortality. That said, there are common trends among specific constituencies in both developed and developing countries. For example, in the US, firearm injury is already the leading cause of death among adult Afro-Americans; given mid-1990s trends, the prognosis is that it will surpass automobile accidents for the entire population by 2003 (CDC, 2000). In Brazil, rapid urbanization, combined with high levels of unemployment and the breakdown of family structures, are purported to have contributed to a situation where almost 60 per cent of deaths among youths are caused by firearms (ISER, 2000).

It is worth recalling that, partly as a result of the reach of media, the international community is today more informed and acutely aware of the effects of armed violence than ever before. For this reason, many communities are intensely concerned about the direct effects of small arms use, even though homicide and suicide rates may actually be declining in real terms.

In industrialized countries, suicide committed with firearms occurs more frequently than firearm-related homicide.[31] The graphic (see Figure 6.4) provides a snapshot of the proportional impacts of firearm-related homicide and suicide in a sample of developed and developing countries. Though only the most tentative conclusions may be drawn, the figure suggests that lesser developed countries are confronted with a relatively higher incidence of firearm-related homicide while more developed states are grappling with firearm-related suicide. For example, Colombia has an aggregate firearm homicide rate 500 times higher than the UK but a firearm suicide rate only six times greater. Brazil has a firearm homicide rate 125 times higher than Denmark, but a firearm suicide rate five times less.

Colombia has a firearm homicide rate 500 times higher than the UK and a firearm suicide rate only six times greater.

Figure 6.4 Proportional rate of firearm deaths: Homicide and suicide in the North and the South

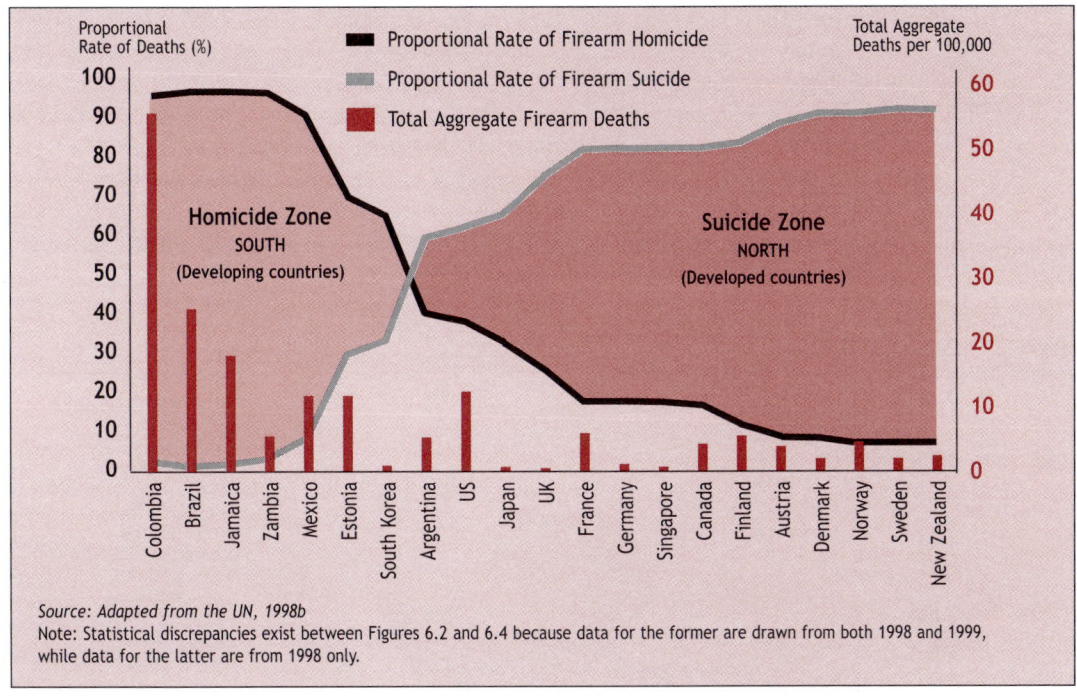

Source: Adapted from the UN, 1998b
Note: Statistical discrepancies exist between Figures 6.2 and 6.4 because data for the former are drawn from both 1998 and 1999, while data for the latter are from 1998 only.

The proportion of 'successful' homicides and suicides carried out with firearms is particularly illuminating: 98 per cent of Jamaica's and Brazil's homicides were carried out with firearms. Well over 75 per cent of all reported firearm deaths among Southern countries are a result of homicide. In contrast, only seven per cent of all firearm deaths were a result of homicide in Sweden and New Zealand.

It should be noted that, while included in the figure above, overall rates of firearm homicide and suicide remained dramatically low in East Asia (see Appendix 6.3).[32] While not included in the figure, in Australia, more than 70 per cent of all firearm deaths in 1998 were suicides. Of these, most were men aged over 65.

Armed conflict

Armed conflict and post-conflict environments result in high levels of firearm-related mortality and morbidity. 'Conflicts' are defined by the Stockholm International Peace Research Institute (SIPRI, 1999) as 'armed confrontations resulting in over one thousand battle-related deaths per annum'.[33] This threshold is set deliberately low because of the unreliability of data on casualties and the fact that governments and non-state actors often under-report deaths and injuries.

Defining conflict:
*'Armed confronta-
tions resulting in
over one thousand
battle-related
deaths per annum'.*
SIPRI, 1999

The magnitude of conflict-induced deaths is particularly great in Africa, although it is difficult to determine the extent to which all of them are directly attributable to small arms (see Map 6.3).[34] Since the independence wars of the 1960s, millions of formal and irregular combatants and civilians have been killed or severely injured by small arms—the weapon of choice in Africa's conflicts. This is not necessarily a new phenomenon. But, while the post-Cold War period may not be qualitatively more violent, there is a 'new and wider awareness of the extent of prevailing brutality and of the difficulties in gainsaying the forces of inhumanity' (Frohardt *et al,* 1999, p. 13).

Prior to the 20th century, an estimated 90 per cent of conflict casualties were combatants. One in five soldiers fighting in World War I—a total of 12 million—were killed, and an additional 21 million injured. A function of changing technology and military strategies, approximately 35 million combatants died in World War II, with just under 50 per cent of them civilians. According to the ICRC's *People on War Report (2000b)*, well over one in four of all combatants in contemporary conflict, including those of Sub-Saharan Africa, has been injured.[35] With an estimated 110 million people dying as a result of conflict, the last 100 years have been described as the 'mega-death' century (Sivard, 1997).

According to some estimates, small arms have been the exclusive weapons used in 90 per cent of the 49 conflicts started since 1990.[36] During this same decade, approximately six million civilians

Map 6.3 Africa's killing fields

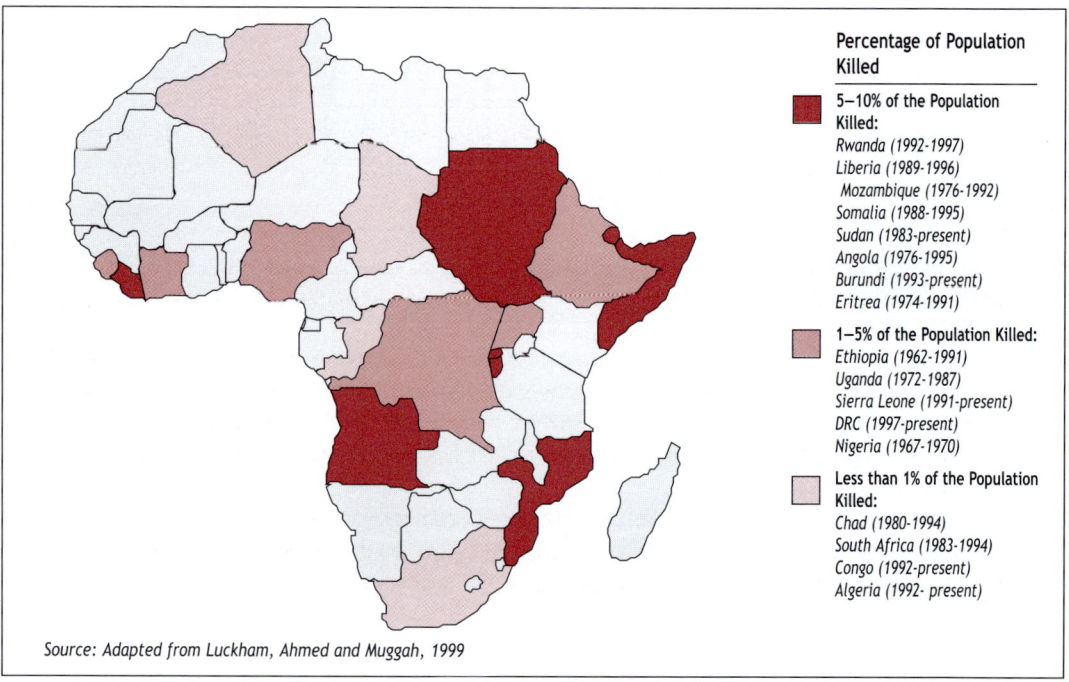

Percentage of Population Killed

5–10% of the Population Killed:
Rwanda (1992-1997)
Liberia (1989-1996)
Mozambique (1976-1992)
Somalia (1988-1995)
Sudan (1983-present)
Angola (1976-1995)
Burundi (1993-present)
Eritrea (1974-1991)

1–5% of the Population Killed:
Ethiopia (1962-1991)
Uganda (1972-1987)
Sierra Leone (1991-present)
DRC (1997-present)
Nigeria (1967-1970)

Less than 1% of the Population Killed:
Chad (1980-1994)
South Africa (1983-1994)
Congo (1992-present)
Algeria (1992- present)

Source: Adapted from Luckham, Ahmed and Muggah, 1999

were killed in conflict. While statistical breakdowns between military and civilian fatalities are not always available, civilians constitute between 30 and 90 per cent of all conflict-related deaths.[37] Indeed, the proportion of civilians killed in the 'crossfire', in violation of international humanitarian law, is increasing, though not necessarily in real terms.[38] It is these changing trends that prompted Justice Richard Goldstone of South Africa to observe, 'if you want to be safe in a modern world, join an army'.[39]

According to some estimates, small arms have been the exclusive weapons used in 90 per cent of the 49 conflicts started since 1990.

Analysts have long noted the rising rates of retributive activity during (and following) armed conflict, and the concomitant reductions in suicide. However, a recent study in Croatia challenges Durkheim's classic theory that populist wars strengthen social integration and thus result in lower suicide rates.[40] In South Croatia, both figures went up: '... there was an increased number of homicides and suicides during the war, especially among the younger population and the military' (Gojanovic *et al,* 1996, p. 5). While high blood alcohol levels figured prominently among perpetrators and victims alike, small arms constituted the primary weapon of choice for committing homicide (61 per cent) and suicide (30 per cent).

Even during the post-conflict period, an increasing frequency of homicides and suicides in Croatia was observed—a tragic consequence of the availability and abuse of large amounts of handguns, rifles, hand grenades, mortars, and other military weapons. The situation is analogous to post-conflict Cambodia, Guatemala, El Salvador, and even the 19th century post-civil war US.[41] Civilian death rates are known to remain constant or even rise in post-conflict situations, largely because the boundaries between war and peace, as between war and crime, tend to be blurred.

As for the weapons themselves, it should be stressed that the mortality and morbidity associated with any given injury vary, according to both the weapon's design (e.g. type) and the context (e.g. environment) in which it is used. Weapons can kill, maim, or contribute to various forms of long-lasting secondary effects. The design of weapons determines their killing and stopping power: a function of ammunition type and twist, propulsion and the amount of kinetic energy distributed throughout the body (see Appendix 6.4). Similarly, the context of use—whether in close proximity to the victim or from afar, whether close to a health clinic or not—invariably influences the outcome (see Commentary 6.1).

Intentional deaths resulting from small arms can be positioned on a continuum that runs from flagrant violations of human rights and international humanitarian law to compliance with existing and legitimate police norms. Studies indicate, however, that non-combatants are frequently killed or injured from fragmenting munitions (e.g. bombardments or artillery) during conflict while those killed outside of conflict are more likely to have been intentionally attacked with firearms.[42]

Brazil has one of the highest firearm-related death rates in the world. With only three per cent of the global population, it accounted for between 9 and 13 per cent of the world's firearm deaths in the 1990s

On the other hand, legitimate police and military actors, who kill criminals or insurgents in self-defence or within the parameters of the Laws of War[43] (a proportional judgement of military utility versus human cost), are often considered to be operating within their legal jurisdiction (De Mulinen, 1987). However, there are clearly exceptions to this rule.

Take the case of Brazil. While not at war, Brazil has one of the highest firearm-related death rates in the world. With only three per cent of the global population, Brazil accounted for between 9 and 13 per cent of the world's firearm deaths in the 1990s. According to the Institute for Religious Studies and Viva Rio in Rio de Janeiro (ISER, 2000, p. 12), ' ... Brazil lives under conditions of micro conflicts of criminality'. Similarly, studies on Afghanistan demonstrate that, in regions experiencing intermittent peace and conflict, 'weapons injuries not attributable to combat are common ... social changes accompanying conflict and the widespread availability of weapons may be predictive of use of weapons that persists independently of conflict' (Michael *et al,* 2000, p. 415).

Commentary 6.1 Why are guns so lethal?

Television screens the world over are saturated with images of males of all ages brandishing deadly arrays of military hardware. Lurid tales of the destruction wrought by armed violence are an omnipresent feature of global news reporting. In many viewers' minds, genocide, armed massacres, and conflict deaths are automatically equated with widespread availability of small arms and light weapons. And yet, military weapons that find their way into civilian hands are notably diverse in their stopping power. A crucial attribute is the weapon's lethality—the degree to which it can inflict damage on one or more vital bodily organs or structures. Factors affecting lethality involve much more than simply the type of weapon; they also include context, vulnerability, and ballistics.

In terms of context, unrestrained arms availability is highly correlated with a pervasive collapse of public institutions and the inability of the state to ensure civilian security. In such an environment, faltering first aid, evacuation capability, and follow-up treatment may increase mortality rates. Other factors are more a function of the location of weapons use and the relative vulnerability of those exposed. For example, organized and formal militaries go to some lengths to protect themselves from the effects of fragmenting munitions—for instance through reinforced bunkers and sandbags. Civilians in areas where such weapons are used and who lack access to protective measures are more vulnerable than military personnel.

Increased vulnerability is another important consideration, since the shelling of civilian inhabited areas is a relatively common feature of many recent conflicts. For example, tribal fighting in Afghanistan appears to have undergone a major qualitative shift away from assaults on individuals and towards a form of combat more typical of organized military factions. Mortars accounted for 90 per cent of injuries in one such tribal clash, and more than 25 per cent of those injured were women or children. In fact, in a number of settings, mortars are the most common cause of civilian death or injury resulting from inter-factional combat. On the other hand, assault rifles are responsible for most deaths and injuries in other situations outside the context of inter-factional combat (e.g. domestic disputes and banditry).

Analyzing non-combat use of assault rifles reveals that the weapon was frequently being used at close range to resolve an interpersonal dispute. Another common scenario is the accidental discharge of an assault rifle while being (mis)handled. In either case, with the victim in non-combat situations much closer to the weapon, the increased kinetic energy carried by the projectile inflicts greater tissue damage and there is increased probability of lethal injury.

Ballistics also has a bearing on weapon lethality. Like all rifles, military assault rifles have a twisting series of grooves within the barrel referred to as rifling. This imparts a twist to the projectile in flight in order to ensure aerodynamic stability. The amount of twist per unit of barrel length changes with different models of assault rifle, even those of the same calibre or within different series of the same model. Organized militaries are outfitted with ammunition specifically designed to match the rifling within the barrel of their assault rifle. This is not always the case with informal militia.

A mismatch between barrel rifling and ammunition means that the projectile has less stability in flight and creates larger bullet wounds. Not surprisingly, stocks of assault rifles, produced at different times in different places and circulating in many parts of the world, are unlikely to be matched with appropriate ammunition. The resultant tendency towards large bullet wounds is yet another factor in the increased lethality associated with widespread weapons availability.

Source: Meddings, 2000a
The opinions expressed above are those of the author and are not in any way to be attributed to the ICRC.

A question of gender?

Consideration of gender is particularly relevant in the discussion of direct effects since a dispro-portionately large percentage of both aggressors and victims (during conflict or peace) are men. An analysis of deaths from the use of firearms in Rio de Janeiro illustrates that the male-female mortality ratio is similarly unbalanced (ISER, 2000). For example, of Rio residents who died in 1998 from firearms, approximately 94 per cent were male and only six per cent female. Among young people in Rio over the same period, males between the ages of 15 and 29 were approximately 24 times more likely to die from the use of firearms than were females of the same age group.

And yet women are explicit targets of certain types of armed violence—simply because they are women. Some forms of violence—like domestic abuse, sexual assault, and rape—are uniquely conditioned by gender-based relations, which means that understanding their dynamics is critical for effective intervention (see Commentary 6.2). For example, women are frequently symbolic targets in conflict—an offensive gesture designed to disgrace and undermine the morale of enemies.

Consider the circumstances of sexual assault. Women constitute the vast majority of victims. For example, an estimated 20-50,000 women in Bosnia and Herzegovina were systematically raped during the conflict in the fragmenting former Yugoslavia (WHO, 2000; Collins, 1998).

In Burundi, a specific armed faction known as Sans Capotes ('Without Condoms') reportedly raped women at gunpoint before murdering them. Guns are also used extensively as instruments of sexual violence against women in South Africa (Cock, 1997). In northeastern Kenya, women are raped and assaulted indiscriminately; even the threat of small arms possession undermines solidarity among large groups searching for firewood or foodstuffs. Nevertheless, there is considerable evidence that women are not merely passive victims during conflict; their involvement runs the gamut from active combat to peace-building and reconciliation.

Women are more at risk from domestic violence at the hands of intimate partners, while men are more at risk from male acquain-tances. Where arms are readily available, they are the weapons of choice when male spouses kill their partners.

Commentary 6.2 Direct effects of gun violence: What's gender got to do with it?

Most small arms owners and users are male. In the US, it is estimated that 42 per cent of men, as compared to nine per cent of women, own guns. In Canada, 85 per cent of gun owners are male. The fact that there are proportionally few female gun owners in relation to female gun victims has been one of the arguments advanced for positioning the firearms debate in the context of human rights and gender.

Guns also figure prominently in the 'cycle of violence' against women. Even when a gun is not fired, it has the capacity to inflict serious psychological damage on those threatened. For every case in which women are killed or physically injured with firearms, there are many more in which they are threatened. The patterns of intimidation are similar across cultures and include such behaviours as shooting the family pet as a warning or getting the gun out and cleaning it during arguments. Studies of abused women in many parts of the world—Australia, New Zealand, South Africa, and Canada—report similar phenomena.

Public opinion polls in many countries reveal a significant gender split in attitudes towards firearms, as well as in firearm-related electoral voting behaviour. For example, in the US House of Congress during the final vote for the Brady Bill (legislation designed to ensure background checks on prospective gun purchasers), 81 per cent of women voted for passage as against only 51 per cent of men. Another relevant US example is the 1999 'Million Mom March', which dramatically illustrated the power of women to lobby against violence, to raise awareness, and potentially to effect societal change. As Canadian Senator Janice Johnston observed, 'if there were more women in Parliament, we would not even be having this debate'.

Source: Cukier, 2000b

Indirect effects

'There is less
threat and more
insecurity than
ever before'.

Jan Egeland,
UN Special
Representative
for Colombia

The international community is increasingly cognizant of violent crime and the attendant costs of armed insecurity. There is mounting concern over the rising number of peacekeeping missions dispatched to insecure regions, the rates of cross-border and internal displacement, the incidence of child soldiers, and the combined impact of these factors on development.

While the qualitative effects of armed violence on societies include the manifestations of cultures of violence and a heightened sense of personal insecurity, the quantitative impacts are more elusive. They range from direct effects (e.g. numbers of casualties) to indirect externalities (e.g. overextended public health facilities or declining foreign investment). Calculating the indirect effects of the availability and use of small arms and light weapons is an imprecise science. However, an increasing number of approaches, including transaction cost theory, opportunity costing, and proxy analysis, are being applied. For further information on these and other methodologies, please refer to the Small Arms Survey website at http://www.smallarmssurvey.org.

There is a need for an informed and balanced perspective to counteract the temptation to conflate figures and attribute all spiralling crime, humanitarian emergencies, and underdevelopment to the abundance and (mis)use of light weapons. It must be kept in mind that small arms are not the origin of crime, complex emergencies, or underdevelopment. Nor should any narrow strategy focusing solely on their reduction or eliminationbe considered a solution to address these complex challenges.

The following sections will explore a range of overlapping and indirect effects of small arms availability through a variety of disciplinary lenses. The discussion begins with a review of the impacts of small arms on the welfare of individuals and public health systems. It then considers the implications of small arms availability on criminality and the growth of privatized security. The section then turns to the consequences of small arms availability on humanitarian interventions and operational security. Finally, it concludes with a review of the opportunity costs of small arms availability on development initiatives and takes a brief look at the relationships between poverty, inequality, and firearm use.

In sickness and in health

In South Africa and
the US, armed
violence is fast
overtaking
infectious disease
as the principal
cause of ill health
and premature
mortality.

Death and injury resulting from firearms has been classified simultaneously as a 'scourge' (Boutwell *et al*, 1995), an 'epidemic' (ICRC, 1996), a 'disease' (Colletta and Kostner, 2000), and a 'preventable global health problem' (CDC, 1999). The biological analogies are not accidental. In South Africa and the US,[44] armed violence is fast overtaking infectious disease as the principal cause of ill health and premature mortality. Indeed, according to South Africa's National Injury Mortality Surveillance System (Butchart, 2000, p. ii), a registry that captures approximately 25 per cent of the estimated 60,000 fatal injuries a year, 'firearms overshadowed all other external causes [of death]. The total of 3,906 firearm deaths was greater than the 3,684 deaths due to all motor vehicle accident (MVA) categories combined'.

It comes as little surprise that a humanitarian stance on small arms has been embraced by the medical profession. Weapons are designed to wound or kill; health professionals are trained to identify, prevent, and treat factors that contribute to mortality and morbidity. The Open Society Institute (1999), for example, has declared gun violence an international public health and safety hazard, as well as a significant and preventable source of suffering and death. The public health community has already begun to forge a 'neutral bridge' to reconcile highly politicized discussions on firearms and traditional supply-side or militarist theorizing on arms control.[45]

The World Health Organization (WHO) and the International Committee of the Red Cross (ICRC) have taken the lead in rethinking the question of mortality and morbidity as measured by firearm-related violence (see Box 6.3). The wider medical community's efforts to recast the problem as a 'measurable' public health issue amenable to medical intervention has greatly contributed to sensitizing the international community (see Commentary 6.3).[46]

International humanitarian law[47] has been developed to safeguard the welfare of non-combatants and the wounded; humanitarian norms have evolved to limit the excessive and 'injurious' effects of certain weaponry.[48] However, both these initiatives are inadequately applied or monitored. As a result, many concerned with the health impacts of small arms have focused on the importance of universal criteria, appraisal of the military utility of various arms, and the need to achieve proportionality between military benefits and human costs (ICRC, 1997). Still others have focused on raising awareness of the social and economic costs of firearms to population health.

Box 6.3   Defining a role for the public health sector

The proliferation and misuse of small arms exacts a high health toll: injury, disability and death, not to mention mental health consequences for victims and their families and friends. Although precise data on the annual number of small arms-related deaths are not yet available on a global scale, there have been some cross-national studies. The largest one to date involved 36 high- and upper-middle-income countries with a total population of 1.19 billion. This study revealed that, even though none of the countries was engaged in civil conflict, more than 88,000 people had died from firearm injuries in a one year period in the mid-1990s.

The health sector has multiple roles in reducing the adverse impact of small arms on health and longevity. Its most immediate responsibility is the provision of effective care and support for victims and their families. Unfortunately, in many countries where small arms proliferation is high, health care resources are low. In some cases, the surfeit of small arms contributes indirectly to economic decline and decreasing resources available for health care. In others, human and material resources for hospital and surgical care or rehabilitation are lacking.

A second important role for the health sector is data collection on the magnitude, risks, and protective factors for small arms injuries. Evidence and information on deaths, injuries, and disabilities, and on the costs of these health consequences are vital for policy and decision-makers. As previously mentioned, very little is known about mortality rates attributed to specific small arms, and even less on the number and variety of injuries, the types of weapons most involved, and the demographic characteristics of victims and perpetrators and their relationships.

The third role of the health sector is to participate in the design, implementation, and evaluation of interventions to prevent interpersonal, self-inflicted, and gun violence in general. These activities could focus on behavioural issues like reducing the presence of guns in the home, promoting safer gun storage, or decreasing alcohol consumption. The health sector could also contribute to evaluating the impact of interventions implemented by others. Gun buy-back programmes, weapons collection and destruction, or legislation passed to reduce the traffic or illegal possession of small arms should ultimately reduce the number of injuries and deaths they cause. Emergency room and forensic data collection could also make a substantive contribution to assessing the impacts of such programmes.

Finally, in the same way as it does for physically communicable diseases like HIV/AIDS, TB, or malaria, the health sector could advocate increased attention to this 'socially communicable' health issue. It should provide decision-makers with information on the human and financial costs of such problems and demonstrate that, in certain countries and age groups, small arms are a leading cause of death. This information can then be linked to demands for more effective measures to counteract the public health danger.

Sources: Krug, 2000a, 2000b

Commentary 6.3 Violence costs

Health economics has long been used to estimate the direct economic impacts of various threats to health, whether it be tobacco, AIDS, motor vehicle accidents, or bullets. Some studies have focused on tallying the economic burden for public institutions (e.g. to hospitals, clinics, and policing institutions).

Other studies have added indirect costs, such as the value of lost life in terms of earning power. The value or presumed 'quality of life' will vary considerably based on the earning power of the victims, their age, and gender. As Michael Renner notes, the concept of 'value of lost life ... is highly controversial ... it is inherently biased toward the better off in society'.

The cost of firearm-related death and injury (including murder, suicide, and unintentional injuries) in the US, Canada, and Latin America are tremendous. The potential range of secondary effects that could be considered is vast. For example, armed violence affects the blood supply, and the fact that emergency responses to large scale violence often do not perform thorough HIV/AIDS testing can result in additional problems (Coupland, 1996; Sidel, 1995).

Dealing with the health effects of armed violence impedes the provision of basic health care and diverts much needed resources from other health and social services. Similarly, armed violence and the prevalence of weapons also create psychological stress that fuels other health problems and creates insecurity. Living in arms-infested environments yields observable symptoms of post-traumatic stress disorder, such as overwhelming anxiety and a lack of motivation.

Source: Cukier, 2000a

How heavy is the health burden?

Of the hundreds of thousands of victims killed by firearms, millions more survive their injuries but are left with permanent physical disabilities and mental health consequences. Victims of small arms injuries often require resource-intensive surgery, followed by prolonged hospitalization and rehabilitation. These treatments are expensive and often drain resources away from already impoverished health systems.

There are even more victims who are unable to access health services or medical treatment. For example, the conflict and instability generated by the unregulated availability of small arms often hampers civilian travel to and from immunization service centres and affects the coverage of vaccination programmes, all of which ultimately contribute to the spread of infectious disease.

> *The average gun in the US—whether 'fired at targets ... at animals ... at people ... gathering dust ... or under the bed' carries an annual injury tag of US$ 630 per capita.*

The cost of treating firearm injuries is staggering. The most reliable statistics on the financial costs of such injuries are recorded by institutes in the US and Canada. According to Miller (1995, p. 1263), the average gun in the US, whether 'fired at targets ... at animals ... at people ... gathering dust ... or under the bed' carries an annual injury tag of US$ 630 per capita. In 1997, for every person shot and killed with a firearm, there were an additional three others treated for non-fatal firearm injuries. For each adult gunshot victim, the price tag amounted to US$ 154,000, US$ 3 million for child fatalities, and US$ 390,000 for hospitalized individuals.

Medical care and the lost productivity resulting from premature disability and death, firearms injuries, and fatalities cost the US health system approximately US$ 126 billion in 1992 (Miller and Cohen, 1997). A follow-up study by Cook and Ludwig (2000) suggests that the costs were closer to US$ 100 billion per year in the late 1990s. Anrest *et al* (1996) estimates that over 80 per cent of the economic costs of treatment and care were borne by US taxpayers. In Canada, Miller (1995) estimated that the costs of firearm mortality and morbidity exceeded US$ 4.7 billion (CAD 6.5 billion) per year.

The aggregate figure included US$ 54 million (CAD 75 million) in medical and police costs and US$ 1.1 billion (CAD 1.5 billion) in lost work opportunities.[49] The consequences of gunshot wounds cost each Canadian the annual equivalent of US$ 170 (CAD 235).[50]

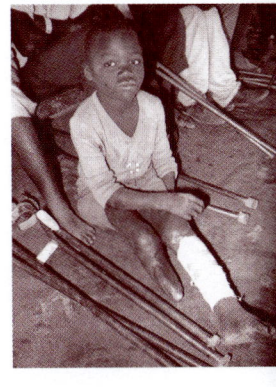

Similar effects are experienced in the South. Though statistics are limited, it is possible to render tentative estimations. In Latin America, the Inter-American Development Bank (IDB) calculated the regional economic costs of violence, since the mid-1990s and including the costs of health, policing, and 'value of life lost', at US$ 140-170 billion per year. In Brazil, approximately 10 per cent of annual GDP is consumed by treating victims of violence and increased policing. In Colombia, the figure rises to 25 per cent. At a more localized level, a 1997 study estimated the cost of treating severe firearm injuries in one South Africa hospital at US$ 2.5 million to US$ 10 million (ZAR 12-47 million) per annum (Burrows *et al*, 2000). Costs to the hospital and clinics in Central America are reported to be similarly high (Godnick, 2000).

For the individual, the repercussions from firearm injury are profound. The costs include treatment, medication, physiotherapy, and counselling, all of which may lead to the need for loans or informal credit and may finally end with the closure of businesses and even repossession of assets. To this economic cost must be added long-term, often permanent, psychological trauma and social marginalization. The indirect effects of small arms on community health, while not captured in the statistics, may be inferred from the diminished quality of life among individuals.

There is a palpable increase in fear among vulnerable sectors of society, which affects their normal domestic and social routines (see Box 6.4). Armed violence creates an atmosphere of anxiety with negative multiplier effects that erode the human, economic, and social capital of communities.

Armed violence creates an atmosphere of anxiety, with negative multiplier effects, that erodes the human, economic, and social capital of communities.

Box 6.4   On being shot in South Africa

People living in contemporary South Africa are at tremendous risk from firearms. Recent statistics reveal that more than 75 per cent of armed robberies with aggravated assault were committed with firearms. The increase in armed violence has had a direct impact on policing and medical facilities, stretching them well beyond normal capacity. It also affects the well being of victims and communities at the physical, psychological, and economic level.

A series of interviews were conducted with six armed robbery survivors (three men, three women) and their friends and family. The victims were all residents of KwaZulu-Natal Province and varied in age, gender, geographic distribution, and economic status. A majority were also small business owners, operating in either the informal or formal sector.

In each case, the victim was approached by two or three armed men, pretending at first to be customers, who then demanded money or goods. All robberies occurred during off-peak hours at either the beginning or end of the day. Each gunshot victim underwent traumatic operations for the removal of bullets.

Though the injuries sustained were not perceived as insurmountable physical obstacles, most victims chose not to return to work for fear of recurrence. The female victims, in particular, felt that their self-image and self-esteem had been damaged and felt uncomfortable interacting outside of their immediate social circle. Their sense of alienation was reflected by their reduced trust in others, with some victims revealing that they had become paranoid about the potential role of other entrepreneurs (or 'competitors') in the incident.

All victims registered acute fear of loud noises and suffered from bouts of anger, flashbacks, and nightmares. They all felt emotionally and psychologically distressed and in need of help from family, friends, and neighbours.

(continued)

Although support was made available by church bodies, nurses, and business entrepreneurs, kin and friendship networks were most sustaining in terms of financial assistance, counselling, and moral support. About half the victims were satisfied with the assistance they received from police and paramedics. As no arrests were made, there was a general feeling of frustration that justice had not been done.

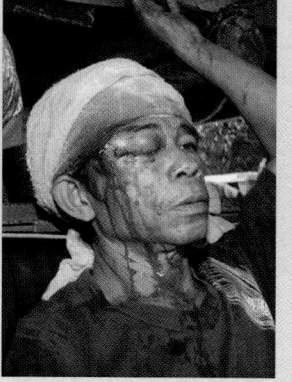

The direct medical costs of the injury did not affect the victims as much as the indirect costs of closing down their businesses. All victims claimed that not only their health, but also their economic status, had been irrevocably damaged as a result of the incident. Each had been the primary house-hold income-earner. Although the initial payments required for emergency hospital bills[51] were covered through loans and donations from kinship networks, the victims ended up using the lion's share of their savings to pay off debts and meet household expenses. As a direct consequence, all victims and households had to adapt their lifestyles and financial manage-ment, resulting in a diminished quality of life. Several had their assets (e.g. household possessions and vehicles) repossessed by the banks soon after the incident.

Testimonies from victims in Natal, South Africa

Respondent	Description of Injuries
Male	' ... Shot at close range with extensive damage to leg leading to amputation. Not taking well to new prosthetic limb. Experiencing further pain and unable to carry articles with his right hand. Development of heart complications and mild epilepsy ...'
Male	' ... Shot at close range. He still suffers from pain—particularly during colder weather. Experiences difficulty getting out of bed. Frequently visiting the hospital to drain puss from his wounds that are not healing on account of diabetes. Suffers from headaches and blackouts ...'
Male	' ... Shot 13 times with one clean wound (no vital organs touched) through the chest. He has recovered physically and experiences occasional pain ...'
Female	' ... Shot at close range. She spent two months in intensive care. Her left side is paralysed and her speech severely affected ...'
Female	' ... Shot three times at close range. Comatose for three weeks losing extensive blood. Her left eye was removed and she suffers from continued limping ...'
Female	' ... Shot three times at close range—two to the stomach and one in the right hand. She has difficulty lifting heavy objects with her right hand. She no longer permits customers to sit inside her house ...'

Source: Arms Management Programme, Institute for Security Studies, 2000a

Crime and punishment

Controlling arms-related violence through appropriate legislation and action is part of a state's inherent obligation to ensure and protect the human rights of its citizens. In the context of structural adjustment, privatization, and the expansion of organized crime,[52] governments the world over have been forced to make difficult decisions regarding public spending priorities. As public expenditures for basic services decline and funding for welfare and social safety nets is diverted to debt servicing, civil societies bear the brunt of the burden and thus become more vulnerable to criminality.[53]

The state's declining control over stockpiles and inventories, in addition to its desire to generate much-needed foreign exchange has resulted in a situation in which the preferred tools of criminals are more readily available than ever before (BROKERS). In many countries there is a fine line between policing and criminality, and guns are often sold to civilians at a premium. As for increasingly at-risk citizens, partly as a consequence of crime and the relative under-capacities of public security, they are resorting to other forms of protection. The privatization of security—that is, the growing tendency of individuals, groups, and organizations to rely on private security forces rather than the state's police and paramilitary formations—is a global phenomenon (Boutwell and Klare, 2000). Increasingly, the provision of security is shifting from the public to the private domain.

Increasingly, the provision of security is shifting from the public to the private domain.

Privatizing security

The widespread availability and trafficking in small arms is creating new security threats. A good indicator of global unease is the proliferation of security firms and private military companies (PMCs). Fear of armed crime and violence has led to enclosed fortress-like communities that are emblematic of the widening divide between the 'haves' and 'have-nots'. Illustrative of the mental militarization and insecurity of communities, those who cannot afford 'protected castles and the … commodification of their security are forced to organise their self-defence outside legal parameters' (Lock, 1999a, p. 31). As a result, we are witnessing 'the evolution of private security into a mutually reinforcing system of multi-polar societal "re-armament" cascading down the social ladder where it amounts to an informal militarization … at the lower end of the social pyramid' (Lock, 1999a, p. 32).

Private commercial actors had been heavily involved in the provision of public security well before the state's so-called monopoly on violence. 'Private Security Companies' (PSCs) emerged as long ago as the 16th century during the era of Italian mercantilism when rival merchants hired security groups as a means of controlling trade routes and protecting their assets. Between the late 16th and 18th centuries, PSCs evolved under the auspices of colonial exploration companies.[54] By the mid-20th century, they came into their own throughout Africa, Asia, and Latin America. As they became better established, PSCs provided services ranging from personnel and installation protection to security training and counter-industrial espionage for corporate clients working in regions of instability and conflict.[55]

Private security is a lucrative growth industry. Analysts predict that it will be worth more than US$ 200 billion per annum in the US alone by 2010.

According to Lock (1999b, p. 9), the 'ideal-type security order with the state fully commanding the monopoly of legitimate coercion … existed, if ever, at the end of the post-World War II boom in social-democratic states in Europe'. Since the beginning of the 1990s, private security has come to represent a lucrative growth industry with significant numbers of corporations and states relying on contracted or in-house services rather than public policing. PSCs represent, not only one of the fastest growing sectors in the global economy, but also a vital sector in the emerging economies of the South.[56]

In 1991, US PSCs employed 1.5 million personnel and spent US$ 52 billion. In contrast, public law-enforcement was employing 600,000 personnel and spending less than US$ 30 billion.

The ratio in 1998 increased to US$ 90 billion (in the case of PSCs) as compared to US$ 40 billion (for public policing). In 1998, for example, PSCs with publicly traded stock in the United States grew at twice the Dow Jones industrial average. American private security and policing companies outspent public policing by 73 per cent and employed more than 4 million personnel. Analysts predict that the industry will be worth more than US$ 200 billion a year in the US alone by 2010 (O'Brien, 2000).

Though the security risks may differ from place to place, the situation is comparable in Europe. For example, since the mid-nineties, Germany's security firms have doubled in number. In the UK, private security personnel have grown from 10,000 in the 1950s to more than 250,000 in the year 2000, outnumbering even the British Army. On a global scale, revenues from the private security market topped US$ 97.6 billion in 1990 and are expected to rise to some US$ 402 billion by 2010 (O'Brien, 2000).

On a global scale, revenues from the private security market topped US$ 97.6 billion in 1990 and are expected to more than quadruple to some US$ 402 billion by 2010.

In the former Soviet Union, a significant proportion of the hundreds of thousands of soldiers demobilized from the armed forces have joined PSCs. Numerous connections between unemployed ex-soldiers and organized crime are becoming apparent. This is taking place at a time when demand for security is growing. By 1994, for example, 6,605 private security enterprises or security services companies were registered, with more than 26,000 private investigation licences issued. This is analogous to the situation in Central Asia and the Pacific Rim, where demobilized combatants, both formal and informal, have sold their services to a variety of organized crime operations involved in small arms trafficking, prostitution, 'human smuggling', and the drug trade.

In Africa, the situation is exceedingly complex owing to the collusion of PSCs and private military companies (PMCs) with the ruling elite, the police, and the army (BROKERS). In South Africa alone, there were 5,939 registered PSCs employing some 136,000 personnel by 1998. Even this figure is considered low, given that the official ratio of private security personnel to police in that country is 9:1. With an estimated 4.2 million registered firearms and a new gun licensing rate of 20,000 per month, PSCs contributed approximately US$ 1.6 billion (ZAR 10 billion) per year to the country's GDP in 1999.

With Central and South America described as among the most heavily militarized regions in the world,[57] it comes as no surprise that in Guatemala City arms are more readily available than telephones. With '1.5 million guns in Guatemala City ... they currently outnumber the population' (Weissert, 2000). As a result of escalating insecurity, between 1999 and 2000, the purchase of private security services and weapons in Guatemala has risen 50 per cent over rates that were already the highest in Central America (CIEN, 2000). There has also been a notable influx of military-style weapons (e.g. hand grenades and mortars) used in common criminal activity.

'Organized Criminal Group': A structured group of three of more persons, existing for a period of time and acting in concert, with the aim of committing one or more serious crimes or offences ... in order to obtain, directly or indirectly, a financial or material benefit.'
UN General Assembly, 2000

The rapid development and influence of private security and PMCs are viewed as a threat to existing democratic and judicial institutions, as they prioritize the profit motive over the public good of communities. They have been accused of lacking accountability and diffusing power away from the state without redistributing it to the people.

Organizing crime

The growth and reach of transnational organized criminal groups dealing in arms have been recorded in banner headlines around the world. A provisional list might include: Russian, Italian, and American *mafiosi*; criminal monopolies in the Golden Crescent and Triangle; triads in China; the decentralization of narco-trafficking and arms dealing in the Northern Andean region; and smuggling operations from South Asia to Central America and the Caribbean. In some cases, particularly among developing countries, criminal elements are better equipped and armed than the state's military, police, or customs apparatus.

The proliferation of globalized criminal markets has contributed to more frequent interactions between major organized crime groups with transnational ambitions (UNDCCP, 2000).

Criminal groups from a range of different countries have established a broad network of illicit businesses, trading goods and services, as well as information and resources across borders. In the Association of South East Asian Nations (ASEAN), for example, transnational crime syndicates, particularly drug traffickers and human smugglers, are perceived as 'the principal recipients of small arms and light weapons and as threats to authority and good governance in the region' (UNDDA, 2000, p. 2).

The presence of international crime networks, coupled with expanding markets and rapidly moving capital, has permitted underground or shadow economies to flourish. As a result, organized crime presents itself simultaneously as both a local and global phenomenon.[58] Transnational criminals are the new venture capitalists, thriving in high-risk markets and unstable or otherwise vulnerable environments. Though only recently recognized, there is a convergence between illicit drug and mineral trafficking[59] with arms proliferation in, among other places, Sierra Leone, Liberia, Angola, Colombia, Pakistan, and Afghanistan[60] (ILLICIT TRANSFERS). In economies weakened by armed conflict, criminal actors may well preside over a territory ripe for money laundering, trafficking in arms, primary commodities (e.g. diamonds, timber, and oil), drugs, abundant and cheap labour, and endless possibilities for exploitation. Though overhead costs can be high, it is a profitable business. Indeed, even where multinational companies and transnational criminal entities devote substantial resources to the provision of private security,[61] the cumulative returns when operating in violent and crime-infested regions often far outweigh the costs.

Transnational criminals are the new venture capitalists.

From the abstract to the concrete

The impact of small arms on criminal violence is difficult to evaluate in the abstract. Crime-related firearm injuries include those caused by interpersonal violence, irrespective of whether the victims were the intended targets. Such injuries can be non-fatal or fatal. While firearms homicide data are, to a certain extent, available, there is little information on non-fatal firearm injuries resulting from crime. Though many countries have laws mandating that gunshot wounds be reported to the law enforcement authorities, there are few national—much less international—registries to monitor trends over time. This is because legislation is rarely consistently implemented at the national level and information is frequently gathered, if at all, in a piecemeal fashion.

Ultimately, the concrete manifestations of criminal and drug-related armed violence are felt locally. These range from the armed protection of interests or 'turf', to armed retribution against drug users unable to pay for their habits, to violence committed by users under the influence of drugs. In London, for example, the homicide rate between 1997 and 1999 was at its highest levels since the mid-eighties.[62] Much of it was drug-related and more than 60 per cent of all cases involved firearms.

According to Thompson (2000), 'modern weapons' (e.g. handguns and automatic weapons) are increasingly being held by young drug dealers to protect themselves and their territories. According to research conducted by Lizotte et al (1994), young males who own guns for protection in the US are six times more likely to carry firearms and eight times more likely to commit a crime with a gun. Also, they are four times more likely to sell drugs, approximately five times more likely to be in a gang and three times more likely to commit serious and violent crimes than youth who do not own guns for protection (Lizotte et al, 1994). In the *favelas* of Brazil, the shantytowns intermingled among and encircling the country's major cities, it is often the poor and marginalized that are affected by armed violence generated out of the drug trade (see Box 6.5). Automatic weapons are also used by young cocaine and crack traffickers in Bogota's South End, Nairobi's Eastleigh district and south-central Los Angeles.

In London, for example, the homicide rate between 1997 and 1999 was at its highest level since the mid-eighties. More than 60 per cent of all cases involved firearms.

Box 6.5   Danger in paradise: Urban criminal violence trends in Rio and Brazil

In Brazil between 1990 and 1999, an estimated 28,000 people died as victims of firearms. The widespread availability and use of small arms is a serious and rapidly growing problem.

A variety of factors contributed to the growth of violence in Brazil in the 1980s and 1990s. Increasing urbanization, coupled with growing socio-economic inequality, the demographic 'bubble' (youth), the erosion of public services, anachronistic laws, and institutional norms regulating public safety and justice—a combination of all these complex factors has created an enabling environment for armed violence. Although it is spurious to single out firearm availability as the only cause of violence, focusing on small arms is important because they are the major instruments of urban violence in Brazil.

In 1997, among young male Brazilians aged 15-19, 'external causes' (e.g. non-natural) leading to death constituted almost 80 per cent of all mortality. Approximately 36 per cent of these youths were killed with firearms. Put another way, a youth in Brazil was 1.6 times more likely to die from gun wounds than as a result of road accidents. The situation did not improve in 1999. In Rio de Janeiro, for example, approximately 40 per cent of all 'externally caused' deaths (and 93 per cent of homicides) were attributed to firearms.

Figure 6.5   Young guns: Risk of firearms death for males aged 15-29 in Rio and Brazil

Population group	Rio de Janeiro (deaths per 100,000)	Brazil (deaths per 100,000)
Total	41.8	17.5
Male, 15–29 years old	198	68.8
Relative risk factor	4.7	3.9

Source: ISER, 2000

Protecting people: A humanitarian imperative

At the centre of the human rights agenda and humanitarian law is protection—the safeguarding of political, economic, social, and cultural rights of all individuals and the upholding of the Geneva Conventions and Protocols. Humanitarian advocacy and action on the small arms issue revolves around three complementary and overlapping policy agendas:

1. Human rights and supply-side controls: Addressing international humanitarian law (IHL) abuses resulting from legal, grey, or 'illegal' shipments to particularly abusive regimes;

2. International humanitarian law and civilians: Addressing violations of IHL and the human rights of civilians during armed conflict; and

3. Deteriorating security: The impact of arms availability on the protection of personnel and the effectiveness of humanitarian relief and development operations.

The recently launched International Action Network on Small Arms (IANSA), a loose coalition of over 250 NGOs working on arms control and violence reduction, is drawing on all three policy agendas.[63] Each perspective, along with its major proponents, is treated in greater detail below.

Human rights and supply-side controls

Spearheaded by a number of like-minded states, international human rights organizations, and non-governmental agencies (NGOs) actively pursuing demilitarization, this perspective highlights the importance of supply-side controls on producer or exporting states to rights-abusing regimes.[64] Proponents of this view contend that a significant majority of arms flows into conflict environments are supplied by governments in direct contravention of international law.

These weapons, it is argued, are frequently used by importing governments to violate the basic human rights of innocent civilians. Thus, efforts should be increased to curb both legal and covert arms trade, since producer and distributor states have an obligation, under Article 1 of the Geneva Conventions, to 'respect and ensure respect' for international humanitarian law. In particular, they argue that the 'provision of arms into situations where serious violations of international law occur or are likely to occur should be condemned' (ICRC, 1999, p. 64). In its strongest form, this perspective suggests that countries that 'distribute to regions of conflict are, by their acts of commission or omission, or sheer neglect, accessories to the abuses that are being committed. If the abuses rise to the level of war crimes, they may be accessories to war crimes, even genocide' (Hilterman and Bondi, 1999).

The humanitarian advocacy community argues that the major and mid-level small arms exporting states, including the US, the Russian Federation, Brazil, Germany, Bulgaria, China, and the UK have an obligation to impose restrictions on licencing arrangements and sales to abusive regimes (LEGAL TRANSFERS). Adopting a rights-first approach, these actors call for increased accountability, governmental scrutiny, and policies on brokering and end-user certification. They also demand ethical policies and codes of conduct on the small arms trade so as to improve transparency on the production, distribution, and receipt of small arms.[65]

Of course, proponents of this rights-based approach recognize the limitations of focusing on transfers and newly produced small arms, particularly in light of the high level of illegal arms circulating or leaking from existing stockpiles. Nevertheless, they seek to situate the debate over small arms transfers within the framework of human rights rather than in the comparatively less politicized arena of global trade.

Significant small arms exporting states—e.g. the US, Brazil, the Russian Federation, China, Germany, Bulgaria, and the UK—have an obligation to impose restrictions on licensing arrangements and sales to abusive regimes.

International humanitarian law and civilians

A second approach—one preferred by the United Nations, some donors, the ICRC, and major international relief agencies—aims to heighten international awareness and, in some cases, actively mitigate the impact of armed violence on non-combatants and vulnerable groups.[66] Operating in the complex realities of the field in regions where demand for small arms is high, they must respond to armed violence on a massive scale. A number of these actors condemn and investigate armed attacks and massacres committed against unarmed civilians by belligerent public authorities and non-state actors. They also campaign against torture, the summary execution of captured victims, and the recruitment of child soldiers.

Humanitarian and development agencies are particularly alarmed that civilians are increasingly the primary target of armed conflict and war. The ICRC (1999, p. 71) for example, notes that, not only do civilian casualties frequently outnumber those of combatants, but that human suffering continues, frequently years after hostilities have ended 'as the widespread availability of arms ... undermines the rule of law and threatens efforts at reconciliation among former warring parties'. In other words, the widespread availability of small arms threatens the foundations of international humanitarian law, 'one of the principal means of protecting civilians in times of armed conflict' (Herby, 1999).

Humanitarian and development agencies are alarmed that civilians are the primary target of armed conflict.

In many cases, the forced displacement of civilians is the object, rather than the by-product, of coercive violence. There are strong indications that availability of small arms is correlated with repeated cycles of cross-border and internal displacement (see Box 6.6).

From the beginning of the 1990s, the deliberate displacement of civilians has been common practice in Angola, Sierra Leone, DRC, and Uganda (see Map 6.4). For example, as a result of the extraordinary availability of military-style arms and 'ground attacks involving far more weaponry' in the Congo, 'relief officials estimate that there are 750,000 refugees, compared with at most 200,000 a year ago' (Fisher, 2000). What with the availability of a seemingly endless supply of weapons in return or resettlement regions, the long-term character of displacement seems assured.

To take another example, the 1994-96 occupation of Rwandan refugee camps in Eastern Zaire by the *Interahamwe* drew the attention of the international media to the problem of militarized refugee camps (see Box 6.7). While the presence of armed elements in refugee camps is by no means a new phenomenon (e.g. the PLO in Palestinian camps, Saharwi rebels in Algeria, and South African members of the ANC's military wing in Mozambique and Tanzania), it has taken on increasing relevance for the international humanitarian community.

With combatants unaware of, avoiding compliance with, or in deliberate contempt of international humanitarian law, the implications for humanitarian agencies seeking to deliver assistance are serious. In conflict and post-conflict settings where small arms remain widely available, there is a combustible mix of recently active or demobilized soldiers, banditry, and in some cases, predatory state activity. Even a single armed person can block supply routes and 'the resulting loss of life is significant ... both from lack of access to relief programs and ... the protection international agencies offer as "witnesses" to deter atrocities' (Greenaway and Harris, 1998, p. 14). For this and other reasons, increased hostage taking, banditry, and violent theft is common in the aftermath of conflict.[67] Consequently, demands for physical protection for both beneficiaries, host communities, and relief/ODA personnel have risen to the top of the humanitarian agenda.

Map 6.4 Violence-induced internal displacement: A growing menace

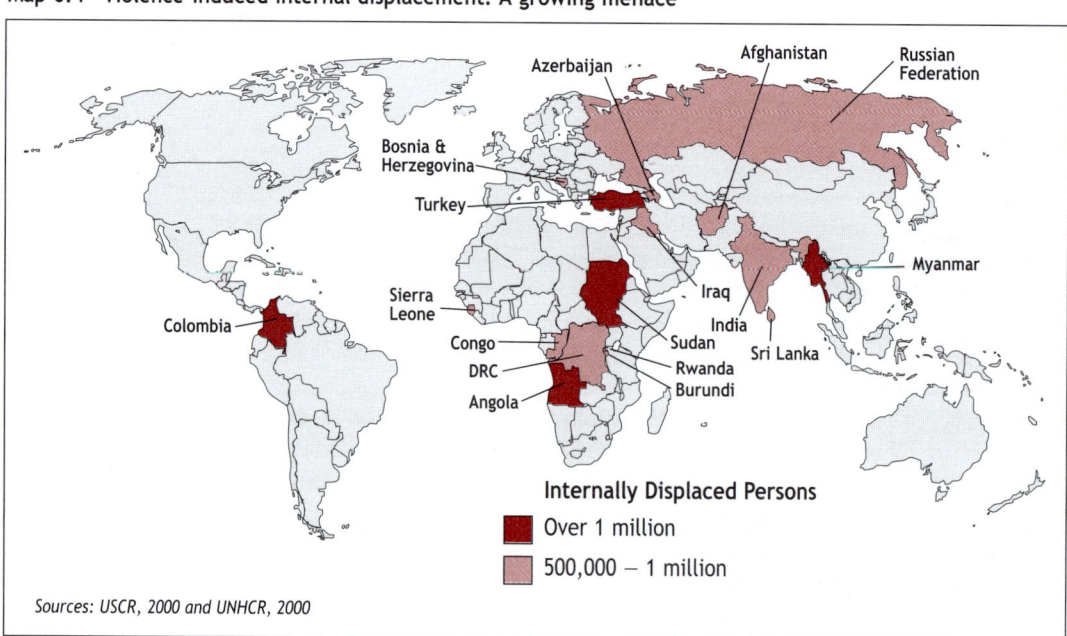

Box 6.6 Flee or perish: The scourge of internal displacement in Africa

For decades, the African continent has witnessed the forcible displacement of civilians as a result of armed conflict. Since the 1980s, however, the number of cross-border refugees has decreased, while the number of people displaced within their own national borders has grown dramatically. The number of internally displaced persons (IDPs) in Africa reached 12 million by mid-2000—an increase of 4 million during the last two years of the century. By contrast, the African refugee population was nearly halved to an estimated 3.6 million between 1994 and 1999.

The proliferation of modern small arms in the Great Lakes Region has been well-documented (see, for instance, Box 6.2). For example, Rwandan soldiers who fled to then-Zaire after having participated in the 1994 Rwandan genocide were able to acquire new arms in spite of a UN embargo. These weapons are fuelling a brutal civil war in the eastern part of the Democratic Republic of Congo (DRC). Referred to as Africa's 'First World War', Burundi, Rwanda, and Uganda deployed troops in the region in support of rebel factions fighting forces loyal to the late DRC President Kabila, while the latter has received support from Angola, Namibia, Chad, and Zimbabwe.

Local militias arms supplies have been regularly replenished by external sources, setting the scene in the eastern DRC for some of the most systemic and widespread violence—and violations of humanitarian law—in Africa. A pattern of reprisal attacks on civilian settlements has been observed since the resumption of civil war in 1998. The complexity of the conflict is illustrated by reports of villagers who, after having been attacked by so many different armed groups, can no longer distinguish between friend and foe. As a result, between 1999 and 2000, the number of IDPs in the area increased by over half a million.

Armed skirmishes between Kenyan pastoralists and their neighbours clearly illustrate the relationship between the availability of small arms and the displacement of civilians (Map 6.5). Tribal conflicts—expressed through livestock raiding—are a custom in the area but, while cattle raids are a key traditional form of 'redistribution', they have come to involve external actors and modern weapons. The Karamojong pastoralists along the Uganda-Kenya border have an inventory of more than 100,000 light weapons, purportedly acquired from fleeing forces loyal to Idi Amin and sustained with purchases from sources in Kenya, Somalia, and Sudan. Between 100,000 and 135,000 people were displaced on the Ugandan side when the Karamojong raided the area during the first half of the year 2000. While looting has characterized past raids, in this instance, systematic rape, killing, and destruction of property was also widespread. The same can be said of the Turkana, the Samburu, and the Sudanese Dinka livestock herders who also live in the region. According to some estimates, 95 per cent of all households possess a firearm (Muggah and Berman, 2001).

Source: Danevad, 2000

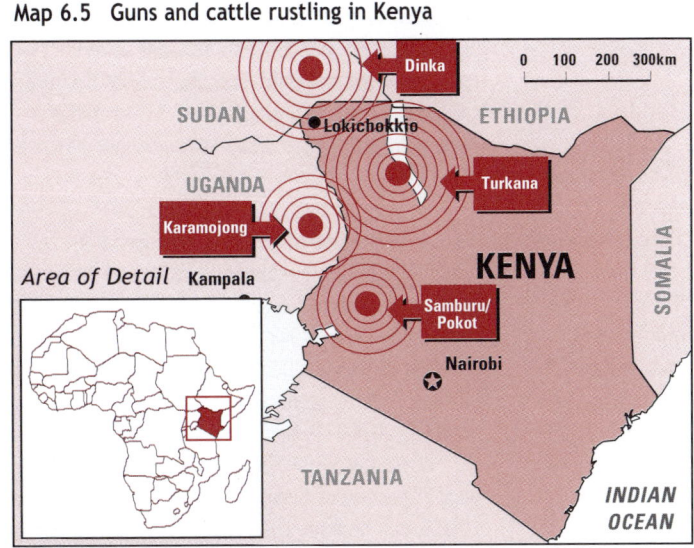

Map 6.5 Guns and cattle rustling in Kenya

Source: Muggah and Berman, 2001

Deteriorating security

The third perspective—the impact of arms availability on the protection of personnel and the effectiveness of relief and development operations—has been explored in great detail by academics, security and policy analysts, governments, multilateral agencies, the ICRC, and the UN. It stresses the deteriorating security environment for peacekeeping and humanitarian operations.[68] It notes that the nature of humanitarian and development work is changing—taking place amidst internal, rather than cross-border, conflict and is tied to a warfare economy. It acknowledges that civilians, and those who are seen to protect and assist them, are now regarded as legitimate targets for extortion, theft, threat, rape, and other brutalities.

By 1997, the UN considered 53 countries—about 25 per cent of all the world's countries— to be insecure.

In the late 1980s and early 1990s, the UN Security Co-ordinator was still able to report that 'security was not an issue' and that 'it was almost unheard of for a staff member to be killed or injured'. By 1997, however, the UN considered 53 countries to be insecure, operations in complex emergencies had increased fivefold, and the working environment for UNHCR and NGO staff had 'altered dramatically' for the worse over the previous half decade (Greenaway and Harris, 1998).

In recent years, United Nations staff and other humanitarian personnel have lost their lives in virtually every corner of our conflict-ridden world: Afghanistan, Albania, Angola, Bosnia and Herzegovina, Burundi, El Salvador, Ethiopia, Georgia, Guinea, Haiti, Indonesia, Iraq, Kenya, Kosovo, the Russian Federation (Chechnya), Rwanda, Sierra Leone, Somalia, Sudan, Tajikistan, and Uganda. Others have been abducted in Bosnia and Herzegovina, Colombia, Georgia, Guatemala, Liberia, Peru, the Philippines, the Russian Federation (Chechnya), Somalia, Tajikistan, and Yemen.

According to a 1997 UN press release, more than 1,500 international and national staff on UN missions have been killed by weapons since the 1945 founding of the United Nations (Dorn, 2000, p. 3). Over the past eight years, the most conservative estimate of the mean homicide rate for UN staff and dependants is approximately 35 per 100,000—on a par with the civilian homicide rates of Lebanon, and higher than in Azerbaijan, Jamaica, Nicaragua, the Russian Federation, or even Sri Lanka.

From January through July 1998, more UN civilian staff died in United Nations' service than soldiers involved in UN peacekeeping operations.

Between January 1992 and March 1997, 131 UN staff were killed with firearms, of which 21 per cent were engaged in humanitarian operations and 52 per cent were killed in societies experiencing state collapse. If international peacekeepers are included, the figure rises to 456. From January to July 1998, more UN civilian staff died in United Nations' service than soldiers involved in UN peacekeeping operations (Deen, 1998). Between January 1994 and March 1997, there were 119 individuals taken hostage, and an additional 500 were taken in 2000. Even now, there are only nine (and rising to 16 by the end of 2001) professional UN staff responsible for co-ordinating and managing the security system covering 70,000 UN staff and dependants at over 70 duty stations.

A recent study by Sheik *et al* (2000) noted that intentional violence was the cause of between 70 and 75 per cent of all deaths among humanitarian personnel between 1992-95. The study emphasizes that it was 'humans with weapons rather than motor vehicles [that] posed the greatest threat' (Sheik *et al,* p. 168). The number of deaths among UN peacekeepers and programme staff broadly follows the changes in the number of refugees and asylum seekers worldwide, providing an indirect measure of the prevalence and violence of conflicts.

The International Committee of the Red Cross (ICRC) reported that, in 1996, its delegates suffered 153 security incidents, including staff members killed or wounded. Between 1990 and 1999, a total of 93 staff members were killed and 280 injured, but trends suggest a general decrease over the past four years.[69] It is reasonable to assume that the UN and the ICRC are more security conscious and risk averse than many field NGOs[70]—and that these figures under-represent the phenomenon in the wider international humanitarian aid community.

Box 6.7   The militarization of refugee camps: A burgeoning security risk

Over the past three decades, the spread of small arms and light weapons, whether as a result of covert or overt criminal activity, has been a contributing factor in forcing people to flee their homes and relocate in makeshift camps. Particularly in countries of asylum, the presence of small arms poses a serious law-and-order problem, threatening the security of civilian refugees both in and outside the camps. According to Milner (2000, p. 2), a perverse outcome of the growing 'security burden' in the region is that offers of 'asylum will become increasingly scarce in countries where hosting refugees is perceived to be a threat to state security'.

Camps have been used to slip rebels surreptitiously across borders to run guns and ammunition, and to establish rear bases or recruiting grounds for rebel forces. In some cases, host governments have supported the use of refugee camps for cross-border, counter-insurgency activities. Examples include Ethiopian refugee camps in Eastern Sudan, Afghan camps in Pakistan, Khmer camps in Thailand, and Salvadoran and Nicaraguan refugee camps in Honduras. What is more, entire 'refugee generations' have grown up within such militarized environments. These and other factors have led to the militarization of many refugee camps.

A case in point is the Tingi-Tingi encampment in Eastern Zaire where an estimated 150-160,000 refugees, including several thousand unaccompanied minors, have been quartered in makeshift camps. According to a UNHCR spokesperson, in 1998 the militarization of the camp put the lives of innocent refugees, IDPs, host communities, and humanitarian workers at risk. According to CNN reports in 1997, about 25 children died each day. A UN assessment (1997) claimed that 'former Rwandan soldiers and militia in the settlement are receiving weapons, ammunition and uniforms by air and are being sent to the front-line … Military elements are being deployed in positions near the camps … and sections of the encampment are being used as storage facilities for arms and ammunition. Young male refugees are being actively recruited.'

Map 6.6   Refugees and arms flows in eastern Democratic Republic of Congo

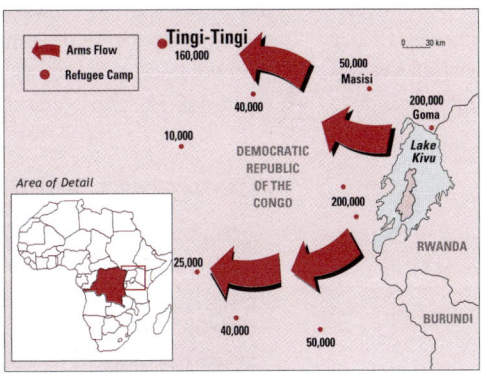

Small arms were frequently shipped under the direct cover of 'humanitarian assistance'. In the refugee camps of the former Zaire, Rwanda, and Burundi, arms were smuggled in by way of NGO aircraft as 'food aid' or 'farm implements'. According to the *East African* (1997), a regional news service, 'so many weapons have been flown into the Tingi-Tingi camp that they have interrupted relief shipments … arms, uniforms and munitions are being supplied daily in the camp itself.' The same phenomenon has reportedly occurred in Sudan, where Christian aid organizations have been repeatedly accused by public authorities of functioning as screens for arms merchants. Similar claims have been levied against camps in Kenya, such as Kakuma and Dadaab, though little substantive evidence exists to back up such claims. To be sure, however, the 'host community' areas surrounding the camps are saturated with arms (Muggah and Berman, 2001).

The UNHCR has a stake in preventing this kind of instability that leads to forced displacement. The organization recognizes that curtailing the production, sale, or transfer of small weapons would contribute to greater stability and security and mitigate the circumstances that cause people to flee. To this end, the UNHCR has adopted a 'security-first' approach, involving the deployment of international police advisors to improve security and law-enforcement capabilities (e.g. to Kosovo Albanian camps in the Former Yugoslav Republic of Macedonia, as well as to Burundian refugee camps in Tanzania). In some cases, the UNHCR has also hired host-country soldiers to provide security in refugee camps, and funded firewood collection programmes to reduce refugee and IDP vulnerability. Further, it has established a Permanent Working Group on Safety, while the Field Safety Section has recently prepared a Camp Security Survey to address this issue in camps and refugee populated areas.

Death, injury or armed harassment of humanitarian personnel has become an almost everyday occurrence (see Commentary 6.4). Relief workers are increasingly forced to negotiate with child soldiers, ex-combatants, and non-state factions. The recent proliferation of agencies in high-risk theatres of operation has resulted, in many cases, in increased 'security incidents'. The UNHCR alone calculates that in 1997 it had 3,000 staff working in areas designated insecure, and an additional 10,000 if associated NGOs were added to the equation. A total of 158 security incidents affected UNHCR staff and property between December 1999 and May 2000. Though they ranged from petty theft to life-threatening events and death, approximately 50 per cent were considered to be serious in nature. Threats were reported in Afghanistan, Colombia, Georgia, Greece, Malaysia, Pakistan, Tajikistan, and Thailand. Convoys and relief activities were explicitly targeted in Kosovo, Sudan, and West Timor.

A recent survey of the international humanitarian aid community concluded that personal safety was a major source of stress for expatriate field staff working in violence-prone areas. Approximately 95 per cent of those interviewed, including development workers recorded varying degrees of on-site security problems. For example, the ICRC estimates that approximately 50 per cent of its international and national staff suffer from emotional difficulties during and following their assignment while an estimated 30 per cent have endured a serious 'security incident' in the field.[71] According to a UN Survey, 'armed conflict, mines, gunfire, murder, banditry, car-jacking, robbery, the narcotics trade, substance abuse and other criminal activities in the … surrounding areas were reported stress factors'.

Personal safety is a major source of stress for expatriate field staff working in violence-prone areas. About 95 per cent of those interviewed cited on-site 'security problems'.

Commentary 6.4 West Timor: A tragic communiqué

'My next post needs to be in a tropical island without jungle fever and mad warriors. At this very moment, we are barricaded in the office. A militia leader was murdered last night—he was decapitated and had his heart and penis cut out. Segments of Timorese society must be some of the most violent and gory people anywhere on Earth: Atambua suddenly shut down when news spread that trucks and buses full of militias were coming from Betun (my former home) to Atambua. The town is suddenly deserted and all the shops were boarded up in a matter of minutes. Traffic disappeared and the streets are strangely and ominously quiet. I'm glad that a couple of weeks ago we bought rolls and rolls of barbed wire.

'I was in the office when the news came out that a wave of violence would soon pound Atambua. We sent most of the staff home, rushing to safety. I just heard someone on the radio saying that they are praying for us in the office. The militias are on the way, and I am sure they will do their best to demolish this office. The man killed was the head of one of the most notorious and criminal militia groups of East Timor. These guys act without thinking and can kill a human as easily (and painlessly) as I kill mosquitoes in my room. You should see this office. Plywood on the windows, staff peering out through openings in the curtains hastily installed a few minutes ago. We are waiting for this enemy, we sit here like bait, unarmed, waiting for the wave to hit. I am glad to be leaving this island for three weeks. I just hope I will be able to leave tomorrow.

'As I wait for the militias to do their business, I will draft the agenda for tomorrow's meeting on Kupang. The purpose of the meeting: to discuss how we are to proceed with this operation.'

These words were written in the last hours of the life of UNHCR staff member, Carlos Caceres, in Atambua, West Timor. Emailed to a UNHCR colleague in the Macedonian city of Skopje on 6 September 2000, this communiqué was sent shortly before he and two colleagues were killed—the most serious incident yet experienced by the UNHCR. This excerpt was read by Sadako Ogata, former High Commissioner for Refugees, at a memorial service for Mr. Caceres on 8 September 2000.

'The world can never be at peace unless people have security in their daily lives … the search for security… lies in development, not in arms'

UNDP *Human Development Report*, 1994

Other surveys of private sector workers in high-risk environments are similar. The psychological stress of working in situations where one's personal safety is continually jeopardized, of enduring extended separation from family who are constantly aware of their loved ones' extreme danger, and of being surrounded on a daily basis by armed violence—all of these factors contribute to critical levels of stress and the potential for psychosocial trauma. Unsurprisingly, real and perceived insecurity adversely impacts the productivity of relief and development operations.[72]

A threat to development

Armed conflict and violence are today concentrated in the world's poorest countries. According to the Organisation for Economic Co-operation and Development (OECD/DAC, 1998), conflict has reduced, even reversed, development gains in the developing world. In 1999, of the thirty countries at the bottom end of the UNDP's Human Development Index (HDI), 22 were engaged in, or just emerging from, some form of complex emergency. In Africa alone, 29 of the 45 UNDP programme countries were experiencing some form of complex humanitarian emergency. The micro and macro impacts of such armed conflicts and widespread violence on development are severe.

At the microeconomic level ...

At a microeconomic level, small arms availability undermines development by inducing some individuals to invest, not in education, but in honing their criminal and combatant skills. Furthermore, arms availability fragments pre-existing social networks, as people feel isolated and increasingly reluctant to leave their homes. The widespread availability and use of small arms disrupts agricultural production, transportation networks, and commercial trading (Luckham, Ahmed and Muggah, 1999) and has therefore contributed to extended food shortages, increasing market prices, and the need for emergency feeding programmes (RGSA, 2000; Collins, 1998).

One particularly vulnerable segment of the population is children. Not only do they suffer as victims of gun violence; they also suffer from being used as soldiers. From Sierra Leone to Afghanistan, in situations of fear and economic insecurity, children often 'receive an AK-47 and little else, leading them to terrorise civilians in their search for food and other material goods' (Colletta & Nezam, 2000, p. 7). Youth excluded from formal markets often adopt a gun-linked livelihood that appears to bestow on them an adult status that commands respect (see Box 6.8). For boys, this practice is particularly potent when combined with the role small arms play in reinforcing patriarchal networks and dominant masculine codes as protector and defender.

In Somalia and northern Kenya, the widespread availability of high-powered weaponry puts gun-toting youths beyond the customary controls exercised by clan elders. In addition, entire generations of young men forced into 'economic apartheid' (e.g. exclusion from the formal market) are increasingly susceptible to the temptation to 'consider armed violence as a means to enforce their inclusion' (Lock, 1999a, p 34). Unemployment and exclusion from educational opportunities among Sinhalese and Tamil youth has been a primary cause of Sri Lanka's bloodshed. Indeed, young men (and women) from country villages and towns join one army or another for lack of anything else to do.

In regions of transit, communities are reported to have adopted new forms of informal trade that involve smuggling and theft, as well as the cultivation of cultures of violence. As a result, entire regions can become economically dependent on conflict and arms; Pakistan's North-West Frontier Province, a main conduit for insurgent arms during the Afghan-Soviet war, is now a significant cottage-industry weapons producer. Due to their abundance, small arms are often acquired at a fraction of their original value. Indicators of their impact on societies include

Twenty-two of the 30 countries at the bottom of the UNDP's 1999 Human Development Index (HDI) were currently engaged in, or just emerging from, some form of complex emergency.

Box 6.8   Children and guns: The tragedy of child soldiers

The spread of inexpensive small arms has had one especially pernicious effect: it has made it much easier to turn children into soldiers. According to the Coalition to Stop the Use of Child Soldiers, there are over 300,000 (both military and insurgent) children under the age of 18 currently taking part in over 30 armed conflicts around the world.

As a continent, Africa is by far the largest recruiter of child soldiers, accounting for approximately 135,000 or 45 per cent of the global total. The principal recruiters operate in Sierra Leone, Sudan, Uganda, Angola, and the Great Lakes countries of Burundi, Congo, and Rwanda.

Asia has an estimated 75-100,000 child soldiers. Afghanistan is the principal recruiter in this region, although its ranking has slipped. The average age of recruits in the late 1990s tended to hover at approximately 14 years of age, whereas, prior to that time, even children between the ages of 10 and 11 were being actively recruited. Militaries and rebel groups in Myanmar and Sri Lanka[73] are also accused of recruiting heavily from among youth—particularly from orphanages, elementary schools, and rural communities.

As for their weapons, due to relatively easy portability, maintenance, and availability, the most popular small arms used by children are the AK-47 and M-16. Testimonies of children familiar with Galils, AR-15s, Uzi sub-machine guns, Ingrams, and 357 Magnums have also been recorded. Moreover, due to their agility and fearlessness, child soldiers are particularly valued in the handling and laying of landmines.

Children are not spared from the horrors of conflict. The most immediate risk is the high likelihood of death or injury as a result of participation in combat. In Chechnya, between February and May 1995, children made up 40 per cent of all civilian casualties. Red Cross field workers found that children's corpses told a grim story; they bore unmistakable marks of having been systematically executed with a bullet through the temple. In the years following Rwanda's genocide, a similar story of systematic executions was repeated again and again. When not killed, children are frequently wounded; in Sarajevo, Bosnia and Herzegovina, almost one child in four has been wounded in the course of the region's long drawn-out conflict.

The most frequent child-specific combat injuries are loss of hearing, sight, and limbs, all of which have permanent or at least long-term repercussions on the victim's future re-integration and 'value' in society. Secondary effects include higher susceptibility to health hazards, such as malnutrition, psychosocial trauma and psychological disorders, skin and respiratory diseases, malaria, as well as sexual exploitation among both sexes laying them open to increased risk of sexually transmitted infections (STI's), HIV/AIDS, pregnancy, abortion, or premature, involuntary childbirth. Other documented non-combat related injuries include beatings, deprivation of food/drink, and bone deformation from carrying heavy loads (Machel, 2000, and World Vision, 1996).

Over the long-term, there are a number of serious challenges for child soldiers in terms of post-conflict rehabilitation. First, there are the obvious problems related to disarmament of children and their reintegration into a civilian society trying to reintroduce peacetime values. These child soldiers may be reluctant to relinquish their weapons, which have also given them a decidedly unchildlike sense of economic and social status, particularly when the local economy has been undermined as a result of prolonged conflict. Additional long-term challenges relate to the lack of vocational and educational training, difficulties of reintegrating children who have committed atrocities, and the particularly sensitive difficulties associated with the reintegration of girls.

Source: Coalition to Stop the Use of Child Soldiers, 1999

In the year 2000, there were over 300,000 children under the age of 18 taking part in over 30 armed conflicts around the world.

Coalition to Stop the Use of Child Soldiers

the heightened militarization of young men, the introduction of voluntary and involuntary restrictions on mobility, and a dwindling confidence in public institutions.

... and at the macroeconomic level

At the macroeconomic level, small arms proliferation discourages foreign and direct investment, as well as domestic savings, as people lose confidence in a country's prospects for growth. Armed conflict, crime, and domestic violence also damage prospects for economic development, affecting school enrolment rates and overall productivity.

According to the UNICEF offices in Burundi, over 200,000 Burundians have been killed since 1993 while some 110,000 children are unable to attend school because of killed and displaced family members. The agency also estimates that, in addition to a deficit of 3,000 primary and secondary school teachers, it will cost approximately US$ 12 million to repair damaged public school infrastructure. To make matters worse, this is happening at a time when public expenditures on health and education are declining and bilateral aid decreasing.[74] The negative multiplier effects of small arms have resulted in lowered incomes, reduced consumption, and the reduction of aggregate demand for goods and services.

Armed conflict and crime impose significant constraints on the ability of affected countries to implement national development programmes. On the one hand, national resources are diverted away from social welfare to purchase arms to protect civilians' security. On the other hand, vital infrastructure needed for development initiatives is put in jeopardy by arms-related anxieties. Foreign-funded development projects are often cancelled or postponed to prevent assets from being diverted towards criminal ends (OECD/DAC, 1998). Though the gross costs of responding to armed violence might be higher in the industrialized world, the proportional impact on GDP and government budgets is higher among developing countries.

During 1998, armed violence cost the equivalent of 12 per cent of Latin America's GDP—a combination of lost human capital, private investment, and property transfer. El Salvador, for example, has been particularly affected by armed violence in the post-conflict period (see Box 6.9). The costs of responding to armed violence (e.g. in terms of expenditures from the health, policing, and judicial sectors) amounted to just under US$ 800 million—approximately 13 per cent of GDP in 1998 (Bunivinic *et al*, 1999). The costs are often higher in countries experiencing on-going conflict.

During 1998, armed violence cost the equivalent of 12 per cent of Latin America's GDP— a combination of lost human capital, private investment, and property transfer.

Similar impacts are apparent in South Asia.[75] In Sri Lanka, for example, military expenditures as a percentage of GDP have increased from 3.8 per cent in 1985 to 6.5 per cent (US$ 867 million) in 1996. As a percentage of health and education expenditures, military spending grew from 17 per cent in 1985 to 107 per cent in 1996. According to the World Bank, the impacts of communal war in Sri Lanka between 1984 and 1996 have cost the national economy approximately US$ 1.18 billion. The Institute of Policy Studies in Colombo estimates that foregone investment, loss of workers to death and emigration, and other attendant costs of the war amount to 200 per cent of GDP in 1999. And yet, throughout this period, Sri Lanka's economy grew at a rate of 4.4 per cent per annum. According to one estimate, the economy of a Sri Lanka at peace would grow at an average annual rate of 9 per cent—thus absorbing 140,000 people entering the workforce each year (Harris, 1996). This is prosperity lost and part of the high price of war.

Indeed, armed conflict 'can no longer be viewed as an externality to development ... rather conflict and its aftermath is one of the key constraints to development and one of the main causes of poverty' (Holtzman, 1999). While the causal relationship is far from straightforward, armed conflict can be seen as a cause and effect of poverty and inequality.

Box 6.9 Central America: Unravelling development

Central America has no uniform system to measure the impact of small arms use on public health systems or other socio-economic and political structures. The regional growth of the private security industry and commercial purchasing of firearms can be interpreted as a response to the insecurities bred out of the large quantities of arms left over from civil wars and now in the hands of civilians, including criminals. Their growth cannot be seen apart from the incomplete process of disarmament and reintegration of ex-combatants, increased drug trafficking throughout the region, pre-existing cultures of gun ownership and violent conflict resolution, growing poverty and inequality, as well as corrupt and inefficient judiciaries and public security institutions.

The experience of Central American countries is varied. Despite Costa Rica's relatively low level of militarization, PSCs are growing in number and commercial firearms sales continue to escalate (STOCKPILES). While Honduras and Panama did not experience outright civil wars, they were militarized through the Cold War strategies promoted by the US. Indeed, the presence of recirculated arms has been documented throughout the region. For example, American M-16s supplied to South Vietnam resurfaced two decades later in Honduras and Nicaragua.

There are high levels of violence and a demonstrated civilian willingness to use armed violence as a form of conflict resolution (see Figure 6.6). According to the Inter-American Development Bank (IDB), 'in postwar El Salvador or Guatemala ... the widespread availability of weapons and attenuation of inhibitions against the use of violence tend to exacerbate such already powerful contributing factors to social and domestic violence as inequality and high levels of poverty' (Buvinic *et al*, 1999).

Source: Godnick, 2000

Figure 6.6 Homicide in Central America

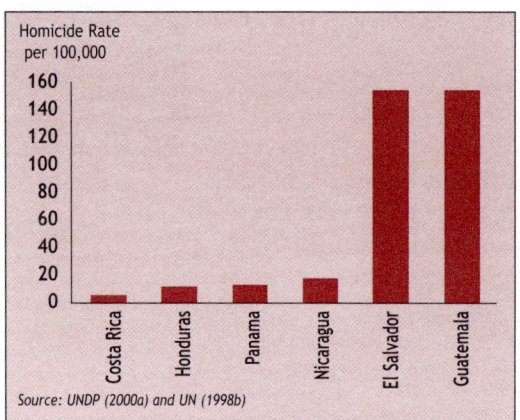

Source: UNDP (2000a) and UN (1998b)

Map 6.7 Focusing on Central America

Guns, poverty, and inequality

The inverse correlation between human development and firearm-related homicide is illustrated in Figure 6.7. Human development indicators are a weighted composite index of variables including life expectancy at birth, adult literacy, gross primary, secondary and tertiary school enrolment, and GDP per capita.[76] Firearm homicide rates are drawn from publicly available information provided to the UN (1998b). They consist of the proportion of reported intentional homicides committed with firearms. While the focus on homicides does not provide a complete picture of firearm use or availability in a given country, it does provide a starting point for comparisons and trends across regions. The point of bringing the two variables together is to begin considering the empirical relationship between levels of development and firearm-related homicide.

Figure 6.7 Is there a relationship between human development and firearm homicide?

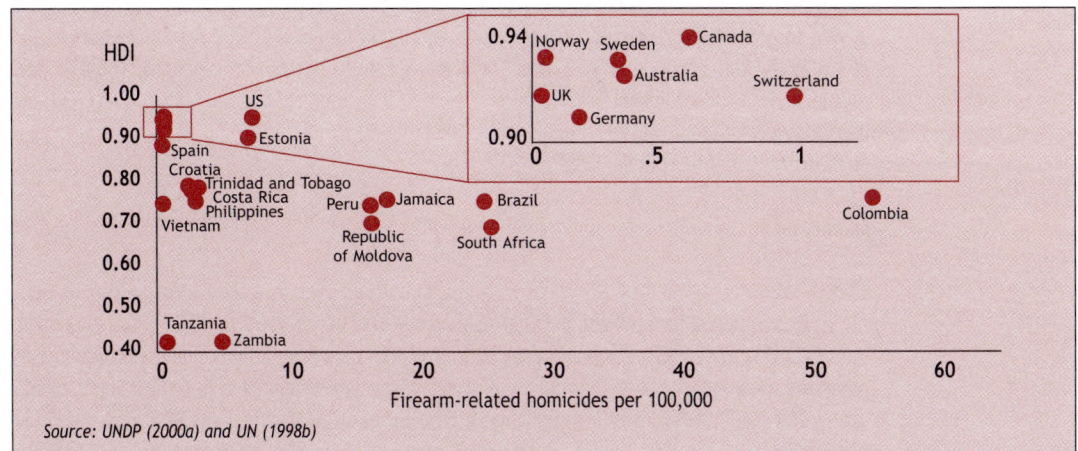

Source: UNDP (2000a) and UN (1998b)

Since Figure 6.7 does not account for rates of firearm availability, whether licit or illicit, only tentative observations may be drawn. However, under certain circumstances, there is some evidence that countries with high levels of development (HDI of 0.90 to 1) experience lower rates of homicide committed with firearms. The institutions of the judiciary and the police, as well as the rule of law, among other things, are presumably working more effectively in such countries than in others. Conversely, states with lower levels of human development (between 0.60 and 0.80) tend to be much more susceptible to high levels of firearms-committed homicides (see Appendix 6.5). Unfortunately, due to the unavailability of data, there is virtually no information on the countries at the lowest end of the HDI scale (between 0 and 0.6). The *Survey* will further assess the empirical association between poverty and inequality with firearm use in subsequent editions.

Human development indicators are a weighted composite index of variables, including life expectancy at birth, adult literacy, gross primary, secondary, and tertiary school enrolment, and GDP per capita.

Human Development Report, UNDP, 2000

Opportunity costs in the field

For multilateral donors, bilateral aid agencies, and development institutions the consequences of small arms availability on their programmes and personnel are severe. Their responses to this increasing atmosphere of insecurity and its implications for development opportunities are twofold:

- **Quantitative:** Funding and commitment to long-term development efforts are shifted to short-term relief-oriented projects, particularly towards conflict-prevention and response.[77] For example, OECD Overseas Development Assistance (ODA) earmarked for emergencies has expanded from two per cent in the mid-1980s to five per cent in 1995.[78] As a proportion of ODA, emergency relief has ballooned to between nine and ten per cent in 1999.[79]
- **Qualitative:** Due to the frequently suspended or delayed operations on account of insecurity, field operations include an increasing number of 'insecure' areas where not even relief workers dare to tread. Even where they do work, the risks of 'danger habituation'[80] among local and expatriate staff and stakeholders are very real. As a result, relief and development personnel are more susceptible to insecurity.

The paradox is that, even as aid workers call for more co-ordination in regions prone to violence, peace-building, rehabilitation, and development activities are not being carried out in regions where they are most urgently needed. At worst, official development programmes close down on account of insecurity and regions are declared 'no-go areas'. Growing insecurity, and risks to government extension workers and aid personnel, force many to seek alternative regions where return on investment and performance indicators may justify continued funding.

Thus, unchecked small arms availability undermines development by encouraging a culture of withdrawal. When development projects are implemented in insecure regions, 'project staff may be at risk, project sites may remain unused by the population for fear of being seen as supporting the government, and sites may attract armed attacks to disturb the transition process' (Colletta and Kostner, 2000). Indeed, recent UNDP reports (1998a; 1998b) indicate that there are few prospects for development without security—highlighting the importance of legitimate local judiciaries and police forces to enforce public order.

Conclusions

There is a growing awareness, across many sectors, that small arms are a serious risk to human security. In recognition of the problem, the analytical appraisal of the effects of small arms has diversified. But the field is undergoing a process of self-definition. The contours of the debate are broadening as more and more actors call for a multidisciplinary and integrated approach to disarmament, recognizing that small arms constitute a challenge, both in terms of supply and demand. Even if one could turn off the small arms tap tomorrow, they would continue to circulate between conflicts, communities, and combatants. This is because the diffusion of small arms takes place at the interface of local and global arenas, in situations of inequality and insecurity, posing intricate challenges to national, regional, and international actors.

Effective responses require reliable information. While far from providing a complete picture, this chapter attempts to tease out a range of methodologies that quantify the effects of small arms proliferation and use. While this chapter has generated only the most tentative of conclusions, subsequent editions of the *Small Arms Survey* will revisit and refine these approaches.

Under certain circumstances, arms availability appears positively associated with armed violence, injury and death. Some societies, especially in the North, are affected by firearm-related suicide. Others, especially in the South, are confronting escalating levels of armed homicide. Though difficult to generalize, the obstacles facing societies are often similar: heavy pressures on public health facilities, increasing rates of criminality, growing humanitarian emergencies, or lost development opportunities.

But there are important differences, not only between countries and regions, but also within individual states and urban centres. Comparative analysis will continue to be hampered by the unreliability and inadequacy or even non-existence of consistent data. Thus, there is an urgent need to undertake site-specific studies with comparable indicators and to generate in-depth quantitative and qualitative research capacities.

The health sector, for example, has been extremely successful in terms of recasting what has been treated as a conventional disarmament issue into a quantitatively measurable threat to people's health and well-being. In bringing the tools of epidemiology, health economics, and human rights to bear, its proponents have usefully highlighted the short- and long-term impacts of small arms and defined preventive measures to reduce their impact.

Social scientists have generated a convincing case for the relationship between small arms and insecurity. The costs of insecurity and its implications for the effectiveness of public institutions have been carefully documented. Relief and development workers, in addition to donors and governments, have also begun reviewing the humanitarian implications of small arms and their real impact on relief and reconstruction efforts in the field. It is now acknowledged that armed violence is a serious impediment to social and economic development. More and more people agree that an environment free from fear and insecurity is a prerequisite for sustainable development.

For further information and current developments on small arms issues please check our website at www.smallarmssurvey.org

6   List of Abbreviations

ANC	African National Congress
ASEAN	Association of South East Asian Nations
CDC	Center for Disease Control
DRC	Democratic Republic of Congo
GDP	Gross Domestic Product
HDI	Human Development Index
HRW	Human Rights Watch
IANSA	International Action Network on Small Arms
ICRC	International Committee of the Red Cross
IDB	Inter-American Development Bank
IDP	Internally Displaced Person
IHL	International Humanitarian Law
IMF	International Monetary Fund
ISER	Institute for Religious Studies
ISS	Institute for Strategic Studies
MVA	Motor Vehicle Accident
NATO	North Atlantic Treaty Organization
NGO	Non-Governmental Organization
NRA	National Rifle Association
ODA	Overseas Development Assistance
OECD	Organization for Economic Co-operation and Development
OSCE	Organization for Security and Co-operation in Europe
PLO	Palestinian Liberation Organization
PMC	Private Military Company
PSC	Private Security Company
RPF	Rwandan Patriotic Front
SALW	Small Arms and Light Weapons
SAP	Structural Adjustment Programme
SIPRI	Stockholm International Peace Research Institute
UK	United Kingdom
UN	United Nations
UNDCCP	United Nations Office for Drug Control and Crime Prevention
UNDP	United Nations Development Program
UNHCHR	United Nations High Commissioner for Human Rights
UNHCR	United Nations High Commissioner for Refugees
US	United States
USCR	United States Committee for Refugees
WHO	World Health Organization
WSF	World Shooting Federation

6   Endnotes

1 See works by Boutwell and Klare (2000), Karp (2000), Klare (1999), Lock (1999a, 1999b), and Willett (1998).

2 See Londono and Guerrero (1999).

3 The population of Latin America and the Caribbean is recorded as 498 million while the combined population of OECD countries accounts for 1.1 billion (UNDP, 2000, p. 226).

4 The most recent *Human Development Report* (UNDP, 2000: 247-250) has tabulated both country homicide rates as a whole and rates in the largest city. Virtually without exception, every urban site cited in the report demonstrates a considerably higher rate than the country average. Although the report does not differentiate between homicide committed with or without firearms, a number of examples are instructive. The US rate was 9.0 per 100,000 and 21.3 in New York City while the Jamaican rate was 29.8 and 62.4 in Kingston.

5 The reverse is also tentatively born out in practice. In a recent study documenting the effects of gun bans in two Colombian cities, preliminary results indicate that homicide rates were lower during periods when the firearm-carrying ban was in effect compared to other periods (Villaveces *et al*, 2000). The reduction of availability and use through strong

disincentives (gun ban) was 'associated with a reduction in homicide rates for Cali and Bogota' (Villaveces *et al,* p. 1205).

6 See, for example, Lott (1998), Lott and Mustard (1997), Kopel (1993), and Mauser (1991).

7 *The Decameron* was written by Boccaccio in the middle of the 14th century.

8 The conclusion of Killias (1993), however, is that the percentage of suicides using firearms is a valid proxy of gun ownership, but not the percentage of homicides using guns, even though this has formed the basis of many evaluative studies.

9 According to the WSF (see, for example, www.worldshootingfederation.org), the organisation 'will NOT [sic] be a political lobbying organization. It will however aim to reinforce the notion that sport shooting is a legitimate recreational activity responsibly practiced by millions of law-abiding participants worldwide. It will set out to establish that there is another legitimate use for firearms in the world other than just Law Enforcement and self-defence'.

10 See, for example, Lott (1997) and Kleck and Gertz (1995).

11 See Klugman (2000), Musah and Thompson (1999); and Miller (1997).

12 Canadians own an estimated one million handguns as compared against the 77 million handguns owned by residents in the United States (Musah and Thompson, 1999, p. 291). But, such figures should be treated with caution because 'no one really knows the actual number'. Personal correspondence with Michael Renner, October 2000.

13 See CBS (2000) at www.cbs.com.

14 As noted in the ICRC's seminal study *Arms Availability and the Situation of Civilians in Armed Conflict* (1999, p. 15), 'concern about the widespread availability of arms is driven by the misuse of the weapon'.

15 For a detailed discussion consult the American Academy of Paediatrics (2000), Dugan (2000), Sherman (2000), Webster and Ludwig (2000), Black and Nagin (1998), Ludwig (1998), Webster *et al* (1998), Hemenway (1997), and Webster *et al* (1997).

16 See Muggah and Berman (2001), Klugman (1999), and Collins (1998).

17 Klare (1999) has also drawn a distinction between the proliferation of major weapons systems and the diffusion of small arms and light weapons (see TRANSFERS).

18 See the Hizbollah and NRA websites at www.hizbollah.org and www.nra.org.

19 See, for example, IISS (2000), ICRC (1999), and Meddings (1999).

20 See Lock (1999a, 1999b), Cock (1997), and Cukier (1991).

21 It should be noted here that the actual perception of a threat is as important as any construction or presence of an objective threat. This is true even if misinterpreted and later proved to be without basis (see Milner, 2000).

22 See Fajnzylber *et al* (1998).

23 According to a WHO report on injury (Krug, 2000), the gross estimate of global deaths from all forms of homicide, war, and suicide in 1998 stood at 2,272,000. For homicides, the number of deaths was 736,000, from war, the number totalled 588,000, and from suicide, it amounted to 948,000.

24 According to an ICRC report (1999, p. 31) 'increased access to firearms make such impulsive acts more likely to be lethal. [I]nternational comparative studies have found a negative correlation between firearm ownership and suicides committed by other means, suggesting that other means are not used to substitute for reduced access to firearms in countries with lower rates of firearm ownership'. See also Zimring and Hawkins (1997).

25 Cornia (2000) and Stewart (1998) have theorized on different forms of inequality. 'Vertical' (e.g. among undifferentiated households) and 'horizontal' (e.g. between social, class, or communal groups) inequality have been empirically proven to cause political instability and social tensions. The UNDP (2000) has pointed to research on complex humanitarian emergencies and concluded that 'horizontal inequalities' between groups —whether communal, religious or social— are the major cause of the current wave of civil conflicts.

26 See, for example, Keen (2000), Lock (1999), and Duffield (1998).

27 See, for example, ICRC (1999), and UNHCR (1997).

28 See, for example, Kaplan (1997), or Ignatieff (1993).

29 See, for example, Cock (2000, 1997), and Cukier (2000c).

30 See, for example, Berdal and Malone (2000), and Collier (2000).

31 While suicides were more likely to be committed with a hunting rifle, homicides were more likely to be committed with a handgun (CDC, 1997).

32 On the other hand, the extremely low levels of homicide and suicide in Asia are frequently attributed to the protective value of cultural and communal homogeneity combined with the preservation of traditional Chinese values and kinship structures. Situational factors such as high levels of natural surveillance and a contained jurisdiction are also regarded as advantageous. In Hong Kong, for example, a city experiencing a homicide rate of 12 per 100,000, the presence of a large colonial-style police and strict gun laws are believed to contribute to lower levels of armed violence.

33 The notion of 'complex humanitarian emergencies' has been advanced to capture the 'total or considerable breakdown of authority resulting from internal or external conflict which requires an international response' (Stewart, 1998, p 1). Complex humanitarian emergencies have been described as profound social crises in which a large number of people die and suffer from war, disease, hunger and displacement owing to man-made or natural disaster (Klugman, 1999; Holtzman, 1999). The idea of 'public violence' also seeks to broaden the frame of reference to capture a range of insecurities including firearm-related mortality. The US Government, for example, lists 74 countries where physical insecurity and public armed violence is endemic—of which approximately 34 endure actual civil war or rebel insurgency.

34 Existing estimates are not only inconsistent with each other, but also are internally inconsistent as to whether they cover only violent deaths, those arising from conflict-induced starvation and disease, or some broader 'guesstimate' of deaths which would not have occurred in the absence of conflict (Keen *et al,* 1996).

35 The number was reported to have been higher among combatants in Afghanistan (46 per cent), Somalia (45 per cent), Bosnians in Bosnia-Herzegovina (43 per cent), and Lebanon

(41 per cent).

36 See Boutwell and Klare (2000).

37 The direct impact of small arms on civilians in Afghanistan, for example, was estimated to account for an average of 45 per cent of injuries requiring hospitalization (Meddings and Connor, 1999).

38 According to studies conducted by Coupland and Meddings (1999), the standard ratio of injuries to death experienced during conflict is in the order of 3:1 (though it can be much higher). But where the rate of death is on par with or exceeds injuries, violations of human rights or international humanitarian law almost certainly have occurred. The ratio is profoundly distorted when firearms are used against people who are immobilised, in a confined space, or unable to defend themselves. UNICEF noted that in Chechnya, between February and May of 1995, 40 per cent of all civilian casualties were children. Red Cross workers found that there was not a large proportion of injured relative to those killed and that childrens' bodies bore marks of having been systematically executed with a bullet through the temple' (Machel, 1996). During what are called 'communal conflicts'—there is evidence that the targeting of children, future generations of the enemy, is increasing (Collins, 1998).

39 The high incidence of civilian deaths could be partly attributed to the fact that the ratio of soldiers to civilians is decreasing despite population growth. For example, there were 5.7 soldiers per thousand people in 1987 but by 1997 this was down to only 3.7 per thousand (BICC, 1999).

40 For a discussion of Durkheim's theory consult Giddens (1986).

41 Indeed, it was the civil war, rather than any inherent belief in the right of individuals to carry guns, that first armed America—and then created the first crime wave to go with it. In the decade immediately following the civil war of 1861-65, murder rates soared and guns became the murder weapon of choice. Fear of crime and the fashionability of hunting spurred production and use. For other countries mentioned above consult CIEN (1999), Moser and McIlwaine (1998), UNDP (1998b), and Romano (1997).

42 This is not always the case. According to statistical records from the one of the world's largest war-hospitals (ICRC Lokichokkio Lopiding Hospital in Kenya)—approximately 98 per cent of Sudanese war-wounded are attributable to small arms. Injuries resulting from landmines, shells, and burns account for less than two per cent of the total (Muggah and Berman, 2001).

43 As defined in the *Hague Conventions* from 1907, the most recent *Geneva Conventions* and the *Hague Cultural Property Convention* dating from 1949 and 1954. This definition also draws on the *Geneva Protocols* and the *Convention on Certain Conventional Weapons* from 1977 to 1980.

44 The annual incidence of firearm injuries in the United States was reported to be 39 per 100,000 in 1997. This was roughly the same rate as demonstrated in Afghanistan during the same period (Michael *et al*, 2000, p. 415).

45 Many gun advocates argue, however, that bridges cannot always be trusted. For example, in 1979 the American public health community adopted the 'objective to reduce the number of handguns in private ownership', the initial target being a 25 per cent reduction by the year 2000. Propelled by leadership from the CDC, pro-gun lobbyists fear that the objective has broadened to the extent that it is calling for the eradication of handguns, restrictive licensing of owners of other firearms, and eventual elimination of firearms from American civil society. Excluded from the ban would be a small elite of extremely wealthy collectors, hunters, or target shooters. This is the case in many European countries (Kates *et al*, 1994).

46 See for example, Krug (2000a), ICRC (1999), Cukier (1998a), Miller and Cohen (1997), and Robinson (1997).

47 For example, the *Universal Declaration of Human Rights* (1948), the *Genocide Convention* (1948) and the first *Geneva Convention* (1949), and *Additional Protocols* (1977).

48 For example, the *Protocol on Superfluous Injury and Unnecessary Suffering* (ICRC, 1997).

49 And an additional US$ 3.6 billion (CAD 5 billion) for pain, suffering and lost 'quality of life'.

50 Another study estimates that the cost of domestic violence against women imposes a further annual cost of US$ 463 million (CAD 684 million) on the criminal justice system and US$ 136 million (CAD 187 million) on policing institutions.

51 Jefferson (2000a, p. 4) writes: 'two victims were able to afford expensive private hospitals (paying between US$ 960-1140 or ZAR 4500-R535) and four victims were admitted to government hospitals (paying between US$ 145-170 or ZAR 680-R800) ... treatment, medication and follow-up visits varied according to the degree of injury and the specific hospitals'.

52 The *United Nations Convention Against Transnational Organised Crime* defines an 'organised criminal group' as '... a structured group of three or more persons, existing for a period of time and acting in concert with the aim of committing one or more serious crimes or offences ... in order to obtain, directly or indirectly, a financial or material benefit' (UNGA, 2000, Article 2).

53 Despite years of analysis, the roots of crime are still misunderstood. Most observers attribute the rise of extreme levels of criminality to a complex interplay of social exclusion, inequality and the demobilization of millions of former combatants with few opportunities for sustainable employment or alternatives.

54 Examples include the Jan Compagnie of VOC in Holland, the British South Africa Company of Cecil Rhodes, and the British East India and Dutch East Indies Companies (see O'Brien, 2000).

55 Examples of contemporary PSCs include Group 4 (UK), Control Risk Group (UK/USA), LifeGuard Management (UK), and Kroll Associates (US/UK). These differ from Private Military Companies (see chapter on BROKERS) in that PSCs rarely engage in sophisticated military operations (see O'Brien, 2000).

56 ISS (1999, p. 256) and Irish (1999).

57 The homicide rate from Latin America and the Caribbean is one of the highest in the world—surpassed only by Sub-Saharan Africa which has an aggregate 40 homicides per 100,000 inhabitants (Murray and Lopez, 1996).

58 The costs of piracy on lost cargo is estimated to be US$ 200 million. If one adds to this the additional costs to shippers, manufacturers, retailers and insurers, the toll rises well above US$ one billion. Certain economies are more vulnerable to piracy than others—of the 285 pirate attacks in 1999, 34 were directed against Japanese-registered vessels. The International Maritime Bureau reports 78 fatalities attributed to pirates with well-organized groups using AK-47s and AK-56s (see Kenkel, 2000).

59 Indeed, studies employing multivariable regression analysis have demonstrated a positive correlation between the abundant presence and exploitation of primary commodities and armed violence (Berdal and Malone, 2000; Fajnzylber *et al* 1998).

60 See, for example, Global Witness (2000), Lock (1999a), Collier (1999), HRW (1999), and Naylor (1995).

61 According to one source, oil firms pay between six and nine per cent of their budgets for security in Colombia and Algeria respectively. Much of this money is spent on crude precautions: 'security firms staffed by ex-soldiers ... houses in crime-torn Lagos or Johannesburg come equipped with a bewildering array of defences: razor wire, panic buttons, pistol-brandishing guards' (*Economist*, 2000).

62 There were 429 homicides in London between 1997-99.

63 The IANSA website is located at www.iansa.org.

64 See, for example, Carle and Lewis (2000), Gillard (2000), Saferworld (1999), DFAIT (1999), ICRC (1999), and Oxfam (1998).

65 This perspective is captured particularly well by UN Secretary General, Kofi Annan (IANSA, 2000): 'an estimated 50 to 60 per cent of the world's trade in small arms is legal—but legally exported weapons often find their way into the illicit market. The task of effective proliferation control is made far harder than it needs to be because of irresponsible behaviour on the part of some states and lack of capacity by others, together with the shroud of secrecy that veils much of the arms trade. Member States must act to increase transparency in arms transfers if we are to make any progress. I would also urge that they support regional disarmament measures, like the moratorium on the importing, exporting or manufacturing of light weapons in West Africa'.

66 See, for example, UNDP (2000), UNHCR (1999), and ICRC (1999).

67 In Jolo, Philippines, in the spring of 2000 approximately twenty foreigners were kidnapped by Abu Sayyaf rebels. Most of the hostages were released over the next five months in exchange for over US$ 15 million in ransom provided by the Libyan government. According to Lamb (2000), 'the Abu Sayyaf has used the money to buy new equipment and weapons ... which has helped the rebels increase the size of their forces tenfold since June ... the rebels recruited more than 2000 young men ... they bought bazookas [and] mortars'.

68 See, for example, Koenraad Van Brabant's (2000) handbook entitled *Operational Security Management in Violent Environments*.

69 Personal communication with representatives of the ICRC in Geneva, October 2000.

70 A UN inter-agency standing committee (IASC) has recently established a reference group (RGSA) to identify the impact of small arms availability and use on security, program design, and operational limitations of agency activities from pre-conflict to post-conflict situations. See also Muggah and Berman (2001).

71 Personal communication with representatives of the ICRC in Geneva, October 2000.

72 The Small Arms Survey, in co-operation with Oxfam-GB, is preparing and implementing a survey on small arms and their impacts on humanitarian staff in 70 countries. The survey will be expanded in 2001 to include humanitarian and development agencies around the world.

73 The journalist Crampton (2000) reported the case of a captured child soldier who began fighting on behalf of the LTTE at the age of seven. According to the CSUCS (1999), child soldiers between the ages of seven and eight have also been recruited throughout Africa.

74 Private communication from UNICEF Burundi to ERD Geneva, April 2000.

75 See also Dasgupta, Hussain, and Shah in Banerjee, ed., (2000).

76 Countries are classified according to three categories: high human development (>0.8), medium human development (0.5-0.79), and low human development (<0.5). Although the concept of human development is much more complex than what can be captured by a composite index, it provides a useful marker from which to gauge a country's progress.

77 An artificial continuum is frequently invoked by policymakers who envision the transition from war to peace as following a smooth linear progression from 'relief' to 'rehabilitation' and 'reconstruction'. In real life, however, humanitarian and development concerns overlap and rarely follow any fixed sequence. See, for example, World Bank (1999) and the OECD/DAC (1998).

78 Overseas Development Assistance (ODA) is declining for two reasons: the movement toward market-driven development and the growing priority attached to peacekeeping and humanitarian assistance. For example, in the first 45 years of the UN's existence, the organisation spent approximately 20 per cent (US$ 3.6 billion) of its budget on peacekeeping. In the last decade, the figure has risen to almost 80 per cent—or roughly US$ 12 billion (Colletta and Kostner, 2000; Macrae and Bradbury, 1997).

79 Personal communication with representatives of OECD/DAC, November 2000.

80 Danger habituation is described as 'a usually unconscious adjustment of one's threshold of acceptable risk resulting from constant exposure to danger; the result is a reduction of one's objective assessment of risk, leading possibly to increased risk-taking behaviour' (Van Brabant, 2000, introduction). See also Bracken and Petty (1997).

6 Appendices

Appendix 6.1 Firearm ownership and deaths in industrialized countries (Figure 6.2)

Country	Firearm Availability per 100,000	Firearm Deaths per 100,000
Australia	16.00	2.74
Belgium	16.60	3.30
Canada	26.00	3.95
Denmark	16.00	0.80
Finland	50.00	6.65
France	22.60	5.40
Germany	8.90	1.44
Greece	8.00	1.80
Japan	0.30	0.07
Netherlands	1.90	0.74
New Zealand	20.00	2.02
Northern Ireland	8.40	4.70
Norway	32.00	4.20
Spain	13.10	0.70
Switzerland	27.20	6.20
UK	4.00	0.46
US	41.00	13.47

Appendix 6.2 Demographics and homicide in the US (Homicide per 100,000) (Figure 6.3)

Dates	National Rates	White Males (18-24)	Black Males (18-24)	White Females (18-24)	Black Females (18-24)
1976	9.00	11.00	89.00	4.00	25.00
1980	10.00	16.00	97.00	5.00	24.00
1984	8.00	12.00	68.00	5.00	18.00
1988	8.00	12.00	109.00	4.00	21.00
1992	9.00	17.00	171.00	4.00	21.00
1996	8.00	17.00	149.00	4.00	17.00
1998	6.00	15.00	117.00	3.00	14.00

Appendix 6.3 Firearm homicide and suicide in the North and the South (Figure 6.4)

	Homicide (%)	Suicide (%)	Total Aggregate per 100,000
Colombia	97	3	55.85
Brazil	98	2	26.22
Jamaica	98	2	18.59
Zambia	97	3	5.52
Mexico	91	9	10.79
Estonia	71	29	11.20
South Korea	66	33	0.60
Argentina	40	60	5.16
US	38	62	11.96
Japan	33	66	0.60
UK	25	75	0.44
France	17	83	6.26
Germany	17	83	1.39
Singapore	17	83	0.24
Canada	16	84	4.48
Australia	15	85	2.79
Finland	12	88	6.64
Austria	9	91	4.48
Denmark	9	91	2.48
Switzerland	9	91	6.20
Norway	7	93	4.25
Sweden	7	93	2.27
New Zealand	7	93	2.21

Appendix 6.4 Lethal impact-terminal ballistics and health effects

Terminal ballistics is the study of what happens when projectiles hit their targets. Wound ballistics is a science that assesses the interaction of projectiles with living tissue. It can relate to other disciplines such as law, the design of weapons, forensic pathology, and surgery. Coupland et al (2000) has sought to make the complex subject accessible to and understandable to health professionals. There are two major contributions made by the science of wound ballistics to the surgical management of war-wounded people.

The first is the demonstration of the transfer of kinetic energy from the projectile to the tissues along the projectile's track ('down track'); this explains the heterogeneity of war wounds. A projectile damages tissue by accelerating the tissues away from the front of the projectile representing the transfer of kinetic energy that the projectile carries. This kinetic energy is arrived at by the equation:

$$E \text{ (joules)} = mv2/2$$

(where m = mass in kg and v = velocity in m/s). The down track deposit of energy of a projectile is determined principally by the mass and velocity of the projectile and also, in the case of a bullet, by its construction and sta-

bility in flight. The location and rate with which energy is transferred determines the amount of tissue damage. If surgeons recognise the heterogeneity of wounds they can adopt management strategies for each individual wounded person. The second contribution relates to fractures; the transfer of energy from the projectile to the bone and its surrounding soft tissues has important implications for fracture management.

In the context of the Laws of War and, in particular, the Hague Declaration of 1899, the ICRC study proposes that down track deposits of energy as opposed to technical consideration of bullet construction should be the starting point for the legal debate about weapons. Certain bullets have been prohibited in warfare by international treaties, not because of their ability to cause tissue damage, but because of their ability to cause tissue damage near their entry—when the energy deposited is early in the track. Following this argument, legislation supplementing existing law should be based on the wounding potential of a weapon system and not around the construction of the bullet.

Source: Coupland et al., 2000

Appendix 6.5 A relationship between human development and homicide? (Figure 6.7)

Country	Firearm Homicide (per 100,000)	Human Development Index Ranking	Country	Firearm Homicide (per 100,000)	Human Development Index Ranking
Canada	0.60	0.94	Costa Rica	2.57	0.79
US	6.24	0.93	Trinidad & Tobago	3.42	0.79
Australia	0.36	0.93	Colombia	53.99	0.76
Germany	0.21	0.91	Brazil	25.78	0.75
Estonia	6.12	0.90	Philippines	3.60	0.74
UK	0.13	0.92	Vietnam	0.12	0.74
Sweden	0.31	0.93	South Africa	26.60	0.69
Switzerland	0.90	0.92	Rep. of Moldova	17.06	0.70
Spain	0.19	0.89	Jamaica	18.23	0.74
Norway	0.16	0.93	Peru	17.00	0.74
Croatia	2.51	0.79			

6 Bibliography

Africa Confidential. 2000. 'South Africa: Policemen Plod On.' Vol. 41, No. 20.

Ball, Nicole and Tammy Halevy. 1996. *Making Peace Work: the Role of the International Development Community*. Overseas Development Council, Policy Essay 18. Washington, DC: Johns Hopkins Press.

Banatvala, Nicholas and Anthony Zwi. 2000. 'The Public Health and Humanitarian Interventions: Developing the Evidence Base.' *British Medical Journal,* Vol. 321, pp. 101-105.

Banerjee, Dipankar, ed. *South Asia at Gun Point: Small Arms and Light Weapons Proliferation*. Colombo: Regional Centre for Strategic Studies.

Berdal, Mats and David Malone, eds. 2000. *Greed and Grievance: Economic Agendas in Civil Wars*. London: Lynne Rienner.

Le Billon, Philip. 2000. *The Political Economy of War: What Relief Agencies Need to Know*. Network Paper 33 HPN. London: ODI.

Black, Dan and Daniel Nagin. 1998. 'Do Right-to-Carry Laws Deter Violent Crime.' *Journal of Legal Studies,* Vol. 27, pp. 209-219.

Blumestein, Alfred, Frederick Rivera and Richard Rosenfeld. 2000. 'The Rise and Decline of Homicide – and Why.' *Annual Review of Public Health,* Vol. 21, pp. 505-541.

Boccaccio, Giovanni. 1921. *The Decameron*. Translated by M. Rigg. London: David Campbell.

Bonn International Center for Conversion. 1999. *Conversion Survey 1999: Global Disarmament, Demilitarisation and Demobilisation*. Baden-Baden: Nomos Verlagsgesellschaft.

Boutwell, Jeffrey, Michael Klare and Laura Reed. 1995. *Lethal Commerce: The Global Trade in Small Arms and Light Weapons*. Cambridge, MA: Committee on International Security Studies.

Boutwell, Jeffrey and Michael Klare. 1999. *Promoting an International Regime to Control Light Weapons*. Discussion Paper. Washington, DC: World Bank.

____. 2000. 'Waging a New Kind of War: A Scourge of Small Arms.' *Scientific American*. June.

von Brabant, Koenraad. 2000. *Operational Security Management in Violent Environments*. Good Practice Review 8. London: Overseas Development Institute and Humanitarian Practice Network. June.

Bracken, Patrick and Celia Petty, eds. 1998. *Rethinking the Trauma of War*. London: Free Association Books/SCF.

British American Security Information Council. 1998. *Combating Illicit Weapons Trafficking: Developments and Opportunities: Research Report*. London: British American Security Information Council.

Broadhurst, Roderick. 1999. *Homicide in Hong Kong*. Draft paper for the Conference of the Hong Kong Sociology Association. Hong Kong: University of Hong Kong.

Brunei, Sylvie and Jean-Luc Bodin. 2000. 'Humanitarianism Should Not Eclipse Humanity.' In International Committee of the Red Cross, ed. *Forum: War Money and Survival*. Geneva: International Committee of the Red Cross.

Buck, Andrew, Simon Hakim and Uriel Speigle. 1993. 'Endogenous Crime Victimization, Taxes.' *Social Science Quarterly,* Vol. 73, No. 2.

Bunvinic, Mayra, Andrew Morrison and Michael Shifter. 1999. *Violence in Latin America and the Caribbean: A Framework for Action.* Technical Study for the Inter-American Development Bank. Washington, DC: IDB.

Canada. Department for Foreign Affairs and International Trade. 1999. *Notes for an Address by Honourable Lloyd Axworthy, Minister of Foreign Affairs to the National Forum.* Montreal. 22 January.

Carle, Christophe and Patricia Lewis. 2000. *Removing Military Weapons from Civilian Hands: A Draft Discussion Paper Circulated for Comment.* Geneva: United Nations Institute for Disarmament Research.

Castellanos, Julieta. 2000. 'Honduras: Armamentismo y Violencia.' Paper presented to the Primer Foro Centroamericano Sobre la Proliferacion de Armas Livianas. Antigua, Guatemala, 26-29 June.

Center for Disease Control. 1997. 'Rates of Homicide, Suicide and Firearm Related Death Among Children: 26 Industrialized Countries.' *CDC Weekly Report,* Vol. 46, No. 5.

____. 1999. *United States: Injury Surveillance, Research and Preventative Activities.* Atlanta: National Center for Injury Prevention and Control/CDC.

Centro de Investigaciones Economicas Nacionales. 1999. 'Diagnostico de la Violencia en Guatemala.' Paper presented to a seminar on the Magnitude and Costs of Violence in Guatemala sponsored by the Program on Security and Development, Monterey.

Chaffee, Wilber. 1992. *The Economics of Violence in Latin America: A Theory of Political Competition.* New York: Praeger.

Chetty, Robert, ed. 1999. *Firearm Use and Distribution in South Africa.* Pretoria: National Crime Prevention Centre.

Child Safety Network. 1997. *Childhood Injury: Cost and Prevention Facts.* Landover, MD: Child Safety Network/Economics and Insurance Resource Centre.

Chinchilla, Laura, ed. 1999. *Seguridad Ciudadana y Justicia Penal: Perspectiva de la Sociedad Civil.* San José: UNDP.

Coalition to Stop the Use of Child Soldiers. 1999. *The Use of Children as Soldiers in Africa: A Country Analysis of Child Recruitment and Participation in Armed Conflict.* London: Coalition to Stop the Use of Child Soldiers.

Cock, Jacklyn. 1995. 'A Sociological Account of Light Weapons Proliferation in Southern Africa.' In Jasjit Singh. ed. *Light Weapons and International Security.* New Delhi: Pugwash Conferences on Science and World Affairs.

____. 1997. 'Fixing our Sites: A Sociological Perspective on Gun Violence in Contemporary South Africa.' *Society in Transition,* Vol. 1, No. 4, pp.70-81.

____. 2000. 'Weaponry and Culture of Violence in South Africa.' In Virginia Gamba, ed. *Society Under Siege: Managing Arms in South Africa.* Pretoria: Institute for Security Studies.

Colletta, Nat and Markus Kostner. 2000. 'Reforming Development Co-operation: from Reconstruction to Prevention.' In International Committee of the Red Cross, ed. *Forum: War, Money and Survival.* Geneva: ICRC

Collier, Paul. 1998. *On the Economic Consequences of War.* World Bank Working Paper. Washington, DC: World Bank.

____. 2000. 'The Economic Causes of Civil Conflict and their Implications on Policy.' In Chester Crocker, Fen Hampson and Pamela Aall, eds. *Managing Global Chaos.* Washington, DC: US Institute of Peace.

Collier, Paul, Ibrahim Eldabawi and Norman Loayza. 1998. *The Economics of Civil Wars and Crime and Violence: An Outline of Main Issues and Tentative Schedule of Activities.* Washington, DC: DECRG/World Bank.

Collins, Cindy. 1998. *Humanitarian Implications of Small Arms Proliferation.* Unpublished Paper. New York: Organization for the Coordination of Humanitarian Affairs.

Cook, Philip and Jens Ludwig. 1997. *Guns in America: National Survey on Private Ownership and Use of Firearms.* National Institute of Justice Research Brief. Washington, DC: US Department of Justice. May.

Cornia, Anrea. 2000. 'Inequality and Poverty Eradication: Toward a Post-Washington Consensus.' *UNU Nexions.* Helsinki: UNU/WIDER.

Coupland, Robin. 1993. 'Hand Grenade Injuries Among Civilians.' *Journal of the American Medical Association (JAMA),* Vol. 270, No. 5, pp. 624-625.

Coupland, Robin, Beat Kneubuehl, David Rowley and Gavin Bowyer. 2000. 'Wound Ballistics, Surgery and the Law of War.' *Trauma,* Vol. 2, pp. 1-10.

Coupland, Robin and David Meddings. 1999. 'Mortality Associated with Use of Weapons in Armed Conflict, Wartime Atrocities and Civilian Mass Shootings.' *British Medical Journal,* Vol. 319. pp, 407 - 410.

Cranna, Michael. 1994. *The True Cost of Conflict.* London: Earthscan.

Cruz, Jose Miguel, Alvaro Trigueros Arguello and Francisco Gonzales. 1999. *The Social and Economic Factors Associated with Violent Crime in El Salvador.* Report. Washington, DC: World Bank.

Cruz, Jose Miguel and Francisco Gonzales. 1997. 'Magnitud de la Violencia en El Salvador.' *Estudios Centroamericanos,* Revista 588, pp. 953-966.

Cukier, Wendy. 1991. *Ceasefire: Guns and Violence Against Women.* Ottawa: Canadian Advisory Council on the Status of Women.

___. 1998. 'International Firearms Control.' *Canadian Foreign Policy,* Vol. 6, No. 1.

___. 2000a. *Economic Effects of Small Arms Proliferation and Misuse.* Background Paper. Geneva: Small Arms Survey.

___. 2000b. *Gender and Small Arms.* Background Paper. Geneva: Small Arms Survey.

Cukier, Wendy, Antoine Chaptelaine and Cindy Collins. 2000. *Globalisation and Firearms: A Public Health Perspective.* Policy Paper. Ottawa: Canadian Centre for Foreign Policy Development.

Cummings, Peter and Thomas Koepsell. 1998. 'Does Owning a Firearm Increase or Decrease the Risk of Death?' *Journal of the American Medical Association,* Vol. 280, No. 5, pp. 471-475.

Dandurand, Yvon. 1998. *Firearms, Accidental Deaths, Suicides and Violent Crime: An Updated Review of the Literature with Special Reference to the Canadian Situation.* Ottawa: Canadian Firearms Centre/Department of Justice.

Davenad, Andreas. 2000. *Flee or Be Shot: How Small Arms Have Contributed to Unprecedented Internal Displacement in Africa.* Background Paper. Geneva: Small Arms Survey.

Deen, Thalif. 1998. 'Politics-UN: UN Personnel Killed with Impunity.' *Inter Press Service.*

van Dijk, Jan. 1997. *Criminal Victimisation and Victim Empowerment in an International Perspective.* 9th International Symposium on Victimology. Amsterdam, August 25-29.

Dorn, Walter. 2000. *Small Arms, Human Security and Development.* Draft for Development Express. Ottawa: CIDA.

Duffield, Mark. 2000. 'Globalisation, Trans-border Trade and War Economics.' In Mats Berdal and David Malone, eds. 2000. *Greed and Grievance: Economic Agendas in Civil Wars.* London: Lynne Rienner.

Dugan, Julie. 2000. *Violent Injury and Firearm Availability.* Background Paper. Geneva: Small Arms Survey.

The East African. 1997. 'Zaire: Deeper US Involvement in the Peace Process was Reflected by a Request to Assist Rebel Leader Kabila.' 15 February.

The Economist. 2000. 'Business in Difficult Places.' 20-26 May, pp. 101-103.

Fajnzylber, Pablo, Daniel Lederman and Norman Loayza. 1998. 'Que Causa el Crimen Violento?' In Roberto Steiner and Mauricio Cardenas, eds. *Crimen y Violencia.* Bogotá: Fedesarrollo.

Faltas, Sami. 2000. *Firearm Availability and Firearm Violence.* Background Paper. Geneva: Small Arms Survey.

Fisher, Ian. 2000. 'New Risks in Congo? Rebel Leader Challenges Kabila on Accord.' *International Herald Tribune.* 21 September.

Frattaroli, Shannon and Stephen Teret. 1998. 'Why Firearm Injury Surveillance?' *American Journal of Preventative Medicine,* Vol. 15, No. 3S, pp. 2-5.

Frohardt, Mark, Diane Paul and Larry Minear. 1999. *Protecting Human Rights: The Challenge to Humanitarian Organizations.* Occasional Paper 35. Providence: Brown University/IIS.

Gallagher, Tom. 1997. 'This is no Time for Western Powers to Sit on their Hands.' *The Sunday Times.* 16 March.

Gamba, Virginia, ed. 2000. *Society Under Siege: Managing Arms in South Africa.* Pretoria: Institute for Security Studies.

Gartner, Rosemary. 2000. 'Cross Cultural Aspects of Interpersonal Violence: A Review of the International Empirical Evidence.' Paper presented at the International Conference on Crime and Violence: Causes and Policy Responses sponsored by the World Bank. Washington, DC, May.

Giddens, Anthony 1986. *Durkheim on Politics and the State.* Stanford: Stanford University Press.

Gillard, Emanuela-Chiara. 2000. 'What's Legal? What's Illegal?' In Lora Lumpe, ed. *Running Guns: The Global Black Market in Small Arms*. London: Zed Books.

Gissinger, Ranveig and Nils Petter Gleditsch. 2000. *Globalisation and Conflict: Welfare, Distribution and Political Unrest*. Oslo: NTNU.

Godnick, Bill. 2000. *Small Arms in Central America*. Background Paper. Geneva: Small Arms Survey.

Gojanovic, Marija Definis, Vesna Capkun and Ankica Smoljanovic. 1996. 'Influence of War on Frequency and Patterns of Homicides and Suicides in South Croatia 1991-1993.' *Canadian Medical Journal*, Vol. 3081.

Greene, Owen. 1999. 'Tackling Illicit Arms Trafficking and Small Arms Proliferation: Developing Legal and Regulatory Controls.' Paper presented at the Conference on Microdisarmament, Security and Development. March 18-20.

Greenaway, Sean and Andrew Harris. 1998. 'Humanitarian Security: Challenges and Responses.' Paper presented to the Forging Peace Conference. Harvard University, MA, March.

Harris, Paul. 1996. 'The Economic Costs of Armed Conflict: The Iran-Iraq War and the Sri Lankan Civil War.' Paper presented to the Development Studies Association Conference sponsored by the University of Reading.

Heis, Lori. 1993. 'Violence Against Women.' *World Health Statistics Quarterly*, Vol. 56, No. 1.

Hemenway, David. 1997. 'Survey Research and Self Defence Gun Use: An Explanation of Extreme Overestimates.' *Journal of Law and Criminology*, Vol. 87, No. 4, pp. 1430-1445.

Herby, Peter. 1999. *Developing a Humanitarian Law Approach to the Problem of Arms Availability*. Geneva: ICRC.

Hiltermann, Joost and Loretta Bondi. 1999. *State Responsibility in the Arms Trade and the Protection of Human Rights*. Washington, DC: Human Rights Watch.

Holsti, Kevin. 1996. *The State, War and the State of War*. Cambridge: Cambridge University Press.

Holtzman, Steve. 1999. *Rethinking Relief and Development in Transitions from Conflict*. Brooking Institution Project on Internal Displacement, Occasional Paper. Washington, DC: Brookings Institute.

Human Rights Watch. 1994. *Arming Rwanda: The Arms Trade and Human Rights Abuses in the Rwandan War*. Vol.6, No. 1. New York: Human Rights Watch.

Ignatieff, Michael. 1993. *Blood and Belonging: Journey's Into the New Nationalism*. New York: Farrar, Straus and Giroux.

Institute for Religious Studies (ISER). 2000. *The impact of firearm injuries on public health in Brazil*. Background Paper. Geneva:Small Arms Survey.

Institute for Security Studies, Arms Management Programme. 2000a. *The Effects/Impacts of Firearm-Injury*. Background Paper. Geneva: Small Arms Survey.

____. 2000b. *The Relationship Between Crime and Firearms in South Africa*. Background Paper. Geneva: Small Arms Survey.

Instituto Universitario de Opinion Publica de la Universidad Centroamericana. 2000. 'Diagnostico sobre las Armas en El Salvador.' Paper presented to the Primer Foro Centroamericano Sobre la Proliferacion de Armas Livianas. Antigua, Guatemala, 26-29 June.

International Action Network on Small Arms. 2000. *IANSA Newsletter*, Vol. 4.

International Committee of the Red Cross. 1997. *The SIRUS Project: Toward a Determination of Which Weapons Cause 'Superfluous Injury or Unnecessary Suffering*. Geneva: ICRC.

____. 1999. *Arms Availability and the Situation of Civilians in Armed Conflict*. Geneva: ICRC.

____. 2000a. *Forum: War, Money and Survival*. Geneva: ICRC.

____. 2000b. *The People on War Report*. Geneva: ICRC.

Irish, Jenny. 1999. *Policing for Profit: The Future of South Africa's Private Security Industry*. ISS Monograph Series 39. Pretoria: Institute for Security Studies.

Kaldor, Mary. 1999. *New and Old Wars: Organised Violence in a Global Era*. Stanford: Stanford University Press.

Kaplan, Mark and Olga Geling. 1998. 'Firearm Suicides and Homicides in the United States: Regional Variations and Patterns of Gun Ownership.' *Social Science Medicine*, Vol. 46, No. 9, pp. 1227-1233.

Kaplan, Robert. 1997. *The Ends of the Earth: A*

Journey at the Dawn of the Twenty First Century.
London: Papermac.

Karp, Aaron. 2000. 'Negotiating Small Arms Restraint:
The Boldest Frontier for Disarmament?'
Disarmament Forum, Vol. 2. pp. 5-12.

Kartha, Tara. 2000. *South Asia: A Rising Spiral of
Proliferation.* Background Paper. Geneva: Small
Arms Survey.

Kates, Don, Henry Schafer, John Lattimer, George
Murray and Edwin Cassum. 1994. 'Guns and Public
Health: Epidemic of violence or Pandemic of
Propaganda.' *Tennessee Law Review*, pp. 513-596.

Keen, David, John Ryle and Mark Duffield. 1996. 'The
Fate of Information in a Disaster Zone.' *Disasters*,
Vol. 20, No. 3, pp. 169-183.

Kellermann, Arthur, Frederick Rivera, Norman
Rushforth, Joyce Banton, Donald Reay, Jerry
Francisco, Ana Locci, Janice Prodzinski, Bela
Hackman and Grant Somes. 1993. 'Gun Ownership
as a Risk Factor for Homicide in the Home.' *New
England Journal of Medicine,* Vol. 329, No. 15,
pp. 1084-1091.

Kellermann, Arthur, Frederick Rivara and Grant
Somes. 1992. 'Suicide in the Home in Relation to
Gun Ownership.' *New England Journal of
Medicine,* Vol. 327, No. 7, pp. 457-72.

Killias, Martin. 1993. 'International Correlation's
Between Gun Ownership and Rates of Homicide and
Suicide.' *Canadian Medical Association Journal,*
Vol. 148, pp. 1721-1725.

King, Jeremy. 2000. *The Albania Turmoil of 1997:
Foreshadowing the Kosovo Conflict of 1998.*
Background Paper. Geneva: Small Arms Survey.

Kingma, Kees. 1999. *Post-War Demobilisation,
Reintegration and Peace-Building.* Draft. Bonn:
Bonn International Center for Conversion.

Kleck, Gary and Mark Gertz. 1995. 'Armed Resistance
to Crime: The Prevalence and Nature of Self-
Defence with a Handgun.' *Journal of Criminal
Law and Criminology*, Vol. 86, No. 1.

Koop, Everett and George Lundberg. 1992. 'Violence
in America: A Public Health Emergency.' *JAMA,* Vol.
267, No. 22, pp. 3075-3076.

Kopel, David. 1993. 'Peril or Protection: The Risks
and Benefits of Handgun Prohibition.' *Public Law
Review*, Vol.12.

Krause, Keith. 1999. *Small Arms and Light
Weapons: The Human Security Dimension*.
Unpublished Paper. Geneva: Graduate Institute of
International Studies.

Krug, Etienne. 2000a. *A Growing Threat to Public
Health*. Background Paper. Geneva: Small Arms
Survey.

____. 2000b. *Methods for Data Collection on the
Impact of Small Arms and Health*. Background
Paper. Geneva: Small Arms Survey.

Krug, Etienne, ed. 2000c. *Injury: A Leading Cause of
the Global Burden of Disease*. Geneva: World
Health Organization.

Krug, Etienne, Linda Dahlberg and Kenneth Powell.
1996. 'Childhood Homicide, Suicide and Firearm
Deaths: An International Comparison.' *World
Health Statistics Quarterly,* Vol. 49, pp. 230-235.

Krug Etienne, Kenneth Powell and Linda Dahlberg.
1998. 'Firearm-Related Deaths in the United States
and 35 Other High and Upper-Middle-Income
Countries.' *International Journal of
Epidemiology.* Vol. 27, No.2, pp. 214-221.

Lamb, David. 2000. 'Kidnappers Lived High on
Ransom Cash.' *International Herald Tribune.* 21
September.

Laurance, Edward. 1999. *'The Role of the Business
Community in Alleviating the Problems
Associated with the Proliferation, Availability and
Misuse of Light Weapons.'* Paper prepared for the
World Bank Conference on Micro-disarmament,
Security and Development. Washington DC, March
18-20.

Leon, Carmon Rosa, Carlos Ogaldes and Oscar Lopez.
1999. 'Guatemala: Diagnostico de la Problematica
Postconflicto.' In CRIES, ed. *Violencia Social en
Centroamerica*. Managua: CRIES.

Lizotte, James Tesoriero, Terene Thornberry and
Marin Krohn. 1994. 'Patterns of Adolescent
Firearms Ownership and Use.' *Justice Quarterly*,
Vol. 11, pp. 51-73.

Lock, Peter. 1999a. 'Light Weapons and Conflict in
Africa.' *Peace and Security*, Vol. 31.

____. 1999b. *Pervasive Illicit Small Arms
Availability: A Global Threat*. HELINI Papers.
Helsinki: the European Institute for Crime
Prevention and Control.

Londono, Juan and Rodrigo Guerrero. 1998.
*Epidemiologia y Costos de la Violencia en
Colombia en Comparacion con America Latina*.
Bogota: DNP.

Loría, Max Alberto. 2000. 'Costa Rica: Diagnóstico de
Armas de Fuego'. *2000*. Paper presented to the

Primer Foro Centroamericano Sobre la Proliferacion de Armas Livianas. Antigua, Guatemala, 26-29 June.

Lott, John. 1998. *More Guns, Less Crime*. Chicago: University of Chicago Press.

Lott, John and David B. Mustard. 1997. 'Crime Deterrence and the Right to Carry a Concealed Handguns.' *Journal of Legal Studies*, Vol. 26.

Louise, Chris. 1995. *Social Impact of Light Weapons Availability and Proliferation*. Geneva: UNRISD.

Louw, Antoinette. 1998. *Looking Forward: Using Socio-economic Data to Determine Crime Trends*. NEDCORE ISS Crime Index 3. Pretoria: Institute for Security Studies.

Loyd, Anthony. 1997. 'Albanian Townsfolk Seize Army Base.' *The Sunday Times*. March 10.

Luckham, Robin, Ismael Ahmed and Robert Muggah. 1999. *Conflict and Development in Sub-Saharan Africa*. Background Paper for the World Bank Poverty Status Report: Africa. Brighton: IDS.

Ludwig, Jens. 1998. 'Concealed Gun-Carrying Laws and Violent Crime: Evidence from State Panel Data.' *International Review of Law and Economy*, Vol. 18, pp. 239-254.

Machel, Graca. 1996. *United Nations Study on the Impact of Armed Conflict on Children*. A/51/306. New York: United Nations.

____. 2000. *The Impact of Armed Conflict on Children: A Critical Review of the Progress Made and Obstacles Encountered in Increasing Protection for War-Affected Children*. Winnipeg: International Conference on War-Affected Children.

Macrae, Joanna and Mark Bradbury. 1997. *Tackling Transition: A Critical Analysis of Relief-Development Linkages in Situations of Chronic Instability*. London: Overseas Development Institute/UNICEF/Humanitarian and War Project, Brown University.

Malone, Jim. 'Albania Falls to Mob Rule.' *The Sunday Times*. March 16.

Mauser, Gary. 1996. 'Are Firearms a Threat to Public Health? The Misuse of Science in Medical Research.' Presented to the Canadian Law Society Association. Brock University, June 1-4.

Meddings, David. 1997. 'Weapons Injuries During and After Periods of Conflict: A Retrospective Analysis.' *BMJ*, Vol. 315, pp. 1417-1420.

____. 1998. 'Health Effects of Weapons: Issues and ICRC Experience.' Presented at the Conference The

Human Costs of Unrestrained Arms Transfers and the Response to Date sponsored by NISAT. Oslo, May.

____. 2000a. *Factors Affecting Availability and Use*. Background Paper. Geneva: Small Arms Survey.

____. 2000b. *Human Security: A Prerequisite for Health*. Draft Paper. Geneva: ICRC.

Meddings, David and Stephanie O'Conner. 1999. 'Circumstances Around Weapon Injury in Cambodia After Departure of a Peacekeeping Force: Prospective Cohort Study.' *BMJ*. Vol. 319, pp. 412-415.

Melvern, Linda. 2000. *A People Betrayed: the Role of the West in the Rwanda Genocide*. London: Zed Books.

Mercy, James, Robin Ikeda, and Kenneth Powell. 1998. 'Firearm Related Injury Surveillance: An Overview of Progress and the Challenges Ahead.' *American Journal of Preventative Medicine*. Vol. 15, No. 3S, pp. 6-16.

Michael, Markus, David Meddings, Salah Ramez and Juan Luis Gutiérrez-Fisac. 1999. 'Incidence of Weapon Injuries to Inter-factional Combat in Afghanistan in 1996: Prospective Cohort Study.' *BMJ*, Vol. 319, pp. 415-417.

Miller, Mark and David Hemenway. 1999. 'The Relationship Between Firearms and Suicide: A Review of the Literature.' *Aggression and Violent Behaviour*, Vol. 4, No. 1, pp. 59-75.

Miller, Ted. 1995. 'Incidence and Costs of Gunshot Wounds in Canada.' *Canadian Medical Journal*, Vol. 159, No. 9, pp. 1261-1268.

Miller, Ted and Mark Cohen. 1997. 'Costs of Gunshot and Cut/Stab Wounds in US with Some Canadian Comparisons.' *Accident Analysis and Prevention*, Vol. 29, No. 3, pp. 329-341.

Milner, James. 2000. *Sharing the Security Burden: Toward the Convergence of Refugee Protection and State Security*. RCS Working Paper 4. Oxford: QEH/RSC.

Morales, Ninette. 1999. 'Repuestas Locales Frente a los Procesos de Desplazamiento de Poblacion Nicaraguense a Costa Rica.' *Dialogo Centroamericano,* Vol. 40.

Morrison, Andrew and Loreto Biehl. 1999. *Too Close to Home: Domestic Violence in the Americas*. Washington, DC: Inter-American Development Bank/Johns Hopkins University.

Moser, Caroline. 1999. *Guatemala: Paz Urbana*. Washington, DC: World Bank /CIEN/SEPREDI/AVANSCO/FUNDESCO/AMVA.

Muggah, Robert and Eric Berman. 2001. *The Humanitarian Impacts of Small Arms*. A Report for the IASC/RGSA. New York: UNICEF/UNDP/UNHCR/OCHA.

De Mulinen, Frederic. 1987. *Handbook of the Law of War for Armed Forces*. Geneva: ICRC.

Murray, Christopher and Alan Lopez, eds. 1996. *The Global Burden of Disease: A Comprehensive Assessment of Mortality and Disability from Disease, Injuries and Risk Factors in the 1990s with Projections to 2020*. Boston, MA: Harvard University Press.

Musah, Abdel-Fatau and Niobe Thompson, eds. 1999. *Over a Barrel: Light Weapons and Human Rights in the Commonwealth*. London: Commonwealth Human Rights Initiative.

Naraghi-Anderlini, Sanam, Rita Manchanda and Shereen Karmali. 1999. *Women, Violent Conflict and Peace-building: Global Perspectives*. London: International Alert.

Naylor, Tom. 1995. 'The Structure and Operation of the Modern Arms Black Market.' In Jeffrey Boutwell, Michael Klare and Laura Reed. 1995. *Lethal Commerce: The Global Trade in Small Arms and Light Weapons*. Cambridge MA: Committee on International Security Studies.

Novello, Antonia, John Shosky and Robert Froehlke. 1992. 'From Surgeon General, US Public Health Service: a Medical Response to Violence.' *JAMA*. Vol. 267, No. 22.

O'Brien, Kevin. 2000. *A History of Private Security*. Background Paper. Geneva: Small Arms Survey.

Office of Naval Intelligence. 1999. *Threats and Challenges to Maritime Security 2020*. Washington, DC: Office of Naval Intelligence.

Open Society Institute. 1999. *Gun Control in the United States*. New York: OSI.

Organization for Economic Co-operation and Development/Development Assistance Committee. 1998. *Conflict, Peace and Development Co-operation on the Threshold of the 21st Century*. Paris: OECD.

Oxfam. 1998. *Small Arms, Wrong Hands: A Case for Government Control of Small Arms Trade*. London: Oxfam.

Pan-American Health Organization. 1997. *Health Situation Analysis Program*. New York: Pan-American Health Organization.

Paediatrics. 2000. 'Firearm-related Injuries Affecting the Paediatric Population.' Vol. 105, No. 4.

Phebo, Luciana, Rubem Fernandes and Marcelo Nascimento. 2000. *The Impact of Firearm Injuries on Public Health in Brazil*. Background Paper. Geneva: Small Arms Survey.

Planck, Nina. 1998. 'Proliferation Dealers in Death.' *Time*. 2 November.

Ramsbotham, David. 1995. 'The Changing Nature of Intervention: the Role of UN Peacekeeping.' *Conflict Studies*, No. 282, pp. 28.

Reno, William. 1998. 'Humanitarian Emergencies and Warlord Economies in Liberia and Sierra Leone.' Paper presented at conference sponsored by UNU/WIDER/Queen Elizabeth House. Stockholm, 15-16 June.

Reference Group on Small Arms. 2000. *Reference Group on Small Arms: Thematic Guidance Working Paper*. Geneva: RGSA.

Romano, Luis. 1997. 'Los Costos de la Violencia en El Salvador.' *Estudios Centroamericanos,* Revista 588, pp. 967-977.

Saferworld. 1999. *Light Weapons Controls and Security Assistance: A Review of Current Practice*. London: Saferworld.

Schonteich, Martin. 1999. *Sentencing in South Africa: Public Perceptions and the Judicial Process*. ISS Paper 43. Pretoria: Institute for Security Studies.

Sherman, Lawrence. 2000. 'Gun Carrying and Homicide Prevention.' *JAMA*, Vol. 283, No. 9, pp. 1193-1195.

Sidel, Victor. 1995. 'Towards a Better World: The International Arms Trade and its Impact on Health.' *BMJ*, Vol. 311, pp. 1677-1680.

Singh, Jasjit, ed. 1995. *Light Weapons and International Security*. New Delhi: Pugwash Conferences on Science and World Affairs.

Sivard, Ruth. 1996. *World Military and Social Expenditures.* New York: Institute for World Order.

Sloan, John. 1988. 'Handgun Regulations, Crime, Assaults, and Homicide: A Tale of Two Cities.' *New England Journal of Medicine*, Vol. 319, pp. 1256-1262.

Smith, Chris. 2000. 'Small Arms Trafficking May Export Albania's Anarchy.' *Jane's Intelligence Review.* January, pp. 24-28.

Smith, Dan. 1997. *The State of War and Peace: Atlas 3rd Edition*. London: Penguin Books.

Stewart, Frances. 1993. 'War and Underdevelopment:

Can Economic Analysis Help Reduce the Costs.' *Journal of International Development*, Vol. 5. No. 4, pp. 357-380.

Stockholm International Peace Research Institute. 1999. *SIPRI Yearbook: Armaments, Disarmament and International Security*. New York: Oxford University Press.

____. 2000. *SIPRI Yearbook: Armaments, Disarmament and International Security*. New York: Oxford University Press.

Swift, Jeremy, ed. 1996. 'War and Rural Development in Africa.' *IDS Bulletin*, Vol. 27, No. 3.

Teret, Stephen, Garon Wintemute and Peter Beilenson. 1992. 'The Firearm Fatality Reporting System.' *JAMA*, Vol. 267, No. 22, pp. 3073-3074.

Thompson, Niobe and Devashish Krihnan. 1999. 'Small Arms in India and the Human Costs of Lingering Conflict.' In Abdel-Fatau Musah and Niobe Thompson. 1999. *Over a Barrel: Light Weapons and Human Rights in the Commonwealth*. London: Commonwealth Human Rights Initiative.

Thompson, Tony. 2000. 'One in Three Young Criminals is Armed.' *Observer*. 3 September.

Toth, M. 1997. OSCE Mission Liaison, Conflict Prevention Centre, Vienna, Austria, electronic mail correspondence.

Travassos, Cláudia and Maria Lebrào. 1998. *Morbidade Hospitalar nos Jovens: Jovens Acontecendo na Trilkha das Politicas Publicas*. Rio de Janeiro: Comissào Nacional de Populacào e Desnvolvimento.

United Nations. 1997. *Report on the Conference of Disarmament to the United Nations*. CD/1476. 9 Sept.

____. 1998a. *The Causes of Conflict and the Promotion of Durable Peace and Sustainable Development in Africa: Report of the Secretary General*. S/1998/318. 13 April.

____. 1998b. *United Nations International Study on Firearm Regulation*. New York: United Nations.

____. 1999a. *Relationship Between Disarmament and Development: Report of the Secretary-General*. GA/54/150.

____. 1999b. *UN Security Council Press Release*. SG/SM/7145, SC/6733.

____. 1999c. *Report of the Panel of Governmental Experts on Small Arms*. A/52/298. 27 August.

____. 2000. *Meeting the Challenge: The Role of the UNDP in Crisis, Post-Conflict and Recovery Situations, 2000-2003*. DP/2000/18. 20 March.

United Nations Department for Disarmament Affairs. 2000. *Summary of the UNDDA Conference on Illicit Trafficking in ASEAN*. Jakarta: UNDDA/Small Arms Survey.

United Nations Development Program. 1994. *Human Development Report*. New York: UNDP/Oxford University Press.

____. 1998. *Violencia e Inseguridad Ciuadana*. Guatemala: PNUD.

____. 1999a. *Development, Peace and Security*. <http://www.undp.org/erd/archives/dps.htm.

____. 1999b. *Human Development Report*. New York: UNDP/Oxford University Press.

____. 2000 *Human Development Report*. New York: UNDP/Oxford University Press.

United Nations General Assembly. 2000. *Draft United Nations Convention Against Transnational Organised Crime*. Vienna: UNGA.

United Nations High Commissioner for Refugees. 1997. *The State of the Worlds Refugees: A Humanitarian Agenda*. Oxford: Oxford University Press.

____. 2000. *The State of the Worlds Refugees: The Last Fifty Years*. Oxford: Oxford University Press.

United Nations Interregional Crime and Justice Research Institute. 1997. *International Crime Victim Survey*. Rome/Turin: UNICRI.

United Nations Office for Drug Control and Crime Prevention. 2000. *Global Studies on Organised Crime: Transnational Organised Crime: Dangerousness and Trends*. Vienna: UNCICP.

United Nations Statistical Division. 1970. *Demographic Yearbook*. New York: UNSTAT.

____. 1980. *Demographic Yearbook*. New York: UNSTAT.

____. 1990. *Demographic Yearbook*. New York: UNSTAT.

____. 1998. *Demographic Yearbook*. New York: UNSTAT.

United States. United States Department of Justice. Bureau of Justice Statistics. 2000a. *Serious Violence Crime Levels Continued to Decline in 1998*. <http://www.ojp.usdoj.gov/bjs/glance.htm>

____. 2000b. *Direct Expenditure for Each of the Major Criminal Justice Functions*. <http://www.ojp.usdoj.gov/bjs/glance/exptyp.htm>

____. 2000c. *Homicide Trends in the U.S.*

<http://www.ojp.usdoj.gov/bjs/homicide/totals.txt>

United States Committee for Refugees. 2000. *World Refugee Survey*. Washington, DC: Immigration and Refugee Services of America.

Valdez, A. 1999. 'Es Como Una Pelicula se Repite.' *La Prensa Grafica*.

Villaveces, Andrés, Peter Cummings, Victoria Espitia, Thomas Koespell, Barbara McKnight and Arthur Kellermann. 2000. 'Effect of a Ban on Carrying Firearms on Homicide Rates in 2 Colombian Cities.' *JAMA*, Vol. 283, No. 1, pp. 1205-1209.

Wallensteen, Peter and Margareta Sollenberg. 'Armed Conflicts and Regional Conflict Complexes, 1989-97.' *Journal of Peace Research*, Vol. 35, No. 5, pp. 621-634.

Webster, Daniel and Jens Ludwig. 2000. *Myths About Defence Gun Use and Permissive Gun Carrying Laws*. Berkeley, CA: Berkeley Media Studies Group.

Webster, Daniel, Jon Vernick and Jens Ludwig. 1998. 'Webster and Colleagues Respond: No Proof that Shall-issue Laws Reduce Violence.' *American Journal of Public Health*, Vol. 886, pp. 982-983.

Webster, Daniel, Jon Vernick, Jens Ludwig and Kathleen Lester. 1997. 'Flawed Gun Policy Research Could Endanger Public Safety.' *American Journal of Public Health*, Vol. 87, No. 6, pp. 918-921.

Weissert, Will. 2000. 'Guatemalans Fear Crime Wave.' *New York Times*. 17 June.

Wilkinson, Tracy. 2000. 'Palestinians Gun Culture Poses Political, Social Perils: Proliferation of Weapons Frustrates Efforts at Law and Order and Leaves Civilians Living in Fear.' *Los Angeles Times*.

18 August.

Wintemute, Garen, Carrie Parham, James Beaumont, Mona Wright and Christiana Drake. 1999. 'Mortality Among Recent Purchasers of Handguns.' *New England Journal of Medicine*, Vol. 341, No. 21, pp. 1583-1589.

Working Group for Weapons Reduction. 1998. *WGWR Newsletter*. July.

World Almanac. 1998. *Military and Veteran Affairs*. New York: St. Martin's Press.

World Bank. 1997a. *From Civil War to Civil Peace*. Washington, DC: World Bank/Carter Center.

____. 1997b. *Crime and Violence as a Development Issue in Latin America*. Washington, DC: World Bank.

____. 1998. *Post-Conflict Reconstruction: The Role of the World Bank*. Washington, DC: World Bank.

____. 1999. *Security, Poverty Reduction and Sustainable Development: Challenges for the New Millennium*. Washington, DC: World Bank.

World Health Assembly. 1996. *Prevention of Violence: Public Health Priority*. Resolution WHA 49.25. Geneva: World Health Organization.

World Health Organization. 2000. *Information Kit on Violence and Health*. <http://www.who.int/eha/pvi/index.html>

World Vision. 1996. *The Effects of Armed Conflict on Girls*. World Vision Staff Working Paper 23. Geneva: World Vision.

Zimring, Franklin and Gordon Hawkins. 1997. *Crime is not the Problem: Lethal Violence in America*. Oxford: Oxford University Press.

7

Tackling the Small Arms Problem:
Multilateral Measures and Initiatives

Introduction

Given the magnitude of the small arms problem, what—if any—counteracting measures and initiatives are being undertaken? This chapter reviews recent multilateral action tackling the proliferation and misuse of small arms and light weapons. It uses a largely descriptive approach, since the current lack of effective implementation in this area precludes any real analysis of best practice. Nevertheless, broader themes relating to the scope and effectiveness of action taken are raised throughout the chapter.

Box 7.1   UN definitions—a reminder

Small arms: Revolvers and self-loading pistols, rifles and carbines, assault rifles, and sub-machine and light machine-guns.

Light weapons: Heavy machine-guns, hand-held and mounted grenade launchers, portable anti-tank and anti-aircraft guns, recoilless rifles, portable launchers of anti-tank and anti-aircraft missile systems, and mortars of less than 100mm calibre.

UN Secretary General, 1997

The chapter is divided into two broad sections, focusing first on multilateral activity at the regional and sub-regional levels, then on progress made at the global level. As indicated throughout the chapter, the links between the three levels have been strong, with progress at one level spurring progress at another.

By no means comprehensive in its coverage, this chapter of the *Survey* does attempt to reflect the most significant recent developments in the field. No regional bias is intended; however, Asia's relative inactivity on the small arms question precludes the same level of treatment accorded to the other regions. Certain sub-regions, such as South Asia and the Middle East, go unmentioned for the same reason. However, the serious proliferation problems that affect them are described elsewhere (PRODUCERS, BROKERS, ILLICIT TRANSFERS, EFFECTS).

The emergence of the small arms issue

Section author: Ed Laurance, Monterey Institute of International Studies

It is only very recently that small arms have emerged onto the international agenda as an issue in their own right. Although there was virtually no momentum around the problem at the beginning of the 1990s, a short decade later, a host of actors are becoming involved—the United Nations, national governments, regional organizations, NGOs, research institutes, and civil society. Efforts to contend with the proliferation and misuse of small arms and light weapons have been accelerating since 1997. How did this policy issue emerge and grow?

The small arms issue initially arose in the wake of the Cold War. While such weapons were plentiful during that period—produced and exported by various governments and transferred to the superpowers' armed clients—they were controlled, more or less effectively, by both sides. However, as the bi-polar political system disintegrated, so did control of these arms.

On the *supply* side, this decline in control led to an unprecedented availability, flooding the global market place with massive amounts of small arms. As the industrial powers trimmed their defence forces, surplus weapons found their way to arms dealers and zones of conflict. In addition, in the early 1990s, several major wars ended in Africa, Central America, and other regions; yet incomplete arms collection left hundreds of thousands of lethal military weapons in circulation in these areas. Instability in newly independent or emerging states also resulted in many arms being 'lost' or stolen from police and military forces.

At the same time, the nature of the *demand* for arms shifted significantly in the 1990s. The Gulf War alerted the international community to the dangers of arms build-ups. The UN's establishment of a *Register of Conventional Arms,* in January 1992, was but one indicator that it viewed major conventional weapons differently than in the past. At the same time, there were few budding *inter-state* conflicts to sustain demand for major weapons systems. Declining defence budgets and the Asian financial crisis of the late 1990s further reduced demand for this class of weapon.

However, the 1990s also saw a sudden upsurge of new *intra-state* conflicts. Such wars are characterized by the use of irregular forces with little or no training, no need for supply lines, and minimal logistics and maintenance support. These new localized conflicts created a demand for exactly the types of weapon that had become readily available—assault rifles, grenades, rocket launchers, mortars, and other weapons designed for use by a single soldier or a small crew.

With the acceleration of globalization during the 1990s, especially its increasing volumes of cross-border trade, it was not long before small arms suppliers and users connected. NGOs, the academic community, and the UN began to produce empirical evidence of a link between increased proliferation and such negative effects as increased violence and loss of life—especially affecting non-combatants—and the serious impairment of much-needed economic development. Thus, the stage was set for a series of efforts conducted at the sub-regional, regional, and global levels to address the problem of small arms proliferation and misuse.

Regional and sub-regional measures

Certain regions have been at the forefront of efforts to combat small arms proliferation and mis-use. This section begins with a discussion of the precedent-setting Organization of American States' (OAS) firearms instruments and other small arms initiatives in the Americas. The focus then shifts, in turn, to significant multilateral activity in Africa, the Asia-Pacific region, Western Europe, and the Euro-Atlantic region. As explained earlier, the following review of regional and sub-regional activity is not intended to be comprehensive in scope. The aim, rather, is to high-light the most significant initiatives at this level. Important links to global measures are also noted throughout the text.

The OAS firearms instruments
Section prepared with information and analysis supplied by: UN-LiREC; Geraldine O'Callaghan, BASIC; and Camilla Waszink, SAND and BICC

Since the mid-1990s, the Americas have played a pioneering role in the fight against small arms proliferation. Growing concern with international drug trafficking and organized crime, coupled with a recognition of their links to illegal arms trafficking, led the member states of the OAS—under the leadership of Mexico, Colombia, and the United States—to negotiate two instruments designed to combat the illicit trade in firearms, ammunition, and explosives. Adopted by the OAS over the 1997-98 period, these represented the first steps taken at the regional level to curb the illicit arms trade and improve controls over the movement of firearms generally. The two

> *With the acceleration of globalization during the 1990s, it was not long before small arms suppliers and users connected.*

> *The Americas have played a pioneering role in the fight against small arms proliferation.*

instruments have, in fact, influenced other small arms processes at both regional and global levels.[1]

The Inter-American Convention: The *Inter-American Convention against the Illicit Manufacturing of and Trafficking in Firearms, Ammunition, Explosives, and Other Related Materials* (OAS, 1997) was adopted in Washington, DC on 14 November 1997 and entered into force on 1 July 1998 after having been ratified by two OAS states. The Convention sets out various operational and legal measures designed 'to prevent, combat, and eradicate the illicit manufacturing of and trafficking in firearms, ammunition, explosives, and other related materials' (OAS, 1997, art. II). Its broad definition of 'firearms', in article I (3)—which includes rockets, missiles, and their delivery systems—ensures coverage of a wide range of small arms and light weapons.

The *Convention's* operational measures aim at improving the monitoring and control of the manufacture and trans-border movement of firearms, ammunition, explosives, and other related materials. Significant provisions include the marking of all firearms at the time of manufacture and import (art. VI), record-keeping (art. XI), the establishment or maintenance of effective export, import and international transit license systems (art. IX), and the strengthening of controls at export points (art. X). The *Convention* also mandates the strengthening of certain legal norms, specifically obliging States Parties to criminalize illicit arms manufacturing and trafficking (art. IV), and provides for mutual legal assistance (art. XVII) and extradition rights (art. XIX).

In tandem with these efforts, the *Convention* seeks 'to promote and facilitate cooperation and exchange of information and experience among States Parties' in respect of illicit arms manufacturing and trafficking (art. II). Relevant provisions cover the exchange of information, including tracing information (art. XIII), and the exchange of experience and training in identification and tracing of weapons, intelligence gathering, and related activities (art. XV). The aim is to enhance the capacity of law enforcement authorities to combat the illicit firearms trade.

The Model Regulations: The *Model Regulations for the Control of the International Movement of Firearms, Their Parts and Components, and Ammunition* (OAS, 1998) were developed parallel to the *Inter-American Convention* by the OAS Inter-American Drug Abuse Control Commission (CICAD) on the basis of a 1992 OAS General Assembly mandate (AG/RES. 1197 (XXII-O/92)). The draft regulations were completed in September 1997, approved by CICAD in Lima, Peru, in November 1997, and adopted by the OAS General Assembly in June 1998 (AG/RES. 1543 (XXVIII-O/98)).

Map 7.1   OAS Member States

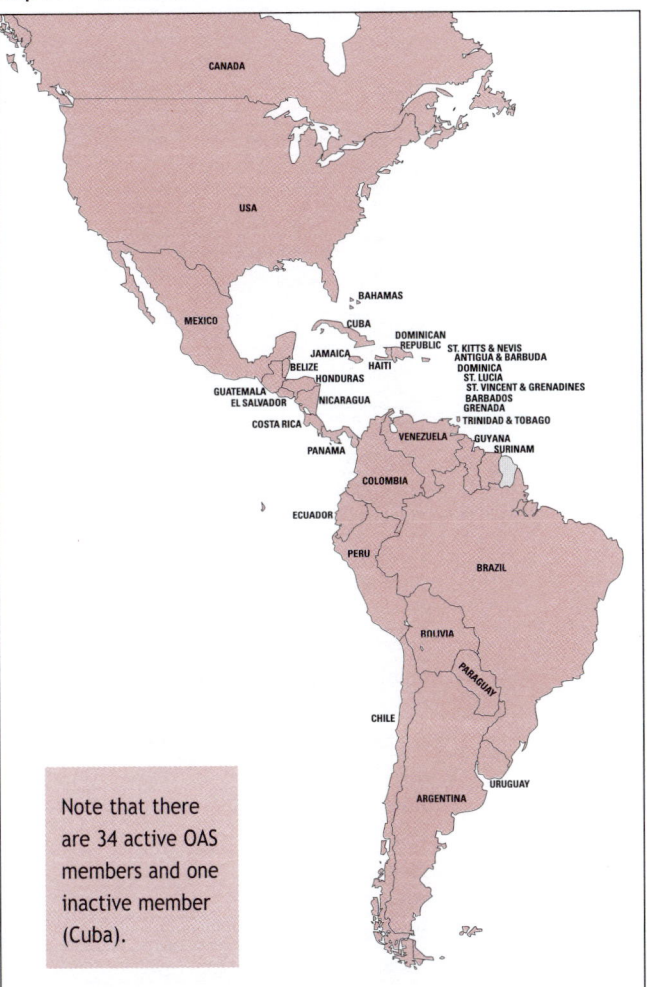

Note that there are 34 active OAS members and one inactive member (Cuba).

The Inter-American Convention aims to 'prevent, combat, and eradicate the illicit manufacturing of and trafficking in firearms, ammunition, explosives, and other related materials'.

Table 7.1   Implementation of the OAS firearms instruments in Latin America and the Caribbean

State	Inter-American Convention Ratification	Model Regulations Adoption	Responsibility for Import and Export Permits
Antigua and Barbuda	no	–	–
Argentina	no	yes	–
Bahamas	yes	under way	–
Barbados	no	under way	Commissioner of Police
Belize	yes	yes	Commissioner of Police
Bolivia	yes	under way	Ministry of Defence
Brazil	yes	–	–
Canada	no	yes	Department of Foreign Affairs and International Trade
Chile	no	–	Ministry of Defence
Colombia	no	partially	Ministry of Defence
Costa Rica	no	under way	Ministry of Public Security
Cuba	–	–	–
Dominica	no	–	–
Dominican Republic	no	under way	Ministry of the Interior/ Police
Ecuador	yes	–	Ministry of Defence
El Salvador	yes	yes	–
Grenada	no	under way	–
Guatemala	no	–	–
Guyana	no	under way	Commissioner of Police
Haiti	no	under way	Commissioner of Police
Honduras	no	–	–
Jamaica	no	under way	–
Mexico	yes	–	Armed Forces
Nicaragua	yes	under way	The National Police
Panama	yes	yes	–
Paraguay	no	under way	Ministry of Defence
Peru	yes	partially	–
Saint Lucia	no	partially	Commissioner of Police
Saint Vincent and the Grenadines	no	–	Commissioner of Police
St. Kitts and Nevis	no	–	Commissioner of Police
Suriname	no	–	–
Trinidad and Tobago	no	partially	Commissioner of Police
United States of America	no	yes	Departments of State, Commerce, and Treasury
Uruguay	no	–	Ministry of Defence
Venezuela	no	–	–
Total Ratifications	**10**		

Source: UN-LiREC, September 2000

The *Model Regulations* consist of a series of harmonized measures and procedures for monitoring and controlling the international movement of firearms, their parts and components, and ammunition[2] among OAS states. Through the adoption of common, high standards in this area, the instrument seeks to prevent the diversion of these weapons to illegal markets and activities (OAS, 1998, section 1.2). The *Model Regulations* set out export, import, and in-transit procedures and documentation for firearms, their parts and components (chapters I and III), and ammunition (chapters II and III). Other responsibilities of member states include record-keeping, information exchange, training and technical assistance, and the notification of shipment irregularities (chapter IV).

The scope of the *Model Regulations* is, however, limited to 'all classes of commercially-traded firearms, their parts and components and commercially traded ammunition.' Expressly excluded are 'state-to-state transactions or transfers for purposes of national security.' (section 1.2)

The *Model Regulations'* goal of strengthening the monitoring and control of the international movement of firearms and ammunition to prevent the diversion of these weapons to the illicit market complements the *Inter-American Convention's* efforts along such lines, including the latter's provisions on marking and record-keeping (OAS, 1997, arts. VI and XI), as well as those for enhanced export, import, and in-transit controls (arts. VIII–X).

Implementing the Inter-American Convention: As a formal legal instrument, the *Inter-American Convention* binds only those OAS member states that have ratified it. The instrument entered into force on 1 July 1998, after the second ratification; yet it is still in its infancy. As of October 2000, ten states—just under one-third of the total, active membership of 34 states—had ratified the Convention.[3] Table 7.1 provides an overview of implementation of the two firearms instruments by OAS states.

The first regular meeting of the Convention's Consultative Committee, consisting of representatives of the States Parties, was held in Washington, DC on 9–10 March 2000. The recommendations of the Committee serve to promote and facilitate implementation of the Convention through the exchange of information, knowledge and experience, the encouragement of co-operation, and the promotion of training, technical assistance, and other measures (OAS, 1997, arts. XX and XXI). The Consultative Committee is assisted in its work by the General Secretariat of the OAS.

Outside the formal treaty framework, it appears that the *Inter-American Convention* has spurred bilateral and sub-regional co-operation among OAS states in such areas as weapons tracing and identification. Following the Convention's adoption, the US stepped up co-operation with, and provided training to, police and customs administrations in several Latin American countries. However, as will be discussed in the next section on the implementation of the OAS firearms instruments in Central America, many of the hemisphere's poorer countries currently lack the resources needed to effectively implement the Convention.

Implementing the Model Regulations: In contrast to the *Inter-American Convention*, the *Model Regulations* are not legally binding and, therefore, do not require ratification by OAS states. Information obtained from the UN Regional Centre for Peace, Disarmament and Development in Latin America and the Caribbean (UN-LiREC) indicates that, as of September 2000, six of 34 active OAS member states[4] had adopted the *Model Regulations*,[5] while another eleven were preparing to do so. Four other active member states had partially adopted them. Criteria used to determine implementation include changes to, or adoption of, new national legislation and regulations, and practical co-operation and exchange of information between member states. Information was not available for the 13 other active members.

Several initiatives are now underway to facilitate adoption and implementation of the *Model Regulations* in line with the recommendations of the Group of Experts that drafted them.[6] CICAD and UN-LiREC have hosted two workshops designed to brief government officials on the practical

The scope of the Model Regulations is limited—expressly excluding 'state-to-state transactions or transfers for purposes of national security.'

The Inter-American Convention is still in its infancy.

implementation of the *Model Regulations* and provide a forum for information-sharing on national policies, practices, and inter-agency co-ordination. The first workshop was held in Lima, Peru, in November 1999, for the countries of South America and Mexico, while the second was organized in co-operation with the Inter-Ministerial Anti-Drug Training Centre of France (CIFAD), in Martinique, French West Indies, in May 2000, for Central American and Caribbean states.

As of September 2000, six of 34 active OAS member states had adopted the Model Regulations, while another eleven were preparing to do so.

A training manual to assist law enforcement officials in the implementation of the *Model Regulations* is being prepared by CICAD and UN-LiREC for dissemination to member states by the end of the year 2000. In addition, a Memorandum of Understanding (MoU) on future co-operation between the two institutions was prepared for signature during the UN Millennium Assembly. It provides, *inter alia*, for the joint development of initiatives supporting national efforts to enhance administrative effectiveness in dealing with firearms. Both CICAD and UN-LiREC have initiated discussions with Interpol Americas to sign similar MoUs with a view to tripartite collaboration in training government officials in the region.

Central America: A proving ground for the OAS firearms instruments
Section author: Camilla Waszink, SAND and BICC

The eventual success or failure of the OAS firearms instruments will be decided, in large measure, in those parts of the Americas especially hard hit by the small arms problem—for example, Central America.

Especially hard hit by the small arms problem, Central America will be a proving ground for the OAS firearms instruments.

The current proliferation of small arms and light weapons in the sub-region has several causes. Many of these weapons remained in circulation after the Cold War and the sub-region's several civil wars ended at the start of the 1990s. In addition, Central America's geographic position—wedged between the largest drug-producing countries in South America and the primary markets in North America—has made it a principal transit point for illicit arms and drug traffickers. Much illicit arms trafficking in the sub-region is also driven by the armed conflicts in Colombia and certain parts of Mexico. Combined with economic weakness and persistent inequality, the resulting abundance of weapons has generated high levels of violence and citizen insecurity throughout the sub-region (BROKERS, ILLICIT TRANSFERS, EFFECTS).

All the countries of Central America have signed the *Inter-American Convention*, while Belize, El Salvador, Nicaragua, and Panama have ratified it. El Salvador's ratification, on 18 March 1999, influenced the passage of national legislation on firearms and money laundering. Four months in advance of Panama's September 1999 ratification of the *Convention*, its legislature approved a 30-article bill setting out comprehensive measures to control illicit trafficking of arms and explosives. Legal and political obstacles, as well as a lack of resources, have, however, prevented some Central American countries from ratifying the *Convention*. For example, in Guatemala, constitutional changes are considered a prerequisite.

It is feared that insufficient resources will also limit the implementation of the *Convention* in the sub-region. Many of the practical measures it mandates, such as marking, record-keeping, and strengthened export controls, require substantial human and financial resources. Yet, Central America is burdened by endemic poverty, underdevelopment, and external debt. The assistance of the OAS, its Member States, and other actors will be needed if the *Convention* is to be effectively implemented in the sub-region, though obviously nothing can be done unless the countries of Central America themselves set *Convention* implementation as a priority.

Some analysts' critiques of the *Convention* appear especially relevant in the Central American context.[7] For example, although it requires States Parties to confiscate illicit arms and ensure that they 'do not fall into the hands of private individuals or businesses', it does not mandate their destruction (OAS, 1997, art. VII). In Central America, many weapons enter the illegal market as a result of theft from insecure government arsenals or sale by corrupt government officials.

Further, while the *Inter-American Convention* is based on the realization that the security threats facing the region are interrelated and must be addressed multilaterally, the law enforcement approach it applies to the problem of illicit trafficking ignores the important relationship between illicit arms and armed conflict. As described earlier, this relationship accounts for much of the small arms proliferation in Central America. Thus, while the *Convention* could potentially constitute part of the solution to the sub-region's small arms problem, it is far from sufficient. Other measures which would complement the OAS instruments are, however, being developed and, in some cases, implemented.[8]

Although the political, legal, and resource constraints hindering implementation of the *Model Regulations* in Central America are similar to those for the *Inter-American Convention*, it has been suggested that the former might be easier and less costly to implement. This, coupled with their practical, specific nature, might ultimately make the *Model Regulations* the more effective of the two OAS instruments (Meek 1998, pp. 53-54). It is, however, too early to judge whether this is the case in Central America, since neither measure has had much practical impact to date.

In a region burdened by endemic poverty, underdevelopment, and external debt, it is feared that insufficient resources may limit implementation of the Inter-American Convention.

Central American measures

Section author: Camilla Waszink, SAND and BICC

This section examines small arms measures adopted in Central America. At least potentially, these address aspects of the sub-region's small arms problem left untouched by the OAS instruments.

The Framework Agreement for Democratic Security in Central America (SICA, 1995), signed in December 1995 and in force since December 1997, was developed under the System for Central American Integration (SICA), an organ established to support the process of integration within the sub-region. As of October 2000, the agreement had been ratified by only four countries: El Salvador, Guatemala, Honduras, and Nicaragua. While Costa Rica and Panama have signed the treaty, they have made a series of reservations on its arms control and regional security provisions.

The agreement aims to establish a new model of regional security that is 'unique, holistic and indivisible' (second preambular para.). Of its 78 articles, articles 30-37 are most relevant to the issue of small arms control and basically complement the OAS Convention. Thus, the parties commit themselves to combat the illicit trafficking of both military-style weapons and handguns and to implement modern and harmonized legislation in this area. The agreement also provides for co-operation between relevant authorities, confidential exchange of information on military inventories and military expenditures, and the establishment of a Central American register for arms and arms transfers.

The Framework Agreement for Democratic Security in Central America aims to establish a new model of regional security that is 'unique, holistic and indivisible'.

Implementation of the Framework Agreement has, however, been minimal to date, apparently partly because of insufficient institutional capacity. Several unresolved border disputes in Central America, including the Gulf of Fonseca maritime boundary dispute between El Salvador, Honduras, and Nicaragua, are also adversely affecting these countries' willingness and ability to co-operate.

The Arias Code of Conduct (*International Code of Conduct on Arms Transfers, 1997*) also springs from Central America, though the proposal targets the international arms trade as a whole. Drafted and promoted by a group of Nobel Peace Prize laureates led by former Costa Rican President Oscar Arias, the Code has been formally backed by the Costa Rican Government and, as of October 2000, was being revised with a view to increasing its operational range and flexibility.

At the same time, Central American citizens are launching initiatives to tackle the small arms problem at the community level. For example, throughout Honduras, 563 'Citizen Security Committees' have been established to provide support to local police forces. Some Honduran communities have also held local plebiscites to ban or control the sale of alcohol, thereby reducing violence and delinquency (Castellanos, 2000). Many reforms conducted in the context of the region's various peace-building processes, including the restructuring of national police forces and the strengthening of democratic institutions, can also contribute to small arms control.

The issue of small arms proliferation is now high on the public agenda in Central America ... but lack of political commitment, institutional weakness, corruption, and inadequate resources remain major stumbling blocks.

The issue of small arms proliferation is now high on the public agenda in Central America. A large number of organizations have taken up the question and civil society is increasingly involved. The final declaration of the sub-regional conference held on the subject in Antigua, Guatemala, in June 2000, emphasizes the need to combine initiatives. The actions listed in the declaration include: co-operation and information exchange between law enforcement agencies and judicial bodies; ratification and implementation of regional treaties; weapons collection and destruction programmes; and the development of measures addressing the legal trade (*Antigua Declaration*, 2000).

Yet, such efforts may well be stymied by the same obstacles that have so far hampered ratification and implementation of the OAS firearms instruments: lack of political commitment, institutional weakness, corruption, and inadequate human and financial resources.

The West African Moratorium
Section author: Anatole Ayissi, UNIDIR

The idea of a West African moratorium on small arms grew out of 1990s efforts for conflict resolution in Northern Mali and a 1996 proposal of Malian President Alpha Oumar Konaré. The Economic Community of West African States (ECOWAS) endorsed the concept, and the *Declaration of a*

Box 7.2 The MERCOSUR Joint Mechanism[9]

MERCOSUR is a customs union comprising Argentina, Brazil, Paraguay, and Uruguay. The MERCOSUR states agreed, in July 1998, on the creation of a Joint Mechanism (MERCOSUR 1998a) to share information on companies and individuals involved in the commercial trade in firearms, ammunition, explosives, and related materials. The agreement involves the creation of a mechanism for sharing information contained in existing national registers.

Application of the Joint Mechanism was extended to MERCOSUR associate members Bolivia and Chile through the signature of a separate Entente (MERCOSUR, 1998b).

Information requests and responses are to be processed through MERCOSUR's System of Security Information Exchange (SISME), a computerized system for the exchange of police and public security information among MERCOSUR's four full and two associate members.

While agreement in principle on SISME was reached in 1998, with an accord on organizational structure and functions following in 1999, as of August 2000, it had not yet become operational due to compatibility problems among national computer systems. Until SISME is operational, the Joint Mechanism cannot function.

Map 7.2 MERCOSUR countries

Member countries

Associate members

BRAZIL

BOLIVIA

PARAGUAY

CHILE

URUGUAY

ARGENTINA

Moratorium on Importation, Exportation and Manufacture of Light Weapons in West Africa (ECOWAS, 1998) was signed by the Heads of State of all 16 ECOWAS members, on 31 October 1998, at their 21st Summit in Abuja, Nigeria. The agreement took effect the following day for a renewable period of three years.

The Moratorium Regime: The Moratorium regime consists of three basic instruments:

1. The **Moratorium Declaration** (October 1998): In addition to the text of the Declaration itself, this instrument provides for 'a meeting of Ministers of Foreign Affairs to assess and evaluate the moratorium at the end of the initial three-year period' of implementation, i.e. October 2001 (ECOWAS, 1998, last operative para.).

2. The **Plan of Action for the Implementation of the Programme for Coordination and Assistance for Security and Development (PCASED)** (March 1999): The PCASED project, established and operated by the UN Development Programme (UNDP), is intended to support the implementation of the Moratorium and assist with its practical development and security-related objectives (e.g. weapons collection) in West Africa and other African sub-regions. The Director of the UN Regional Centre for Peace and Disarmament in Africa (Lomé) also acts as the Director of PCASED. The *Plan of Action* for PCASED (ECOWAS, 1999c), adopted by ECOWAS Foreign Ministers in March 1999 (ECOWAS, 1999b), targets nine 'priority areas' which mirror various provisions of the *Code of Conduct*, including several mentioned below.

3. The **Code of Conduct** (December 1999): This document (ECOWAS, 1999d), adopted by ECOWAS Heads of State at their Lomé Summit, on 10 December 1999, tackles the details of Moratorium implementation. It specifies the types of weapons covered by the Moratorium[10] and extends the latter's scope to include 'components and ammunition' for these weapons (art. 3). Key institutional and operational mechanisms envisaged in the Code include:

- The establishment of 'National Commissions' in each member state to 'promote and ensure coordination of concrete measures for effective implementation of the Moratorium at national level' (art. 4);[11]

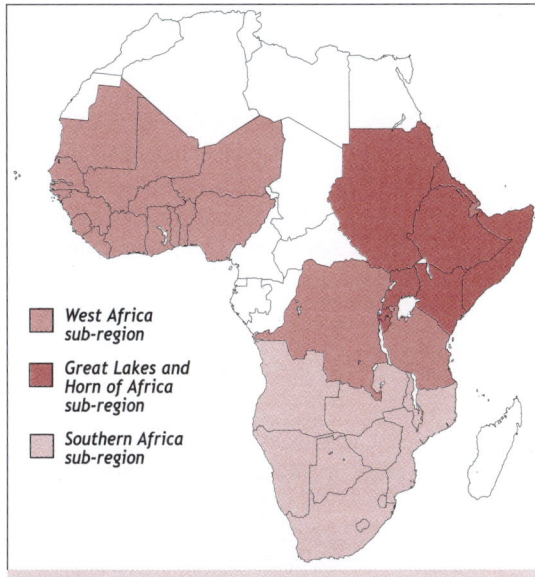

Map 7.3   African sub-regions

- ■ West Africa sub-region
- ■ Great Lakes and Horn of Africa sub-region
- □ Southern Africa sub-region

West Africa sub-region: Benin, Burkina Faso, Cape Verde, Côte d'Ivoire, Gambia, Ghana, Guinea, Guinea-Bissau, Liberia, Mali, Mauritania, Niger, Nigeria, Senegal, Sierra Leone, and Togo.

Great Lakes and Horn of Africa sub-region: Burundi, Democratic Republic of Congo, Djibouti, Eritrea, Ethiopia, Kenya, Rwanda, Somalia, Sudan, Tanzania, and Uganda.

Southern Africa sub-region: Angola, Botswana, Democratic Republic of Congo, Lesotho, Malawi, Mauritius, Mozambique, Namibia, Seychelles, South Africa, Swaziland, Tanzania, Zambia, and Zimbabwe.

Note: Democratic Republic of Congo and Tanzania are included in the two sub-regions (Great Lakes and Southern Africa).

Figure 7.1   West African Moratorium timeline

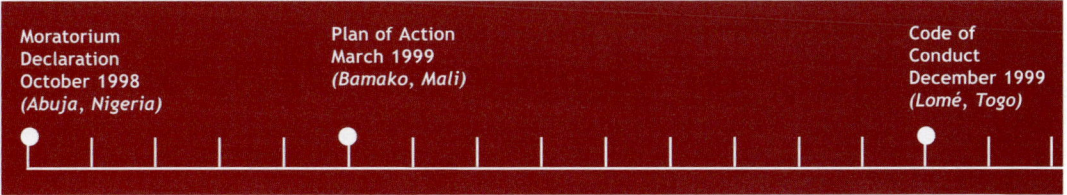

Moratorium Declaration
October 1998
(Abuja, Nigeria)

Plan of Action
March 1999
(Bamako, Mali)

Code of Conduct
December 1999
(Lomé, Togo)

- The development of '[s]tructures, staff, and procedures' within the ECOWAS Secretariat to support member states' implementation of the Moratorium and monitor compliance with it (art. 5);
- The preparation of annual reports by member states 'on the ordering or procurement of weapons, components and ammunition covered by the Moratorium' (art. 6);
- The development of a regional arms register and database (art. 6);
- The harmonization (and adoption) of legislation and administrative measures 'necessary for exercising control of cross-border' small arms transfers (art. 7); and
- The declaration of weapons and ammunition used in regional peace operations (art. 8).

The *Code of Conduct* sets out procedures for obtaining 'exemptions' to the Moratorium 'to meet legitimate national security needs or international peace operations requirements' (art. 9). At the same time, ECOWAS states undertake to collect, register, and destroy weapons and ammunition, covered by the Moratorium, 'that are surplus to national security requirements' or retrieved in the context of peace processes (art. 13).

The Code also calls for the development of procedures for inter- and intra-state co-operation between officials involved in monitoring and implementing the Moratorium (art. 11) and the development of 'more effective border control mechanisms' (art. 12). The key organs involved in these efforts are the Executive Secretariat of ECOWAS, the National Commissions, and PCASED.

Implementing the Moratorium

On the face of it, the West African Moratorium constitutes something of a watershed, suggesting, as it does, an important perceptual shift towards acknowledgement of 'human security' alongside 'national security' as an essential component of the broad African security equation. It also implies recognition of the need to pursue these goals within a regional framework. Still, these conceptual advances mean little if left unimplemented.

As of October 2000, the Moratorium had been in effect for almost two years. Yet, implementation is proving difficult. So far, only three of 16 ECOWAS states—Liberia, Mali, and Niger—had set up the National Commissions envisaged in the *Code of Conduct*. The establishment of other critical Moratorium support structures has also lagged. PCASED reached its full complement of staff only in May 2000. At the same time, the ECOWAS Executive Secretariat, with limited staff and resources, has not been able to support the Moratorium process as fully as had been hoped (PCASED 2000, p. 18).

The Moratorium has been in effect since November 1998, but implementation is proving difficult.

Nevertheless, modest progress in Moratorium implementation is being achieved. Although, as mentioned, only three countries have established National Commissions, several others have taken 'preliminary steps' to this end (PCASED 2000, p. 7).[12] At the end of August 2000, the ECOWAS Executive Secretary announced that a liaison office for PCASED would be established at ECOWAS headquarters in Abuja, giving the latter, for the first time, a dedicated small arms organ. As for the regional arms register and database, a prototype has been approved by ECOWAS member states, with the necessary infrastructure being designed and set up by PCASED. Preliminary work on the enhancement of border controls and on the review and harmonization of national legislation is also being undertaken.[13] At the same time, PCASED has provided support for weapons collection efforts throughout West Africa.[14] Efforts to build support for the Moratorium within African civil society are also underway.[15]

The support of supplier countries is important, including the decision by individual Participating States of the Wassenaar Arrangement to actively back the Moratorium. Germany, for example, has indicated in writing that it will not authorize any exports of small arms or light weapons to ECOWAS countries before receiving confirmation from the ECOWAS Secretariat that these have been approved under *Code of Conduct* exemption procedures. And on several occasions, the UK has checked the legitimacy of export orders received from ECOWAS states with the ECOWAS Secretariat and PCASED.[16]

Yet, external support can be effective only where local conditions permit. On the crucial question of whether West African states are abiding by their commitment to stop importing, exporting, and manufacturing small arms there is cause for real concern. Several ECOWAS states and other actors have applied for exemptions for specific arms transactions, in some cases even before the relevant procedures had been finalized in the December 1999 *Code of Conduct*.[17] Nevertheless, evidence of Moratorium violations by some West African states, notably in relation to the Sierra Leone conflict, is mounting.[18]

As a regional instrument, the Moratorium's effectiveness depends on conditions prevailing across the region as a whole. At the end of the year 2000, the situation, as already suggested, was not good. Armed conflict and/or instability prevailed in several areas, while some West African states were apparently flouting the formal commitments they had made to the Moratorium process. The support of external actors, including arms suppliers, is no doubt important to the measure's eventual success or failure. Yet, ultimately, its fate depends on West Africa itself.

Developing a small arms programme for Southern Africa
Section author: Virginia Gamba, Arms Management Programme, ISS

The problem of small arms proliferation and misuse has been on the Southern African agenda for several years now. While progress in translating shared concerns into operational mechanisms has been slow, this derives from the conviction that an effective small arms policy must be based on a strong, pre-existing consensus, coupled with a viable implementation strategy. Before discussing the small arms process that is specific to, and being developed by, the Southern African sub-region itself, we will look at the sub-region's links to the EU on the issue in the context of the latter's *Programme for Preventing and Combating Illicit Trafficking in Conventional Arms*.[19]

The main forum for policy debate and development in Southern Africa is the 14-member Southern African Development Community (SADC).[20] A May 1998 conference, hosted by the Institute for Security Studies (ISS) and Saferworld at Halfway House near Pretoria, brought together officials from SADC member states and the European Union (EU) and its member states to develop the main elements of a regional action programme for small arms.

The resulting *Southern Africa Regional Action Programme on Light Arms and Illicit Arms Trafficking* (SADC, 1998) was formally endorsed at a November 1998 EU-SADC Ministerial Meeting. It tackles the small arms problem in comprehensive fashion, listing measures which the countries of the sub-region can take and identifying areas of potential EU assistance across four broad areas:

1. Combating illicit trafficking;
2. Strengthening regulation and controls on accumulation and transfers of arms;
3. Promoting the removal of arms from society and the destruction of surplus arms; and
4. Enhancing transparency, information exchange, and consultation on arms in Southern Africa (SADC, 1998).

A dedicated EU-SADC working group on small arms was established in late 1999 to facilitate the small arms dialogue between the two regions and to allow for regular review of progress in implementing the *Action Programme*.

Although programme implementation has been modest to date, this stems from SADC's preference for region-to-region, as opposed to bilateral, assistance. Perhaps the main significance of the EU-SADC process to date has been the impetus given to the purely sub-regional small arms process. Development of the implementation plan to the *Draft Protocol*, discussed below, has been premised on the expectation of eventual EU support.

Evidence of Moratorium violations by some West African states, notably in relation to the Sierra Leone conflict, is mounting.

The Moratorium's fate ultimately depends on West Africa itself.

The Southern Africa Regional Action Programme tackles the small arms problem in comprehensive fashion.

The sub-regional process was launched at the August 1999 SADC Summit, in Maputo, with agreement on the establishment of a SADC small arms working group (SADC, 1999).[21] At its first meeting, in October 1999, the working group asked the Southern African Regional Police Chiefs Co-operation Organisation (SARPCCO)[22] to prepare a *Draft Protocol on Firearms and Ammunition*, together with an accompanying implementation plan. This work, subsequently assigned to SARPCCO's Legal Subcommittee, was completed in March 2000. As of August 2000, the draft documents were being discussed at the national level, prior to their expected adoption at the 2001 SADC Summit.

The draft documents cover a broad range of areas, including: national controls over firearms; marking and record-keeping systems; the collection and disposal of surplus or confiscated firearms; mutual legal assistance; improved policing; and transparency and information exchange mechanisms. Significantly, the drafts recognize the need to combat corruption and control arms brokering activities. The overall approach is comprehensive with provision made for long-term prevention strategies, as well as short-term reduction measures. The *Draft Protocol*, when finalized, is also intended to be legally binding.

Once finalized, Southern Africa's Draft Protocol on Firearms and Ammunition is intended to be a comprehensive, legally binding instrument.

With civil society organizations in a facilitating role, the draft documents are being shaped through discussion between the sub-region's developmental-political organization, SADC, and its police organization, SARPCCO, the envisaged implementing agency. This collaboration is being followed with interest elsewhere, including in the Great Lakes/Horn of Africa sub-region, the subject of the next section.

Recent initiatives in the Great Lakes and Horn of Africa
Section author: Andrew McLean, Saferworld and ISS

The Great Lakes region[23] and the Horn of Africa[24] are both severely affected by the proliferation and misuse of small arms and light weapons (ILLICIT TRANSFERS, BROKERS, EFFECTS). Yet, until recently, little had been done to address this issue.

The initiatives described below are prompted by the growing realization that small arms lie at the heart of many of the problems facing the two sub-regions. The conflicts in Burundi, Democratic Republic of Congo (DRC), Northern Uganda, Southern Sudan, and Somalia are all fuelled by these weapons, as is the increasingly violent practice of cattle-rustling in such border districts as Wajir (Kenya) and Karamoja (Uganda)(EFFECTS). Small arms are also driving high levels of crime, violence, and insecurity in cities like Kigali, Nairobi, and Mogadishu.

Small arms proliferation lies at the heart of many of the problems facing the Great Lakes and Horn of Africa. Dealing with it requires joint action.

Porous borders and conflict dynamics mean that the security and stability of the Great Lakes and Horn sub-regions are closely intertwined. For example, the conflict in DRC fuels the illicit trafficking of weapons in and through the Horn. Dealing with small arms proliferation in the two sub-regions requires joint action.

Developing a draft action programme: The experience of Southern Africa shows the important role the police can play in developing comprehensive, viable strategies for combating small arms. It also demonstrates the value of civil society organizations leading a 'track two' initiative parallel to the official governmental process.

With this in mind, four NGOs from Africa and the UK—ISS, Saferworld, the Security Research and Information Centre (SRIC), and the UN African Institute for the Prevention of Crime and the Treatment of Offenders (UNAFRI)[25]—organized a meeting in Kampala, Uganda, on 31 January-1 February 2000. It brought together senior police officers from across the Great Lakes and Horn sub-regions and representatives of the Interpol sub-regional bureau in Nairobi, the East African Co-operation (EAC),[26] and the Inter-Governmental Authority on Development (IGAD)[27] to map out a possible policy agenda. A second objective of the meeting was to engage the Interpol sub-regional bureau as a partner. The latter is important as it acts as the secretariat to the Eastern Africa Police Chiefs Committee (EAPCCO). Eleven countries are members of EAPCCO[28] and so it is the only structure which covers the entire Great Lakes and Horn of Africa sub-region.[29]

The Kampala meeting document (*Draft Proposal for Elements of a Subregional Action Programme*, 2000) identified four areas or 'pillars':

1. *Strengthening legal controls on weapons possession and transfer,* including regulating civilian ownership, marking, controlling manufacturing, increasing transparency, regulating arms dealers and brokers, and controlling small arms transfers into the sub-region;

2. *Enhancing operational capacity to combat illicit arms trafficking,* including establishing a regional illicit trafficking database, enhancing the capacity of law enforcement agencies, improving co-ordination, exchanging intelligence, strengthening border controls, and establishing cross-border operations;

3. *Removing and destroying surplus weapons and developing education programmes,* including demobilizing and reintegrating former combatants, taking inventories of state-held small arms, introducing community policing, protecting witnesses and sources, and working with community structures and civil society; and

4. *Enhancing the capacity of sub-regional institutions for implementation,* including proposals to build the capacity of the EAC, EAPCCO, and IGAD.

The draft action programme also indicates areas in which donor governments could provide financial and technical assistance to facilitate its implementation.

Adopting the Nairobi Declaration: The Kampala proposals were discussed at a conference hosted by the Kenyan Government in Nairobi, on 12–15 March 2000, and attended by foreign ministers from ten countries in the Great Lakes and Horn sub-regions.[30] The resulting agreement (*Nairobi Declaration*, 2000) represents a significant statement of intent on an issue which, until recently, states have considered highly sensitive.

The signatories undertake to share information and co-operate 'in all matters relating to illicit small arms and light weapons' (*Nairobi Declaration,* 2000, operative para. iii) and express their intention 'to exercise effective control over the possession and transfer of small arms and light weapons' through such measures as the strengthening (or adoption) and co-ordination of controls on civilian arms possession and the strengthening of sub-regional co-operation among police, intelligence, customs, and border control officials (operative para. iv).

In addition, the signatories '[u]rge source countries to ensure that all manufacturers, traders, brokers, financier, and transporters of small arms and light weapons are regulated through licensing' (operative para. iv). They also mandate the Kenyan government to co-ordinate follow-up activities (operative para. v). In fact, Kenya has since established a small arms secretariat in its Ministry of Foreign Affairs for this purpose.

Moving towards implementation: ISS, Saferworld, SRIC, and UNAFRI, in association with the Interpol sub-regional bureau in Nairobi, held a seminar in Dar-es-Salaam, on 7–8 May 2000, to discuss how the proposals in the draft Kampala *Subregional Action Programme* could help build upon and implement the *Nairobi Declaration*. The conference was attended by senior police officers, government officials, and representatives from sub-regional organizations, as well as NGOs from ten countries in the Great Lakes and Horn sub-regions.[31]

This was the first time that all these actors had come together to discuss small arms issues.[32] The main focus was on enhancing the capacity of the sub-regional organizations to implement an action programme. Participants discussed the comparative strengths and potential roles of the EAC, EAPCCO, and IGAD. They also looked at how these organizations will link to the small arms secretariat that the Kenyan Government has established to co-ordinate follow-up activities to the *Nairobi Declaration*.

Developing an effective division of labour between these myriad organizations will be crucial

The Nairobi Declaration represents a significant statement of intent on an issue which, until recently, states have considered highly sensitive.

to the success of small arms initiatives in the Great Lakes and Horn sub-regions. The following proposals are now beginning to gain acceptance:

- EAPCCO could focus on operational matters, generally, and, more specifically, on the implementation of the measures outlined in the second pillar of the Kampala draft programme;
- EAC could work towards establishing and strengthening the legal controls and measures outlined in the first pillar of the Kampala draft programme;
- IGAD could focus on the developmental, educational, and demobilization tasks outlined in the third pillar of the Kampala draft programme; and
- The Nairobi secretariat could play a co-ordinating and facilitating role.

Finalizing an Agenda for Action: Experts from all the *Nairobi Declaration* signatory countries (excepting DRC) met again in Nairobi on 6–8 November 2000 to discuss how to implement the agreement. They agreed on three key documents for this purpose. Building upon the *Nairobi Declaration*, the first document (*Coordinated Agenda for Action*, 2000) articulates a comprehensive and concrete framework for action on the small arms problem, committing the states of the Great Lakes and Horn of Africa sub-regions to a series of practical measures in the following areas:

- Institutional framework;
- Regional co-operation and co-ordination;
- Legislative measures;
- Operational and capacity building;
- Control, seizures, forfeiture, distribution, collection and destruction;
- Information exchange and record-keeping; and
- Public awareness.

The second document (*Implementation Plan*, 2000) sets out the specific measures needed to turn the *Coordinated Agenda* into a working reality in each of the agreed areas. Meetings, training, and information exchanges are proposed for this purpose. In the third document (*Annex A to International Assistance,* 2000), the countries of the Great Lakes and Horn sub-regions call upon the international community for support in implementing the *Coordinated Agenda* and its *Implementation Plan*. General assistance is requested in the following areas: ensuring responsible controls on weapons transfers; abiding by international sanctions; supporting peace processes, and conflict prevention and resolution efforts; and implementing social and economic programmes. Financial and technical assistance is also sought in support of specific needs identified in the *Implementation Plan*.

These documents, offering a comprehensive basis for action on small arms in the sub-regions, were to be submitted for signature at the OAU Ministerial Conference, scheduled for Bamako, Mali, on 30 November–1 December 2000.

Involving East Africa's police chiefs: Significant progress is also being made at the operational level. Small arms was one of the main agenda items at the EAPCCO annual general meeting, held in Khartoum from 19–21 June 2000. The Police Chiefs agreed on a constitution for EAPCCO and a number of resolutions tackling firearms trafficking. They agreed specifically to: strengthen national laws, regulations, and procedures on the control, licensing, and use of arms; establish a regional database on firearms to facilitate sharing of information; and utilize the Interpol Weapons and Explosives Tracking System (IWETS) database. The Police Chiefs also agreed on measures to deal with cattle-rustling and resolved to develop an agreement for co-operation and mutual assistance to combat crime. These steps show that EAPCCO is developing teeth and has the potential to play a key role in sub-regional efforts to address the illicit trafficking of small arms.

Galvanizing civil society: An increasing number of NGOs in the Horn of Africa are realizing the need for action to combat small arms because of the impact the problem is having on their work. This is important since these organizations can help spur political action, monitor the implementation of initiatives, and provide a link from the local to the national and sub-regional levels.

A national network of NGOs working on the small arms issue in Uganda has already been established by People with Disabilities. SRIC has organized two workshops for Kenyan NGOs in Nairobi, while the Africa Peace Forum, in association with the EAC and the Norwegian Initiative on Small Arms Transfers (NISAT), organized a seminar for civil society organizations from Kenya, Tanzania, and Uganda in Arusha, Tanzania on 23-25 March 2000.[33] These organizations are now working together to develop a sub-regional network of NGOs which will be affiliated to the International Action Network on Small Arms (IANSA).

Forging links to other African initiatives: Eastern Africa's potential division of labour between a sub-regional developmental organization, IGAD, and a sub-regional police chiefs organization, EAPCCO, is similar to that adopted in Southern Africa, described in the preceding section. IGAD, however, does not include Burundi, DRC, Rwanda, the Seychelles, and Tanzania. The omission of DRC, Tanzania, and the Seychelles is not crucial as these countries are all in SADC and the Seychelles do not have a significant small arms problem. But Burundi and Rwanda are clearly significant absentees. This shows the potential importance of the new small arms secretariat in the Kenyan Ministry of Foreign Affairs in serving to link the different sub-regional organizations.

At the same time, the Great Lakes/Horn initiatives tie in with the Organization of African Unity (OAU) and UN processes described below. These are mutually reinforcing. To the extent that the sub-region continues to move forward on small arms issues, it could help spur the development of concrete measures at the continent-wide level.

Assessing prospects for the sub-region: The countries of the sub-region have expressed a clear desire to effectively address the small arms problem. A broad network of institutions, including sub-regional institutions, is fully engaged on the issue, with increasingly strong links being established between political and operational entities (e.g. departments of foreign affairs and police). Civil society organizations have also been accepted by all sides as important partners. The sub-region has thus made considerable progress on the small arms question in 2000. Yet, the existing agreements and broad momentum remain to be translated into effective action.

'An African common approach' to small arms
Section author: Virginia Gamba, Arms Management Programme, ISS

While the consequences of small arms and light weapons proliferation have been acutely felt on the African continent, the countries of the region have seldom spoken with one voice. Despite isolated, earlier requests on the part of member states that the OAU take up the issue, it was only in July 1999 that the organization's highest policy-making organ launched efforts for the development of 'an African common approach' in advance of the July 2001 *UN Conference on the Illicit Trade in Small Arms and Light Weapons in All Its Aspects*. The focus of this initiative was the convening of a 'ministerial preparatory conference' (OAU, 1999, para. 13).[34]

The work undertaken by the OAU Secretariat to prepare for the ministerial conference had two main components: first, an ongoing awareness-raising programme targeted at OAU member states[35] and, second, the convening of meetings, in Addis Ababa, in May and June 2000, of experts from African states (OAU, 2000a) and representatives of African and international organizations (OAU, 2000b).

The OAU Ministerial Conference, held in Bamako, Mali on 30 November-1 December 2000, served both to consolidate an African common position for the *2001 UN Conference* and to articulate, for the first time, a continent-wide strategy for tackling the small arms problem. The *Bamako Declaration* (OAU, 2000c), adopted by the OAU ministers on 1 December 2000, takes a comprehensive approach to its subject. While it stresses the need for action on the part of supplier countries, it also addresses the demand aspect of the small arms question. The importance of prevention is recognized, together with control and reduction. The provisions of the *Declaration* target both the licit and illicit dimensions of the problem.

At a general level, the *Bamako Declaration* calls for the 'institutionalization' of programmes for action on small arms at the national and sub-regional levels (OAU, 2000c, subpara. 2.viii). Specific recommendations for action at the national level include:

- Creation of national co-ordination agencies for small arms (subpara. 3.A.i);
- Enhancement of the capacity of national law enforcement and security agencies and officials, including training and upgrading of equipment and resources (subpara. 3.A.ii);
- Destruction of surplus and confiscated weapons (subpara. 3.A.iv);
- Development and implementation of public awareness programmes (subpara. 3.A.v); and
- The conclusion of bilateral arrangements for small arms control in common frontier zones (subpara. 3.A.ix).

The 2000 Bamako Conference articulated, for the first time, a continent-wide approach to the small arms problem.

Among the Declaration's recommendations for action at the sub-regional level are the codification, harmonization, and standardization of national norms governing small arms and ammunition (subpara. 3.B.ii) and the strengthening of sub-regional and Africa-wide co-operation among police, customs, and border control services (subpara. 3.B.iii).

African nations also seek the commitment of states beyond the continent—especially arms supplier countries—to, *inter alia*, improve controls over the small arms trade, 'discourage and eliminate the practice of dumping excess weapons in African countries', and limit trade in small arms to governments and authorized traders (para. 4). In addition, OAU countries call upon international donors to provide financial, technical, and other support for African efforts to address the continent's small arms problem, including for 'the reintegration of demobilized youths and those in illegal possession of small arms' (subpara. 4.ii and para. 5).

The important supporting role of civil society in developing and implementing small arms measures is stressed throughout the *Bamako Declaration*. So is the need for strong co-operation among states, regional, and international organizations, and NGOs in tackling a problem that, OAU ministers emphasize, 'transcends borders' (subpara. 1.vii). The ministers have also committed themselves to 'promote and defend this African common position', reflected in the *Declaration,* at the July 2001 *UN Conference* and 'call for a realistic and implementable programme of action' as its outcome (paras. 6-7).

The Bamako Declaration is a statement of political commitment, not a legally binding instrument. Its impact remains to be seen.

The *Bamako Declaration* is a statement of political commitment, not a legally binding instrument. In fact, the expression of that commitment is quite muted. Those provisions which concern African nations themselves are cast in the form of recommendations[36] that, implicitly, individual states are free to follow or not, as they see fit. It remains to be seen what impact the *Declaration* will have. It could lend important momentum to sub-regional initiatives on the continent and to the July 2001 *UN Conference*. Its adoption by all OAU states, without reservation, is in itself important. However, the *Declaration* makes only modest provision for follow-up, with the OAU Secretary-General simply requested 'to follow up on the implementation of the present Declaration and to present regular progress reports to the Council of Ministers' (para. 8).

The next step in the development of a continent-wide strategy to combat small arms would be agreement on an implementation plan fleshing out the *Bamako Declaration* with specific, practical measures. The OAU's successful management of the process leading to Bamako has prepared it to take the process forward from there. Meanwhile, concrete action for the implementation of the *Declaration* has been left to the discretion of individual OAU states.

ASEAN's first steps on small arms

Section author: Katherine Kramer, Small Arms Survey in partnership with Nonviolence International Southeast Asia

The Association of Southeast Asian Nations (ASEAN) has, to date, avoided consideration of controls on small arms and light weapons for fear of compromising national sovereignty and security. A partial exception has been the question of illicit small arms trafficking, specifically in the context of transnational crime.

ASEAN's 1997 ministerial meeting in Malaysia set a cautious tone on the small arms issue, emphasizing the need for regional co-operation in combating transnational crime. Small arms and their illicit smuggling were seen as an integral part of terrorism, drug trafficking, money laundering, trafficking of persons, and piracy.[37] The 1997 *ASEAN Declaration on Transnational Crime* (ASEAN, 1997), setting out the basic framework for regional co-operation on this issue, was followed by the 1999 *ASEAN Plan of Action to Combat Transnational Crime* (ASEAN 1999, paras. 8-12), that envisages 'a cohesive regional strategy to prevent, control and neutralise transnational crime'. ASEAN Ministers also agreed in principle to the establishment of an ASEAN Centre for Combating Transnational Crime (ACTC) with a mandate to:

- Promote data sharing on matters relating to transnational crime;
- Act as a repository of information on national legislation, regulatory measures, and jurisprudence of member states;
- Conduct in-depth analysis of transnational crime activities;
- Recommend appropriate regional strategies to fight such activities; and
- Assist in the implementation of *Plan of Action* programme activities (paras. 13-14).

As of August 2000, the Philippine government, whose offer to host the ACTC was 'welcomed' at the 1999 Yangon ministerial meeting (para. 15), had already begun to construct the building intended to house it. However, final approval for the Centre had yet to be granted, with some member states reluctant to share certain types of information.[38] Thus far, ASEAN initiatives in the area of transnational crime, aimed primarily at criminal syndicates operating across borders, have involved written or verbal agreements, with no concrete action taken.

Small arms, as a distinct topic, was considered by ASEAN member states[39] for the first time at the *Jakarta Regional Seminar on Illicit Trafficking in Small Arms and Light Weapons*, in May 2000,[40] yet collectively they kept to a narrow, transnational crime perspective.

ASEAN's continuing reluctance to tackle small arms issues head-on has a variety of sources. An acute aversion to outside interference in matters seen as strictly internal is one. At the same time, member countries are affected by small arms in different ways and to different degrees. Currently, the only point of agreement is the transnational crime

Map 7.4   ASEAN countries

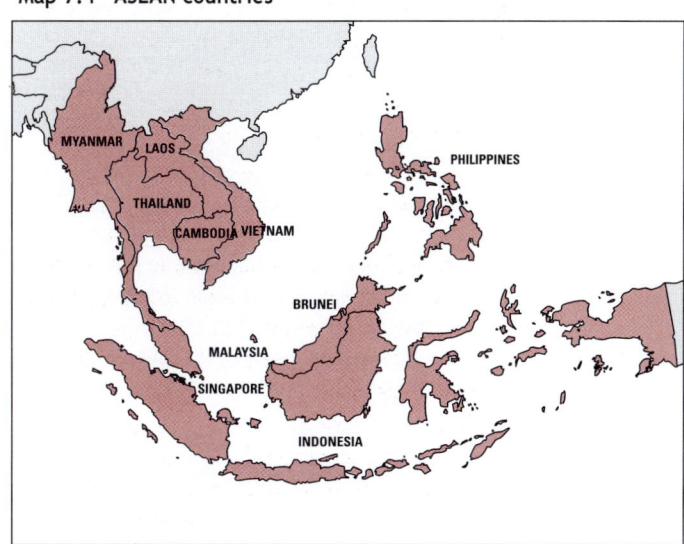

aspect, in which small arms are intertwined with other cross-border crimes. Yet, where small arms issues are subsumed under other topics, they risk being overlooked. A limited perspective on the small arms problem also ignores the important links that exist between the licit and illicit trades, as well as the destabilizing effects small arms have outside the context of transnational crime.

ASEAN states have, to date, shown little inclination to use the organization to shape regional policy, consistently opting for bilateral agreement over broader regional norms. Thus, while five member states have bilateral extradition agreements, no regional agreement yet exists. ASEAN's potential as a vehicle for regional policy-making is currently undermined by its members' sensitivity to perceived infringements of national sovereignty. Unless their recent willingness to discuss small arms as a distinct issue signals a new approach, this will constitute a serious handicap in addressing the complex problem of small arms proliferation.

EU measures

Section author: Elizabeth Clegg, Saferworld

Co-operation among EU member states to combat small arms proliferation is relatively recent.[41] However, since mid-1997, the EU has shown an increasing willingness to tackle the causes and effects of this phenomenon. Several agreements have been concluded, focusing on the control of legal transfers, tackling illicit trafficking, and reducing levels of small arms in affected regions. The EU is thus well-placed to make a meaningful contribution to international efforts to control the

---

Box 7.3   The Pacific Islands Forum

The South Pacific region has not escaped the small arms problem. On the contrary, armed conflict has fueled demand for weapons in several Pacific island nations—a demand which is being met by the transfer of newer weapons and the recycling of older ones dating, in some cases, back to World War II.

The Pacific Islands Forum (formerly the South Pacific Forum), brings together Australia, New Zealand, and smaller Pacific island nations on a broad range of issues, including small arms—first discussed by the Forum in mid-1996. The task of developing a common approach to weapons control for the region was initially delegated to a sub-committee of the South Pacific Chiefs of Police Conference (SPCPC) and the Oceania Customs Organisation (OCO).

In October 1998, the sub-committee drafted the 'Honiara Initiative', setting out a weapons control strategy covering firearms and their parts and the questions of illicit manufacture, illicit trafficking, and firearms licensing. The 'Nadi Framework', produced by the SPCPC/OCO sub-committee in March 2000, expands the 'Honiara Initiative' to a wider range of weapons, including knives, traditional weapons (clubs, bows and arrows, and spears), stun guns, martial arts equipment, military-style ordnance and explosives, and incapacitating gases and liquids.

The 'Nadi Framework' includes the following core principles:

• that the possession and use of firearms, ammunition, other related materials, and prohibited weapons is a privilege that is conditional on the overriding need to ensure public safety; and

• that the improvement of public safety requires the imposition of strict controls on the importation, possession, and use of firearms, ammunition, other related materials, and prohibited weapons.

As of November 2000, the Pacific Islands Forum Secretariat, at the request of Forum Leaders, was working to develop model legislation on weapons controls.

Sources: Pacific Islands Forum Secretariat, 2000; UN Secretary-General 2000.

---

spread and misuse of small arms. For a variety of reasons, however, implementation has not followed as swiftly as might have been anticipated. As a result, the impact of these various initiatives
has, to date, been limited.

The EU programme on illicit trafficking: The first substantive EU initiative to control small
arms was agreed by its member states (the Council of the European Union) in June 1997 in the form
of the *European Union Programme for Preventing and Combating Illicit Trafficking in
Conventional Arms* (EU Council, 1997).

This programme translates the member states' desire to 'take concrete measures to curb the
illicit traffic and use of conventional arms' (5th preambular para.), mandating action in three main
areas:

1. Strengthening collective efforts to prevent and combat the illicit trafficking of arms from their
   territories through co-ordination and co-operation among intelligence, customs, and law
   enforcement agencies, and through the exchange of information on illicit arms trafficking
   (para. 1);

2. Assisting affected countries by building the capacity of national police, customs, and immigration authorities and by promoting sub-regional and national co-operation among relevant
   agencies with respect to arms trafficking (para. 2); and

3. Seeking to reduce the number of arms in circulation through such measures as weapons collection and destruction programmes (para. 3).

The most significant effort in the implementation of the EU Programme to date has been the
development and endorsement by the EU and SADC of a *Southern Africa Regional Action
Programme on Light Arms and Illicit Arms Trafficking* (SADC, 1998) and the establishment of an
EU-SADC working group on this issue—described above in the section on Southern Africa.

The EU Code of Conduct: In June
1998, the Council of the EU agreed on a
*European Union Code of Conduct on
Arms Exports* (EU Council, 1998a),
marking a new phase in co-operation on
arms issues among EU states. An initiative of the UK Presidency of the EU, the
Code involved significant political movement on the part of EU governments and
a recognition of the need for 'high common standards which should be regarded
as the minimum for the management of,
and restraint in, conventional arms
transfers by all Member States' (3rd preambular para.).

The *Code of Conduct* governs transfers of all types of conventional arms—
including small arms and light
weapons—as well as the export of dual-
use equipment (i.e. technology with

Map 7.5   European Union countries

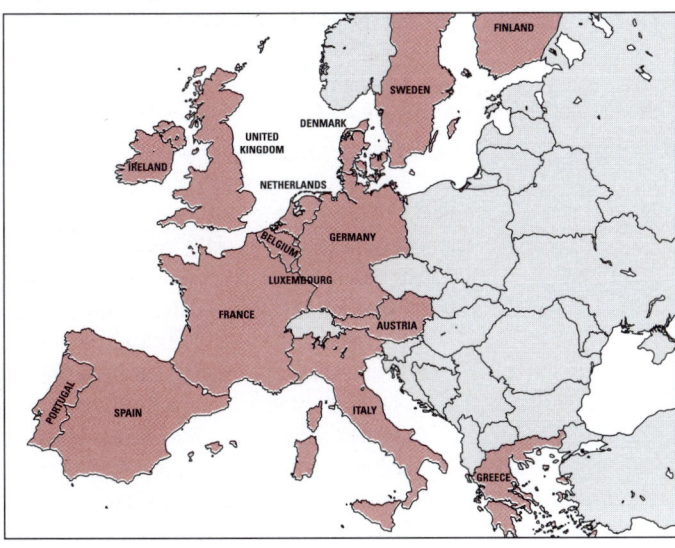

potential civilian and military applications) destined for the armed forces or other security forces of
the recipient state. The development of a 'Common Control List' was identified as a priority when the
Code was agreed in June 1998, though it was finalized only at the end of the Portuguese Presidency,
in June 2000.

It consists of guidelines of varying detail—based on the eight criteria for conventional arms exports agreed by the member states in 1991 and 1992[42]—which should be factored into export licensing decisions. These include the human rights record of the recipient, its internal situation, its external behaviour, including respect for international law, and its expenditure on arms as compared with social and economic development.

The Code also contains a series of 'Operative Provisions' which provide for information exchange and review. With respect to export licensing, the most significant provision is the mechanism whereby member states inform each other if they deny an export licence. If, less than three years after such a denial has been issued, an EU state wishes to issue a licence for 'an essentially identical transaction', it must first consult with the member state which issued the original denial (EU Council, 1998a, Operative Provision 3). The Code also provides for an annual review process in which member states present a report on their arms exports and implementation of the Code for discussion at an annual meeting. This meeting then leads to the production of a 'consolidated report' by all 15 EU states (Operative Provision 8). The first review was conducted in the second half of 1999, under the Finnish Presidency; the next was scheduled for November 2000, under the auspices of the French Presidency.

The EU Code of Conduct has been welcomed as an important first step in the development of responsible controls over the European arms trade.

Finally, the EU Code contains a commitment by the member states to 'use their best endeavours to encourage other arms exporting states to subscribe to the principles of the Code of Conduct' (Operative Provision 11). The EU Associate countries of Central and Eastern Europe have already signed up to the principles of the Code, while the US and Canada have also expressed their support.

The EU Code has been welcomed as an important first step in the development of responsible controls over the European arms trade, however a number of weaknesses have been identified by parliamentarians, NGOs, and even some EU governments. One criticism concerns the guidelines which, while involving a significant elaboration of the eight criteria, are quite vague and subject to differing interpretations. The consultation provisions of the EU Code are also the subject of controversy. In particular, the provision for bilateral notification of intention to undercut has been criticized by a number of EU governments as insufficient to ensure a common approach. While most governments earlier appeared to support the principle that all 15 member states be notified in such cases, this did not receive the unanimous support required. Finally, the EU Code has also been criticized for a lack of transparency, its emphasis clearly being on the exchange of information between member states rather than on public transparency. While no specific commitment has been made that either the national reports or the 'consolidated report' would be made public, the first annual review did, in fact, lead to the publication of the 'consolidated report' (EU Council, 1999b). The adoption of the EU Code has undoubtedly been beneficial in several respects:

- **Information sharing:** Even its relatively limited information exchange provisions—especially, the circulation of denials to all member states—are an important source of information to those EU states who lack substantial intelligence resources. Such information should prevent governments from unwittingly licensing the export of arms where there is a serious risk of misuse.
- **Objective criteria:** The Code has also helped increase international acceptance of the need to assess arms export licences using objective criteria.
- **Human rights and other considerations:** The support the Code has received from non-EU arms exporters points to widespread acknowledgement of the need to put concerns relating to human rights, regional and international stability, and development at the centre of decisions on arms export licences. This is especially significant against the backdrop of the July 2001 *UN Conference on the Illicit Trade in Small Arms and Light Weapons in All Its Aspects.*

Still, in practical terms, the effect of the EU *Code of Conduct* on member states' small arms trade is difficult to judge. While the guidelines relating to internal repression and instability are potentially very significant, their actual impact is unclear because of a lack of information on EU member states' arms exports, both before and after the adoption of the Code.

Indeed, across the EU, there still exist widely different standards of transparency in the arms trade. Some governments publish very detailed information (e.g. United Kingdom, 2000 and Italy, 2000), while others have yet to publish any form of annual report on their arms sales. While the introduction of the EU Code does seem to have prompted moves towards greater transparency in a number of EU states—notably with the publication of the first reports by France in March 2000 (France, 2000) and Germany in September 2000 (Germany, 2000)—in general, the information provided by EU governments does not allow a clear assessment of how the Code is being implemented.

The EU Joint Action: On 17 December 1998, the Council of the European Union agreed on a *Joint Action* on small arms (EU Council, 1998b), motivated, in large measure, by the German government's desire for a comprehensive EU mechanism that addressed both control and reduction aspects of small arms proliferation. Its stated objectives are:

- To combat and contribute to ending the destabilizing accumulation and spread of small arms;
- To contribute to the reduction of existing accumulations of these weapons to levels consistent with countries' legitimate security needs; and
- To help solve the problems caused by such accumulations (EU Council, 1998b, art. 1).

Thus, the *Joint Action* sets out a comprehensive programme comprising:
- Preventive measures, which seek to limit the build-up of further destabilizing accumulations of small arms, for example, by establishing and maintaining national inventories of small arms and through a commitment to export small arms in accordance with restrictive criteria (art. 3);
- Reactive measures designed to help reduce existing accumulations of small arms, through, for example, the effective removal of surplus small arms, including their safe storage and destruction, and the demobilization, rehabilitation, and reintegration of former combatants (arts. 4-5); and
- Provision of financial and technical assistance which makes 'a direct and identifiable contribution' to the achievement of the measures described above (art. 6).

Introduction of the EU Code of Conduct seems to have prompted moves towards greater transparency.

An Annex to the *Joint Action* lists the equipment it covers, including a range of small arms and light weapons extending from machine guns to anti-aircraft missiles, but—crucially—not ammunition. The fact that measures to remove and destroy ammunition do not fall within its scope has been cited as a major weakness of the agreement.

The *Joint Action* is premised upon the need for a partnership approach, between the EU and affected countries, in order to effectively tackle the problem of small arms proliferation. The first step in the establishment of a partnership involves recognition of the principles espoused within the *Joint Action*. To this end, the EU has encouraged partner countries to endorse its objectives. A request for assistance in addressing a particular problem then has to be received by the EU before a practical course of action can be initiated or funds disbursed.

While the *Joint Action* has received considerable support, including from the EU Associate countries and the members of ECOWAS, implementation thus far has focused on just a few countries, including Albania and Cambodia. Following a request for assistance from the Cambodian government, the EU sent a delegation in July 1999 to explore possibilities for supporting the weapons collection and destruction programmes previously initiated by the Cambodian authorities. This mission led to a December 1999 agreement on a joint EU-Cambodia programme to tackle small arms proliferation, including assistance in the development of legislation, in the management of small arms stockpiles, and for initiatives to raise awareness within civil society of the small arms problem.

Through the *Joint Action*, the EU has also sought to support weapons collection efforts in Albania. However, the original Gramsh Pilot Programme, elaborated by UNDP in collaboration with the Albanian authorities, made no provision for the destruction of collected weapons—a prerequisite for EU assistance. As a result of negotiations conducted in 1999, the EU has, in principle, agreed to support the latest phase of the 'weapons for development' initiative in Albania, involving two new districts and comprising a weapons destruction component.

The partnership orientation of the EU *Joint Action* represents a potentially productive means of tackling accumulations of small arms in affected regions. However, the experience of the Cambodian, and particularly the Albanian, initiatives shows that the *Joint Action* does not necessarily offer a prompt response to particular small arms problems. Accordingly, the implementation of the *Joint Action* has been limited to date; the potential impact of its wide-ranging approach towards accumulations of small arms has yet to be realized.

The EU Joint Action is premised upon the need for a partnership approach.

The EU Development Council Resolution: In May 1999, the Development Council of the EU Council of Ministers agreed on a small arms resolution (EU Council, 1999a) that builds upon the commitments already made by EU member states. It asserts that:

> *An integrated and comprehensive approach is required by the international community which adequately addresses the complexity of the small arms problem and its political, economic and social causes and takes account of the aspect of security as a prerequisite for development* [EU Council, 1999a, para. 4].

Measures deserving particular attention include: encouraging countries to eliminate surplus weapons; combating illicit trafficking; ensuring effective demobilization; and challenging cultures of violence. The Resolution also points to the SADC and ECOWAS sub-regions as especially worthy of EU attention, given the progress already made there on frameworks for combating small arms proliferation (para. 5). It also stresses the importance of continued consultation and co-operation with relevant agencies at global, regional, and national levels, as well as adequate co-ordination within the EU itself (para. 7).

The Council Resolution is important in that it constitutes an acknowledgement by EU development co-operation ministries that it is appropriate to use development aid for tackling the problem of small arms proliferation. It also recognizes the EU Commission's role in combating small arms accumulations by inviting 'the Commission, together with the relevant experts of the Member States, to define the conditions and guidelines for specific development cooperation activities relevant to the matter'. Efforts to tackle small arms should now be at the heart of EU development assistance programmes. However, despite the commitments made in the Council Resolution, it is unlikely that new funds will be made available to tackle small arms issues. These will instead have to be found from existing budgets and within the context of EU development programmes.

The 1999 EU Development Council Resolution endorses the use of development aid to tackle the problem of small arms proliferation.

Conclusions on EU measures: EU co-operation on small arms has advanced steadily since the late 1990s with agreement on a range of initiatives to tackle the supply of and demand for these weapons. Yet, if the objectives of these agreements are to be realized, the focus now needs to be on implementation.

In terms of efforts to reduce the levels of small arms in circulation, work has to be done to bridge the gap between the needs of countries in affected regions and the disbursement of EU assistance within the frameworks of the Programme on illicit trafficking and the *Joint Action*. EU member states also need to reinforce the *Code of Conduct* to achieve a more transparent export control policy and ensure that restraint in the export of small arms is clearly demonstrated. Finally, additional measures are required to prevent the circumvention of existing EU restrictions. These could include strict controls on the end use of EU arms, increased scrutiny of licensed production arrangements, and registration and licensing requirements for EU arms brokers and their transactions.

Tackling small arms in the Euro-Atlantic region
Section authors: Geraldine O'Callaghan and Dan Plesch, BASIC

The North Atlantic Treaty Organization (NATO) and the Organization for Security and Co-operation in Europe (OSCE) are the two leading multilateral security organizations in the Euro-Atlantic region. Until recently, neither had been involved in efforts to combat the proliferation and misuse of small arms and light weapons. Although a number of their member states had leading roles in these initiatives, they had been pursued in other regional fora.

The EU's focus now needs to be on implementation.

However, in 1998 and 1999, both NATO and the OSCE began to examine small arms issues. Several factors appear to have contributed to this. The supply of weapons from the Euro-Atlantic region was identified as a critical component of the global proliferation problem (PRODUCERS, BROKERS, ILLICIT TRANSFERS). Ironically, peacekeeping commanders found their forces facing weapons exported by their own or allied governments.[43] The looting and partial re-circulation of some 650,000 Albanian government weapons during that country's 1997 crisis contributed to instability in Kosovo and concentrated policy makers on problems within Europe[44] (EFFECTS). Finally, a number of governments, already engaged in combating illicit trafficking and the criminal use of guns in other regional fora, saw no reason to exclude NATO and the OSCE from what increasingly looked like an evolving, global process of control. NGOs have also helped advance the consideration of the small arms issue by both of these organizations.[45]

The importance of engaging NATO: The NATO/Euro-Atlantic Partnership Council (EAPC) Work Programme was adopted only in July 1999 (EAPC, 1999a). Although the Alliance had previously been sceptical of small arms initiatives, insisting that responsibility for stockpile security, export controls, and transparency lay with member governments, by the time of the April 1999 Washington summit, NATO had extended its traditional defence and deterrence role to include a range of responsibilities from conflict prevention to crisis management.[46]

In many respects, NATO is well-placed to take up the challenge of small arms control—in both political and practical terms. Politically, the 46 members of the EAPC, comprising the 19 NATO states and 27 'partner' countries, include many of the world's most important suppliers of small arms and light weapons to regions of conflict, several of which are not parties to the arms control regimes of the EU or Wassenaar Arrangement. NATO can therefore play a key role in setting the arms control standards for the EAPC countries, especially those seeking to join the Alliance.

In practical terms, NATO is a well-resourced organization, equipped with established military structures and technical expertise that outstrips other multilateral organizations working on small arms issues. In addition, NATO can draw the perspectives and expertise of military officers and defence officials—with direct experience in managing weapons and working with the arms industry—into a policy area thus far dominated by officials working for foreign affairs, development, and justice departments.

Developing a NATO work programme: Led by Canada, Norway, and the US, the EAPC began to consider the small arms issue in March 1999.[47] One month later, the EAPC formed an Ad Hoc Working Group on small arms charged with setting a work programme for the Council, which was drafted by July 1999 (EAPC, 1999a).

The July 1999 NATO/EAPC programme sought to 'identify ways in which EAPC/PfP might contribute to the challenge of small arms and light weapons' (EAPC, 1999a, para. (1)).[48] Emphasis was placed on reinforcing existing initiatives rather than duplicating them, taking advantage of NATO/EAPC's specific knowledge and expertise. The programme identified three areas for examination:

1. Stockpile management and security, and destruction of surplus stocks;
2. National export control, mechanisms, enforcement and arms embargoes; and
3. Peacekeeping training and development.

Following a series of workshops, held in September 1999, the Working Group identified the following 'three broad areas where there is significant potential for an enhanced contribution' (EAPC,1999b, para. 4) to small arms control:

1. **Generic training:** Dialogue and training on 'best practices' in respect of stockpile management and security, the collection, disposal, and destruction of weaponry, and small arms control in the context of peace missions (para. 4.1);

2. **Tailored assistance and co-operation:** Support for individual countries in such areas as border controls, stockpile management and security, export control regimes, and customs and police enforcement (para. 4.2); and

3. **Best practices:** Further information exchange and consultation on such matters as transparency and weapons marking regimes (para. 4.3).

NATO is well-placed to take up the challenge of small arms control. It has the potential to make a significant impact on the problem.

The Working Group further called for the elaboration of a Partnership Work Programme 'Chapter' on small arms and light weapons to 'consolidate all of the related PfP activities' and 'provide an appropriate political focus for subsequent SALW [small arms and light weapons] initiatives' (EAPC, 1999b, para. 8.1). Subsequent workshops have attempted, with some success, to build consensus in such areas as best practice in export control and common systems of marking and tracing weapons.[49]

Moving from words to action: NATO's work programme has, to date, been short on concrete action. In an attempt to address this, a new Partnership Work Program (PWP) Chapter, *The Challenge of Small Arms and Light Weapons,* was agreed upon in February 2000. The Chapter aims to involve EAPC countries in small arms issues through the elaboration of specific, practical activities and guidelines, focusing on such areas as stockpile management and security, destruction of surplus stocks, and the collection and destruction of small arms in peace missions (EAPC, 2000a).

As of August 2000, six months after the publication of the PWP Chapter, candidate countries' response to the initiative has been cautious. Although many have acknowledged its potential importance, only Lithuania and Romania have so far indicated they intend to take up NATO's offer of assistance.[50] For the moment, it is unclear how far NATO will go in implementing its small arms programme and, crucially, whether programmes designed for partner nations will also be implemented by the Alliance's existing members.

Building consensus around small arms issues in the OSCE: The OSCE faced considerable hurdles in its efforts to agree on a concrete programme of work on small arms control and reduction measures. As of December 2000, the organization comprised 55 participating States spanning a huge geographical area with widely divergent small arms problems and political perspectives. Yet, it can secure agreements only through a lengthy process of consensus building.

The OSCE began to explore small arms issues in November 1998, when the governments of Canada, the Netherlands, Norway, and Switzerland, in association with the British American Security Information Council (BASIC), organized an exploratory workshop on small arms at the organization's Vienna headquarters. By the time of the November 1999 OSCE Summit in Istanbul, small arms control was squarely on the organization's agenda.

Decision No. 6/99 of the Summit mandated the Forum for Security Co-operation (FSC) to initiate 'a broad and comprehensive discussion' on the question of small arms proliferation and convene a seminar 'devoted to the examination of concrete measures' in this area (OSCE/FSC, 1999). While some OSCE participating States, leading other small arms efforts, were disappointed that the Istanbul Summit did not yield more concrete results, this high-level commitment to addressing the problem represented important progress.[51]

The subsequent seminar, held in April 2000, explored a range of control, reduction, and prevention measures which the OSCE could pursue.[52] Following the seminar, it was generally agreed that a consensus document should be developed for endorsement by OSCE foreign ministers at their November 2000 meeting in Vienna (Eighth 'Ministerial Council'). The resulting *OSCE Document on Small Arms and Light Weapons* was adopted by the FSC on 24 November 2000 (OSCE/FSC, 2000b). While not formally endorsed by the Ministerial Council at its 27–28 November meeting, because of a dispute over other issues, the Document had the support of OSCE ministers.[53] It is now OSCE policy.

The OSCE Document on Small Arms and Light Weapons: While the *OSCE Document* is a statement of political commitment rather than a legally binding instrument (OSCE/FSC, 2000b, sec. VI, para. 6), it has considerable importance. OSCE participating States account for just over half of the world's legal exporters of small arms, including three of the four biggest exporters—the US, the Russian Federation, and Germany (LEGAL TRANSFERS). At the same time, several OSCE countries— especially in Central Asia, the Caucasus, and southeastern Europe—are directly affected by the problem of small arms proliferation. Of equal significance is the Document's comprehensive nature. The definition expressly accords the term 'small arms and light weapons' (3rd preambular para.), and mirrors that of the 1997 UN Experts Panel,[54] while the Document's various norms, principles, and measures address many of the key aspects of the small arms problem.

Sections II and III of the *OSCE Document* both aim at 'combating illicit trafficking in all its aspects' (section titles). In line with the approach taken by the OAS, there is a strong focus on improving controls over legal manufacture and transfer, with provision made for marking, record-keeping, and the harmonization of import, export, and in-transit procedures and documentation. Yet, in contrast to the narrower OAS approach, OSCE efforts to combat illicit trafficking also target the problem of supply, subordinating the export of small arms and related technology to a series of common criteria that are derived from and elaborate upon the 1993 OSCE 'Principles Governing Conventional Arms Transfers' (subsec. III (A)). Participating States also undertake to 'make every effort within their competence' to extend these criteria to licensed small arms producers located outside their territory (subsec. III (A), para. 3). In addition, the *OSCE Document* includes language acknowledging the need to regulate international brokering activities, though it leaves the adoption of specific measures to the discretion of participating States (subsec. III (D)). Preceding drafts of the Document had included agreement on certain minimum standards in this area.

The question of stockpile management, reduction of surpluses, and destruction is addressed in section IV of the *OSCE Document*. Key decisions in this area, including the determination of the existence of a surplus, are left to individual participating States, though the section does indicate that destruction is 'the preferred method for the disposal of small arms' (subsec. IV (C), para. 1) and, generally, seeks to promote 'best practice' in relation to stockpile management. Section V of the Document seeks to integrate OSCE small arms initiatives into the organization's broader efforts for conflict prevention and post-conflict rehabilitation. In principle, participating States agree to provide assistance *inter alia*, for stockpile management, weapons collection, and border control, and to incorporate small arms-related measures—including the disarmament, demobilization, and reintegration of ex-combatants—into future OSCE missions and peacekeeping operations (subsecs. V (C)–(D)).

Implementation of sections II to IV of the *OSCE Document* is supported by a series of transparency measures. These include the 'restricted' annual exchange of information among participating States on small arms exports to, and imports from, other participating States (subsec. III (F), para. 1 and Annex). While an improvement over existing practice, the latter measure will not require full (public) transparency under prevailing OSCE rules.[55]

Dividing the responsibilities: While the progress made by NATO and the OSCE to develop small arms work programmes is welcome, their comprehensive nature threatens a duplication of efforts in such areas as export controls, weapons marking, and stockpile management and security. At the same time, these programmes overlap with the EU and the UN, especially in the area of illicit trafficking. While only a comprehensive approach can effectively address the small arms problem, it

The OSCE comprises 55 participating States spanning a huge geographical area with widely divergent small arms problems and political perspectives.

The OSCE's participating States account for just over half of the world's legal exporters of small arms, including three of the four biggest exporters— the US, the Russian Federation, and Germany.

is critical that NATO and the OSCE, whose programmes cover many of the same countries, co-operate in developing relevant and complementary initiatives.

The November 2000 *OSCE Document* confirms the organization's strength in developing norms and principles. Following its adoption, the OSCE appears well-placed to increase transparency in a wide range of small arms-related areas, including transfers. NATO's considerable resources and military expertise would suggest a potential focus on the problems of stockpile management and security along with the destruction of surplus weapons stocks. In addition, the two organizations could extend their nascent collaboration in the area of conflict prevention and management, and post-conflict rehabilitation. Both the OSCE and NATO have acquired considerable expertise in the conduct of peace missions and could develop joint programmes for small arms control in this context.

In contrast to the narrower OAS approach, OSCE efforts to combat illicit trafficking also target the problem of supply.

Global measures

The need for a global component to the fight against small arms proliferation was recognized at an early stage. The two key initiatives in this respect—the *UN Firearms Protocol* and the July 2001 *UN Conference on the Illicit Trade in Small Arms and Light Weapons in All Its Aspects*—are highlighted in this section, with a broader, though not comprehensive, picture of global activity offered immediately below. Important links to activity at other levels (regional and sub-regional) are again noted where appropriate.

The global small arms process
Section author: Ed Laurance, Monterey Institute of International Studies

Even when states have the economic and political resources to address the problems posed within their borders by the proliferation and misuse of small arms, their efforts are invariably inadequate to the task if conducted in isolation. Bilateral or regional solutions have often been pursued. Yet, by the mid-1990s, it was increasingly evident that the small arms problem had important global aspects that required a global process as well.

The global nature of the small arms problem: The global dimensions of the small arms problem were initially brought home in the context of UN efforts to tame a series of intra-state conflicts in the first half of the 1990s. Peacekeeping troops from many nations, along with their political leaders, were suddenly confronted with the reality of small arms proliferation. The UN's increasing willingness to circumvent the principle of non-intervention in the internal affairs of states also helped legitimize the idea of global action on a still-sensitive issue.

Research confirmed that the supply of small arms was global in scope. States and armed opponents looked to the whole world for the sources and transit routes of their weapons. At the same time, many of the states worst hit by small arms proliferation were asking the international community for assistance. As the problem's global dimensions became clear, the landmine campaign, and its resulting treaty banning antipersonnel mines, demonstrated the potential of global action centred on a particular type of weapon.

Small arms as an international security and disarmament issue: By the mid-1990s, small arms were viewed as a problem of international security and disarmament. UN Secretary-General Boutros Boutros-Ghali helped direct attention to the issue, in these terms, in his 1995 *Supplement to An Agenda for Peace*. He challenged the international community to 'find effective solutions' to the problem of small arms proliferation and misuse illustrated by the conflicts the UN was grappling with at that time.[56]

This call for global action was soon answered. In December 1995, the General Assembly authorized the first small arms Panel of Experts to prepare a report on the types of weapons being used and the nature and causes of their accumulation and transfer, and to make recommendations for appropriate action (UNGA, 1995, para. 1). The resulting August 1997 report of the Panel recommended, *inter alia,* that the UN consider convening a global conference on the small arms issue (UN Secretary-General, 1997, Annex, para. 80(k)). A second small arms Group of Experts produced a report in August 1999 which set out objectives for an International Conference on the Illicit Trade in Small Arms and Light Weapons in All Its Aspects.

The law enforcement approach: At the same time that the UN was pursuing the international security aspect of small arms, a parallel and unconnected UN effort was underway that dealt with the problem as one of law enforcement, with transnational crime and illicit trafficking the focus of attention.

The Economic and Social Council's (ECOSOC's) Commission on Crime Prevention and Criminal Justice (CCPCJ) has dealt with the question of firearm regulation since 1995. Its initial efforts were directed towards an assessment of the firearms situation based on a survey completed by 69 countries.[57] Although the Firearms Study focused on domestic aspects of the small arms problem, it also uncovered evidence pointing to its international dimensions. These findings inspired negotiations on a legally binding *Firearms Protocol*, described in the next section.

The UN organizes for action: In 1998, the global process was further advanced when the UN Department for Disarmament Affairs (UNDDA) was designated as focal point for all action on small arms within the UN system. Under its leadership, a mechanism called the *Coordinating Action on Small Arms* (CASA) was created and began to integrate the developmental, criminal, and humanitarian features of the problem with its security aspect.[58]

The role of civil society: By 1997, the NGO community had joined both of these UN tracks, with an emphasis on global action. At a meeting in December 1997, after four years of research and conferences, these groups agreed that the time was right to begin developing a global action plan. In January 1998, a website was developed which, in May 1999, became the basis for the establishment of the International Action Network on Small Arms (IANSA). With over 300 members, IANSA has become the main co-ordinating body for NGO efforts to raise the awareness of civil society, media, and governments, to encourage the development of global policy initiatives, and to work with governments, regional organizations, and the UN to combat the small arms problem.

Concerned NGOs are increasingly focusing on the *2001 UN Conference*. These organizations are active participants in the process and will seek to convince governments of the global nature of the problem, of its devastating effects throughout the world, and of the considerable potential for effective action. To illustrate this last point, they will be highlighting the wide variety of programmes they have implemented—from awareness raising to weapons collection and destruction.

Using global resources: As the efforts described above advance, often slowly, towards fruition, several global institutions have begun to fund programmes which seek to address the small arms problem at local and national levels. A 1997 UN General Assembly resolution (UNGA, 1997a) established a process known as the Group of Interested States whereby donor countries meet with states especially hard hit by small arms to identify promising 'practical disarmament' projects for funding. UNDP has established a similar fund. Despite its reluctance to get involved in 'security issues', recognition of the negative effects of small arms on development has also led the World Bank's Post-Conflict Unit to explore how it can help.

Testing the global process: These diverse threads of the global process—including national and regional action, reports and studies, resolutions, and co-ordination mechanisms, pursued by the UN, concerned governments, and civil society—are drawing together in advance of the *2001 UN Conference.*

Although national governments will be the central players at the Conference, a wide range of actors will be involved. Regional organizations will be there. Civil society will also participate, having

The landmine campaign demonstrated the potential of global action centred on a particular type of weapon.

been recognized as crucial to the solution of the problem in the December 1999 resolution authorizing the Conference (UNGA, 1999a, 3rd preambular para.). Since one of the Conference's potential outcomes is a global funding initiative, the experience of the Group of Interested States and other funding efforts will also be essential.

The UN Firearms Protocol
Section author: Geraldine O'Callaghan, BASIC

While multilateral efforts to curb the proliferation of small arms and light weapons are still relatively new and untested, the 'law enforcement approach' to the problem, with its corresponding focus on illicit weapons trafficking, has had relative success, gaining the high-level political support of a diverse group of states. This approach—whereby controls on the movement of small arms generally are strengthened in order to isolate and combat the illicit trade—has been adopted by both the OAS and ECOSOC.

The initiative shepherded by ECOSOC's Crime Commission for a binding international agreement to combat the illicit arms trade is the focus of this section. Negotiations for a *Protocol against the Illicit Manufacturing of and Trafficking in Firearms, Their Parts and Components and Ammunition ('Firearms Protocol')* have been underway since early 1999. If and when it is finalized, the *Firearms Protocol*, a supplement to the overarching *United Nations Convention against Transnational Organized Crime* (UNGA, 2000d), will have the potential to make a significant impact on the illicit manufacture of and trade in small arms.

The OAS precedent: The negotiators of the global *Firearms Protocol* have taken the pre-existing *Inter-American Convention* (OAS, 1997) as its model. The OAS Convention, described earlier, has significant strengths. Perhaps most important, it reflects specific regional concerns surrounding drug trafficking and transnational crime and focuses on increasing co-operation, rather than employing sanctions against countries seen to facilitate the illicit arms trade in the region. It is also a very practical instrument, setting out clear obligations for states to follow in combating illicit trafficking. However, there are concerns that some of the Convention's inherent limitations may also weaken the global instrument modelled upon it. In particular, the OAS Convention emphasizes the enforcement of *existing* laws alongside the improved implementation of import and export procedures. It does little to change current policies and the impact these may have on the broader small arms problem.

The Firearms Protocol:[59] There is little to distinguish the May 2000 draft version of the *Firearms Protocol* from the OAS Convention which inspired it. Like the OAS Convention, the stated purpose of the Protocol is to:

> *promote, facilitate and strengthen cooperation among States Parties in order*
> *to prevent, combat and eradicate the illicit manufacturing of and trafficking*
> *in firearms, their parts and components and ammunition* [UNGA, 2000c, art. 3].

One significant, and initially very controversial, distinction between the regional and international agreements is the omission of explosives from the Protocol. Although Mexico fought hard for their inclusion, both Canada and the US, citing the difficulties faced by the OAS in developing precise definitions, argued that this could hinder ratification. Therefore, although explosives will not fall within the scope of the finalized Protocol, ECOSOC is setting up an Experts Group to determine the feasibility of controlling them.[60] If the Group can make a convincing case, ECOSOC is committed to drafting a separate protocol which will be attached to the umbrella convention at a later date.

However, apart from this omission, many of the measures outlined in the Protocol mirror corresponding articles in the OAS Convention. In broad terms, the Protocol commits states to:

- Promote common international standards for the import, export, and in-transit international movement of firearms, their parts and components, and ammunition;
- Encourage co-operation and information exchange at the national, regional, and global levels, including on firearms identification, tracking, and tracing; and
- Further international co-operation on firearms, their parts and components, and ammunition by developing an international regime for the management of commercial shipments.

The emphasis placed on co-operation, information exchange, and transparency will enable governments to identify trafficking routes and enhance their understanding of the illicit trade. The development of harmonized marking, licensing, and record-keeping systems will help law enforcement and customs officials distinguish between legal and illegal weapons shipments—often difficult in regions of armed conflict.

Yet, although the draft Protocol contains many detailed and effective provisions for developing harmonized international standards to control the movement of weapons, as of August 2000, some of the most critical aspects of the agreement remained unresolved. These included the definition of firearms, weapons marking, controls on arms brokers, and the disposal of seized illicit weapons.

A prime concern, as mentioned earlier, is that the priorities of the Americas will be transplanted wholesale into the international arena. Although organized crime and drug trafficking remain pressing issues in many parts of the world, measures suited to the phenomenon of illicit weapons trafficking in regions of conflict and post-conflict reconstruction—such as a reasonably broad definition of firearms and the adoption of comprehensive controls on arms brokers—are necessary elements of the broader, global *Firearms Protocol*. Moreover, the relevance of the finalized Protocol to countries in conflict and developing countries could be limited further were their needs for material and technical assistance in effectively implementing the Protocol left unaddressed.

The road towards implementation is expected to be a long one. Before becoming parties to the *Firearms Protocol*, states will first have to ratify the umbrella convention, as many of the Protocol's articles (e.g. mutual legal assistance and law enforcement co-operation) hinge upon provisions in the main convention. Forty ratifications of the main convention are required before it enters into force (UNGA, 2000d, art. 38). Under current proposals, the Protocol will need the same number of ratifications before it, independently, enters into force. The problem of insufficient resources, mentioned above, is also being addressed to some extent. Under article 30 of the umbrella convention, States Parties undertake to 'make concrete efforts to the extent possible' to assist developing countries in implementing the Convention. ECOSOC is already encouraging UN member states to commit funds to this process.

Conclusions on the UN Firearms Protocol: A combination of significant resources and political will are prerequisites to the transformation of the *UN Firearms Protocol* from lofty agreement to working mechanism. Yet, even then, the Protocol will not be a panacea for all the problems associated with small arms proliferation and misuse. Complementary measures, which embed small arms control within the broader context of human security, security sector reform, post-conflict reconstruction, and long-term development, must be pursued if the Protocol is to have any impact on 'the well-being of peoples, their social and economic development and their right to live in peace' (UNGA, 2000c, Preamble, Option 2 (a)). The July 2001 *UN Conference on the Illicit Trade in Small Arms and Light Weapons in All Its Aspects* will provide states with an opportunity to pursue a more integrated approach to small arms control.

However, the successful conclusion of the *Firearms Protocol* negotiations could constitute a significant step forward—not least in consolidating international consensus around the need to combat illicit weapons trafficking and manufacturing. Much will depend on the form which the finalized Protocol takes. Any loopholes or exemptions will quickly be exploited by weapons traffickers. Yet, the impact of a strong, comprehensive Protocol could be quite far-reaching. In the short-term, such an agreement would initiate a process of meaningful change and inter-governmental co-operation. In the longer-term, it could help reduce the number of weapons reaching the streets and battlefields of the future.

The road towards implementation of the UN Firearms Protocol is expected to be a long one.

The United Nations Conference on the Illicit Trade in Small Arms and Light Weapons in All Its Aspects

Section author: Ed Laurance, Monterey Institute of International Studies

In July 2001, the United Nations is scheduled to convene the largest conference held to date for the purpose of addressing the problem of small arms proliferation and misuse—the *United Nations Conference on the Illicit Trade in Small Arms and Light Weapons in All Its Aspects*. UN member states, UN specialized agencies, regional and international organizations, NGOs, and civil society will gather for the purpose of developing a global response to the small arms problem.

Background to the Conference: As described earlier, the Conference emerged from the widespread recognition that the small arms problem is *global* in nature and requires global action. The success of the *International Campaign to Ban Landmines* in achieving a ban on anti-personnel land-mines (APMs) was a key precedent in this regard. While some of the organizations and individuals working on small arms also saw a legal treaty as the primary goal of their efforts, many others concluded that the complex nature of the problem called for a multifaceted approach. The UN was also influenced by the landmine campaign—specifically by the failure to secure an APM ban under the auspices of the UN Conference on Disarmament.[61] Determined to avoid a repeat of this experience in the case of small arms, a major effort was to be mounted to devise a global response within the UN framework.

The impact of a strong, comprehensive Firearms Protocol could be quite far-reaching.

However, there was no existing global mechanism clearly suited to the task. The UN *Register of Conventional Arms* only dealt with major weapons systems. Several reviews of the Register revealed that UN member states did not want to expand it to include small arms. The option of the Certain Conventional Weapons (CCW) Treaty (UNGA, 1980) had failed in the case of APMs and there seemed little chance that the more controversial category of small arms and light weapons could be addressed through this global convention.

Such issues were discussed during the deliberations of the first UN Panel on Small Arms in 1996-1997. The concept of a global conference emerged at this time, yet sustained efforts to develop an agenda failed. Among the contentious issues were the possibility of considering the question of legal, as well as illegal, transfers, the form of the final conference document, the development of a code of conduct for small arms transfers, and the collection and destruction of weapons surplus to the security needs of states. The Panel's failure to agree on these questions led to its recommendation, in its August 1997 report, that '[t]he United Nations should consider the possibility of convening an international conference on the illicit arms trade in all its aspects, based on the issues identified in the present report' (UN Secretary-General, 1997, Annex, para. 80(k)). The phrase 'in all its aspects' was deliberately vague. In essence, the hard decisions were passed on to those who would take the next step in the process.

The idea of concrete UN action on small arms proved controversial.

The idea of concrete UN action on small arms proved controversial. Despite the efforts of those who advocated action at the global level (essentially the same coalition of states that had spurred action on the APM issue), the fall 1997 session of the General Assembly did not produce a resolution establishing a firm date for the global conference, calling instead for the views of member states on its convening. At the same time, the General Assembly requested the Secretary-General to review action on the first small arms report in a second report to be prepared with the assistance of a group of governmental experts (UNGA, 1997b, paras. 4 and 5).

The resulting *Report of the Group of Governmental Experts on Small Arms* set out the aims of the Conference as follows:

- To strengthen or develop **norms** at the global, regional, and national levels that would reinforce and further co-ordinate efforts to prevent and combat the illicit trade in small arms and light weapons in all its aspects;
- To develop agreed international **measures** to prevent and combat illicit arms trafficking in and manufacturing of small arms and light weapons and to reduce excessive and destabilizing accumulations and transfers of such weapons, throughout the world, with particular emphasis on the regions of the world where conflicts come to an end and where serious problems with the proliferation of small arms and light weapons have to be dealt with urgently;
- To mobilize the **political will** throughout the international community to prevent and combat illicit transfers in and manufacturing of small arms and light weapons in all their aspects, and raise awareness of the character and seriousness of the interrelated problems associated with illicit trafficking in and manufacturing of small arms and light weapons and the excessive and destabilizing accumulation and spread of these weapons; and
- To promote **responsibility** by states with regard to the export, import, transit, and retransfer of small arms and light weapons (UN Secretary-General, 1999, para. 126).

While the Group of Experts left most of the substantive and procedural issues to the Conference Preparatory Committees and the Conference itself, it did agree on certain points that were intended to shape the development and execution of the Conference:

- The primary focus should be on small arms and light weapons manufactured to military specifications.
- The illicit manufacture, acquisition, possession, use, and storage of these weapons should be considered in addition to transfers.
- Legal transfers should be considered insofar as they are directly related to illicit trafficking in and manufacture of small arms and light weapons (UN Secretary-General, 1999, paras. 130-32).

The Conference Preparatory Committee held its first session from 28 February to 3 March 2000, yet made scant progress—deferring decisions on the dates and venue of the Conference, the modalities of NGO participation, and Conference objectives, agenda, and rules of procedure. It did, however, decide to hold further Preparatory Committee meetings on 8-19 January and 19-30 March 2001 (UNGA, 2000b, paras. 15-16 and 18). In October 2000, the UN General Assembly's First Committee decided the Conference would be held from 9-20 July 2001 in New York (UNGA, 2000e).

Conclusions

A wide range of multilateral measures and initiatives has been launched in recent years to combat the proliferation and misuse of small arms and light weapons. This activity is occurring at several different levels—sub-regional, regional, and global—with substantial cross-fertilization between them. Thus, the OAS *Inter-American Convention*, a regional instrument, is serving as a model for the global *UN Firearms Protocol*. At the same time, the July 2001 *UN Conference on the Illicit Trade in Small Arms and Light Weapons in All Its Aspects* is prompting action on the small arms question at regional and sub-regional levels. In some cases, such action simply involves discussion of the question and the initial elaboration of a common position (e.g. ASEAN). In other cases, the regional process is doing more than merely prepare for the 2001 Conference, developing, at the same time, a region-wide policy on small arms (e.g. the OAU). Co-operation between regions—as with the EU-SADC initiative or in the context of NATO and OSCE measures—is another important feature of current efforts to address the small arms problem.

Activity on small arms is also engaging a broad range of actors: intergovernmental organizations, the UN system as a whole, NGOs, civil society, concerned governments, and coalitions between them. Partnership between NGOs and regional organizations has been instrumental in the development of important small arms initiatives in Africa and Europe. Collaboration between the UN, concerned governments, and civil society is proving equally important to the development of global small arms initiatives, especially the *July 2001 UN Conference*. These same actors are also producing the

---

Box 7.4   Issues for the 2001 UN Conference on the Illicit Trade in Small Arms and Light Weapons in All Its Aspects

As of October 2000, with preparations for the Conference accelerating, a series of substantive issues have emerged as its likely focus:

- **Licit versus illicit small arms manufacture and transfer:** One group of states contends that the Conference should restrict itself to a consideration of illicit small arms manufacture and trade, narrowly defined. Others maintain that effective constraints on the illicit trade can only be achieved through increased transparency and better control of the legal trade.
- **Stockpile security and management:** There is growing consensus on the need for states to safeguard weapons against loss through theft or corruption. More controversial is the question of destroying all weapons that are surplus to a state's national and internal security requirements, along with those illegally held by civilians.
- **Control and restraint in weapons manufacture and transfer:** Many states want the Conference to produce some kind of governmental commitment to national legislation that controls and criminalizes the illicit manufacture and export of weapons. Some states are also calling for the adoption of a binding set of international guidelines that would govern small arms exports. Another option is to develop a set of non-binding model regulations for application by states, along with other measures designed to improve the standardization and harmonization of the arms trade.
- **Arms brokering:** Few countries regulate this important part of the supply chain. Suggestions for action include a commitment by states to register arms brokers and transport agents, the insertion of clauses on arms brokering activities into UN Security Council embargo resolutions, and the development of model national brokering legislation (BROKERS).
- **Marking, record-keeping, and tracing:** There is increasing support for the development of international standards for marking small arms, light weapons, and explosives and for associated record-keeping and tracing mechanisms.
- **Civilian possession of small arms:** Although it is widely held that states should strictly regulate the possession and use of military weapons by their citizens, many states are opposed to any discussion of national gun control legislation in multilateral fora.
- **Funding Conference follow-up:** The Conference will also consider how to fund the various measures which are agreed upon and, generally, how to build the capacity of states to address the small arms problem. Options range from improved co-ordination of existing mechanisms to a new global mechanism designed specifically to assist states in preventing, reducing, and eradicating the illicit trade and manufacture of small arms and light weapons.
- **Conference outcome:** One possible, though improbable, outcome of the Conference is a legally binding instrument. More likely is the adoption of a multifaceted programme of action that could include a set of political commitments, as well as recommendations for the negotiation of legally binding instruments that address specific aspects of the small arms problem—for example, a convention on marking.[62]

Ed Laurance, Monterey Institute of International Studies

---

evidence that demonstrates the nature and effects of the small arms problem, along with the possibility of effective action, at all levels, for addressing it.

While the *implementation* of existing small arms instruments has scarcely begun, effective collaboration appears key here as well. Close co-operation between states and between their respective operational agencies, as practiced and envisaged in southern and eastern Africa, is clearly important. Co-ordination and co-operation among relevant government departments and ministries within individual states seem equally essential—as recognized by ECOWAS states in the context of the operational mechanisms agreed for the Moratorium.

The multilateral small arms process has also seen the adoption of somewhat contrasting approaches to the problem. One divide separates the law enforcement approach, with its emphasis on transnational crime and illicit arms trafficking (e.g. the OAS firearms instruments and the *UN Firearms Protocol*), from broader efforts to integrate the security, disarmament, developmental, and humanitarian aspects of the small arms problem (e.g. the EU). Various small arms initiatives can also be distinguished according to whether they are designed to address the supply side of the small arms problem (e.g. the EU *Code of Conduct*) or its demand aspect (e.g. the West African Moratorium).

While *comprehensive* approaches to the small arms problem have been adopted or are being developed in some regions, including the euro-Atlantic region and Africa, other parts of the world are characterized by partial or total inactivity (e.g. South East Asia and South Asia, respectively). The present reality is one of sharply different levels of regional activity, coupled with a definite emphasis, in the few concrete measures developed to date, on the law enforcement approach to the problem. The focus, in this approach, on transnational crime ignores the far broader and more difficult problem of the availability of small arms *per se*, including the legal trade's role in this proliferation.

The *July 2001 UN Conference* could begin to close this gap by initiating or stimulating practical action spanning the entire small arms spectrum—including its security, disarmament, developmental, and humanitarian aspects. Yet, as of November 2000, such an outcome is far from certain. While the potential impact of the Conference on regional activity could be very positive, its failure could well hinder progress in the regions.

Whereas a growing body of practice probably allows for a few tentative inferences as to what works well in the field of weapons collection,[63] it is too early to assess the efficacy of the small arms instruments described in this chapter. Very few concrete instruments have been developed for the purpose of curbing or controlling small arms proliferation and misuse, while the effective implementation of those that have been finalized is lagging.

It is clear that effective small arms measures require viable implementation mechanisms. The need to involve, in their design, those operational agencies that will eventually be charged with implementation, as in southern and eastern Africa, seems equally important. It is also apparent that the shortfall of human and material resources that many developing countries face, for example in Central America, must be addressed if they are to participate fully in the implementation of small arms measures. At the same time, West Africa demonstrates the limits of subregional processes confronted with uneven political commitment and armed conflict.

The lack of effective implementation of those few small arms instruments now in existence precludes any analysis extending beyond such considerations of basic design and application. The multilateral small arms process, with its different levels, actors, and approaches, is clearly in its infancy. Nevertheless, as illustrated throughout this chapter, considerable work has been accomplished. It will take much time to develop and implement effective remedies to the small arms problem. Yet, the first steps on this long, but crucial, road have now been taken.

For further information and current developments on small arms issues please check our website at www.smallarmssurvey.org

There is substantial cross-fertilization occurring between the various measures and initiatives launched in recent years.

The July 2001 UN Conference could stimulate practical action spanning the entire small arms spectrum—including its security, disarmament, developmental, and humanitarian aspects.

7   List of Abbreviations

ACTC	ASEAN Centre for Combating Transnational Crime
APM	Anti-personnel landmine
ASEAN	Association of Southeast Asian Nations
BASIC	British American Security Information Counci (UK, US)
BICC	Bonn International Center for Conversion (Germany)
CASA	Coordinating Action on Small Arms
CCPCJ	Commission on Crime Prevention and Criminal Justice
CCW	Certain Conventional Weapons
CICAD	Inter-American Drug Abuse Control Commission
CIFAD	Inter-Ministerial Anti-Drug Training Centre (France)
CSH	Committee on Hemispheric Security
DRC	Democratic Republic of Congo
EAC	East African Co-operation / East African Community
EAPC	Euro-Atlantic Partnership Council
EAPCCO	Eastern Africa Police Chiefs Committee
ECOSOC	Economic and Social Council
ECOWAS	Economic Community of West African States
EU	European Union
FSC	Forum for Security Co-operation
IANSA	International Action Network on Small Arms (UK)
IGAD	Inter-Governmental Authority on Development (Kenya)
Interpol	International Criminal Police Organization
ISS	Institute for Security Studies
IWETS	Interpol Weapons and Explosives Tracking System
MERCOSUR	Mercado Commún del Sur
MoU	Memorandum of Understanding
NATO	North Atlantic Treaty Organization
NGO	Non-governmental organization
NISAT	Norwegian Initiative on Small Arms Transfers
NUPI	Norwegian Institute of International Affairs
OAS	Organization of American States
OAU	Organization of African Unity
OCO	Oceania Customs Organisation
OSCE	Organization for Security and Co-operation in Europe
PCASED	Programme for Coordination and Assistance for Security and Development
PfP	Partnership for Peace (NATO)
PWP	Partnership Work Program
SADC	Southern African Development Community
SALW	Small arms and light weapons
SAND	Program on Security and Development (Monterey Institute of International Studies, US)
SARPCCO	Southern African Regional Police Chiefs Co-operation Organisation
SICA	System for Central American Integration
SIPRI	Stockholm International Peace Research Institute
SISME	System of Security Information Exchange

SPCPC	South Pacific Chiefs of Police Conference
SRIC	Security Research and Information Centre (Kenya)
UK	United Kingdom
UN	United Nations
UNAFRI	United Nations African Institute for the Prevention of Crime and the Treatment of Offenders (Uganda)
UNDDA	United Nations Department for Disarmament Affairs
UNDP	United Nations Development Programme (US)
UNGA	United Nations General Assembly
UNIDIR	United Nations Institute for Disarmament Research (Switzerland)
UN-LiREC	United Nations Regional Centre for Peace, Disarmament and Development in Latin America and the Caribbean (Peru)
UNRCPDA	United Nations Regional Centre for Peace and Disarmament in Africa (Togo)
US	United States

7   Endnotes

1 With respect to the global level, see the separate section in this chapter on the *UN Firearms Protocol*.

2 The Group of Experts which drafted the *Model Regulations* recommended that a separate experts group be convened to study the question of explosives and develop model regulations for their control. See the 'Recommendations of the Group of Experts to CICAD', appearing at the end of the *Model Regulations* document (OAS, 1998).

3 As of the same date, 32 states had signed the Convention. For an up-to-date list of signatory and ratifying countries, see: http://www.oas.org. Note that while Cuba technically remains a member of the OAS, it has been excluded from voting or participating in the organization's activities since 1962. Active OAS members thus number 34.

4 With respect to Cuba, technically the 35th member state, see preceding note.

5 US implementation of the *Model Regulations* has been realized through a series of three amendments to pre-existing rules. See: US Department of State, 1999; US Department of Commerce, 1999; US Department of the Treasury, 2000.

6 See the 'Recommendations of the Group of Experts to CICAD', appearing at the end of the *Model Regulations* document (OAS, 1998).

7 See Dyer and O'Callaghan, 1999.

8 Some of these measures are discussed in the next section. See also in this chapter the section on the *July 2001 UN Conference*.

9 This section was finalized in August 2000 on the basis of information supplied by Pablo Dreyfus, Small Arms Survey.

10 These include pistols, rifles, sub-machine guns, machine guns, mortars, and howitzers. ECOWAS, 1999c, art. 2 and Annex I.

11 A decision adopted on 10 December 1999 by ECOWAS Heads of State sets out the functions of the National Commissions in some detail. These include assisting governments in the design and implementation of national policies for small arms control. See ECOWAS, 1999e.

12 See also: PCASED, 2000, pp. 7-8 and 18; UNRCPDA, NUPI, and NISAT, 2000, p. 77.

13 See PCASED, 2000, pp. 8 and 12.

14 See PCASED, 2000, pp. 9-11.

15 See: PCASED, 2000, pp. 6-7 and 15; UNRCPDA, NUPI, and NISAT, 2000, p. 81. These efforts include the UNIDIR project 'Peacebuilding and Practical Disarmament in West Africa'.

16 See: PCASED, 2000, pp. 11-12; UNRCPDA, NUPI, and NISAT, 2000, pp. 77-78.

17 See: PCASED, 2000, pp. 22-23; UNRCPDA, NUPI, and NISAT, 2000, pp. 82-83.

18 See: Berman, 2000, pp. 13-17 and 27; Harden, 2000; PCASED, 2000, p. 23; UN Security Council, 2000, Annex, Enclosure, Part Two (especially paras. 252-54).

19 Described in the section of the chapter dealing with EU measures.

20 Members are: Angola, Botswana, Democratic Republic of Congo, Lesotho, Malawi, Mauritius, Mozambique, Namibia, Seychelles, South Africa, Swaziland, Tanzania, Zambia, and Zimbabwe.

21 Note that the membership of the working group, initially five SADC states along with the secretariats of SADC and SARPCCO, has since been expanded to include all SADC countries.

22 Members are: Angola, Botswana, Lesotho, Malawi, Mauritius, Namibia, South Africa, Swaziland, Tanzania, Zambia, and Zimbabwe.

23 i.e. Burundi, Democratic Republic of Congo, Rwanda, Tanzania, and Uganda.

24 i.e. Djibouti, Eritrea, Ethiopia, Kenya, Somalia, Sudan, and Uganda.

25 The four NGOs have worked in partnership to facilitate

action on small arms in the Great Lakes and Horn sub-regions.

26 EAC member states are Kenya, Tanzania, and Uganda. Burundi and Rwanda have also applied to join. A treaty paving the way for the transformation of the EAC into the East African Community was signed on 30 November 1999 and entered into force on 7 July 2000 following the completion of member state ratification processes. An Inter-State Security Committee, comprised of representatives from national departments of defence, state security, and immigration, will have primary responsibility for small arms issues in the revamped organization.

27 Member countries are those listed in the note defining the Horn of Africa sub-region.

28 Burundi, Djibouti, Eritrea, Ethiopia, Kenya, Rwanda, the Seychelles, Somalia, Sudan, Tanzania, and Uganda.

29 With the exception of DRC, which is not a member, and Somalia, which has no central government.

30 Burundi, DRC, Djibouti, Eritrea, Ethiopia, Kenya, Rwanda, Sudan, Tanzania, and Uganda.

31 Burundi, Djibouti, Eritrea, Ethiopia, Kenya, Rwanda, Somalia, Sudan, Tanzania, and Uganda.

32 The meeting report has been published as McLean, 2000c.

33 'Conference on Improving Human Security through the Control and Management of Small Arms', Africa Peace Forum/International Resource Group, July 2000.

34 See OAU, 1999, paras. 8-10.

35 The main instrument of this programme is a newsletter, jointly produced by the OAU Secretariat and ISS, entitled *Small Arms Proliferation and Africa*.

36 'WE RECOMMEND that Member States should: …' (OAU, 2000c, para. 3, opening phrase).

37 'Japanese Premier, ASEAN Issue Joint Statement Following Meeting,' *BBC Summary of World Broadcasts*, 18 December 1997.

38 Communication with the ASEAN Secretariat.

39 Vietnam was the only ASEAN member state not attending.

40 See UNDDA, 2000.

41 Note that article 296 of the Treaty establishing the European Community (ex art. 223 of the Treaty of Rome) stipulates that matters relating to arms production and trade remain the competence of the member states (EU, 1997). As a result, arms related issues must be dealt with by the EU's intergovernmental body, the Council of the European Union, also known as the Council of Ministers.

42 See the conclusions of the Presidency of the European Council, Luxembourg, 28-29 June 1991, and Lisbon, 26-27 June 1992.

43 See, for example, Beach, Eberle, and Rose, 1998.

44 See Ter-Velde, 1999.

45 With respect to NATO, see: testimony of Daniel Plesch, Director, BASIC, before the Committee on Foreign Relations, US Senate, 5 November 1997; Hilterman, 1998. With respect to the OSCE, see text (November 1998 workshop).

46 See NATO, 1999.

47 See Bondi, 1999.

48 Note that the acronym 'PfP' stands for 'Partnership for Peace', the operational component of the broader, more political EAPC framework.

49 See EAPC, 2000b.

50 Correspondence with Amb. Lazar Comnescu of the Romanian Mission to NATO, April 2000, and Vaclovas Semakevicius of the Lithuanian Weapons Fund, 15 May 2000.

51 See Joseph, 2000.

52 See OSCE/FSC, 2000a.

53 See: OSCE, 2000b; OSCE, 2000a; Agarkov, 2000; 'OSCE Talks Fail as West and Russia Trade Barbs,' *International Herald Tribune* (Associated Press), 29 November 2000, p. 6.

54 See UN Secretary-General, 1997, Annex, paras. 24-26.

55 These prevent the OSCE Secretariat from releasing 'restricted information'. Individual participating States will, however, be able to disclose this information if they want to—including that received from other participating States.

56 See UN Secretary-General, 1995, paras. 60-63 and 65.

57 See UN, 1998. Note that an updated version of the study, with information from additional countries, is available from the website of the UN Crime and Justice Information Network (http://www.uncjin.org/Statistics/firearms/index.htm).

58 The key documents are available from the UNDDA website (http://www.un.org/Depts/dda/CAB/action.htm).

59 The following analysis was prepared in August 2000 using the most recent version of the draft Protocol text then available: UNGA, 2000c.

60 See: UNGA, 1999b, paras. 5-8; UNGA, 2000c, nn. 1 and 3.

61 Initial efforts to secure such a ban were aimed at the conclusion of a landmine protocol to the CCW Treaty (UNGA, 1980).

62 See, for example, the joint proposal of the French and Swiss governments for 'a convention on marking, identification and control of small arms and light weapons', reproduced in UNGA, 2000a.

63 See the forthcoming Small Arms Survey *Occasional Paper* on this subject.

7   Bibliography

Agarkov, Valery. 2000. 'Russia Hails OSCE Efforts to Control Spread of Firearms.' ITAR-TASS News Agency. 27 November.

Annex A to International Assistance to the Implementation Programme of the Agenda for Action on the Problem of the Proliferation of Small Arms and Light Weapons in the Great Lakes Region and the Horn of Africa ('Annex A to International Assistance'). 2000. Nairobi, 6-8 November.

Antigua Declaration on the Proliferation of Light Weapons in the Central American Region ('Antigua Declaration'). 2000. Adopted at the Primer Foro Centroamericano sobre la Proliferación de Armas Livianas, Antigua, Guatemala, 26-29 June.

Association of Southeast Asian Nations (ASEAN). 1997. *ASEAN Declaration on Transnational Crime*. Manila, 20 December. <http://www.aseansec.org/politics/adtc97.htm>

____. 1999. *Joint Communiqué of the Second ASEAN Ministerial Meeting on Transnational Crime*. Yangon, Myanmar, 23 June. <http://www.aseansec.org/politics/jc_cri02.htm>

____. 2000. *ASEAN Cooperation in Combating Transnational Crime*. ASEAN Secretariat Information Paper. 31 March.

Beach, General Sir Hugh, Admiral Sir James Eberle and General Sir Michael Rose. 1998. 'Arms Guidelines Must Be Tightened.' *The Daily Telegraph*. 16 February.

Berman, Eric. 2000. *Re-Armament in Sierra Leone: One Year After the Lomé Peace Agreement*. Occasional Paper No. 1. Geneva: Small Arms Survey.

Bondi, Loretta. 1999. *NATO Ambassadors Tackle Small Arms Problem*. BASIC Report No. 69. 29 March.

British American Security Information Council. 1999. *Small Arms and Light Weapons: An Issue for the OSCE?* London/Washington: BASIC. June.

Castellanos, Julieta. 2000. 'Honduras: Armamentismo y Violencia.' Paper presented to the Primer Foro Centroamericano sobre Proliferación de Armas Livianas, Antigua, Guatemala, 26-29 June.

Coordinated Agenda for Action on the Problem of the Proliferation of Small Arms and Light Weapons in the Great Lakes Region and the Horn of Africa ('Coordinated Agenda for Action'). 2000. SAEM/GLR.HOA/1. Nairobi, 6-8 November.

Draft Proposal for Elements of a Subregional Action Programme to Combat Small Arms Proliferation in Eastern Africa and the Greater Horn ('Draft Proposal for Elements of a Subregional Action Programme'). 2000. Adopted at the Kampala Preparatory Meeting, Uganda, 31 January - 1 February. Reproduced in Andrew McLean ed. 2000. *Tackling Small Arms in Eastern Africa and the Greater Horn: Meeting Report*. Pretoria: Institute for Security Studies.

Dyer, Susannah and Geraldine O'Callaghan. 1999. *One Size Fits All? Prospects for a Global Convention on Illicit Trafficking by 2000*. BASIC Research Report 99.2. London/Washington: BASIC. April.

Economic Community of West African States (ECOWAS). 1998. *Declaration of a Moratorium on Importation, Exportation and Manufacture of Light Weapons in West Africa*. Abuja, 31 October. Reproduced in UN doc. A/53/763 – S/1998/1194 (Annex). 18 December.

____. 1999a. *Declaration by ECOWAS Ministers of Foreign Affairs on Child Soldiers*. Bamako, 24 March. Reproduced in Jacqueline Seck, ed. 2000. *West Africa Small Arms Moratorium: High-Level Consultations on the Modalities for the Implementation of PCASED*. Geneva/Lomé: United Nations Institute for Disarmament Research/The UN Regional Centre for Peace and Disarmament in Africa, pp. 27-30.

____. 1999b. *Meeting of Ministers of Foreign Affairs on the Modalities for the Implementation of the Programme for Coordination and Assistance for Security and Development (PCASED): Final Communiqué*. Bamako, 25 March. Reproduced in Jacqueline Seck, ed. 2000. *West Africa Small Arms Moratorium: High-Level Consultations on the Modalities for the Implementation of PCASED*. Geneva/Lomé: United Nations Institute for Disarmament Research/The UN Regional Centre for Peace and Disarmament in Africa, pp. 21-25.

____. 1999c. *Plan of Action for the Implementation of the Programme for Coordination and Assistance for Security and Development (PCASED)*. Bamako, 25 March. Reproduced in

Jacqueline Seck, ed. 2000. *West Africa Small Arms Moratorium: High-Level Consultations on the Modalities for the Implementation of PCASED*. Geneva/Lomé: United Nations Institute for Disarmament Research/The UN Regional Centre for Peace and Disarmament in Africa, pp. 31-45.

——. 1999d. *Code of Conduct for the Implementation of the Moratorium on the Importation, Exportation and Manufacture of Light Weapons*. Lomé, 10 December. Reproduced in Jacqueline Seck, ed. 2000. *West Africa Small Arms Moratorium: High-Level Consultations on the Modalities for the Implementation of PCASED*. Geneva/Lomé: United Nations Institute for Disarmament Research/The UN Regional Centre for Peace and Disarmament in Africa, pp. 53-62.

——. 1999e. *Decision Establishing National Commissions for the Control of the Proliferation and Illicit Circulation Of Light Weapons*. A/DEC/12/99. 10 December.

Euro-Atlantic Partnership Council (EAPC). 1999a. *EAPC/PFP and the Challenge of Small Arms and Light Weapons*. EAPC(PC)(SALW)WP(1)(Final). 9 July.

——. 1999b. *EAPC/PFP and the Challenge of Small Arms and Light Weapons (SALW): Report*. EAPC(C)D(1999)23. 4 November.

——. 2000a. *Small Arms and Light Weapons*. EAPC(C)D(2000)11. 22 March.

——. 2000b. *Consideration of EAPC Activity on Small Arms and Light Weapons (SALW)*. EAPC(PC-SALW)D(2000)8. 19 April.

European Union (EU). 1997. *Consolidated Version of the Treaty Establishing the European Community*. Reproduced in Official Journal C 340. 10 November.

European Union. Council of the European Union. 1997. *European Union Programme for Preventing and Combating Illicit Trafficking in Conventional Arms*. 26 June. Reproduced in UN doc. A/CONF.192/PC/3 (Annex I). 13 March.

——. 1998a. *European Union Code of Conduct on Arms Exports*. 8 June. Reproduced in UN doc. A/CONF.192/PC/3 (Annex II). 13 March.

——. 1998b. *Joint Action of 17 December 1998 Adopted by the Council on the Basis of Article J.3 of the Treaty on European Union on the European Union's Contribution to Combating the Destabilising Accumulation and Spread of Small Arms and Light Weapons*. 1999/34/CFSP. 17 December. Reproduced in Official Journal L 9. 15 January 1999.

——. 1999a. *Council Resolution on Combating the Excessive and Uncontrolled Accumulation and Spread of Small Arms and Light Weapons as Part of the EU's Emergency Aid, Reconstruction and Development Programmes*. 21 May.

——. 1999b. *Annual Report in Conformity with Operative Provision 8 of the European Union Code of Conduct on Arms Exports*. Press release: 296 - Nr: 11651/99. Approved at the 2206th Meeting of the EU Council, Luxembourg, 11 October.

France. Ministère de la défense. 2000. *Rapport au Parlement sur les exportations d'armement de la France: Résultats 1998*. March.

Gamba, Virginia, ed. 1998. *Society under Siege: Licit Responses to Illicit Arms*. Pretoria: Institute of Security Studies.

——. 2000. *Governing Arms: the Southern African Experience*. Pretoria: Institute of Security Studies.

Germany. Bundesministerium für Wirtschaft und Technologie. 2000. *Rüstungsexportbericht 1999*. September.

Harden, Blaine. 2000. '2 African Nations Said to Break U.N. Diamond Embargo.' *The New York Times*. 1 August.

Hilterman, Joost. 1998. 'NATO as Weapons Proliferator.' *International Herald Tribune*. 11 June.

Human Rights Watch. 1999. *Arsenals on the Cheap: NATO Expansion and the Arms Cascade*. April.

Implementation Plan of the Coordinated Agenda for Action on the Problem of the Proliferation of Small Arms and Light Weapons in the Great Lakes Region and the Horn of Africa ('Implementation Plan'). 2000. SAEM/GLR.HOA/2. Nairobi, 6-8 November.

International Code of Conduct on Arms Transfers. 1997. Reproduced in UN doc. A/54/766 – S/2000/146. 24 February 2000.

Italy. 2000. *Relazione sulle operazioni autorizzate e svolte per il controllo dell'esportazione, importazione e transito dei materiali di armamento nonche dell'esportazione e del transito di prodotti ad alta tecnologia (anno 1999)*. Camera dei Deputati – Atti Parlamentari XIII Legislatura – Doc. LXVII No. 4. Presented to the Presidency of the House of Deputies, 4 April.

Joseph, Kate. 2000. *OSCE and NATO Take Aim at Small Arms*. BASIC Report No. 73. London/Washington: BASIC. January.

Lodgaard, Sverre and Carsten Ronnfeldt, eds. 1998. *A

Moratorium on Light Weapons in West Africa.
Oslo: NISAT/NUPI.

McLean, Andrew. 2000a. 'Small Arms – Big Challenge:
Can Southern Africa Show the Way for the 2001 UN
Conference?' In Virginia Gamba, ed. 2000.
Governing Arms: the Southern African Experience.
Pretoria: Institute for Security Studies.

McLean, Andrew, ed. 2000b. *Tackling Small Arms in
Eastern Africa and the Greater Horn: Meeting
Report.* Pretoria: Institute for Security Studies.

_____. 2000c. *Tackling Small Arms in the Great Lakes
Region and the Horn of Africa: Strengthening the
Capacity of Subregional Organisations.* Pretoria:
Institute for Security Studies

McLean, Andrew and Elizabeth Clegg, eds. 1999.
*Towards Implementation of the Southern Africa
Regional Action Programme on Light Arms and
Illicit Trafficking, 8-9 September 1999, Pretoria,
South Africa: Seminar Report.* Pretoria: Institute for
Security Studies.

Meek, Sarah. 1998. 'The Organisation of American
States.' In Virginia Gamba, ed. 1998. *Society under
Siege: Licit Responses to Illicit Arms.* Pretoria:
Institute for Security Studies.

Mercado Commún del Sur (MERCOSUR). 1998a.
*Mecanismo Conjunto de Registro de Compradores
y Vendedores de Armas de Fuego, Municiones,
Explosivos y otros Materiales Relacionados para el
MERCOSUR.* MERCOSUR/CMC/DEC No. 7/98.
Buenos Aires, 23 July.

_____. 1998b. *Entendimiento entre el MERCOSUR, la
República de Bolivia y la República de Chile, rel-
ativo al Mecanismo Conjunto de Registro de
Compradores y Vendedores de Armas de Fuego,
Municiones, Explosivos y otros Materiales
Relacionados.* MERCOSUR/CMC/DEC No. 8/98.
Buenos Aires, 23 July.

*Nairobi Declaration on the Problem of the
Proliferation of Illicit Small Arms and Light
Weapons in the Great Lakes Region and the Horn
of Africa ('Nairobi Declaration').* 2000. Nairobi, 15
March. Reproduced in Andrew McLean. 2000.
*Tackling Small Arms in the Great Lakes Region
and the Horn of Africa: Strengthening the Capacity
of Subregional Organisations.* Pretoria: Institute for
Security Studies, pp. 74-77.

North Atlantic Treaty Organization. North Atlantic
Council. 1999. *Washington Summit Communiqué.*
NAC-S(99)64. 24 April.

Organization for Security and Co-operation in Europe

(OSCE). 2000a. *Interpretative Statement under
Paragraph 79 (Chapter 6) of the Final
Recommendations of the Helsinki Consultations;
Statement by the Deputy Minister for Foreign
Affairs of the Russian Federation, E.P. Gusarov, at
the Eighth Meeting of the OSCE Ministerial Council.*
MC.DEL/148/00. 28 November.

_____. 2000b. *Statement by Dr. Benita Ferrero-
Waldner, Chairperson-in-Office of the
Organization for Security and Co-operation in
Europe, at the Closing Plenary Session of the
Eighth Meeting of the OSCE Ministerial Council.* 28
November. MC.DEL/149/00. 29 November.

Organization for Security and Co-operation in Europe.
Forum for Security Co-operation. 1999. 269th
Plenary Meeting. FSC.DEC/6/99. 16 November.
Reproduced in FSC Journal No. 275.

_____. 2000a. *Seminar on Small Arms and Light
Weapons: Summary.* Vienna, 3-5 April 2000.
FSC.GAL/42/00. 10 April.

_____. 2000b. *OSCE Document on Small Arms and
Light Weapons.* 308th Plenary Meeting.
FSC.DOC/1/00. 24 November.

Organization of African Unity (OAU). 1999. *Decision
on the Illicit Proliferation, Circulation and
Trafficking of Small Arms and Light Weapons.*
AHG/Dec.137 (LXX). Adopted by the OAU Assembly of
Heads of State and Government at its 35th ordinary
session, Algiers, 12-14 July. Reproduced in UN doc.
A/54/424. 5 October.

_____. 2000a. *Report of the First Continental Meeting of
African Experts on Illicit Proliferation, Circulation
and Trafficking of Small Arms and Light Weapons.*
CM/2165 (LXXII), Annex. Addis Ababa, 17-19 May.
Reproduced in Eunice Reyneke. 2000. *The Illicit Trade
in Small Arms in All Its Aspects: Proceedings of the
OAU Experts Meeting and International
Consultation, May-June 2000.* Institute for Security
Studies/Organization of African Unity.

_____. 2000b. *Final Report of the International
Consultation on the Illicit Proliferation,
Circulation and Trafficking in Small Arms and
Light Weapons.* Addis Ababa, 22-23 June. Reproduced
in Eunice Reyneke. 2000. *The Illicit Trade in Small
Arms in All Its Aspects: Proceedings of the OAU
Experts Meeting and International Consultation,
May-June 2000.* Institute for Security
Studies/Organization of African Unity.

_____. 2000c. *Bamako Declaration on an African
Common Position on the Illicit Proliferation,*

Circulation and Trafficking of Small Arms and Light Weapons ('Bamako Declaration'). SALW/Decl.(I). Bamako, Mali, 1 December.

Organization of American States (OAS). 1997. *Inter-American Convention against the Illicit Manufacturing of and Trafficking in Firearms, Ammunition, Explosives, and Other Related Materials* ('*Inter-American Convention*'). Washington, DC, 14 November. Reproduced in UN doc. A/53/78. 9 March 1998.

——. 1998 *Model Regulations for the Control of the International Movement of Firearms, Their Parts and Components, and Ammunition* ('*Model Regulations*'). Adopted 2 June (AG/RES. 1543 (XXVIII-O/98)).

Pacific Islands Forum Secretariat. 2000. Correspondence with Shaun Evans, Law Enforcement Liaison Officer. December.

Poulton, Robin-Edward and Ibrahim ag Youssouf. 1998. *A Peace of Timbuktu: Democratic Governance, Development and African Peacemaking*. New York/Geneva: United Nations Institute for Disarmament Research.

Programme for Coordination and Assistance for Security and Development (PCASED). 2000. *Annual Report of the Director: March 1999 – May 2000*. Third Advisory Group Meeting, Bamako, Mali, 26-27 June 2000.

Reyneke, Eunice. 2000. *The Illicit Trade in Small Arms in All Its Aspects: Proceedings of the OAU Experts Meeting and International Consultation, May-June 2000*. Institute for Security Studies/Organization of African Unity.

Seck, Jacqueline, ed. 2000. *West Africa Small Arms Moratorium: High-Level Consultations on the Modalities for the Implementation of PCASED*. Geneva/Lomé: United Nations Institute for Disarmament Research/The UN Centre for Peace and Disarmament in Africa.

Sistema de la ingegración Centroamericana (SICA). 1995. *Tratado Marco de Seguridad Democrática en Centroamérica*. San Pedro Sula, Honduras, 15 December.

Southern African Development Community (SADC). 1998. *Southern Africa Regional Action Programme on Light Arms and Illicit Arms Trafficking*. November. Reproduced in Andrew McLean and Elizabeth Clegg, eds. 1999. *Towards Implementation of the Southern Africa Regional Action Programme on Light Arms and Illicit*

Trafficking, 8-9 September 1999, Pretoria, South Africa: Seminar Report. Pretoria: Institute for Security Studies, pp. 71-85.

——. 1999. *SADC Council Decisions, 13-14 August 1999: Prevention and Combating of Illicit Trafficking in Small Arms and Related Crimes*. Reproduced in UN doc. A/54/488 – S/1999/1082 (Annex). 21 October.

Ter-Velde, Willem. 1999. 'OSCE Presence in Albania: Lesson Learnt.' In British American Security Information Council. 1999. *Small Arms and Light Weapons: An Issue for the OSCE?* London/Washington: BASIC. June.

United Kingdom. Ministry of Defence, Foreign and Commonwealth Office, and Department of Trade and Industry. 2000. *Strategic Export Controls: Annual Report 1999*. 21 July.

United Nations. 1998. *United Nations International Study on Firearm Regulation*. New York: United Nations.

United Nations Department for Disarmament Affairs and the United Nations Regional Centre for Peace and Disarmament in Asia and the Pacific. 2000. *Summary Highlights: Jakarta Regional Seminar on Illicit Trafficking in Small Arms and Light Weapons*. Jakarta, 3-4 May.

United Nations General Assembly. 1980. *Convention on Prohibitions or Restrictions on the Use of Certain Conventional Weapons Which May Be Deemed to Be Excessively Injurious or to Have Indiscriminate Effects* ('*CCW Treaty*'). 10 October. Reproduced in UN doc. A/CONF.95/15. 27 October.

——. 1995. Resolution 50/70 B, adopted 12 December 1995. A/RES/50/70. 15 January 1996.

——. 1997a. Resolution 52/38 G, adopted 9 December 1997. A/RES/52/38. 8 January 1998.

——. 1997b. Resolution 52/38 J, adopted 9 December 1997. A/RES/52/38. 8 January 1998.

——. 1999a. Resolution 54/54 V, adopted 15 December 1999. A/RES/54/54. 10 January 2000.

——. 1999b. Resolution 54/127, adopted 17 December 1999. A/RES/54/127. 26 January 2000.

——. 2000a. *Note Verbale Dated 1 March 2000 from the Permanent Mission of France to the United Nations and Note Verbale Dated 2 March 2000 from the Permanent Observer Mission of Switzerland to the United Nations Transmitting the 'Food-for-thought Paper' Entitled 'Contribution to the Realization of an International Plan of Action in the Context of* the 2001 Conference: Marking, Identification, and Control of Small Arms and Light Weapons. A/CONF.192/PC/7. 17 March.

___. 2000b. *Report of the Preparatory Committee for the United Nations Conference on the Illicit Trade in Small Arms and Light Weapons in All Its Aspects.* A/CONF.192/PC/9. 21 March.

___. 2000c. *Revised Draft Protocol Against the Illicit Manufacturing of and Trafficking in Firearms, Their Parts and Components and Ammunition, Supplementing the United Nations Convention against Transnational Organized Crime.* A/AC.254/4/Add.2/Rev.5. 5 May.

___. 2000d. *United Nations Convention against Transnational Organized Crime.* Finalized in July. A/55/383 (Annex I). 2 November.

___. 2000e. Decision of the 1st Committee. A/C.1/55/L.28/Rev.1. 27 October.

United Nations Regional Centre for Peace and Disarmament in Africa (UNRCPDA), in co-operation with The Norwegian Institute of International Affairs (NUPI) and The Norwegian Initiative on Small Arms Transfers (NISAT). 2000. *The Making of a Moratorium on Light Weapons.* Lomé/Oslo: UNR-CPDA/NUPI/NISAT.

United Nations Secretary-General. 1995. *Supplement to An Agenda for Peace: Position Paper of the Secretary-General on the Occasion of the Fiftieth Anniversary of the United Nations.* A/50/60 – S/1995/1. 25 January.

___. 1997. *Note by the Secretary-General: General and Complete Disarmament: Small Arms.* A/52/298. 27 August.

___. 1999. *Note by the Secretary-General: Small Arms.* A/54/258. 19 August.

___. 2000. *Report of the Secretary-General: Illicit Traffic in Small Arms.* A/55/323. 25 August.

United Nations Security Council. 2000. *Note by the President of the Security Council.* S/2000/1195. 20 December.

United States. Department of Commerce. Bureau of Export Administration. 1999. *Exports of Firearms.* Reproduced in the Federal Register, Vol. 64, No. 70, Rules and Regulations. 13 April, pp. 17968-75.

United States. Department of State. 1999. *Amendments to the International Traffic in Arms Regulations.* Reproduced in the Federal Register, vol. 64, No. 69, 12 April, Rules and Regulations. pp. 17531-35.

United States. Department of the Treasury. Bureau of Alcohol, Tobacco and Firearms. 2000. *Implementation of the Model Regulations for the Control of the International Movement of Firearms, Their Parts and Components, and Ammunition (99R-281P).* Reproduced in the Federal Register, Vol. 65, No. 119, Rules and Regulations. 20 June, pp. 38194-201.

Notes to Readers

Abbreviations: Topic-specific lists of abbreviations are placed at the end of each chapter.

Chapter cross-referencing: Chapter cross-references appear capitalized in parenthesis throughout the text. For example in Chapter 6:

'Defence economists and political analysts have documented how small arms availability has increased as a result of state manufacturers attempting to reconcile surplus production with decreased demand (PRODUCERS).'

Exchange rates: All monetary values are expressed in current US dollars (US$). When other currencies are additionally cited, unless otherwise indicated, they are converted to US$ as of January 2000.

Small Arms Survey: The plain text—Small Arms Survey—is used to indicate the overall project, while the italicized version—*Small Arms Survey*—refers to the publication itself.

Website: For more detailed information and current developments on small arms issues, readers are invited to check our website at *http://www.smallarmssurvey.org*

Photo Credits

Photos in the chapters are from the following sources:

Associated Press: Pages 11, 15, 17, 19, 25, 29, 37, 45, 97, 103, 105, 109, 115, 117, 119, 121, 122-23, 149, 151,159, 187, 265, 271, 277, 279, 281.

Reuters Media Services: Pages 61, 65, 69, 79, 83, 87, 169, 218, 221, 225, 231.

Gérard Klijn (Independent photojournalist): Pages 173, 175, 207, 215, 217, 229.

International Committee of the Red Cross Photo Library: Pages 177, 189.